Eye-Tracking Technologies: Theory, Methods and Applications

Eye-Tracking Technologies: Theory, Methods and Applications

Guest Editors

Zbigniew Gomolka
Damian Kordos
Ewa Dudek-Dyduch
Bogusław Twaróg

MDPI

Basel • Beijing • Wuhan • Barcelona • Belgrade • Novi Sad • Cluj • Manchester

Guest Editors

Zbigniew Gomolka
College of Natural Sciences
University of Rzeszow
Rzeszow
Poland

Damian Kordos
The Faculty of Mechanical Engineering and Aeronautics
Rzeszow University of Technology
Rzeszow
Poland

Ewa Dudek-Dyduch
Faculty of Electrical Engineering, Automatics, Computer Science, and Biomedical Engineering
AGH University of Science and Technology in Krakow
Krakow
Poland

Bogusław Twaróg
College of Natural Sciences
University of Rzeszow
Rzeszow
Poland

Editorial Office
MDPI AG
Grosspeteranlage 5
4052 Basel, Switzerland

This is a reprint of the Special Issue, published open access by the journal *Applied Sciences* (ISSN 2076-3417), freely accessible at: https://www.mdpi.com/journal/applsci/special_issues/211I9C9N2P.

For citation purposes, cite each article independently as indicated on the article page online and as indicated below:

Lastname, A.A.; Lastname, B.B. Article Title. *Journal Name* **Year**, *Volume Number*, Page Range.

ISBN 978-3-7258-6047-0 (Hbk)
ISBN 978-3-7258-6048-7 (PDF)
https://doi.org/10.3390/books978-3-7258-6048-7

Cover image courtesy of Gomolka Zbigniew

Contents

About the Editors

Zbigniew Gomolka

Zbigniew Gomolka is with the Institute of Computer Science, Faculty of Exact and Technical Sciences, University of Rzeszow (Poland). His research focuses on eye-tracking, image-processing, and neural networks, with applications in pilot attention analysis, control, and state estimation. He has led projects on gaze-based instrumentation awareness and contributed to hybrid AI methods in engineering contexts, in addition to co-editing Special Issues on applied AI and attention analytics.

Damian Kordos

Damian Kordos is with the Faculty of Mechanical Engineering and Aeronautics, Rzeszow University of Technology (Poland). His interests include aircraft systems, vision systems, flight simulators, and HMI. He has worked on integrating eye-tracking with simulator platforms to study operator workload and decision-making, and he has co-organized editorial projects bridging control, image-processing, and neural network techniques for aerospace applications.

Ewa Dudek-Dyduch

Ewa Dudek-Dyduch is with the Faculty of Electrical Engineering, Automatics, Computer Science, and Biomedical Engineering, AGH University of Science and Technology in Krakow (Poland). Her work covers the scheduling of discrete processes, control algorithms, neural networks, and knowledge-based decision systems. She has advanced methods for attention modelling and 3-D scene analysis and has co-edited initiatives on engineering applications of hybrid AI tools.

Bogusław Twarog

Bogusław Twarog is with the Institute of Computer Science, Faculty of Exact and Technical Sciences (Poland). His research spans eye-tracking, image-processing, human–computer interaction, and ontology-based solvers. He has co-authored studies on deep neural networks for instrument detection and attention analysis in aviation and other transportation domains, contributing to the design of robust measurement protocols in realistic environments.

Preface

Eye-tracking has matured from a laboratory instrument into a versatile platform for cognitive science, engineering, and applied AI. In curating this reprint, our aim was to present a coherent snapshot of current capabilities and open questions. The chapters span algorithmic innovation, validation methods, and use cases in transportation, reading and learning, and ophthalmic assessment. We especially valued studies conducted in realistic settings, as these reveal the constraints that shape robust measurement and interpretation. We hope this collection serves both newcomers and experienced readers as a practical entry point into methods, datasets, and evaluation practices that will inform the next generation of human-centred systems.

Zbigniew Gomolka, Damian Kordos, Ewa Dudek-Dyduch, and Bogusław Twaróg
Guest Editors

applied sciences

MDPI

Editorial

New Perspectives on Eye-Tracking: Theory, Methods, and Applications

Zbigniew Gomolka [1,*], Damian Kordos [2], Ewa Dudek-Dyduch [3] and Boguslaw Twarog [1]

1 College of Natural Sciences, University of Rzeszow, Pigonia St. 1, 35-959 Rzeszow, Poland; btwarog@ur.edu.pl
2 The Faculty of Mechanical Engineering and Aeronautics, Rzeszow University of Technology, 35-959 Rzeszow, Poland; d.kordos@prz.edu.pl
3 Faculty of Electrical Engineering, Automatics, Computer Science, and Biomedical Engineering, AGH University of Science and Technology in Krakow, 30-059 Krakow, Poland; edd@agh.edu.pl
* Correspondence: zgomolka@ur.edu.pl

1. Introduction

Eye-tracking technology has evolved into a cornerstone of modern behavioral and cognitive research, providing precise insight into how individuals perceive, interpret, and interact with their visual environments. Rapid progress in computer vision, artificial intelligence, and sensor miniaturization has transformed traditional gaze-tracking systems into robust analytical platforms capable of real-time monitoring and multimodal integration [1–4]. Recent transformer-based and semi-supervised architectures have markedly improved the accuracy of gaze-estimation pipelines [1,5,6], while deep learning has enabled joint modeling of eye landmarks, states, and visual context [2,6,7]. These developments expand the applicability of eye-tracking to a wide spectrum of domains, from clinical diagnostics [7–11] and neuroergonomics [12,13] to transportation safety [14–18] and immersive virtual environments [4,19–22].

In the biomedical sphere, gaze-pattern analysis and oculomotor metrics have become valuable tools for detecting visual and cognitive disorders. Studies have demonstrated the potential of fixation-based modeling for the early detection of dyslexia [8,9], schizophrenia [10], and diabetic retinopathy [23]. Deep-learning classifiers and recurrent neural networks increasingly interpret complex eye-movement data for cognitive screening [6,8,11,23]. Simultaneously, advances in neuro-optometric research have connected pupillometric dynamics with cortical plasticity and perceptual dominance [24,25], offering promising biomarkers for neurological adaptation and rehabilitation. Similar bio-signal fusion approaches, such as hybrid electrooculogram networks [7,11], reveal that eye-tracking can complement physiological sensing in healthcare monitoring.

In applied psychology and ergonomics, eye-tracking serves as a direct window into attention, situational awareness, and decision-making [12–18]. Studies focusing on pedestrians [14], drivers [15–18], and operators in complex human–machine interfaces reveal that gaze behavior encodes both task-load distribution and hazard anticipation. Combining gaze metrics with EEG or vehicle telemetry yields comprehensive measures of cognitive load and safety risk [12,13,15,17]. These insights have inspired new approaches to automation design, intelligent driver-assistance systems, and augmented interfaces that respond dynamically to user intent [19–22].

Parallel progress has emerged in virtual- and augmented-reality environments, where gaze data enrich interactivity and immersion [4,19–22,26]. Applications range from retail analytics and avatar-mediated communication [19,27] to clinical training and digital pathology [7,28]. The fusion of real-time gaze tracking with spatial computing enables adaptive rendering, attention-aware simulation, and context-sensitive learning systems [21,22,26]. As vision science, machine learning, and interface design converge, eye-tracking is transitioning from a diagnostic and observational tool to an active component of intelligent perception systems.

This Special Issue of Applied Sciences, entitled "Eye-Tracking Technologies: Theory, Methods and Applications," was conceived to reflect this interdisciplinary momentum. It brings together contributions addressing both the methodological foundations and the practical implementations of contemporary eye-tracking research. The articles encompass computational modeling of gaze patterns, multimodal integration in human–machine systems, clinical assessment using oculomotor data, and application-driven innovations in immersive and assistive technologies. Collectively, these studies highlight the dual role of eye-tracking as a research instrument and as a core enabler of next-generation adaptive interfaces.

This Special Issue gathers contributions published between 2022 and 2024 from research groups across Europe, Asia, and the Americas. The papers span core methodological advances and diverse application domains. On the methodological side, this Special Issue includes studies on stimulus-dependent oculomotor responses, remote and video-based gaze detection for oculomotor assessment, event-camera imaging for robust pupil tracking, and machine-learning pipelines tailored to eye-movement analysis. On the application side, contributions address HMIs and operator monitoring, transportation (driver attention and distraction, situational awareness), aeronautics (documentation use and maintenance procedures), visual ergonomics and lens design, reading and educational assessment in children, and clinical or pre-clinical screening (e.g., early indicators relevant to learning difficulties). Collectively, they demonstrate how eye-movement data can inform design decisions, support objective evaluation, and unlock new forms of human-centered automation.

In curating this Special Issue, our aims were to (i) showcase instrumentation and signal-processing solutions that improve robustness and reproducibility in real-world contexts; (ii) highlight analytics and machine learning methods that transform raw gaze signals into actionable metrics; and (iii) present application case studies that connect those metrics to outcomes in safety, training, usability, and health. Across the contributions, common themes emerge: the need for principled handling of missing or noisy data; careful task and stimulus design to elicit diagnostic oculomotor patterns; integration of gaze with complementary modalities; and transparent evaluation protocols that enable cross-study comparison and deployment.

The remainder of this editorial provides a concise overview of each paper, emphasizing methodological innovations, datasets and experimental designs, and the implications of the reported findings for future research and practice. We conclude by outlining open challenges and opportunities for translating eye-tracking advances into reliable, ethical, and scalable solutions across domains.

2. An Overview of Published Articles

In the paper by Gomolka et al. (contribution 1), the authors investigate how deep neural networks can enhance the recording and interpretation of operator attention within advanced human–machine interfaces. Combining high-resolution eye-tracking with artificial-intelligence-based pattern recognition, they model cognitive states under varying workload conditions. Through controlled experiments, the team demonstrates that neural representations can capture subtle variations in fixation duration, saccadic dynamics, and visual focus stability corresponding to fluctuations in attention and fatigue. This integration of gaze analytics and deep learning reflects wider advances in real-time cognitive-state estimation [1–6,12,13]. The authors argue that such adaptive systems will play a key role in next-generation industrial automation, safety monitoring, and decision-support environments-domains in which intelligent gaze-based feedback can significantly improve operator performance and reliability [12,13,15,16].

The manuscript by Essig et al. (contribution 2) explores how optokinetic nystagmus (OKN) parameters depend on specific stimulus properties. Using a precision eye-tracking setup, the authors systematically vary contrast, motion direction, and texture to analyze corresponding changes in OKN amplitude, frequency, and latency. Their results reveal consistent modulation of reflexive eye movements by the physical structure of visual input, complementing recent studies on predictive oculomotor control and perceptual coherence [4,24,25]. The work contributes to both theoretical neuroscience and applied vision technology by providing methodological guidance for designing visual environments that elicit reliable involuntary eye responses-important for medical diagnostics and calibration protocols in oculomotor research.

In the study by Madlenak et al. (contribution 3), eye-tracking methods were applied to analyze the visual behavior of train drivers during real driving scenarios. The authors measured fixation points, saccade paths, and gaze dispersion to assess how attention is distributed among track signals, control elements, and the external environment. Their findings confirm that visual focus is predominantly directed toward safety-critical areas such as signals and speed indicators, while peripheral elements attract limited attention results consistent with earlier studies on operator attention and visual load dynamics in transport systems [29–32]. The discussion further considers how workload, environmental complexity, and route familiarity influence visual scanning strategies, aligning with cognitive-ergonomic models of driver monitoring and vigilance [33–35]. Overall, this contribution underscores the relevance of gaze analytics for enhancing driver training, cab-interface design, and real-time safety assessment in railway operations.

In the study by Lin et al. (contribution 4), the authors explored how stereoscopic 3D visual displays influence both ocular activity and motor performance. Using a controlled laboratory setting, participants were exposed to 2D and 3D stimuli while their saccade dynamics, fixation durations, and manual-response times were recorded. The results revealed measurable differences in gaze stability and reaction accuracy when interacting with 3D content, indicating an increased cognitive and oculomotor load. These findings are consistent with prior investigations into depth perception, visual fatigue, and sensorimotor coordination under immersive display conditions [29–32], which emphasize the complex interplay between binocular disparity and attention control. The authors discuss the ergonomic implications for prolonged use of 3D technologies in entertainment, education, and simulation, aligning with broader research on visual comfort optimization and adaptive display design [33–35]. Overall, the work contributes valuable insights into how advanced visual media affect human performance and perception.

In the work of Concepcion-Grande et al. (contribution 5), an innovative eye-tracking-based methodology is presented for assessing visual performance in users of progressive lens designs. The authors developed a quantitative evaluation framework linking fixation stability, gaze trajectory, and spatial attention metrics to optical lens parameters. Their controlled experiments demonstrate that the proposed system can identify subtle differences in visual adaptation and comfort between lens types, offering a reproducible, objective complement to conventional subjective testing. The study's approach resonates with recent advances in visual behavior analytics and adaptive optics modeling [3,9,17,30], which emphasize the importance of integrating physiological data into optical-product validation. Moreover, the authors discuss how eye-movement signatures can inform ergonomic lens design and user-specific calibration [26,33,34], highlighting the broader applicability of gaze-based diagnostics in visual science research and ophthalmic engineering. This contribution provides a robust foundation for bridging laboratory-based measurements with practical applications in the optical wear industry.

In the study by Madlenak et al. (contribution 6), an integrated eye-tracking and A/B-testing approach is used to examine how outdoor advertising influences the visual attention and decision-making of car drivers in realistic driving scenarios. The authors collected gaze-distribution data from drivers exposed to various billboard designs differing in color, message complexity, and placement, and correlated these findings with recall and preference measures. The results indicate that vivid colors and concise message layouts elicit stronger fixation density and higher recall, whereas complex or text-heavy content tends to divert attention from the roadway. These outcomes correspond with earlier research on driver distraction and gaze-allocation behavior in dynamic visual environments [4,10,16,29,32], confirming the sensitivity of ocular metrics to perceptual load. The paper further discusses implications for traffic-safety policy, advertising ergonomics, and human-factors modeling [11,26,34], emphasizing the need to balance promotional effectiveness with attentional safety requirements in transport contexts.

In the study by Kang et al. (contribution 7), a novel event-camera imaging framework is evaluated as an emerging approach for remote pupil-tracking. Event cameras, or neuromorphic sensors, register only brightness changes at microsecond resolution, enabling high-speed, low-power acquisition of dynamic visual information. The authors demonstrate that this asynchronous imaging principle effectively captures rapid ocular movements and luminance variations even under variable lighting and head motion, outperforming conventional frame-based trackers. Their results are consistent with current advances in high-frequency gaze-sensing architectures and neuromorphic vision modeling [3,4,12,17,29], which seek to minimize latency and energy consumption. The paper highlights the potential of these sensors for automotive, mobile, and extended-reality systems, where motion blur and environmental variability often degrade optical performance. By integrating hardware efficiency with temporal precision, this contribution sets a technical foundation for next-generation real-time human–machine-interface and assistive-vision applications [11,33,34].

In their research, Kim et al. (contribution 8) analyzed how different reading modalities (such as digital and printed text) and text types influence the reading behavior of school-aged children through eye-tracking techniques. The study recorded fixation durations, saccade amplitudes, and regression frequencies to compare visual and cognitive processing across narrative and informational materials. Results revealed that digital formats elicited shorter fixations and more frequent regressions, indicating differences in comprehension strategies and visual strain. These findings correspond with prior work on reading fluency, visual ergonomics, and cognitive adaptation in digital literacy environments [15,17,25,30,32], highlighting developmental and media-related effects on reading efficiency. The authors further discuss pedagogical implications, suggesting that adaptive presentation and font optimization could mitigate ocular fatigue and support individualized learning. This contribution broadens the application of eye-movement analysis to educational technology and developmental psychology, offering a data-driven foundation for improving reading interfaces and cognitive-assessment tools [18,33,35].

In the study by Paris et al. (contribution 9), eye-tracking technology was applied to investigate how expertise level influences visual information processing during the use of aircraft maintenance documentation. The authors compared professional engineers and novice trainees as they performed diagnostic and procedural tasks, analyzing fixation density, gaze sequences, and information-search efficiency. Results show that experts exhibited shorter fixations and more structured visual patterns, indicating greater task familiarity and mental-model integration, whereas novices relied heavily on text scanning and repetitive verification. These outcomes align with established findings on expert–novice differences in cognitive workload, attention control, and domain-specific visual search [13,14,17,30,34], emphasizing how experience shapes perceptual organization. The paper concludes that eye-movement metrics can serve as objective indicators of technical proficiency and training effectiveness [7,18,35], supporting the development of adaptive instruction systems and digital maintenance interfaces optimized for safety and performance consistency.

In their work, Harpaz et al. (contribution 10) present an advanced video-based gaze-detection system designed to identify and quantify oculomotor abnormalities through precise, non-invasive measurement. The method combines high-resolution video acquisition with feature-tracking algorithms that automatically extract pupil position, velocity, and microsaccade parameters. The authors validated their approach using datasets from clinical and control populations, demonstrating high sensitivity in detecting subtle irregularities associated with neurological or visual motor disorders. The proposed framework aligns with ongoing developments in computer-vision-based diagnostics and medical eye-movement analytics [9,12,25,26,32], offering a practical balance between accessibility and diagnostic accuracy. Beyond its clinical relevance, the system contributes to broader applications in neuroergonomics, human–machine interaction, and rehabilitation monitoring [11,29,34], where reliable eye-movement assessment supports real-time evaluation of cognitive and sensorimotor functions. This study thus reinforces the potential of gaze-tracking technologies as robust, scalable tools for both research and applied health domains.

In their comprehensive literature review (contribution 11), Arias-Portela et al. analyze the role of eye-tracking metrics in assessing and enhancing drivers' situational awareness within road-safety and human-factors research. The authors systematically synthesize prior empirical findings on fixation behavior, gaze entropy, and attention distribution under diverse environmental and cognitive-load conditions. Their review highlights that gaze-based indicators-such as fixation duration, saccade variability, and visual search efficiency can serve as reliable proxies for situational awareness, complementing subjective workload and reaction-time measures. The paper emphasizes methodological challenges related to dynamic-scene calibration, inter-subject variability, and cross-task comparability, echoing concerns raised in earlier studies on driver monitoring, vigilance assessment, and cognitive state estimation [4,8,10,29,32]. By outlining consistent analytical frameworks and integrating results from both simulator and on-road experiments, the authors establish a solid reference for future model development in adaptive driver-assistance systems and intelligent-transport interfaces [11,17,26,34].

In their experimental study, Gugerell et al. (contribution 12) investigated how visuospatial attention is distributed and managed during multitasking using the Multi-Attribute Task Battery II (MATB-II) framework. Participants performed concurrent flight-control, system-monitoring, and tracking tasks while their gaze patterns and response accuracy were analyzed to quantify attentional resource allocation. Results revealed that increased task complexity and switching frequency significantly altered fixation dwell times and scan-path organization, confirming that visuospatial attention dynamically adapts to workload and task prioritization. These findings correspond with prior work on attention management, visual cognitive control, and situational awareness in multitasking environments [3,8,10,17,29,32], emphasizing the interdependence between gaze dynamics and performance efficiency. The authors discuss implications for aerospace ergonomics and cognitive modeling, noting that eye-tracking data can serve as a real-time indicator for adaptive workload balancing in mission-critical systems. This contribution strengthens the empirical basis for designing attention-aware operator-support tools [11,26,34] in complex human–machine environments.

In their study, Nagy et al. (contribution 13) proposed and evaluated advanced area-of-interest (AOI) tracking techniques to detect and quantify visual distraction in simulated driving environments. The authors developed algorithms capable of dynamically segmenting gaze data into functional regions, such as road center, mirrors, dashboard, and peripheral zones, to capture momentary attention shifts and lapses. The method enables real-time identification of distraction events based on fixation duration and gaze-transition entropy, offering improved sensitivity over traditional AOI mapping. Results demonstrate that subtle deviations in visual behavior correlate with delayed response times and decreased situational awareness. These findings align with prior research on driver-attention modeling, visual load assessment, and gaze-based hazard prediction [6,10,16,17,29,32], highlighting the diagnostic potential of eye-movement analytics for intelligent transport safety. The study concludes that integrating AOI-driven metrics into driver-monitoring systems [7,11,26,34] can enhance the early detection of cognitive distraction and support adaptive vehicle-assistance technologies.

In their contribution, Zeslawska et al. (contribution 14) developed a hybrid diagnostic framework for early dyslexia detection that integrates eye-tracking metrics with long short-term memory (LSTM) neural networks. The approach captures detailed gaze trajectories and temporal features during children's reading tasks, transforming them into sequential data suitable for deep-learning analysis. The trained LSTM model successfully distinguished dyslexic readers from typically developing peers with high classification accuracy, demonstrating the diagnostic power of combining physiological and computational methods. These results extend current research in machine-learning-assisted cognitive assessment and reading analytics [3,4,8,10,29,32], illustrating how data-driven techniques can complement traditional educational testing. The authors also discuss implications for early intervention, individualized therapy, and digital screening tools [11,17,26,33,34], emphasizing that integrating neural modeling with eye-tracking provides a scalable, non-invasive approach to developmental learning evaluation. This study concludes the collection by showcasing how modern AI- and vision-based analytics converge in applied cognitive science.

3. Conclusions

This Special Issue, "Eye-Tracking Technologies: Theory, Methods and Applications," brings together a rich collection of studies that collectively illustrate the rapid maturation and diversification of modern eye-tracking research. Across the contributions, the papers reveal a strong convergence between technological innovation, cognitive modeling, and applied engineering. The works presented here address a wide spectrum of topics, ranging from fundamental investigations of visual physiology and oculomotor behavior to highly practical applications in transportation safety, industrial ergonomics, clinical diagnostics, and educational assessment. Taken together, they demonstrate that eye-tracking has evolved from a laboratory instrument for psychological inquiry into a multidisciplinary framework for understanding and augmenting human performance in complex environments [1–4,8,12].

Several contributions, including those by Gomolka et al., Kang et al., and Harpaz et al., show how deep-learning architectures, convolutional, recurrent, or attention-based can extract meaningful patterns from gaze dynamics in real time. These developments move eye-tracking beyond descriptive statistics toward predictive and adaptive modeling, mirroring advances in transformer-based architectures, semi-supervised learning, and neuromorphic sensing [1–7,12,13]. The resulting systems can automatically recognize cognitive states, detect anomalies, and infer task intent. Such capabilities open new possibilities for human–machine interaction, enabling interfaces that dynamically respond to the user's level of attention, fatigue, or comprehension [12–18]. In parallel, improvements in computational efficiency and the use of consumer-grade imaging hardware lower the barriers to deployment, expanding the reach of gaze-based analytics beyond specialized laboratories.

Another recurrent topic concerns visual attention and situational awareness in transport and control domains. Papers by Madlenak et al., Nagy et al., and Arias-Portela et al. collectively demonstrate the practical value of eye-tracking for monitoring operator performance in driving, railway, and pedestrian-safety contexts. These studies show how fixation sequences, scanning strategies, and AOI distributions correspond to safety-critical behaviors [14–18]. The insights gained have direct implications for the design of dashboards, driver-assistance systems, and training programs, contributing to a deeper understanding of human reliability in dynamic multitasking environments. At the same time, the systematic review by Arias-Portela et al. underscores the importance of methodological consistency and multimodal data fusion to ensure comparability and reproducibility across driver-monitoring studies [12–18].

A third important line of research relates to visual ergonomics, perceptual comfort, and human factors. The papers by Essig et al., Lin et al., and Concepcion-Grande et al. explore how specific visual stimulus properties contrast, motion, stereoscopic depth, and calibration strategy-shape ocular behavior and influence comfort, accuracy, and fatigue. These results demonstrate that quantitative gaze analysis provides objective, reproducible indicators of user experience, complementing subjective ratings and self-reports. Such evidence-based assessment supports innovation in optical design, extended-reality visualization, and human–machine interfaces [4,19–22,26]. More broadly, it illustrates how eye-tracking contributes to the ergonomics of perception, offering measurable insight into how humans adapt to increasingly immersive digital environments.

Equally prominent is the use of eye-tracking in education, training, and clinical diagnostics. The studies by Kim et al. and Gomolka et al. highlight how gaze metrics can identify early indicators of dyslexia and other reading-related difficulties, while Harpaz et al. and Madlenak et al. demonstrate how oculomotor and behavioral data can monitor cognitive workload, fatigue, and attention dynamics [7–11,13,16]. These examples show the transformative potential of gaze analytics in supporting individualized learning, adaptive training, and accessible healthcare diagnostics. The integration of deep-learning methods with biomedical signal processing [7–9,11,23] points toward a future where eye-tracking acts as a non-invasive window into neurological and cognitive function, bridging neuroscience, education, and clinical practice.

Beyond these thematic clusters, several cross-cutting methodological trends emerge. A clear movement toward real-world data collection using wearable, mobile, or vehicle-mounted sensors enables authentic behavioral monitoring in ecological contexts [4,14–17]. Simultaneously, the field is transitioning from purely descriptive analyses toward model-based frameworks capable of linking gaze dynamics to decision processes, workload, and affective states [12,13,16,21,22,26]. Contributions throughout the issue emphasize the need for standardized data formats, transparent evaluation protocols, and ethical handling of biometric information. Addressing these challenges will be vital for ensuring reproducibility, privacy, and the responsible integration of eye-tracking into daily life.

Looking forward, future eye-tracking systems are expected to benefit from continued advances in sensor miniaturization, neuromorphic imaging, and multimodal fusion with physiological and behavioral data streams [3,4,7,11]. These innovations will support new forms of intelligent, context-aware systems capable of continuous interpretation of user intent and affect. At the same time, the democratization of hardware and software calls for heightened attention to data governance, interpretability of machine-learning models, and safeguards against misuse. Sustained interdisciplinary collaboration among engineers, neuroscientists, psychologists, clinicians, and educators remains essential for translating technological progress into socially beneficial outcomes.

In conclusion, the contributions assembled in this Special Issue demonstrate both the maturity and vitality of contemporary eye-tracking research. They collectively point toward a future in which gaze-based sensing forms a cornerstone of human-centered design, adaptive automation, and cognitive-health assessment. By bridging theoretical insight with applied innovation, this volume highlights the enduring relevance of eye-tracking as a means of exploring the interface between perception, cognition, and intelligent technology.

Funding: This research received no external funding.

Conflicts of Interest: The author declares no conflicts of interest.

List of Contributions:

1. Gomolka, Z.; Zeslawska, E.; Twarog, B.; Kordos, D.; Rzucidlo, P. Use of a DNN in Recording and Analysis of Operator Attention in Advanced HMI Systems. *Appl. Sci.* **2022**, *12*, 11431. https://doi.org/10.3390/app122211431.
2. Essig, P.; Müller, J.; Wahl, S. Parameters of Optokinetic Nystagmus Are Influenced by the Nature of a Visual Stimulus. *Appl. Sci.* **2022**, *12*, 11991. https://doi.org/10.3390/app122311991.
3. Madlenak, R.; Masek, J.; Madlenakova, L.; Chinoracky, R. Eye-Tracking Investigation of the Train Driver's: A Case Study. *Appl. Sci.* **2023**, *13*, 2437. https://doi.org/10.3390/app13042437.
4. Lin, C.; Widyaningrum, R.; Prasetyo, Y. The Effect of 3D TVs on Eye Movement and Motor Performance. *Appl. Sci.* **2023**, *13*, 2656. https://doi.org/10.3390/app13042656.
5. Concepcion-Grande, P.; Chamorro, E.; Cleva, J.; Alonso, J.; Gómez-Pedrero, J. Evaluation of an Eye-Tracking-Based Method for Assessing the Visual Performance with Progressive Lens Designs. *Appl. Sci.* **2023**, *13*, 5059. https://doi.org/10.3390/app13085059.
6. Madlenak, R.; Chinoracky, R.; Stalmasekova, N.; Madlenakova, L. Investigating the Effect of Outdoor Advertising on Consumer Decisions: An Eye-Tracking and A/B Testing Study of Car Drivers' Perception. *Appl. Sci.* **2023**, *13*, 6808. https://doi.org/10.3390/app13116808.
7. Kang, D.; Lee, Y.; Jeong, J. Exploring the Potential of Event Camera Imaging for Advancing Remote Pupil-Tracking Techniques. *Appl. Sci.* **2023**, *13*, 10357. https://doi.org/10.3390/app131810357.
8. Kim, W.; Yoon, S.; Nam, S.; Lee, Y.; Yim, D. The Impact of Reading Modalities and Text Types on Reading in School-Age Children: An Eye-Tracking Study. *Appl. Sci.* **2023**, *13*, 10802. https://doi.org/10.3390/app131910802.
9. Paris, F.; Casanova, R.; Bergeonneau, M.; Mestre, D. Differences between Experts and Novices in the Use of Aircraft Maintenance Documentation: Evidence from Eye Tracking. *Appl. Sci.* **2024**, *14*, 1251. https://doi.org/10.3390/app14031251.
10. Harpaz, E.; Bar-Or, R.; Rosset, I.; Ben-Ami, E. Video-Based Gaze Detection for Oculomotor Abnormality Measurements. *Appl. Sci.* **2024**, *14*, 1519. https://doi.org/10.3390/app14041519.
11. Arias-Portela, C.; Mora-Vargas, J.; Caro, M. Situational Awareness Assessment of Drivers Boosted by Eye-Tracking Metrics: A Literature Review. *Appl. Sci.* **2024**, *14*, 1611. https://doi.org/10.3390/app14041611.
12. Gugerell, D.; Gollan, B.; Stolte, M.; Ansorge, U. Studying the Role of Visuospatial Attention in the Multi-Attribute Task Battery II. *Appl. Sci.* **2024**, *14*, 3158. https://doi.org/10.3390/app14083158.
13. Nagy, V.; Földesi, P.; Istenes, G. Area of Interest Tracking Techniques for Driving Scenarios Focusing on Visual Distraction Detection. *Appl. Sci.* **2024**, *14*, 3838. https://doi.org/10.3390/app14093838.
14. Gomolka, Z.; Zeslawska, E.; Czuba, B.; Kondratenko, Y.; Diagnosing Dyslexia in Early School-Aged Children Using the LSTM Network and Eye Tracking Technology. *Appl. Sci.* **2024**, *14*, 8004. https://doi.org/10.3390/app14178004.

References

1. Gou, C.; Zhang, H.; Chen, Y.; Li, H.; Yuan, X. Cascaded learning with transformer for simultaneous eye landmark, eye state and gaze estimation. *Pattern Recognit.* **2024**, *156*, 110760. [CrossRef]

2. Zhao, H.; Li, X.; Wang, Y.; Liu, J.; Sun, Z. Real-time dual-eye collaborative eyeblink detection with contrastive learning. *Pattern Recognit.* **2025**, *162*, 111440. [CrossRef]
3. Kang, D.; Kang, D. An adaptive learning framework for event-based remote eye tracking. *Expert Syst. Appl.* **2025**, *286*, 128038. [CrossRef]
4. Burch, M.; Kurzhals, K.; Weiskopf, D. Eye Tracking Studies in Visualization: Phases, Guidelines, and Checklist. In Proceedings of the ETRA '25, Tokyo, Japan, 26–29 May 2025; ACM: New York, NY, USA, 2025; pp. 1–7. [CrossRef]
5. Sun, Y.; Wang, J.; Ren, L.; Li, Z. Gaze estimation with semi-supervised eye-landmark detection. *Pattern Recognit.* **2024**, *146*, 109980. [CrossRef]
6. Tao, J.; Zhou, F.; Huang, H.; Zhang, Y. FocTrack: Focus-attention mechanism for visual tracking. *Pattern Recognit.* **2025**, *160*, 111128. [CrossRef]
7. Khan, W.; Rahman, S.; Alam, M.; Patel, V.M. Deep Face Profiler (DeFaP): Towards explicit non-invasive gaze comprehension. *Expert Syst. Appl.* **2024**, *254*, 124425. [CrossRef]
8. JothiPrabha, A.; Asha, G.; Aruna, M.; Ravi, S. Prediction of dyslexia severity levels from fixation and saccadic eye movement using machine learning. *Biomed. Signal Process. Control* **2023**, *79*, 104094. [CrossRef]
9. Liu, F.; Zhou, Q.; Chen, Y.; Wang, C. Small-world properties of eye-movement time series assist in identifying dyslexia risk. *Biomed. Signal Process. Control* **2024**, *93*, 106148. [CrossRef]
10. Yang, H.; Zhang, L.; Wu, Y.; Wang, J. Automatic detection of schizophrenia from eye movements in reading tasks. *Expert Systems with Applications* **2024**, *238*, 121850. [CrossRef]
11. Eraslan, S.; Yılmaz, A.; Akın, B. Systematic evaluation of autism-spectrum-disorder identification with scanpath trend analysis. *Biomed. Signal Process. Control* **2025**, *103*, 107414. [CrossRef]
12. Liu, Y.; Chen, F.; Zhang, R.; Li, K. Recognizing drivers' turning intentions via EEG and eye movement. *Biomed. Signal Process. Control* **2025**, *101*, 107218. [CrossRef]
13. Ezzati Amini, R.; Rahman, F.; Ahn, S. Driver distraction and in-vehicle interventions: Visual attention and driving performance. *Accid. Anal. Prev.* **2023**, *191*, 107195. [CrossRef]
14. Krishna, K.V.; Choudhary, P. Unravelling situational awareness of multitasking pedestrians through average gaze fixation durations. *Accid. Anal. Prev.* **2025**, *211*, 107912. [CrossRef]
15. Vijay, N.C.; Shankar, R.; Joshi, S. Do automation and digitalization distract drivers? A systematic review. *Accid. Anal. Prev.* **2025**, *211*, 107888. [CrossRef]
16. Huang, W.-C.; Lin, C.-H.; Yu, P. Enhancing safety in conditionally automated driving: Visual information and hazard visibility. *Accid. Anal. Prev.* **2024**, *205*, 107687. [CrossRef]
17. AlKheder, S. Naturalistic road advertisements and driver attention: An eye-tracking and ML approach. *Expert Syst. Appl.* **2024**, *252*, 124222. [CrossRef]
18. Yu, Z.; Xu, G.; Jiang, K.; Feng, Z.; Xu, S. Constructing the behavioral sequence of the takeover process—TOR, behavior characteristics and phases division: A real vehicle experiment. *Accid. Anal. Prev.* **2023**, *186*, 107040. [CrossRef]
19. Li, C.; Wang, T.; Zhou, L.; Xu, M. Avatar-mediated communication in collaborative virtual environments. *Comput. Hum. Behav.* **2025**, *167*, 108598. [CrossRef]
20. Bigné, E.; Ruiz, C.; Andreu, L.; Hernández, B. Furnishing your home? The impact of voice-assistant avatars in VR shopping. *Comput. Hum. Behav.* **2024**, *153*, 108104. [CrossRef]
21. Tang, T.; Zhang, Q.; Li, J.; Xu, P. eHMI designs for automated vehicles: Decisions, comprehension, and safety effects. *Accid. Anal. Prev.* **2025**, *222*, 108227. [CrossRef]
22. Gomolka, Z.; Kordos, D.; Zeslawska, E. The Application of Flexible Areas of Interest to Pilot Mobile Eye Tracking. *Sensors* **2020**, *20*, 986. [CrossRef]
23. Jiang, H.; Zhao, J.; Chen, X.; Li, S. Eye-tracking-based deep learning analysis for early diabetic-retinopathy detection. *Biomed. Signal Process. Control* **2023**, *84*, 104830. [CrossRef]
24. Acquafredda, M.; Binda, P. Pupillometry indexes ocular-dominance plasticity. *Vis. Res.* **2024**, *222*, 108449. [CrossRef] [PubMed]
25. Mairon, R.; Ben-Shahar, O. Polar saccadic-flow model: Re-modeling center bias from fixations to saccades. *Vis. Res.* **2025**, *228*, 108546. [CrossRef]
26. Yang, F.-Y.; Wang, H.-Y. Tracking Visual Attention during Learning of Complex Science Concepts with Augmented 3D Visualizations. *Computers & Education* **2023**, *193*, 104659. [CrossRef]
27. Lopes, A.; Pereira, M.; Batista, J.; Rodrigues, F. Eye tracking in digital pathology: A comprehensive review. *J. Pathol. Inform.* **2024**, *15*, 100189. [CrossRef] [PubMed]
28. Garlichs, A.; Lustig, M.; Gamer, M.; Blank, H. Expectations guide predictive eye movements and information sampling during face recognition. *iScience* **2024**, *27*, 110920. [CrossRef]
29. Chakravarthula, P.N.; Suffridge, J.E.; Wang, S. Gaze dynamics during natural-scene memorization and recognition. *Cognition* **2025**, *259*, 106098. [CrossRef] [PubMed]

30. Gurtner, L.M.; Laeng, B.; Kowler, E. Eye movements during visual imagery and perception. *Cognition* **2021**, *212*, 104693. [CrossRef]
31. Goodwin, S.; Prouzeau, A.; Whitelock-Jones, R.; Hurter, C.; Lawrence, L.; Afzal, U.; Dwyer, T. VETA: Visual eye-tracking analytics for exploration of gaze behavior. *Vis. Inform.* **2022**, *6*, 1–13. [CrossRef]
32. Luo, Z.; Shen, Y.; Xu, L.; Chen, H. Eye-tracking in identifying visualizers and verbalizers in learning. *Data Brief* **2019**, *25*, 104240. [CrossRef]
33. Kurzhals, K Anonymizing eye-tracking stimuli with stable diffusion. *Comput. Graph.* **2024**, *119*, 103898. [CrossRef]
34. Monier, F.; Durand, M.; Priot, A.-E. Ocular vergences measurement in virtual reality: A pilot study. *Vis. Res.* **2025**, *234*, 108658. [CrossRef] [PubMed]
35. Huang, L.; Chen, P.; Li, Z.; Wang, S. Eye-tracking analysis of expressway guide-sign recognition. *Accid. Anal. Prev.* **2024**, *205*, 107637. [CrossRef]

applied sciences

MDPI

Review

Situational Awareness Assessment of Drivers Boosted by Eye-Tracking Metrics: A Literature Review

Claudia Yohana Arias-Portela [1,*], Jaime Mora-Vargas [1] and Martha Caro [2]

1 Tecnologico de Monterrey, Departamento de Ingenieria Industrial, Mexico City 52290, Mexico; jmora@tec.mx
2 Departamento de Ingeniería Industrial, Pontificia Universidad Javeriana, Bogotá 110321, Colombia; mpcaro@javeriana.edu.co
* Correspondence: a00834073@tec.mx

Abstract: The conceptual framework for assessing the situational awareness (SA) of drivers consists of three hierarchical levels: perception of the elements of the environment, comprehension of the elements, and decision-making in the near future. A common challenge in evaluating SA is the determination of the available subjective and objective techniques and their selection and integration into methodologies. Among the objective techniques, eye tracking is commonly used, considering the influence of gaze behavior on driving. This review is presented as an innovative approach to the subject matter, introducing physiological metrics based on eye tracking and investigating their application in assessing the SA of drivers. In addition, experiments and methodologies that revealed patterns at the three levels of SA were identified. For this purpose, databases were searched, and 38 papers were considered. Articles were clustered according to prevalent themes such as eye-tracking metrics, eye-tracking devices, experiment design, and the relationship between SA and eye-tracking. This review summarizes the main metrics and key findings for each article and reveals a wide relationship between the eye-tracking metrics and SA. The influence of appropriately calibrated equipment, refined data collection protocols, and adequate selection of the eye-tracking metrics was examined. Further reviews are needed to systematically collect more evidence.

Keywords: situational awareness; eye tracking; driving; gaze behavior; naturalistic driving; simulation-based experiments

1. Introduction

Understanding human cognitive capabilities and limitations in work environments are the essential objectives and main requirements specified by the International Labor Organization (ILO) for the design and management of work systems [1,2]. Among the cognitive determinants that proficiently influence human behavior are some factors pertaining to knowledge and strategic considerations. These factors play a pivotal role in realizing the primary objectives of a given task despite the conflicting demands and attentional fluctuations that govern the allocation of cognitive resources. The concept of situational awareness (SA) is relevant in the realm of the aforementioned attentional dynamics [3].

"SA refers to the perception of the elements in the environment within a volume of time and space, the comprehension of their meaning and the projection of their status of the near future" [4]. This domain encompasses the examination of diverse cognitive mechanisms, including the discernment of surroundings, assimilation of information, and anticipation of choices. From the viewpoint of human factors engineering (HFE), SA emerges as a focal point within an expansive realm of investigation pertaining to interactive human–machine systems [5,6].

SA may be assessed through both subjective and objective methodologies. In the former type, evaluations by observers or self-assessments by participants constitute the primary metrics; an example is the utilization of the situational awareness rating technique.

In the latter type, freeze-probe methods are commonly used. In this latter approach, participants are prompted to respond to a series of queries at a specific juncture during task execution; the task is then momentarily suspended, with or without prior notification, and the provided responses are juxtaposed with the prevailing circumstances; an example of a freeze-probe method is the situational awareness global assessment technique. Eye tracking is another objective technique that is conducive to real-time participant analysis and involves physiological measurements.

Eye tracking has been extensively employed for quantifying human performance and behavior. It presents a promising and viable alternative for appraising SA, and it can overcome the constraints associated with alternate approaches. This technique offers the distinct advantage of facilitating real-time measurements or assessments within simulated contexts while minimizing disruptions [7]. It mitigates problems such as participants resorting to long-term memory utilization, which is encountered in freeze-probe methods, to elucidate subtasks or elaborate on task-specific details [8]. Eye tracking is one of the most commonly used techniques in SA research [9].

In HFE, operational difficulties can occur during an activity when SA is lost or when mental breakdowns occur during complex tasks [3]. SA assumes a pivotal role in the examination of performance in intricate tasks. It is characterized by the swift assimilation of stimuli and environmental information, coupled with the demand for long-term memory utilization. Thus, SA plays a particularly salient role in scenarios marked by persistent disruptions that originate from shifting surroundings and necessitate a discerning decision-making process about impending events. An important example of such multifaceted tasks is the act of driving [5,10–12].

SA has received immense attention over the past years in different fields of study, particularly in the field of driving [5,13]. The cognitive functioning and measurement of the SA is a key field of study of the performance and behavior of drivers. For instance, a previous study reported that 87.5% of drivers identified distracted driving as a greater concern compared to the past, while 87.9% perceived drowsiness as a safety threat [14].

The utilization of an eye-tracking device is a prevalent and extensively employed methodology for quantifying user performance and behavior. This technology facilitates capturing the human eye movement via pupillometry and a dedicated sensor; thus, the gaze points that signify the focal points within a given stimulus environment are recorded. This mechanism further permits quantification of the frequency of gaze point registrations per unit of time and is often measured in gaze points per second [15–17].

Eye tracking has been commonly used to identify the area of interest (AOI) of the gaze, behavior, and attention of drivers. In naturalistic driving, eye tracking has been used by harvester operators in the field of forestry and to track mine workers and train traffic monitoring; it has also been applied in autonomous vehicles [18]. Simulation driving presents boundless opportunities to measure the three levels of SA using, for instance, remotely controlled cars, commercial vehicles, autonomous vehicles, truck platooning, and crawler and wheeled excavators.

Considering the lacunae in research on the relation between eye-tracking metrics and SA in the domain of driving, this study conducted a novel approach to this domain. The principal aim was to provide a substantive contribution to this field of study by elucidating the discernible relationship between eye-tracking metrics and SA in the context of driving, as well as the principal eye-tracking devices used, experimental designs, and a discussion.

The rest of the paper is organized as follows: Section 2 describes the methodology used for selecting the studies for review, the exclusion criteria, and the information that was extracted for this review. Section 3 discusses scientometric and demographic analyses, the physiological measures and oculomotor events, experimental environments, definitions and types of eye trackers, and the relationship between SA and eye tracking in the field of driving. The final section concludes the article.

2. Materials and Methods

For this review, this study performed a systematic and descriptive analysis to identify the most relevant literature. The methodology employed in selecting noteworthy studies is graphically depicted in Figure 1. The review comprises three phases: identification, screening, and inclusion of records. In the first phase of identification, the preliminary search generated a list of 190 documents, and two records were removed before screening. In this phase, the strategy involved formulating a guiding question to facilitate the identification, evaluation, and synthesis of research in the domain of driving while assessing its relevance throughout the review process. The search strategy employed allowed us to potentially identify as many eligible studies as possible. In identification phase, all reviewers actively participated in determining the eligibility of a record for inclusion in the review. Scopus and Web of Science databases were systematically queried to source a spectrum of the current research, encompassing diverse domains and potential areas of inquiry [19].

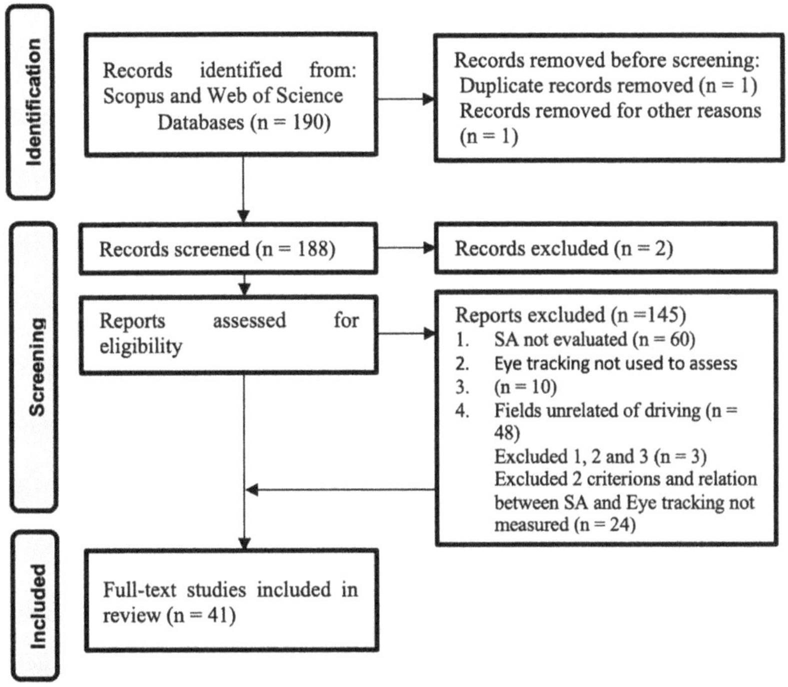

Figure 1. Process used to identify and select relevant studies [20].

To curate the search terms for the databases, we adopted a bifurcated approach. First, the recent literature review of [9] was used to extract multiple variations and acronyms of the keyword "situational awareness", i.e., "SA", "situation awareness" and "awareness state"; similarly, for the second keyword, i.e., "eye-tracking", we used multiple variations: "eye-tracking", "eye-tracker", "eye movements", "gaze patterns", "eye moves", "eye track", and "gaze behavior" (including those that assess visual attention, gaze behavior, and perception).

Psychological measurements or data obtained from humans by using sensors [9] and oculomotor events were defined and classified based on the recent reviews by [9,21].

Second, we focused on keywords covering the scope of study delineated in this review—specifically, the domain of driving. Hence, we considered terms such as "driving", "drive", "drives", "automobilist", "chauffeur", and "vehicle operator", among others, across contexts that included autonomous, semiautonomous motor, commercial, and heavy vehicles, within the realms of both naturalistic driving and driving simulation. The terminology "naturalistic driving" refers to experiments conducted in authentic field settings, while "driving simulation" refers to experiments conducted via laboratory simulations or virtual reality. To facilitate the bibliographic exploration within the databases, the Boolean operators "AND" and "OR" were judiciously employed.

For the screening phase, 188 reports were assessed for eligibility, and the citations and bibliographical information, abstracts, and keywords were extracted and screened. The following inclusion criteria were used: articles dealing with (1) assessment of SA in humans, (2) assessment of SA with eye tracking (these may contain additional assessment tools, i.e., questionnaires, encephalograms, etc.), and (3) application of assessment of SA in the domain of driving. Restrictions on eligibility criteria, such as language, were considered; only records in English were kept in the sample, and access restrictions (publication status) were considered.

Furthermore, we used the following exclusion criteria: (1) SA was not evaluated; instead, only the stress or mental workload was measured. However, these articles were included if they measured a psychological variable other than SA. (2) Eye tracking was not used to assess SA. (3) The study pertained to fields unrelated to driving. Throughout this phase, all reviewers participated in addressing selection bias as part of adherence to eligibility criteria. Any disagreements regarding adherence were reviewed and discussed among the reviewers to reach consensus. Similarly, an author took samples from the excluded records to verify that the eligibility criteria had been applied correctly. Records selected were organized in an Excel spreadsheet and shared with the author reviewers for subsequent reading. In total, 145 reports were excluded, and 41 documents were selected for full-text review. In the review, each selected document was studied, and the following information was extracted:

1. Citation and bibliographical information, keywords, and sources (for the scientometric analysis);
2. Demographic information of the experiments, i.e., sample size, gender, age, and the field of application;
3. Eye-tracking metrics and oculomotor events;
4. Experimental environment, i.e., naturalistic driving or driving simulation
5. Type of eye trackers used;
6. Discussion of the relationship between SA and eye tracking in the context of driving.

The selected papers were managed using Mendeley Reference Manager. To conduct the citation in the desired style, the Zotero Reference Manager was employed. Furthermore, in the final stages of the review, we included three records through the use of additional search query combinations for a total of 41 documents selected for full-text review. Throughout this phase, the review authors actively engaged in independent reading of the articles and shared their findings during meeting sessions to resolve discrepancies.

In the total documents selected for a full-text review, efforts were made to ensure that the collected data were sufficient for both the review authors and readers, aligning the extracted information with the research question. Additionally, all data were systematically collected and cataloged in an Excel spreadsheet for easy reference.

3. Results

A total of 41 reports were selected for this literature review. These pertained to various topics such as the evaluation of SA, use of eye tracking, main physiological variables measured in gaze behavior, and experimental designs. Furthermore, these reports also describe the methodologies that revealed patterns in the three levels of SA.

3.1. Scientometric Analysis

Based on the analysis of the 41 documents selected for full-text review and using the freely accessible software Bibliometrix version 4.1.4 [22], we described the growth trend of the study of SA with eye tracking in the field of driving in terms of citation and bibliographical information.

The line chart in Figure 2 gives information on the annual scientific production in the study of SA based on eye tracking in the field of driving for the period 2011–2023. Annual scientific production over five years from 2011 remained steady, while it underwent an irregular fluctuation in the period 2016–2018. However, for 2018, we see a steady but remarkable rise in the number of articles. This is also seen in Figure 3, which shows the accumulated rise in the number of occurrences of the keywords "SA", "eye-tracking", and "driving" within the literature. Eye tracking related to the study of physiological measures of SA experienced a rapid surge in 2015 and reached a point of inflection in 2019.

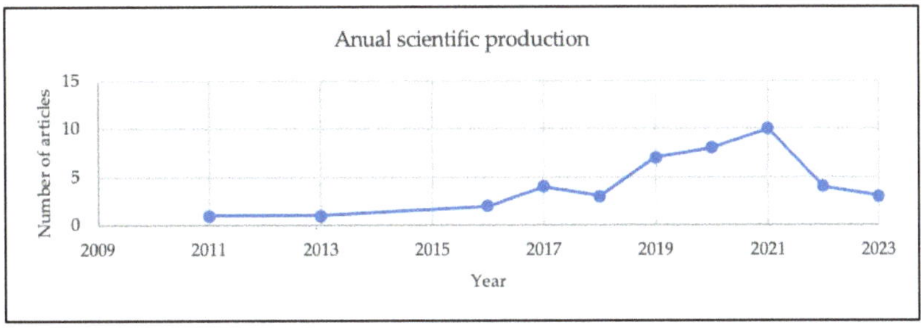

Figure 2. Annual scientific production in the study of SA based on eye tracking in the field of driving.

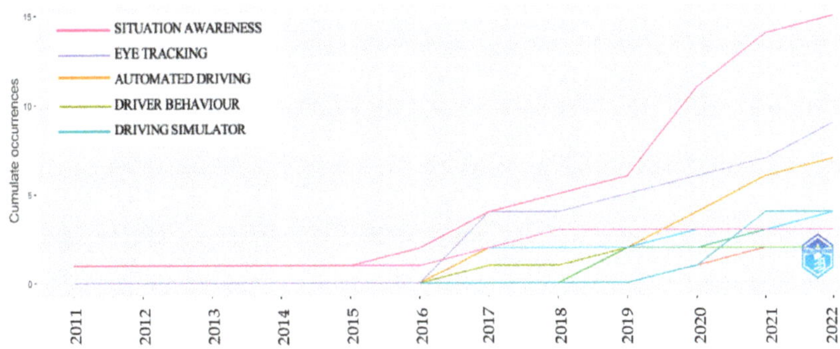

Figure 3. Rise in the occurrences of keywords. Source: own elaboration using Bibliometrix.

Moreover, out of the 41 selected documents, 29 were published in different scientific journals and 12 in conference proceedings. The most relevant sources are summarized in Table 1; *Human Factors* and *Transportation Research Part F: Traffic Psychology and Behavior* are the main journals in which the research was published. In all, 97% of the articles belong to quartiles of scientific journals Q1 and Q2, and the review included an average of 3.5 authors per document, with 40 multi-author papers and one single-authored article.

Table 1. Most relevant sources (top 5) from among the 41 selected documents.

Sources (Journal)	Articles
Human Factors	6
Transportation Research Part F: Traffic Psychology and Behavior	5
Lecture Notes in Computer Science	5
Accident Analysis and Prevention	2
IEEE Intelligent Vehicles Symposium Proceedings	2

Furthermore, about 133 authors were devoted to the study of SA with eye tracking in the context of driving. The most relevant and cited authors who have contributed to this topic are Curry R., de Winter J., Gabbard J., Happe R., and Katrahmani A. Furthermore, the number of citations of each article was reviewed to identify papers with major impacts; these papers include those of [23–25], with 358 citations in total. The most relevant affiliations and countries are listed in Table 2 and Figure 4, with Purdue University (USA) as the predominant institution, followed by the Delft University of Technology (the Netherlands), reporting on this topic. Only two studies originated from developing nations.

Table 2. Most relevant affiliations (top 5) from among the 41 selected documents.

Affiliations	Articles
Purdue University (USA)	11
Delft University of Technology (Netherlands)	10
Beihang University (China)	5
Institute for Occupational Safety and Health of the German Social Accident Insurance (IFA) (Germany)	5
Mälardalen University (Sweden)	5

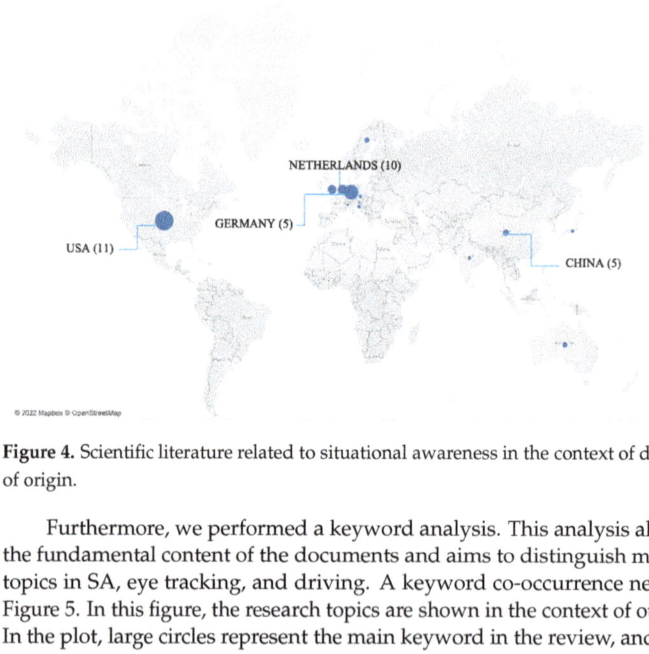

Figure 4. Scientific literature related to situational awareness in the context of driving by the country of origin.

Furthermore, we performed a keyword analysis. This analysis allows us to capture the fundamental content of the documents and aims to distinguish meaningful research topics in SA, eye tracking, and driving. A keyword co-occurrence network is shown in Figure 5. In this figure, the research topics are shown in the context of our literature review. In the plot, large circles represent the main keyword in the review, and the lines between keywords show the strengths of their correlation [26].

In Figure 5, four keyword clusters show the relationship among the main keywords, and synonyms and keywords with common meanings were identified in the review. The first category encompasses the examination of SA, delving into physiological measurement and the apprehension of driver behavior (indicated in red). Similarly, the second category pertains to eye tracking, encompassing driver behavior, pupillometry, and visual perception (represented in blue). The third category deals with driver gaze behavior, encompassing human–vehicle interactions and accidents (indicated in orange). Finally, the fourth category deals with real-time SA in conjunction with human factors and driver support (represented in green).

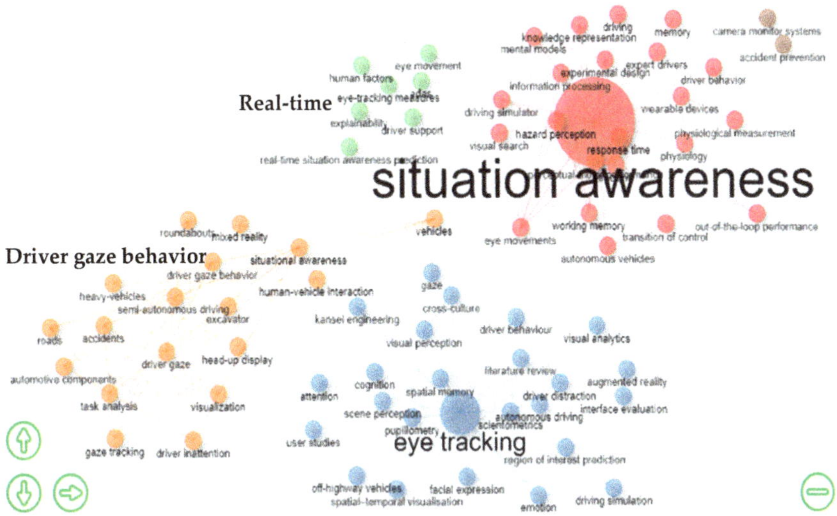

Figure 5. Keywords co-occurrence analysis publications. The first category (red) deals with the examination of SA, physiological measurement, and driver behavior. The second category (blue) deals with eye tracking, driver behavior, pupillometry, and visual perception. The third category (orange) deals with driver gaze behavior, human–vehicle interactions, and accidents. The fourth category (green) deals with real-time SA, human factors, and driver support. Source: own elaboration using Bibliometrix.

3.2. Demographic Analysis of the Experiments

Within the compiled body of studies, a discernible pattern emerged: experiments pertaining to the measurement of SA in drivers via eye tracking, along with metrics analyzing driver behavior covering aspects such as hazard perception, attention allocation, driver distraction, visual perception, and vigilance, consistently featured a selection of two distinct vehicle categories for experimental trials—commercial and industrial vehicles.

For the scope of this review, commercial vehicles refer to vehicles designed to transport products or passengers with or without business purposes, and industrial vehicles refer to any vehicle that is used to lift, stow, load, push, or stack materials. Within the sample of 35 articles that dealt with driving experiments, 29 of them were based on commercial vehicles, which represent 85.4% of the sample; the remaining 14.6% of the sample dealt with industrial vehicles.

The primary category of industrial vehicles considered in studies on SA included covered forestry harvesters, wheel loaders, excavators, dump trucks, wheeled excavators, mobile cranes [18], truck platooning [27], forklifts [28], and crawler and wheeled excavators [29,30]. The commercial vehicles were mainly passenger and goods vehicles [31–34], school vehicles [35], and automated vehicles [36–38].

Conversely, with regard to the gender-based distribution of participation, a discernible and noteworthy trend was observed in the significant involvement of male participants. All the selected studies taken together involved 906 participants. In the experiments on commercial vehicles, the participants were composed of 543 men and 334 women. Similarly, the participants in the experiments on industrial vehicles comprised three women and 26 men, as presented in Figure 6.

The age range of participants revealed that the average ages of male and female drivers were 26.44 and 27.94 years, respectively. In some of the studies, participant eligibility criteria included being the age of 18 years or more and holding a valid driver's license, as per the data collection protocol in those studies [36,39].

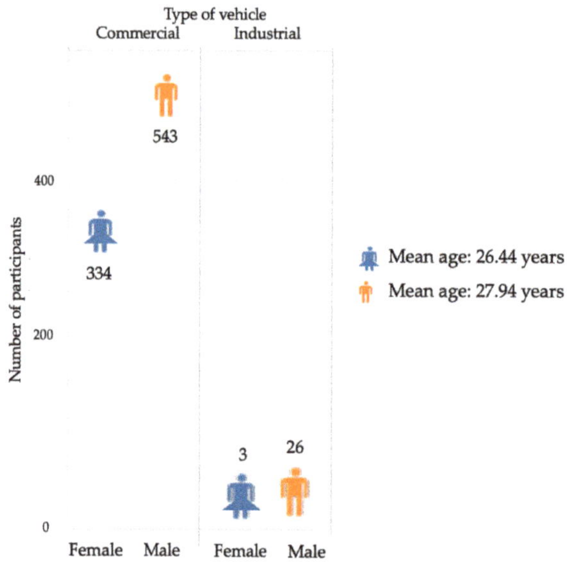

Figure 6. Participants by gender and types of vehicles.

3.3. Eye-Tracking Metrics and Oculomotor Events

Appendix A succinctly encapsulates the collective scholarly contributions of authors within the realm of the investigated eye-tracking metrics, as delineated and covered within this comprehensive literature review. The importance of their contributions has been reported in the literature [9,21].

Eye tracking has been increasingly used in studies on human behavior since 2002, perhaps following one of the largest studies on human behavior in the analysis of gaze patterns carried out by [40], with a significant rise in the field of study of driver behavior in 2013 [41]. Similarly, the use of eye tracking as an objective method and its rise as the commonly used method in studies on SA has witnessed a significant rise [9].

Among the selected studies in this review, 41 studies dealt with the use of eye tracking to investigate SA in drivers. In these studies, a total of 36 distinct oculomotor events—events pertaining to activities governed by the ocular motor system, facilitating the preservation of visual stability, and orchestrating gaze-oriented motions—were discerned and cataloged. For categorizing the metrics, we considered the classification and studies of [21] and [9], which were used as a reference. The oculomotor events that we examined are fixation, saccade, smooth pursuit, blinking, pupillometry measures, gaze, peripheral vision, tremors, microsaccade, and drift, with their respective metrics.

Figure 7 shows the proportion of eye-tracking measures in relation to the comprehensive scope of this review. Among the 41 studies incorporated within the review, 31 studies used the fixation metric as the fundamental component to study SA; 29 used count fixation and 25 used duration fixation for SA measurement; 17 studies used gaze direction; and 8 studies used the amplitude and rate of the saccade.

These studies revealed a direct relationship between physiological measures obtained through eye tracking and its emergence as the commonly used method in studies assessing SA. For instance, ref. [12] built a prediction model named light gradient boosting machine from the data collected with eye tracking to predict SA during the takeover transition period in conditionally automated driving; they recreated simulated driving scenarios with videos and by using PreScan 8.0.0. They found that fixations, followed by pupil diameter and saccades, had the highest importance in predicting SA. Reference [21] reported in their review that distracted drivers had higher fixation durations and lower fixation counts on the mirror or speedometer.

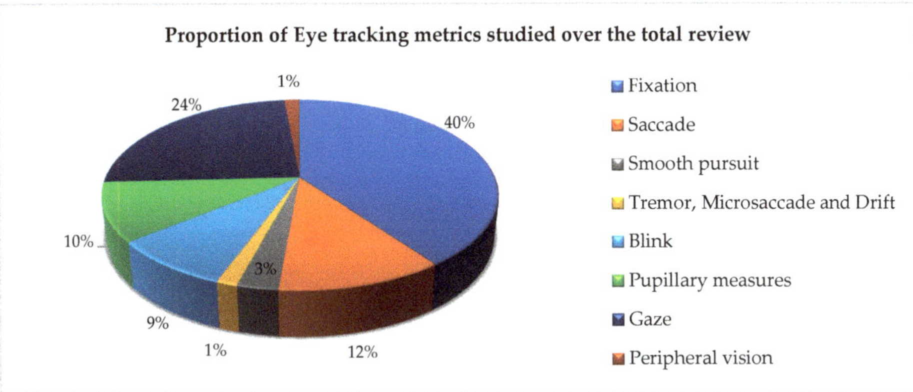

Figure 7. Proportion of eye-tracking measures over the total papers reviewed.

Likewise, ref. [32] observed that in a traffic scenario at an intersection in which the participants were instructed to memorize information and to build an understanding of the situation, commonly, participants fixed deflated spatial locations associated with the relevant information (level 3 of SA); in addition, when retrieving information associated with other road users, participants made considerably more saccades between empty locations on the screen.

Furthermore, ref. [31] examined instances in which drivers exhibited diminished awareness when approaching and entering a roundabout. They used three distinct eye-tracking devices and relied on metrics such as fixation duration, fixation count, and gaze direction to reveal that drivers, on average, allocated approximately 28.36% of their temporal focus to non-driving-related areas (NDRAs). Likewise, ref. [42] revealed consistency between fixation count and fixation duration on an object and showed that SA during simulated automated driving might be attributed to visual fixation patterns for various traffic scene elements. Similarly, ref. [43] investigated the safety implications of environment self-explaining design on drivers' situational awareness; it was noted that drivers exhibited the highest percentage of fixation number and fixation duration while traversing the yellow-green adorned sidewall tunnel.

Eight studies used pupillary measures for oculomotor movements. Reference [12] commented on the need for further research to understand the relationship between pupil diameter and SA and ranked pupil diameter as one of the most important measures for predicting SA when drivers scan their driving scenarios. In addition, ref. [32] measured pupil dilation during a memory task to evaluate the effects of mental workload in SA. Reference [44] developed assessments of driver situational awareness utilizing sensor-based methods, especially focusing on road signs. For this experiment, eye-tracking metrics such as average pupil size, eye blinks, and gaze-related features, including gaze visits and total fixation time, were employed. This method allowed AI systems to predict driver situational awareness in relation to levels 1 and 2 of the Endsley model (perception and comprehension). Reference [45], in their literature review, additionally highlighted that pupil measurements, specifically focusing on pupil diameter, may serve as an indication of the user's emotional arousal.

Additionally, ref. [34] established a safety analysis of work zone complexity with respect to driver characteristics by using fixations and pupillary measures and situation awareness, with longitudinal control, lateral control, gaze behavior, and daze behavior in the event of changes in SA because of the involvement of secondary visual tasks, for instance, text entry into a GPS unit in an active work zone and a lower perception of hazards.

Similarly, ref. [46] reported a relationship between the increase in pupil diameter and situations perceived as risky, showing that danger provokes a stress response that can be represented in terms of pupil diameter. However, it is not possible to establish this conclusively since videos on monitors were used in the experiment, and the pupil is sensitive to changes in light. Nonetheless, it is possible to measure whether these hazardous situations can be qualified as more dangerous than the nonhazardous situations from oculomotor metrics such as pupil diameter [46]. In addition, ref. [47] considered the effects of pre-takeover visual engagement or takeover request (TOR) warning and risk perception and revealed a correlation between the change in pupil diameter and visual attention—the more dispersed the visual attention, the greater the SA.

Other metrics included the blink rate, pupil position, and gaze angle, each of which was utilized in six studies. For instance, ref. [39] studied the role of an in-vehicle digital voice-assistant in conditionally automated vehicles; they stated that drivers could trust driving by an automatic vehicle and tend to fall asleep, thereby suspending the process of becoming alert, as measured by the rate and duration of saccades, as well as the pupil diameter.

Reference [48] examined the implications of uncertainty communication for automation and saccades and fixations with eye tracking. They reported that, presumably, operators could adjust their gaze behavior to the level of uncertainty. Reference [49] explored gaze prediction for drivers and used the probability for motion hypotheses and an approach based on a dynamic Bayesian network of fixations and saccades considering human gaze motion characteristics. Similarly, metrics such as smooth pursuit direction, blink rate and duration, pupil dilation, gaze velocity, and peripheral vision were used in studies on driver's gaze prediction in dynamic environments and in the study on driver distraction.

In Figure 8, we provide an overview of the eye-tracking metrics systematically categorized and identified within the context of this review. Orange bars indicate the primary metric associated with each distinct oculomotor event. In a majority of the studies, the assessment of SA in drivers was based on the deployment of metrics related to gaze fixation, gaze direction, pupil measurements, and saccades. In a relatively smaller proportion, relatively less importance was given to metrics such as smooth pursuit and blink measures. Furthermore, notably, the joint measurement of fixation and saccades was employed in 30% of the studies; a similar distribution was observed in the case of the joint measurement of pupil diameter and gaze fixation metrics.

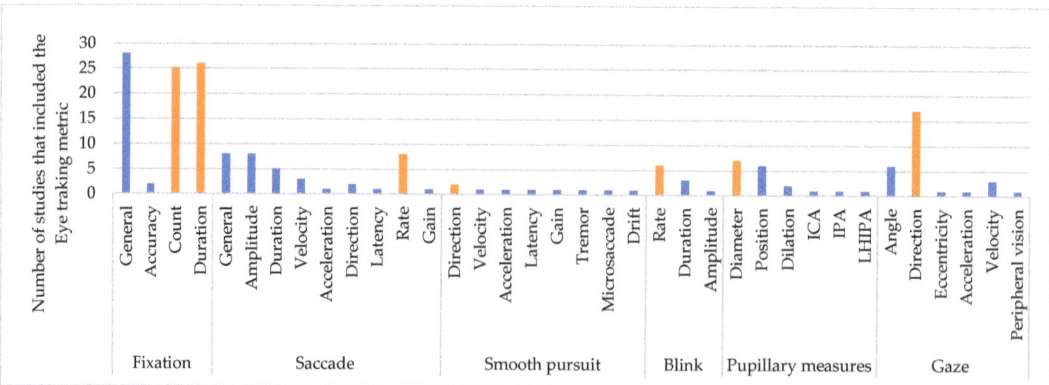

Figure 8. Comparison of the eye-tracking metrics in this review. Orange bars indicate the primary metric associated with each distinct oculomotor event.

In the experiments on industrial vehicles, 100% of the cases involved the use of gaze fixation in AOI, followed by the gaze direction, and finally, the position of the pupil and general evaluation of the saccade. In commercial vehicles, gaze fixation was used in 82% of the studies; this metric was followed by saccades, gaze direction, and pupillary measurements. Likewise, in experiments on automated vehicles, the amplitude and rate of the saccade, as well as the diameter of the pupil, were used as additional metrics along with gaze fixation to analyze differences in driver's SA and mental stress over time (level 1 of SA).

3.4. Experimental Environment: Naturalistic or Driving Simulation

Among the diverse factors contributing to the potential variance in assessing SA in drivers based on eye tracking, the contextual environment within which the experiment was conducted assumes pronounced importance. In this review, studies were categorized into driving simulation and naturalistic driving. Of the total number of studies reviewed, 76% were simulated driving experiments, and 24% were naturalistic driving experiments. Table 3 lists the driving simulators or simulation software used in the studies.

Table 3. Driving simulators or simulation software used in the studies.

Author	Driving Simulator or Simulation Software
[12]	Prescan 8.0.0
[32]	VicomEditor
[36]	AVSimulation
[50]	Lab CARRS-Q, QUT
[47]	National Advanced Driving Simulator—NADS, miniSim™
[39]	STISIM Drive 3 software (Version 2.8)
[51]	Ergonomics lab of the University of Missouri-Columbia, OpenDS driving simulation
[52]	CARLA simulator
[53]	Vicom Editor©
[23]	Prescan 8.0.0
[34]	IniSim (NADS)
[54]	Not present in the report
[55]	Not present in the report
[56]	Honda Research Institute, augmented reality (AR) head-up display (AR HUD)
[48]	TISIM Drive system
[30]	CAVE-like room
[57]	AR and pedestrian collision warnings
[58]	ST-Software platform
[49]	Not present in the report
[42]	Not present in the report
[46]	PreScan 7.0
[24]	University of Leeds Driving Simulator, Jaguar S-type cab
[59]	MODATS
[60]	Motion system of the WIVW
[25]	Not present in the report
[43]	3D Max software 2023
[44]	A3 motion simulator

Of the studies that used a driving simulator, 94% were simulated driving scenarios comprising video-based laboratory experiments, and 6% were a mix of virtual reality (VR) for instance [44], augmented reality (AR), and driving simulator experiments [30,56,57]. For the simulations, the authors used different types of software to recreate simulated driving scenarios with videos in testing laboratories.

Similarly, ref. [12] tested 32 simulated driving scenarios with six lengths for durations of 1–20 s using PreScan 8.0.0. The purpose of their study was to create a model that allowed real-time monitoring and predicting of SA in automated driving. It is significant that the study recommends conducting the study in high-fidelity driving simulators or naturalistic driving based on data collection in a low-fidelity setup [47].

Moreover, ref. [32] conducted a video-based laboratory experiment to evaluate the SA and its effects on working memory. In all, 18 traffic scenarios and three practice videos were used; the total duration was 7000 ms, and the scenarios were created by Vicom Editor. Dynamic traffic scenarios were designed, and participants were trained to memorize the information and interpret the situation. Nonetheless, the study suggests that further studies can be realized in a dynamic situation. Likewise, ref. [50] performed a high-fidelity simulator study in the Advanced Driving Simulator of the Center of Accident Research and Road Safety, Queensland (CARRS-Q, QUT). They evaluated three interventions, namely, uncertainty display, interruption of non-driving-related tasks (NDRTs), and a combination of both, to evaluate the interfaces that address the difficulty of missing the SA or being out-of-the-loop.

Reference [47] used a medium-fidelity fixed-base driving simulator of the National Advanced Driving Simulator (NADS), miniSim™, to evaluate the relation of the pre-takeover state of drivers in the context of NDRTs and to evaluate how this state affects level 3 SA. The study highly recommends validating the results in an automated driving vehicle in real time in more naturalistic environments. Further, reference [51] analyzed the driver's emotional state and physiological feelings using OpenDS driving simulation software in the Ergonomics lab of the University of Missouri (Columbia). The simulation can contribute to advanced driver assistance systems in the future; nevertheless, it remains subjective and does not capture the feelings induced in the driver by simulated surrounding road environments in real time.

Research conducted in authentic, real-world environments is regarded optimal for validating study variables. While it can be posited that such an approach incurs high costs and necessitates more extensive investment in the formulation of ethical, safety, and data collection protocols, the advantages are notable. The advantages include the capacity to capture the nuanced dynamics of the environment and the real-time analysis of driver emotions, reactions, attentional patterns, and perceptions of the contextual elements. In doing so, this approach counters the potential subjectivity inherent in simulations, while also examining the prospective trajectory of research within the majority of studies included in this review.

Amid the array of naturalistic studies incorporated within the scope of this review, reference [18] evaluated SA in diverse industrial vehicles in naturalistic driving scenarios. The vehicles considered include a forestry harvester, a wheel loader, an excavator, a dump truck, a wheeled excavator, and a mobile crane. The study evaluates how eye tracking can be used to evaluate the attention of operators. The major activities evaluated and measured were cutting, unloading, reversing, and lifting. These activities were evaluated using cameras and sensors to range visualization around the vehicle. The study highlights the need for more studies focused on the industrial environment since such studies are rare; there are considerable advantages of being able to use real data without interfering with the work being carried out.

Furthermore, ref. [37] studied the visual load and the associated loss of SA by examining the takeover and driving NDRT performance. A relevant conclusion of the study validates that in the real world, drivers' responses are primarily instinctive and swifter than those observed in simulators, whereas physical and cognitive loads may not have a significant impact on reaction times, as suggested in some simulated studies.

On the other hand, ref. [27] evaluated the SA and perceived sleepiness of 10 professional truck drivers who worked with a two-vehicle platooning system. One of the discussions deals with the number of participants since, although the experiment was conducted under naturalistic conditions, it also dealt with a smaller sample compared to laboratory experiments, and the eye-tracking measurement was less reliable than in laboratory settings because of variable light conditions.

In a notable study by [61], emphasis was placed on the examination of natural gaze patterns within street intersections. The primary objective was to glean insights into the capacity of gaze behavior to serve as an indicator of driver awareness, thereby facilitating predictions of SA. They examined the potential utility of gaze metrics in relation to distinct road users while also highlighting the significance of obtaining pertinent information of the entirety of the visual field. The study underscored the challenges associated with recreating the dynamic real-world environment and authentic AOIs within experimental methodologies.

Likewise, ref. [33] found that the relevance of data collection from experiments in real environments relapses; for instance, in the design of future advanced driver assistance systems (ADAS), if the SA of the driver is known, the ADAS will administer critical information to the driver in risky situations or when required. Thus, the driver's SA can be regained more rapidly and confidently. Reference [58] also demonstrated that the driver first tries to obtain a mental map of the situation by looking around rather than by paying attention to the road and its risks, as predicted by the recovery of SA theory.

Let us discuss the naturalist experiments to explore two phases, the training and the assessment of the participants, as conducted by [35]. For instance, a 30 min long training session was completed at the Center for Advanced Training Research and Naturalistic Studies; this training system is called the engaged driver training system (EDTS), and it allows us to elevate the hazard perception skills of the drivers and helps examine the effectiveness of the EDTS training program on drivers.

Finally, in the study of [29] relevant information was obtained for reversing movements in crawlers and wheeled excavators by using mirrors during regular work on construction; most of the studies in their review dealt with the importance of helping workers become accustomed to the measurement equipment prior to data collection, the use of written informed consents, and approval of data collection protocols; thus, they explored the means that allow establishing safer behaviors and helping to reduce accidents by increasing levels of SA in drivers via assistance tools.

3.5. Eye Trackers: Definition and Types

In this review, we identified and examined a total of 24 distinct eye-tracking devices, each playing a role in the conducted experiments. These findings are documented in Table A2 of Appendix A; these findings are further shown in Figure 9. Tobbi Pro and X2-60 glasses were the most used eye trackers in all the studies considered in this review, and Pupil Lab using Python API was the second most used eye tracker. SmartEye Pro and DR120 were the third most used eye trackers, and Fovio and Eyelink with Eye Works Suite were used, albeit less frequently, within studios.

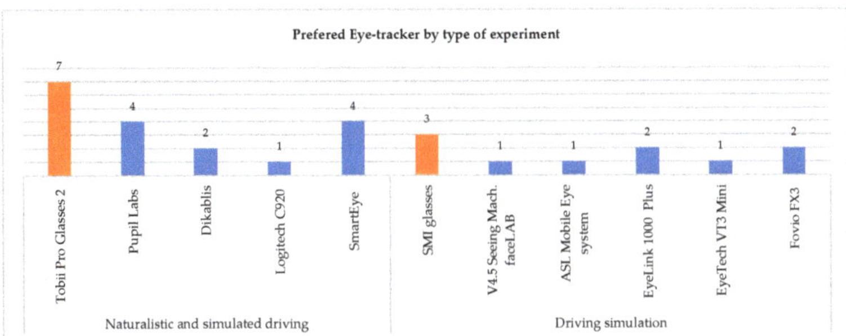

Figure 9. Preferred eye trackers by number of experiments in which their use is reported. Orange bars indicate the primary eye tracker associated with each experiment.

An eye tracker is a device based on pupillometry, and a sensor captures the human eye movement by recording gaze points that indicate where a human is looking in an environment with a stimulus and measuring how many gaze points are registered per second [15–17].

The advantages of each eye tracker are interpreted by the communication between the device and data storage, analysis software, ease of interpreting the data, and data visualization, as well as the fact that the equipment is as less intrusive as possible for the operator; less intrusive equipment allows the process to continue without interruptions and ensure proper calibration time. With regard to demographics and cultural characteristics, reference [31] considered the difference in pupil color between Asians and Caucasians, and [42] reported large cultural SA differences between drivers hailing from Japan and the USA. In addition, reference [59] found that teenage drivers have a lower level of SA than adults while driving.

In the experiments, particularly in naturalistic driving experiments, daylight can be unpredictable because of dynamic conditions and can cause difficulties in reading the device data by the human eye; hence, reference [31] used illuminators to illuminate the driver's retina to compensate for the dim ambient light. Reference [33] used an infrared (IR) illuminator to reduce the effects of poorly illuminated environments; because IR is not visible to the human eye, it does not distract the driver. Additionally, note that several of the eye trackers generate some interference with the equipment used by the operator, and frequencies greater than 50 Hz are preferable for eye trackers.

Finally, it is noteworthy that, for the assessment of potential biases arising from incomplete or unavailable data, a manual approach was employed for the total of reviewers. At the outset, a comprehensive search strategy was accomplished within the literature review to minimize the risk of overlooking relevant studies. The use of databases and conference proceedings contributed to this endeavor. In some instances, authors were contacted to gain access to their studies. For instance, Gwangbin Kim [44] affably provided complete access to his publication.

Additionally, the reviewers systematically categorized the criteria used to determine which results were eligible for inclusion. In this context, the criteria were grouped into the following: (1) Keywords and co-occurrence analysis in publications for scientometric analysis. (2) Demographic information, including sample size, gender, age, and any other relevant factors such as experience in the function. (3) The type of vehicle used in the experiment, categorized as either commercial or industrial. Metrics that were collected through eye tracking and reported included fixations, saccades, smooth pursuit, tremor, microsaccades, drift, blinks and their classifications, pupillary measures, gaze, and peripheral vision.

Furthermore, the reviewers included a synthesis of the experimental environment in the results. These were grouped into naturalistic driving or driving simulations, selected from the reports, and documented the specifics of each experiment. For naturalistic settings, details included the type of activity conducted, while for simulated settings, information covered the types of simulators used and the software supporting data analysis. In the reporting of the types of eye trackers used, it was necessary to mention the brand and analysis software, but only if reported. Certainly, attention was paid to the points where the authors focused their efforts to demonstrate or present the existing relationships between eye-tracking metrics for the subjective assessment of situational awareness in the driving experiment. This compilation of categorizations and criteria allowed us to define which results were eligible for inclusion in each synthesis.

Lastly, regarding the selected studies, data were available either in the main article or appendices. Within this study, it is crucial to consider that minimizing biases in studies can also be achieved by exploring metrics different from the common ones, as reported in this literature review, aligning with the objectives of research designs in evaluating situational awareness in the field of driving.

4. Discussion

In this literature review, one of the principal aims was to investigate the objective assessment of situational awareness in drivers based on physiological metrics obtained through eye tracking. Our approach utilized a systematic literature review, and papers dealing with the assessment of SA in humans with eye tracking in the domain of driving were incorporated. Furthermore, our literature review encompassed a scientometric analysis, which identified prevalent authors and topics in the field. Similarly, we conducted a demographic analysis of the experiments and a compiled and comprehensive list of the eye-tracking metrics employed in these experiments. Additionally, we incorporated a compilation of experimental environments, classifying them into real (naturalistic) and simulated environments, and documented the primary devices utilized in these studies. The potential utility of gaze metrics in the assessment of SA was observed.

Several explanations included in this review substantiate the robust relation between gaze behavior and SA, particularly within the context of driving activities that are characterized by their predominantly visual nature. These relationships are consistent with literature reviews such as that conducted by [9], where, among all the identified physiological measures, the eye-tracking technique is the most prevalent to assess SA.

This alignment could enable the authors to explore how gaze behavior can signify various cognitive aspects of driver awareness and behavior, such as visual attention distribution, attentional patterns, distraction, remembered information, mental workload, decision-making, and prediction models of SA.

Central to this understanding is the exploration of visual attention and attentional patterns inherent in the execution of complex tasks by individuals [8]. The first investigations of patterns in driving and visual attention with the use of eye trackers date back to the works of Mourant and Rockwell (1970, 1972) using an eye-marker camera and a stabilization unit [11].

Reference [18] performed research on measuring attention in the visualization of the graphical interface in different industrial vehicles and reported that by measuring the pupil position and the duration and count of fixations on and off the screen, it is possible to observe the spatial awareness and monitor the points of attention of the operator.

For example, ref. [29] investigated the use of mirrors for eye tracking during work at construction sites. Surprisingly, they found something different than expected: the operator spent less than 7% of his attention on the display. Studies on eye tracking open the door to obtaining objective information from the operator to make decisions regarding display design, for example, the use of head-up displays in the driver's line of sight and support training of the operators to increase the SA of the driver as demonstrated by [35], who reported that trained drivers had better performance and SA.

Reference [24] performed a similar study and evaluated the visual attention distribution of drivers during automation and examined the influence of the scenarios around the driver on the increase in SA. These studies show that gaze fixation, pupil diameter, and saccades are the major metrics for predicting SA. As evidence, the study finds that a high number of fixations can be associated with the difficulty of gathering information, and additionally, saccade amplitudes are negatively correlated with SA, and the results have a high similitude to the study of [62]. The observations further underscore the intricate interplay between visual search patterns and error reduction.

Similarly, ref. [47] investigated adaptable systems. They examined the effects of pre-takeover visual engagement on situation awareness during automated driving. Their results suggested that natural driving without previously marked tasks benefits drivers' SA more than asking drivers to pay more attention to the path when driving. The eye-tracking metrics, such as peripheral vision, pupil diameter, rate of saccades, and general fixation, suggest differences in the SA of drivers in observation windows of 7 s. They concluded that dispersed visual attention has a positive correlation with better SA. Studies such as those of [62] support and validate the idea that SA in humans is related to the fixation of their eyes on relevant objects [11], and various studies revealed a positive relationship between eye-tracking metrics and SA [9].

Regarding distraction, reference [21] presented the research of Recarte and Nunes (2000), who studied the relationship of SA with eye tracking to identify patterns in driver distraction. The review reported that higher fixation durations, higher pupil dilations, and lower fixation counts in the display of the vehicle or mirror are related to driver distraction. Likewise, the review also explained how fixations allow us to understand the visual perception processes and how much of the visual gaze is retained.

Concerning remembered information and mental workload, reference [32] studied the count and duration of the fixations and their relation with different information retrieval patterns through the gaze; they also examined how the metrics are related to the information remembered by the driver and the behavior, as a part or due to the mental interpretation of the trajectory traversed rather than based on retrieving individual pieces of information.

Other studies [30,34,54] explored the safety analysis of work zone complexity and the influence of different attention allocation strategies under mental workloads on SA based on the metrics of count and duration of fixations, diameter and position of the pupil, and gaze direction. These studies showed that an increase in the complexity of the driving zones increases the mental workload and decreases SA. Furthermore, the mental workload can increase by 37% if a secondary visual task is involved; this has immediate repercussions on the gaze behavior, leading to a lower perception of risks and a lower level of safety perception of the situation.

Additionally, ref. [50] made an interesting statement regarding the construction of new adaptable systems that include the human–machine relationship with SA. They reported the ability of the operator to be prepared to "fallback-ready user", even performing secondary tasks and recovering awareness in the main operation by studying SA with real-time data from eye trackers. Likewise, reference [12] built a prediction model of SA during takeover transitions in conditionally automated driving with only eye-tracking data.

In terms of the metrics used, specifically, 89% of authors using at least three commonly employed eye-tracking metrics, such as gaze fixation, pupil diameter, and saccades, found eye tracking to be an objective indicator of SA. Fixations were the most utilized metric in the experiments, aligning with studies such as the one conducted by [12]. It was found that within the relationships with the measurement of situational awareness in drivers, at the perceptual level (level 1), an excessive number of fixations might be associated with difficulty in gathering information during demanding tasks. Additionally, it was observed that distracted drivers had higher fixation durations. Furthermore, the mean fixation time of eye movement was noted to have the potential to measure situational awareness, as presented by [54]. Combining saccades with fixations is the second most used metric for measuring SA, although saccade amplitudes were found to be negatively correlated with SA, as reported by [12].

However, it is crucial to consider the limitations of using eye-tracking metrics. Certain metrics may excel in measuring perception (level 1 of SA) but may have less relevance to comprehension (level 2) and projection (level 3), as presented in the research by [59].

In terms of the scientometric analysis, eye-tracking-related research on physiological measures of SA has experienced a rapid surge since 2015. Common themes associated with eye-tracking studies include automated driving, driver behavior, driving simulation, and SA. Most studies are concentrated on transportation research and human factors, with a higher concentration in countries such as the Netherlands, the USA, and China. This concentration provides an opportunity to delve into further research investigations from regions of the Americas. Regarding the demographic study within the compiled body of studies, a noteworthy trend was observed in the significant involvement of male participants, with a maximum of 1% being female. This gender imbalance could be a limitation and bias when generalizing outcomes predominantly from male samples. Moreover, the average age of participants is around 27 years, a factor that needs consideration in studies of assessment of SA requiring analysis of novice versus expert populations.

Furthermore, only 12.1% of studies on the assessment of SA with eye-tracking measures were conducted in real environments with industrial vehicles, presenting an opportunity for future research, such as studying industrial vehicle operators like forklift drivers. Likewise, the results suggest a need for more effort in conducting research in real-world environments for optimal validation of study variables. Although this approach may incur higher costs and require more extensive investment in ethical, safety, and data collection protocols, the advantages are notable. Similarly, the review uncovered the need for future research focused on the industrial environment, as such studies are scarce.

Likewise, concerning the measurement equipment and software used, Tobii Pro Lab, Lab version 1.232 and Tobii Pro X2-60 glasses (discontinued) were the preferred eye trackers, as reported in the majority of experiments. It is essential to note that some eye trackers may generate interference with operator equipment, and frequencies greater than 50 Hz are preferable. Additionally, in real environments, the use of wireless equipment may encounter interference due to the company's infrastructure, potentially leading to signal loss and data loss. It is also crucial to consider the presence of natural light in the data collection space, as sunlight could interfere with data collection. Moreover, in experiment design, demographic and cultural characteristics should be considered due to differences in pupil color [31].

Concerning the review process, the results demand a discussion regarding criteria such as validity and reliability. In terms of viability, this review presents outcomes similar to those found in existing reviews, for instance, by [21,41], particularly in terms of the relationships observed between physiological metrics measured with eye tracking and the assessment of SA.

Finally, regarding reliability, this review presents a systematic methodology that allowed us to compile demographic, statistical, and experimental design data, showing that the information collection remains consistent. However, further studies are necessary to identify variations across different study domains, distinct from those related to driving.

5. Conclusions

Collectively, the applications of SA evaluation have become extremely popular; however, this expansion of applications is accompanied by a wide range of challenges stemming from methodological intricacies and precision-related considerations in estimating driver awareness. In response, a combination of objective and subjective methodologies has become imperative to harmonize and align with the distinct requirements of each study. This synergy should aim to evolve into robust frameworks that can enhance the seamless integration of monitoring, measurement, and assessment of driver awareness, thereby fostering a more comprehensive and advanced approach.

In this review, we introduced driver SA assessment by the eye-tracking metrics framework and examined this framework based on a scientometric analysis, demographic comparison of experiments (sample size, gender, age, and the field of application), eye-tracking metrics, oculomotor events, the effects of the environment surrounding the experiments (naturalistic or simulated driving), the preferred type of eye-tracker devices, and emphasis on the discussion of the relationship between SA and eye tracking in the field of driving. We showed that keyword clusters for physiological measures and comprehension of driver behavior are the most used approaches in the literature reviewed.

Our results also revealed a relationship between eye-tracking metrics and SA, especially at perception level 1; furthermore, the results revealed how eye-tracking metrics contribute objectively to the assessment of the driver's gaze behavior, mainly in simulated environments and less so in naturalistic environments.

The most popularly used eye-tracking metrics for the study of SA are fixation, saccade, and pupillary metrics. The preferred eye trackers for the experiments are those that are less intrusive for the operator and those that possess a wireless connection. These results can support decision makers in selecting appropriate eye-tracking metrics to integrate into experiments, eye-tracker types, and information for designing data collection protocols.

Future research will be based on the challenges in the studies of driver awareness, the need for efforts in the study of driver awareness in industrial environments, the inclusion of bigger samples of women drivers, and more studies in naturalistic driving environments that allow the study of real-time data from actual environments. Likewise, the review aspires to clarify the relation between SA and eye tracking toward future work in the design of driving assistance solutions based on the study of driver behavior in risk situations or situations with mental workload and by using support alert systems. Thus, safer behavior can be realized, and accidents can be reduced by improving the SA of the driver.

Author Contributions: Conceptualization, C.Y.A.-P.; methodology, C.Y.A.-P.; validation, C.Y.A.-P., J.M.-V. and M.C.; formal analysis, C.Y.A.-P.; investigation, C.Y.A.-P.; resources, C.Y.A.-P.; data curation, C.Y.A.-P., J.M.-V. and M.C.; writing—original draft preparation, C.Y.A.-P.; writing—review and editing, C.Y.A.-P., J.M.-V. and M.C.; visualization, C.Y.A.-P.; supervision, J.M.-V. and M.C.; project administration, J.M.-V. and M.C.; funding acquisition, J.M.-V. All authors have read and agreed to the published version of the manuscript.

Funding: At the time of writing, C.Y.A.-P., was supported by Tecnologico de Monterrey scholarship and was supported by CONACYT scholarship.

Institutional Review Board Statement: Not applicable.

Informed Consent Statement: Not applicable.

Data Availability Statement: No new data were created or analyzed in this study. Data sharing is not applicable to this article.

Conflicts of Interest: The authors declare no conflicts of interest. The funders had no role in the design of the study; in the collection, analysis, or interpretation of data; in the writing of the manuscript; or in the decision to publish the results.

Appendix A

Table A1. Eye-tracking metrics (Oculomotor events).

		Eye-Tracking Metrics (Oculomotor Events)																																	
		Fixation				Saccade									Smooth Pursuit						Blink			Pupillary Measures						Gaze					
Author	Year	General	Accuracy	Count	Duration	General	Amplitude	Duration	Velocity	Acceleration	Direction	Latency	Rate	Gain	Direction	Velocity	Acceleration	Latency	Gain	Tremor; Microsaccade; Drift	Rate	Duration	Amplitude	Diameter	Position	Dilation	ICA *	IPA *	LHIPA *	Angle	Direction	Eccentricity	Acceleration	Velocity	Peripheral Vision
[18]	2017	x		x	x																				x										
[12]	2021			x	x		x						x											x											
[21]	2022	x		x	x	x	x	x	x			x	x	x	x	x	x	x	x	x	x		x	x	x		x	x	x						
[32]	2022			x	x		x																			x									
[36]	2021	x		x	x																														
[50]	2021																																		
[47]	2021	x		x	x								x											x											x
[39]	2021			x	x																x	x		x											
[11]	2021																																		
[37]	2021	x		x	x								x																						
[51]	2021			x	x		x	x	x	x	x		x																				x	x	
[31]	2021	x		x	x																										x				
[27]	2021	x		x	x	x																													
[52]	2020	x				x																													
[53]	2020	x	x	x	x																														
[46]	2020																							x							x				
[34]	2020			x	x																			x	x						x				
[54]	2020	x			x																														
[55]	2020	x																							x					x	x			x	
[9]	2020	x	x	x	x		x						x								x					x				x	x			x	
[61]	2020	x		x	x	x		x			x		x																	x		x			
[33]	2019	x																							x					x	x			x	
[56]	2019	x		x	x																										x				
[48]	2019	x		x	x																x	x													
[41]	2019	x		x	x	x	x	x													x	x		x						x	x				
[30]	2019	x		x																											x				
[57]	2019	x			x																										x				
[58]	2018	x		x	x																				x						x				
[49]	2018	x		x		x		x	x						x						x										x				
[35]	2018	x				x																									x				
[42]	2017			x	x																														
[23]	2017	x		x	x	x																									x				
[28]	2023			x	x																														
[24]	2017	x																												x	x				
[59]	2016	x		x																											x				
[29]	2016	x		x	x																										x				
[60]	2013	x			x		x						x																	x	x				
[25]	2011	x			x		x																												
[45]	2022	x			x	x	x	x												x											x				
[44]	2023													x						x				x											
[43]	2024			x	x																														

* Index of pupillary activity (IPA); low/high IPA (LHIPA); index of cognitive activity (ICA).

Table A2. Eye trackers identified in this review.

Author	Year	Experiment	Eye Tracker
[18]	2017	Naturalistic driving	Pupil Labs
[12]	2021	Video-based (driving simulation)	EyeLink 1000 Plus
[21]	2022	Review	NP
[32]	2022	Video-based (driving simulation)	SMI iViewX RED120
[36]	2021	Video-based (driving simulation)	Dikablis Glasses 3
[50]	2021	Video-based (driving simulation)	NP
[47]	2021	Video-based (driving simulation)	FOVIO FX3
[39]	2021	Video-based (driving simulation)	SMI glasses
[11]	2021	Review	NP
[37]	2021	Naturalistic driving	Tobii Pro Glasses 2
[51]	2021	Video-based (driving simulation)	EyeTech VT3 Mini
[31]	2019	Naturalistic driving	SmartEye Pro
[27]	2021	Naturalistic driving	Tobii Glasses 2
[52]	2020	Video-based (driving simulation)	Pupil Corewearable
[53]	2020	Video-based (driving simulation)	Tobii X2-60
[46]	2020	Video-based (driving simulation)	EyeLink 1000 Plus
[34]	2020	Video-based (driving simulation)	Fovio FX3
[54]	2020	Video-based (driving simulation)	NP
[55]	2020	Video-based (driving simulation)	NP
[9]	2020	Review	NP
[61]	2020	Naturalistic driving	SmartEye Pro
[33]	2019	Naturalistic driving	Logitech C920-1080p HD Pro standard webcam with 30 fps
[56]	2019	Video-based (driving simulation)	Tobii Pro Glasses 2
[48]	2019	Video-based (driving simulation)	Tobii Pro Glasses 2
[41]	2019	Review	NP
[30]	2019	Video-based and virtual reality	Pupil Labs
[57]	2019	Video-based and augmented reality	Eyeglasses, with SMI's BeGaze 3.5
[58]	2018	Video-based (driving simulation)	Pupil Lab Pro
[49]	2018	Video-based (driving simulation)	NP
[35]	2018	Naturalistic driving	Tobii Pro Glasses 2
[42]	2017	Video-based (driving simulation)	Tobii X2-60
[23]	2017	Video-based (driving simulation)	Smart Eye DR120 remote
[24]	2017	Video-based (driving simulation)	V4.5 Seeing Machines faceLAB
[59]	2016	Video-based (driving simulation)	ASL Mobile Eye system
[29]	2016	Naturalistic	Dikablis
[60]	2013	Video-based (driving simulation)	SmartEye
[25]	2011	Video-based (driving simulation)	NP
[45]	2022	Review	Review
[44]	2023	Driving simulation	HTC VIVE Pro Eye Head-mounted Display
[43]	2024	Driving simulation	NP

NP: not presented.

References

1. International Ergonomics Association; International Labour Organization. *Principles and Guidelines for Human Factors/Ergonomics (HF/E) Design and Management of Work Systems*; IEA/ILO: Geneva, Switzerland, 2021.
2. World Health Organization; International Labour Organization. *WHO/ILO Joint Estimates of the Work-Related Burden of Disease and Injury, 2000–2016*; Technical report; WHO/ILO: Geneva, Switzerland, 2021.
3. Woods, D.; Johannesen, L.J.; Cook, R.I.; Sarter, N.B. *Behind Human Error: Cognitive Systems, Computers and Hindsight*; Crew Systems Ergonomics: Alexandria, VA, USA, 1994.
4. Endsley, M.R. Design and Evaluation for Situation Awareness Enhancement. In Proceedings of the Human Factors Society Annual Meeting, Anaheim, CA, USA, 24–28 October 1988; pp. 97–101.
5. Endsley, M.R. Situation Awareness Misconceptions and Misunderstandings. *J. Cogn. Eng. Decis. Mak.* **2015**, *9*, 4–32. [CrossRef]
6. Ziemke, T.; Schaefer, K.E.; Endsley, M. Situation Awareness in Human-Machine Interactive Systems. *Cogn. Syst. Res.* **2017**, *46*, 1–2. [CrossRef]

7. Choi, M.; Ahn, S.; Seo, J.O. VR-Based Investigation of Forklift Operator Situation Awareness for Preventing Collision Accidents. *Accid. Anal. Prev.* **2020**, *136*, 105404. [CrossRef] [PubMed]
8. de Winter, J.C.F.; Eisma, Y.B.; Cabrall, C.D.D.; Hancock, P.A.; Stanton, N.A. Situation Awareness Based on Eye Movements in Relation to the Task Environment. *Cogn. Technol. Work.* **2019**, *21*, 99–111. [CrossRef]
9. Zhang, T.; Yang, J.; Liang, N.; Pitts, B.J.; Prakah-Asante, K.; Curry, R.; Duerstock, B.; Wachs, J.P.; Yu, D. Physiological Measurements of Situation Awareness: A Systematic Review. *Hum. Factors* **2023**, *65*, 737–758. [CrossRef] [PubMed]
10. Kass, S.J.; Cole, K.S.; Stanny, C.J. Effects of Distraction and Experience on Situation Awareness and Simulated Driving. *Transp. Res. Part F Traffic Psychol. Behav.* **2007**, *10*, 321–329. [CrossRef]
11. Linkov, V.; Vanžura, M. Situation Awareness Measurement in Remotely Controlled Cars. *Front. Psychol.* **2021**, *12*, 592930. [CrossRef] [PubMed]
12. Zhou, F.; Yang, X.J.; Winter, J.D. Using Eye-Tracking Data to Predict Situation Awareness in Real Time during Takeover Transitions in Conditionally Automated Driving. *IEEE Trans. Intell. Transp. Syst.* **2021**, *23*, 2284–2295. [CrossRef]
13. Stanton, N.A.; Chambers, P.R.G.; Piggott, J. Situational Awareness and Safety. *Saf. Sci.* **2001**, *39*, 189–204. [CrossRef]
14. AAA Foundation for Traffic Safety. *2017 Traffic Safety Culture Index*; Technical Report; AAA Foundation for Traffic Safety: Washington, DC, USA, 2018.
15. Blascheck, T.; Kurzhals, K.; Raschke, M.; Burch, M.; Weiskopf, D.; Ertl, T. Visualization of Eye Tracking Data: A Taxonomy and Survey. *Comput. Graph. Forum* **2017**, *36*, 260–284. [CrossRef]
16. Mao, R.; Li, G.; Hildre, H.P.; Zhang, H. A Survey of Eye Tracking in Automobile and Aviation Studies: Implications for Eye-Tracking Studies in Marine Operations. *IEEE Trans. Human-Mach. Syst.* **2021**, *51*, 87–98. [CrossRef]
17. Palinko, O.; Kun, A.L.; Shyrokov, A.; Heeman, P. Estimating Cognitive Load Using Remote Eye Tracking in a Driving Simulator. In Proceedings of the Eye Tracking Research and Applications Symposium (ETRA), Austin, TX, USA, 22–24 March 2010; pp. 141–144.
18. Wallmyr, M. Seeing Through the Eyes of Heavy Vehicle Operators. In *Human-Computer Interaction—INTERACT 2017, Proceedings of the 16th IFIP TC 13 International Conference, Mumbai, India, 25–29 September 2017*; Springer: Cham, Switzerland, 2017; pp. 263–282. [CrossRef]
19. Vieira, E.S.; Gomes, J.A.N.F. A Comparison of Scopus and Web of Science for a Typical University. *Scientometrics* **2009**, *81*, 587–600. [CrossRef]
20. Moher, D.; Liberati, A.; Tetzlaff, J.; Altman, D.G. Preferred Reporting Items for Systematic Reviews and Meta-Analyses: The PRISMA Statement. *PLoS Med.* **2009**, *6*, e1000097. [CrossRef]
21. Mahanama, B.; Jayawardana, Y.; Rengarajan, S.; Jayawardena, G.; Chukoskie, L.; Snider, J.; Jayarathna, S. Eye Movement and Pupil Measures: A Review. *Front. Comput. Sci.* **2022**, *3*, 733531. [CrossRef]
22. Aria, M.; Cuccurullo, C. Bibliometrix: An R-Tool for Comprehensive Science Mapping Analysis. *J. Informetr.* **2017**, *11*, 959–975. [CrossRef]
23. Lu, Z.; Coster, X.; de Winter, J. How Much Time Do Drivers Need to Obtain Situation Awareness? A Laboratory-Based Study of Automated Driving. *Appl. Ergon.* **2017**, *60*, 293–304. [CrossRef]
24. Louw, T.; Merat, N. Are You in the Loop? Using Gaze Dispersion to Understand Driver Visual Attention during Vehicle Automation. *Transp. Res. Part C Emerg. Technol.* **2017**, *76*, 35–50. [CrossRef]
25. Underwood, G.; Crundall, D.; Chapman, P. Driving Simulator Validation with Hazard Perception. *Transp. Res. Part F Traffic Psychol. Behav.* **2011**, *14*, 435–446. [CrossRef]
26. Tao, J.; Qiu, D.; Yang, F.; Duan, Z. A Bibliometric Analysis of Human Reliability Research. *J. Clean. Prod.* **2020**, *260*, 121041. [CrossRef]
27. Castritius, S.-M.; Schubert, P.; Dietz, C.; Hecht, H.; Huestegge, L.; Christian, M.L.; Haas, T.T. Driver Situation Awareness and Perceived Sleepiness during Truck Platoon Driving-Insights from Eye-Tracking Data. *Int. J. Hum.-Comput. Interact.* **2021**, *37*, 1467–1477. [CrossRef]
28. Kang, Y.; Zhou, X.; Chen, W.; Li, X. Investigating the Relationship between Eye Movements and the Situation Awareness of Forklift Operators for Accident Prevention. *Int. J. Occup. Saf. Ergon.* **2023**, *29*, 1477–1485. [CrossRef]
29. Koppenborg, M.; Huelke, M.; Nickel, P.; Lungfiel, A.; Naber, B. Operator Information Acquisition in Excavators—Insights from a Field Study Using Eye-Tracking. In *HCI in Business, Government, and Organizations: Information Systems, Proceedings of the Third International Conference, HCIBGO 2016, Held as Part of HCI International 2016, Toronto, ON, Canada, 17–22 July 2016*; Lecture Notes in Computer Science (including subseries Lecture Notes in Artificial Intelligence and Lecture Notes in Bioinformatics); Springer: Cham, Switzerland, 2016; Volume 9752, pp. 313–324.
30. Wallmyr, M.; Sitompul, T.A.; Holstein, T.; Lindell, R. Evaluating Mixed Reality Notifications to Support Excavator Operator Awareness. In *Human-Computer Interaction—INTERACT 2019, Proceedings of the 17th IFIP TC 13 International Conference, Paphos, Cyprus, 2–6 September 2019*; Lecture Notes in Computer Science (including subseries Lecture Notes in Artificial Intelligence and Lecture Notes in Bioinformatics); Springer: Cham, Switzerland, 2019; Volume 11746 LNCS, pp. 743–762.
31. Abbasi, J.A.; Mullins, D.; Ringelstein, N.; Reilhac, P.; Jones, E.; Glavin, M. An Analysis of Driver Gaze Behaviour at Roundabouts. *IEEE Trans. Intell. Transp. Syst.* **2019**, *23*, 8715–8724. [CrossRef]
32. Frank, W.; Mühl, K.; Rosner, A.; Baumann, M. Advancing Knowledge on Situation Comprehension in Dynamic Traffic Situations by Studying Eye Movements to Empty Spatial Locations. *Hum. Factors* **2022**, *65*, 1674–1688. [CrossRef]

33. Hijaz, A.; Wing-Yue, G.; Mansour, I. Towards a Driver Monitoring System for Estimating Driver Situational Awareness. In Proceedings of the IEEE International Conference on Robot and Human Interactive Communication, New Delhi, India, 14–18 October 2019.
34. Kummetha, V.C.; Kondyli, A.; Chrysikou, E.G.; Schrock, S.D. Safety Analysis of Work Zone Complexity with Respect to Driver Characteristics—A Simulator Study Employing Performance and Gaze Measures. *Accid. Anal. Prev.* **2020**, *142*, 105566. [CrossRef]
35. Ahmadi, N.; Katrahmani, A.; Romoser, M.R. Short and Long-Term Transfer of Training in a Tablet-Based Teen Driver Hazard Perception Training Program. In Proceedings of the Human Factors and Ergonomics Society, Philadelphia, PA, USA, 1–5 October 2018; Human Factors and Ergonomics Society Inc.: Washington, DC, USA, 2018; Volume 3, pp. 1965–1969.
36. Agrawal, S.; Peeta, S. Evaluating the Impacts of Situational Awareness and Mental Stress on Takeover Performance under Conditional Automation. *Transp. Res. Part F Traffic Psychol. Behav.* **2021**, *83*, 210–225. [CrossRef]
37. Wintersberger, P.; Schartmüller, C.; Shadeghian-Borojeni, S.; Frison, A.K.; Riener, A. Evaluation of Imminent Take-Over Requests With Real Automation on a Test Track. *Hum. Factors* **2021**, *65*, 1776–1792. [CrossRef] [PubMed]
38. Zhou, F.; Yang, X.J.; Zhang, X. Takeover Transition in Autonomous Vehicles: A YouTube Study. *Int. J. Hum.-Comput. Interact.* **2020**, *36*, 295–306. [CrossRef]
39. Mahajan, K.; Large, D.R.; Burnett, G.; Velaga, N.R. Exploring the Benefits of Conversing with a Digital Voice Assistant during Automated Driving: A Parametric Duration Model of Takeover Time. *Transp. Res. Part F Traffic Psychol. Behav.* **2021**, *80*, 104–126. [CrossRef]
40. Sodhi, M.; Reimer, B.; Cohen, J.L.; Vastenburg, E.; Kaars, R.; Kirschenbaum, S. On-Road Driver Eye Movement Tracking Using Head-Mounted Devices. In Proceedings of the Symposium on Eye Tracking Research & Applications—ETRA'02, New Orleans, LA, USA, 25–27 March 2002; ACM Press: New York, NY, USA, 2002; p. 61.
41. Ojsteršek, T.C.; Topolšek, D. Eye Tracking Use in Researching Driver Distraction: A Scientometric and Qualitative Literature Review Approach. *J. Eye Mov. Res.* **2019**, *12*, 1–30. [CrossRef] [PubMed]
42. Shinohara, Y.; Currano, R.; Ju, W.; Nishizaki, Y. Visual Attention during Simulated Autonomous Driving in the US and Japan. In Proceedings of the AutomotiveUI 2017—9th International ACM Conference on Automotive User Interfaces and Interactive Vehicular Applications, Oldenburg, Germany, 24–27 September 2017; Association for Computing Machinery, Inc.: New York, NY, USA, 2017; pp. 144–153.
43. Yan, Y.; Zhang, Y.; Yuan, H.; Wan, L.; Ding, H. Safety Effect of Tunnel Environment Self-Explaining Design Based on Situation Awareness. *Tunn. Undergr. Space Technol.* **2024**, *143*, 105486. [CrossRef]
44. Kim, G.; Lee, J.; Yeo, D.; An, E.; Kim, S. Physiological Indices to Predict Driver Situation Awareness in VR. In Proceedings of the Adjunct Proceedings of the 2023 ACM International Joint Conference on Pervasive and Ubiquitous Computing & the 2023 ACM International Symposium on Wearable Computing, Cancun, Mexico, 8–12 October 2023; ACM: New York, NY, USA, 2023; pp. 40–45.
45. Zheng, T.; Glock, C.H.; Grosse, E.H. Opportunities for Using Eye Tracking Technology in Manufacturing and Logistics: Systematic Literature Review and Research Agenda. *Comput. Ind. Eng.* **2022**, *171*, 108444. [CrossRef]
46. Zhenji, L.; Riender, H.; Winter, J.C.F. de Take over! A Video-Clip Study Measuring Attention, Situation Awareness, and Decision-Making in the Face of an Impending Hazard. *Transp. Res. Part F Traffic Psychol. Behav.* **2020**, *72*, 211–225. [CrossRef]
47. Liang, N.; Yang, J.; Yu, D.; Prakah-Asante, K.O.; Curry, R.; Blommer, M.; Swaminathan, R.; Pitts, B.J. Using Eye-Tracking to Investigate the Effects of Pre-Takeover Visual Engagement on Situation Awareness during Automated Driving. *Accid. Anal. Prev.* **2021**, *157*, 106143. [CrossRef]
48. Kunze, A.; Summerskill, S.J.; Marshall, R.; Filtness, A.J. Automation Transparency: Implications of Uncertainty Communication for Human-Automation Interaction and Interfaces. *Ergonomics* **2019**, *62*, 345–360. [CrossRef] [PubMed]
49. Schwehr, J.; Willert, V. Driver's Gaze Prediction in Dynamic Automotive Scenes. In Proceedings of the IEEE Conference on Intelligent Transportation Systems, Proceedings, ITSC, Yokohama, Japan, 16–19 October 2017; Institute of Electrical and Electronics Engineers Inc.: New York, NY, USA, 2018; Volume 2018-March, pp. 1–8.
50. Gerber, M.A.; Schroeter, R.; Johnson, D.; Rakotonirainy, A. Eye-Gaze Analysis of HUD Interventions for Conditional Automation to Increase Situation Awareness. In Proceedings of the Adjunct Proceedings—13th International ACM Conference on Automotive User Interfaces and Interactive Vehicular Applications, AutomotiveUI 2021, Leeds, UK, 9–14 September 2021; Association for Computing Machinery, Inc.: New York, NY, USA, 2021; pp. 210–212.
51. Mostowfi, S.; Kim, J.H.; Buttlar, W.G. Investigating the Relationship Between a Driver's Psychological Feelings and Biosensor Data. In *HCI International 2021—Late Breaking Papers: HCI Applications in Health, Transport, and Industry, Proceedings of the 23rd HCI International Conference, HCII 2021, Virtual, 24–29 July 2021*; Lecture Notes in Computer Science (including subseries Lecture Notes in Artificial Intelligence and Lecture Notes in Bioinformatics); Springer Science and Business Media: Cham, Switzerland, 2021; Volume 13097 LNCS, pp. 305–321.
52. Hofbauer, M.; Kuhn, C.B.; Püttner, L.; Petrovic, G.; Steinbach, E. Measuring Driver Situation Awareness Using Region-of-Interest Prediction and Eye Tracking. In Proceedings of the 2020 IEEE International Symposium on Multimedia, ISM 2020, Naples, Italy, 2–4 December 2020; Institute of Electrical and Electronics Engineers Inc.: New York, NY, USA, 2020; pp. 91–95.
53. Malone, S.; Brünken, R. Studying Gaze Behavior to Compare Three Different Hazard Perception Tasks. *Hum. Factors* **2020**, *62*, 1286–1303. [CrossRef] [PubMed]

54. Feng, C.; Wanyan, X.; Liu, S.; Chen, H.; Zhuang, D.; Wang, X. Influence of Different Attention Allocation Strategies under Workloads on Situation Awareness. *Acta Aeronaut. Astronaut. Sin.* **2019**, *41*, 123307.
55. Kim, H.; Martin, S.; Tawari, A.; Misu, T.; Gabbard, J.L. Toward Real-Time Estimation of Driver Situation Awareness: An Eye-Tracking Approach Based on Moving Objects of Interest. In Proceedings of the 2020 IEEE Intelligent Vehicles Symposium (IV), Las Vegas, NV, USA, 19 October–13 November 2020; IEEE: New York, NY, USA, 2020; pp. 1035–1041.
56. Merenda, C.; Suga, C.; Gabbard, J.; Misu, T. Effects of Vehicle SimulationVisual Fidelityon Assessing Driver Performance and Behavior. In Proceedings of the IEEE Intelligent Vehicles Symposium, Paris, France, 9–12 June 2019; Coleman, M., Suga, C., Gabbard, J., Misu, T., Eds.; IEEE: New York, NY, USA, 2019.
57. Kim, H.; Gabbard, J.L. Assessing Distraction Potential of Augmented Reality Head-Up Displays for Vehicle Drivers. *Hum. Factors* **2022**, *64*, 852–865. [CrossRef] [PubMed]
58. Vlakveld, W.; van Nes, N.; de Bruin, J.; Vissers, L.; van der Kroft, M. Situation Awareness Increases When Drivers Have More Time to Take over the Wheel in a Level 3 Automated Car: A Simulator Study. *Transp. Res. Part F Traffic Psychol. Behav.* **2018**, *58*, 917–929. [CrossRef]
59. Katrahmani, A.; Romoser, M.; Samuel, S. Investigating a Non-Invasive Method of Measuring the Quality of Latent Hazard Schemas of Novice Teen and Experienced Adult Drivers: A New Perspective Using Traditional Tools. In Proceedings of the Human Factors and Ergonomics Society, Washington, DC, USA, 19–23 September 2016; Human Factors and Ergonomics Society Inc.: Washington, DC, USA, 2016; pp. 711–715.
60. Schömig, N.; Metz, B. Three Levels of Situation Awareness in Driving with Secondary Tasks. *Saf. Sci.* **2013**, *56*, 44–51. [CrossRef]
61. Stapel, J.; El Hassnaoui, M.; Happee, R. Measuring Driver Perception: Combining Eye-Tracking and Automated Road Scene Perception. *Hum. Factors* **2022**, *64*, 714–731. [CrossRef] [PubMed]
62. Moore, K.; Gugerty, L. Development of a Novel Measure of Situation Awareness: The Case for Eye Movement Analysis. In Proceedings of the Human Factors and Ergonomics Society, Queensland, Australia, 31 October–3 November 2010; Human Factors and Ergonomics Society Inc.: Washington, DC, USA, 2010; Volume 3, pp. 1650–1654.

applied sciences

MDPI

Article

Diagnosing Dyslexia in Early School-Aged Children Using the LSTM Network and Eye Tracking Technology

Zbigniew Gomolka [1,*,†], Ewa Zeslawska [1,†], Barbara Czuba [2] and Yuriy Kondratenko [3,4]

1 College of Natural Sciences, University of Rzeszow, 35-959 Rzeszow, Poland; ezeslawska@ur.edu.pl
2 Department of Humanities, State Academy of Applied Sciences in Jaroslaw, 37-500 Jaroslaw, Poland; barbara.a.czuba@gmail.com
3 Intelligent Information Systems Department, Petro Mohyla Black Sea State University, 54003 Mykolaiv, Ukraine; y_kondrat2002@yahoo.com
4 Institute of Artificial Intelligence Problems, 01001 Kyiv, Ukraine
* Correspondence: zgomolka@ur.edu.pl; Tel.: +48-17-851-8755
† These authors contributed equally to this work.

Abstract: Dyslexia, often referred to as a specific reading disability, affects many students around the world. It is a neurological disorder that affects the ability to recognise words, and it causes difficulties in writing and reading comprehension. Previous computer-based methods for the automatic detection of dyslexia in children have had low efficiency due to the complexity of the test administration process and the low measurement reliability of the attention measures used. This paper proposes the use of a student's mobile device to record the spatio-temporal trajectory of attention, which is then analysed by deep neural network long short-term memory (LSTM). The study involved 145 participants (66 girls and 79 boys), all of whom were children aged 9 years. The input signal for the neural network consisted of recorded observation sessions, which were packets containing the child's spatio-temporal attention trajectories generated during task performance. The training set was developed using stimuli from Benton tests and an expert opinion from a specialist in early childhood psychology. The coefficients of determination of $R2 \sim 0.992$ were obtained for the proposed model, giving an accuracy of 97.7% for the test set. The ease of implementation of this approach in school settings and its non-stressful nature make it suitable for use with children of different ages and developmental stages, including those who have not yet learned to read. This enables early intervention, which is essential for effective educational and emotional support for children with dyslexia.

Keywords: recognition of dyslexia; eye tracking for attention analysis; LSTM neural network; BVRT test

1. Introduction

In the information age we live in, technology and data have become key elements of people's daily lives. Two areas that can benefit from data collection are education and early educational diagnostics, especially in the context of the often-occurring problem of dyslexia. Dyslexia, often referred to as a specific reading disorder, affects many students worldwide. It is a neurological disorder that impacts the ability to recognize words, causing difficulties in writing and understanding text. The effects of dyslexia are not limited to the classroom but can also lead to problems with self-esteem, frustration, and social isolation. As experts in dyslexia diagnosis point out [1], it is a neurological disorder affecting the ability to recognize words, which causes difficulties in writing and understanding text. Despite normal levels of intelligence and adequate teaching, children with dyslexia often have difficulty acquiring reading skills at the level of their peers [2]. However, the effects of dyslexia are not limited to the classroom, but can also lead to problems with self-esteem, frustration, and social isolation [3–5]. Dyslexia is a complex disorder that affects reading, writing, and language processing abilities. Although it is most commonly diagnosed in school-aged children, its causes are varied and may include both neurological and genetic factors. Among the hypotheses regarding the causal background of dyslexia, the following are suggested:

- Phonological disorders related to difficulties in processing speech sounds, such as phonemes—the basic sound units of language—are the primary cause of dyslexia. Children with dyslexia struggle with segmenting, blending, and manipulating sounds in words, which directly impacts their reading and writing skills. Research confirms that deficits in phoneme recognition affect reading and writing abilities [2,6].
- Problems with the coordination and automation of cognitive processes related to the cerebellum can lead to difficulties in learning to read, as confirmed by neuroimaging studies [7].
- Deficits in the magnocellular cells responsible for processing rapid visual stimuli can cause difficulties in reading fluency and visual perception [8].
- Improper migration of neurons during brain development can lead to dysfunction in areas responsible for language processing and reading [8].

The symptoms of dyslexia include difficulties in word recognition, spelling problems, slow reading speed, and challenges in segmenting speech sounds. Current methods for diagnosing dyslexia involve reading skills tests, phonological assessments, psychological tests, and interviews with parents and teachers.

The study of dyslexia is crucial due to its significant impact on educational outcomes and social functioning. Dyslexia can affect a child's ability to read and write effectively, leading to broader educational challenges, including lower academic achievements and an increased risk of early school dropout [2]. The economic burden associated with dyslexia is considerable in terms of educational costs, therapy, and the potential loss of productivity due to the challenges faced by individuals with dyslexia.

Dyslexia is a serious issue, not only for individuals but also for society as a whole. It is one of the most common learning disorders, affecting a significant portion of the population. Dyslexia impacts about 5–10% of the global population [9]. In the United States, the National Institutes of Health (NIH) estimate that around 15–20% of the population exhibits symptoms of dyslexia [3]. In Europe, a comprehensive review conducted by the European Dyslexia Association highlights that dyslexia affects about 10% of the population, with varying degrees of severity [10]. These figures underscore the widespread prevalence of the disorder and its impact on educational systems and individual lives.

The standard approach to treating dyslexia does not involve using a drug or an established therapy for all patients, as is the case with treating a specific disease. Dyslexia is not a disease but a developmental disorder that manifests differently in different individuals. Each of us is unique, and depending on the individual characteristics of our bodies, we experience this disorder in various ways. The research presented in this paper responds to a new approach to the diagnostic–therapeutic process, changing the paradigm of therapy and rehabilitation for neurodevelopmental disorders, especially in children and adolescents. The proposed technology for diagnosing dyslexia departs from the traditional approach that applies the same treatment method to all individuals with the same disorder. People differ from each other, and therefore, there is no universal method of therapy.

The last few decades have brought about significant progress in understanding and diagnosing dyslexia, a disorder characterized by difficulties in reading. Research on dyslexia has also shown that it is not a homogeneous disorder but rather a spectrum of difficulties manifesting in various ways, necessitating an individualized approach to diagnosis and therapy. This individualized approach ensures that each person's unique needs are addressed effectively. As highlighted in [3,11], dyslexia is a developmental disorder that requires individualized and adaptive treatment strategies to effectively address the unique needs of each person. Among the methods used to diagnose dyslexia, particular attention has been given to those that allow for the direct observation of behaviors and eye movements during reading [11,12]. Dyslexia, traditionally diagnosed based on assessments of reading and writing skills, has gained new diagnostic tools thanks to the development of digital technologies [6,13–15]. The digitization of tests allows for a detailed analysis of the reading process, providing data that are difficult to obtain in traditional settings [16,17]. Traditional assessment methods, focusing mainly on written and oral tests, are increasingly supplemented by modern technologies such as eye tracking and artificial intelligence, offering new possibilities for objective and precise diagnostics. Diagnostic methods based on brain imaging, such as functional magnetic resonance imaging (fMRI) or diffusion tensor imaging (DTI), provide valuable information about structural and functional differences in the brains of individuals with dyslexia compared to control groups [18,19]. These techniques, supplemented by electroencephalographic (EEG) studies, shed light on the neurobiological basis of dyslexia, explaining the mechanisms responsible for reading difficulties [20–22].

Eye tracking, or tracking eye movements, has become one of the key tools in research on dyslexia. It allows for precise tracking of how individuals with dyslexia read text, including the analysis of eye fixation patterns, saccades (rapid eye movements), and other eye movement characteristics that may indicate difficulties in text processing [23–25]. Innovative studies, such as [26], emphasize the importance of eye movement coordination in children with dyslexia, showing that they may have problems with proper text tracking, directly impacting their reading skills. Conversely, in the work of [27], artificial intelligence is used to predict dyslexia based on reading patterns in children, demonstrating how modern technologies can revolutionize the diagnosis of this disorder. In the work of [28], attention is drawn to the potential of using machine learning and eye tracking to identify individuals with dyslexia, opening new perspectives for precise and rapid diagnosis. Similarly, further research with larger sample sizes and advanced data analysis methods presented in [29,30] demonstrate that the application of sophisticated algorithms can significantly improve the accuracy of dyslexia detection, achieving an effectiveness level of over 95%. The development of deep learning algorithms and their application in eye tracking data analysis opens new possibilities in dyslexia diagnosis. In the works of [31,32], utilizing neural networks for eye tracking data processing, the potential of these technologies for identifying reading disorders is highlighted, offering high efficacy and paving the way for the development of new, even more efficient diagnostic tools. Table 1 presents the main directions of existing research that utilize eye-tracking methods in diagnosing dyslexia [23–32].

Table 1. The review of recent findings in eye tracking for dyslexia diagnosis.

Authors	Subject	Age	Experimental Approach	Main Findings
Christoforou, C.; et al. [23]	30 children with dyslexia and 30 chronological age controls	A mean age of 9.79 years and a range of 7.6 to 12.1 years.	A combined EEG and eye- tracking study on children with dyslexia	Novel framework for integrative analysis of neurophysiological and eye-gaze.
Jakovljevi, T.; et al. [24]	36 children, 18 with dyslexia and 18 control	8–12 years old	The reading task in 13 combinations of background and overlay colours	Findings showed that the dyslexic children have longer reading duration, fixation count, fixation duration average and total, and longer saccade while reading on white and coloured background/overlay.

Table 1. *Cont.*

Authors	Subject	Age	Experimental Approach	Main Findings
Jakovljevi, T.; et al. [25]	25 children, 10 boys and 15 girls	8–9 years	This study investigated the influence of white vs. 12 background and overlay colors on the reading process.	The findings showed a decreasing trend with age regarding EEG power bands and lower scores of reading duration and eye-tracking measures in younger children compared to older children.
Temelturk, R.D.; et al. [26]	Children with dyslexia and typical development	5–17 years	The review through the examination of binocular coordination in children with dyslexia by describing the normative development of stable binocular control.	The studies reviewed provided consistent evidence of poor binocular coordination in children with dyslexia.
Wang, R.; et al. [27]	399, 187 with dyslexia and 212 typically developing children	7–13 years	These studies implemented tests evaluating reading-related cognitive skills.	This study established a genetic algorithm optimized back-propagation neural network model to predict whether Chinese children have dyslexia.
Rello, L.; et al. [28]	97, 49 without dyslexia (28 female, 21 male) and 48 with diagnosed dyslexia (22 female, 26 male)	11–54 years	Each participant read 12 different texts with 12 different typefaces. The texts and the fonts were counter balanced to avoid sequence effects.	The eye movements of readers with dyslexia are different from regular readers. People with dyslexia have longer reading times, make longer fixations, and make more fixations than readers without dyslexia.
M. N. Benfatto, et al. [29]	185, 97 high-risk subjects and a control group of 88 low-risk subjects.	9–10 years	Using eye tracking during reading to probe the processes that underlie reading ability.	It is possible to identify 9–10-year-old individuals at risk of persistent reading difficulties by using eye tracking.
Prabha, A.J.; et al. [30]	185, 97 high-risk subjects, a control group of 88 low-risk subjects.	9–10 years	Using eye tracking during reading to probe the processes that underlie reading ability.	The research focused on identifying features that contribute to better prediction and then build an appropriate prediction model.

Table 1. *Cont.*

Authors	Subject	Age	Experimental Approach	Main Findings
Neruil, B.; et al. [31]	185, 88 with low risk (69 male,19 female) and 97 with high risk of dyslexia (76 male, 21 female)	9–10 years	A new detection method for cognitive impairments is presented utilizing eye tracking signals in a text reading test.	In a series of experiments it was found that the best results provide magnitude spectrum-based representation of the time-interpolated eye-tracking signals recorded.
Vajs, I.; et al. [32]	30 persons (19 female, 11 male), 15 with dyslexia and 15 control subjects.	7–13 years	The children read a text written in Serbian on 13 different color configurations (including background and overlay color variations).	A combination of convolutional neural network and visual encoding of the eye tracking data shows promising results in dyslexia detection with minimal preprocessing effort.

In summary, the dynamic development of research on dyslexia, supported by technological progress, is changing the face of diagnosing this disorder. The use of modern tools such as eye tracking and machine learning not only increases the precision of dyslexia recognition but also helps to better understand the underlying mechanisms, opening new pathways for effective therapeutic intervention and support for individuals with this disorder.

In the research presented in [33–35], the subsequent part of the study builds upon previously conducted hybrid studies in the field of developmental psychology, which involved therapeutic and preventive interventions among children aged 10–14 years old. The author's program consisted of selected elements from various therapeutic interventions, particularly Davis, CBT, SI, hand therapy, and eye training. The aim of the research was to alleviate difficulties in writing/dysgraphia. As a result of the conducted program, participants were observed to exhibit correct muscle tension in the fingers and wrist, proper writing grip, and a correct habit associated with writing technique. The therapeutic interventions were conducted in face-to-face settings. Through the conducted research, a strategy for designing and utilizing/conducting psycho-tests and utilizing attention analysis to assess the effectiveness of therapy and individual therapy selection was developed. Additionally, over the course of several years, the team conducted studies on the attention of pilots during the execution of specific types of aviation tasks in both IFR and VFR conditions, demonstrating that the observer's attention is diffuse, while the shape and trajectory of attention over time–space are indicators of the pilot's training level. It was shown that the chronology of attention is directly linked to the pilot's ability to perceive information from cockpit instruments and directly impacts flight safety [36,37]. It was proven that the shape and dynamics of observation trajectories are directly related to the process of scene recognition and the perception of its individual components. Therefore, there is a strong coincidence between the understanding of a scene and the dynamics of observation, which can serve as a significant source of diagnostic data for a hypothetical neural system. The authors thus combined their experience using human–machine interface (HMI) systems with the new capabilities of recurrent neural networks (LSTM), which are currently an efficient and effective tool for analyzing and recognizing time series [38,39]. Based on this groundwork, the present study aims to develop intelligent technology that will support therapy for neurodevelopmental disorders. The proposed combination of research related to psycho-tests and the measurement of the attention of the subject will allow for the establishment of individualized therapeutic procedures for each patient, minimizing adverse effects.

The proposed hybrid technology for conducting psycho-tests, allowing for result assessment through the use of observer attention, represents an original and innovative approach, adding value to this study. In this article, we propose an innovative approach to diagnosing dyslexia by integrating the Benton Visual Retention Test (BVRT) with advanced analysis of visual attention trajectories using eye-tracking technology and deep neural networks (DNN). This approach not only enhances the effectiveness of dyslexia diagnosis but also makes it more accessible and efficient, especially for children who are not yet able to read. The Benton test is a widely recognized tool for assessing visual memory and perception. Integrating this test with eye-tracking technology allows for detailed analysis of a child's eye movement patterns while performing tasks. Recording the spatiotemporal trajectories of visual attention using mobile devices like Pupil Invisible or Pupil Core provides objective and precise data. The recorded spatiotemporal data, extracted from sessions, are analyzed by an LSTM network, enabling the detection of subtle visual anomalies characteristic of dyslexia. One of the main advantages of the proposed approach is its ability to diagnose dyslexia in children who have not yet mastered reading skills. Traditional diagnostic methods often rely on reading tests, which can be a barrier for younger children or those with severe reading difficulties. The method based on visual perception and eye movement analysis bypasses this obstacle, allowing for the early detection of dyslexia. The proposed solution offers several key advantages over traditional dyslexia diagnostic methods:

- Objectivity and Precision: Utilizing eye tracking for the accurate and objective collection of data related to eye movements and subjecting the gathered data to analysis using LSTM networks allows for the identification of subtle eye movement patterns characteristic of dyslexia. The high correlation coefficient R ($\sim$0.992) achieved in the proposed model indicates its high accuracy and reliability.
- Speed and Efficiency: Traditional diagnostic methods can be time-consuming and require multiple sessions with the child. The proposed approach allows for rapid data collection and immediate analysis of results, significantly reducing the time needed for diagnosis.
- Stress-Free Environment: The BVRT, which does not require reading skills, is less stressful and more natural for younger children. Eye tracking allows for administering the test in a friendly and engaging manner, which can lead to more reliable results.
- Early Intervention: The ability to diagnose dyslexia in children who are not yet able to read enables the early implementation of appropriate educational and therapeutic interventions. Early recognition of dyslexia-related issues allows for the prompt introduction of effective support strategies, which can significantly improve the child's educational and emotional outcomes.

A key added value of this work is the combination of the Benton Visual Retention Test with eye-tracking technology and LSTM deep neural networks, presenting a novel approach to diagnosing dyslexia. The ease of implementing this approach in school settings and its stress-free nature make it suitable for use with children of various ages and developmental stages, including those who have not yet learned to read. This enables early intervention, which is crucial for effective educational and emotional support for children with dyslexia.

2. Materials and Methods

2.1. Participants

The study included 9-year-old children attending the third grade of primary school in Jarosław, southeastern Poland. All participants were primary school students from one geographical region, allowing for a certain level of socioeconomic and educational homogeneity. A total of 145 children participated in the study (66 girls and 79 boys). In 65% of the cases, at least one parent had higher education, 20% had a secondary school education, and 15% of parents had a primary school education. In the studied group, 40% of the children came from families with a middle socioeconomic status, 35% from families with a high status, and 25% from families with a low status. A total of 90% of the children lived in urban areas, while 10% lived in rural areas. In the studied group, a diagnosis of dyslexia was made at the age of 8, following earlier observations (and a diagnosis in the "zero" class—at risk of dyslexia) indicating a risk of dyslexia between the ages of 5 and 7. All children participated in therapy lasting an average of 1.5 years, which included various support methods, including speech therapy and psycho-pedagogical therapy. Some children had coexisting visual impairments that could have affected their performance in visual studies. However, all children underwent appropriate ophthalmological diagnostics and, if necessary, treatment before starting the dyslexia study. The study was approved by the Institutional Review Ethic Board of the PGKICPO, and the ethical approval was granted on 9 November 2022, under the reference number IRB-20221109. Informed consent was obtained from all subjects involved in the study, and written informed consent has been obtained from the patient(s) to publish this paper.

After assembling the group of participants for the experiment, research was conducted on a test group comprising 145 individuals aged 7 to 10 years old. The experiment for each participant lasted no longer than 10 min, with the duration depending on the individual and the time allocated for reproducing the pattern from memory. The summary of the conducted experiments is presented in Table 2.

Table 2. Characteristics of the subjects.

Name	Value
Number of people surveyed	145
Number of women	66 (46%)
Number of men	79 (54%)
Right-handed persons	132 (91%)
Left-handed persons	13 (9%)
People with visual impairment	7 (5%)
Individuals without a visual defect	138 (95%)
Maximum duration of the study	00:08:32
Minimum duration of the study	00:03:37
Average duration of the study	00:04:54

2.2. Research Equipment

For the purposes of the conducted research, a research station was designed and configured, enabling the registration of observer attention. The data collected in this way allow for the processing of the obtained video sequence using DNN, thereby enabling the diagnosis of neurodevelopmental disorders associated with dyslexia. Figure 1 illustrates the utilized research station.

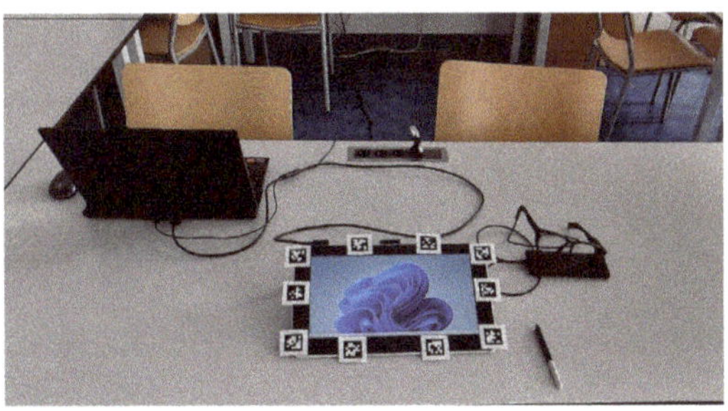

(a)

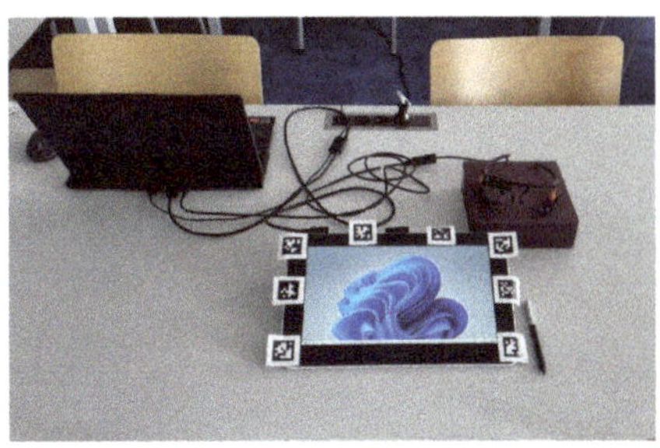

(b)

Figure 1. Stand for attention trajectory acquisition with Pupil Invisible (**a**) and Pupil Core (**b**).

The research was conducted using two eye-tracking systems: Pupil Core v2.0.182 and Pupil Invisible. These systems offer high precision in tracking eye movements, which is crucial for their use in experimental research, human–computer interfaces, and virtual reality. The systems are equipped with dedicated cameras for recording eye movements and a camera for recording the observed scene. Pupil Core, in its initial phase, requires calibration, which allows for precise adjustment of eye movement tracking to a specific user. To ensure high measurement accuracy, a 5-point calibration and natural calibration using Apriltag markers were utilized. Pupil Invisible is an attention-tracking system based on deep learning, which eliminates the need for calibration and significantly increases measurement reliability.

During the measurements, the least-invasive measurement model was adopted, which utilized the Pupil Invisible eye tracker. The recorded video stream for each participant was processed in the Pupil Cloud. In this way, measurement data were obtained, which were used to create a training set. An example of recording observer fixations during the object reproduction task from the Benton test is presented in Table 3. Fixations marked as True indicate that the object of attention is within the observed scene plane defined by the Apriltag set. The value False indicates that the observer's attention momentarily moved outside the field of view. Figure 2 shows a graph for the recorded data obtained during the BVRT survey from Table 3. This data in the form of a time moving window were the input to the LSTM network. In the experiments presented in this work, a sampling frequency of 120 Hz was adopted. The data stream recorded during the experiments was processed in the Pupil Cloud environment. This resulted in observer attention trajectories with a non-uniform time axis, chronologically encompassing the moments of fixation occurrence, their durations, and the coordinates of the detected fixations normalized relative to the adopted coordinates of the observed scene. The resulting non-uniform time series of fixation coordinates was processed using a window size of 256 with a shift step of 2, which considered the lengths of the recorded trajectories in all experiments and allowed for proper balancing of the training dataset. The observation window size was selected heuristically to account for both the lengths of the processed trajectories (the shortest being 387 fixations, and the longest being 574 fixations) and to maximize resistance to temporary measurement disturbances (occlusions, blinks, going outside the controlled field of observation, etc.).

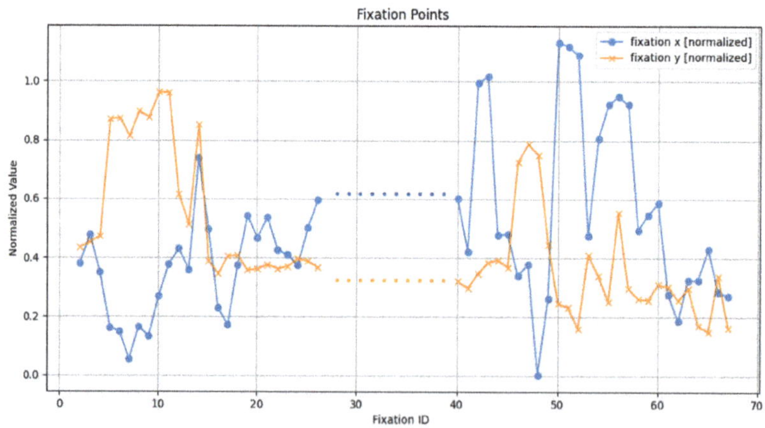

Figure 2. Graph of normalised coordinates recorded by the Pupil Labs eye tracker.

Table 3. Examples of fixation data obtained from eye-tracking measurement.

Fixation id	Duration [ms]	Fixation Detected on Surface	Fixation x [Normalized]	Fixation y [Normalized]
2	350	True	0.381184	0.434751
3	155	True	0.478635	0.452984
4	216	True	0.351071	0.473251
5	79	True	0.164494	0.872142
6	735	True	0.148455	0.874538
7	351	True	0.055462	0.814655
8	371	True	0.166153	0.897663
9	991	True	0.133664	0.877281
10	135	True	0.27131	0.96255
11	220	True	0.377649	0.961936
12	223	True	0.43152	0.615011
13	323	True	0.359779	0.514438
14	251	True	0.740871	0.85324
15	131	True	0.497466	0.389931
16	199	True	0.229441	0.346479
17	152	True	0.173246	0.405854
18	231	True	0.37687	0.408425
19	368	True	0.543391	0.358734
20	167	True	0.468531	0.36243
21	251	True	0.537559	0.377421
22	531	True	0.427361	0.363313
23	91	True	0.409878	0.371664
24	1331	True	0.375001	0.397355
25	240	True	0.502381	0.388864
26	300	True	0.596782	0.367004
⋮	⋮	⋮	⋮	⋮
40	259	True	0.602571	0.321279
41	326	True	0.423158	0.297279
42	319	True	0.995357	0.347378
43	751	True	1.01715	0.383466
44	256	True	0.478577	0.393537
45	159	True	0.48118	0.368611
46	60	True	0.340173	0.727317
47	112	True	0.378526	0.787224
48	291	True	0.001522	0.751218
49	92	True	0.262708	0.446477
50	676	False	1.133303	0.247477
51	375	False	1.120387	0.232185
52	223	False	1.089224	0.161522
53	160	True	0.47592	0.410375
54	168	True	0.80732	0.340732
55	156	True	0.922784	0.25163
56	188	True	0.949428	0.552949
57	208	True	0.921888	0.298959
58	68	True	0.495532	0.261822
59	91	True	0.546163	0.258226
60	227	True	0.585588	0.310388
61	191	True	0.27676	0.302838
62	223	True	0.186211	0.256423
63	156	True	0.324427	0.296805
64	160	True	0.324148	0.17112
65	415	True	0.43132	0.149982
66	136	True	0.285724	0.3394
67	668	True	0.270591	0.162541

2.3. Description of the Task to Be Carried Out

During the execution of individual studies, participants were asked to perform the Benton Visual Retention Test, assessing visual memory. BVRT allows for inferences about potential changes in the overall neurological status of the patient based on obtained results, especially regarding visual perception, visual memory, and visuoconstructive abilities. It is a sensitive diagnostic tool used, among others, in reading difficulties, traumatic brain injuries, and attention deficit disorders. BVRT has three alternative forms: C, D, and E, all of which are equivalent and can be administered in different conditions. In the conducted experiments, version C of the test was used, along with method A: exposure of the pattern for 10 s followed by immediate reproduction from memory. The test material consisted of geometric figures placed on a white background. Views of the test cards are presented in Figure 3.

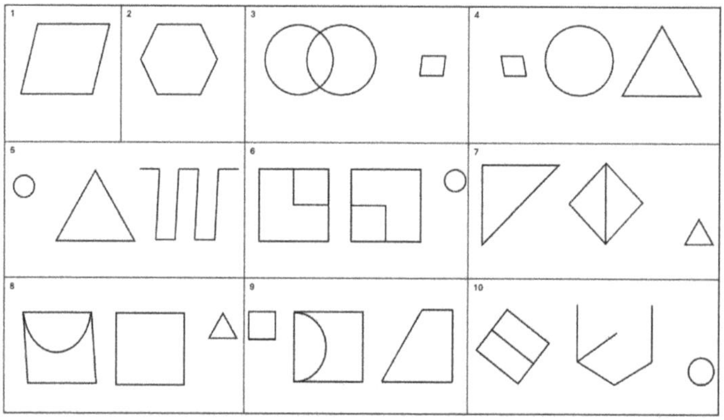

Figure 3. Cards of the BVRT test performed. The numbers of consecutive cards 1–10 indicate the order of their presentation during the test.

Table 4 classifies the relevant risk levels of visual perception disorders, as indicated by the range of errors made by participants. Participants were classified based on the number of errors made and the overall accuracy in reproducing the patterns.

Table 4. Observed dyslexia levels.

Level of Visual Perception Disorder	Range	Quantity	%
Low	1–5	84	58
Average	6–7	35	24
High	8>	26	18

The correctness of copying patterns as well as their reproduction from memory were assessed, considering both the number of correct drawings and the number of errors made. Errors indicating spatial function disturbances involve omitting, distorting, rotating, or repeating (perseverating) memorized figures from the previous pattern.

The visual perception experiment proceeded according to the following steps:

- Taking a seat at the research station, ensuring appropriate measurement conditions, in a position similar to that typically assumed by participants when seated at a desk during lessons or other activities. This ensured the naturalness of the research environment;
- Wearing the necessary glasses for conducting the visual perception test. (In the case of using the Pupil Core system, a calibration process was conducted);
- Familiarizing oneself with the instructions regarding task execution;

- Testing the interactive tool for reproducing pattern exposure;
- Performing the BVRT test face-to-face, consisting of 10 cards (pattern exposure followed by immediate reproduction from memory).

In Figure 4, selected stages from the conducted experiments are presented. In Figure 5, sample shots from the participant's world camera and information recorded by the eye tracker during the experiments are shown.

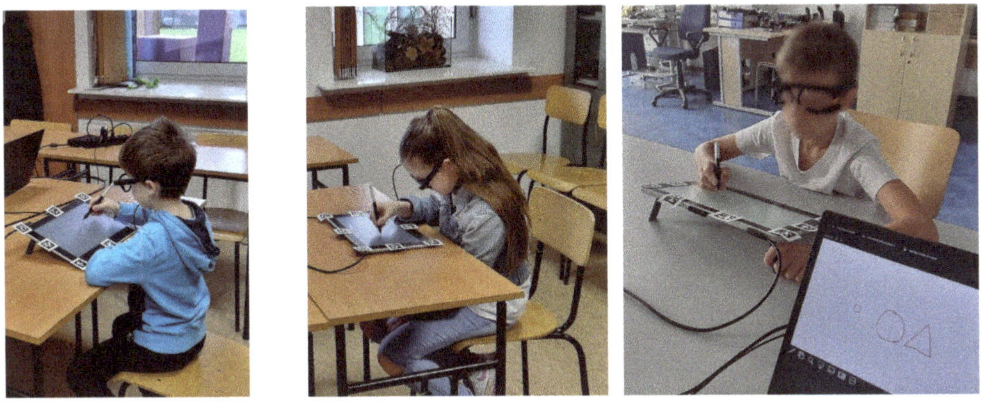

(**a**) Participant P0059. (**b**) Participant P0103. (**c**) Participant P02032

Figure 4. Selected views from the BVRT study.

In the initial phase of the experiments, the team conducted 10 preliminary measurements aimed at demonstrating the existence of distinct features distinguishing attention trajectories depending on the degree of dyslexia risk. Subsequently, a classical assessment of participants' work sheets was performed, determining the dyslexia risk level (DRL) coefficient. The visualization of attention trajectories depicted in Figure 6 indicates that the dispersion of attention for individuals with a high risk of dyslexia is minimal, whereas for those with a low risk, it is greater. This suggests, on the one hand, greater perceptual mobility in healthy individuals and, on the other hand, the existence of characteristic features that can be utilized in the neural network learning process. Preliminary trajectory sets, whose observation durations indicate that healthy individuals focus their attention on the observed scene for a longer period, thus effectively completing the reproduction task, are listed in Table 5.

Table 5. Dyslexia risk level and trajectory length coincidence, the best and the worst case marked with bold respectively.

Registered Attention Trajectory	Dyslexia Risk Level
2 × 461 double	0.4
2 × 574 double	0.3
2 × 506 double	0.2
2 × 637 double	0.4
2 × 576 double	0.4
2 × 548 double	**0.1**
2 × 482 double	0.1
2 × 357 double	0.6
2 × 477 double	0.6
2 × 387 double	**0.8**

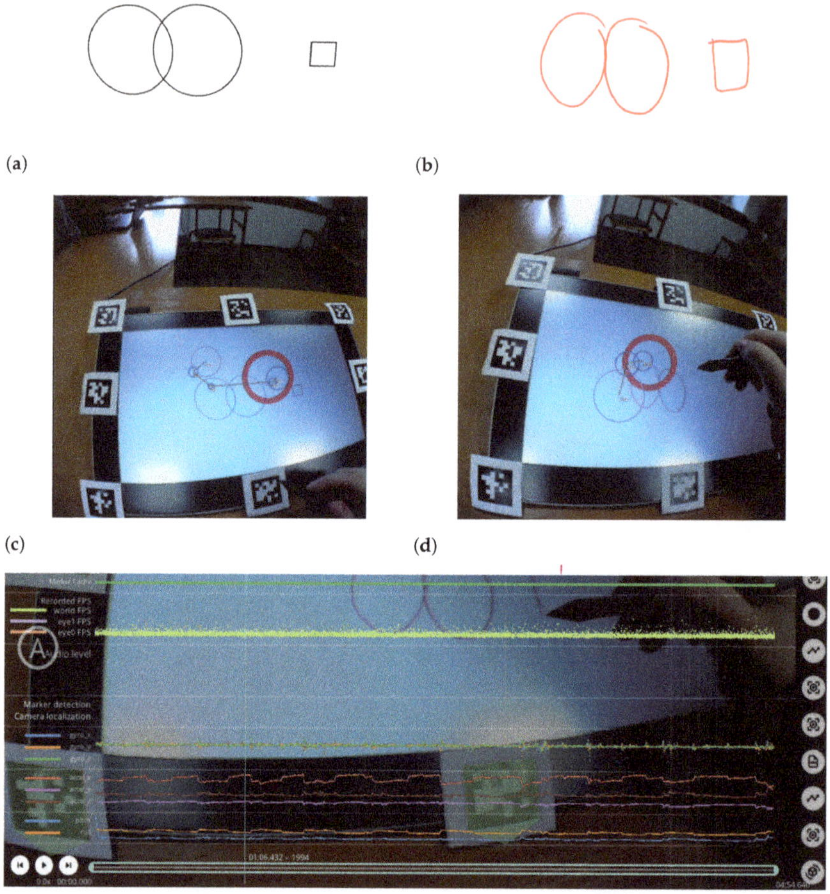

(a) (b) (c) (d) (e)

Figure 5. Sample footage obtained during the conducted work: (**a**) test card image, (**b**) result of reproduced exposure of the figure, (**c**) fixations and saccades during card exposure and (**d**) during the reproduction process, (**e**) chart of fixations obtained from eye-tracking measurement.

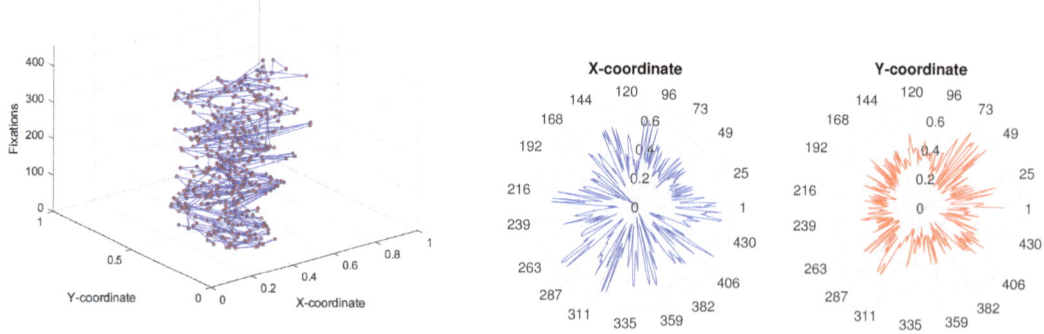

(a) (b)

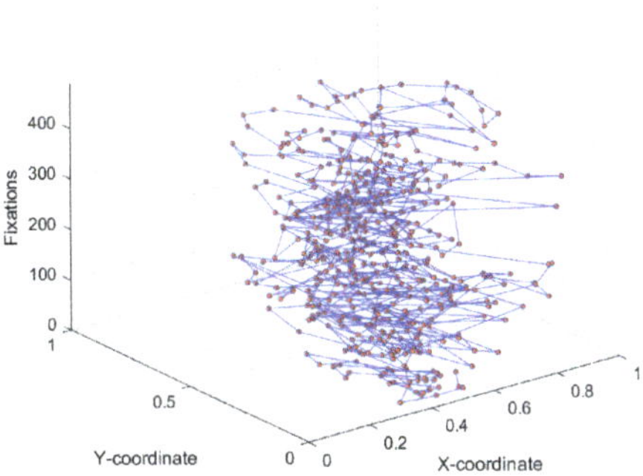
Fixations
400
300
200
100
0
Y-coordinate
1
0.5
0
X-coordinate
0
0.2
0.4
0.6
0.8
1

(c)

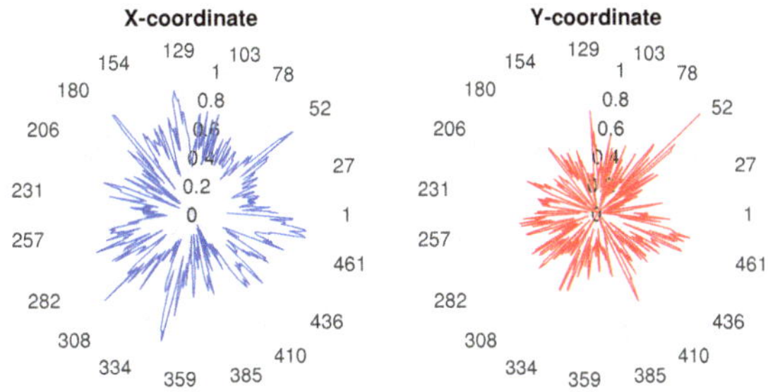
X-coordinate
Y-coordinate
129
103
78
52
27
1
461
436
410
385
359
334
308
282
257
231
206
180
154
0.8
0.6
0.4
0.2
0

(d)

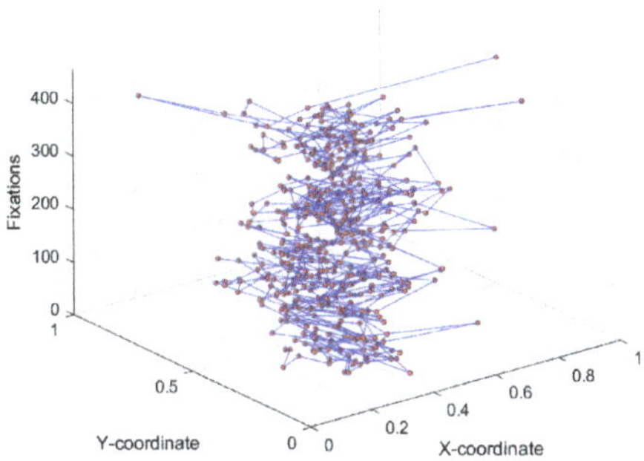
Fixations
400
300
200
100
0
Y-coordinate
1
0.5
0
X-coordinate
0
0.2
0.4
0.6
0.8
1

(e)

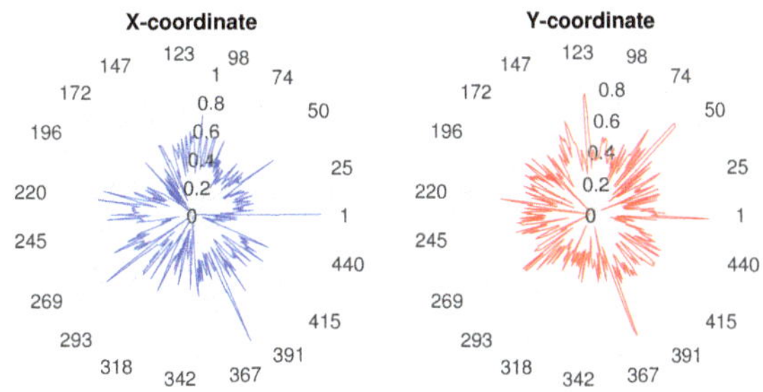
X-coordinate
Y-coordinate
123
98
74
50
25
1
440
415
391
367
342
318
293
269
245
220
196
172
147
0.8
0.6
0.4
0.2
0

(f)

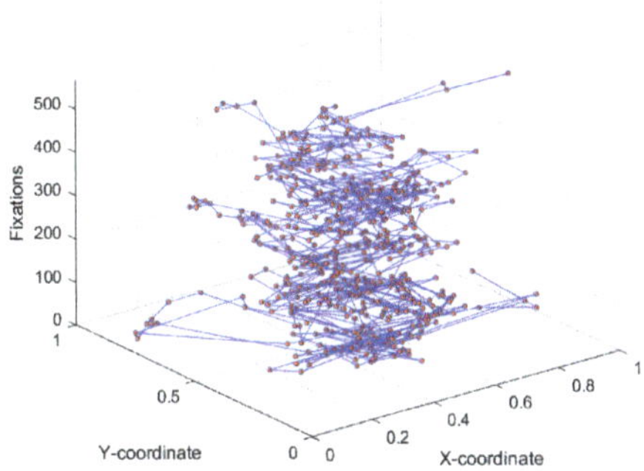
Fixations
500
400
300
200
100
0
Y-coordinate
1
0.5
0
X-coordinate
0
0.2
0.4
0.6
0.8
1

(g)

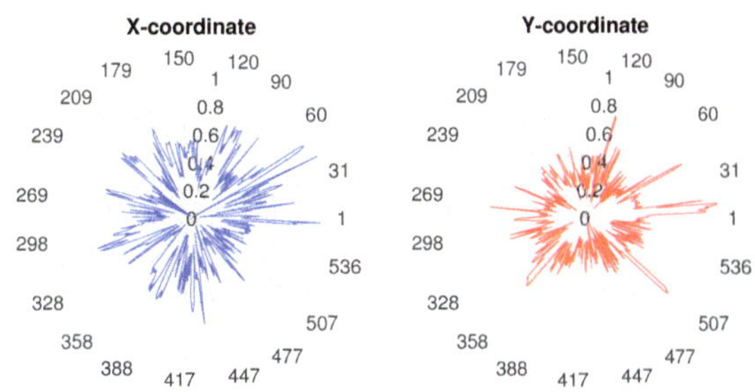
X-coordinate
Y-coordinate
150
120
90
60
31
1
536
507
477
447
417
388
358
328
298
269
239
209
179
0.8
0.6
0.4
0.2
0

(h)

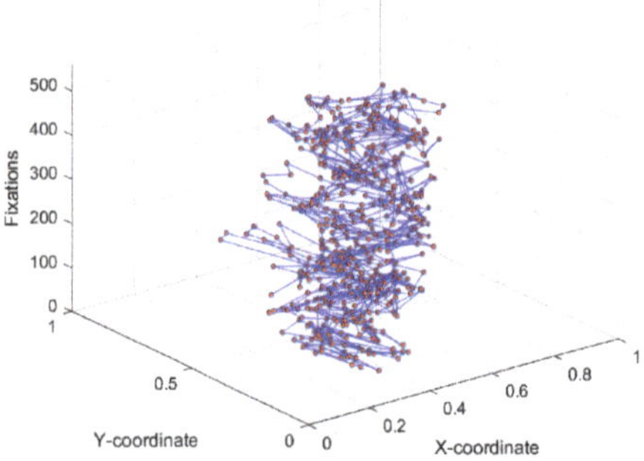

(i)

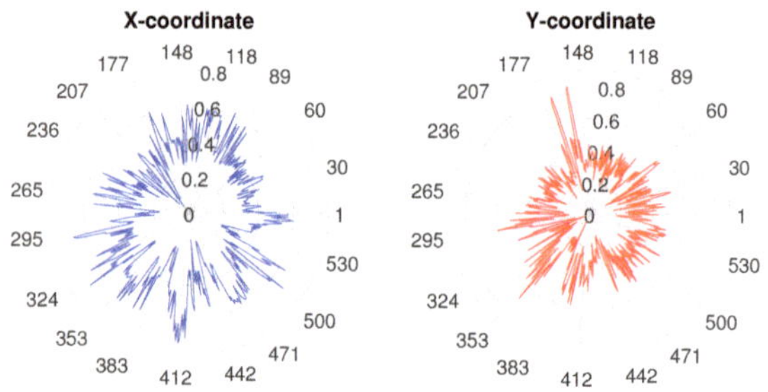

(j)

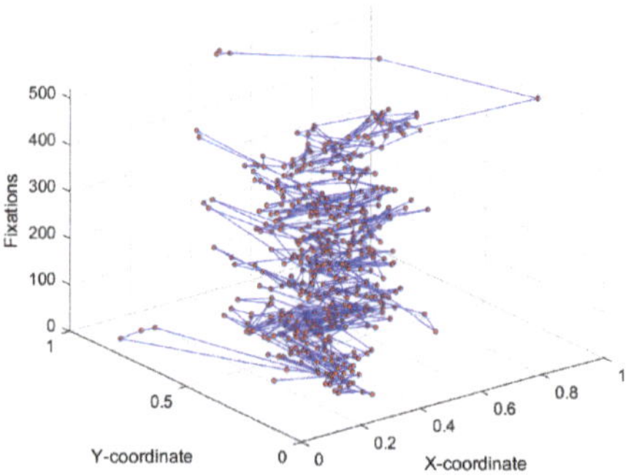

(k)

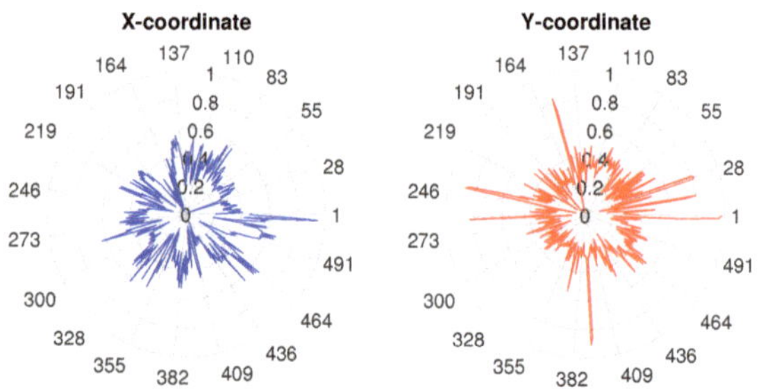

(l)

Figure 6. Dispersion of attention trajectories according to the degree of dyslexia risk and shape of X and Y coordinates in polar plane, left and right side of the figure, presented in the consecutive rows respectively. (**a**) Trajectory length: 454, dyslexia risk level: 0.4; (**b**) polar view of the attention coordinates with 7 occlusion episodes. (**c**) Trajectory length: 487, dyslexia risk level: 0.3; (**d**) polar view of the attention coordinates with 87 occlusion episodes. (**e**) Trajectory length: 464, dyslexia risk level: 0.2; (**f**) polar view of the attention coordinates with 42 occlusion episodes. (**g**) Trajectory length: 566, dyslexia risk level: 0.1; (**h**) polar view of the attention coordinates with 71 occlusion episodes. (**i**) Trajectory length: 559, dyslexia risk level: 0.6; (**j**) polar view of the attention coordinates with 17 occlusion episodes. (**k**) Trajectory length: 518, dyslexia risk level: 0.8; (**l**) polar view of the attention coordinates with 30 occlusion episodes.

Some of the strands of research that have formed in existing methods of detecting dyslexia with AI methods include [13], in which the image analysis of reproduced BVRT test cards was used, but it did not take into account the chronology and dynamics of scene observation or the relationship between observation and drawing tool operation. The coincidence of fixations depending on the complexity of the observed geometric figure is depicted in Figure 7.

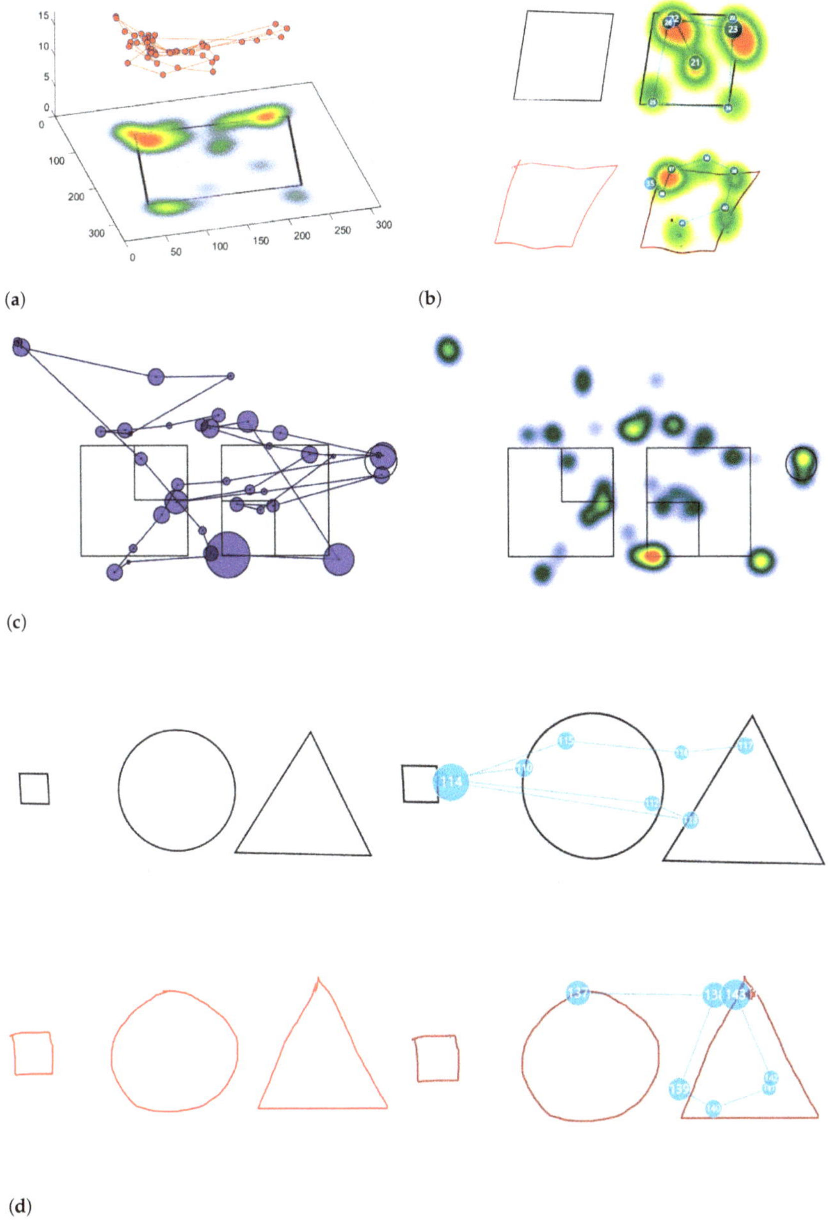

Figure 7. Fixation coincidence with figures' geometry (**a**) 3D appearance of the attention trajectory, (**b**) 2D appearance of the attention trajectory and the fixation heat map, (**c**) figure observation trajectory and accompanying heat map, respectively, (**d**) the coincidence of the geometry of the exposed figures and the observation trajectory.

During task execution, additional parameters of the process are recorded, such as momentary pupil diameter, which may be associated with individual characteristics of the study participant (see Figure 8).

Figure 8. The attention plot of the observer during the reproduction of the shape (square) from memory using the BeGaze Analysis Software (Version 2.4).

In the next chapter, based on the preliminary research conducted and observations, and utilizing the accumulated experience of team members, a measurement setup using a DNN (deep neural network) was proposed.

3. Attention-Tracking System Utilizing DNN to Support Therapy for Individuals with Neurodevelopmental Disorders

In Figure 9, a modular structure of an attention-tracking system supporting therapy for individuals with neurodevelopmental disorders is presented. Module A encompasses a designed research setup for recording the observer's attention during the performance of the BVRT test. This module is responsible for acquiring the video stream of the observed scene and recording the spatial position of the observer's pupils. Module B performs feature extraction (1) related to attention coordinate detection and fixation detection. The obtained data are passed to component (2), where tasks associated with recognizing visual perception disorders using LSTM (long short-term memory) networks are performed. The obtained results are transmitted to module C, and based on them, the therapist decides whether to initiate therapy or refer the subject to additional sessions. In contrast to previous works, which mainly focused on the use of neural networks during the reading and writing process [7,40–44], this study utilizes an LSTM network in the process of diagnosing dyslexia in elementary school-aged children. For implementation purposes, the Matlab environment and dedicated libraries for modeling DNNs were utilized. From the literature, it is known that attention trajectories, which possess a time-series nature, are effectively processed by LSTM networks. Therefore, the authors adopted a 5-layer model of the network, the structure of which is included in Table 6.

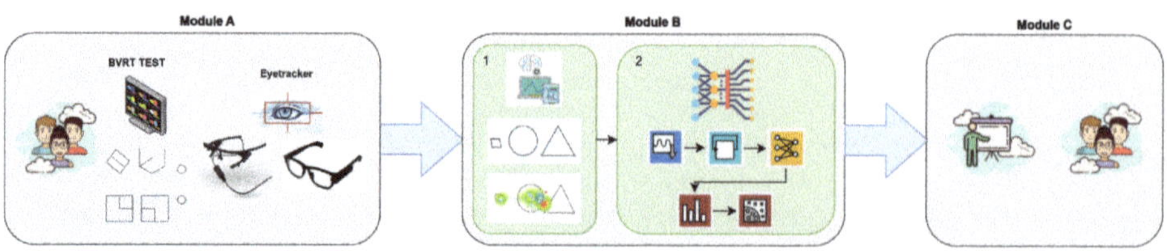

Figure 9. Attention -tracking system to support therapy for people with neurodevelopmental disorders for dyslexia diagnosis.

Table 6. Net structure from the deep learning network analyzer.

Name	Type	Activations	Learnables	
Trajectory series	Sequence input	5		–
Attention analyser	LSTM	16	InputWeights RecurrentWeights In Bias	64 × 12 64 × 16 64 × 1
Encoder	Fully Connected	6	Weights Bias	6 × 16 6 × 1
Softmax normalizer	Softmax	6		–
Dyslexia clasifier	Classification Output	6		–

Within the LSTM layer, the input gates x and y were adopted, respectively, which process successive fixations in the attention trajectory that occur during the measurement process. In the diagram below, h_t denotes the output, also referred to as the hidden state, while c_t denotes its state at time step t (see Figure 10).

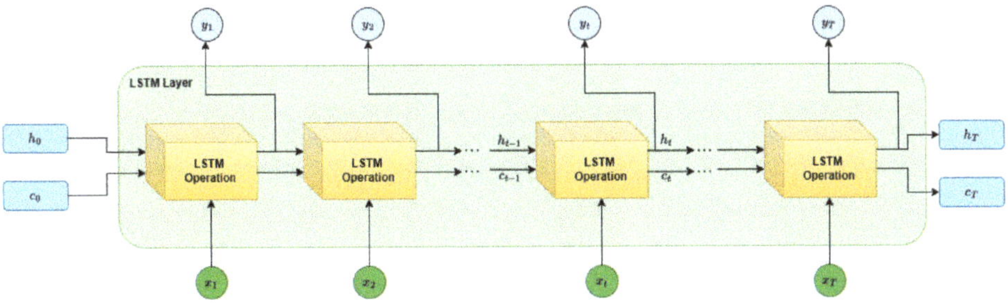

Figure 10. LSTM Layer Diagram.

At the time step t, the consecutive net layer cells use the current state of the RNN (c_{t-1}, h_{t-1}) and the next time step of the sequence to compute the output and the updated cell state c_t. The hidden state at time step t contains the output of the LSTM layer for this time step. The cell state contains information learned from the previous time steps. Each cell controls updates using gates (see Figure 11).

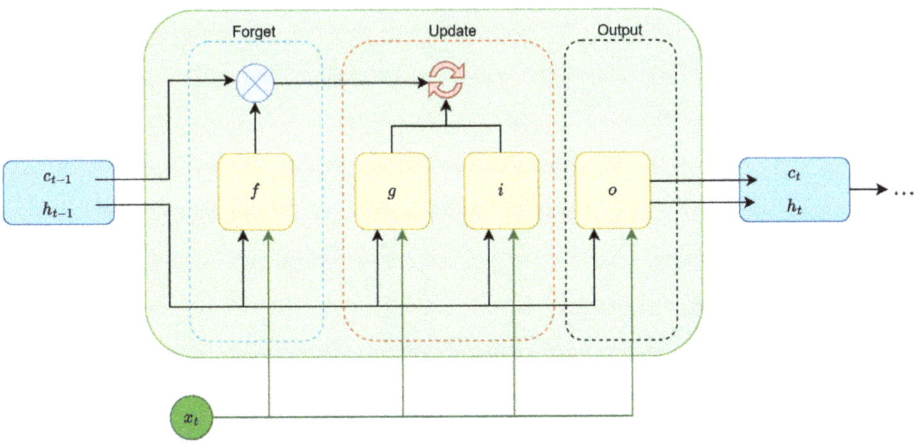

Figure 11. LSTM cell diagram.

The diagram shows how the gates forget, update, and output generate the cell signal and its hidden states, respectively. The learnable weights of an LSTM layer are

$$W = \left[W_i \; W_f \; W_g \; W_o\right]^T \tag{1}$$

$$R = \left[R_i \; R_f \; R_g \; R_o\right]^T \tag{2}$$

$$b = \left[b_i \; b_f \; b_g \; b_o\right]^T \tag{3}$$

where W denotes input weights, R represents recurrent weights, and b indicates bias, respectively. The flow of signal through the net implies that matrices W, R, and b are concatenations of the input weights, the recurrent weights, and the bias of each component, respectively. Additionally i, f, g, and o denote the input gate, forget gate, cell candidate, and output gate, respectively. The cell state at time step t is given by

$$c_t = f_t \odot c_{t-1} + i_t \odot g_t \tag{4}$$

where $\odot$ denotes the Hadamard product. The hidden state at time step t is given by

$$h_t = o_t \odot \sigma_c(c_t) \tag{5}$$

where σ_g denotes the state activation function. We assumed default transfer function as the hyperbolic tangent function to compute the net state at consecutive states [45].

One of the key stages in preparing data for analysis was standardizing the duration of fixations. Due to the large variation in the values of this feature, its standardization was applied, allowing for comparison and analysis of visual behaviors among participants. This stage was necessary to adapt the data for further modeling, considering the diversity of natural visual behaviors in children.

4. Results and Discussion

The analysis of the Benton Visual Retention Test (BVRT) results conducted on a group of early school-age children provided valuable insights into their cognitive abilities and potential learning difficulties, particularly related to dyslexia. The study involved 145 children, each subjected to a series of trials aimed at assessing their ability to reproduce geometric patterns from memory. Based on the obtained results, appropriate risk levels of visual perception disorders were classified, as indicated by the range of errors made (see Table 4). Participants were classified based on the number of errors made and the overall accuracy in reproducing the patterns.

The total number of errors made by the study participants consists of various types of inaccuracies, indicating the complexity of cognitive processes related to visual perception, visual memory, and visual constructional abilities. A statistical summary of the number of correct and incorrect reproductions is presented in Table 7.

Table 7. Summary of errors.

Name	Quantity
Number of correct mappings	746
Number of incorrect mappings	704
Average number of correct mappings	5.14
Average number of misrepresentations	4.86

According to the task assumptions, the correctness of pattern execution and its reproduction from memory were evaluated. Errors indicating spatial function disturbances were mainly related to distortions, omissions, and displacements. A detailed breakdown of errors is presented in Table 8.

Table 8. Summary of error types.

Types of Errors in Subjects	Quantity
Skip	190
Distortion	212
Perseverations	61
Rotation	58
Translation	139
Errors of relative magnitude	44

Analyzing the results obtained from the conducted eye-tracking studies, differences between fixations during memorization and reproduction of figures can be observed. As shown in Figure 7, trajectories during observation and reproduction differ slightly. This can be particularly observed in the attention plots during memorization and reproduction of shapes. The Figure 12 illustrates the convergent learning process for the adopted network architecture. As can be seen, this process is highly unstable due to numerous similarities among individual attention trajectories. Additionally, one must consider the arbitrary manner in which the expert assigns scores in the BVRT test, which generates a locally biased information leakage effect.

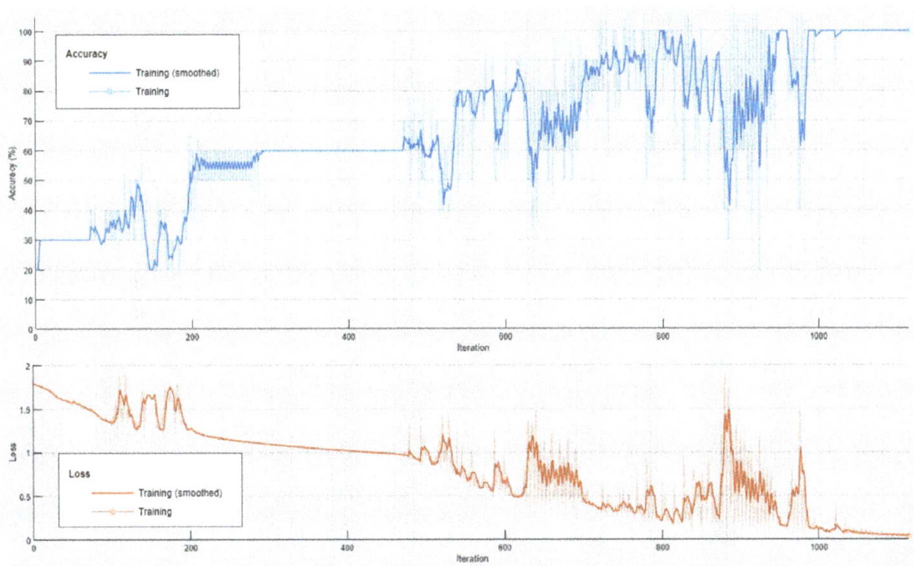

Figure 12. Training efficiency for the assumed net structure model.

For the network used, a fit test of the trained network model was carried out using a linear regression model. The following results, shown in Table 9, were obtained for the designed network during testing mode (train/test ratio: 70%/30%). In Figure 13, a confusion matrix is also presented, which facilitates the final assessment of the determination level of the obtained model. In the test set containing 43 records, 42 records were identified correctly with one incorrect diagnosis, yielding an overall prediction accuracy of the LSTM network of 97.7%, which should be considered a high indicator.

Table 9. Summary of error types.

	Estimate	SE	tStat	*p* Value
(Intercept)	0.03301	0.052743	0.62586	0.53488
×1	0.99709	0.014096	70.734	1.7749×10^{-44}

Number of observations: 43, Error degrees of freedom: 41. Root Mean Squared Error: 0.154. R–squared: 0.992, Adjusted R–Squared: 0.992. F–statistic vs. constant model: 5×10^3, *p*-value = 1.77×10^{-4}.

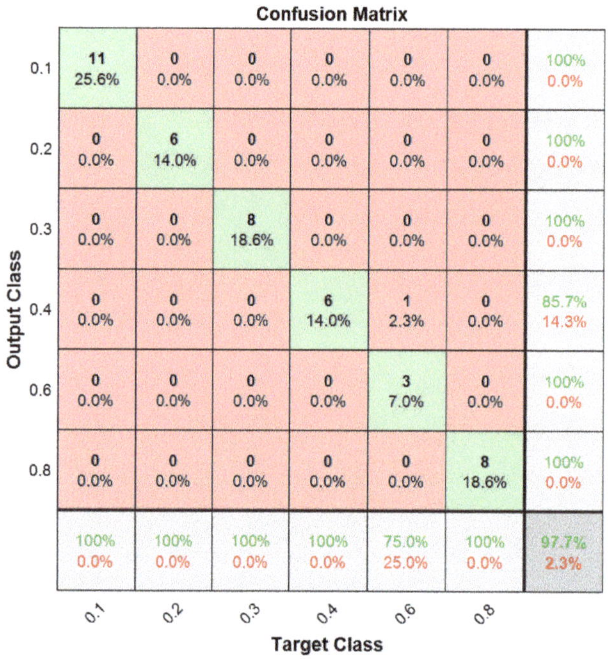

Figure 13. Confusion matrix obtained after the completed learning process. Cells colored with pink indicate the fields of wrong answers given by the network, while green cells indicate the fields of correct answers. The gray color indicates the cells containing the percentages of correct and incorrect network responses for each class, respectively.

Based on this, it can be concluded that the obtained coefficient of determination R^2 indicates the high effectiveness of the proposed method of attentional analysis for diagnosing dyslexia.

Early diagnosis of dyslexia is essential for maximizing the potential of individuals with dyslexia and for creating a more inclusive, educated, and economically stable society. By identifying and addressing dyslexia early, we can ensure that all individuals have the opportunity to succeed and contribute positively to their communities. Early diagnosis of dyslexia is especially essential for providing children with the support they need to succeed academically, emotionally, and socially. It empowers families, educators, and society to create a more inclusive and effective education system, leading to better outcomes for individuals and communities.

Over the past few years, various tools and methods have been developed to achieve relatively high detectability of dyslexia. These include studies of brain activity associated with cognitive processes during specific tasks using highly specialized equipment, such as fMRI imaging. Analysis of these images with convolutional networks has achieved an accuracy of 72.73% [13,19]. Combining fMRI with DTI can provide extended DICOM data, which, when analyzed using PCA, serve as a source of information for neural classifiers, achieving an accuracy of 91.87% [18].

In contrast, other systems [13] (with an accuracy of around 94.73%) are convenient and easy to use, as they require only modules for acquiring graphical task results. This is an important feature that facilitates their application in school settings without the need for an expert's involvement. On the other hand, the age and academic skills of the children being tested may necessitate differentiating the test tasks used for dyslexia detection.

Methods for diagnosing dyslexia that utilize reading process analysis often employ SVM binary classifiers [28], which leverage the properties of fixation and saccade observations, achieving an accuracy of 80.18%. Higher accuracy is achieved by KNN classifiers [30], tested on a relatively large group of children, reaching an accuracy of 95%.

Some reading task analysis methods are tailored to specific languages, such as Serbian [32], where analysis of the geometry of observation trajectories achieves an accuracy of 87%. In methods aimed at individuals with reading and writing skills, both lexicographic and semantic tasks can be used. Efforts to increase dyslexia detection accuracy also focus on acquiring a large number of coordinates representing the state of the perception and scene recognition process. In such cases, the task of extracting relevant information is left to CNNs, achieving an accuracy of 95.6% [31].

5. Conclusions

This study presented significant findings on using deep LSTM networks for dyslexia recognition by analyzing time series data depicting the attention trajectories of individual participants. Among various eye trackers, including Tobii, SMI, and Pupil, the team effectively utilized the Pupil Invisible and Pupil Core models, which facilitated seamless research in school environments.

Based on the conducted experiments, the following conclusions can be drawn:

- The Benton Test, employed to establish the expected values of the training set, proved to be an effective tool for use in intelligent systems aimed at recognizing developmental disorders in early school-age children.
- For dyslexia detection studies in children, non-invasive eye trackers that minimally disrupt the child's attention during measurements are recommended.
- Spatiotemporal measurements of attention trajectories can be effectively utilized to identify anomalies indicative of dyslexia risk.
- A high level of dispersion in attention trajectories correlates with high accuracy in task reproduction during BVRT tests, suggesting a lower risk of dyslexia.
- As with other systems that rely on expert knowledge, the arbitrary assessment method of BVRT test results for constructing a learning sequence is a limitation. It is advisable to involve a larger number of experts for independent result assessments to enhance reliability.
- The definite ease of implementation in a school setting (preferring a Pupil Invisible stand) of the proposed method is a significant advantage and superiority over methods using fMRI measurements [7].
- Analyzing attention trajectories using LSTM networks offers a robust alternative to methods utilizing CNNs for static graphical analysis of the BVRT test forms, as it accounts for the temporal and spatial strategies employed by humans in scene recognition.

Based on the observations and conclusions from the conducted research, several promising directions for further studies on dyslexia recognition can be identified. In particular, it is anticipated that combining LSTM and CNN networks in future research will enhance the accuracy and confidence in dyslexia recognition results for early school-age children. Exploring the creation of a hybrid model that combines various methods of analyzing perception and scene recognition, as well as psychomotor reactions during performing specific tasks, will be a focus for the authors' future work.

Author Contributions: Conceptualization, Z.G.; methodology, Z.G., E.Z. and B.C.; software, Z.G. and E.Z.; validation, Z.G., E.Z., B.C. and Y.K.; formal analysis, Z.G., E.Z., B.C. and Y.K.; investigation, Z.G. and E.Z.; resources, Z.G., E.Z. and B.C.; data curation, Z.G. and E.Z.; writing original draft preparation, Z.G. and E.Z.; writing—review and editing, Z.G. and E.Z.; visualization, Z.G. and E.Z.; supervision, Z.G.; project administration, Z.G.; funding acquisition, Z.G. and E.Z. All authors have read and agreed to the published version of the manuscript.

Funding: This research received no external funding

Institutional Review Board Statement: The study was approved by the Institutional Review Ethic Board of the PGKICPO, and the ethical approval was granted on 9 November 2022, under the reference number IRB-20221109. Informed consent was obtained from all subjects involved in the study and written informed consent has been obtained from the patients to publish this paper.

Informed Consent Statement: Informed consent was obtained from all subjects involved in the study. Written informed consent has been obtained from the patients to publish this paper.

Data Availability Statement: The data presented in this study are available on request from the corresponding author.

Conflicts of Interest: The authors declare no conflicts of interest.

Abbreviations

The following abbreviations are used in this manuscript:

BVRT	Benton Visual Retention Test
CBT	Cognitive Behavioral Therapy
CNN	Convolutional Neural Network
Davis	Ron Davis Method
DNN	Deep Neural Network
DRL	Dyslexia Risk Level
DTI	Diffusion Tensor Imaging
EEG	Electroencephalography
fMRI	Functional Magnetic Resonance Imaging
IFR	Instrument Flight Rules
LSTM	Long Short-Term Memory
RNN	Recurrent Neural Network
SI	Sensory Integration Therapy
VFR	Visual Flight Rules

References

1. Bogdanowicz, M. Specyficzne trudności w czytaniu i pisaniu. In *Dysleksja rozwojowa. Perspektywa psychologiczna*; Krasowicz-Kupis, G., Ed.; Wydawnictwo Harmonia: Gdańsk, Poland, 2006; pp. 7–35.
2. Snowling, M.J. *Dyslexia*; Blackwell Publishers: Oxford, UK, 2000.
3. Shaywitz, S.E. *Overcoming Dyslexia: A New and Complete Science-Based Program for Reading Problems at Any Level*; Alfred A., Ed.; Knopf: New York, NY, USA, 2003.
4. Zoccolotti, P.; de Jong, P.F.; Spinelli, D. Editorial: Understanding Developmental Dyslexia: Linking Perceptual and Cognitive Deficits to Reading Processes. *Front. Hum. Neurosci.* **2016**, *10*, 140. [CrossRef]
5. Vellutino, F.R.; Fletcher, J.M.; Snowling, M.J.; Scanlon, D.M. Specific reading disability (dyslexia): What have we learned in the past four decades? *J. Child Psychol. Psychiatry* **2004**, *45*, 2–40. [CrossRef]
6. Ramus, F. Developmental dyslexia: Specific phonological deficit or general sensorimotor dysfunction? *Curr. Opin. Neurobiol.* **2003**, *13*, 212–218. [CrossRef] [PubMed]
7. Zahia, S.; Garcia-Zapirain, B.; Saralegui, I.; Fernandez-Ruanova, B. Dyslexia detection using 3D convolutional neural networks and functional magnetic resonance imaging. *Comput. Methods Programs Biomed.* **2020**, *197*, 105726. [CrossRef]
8. Scheiman, M. *Understanding and Managing Vision Deficits: A Guide for Occupational Therapists*, 3rd ed.; Routledge: London, UK, 2024.
9. Lyon, G.R.; Shaywitz, S.E.; Shaywitz, B.A. A Definition of Dyslexia. *Ann. Dyslexia* **2003**, *53*, 1–14. [CrossRef]
10. European Dyslexia Association. *Dyslexia: The European Perspective*; European Dyslexia Association: Braine Le Château, Belgium. Available online: https://eda-info.eu/ (accessed on 1 July 2024).
11. Roitsch, J.; Watson, S. An Overview of Dyslexia: Definition, Characteristics, Assessment, Identification, and Intervention. *Sci. J. Educ.* **2019**, *7*, 81–86. [CrossRef]

12. Capin, P.; Gillam, S.L.; Fall, A.M.; Roberts, G.; Dille, J.T.; Gillam, R.B. Understanding the nature and severity of reading difficulties among students with language and reading comprehension difficulties. *Ann Dyslexia.* **2022**, *72*, 249. [CrossRef] [PubMed]
13. Gabor, D.; Doniec, R.; Sieciński, S.; Piaseczna, N.; Duraj, K.; Tkacz, E. Automatic Assessment of Benton Visual Retention Test Results: A Pilot Study. In Proceedings of the Biocybernetics and Biomedical Engineering—Current Trends and Challenges; Warsaw, Poland, 19–21 May 2021; Pijanowska, D.G., Zieliński, K., Liebert, A., Kacprzyk, J., Eds.; Springer: Cham, Switzerland, 2022; pp. 1–8. [CrossRef]
14. Shaywitz, S.; Shaywitz, J. *Overcoming Dyslexia (2020 Edition): Second Edition, Completely Revised and Updated*; Vintage; Knopf Doubleday Publishing Group: Broadway, NY, USA, 2008.
15. Berninger, V.; Richards, T. Inter-relationships among behavioral markers, genes, brain and treatment in dyslexia and dysgraphia. *Future Neurol.* **2010**, *5*, 597–617. [CrossRef] [PubMed]
16. Drigas, A.; Drigas, A.; Politi-Georgousi, S. ICTs as a Distinct Detection Approach for Dyslexia Screening: A Contemporary View. *Int. J. Online Biomed. Eng.* **2019**, *3*, 46–59. [CrossRef]
17. Sood, M.R.; Toornstra, A.; Sereno, M.I.; Boland, M.; Filaretti, D.; Sood, A. A Digital App to Aid Detection, Monitoring, and Management of Dyslexia in Young Children (DIMMAND): Protocol for a Digital Health and Education Solution. *JMIR Res. Protoc.* **2018**, *7*, e135. [CrossRef]
18. Chimeno, Y.G.; Zapirain, B.G.; Prieto, I.S.; Fernandez-Ruanova, B. Automatic classification of dyslexic children by applying machine learning to fMRI images. *Biomed. Mater. Eng.* **2014**, *24*, 2995. [CrossRef]
19. Lobier, M.A.; Peyrin, C.; Pichat, C.; Bas, J.F.L.; Valdois, S. Visual processing of multiple elements in the dyslexic brain: Evidence for a superior parietal dysfunction. *Front. Hum. Neurosci.* **2014**, *8*, 81737. [CrossRef] [PubMed]
20. Arns, M.; Peters, S.; Breteler, R.; Verhoeven, L. Different brain activation patterns in dyslexic children: Evidence from EEG power and coherence patterns for the double-deficit theory of dyslexia. *J. Integr. Neurosci.* **2011**, *6*, 175. [CrossRef] [PubMed]
21. Gonzlez, G.F.; der Molen, M.J.W.V.; Žarić, G.; Bonte, M.; Tijms, J.; Blomert, L.; Stam, C.J.; Molen, M.W.V.d. Graph analysis of EEG resting state functional networks in dyslexic readers. *Clin. Neurophysiol.* **2016**, *127*, 3165. [CrossRef]
22. Spironelli, C.; Penolazzi, B.; Angrilli, A. Dysfunctional hemispheric asymmetry of theta and beta EEG activity during linguistic tasks in developmental dyslexia. *Biol. Psychol.* **2008**, *77*, 123. [CrossRef]
23. Christoforou, C.; Fella, A.; Leppnen, P.H.T.; Georgiou, G.K.; Papadopoulos, T.C. Fixation-related potentials in naming speed: A combined EEG and eye-tracking study on children with dyslexia. *Clin. Neurophysiol.* **2021**, *132*, 2798. [CrossRef]
24. Jakovljevi, T.; Janković, M.M.; Savić, A.M.; Soldatović, I.; Čolić, G.; Jakulin, T.J.; Papa, G.; Ković, V. The relation between physiological parameters and colour modifications in text background and overlay during reading in children with and without dyslexia. *Brain Sci.* **2021**, *11*, 539. [CrossRef] [PubMed]
25. Jakovljević, T.; Janković, M.M.; Savić, A.M.; Soldatović, I.; Todorović, P.; Jere Jakulin, T.; Papa, G.; Ković, V. The Sensor Hub for Detecting the Developmental Characteristics in Reading in Children on a White vs. Colored Background/Colored Overlays. *Sensors* **2021**, *21*, 406. [CrossRef]
26. Temelturk, R.D.; Ozer, E. Binocular coordination of children with dyslexia and typically developing children in linguistic and non-linguistic tasks: Evidence from eye movements. *Ann Dyslexia.* **2022**, *72*, 426. [CrossRef]
27. Wang, R.; Bi, H.-Y. A predictive model for chinese children with developmental dyslexia—Based on a genetic algorithm optimized back-propagation neural network. *Expert Syst. Appl.* **2022**, *187*, 115949. [CrossRef]
28. Rello, L.; Ballesteros, M. Detecting readers with dyslexia using machine learning with eye tracking measures. In Proceedings of the W4A: International Web for All Conference, Florence, Italy, 18–20 May 2015; pp. 1–8. [CrossRef]
29. Benfatto, M.N.; Seimyr, G.Ö.; Ygge, J.; Pansell, T.; Rydberg, A.; Jacobson, C. Screening for Dyslexia Using Eye Tracking during Reading. *PLoS ONE* **2016**, *11*, e0165508. [CrossRef]
30. Prabha, A.J.; Bhargavi, R.; Harish, B. An Efficient Machine Learning Model for Prediction of Dyslexia from Eye Fixation Events. *New Approaches Eng. Res.* **2021**, *10*, 171179. [CrossRef]
31. Neruil, B.; Polec, J.; Škunda, J.; Kačur, J. Eye tracking based dyslexia detection using a holistic approach. *Sci. Rep.* **2021**, *11*, 15687. [CrossRef]
32. Vajs, I.; Kovic, V.; Papic, T.; Savic, A.M.; Jankovic, M.M. Dyslexia detection in children using eye tracking data based on VGG16 network. In Proceedings of the European Signal Processing Conference, Belgrade, Serbia, 29 August–2 September 2022; p. 16011605. [CrossRef]
33. Czuba, B. Psychological and medical aspects of influencing a chronically psychosomatically ill child and his family. *Educ. Ther. Care* **2021**, *3*, 207–217. [CrossRef]
34. Czuba, B.; Król, K. Behavioural and emotional disorders in children and psychological and pedagogical assistance. *Educ. Ther. Care* **2020**, *2*, 198–210. [CrossRef]
35. Czuba, B.; Inglot-Kulas, J.; Król, K. Psychosocial strategies supporting the student's abilities in contemporary education. *Educ. Ther. Care* **2019**, *1*, 163–183. [CrossRef]
36. Gomolka, Z.; Kordos, D.; Zeslawska, E. The Application of Flexible Areas of Interest to Pilot Mobile Eye Tracking. *Sensors* **2020**, *20*, 986. [CrossRef]
37. Gomolka, Z.; Zeslawska, E.; Twarog, B.; Kordos, D.; Rzucidlo, P. Use of a DNN in Recording and Analysis of Operator Attention in Advanced HMI Systems. *Appl. Sci.* **2022**, *12*, 11431. [CrossRef]

38. Choi, W.H.; Kim, J. Unsupervised Learning Approach for Anomaly Detection in Industrial Control Systems. *Appl. Syst. Innov.* **2024**, *7*, 18. [CrossRef]
39. Sidenko, I.; Filina, K.; Kondratenko, G.; Chabanovskyi, D.; Kondratenko, Y. Eye-tracking technology for the analysis of dynamic data. In Proceedings of the 2018 IEEE 9th International Conference on Dependable Systems, Services and Technologies (DESSERT), Kyiv, UKraine, 24–27 May 2018; pp. 479–484. [CrossRef]
40. Aldehim, G.; Rashid, M.; Alluhaidan, A.S.; Sakri, S.B.; Basheer, S. Deep Learning for Dyslexia Detection: A Comprehensive CNN Approach with Handwriting Analysis and Benchmark Comparisons. *J. Disabil. Res.* **2024**, *3*, 202400. [CrossRef]
41. Alqahtani, N.D.; Alzahrani, B.; Ramzan, M.S. Deep Learning Applications for Dyslexia Prediction. *Appl. Sci.* **2023**, *13*, 2804. [CrossRef]
42. Mati-Zissi, H.; Zafiropoulou, M.; Bonoti, F. Drawing performance in children with special learning difficulties. *Percept. Mot. Ski.* **1998**, *87*, 487. [CrossRef] [PubMed]
43. Rankin, Q.; Riley, P.E.H. Exploring the Links between Drawing and Dyslexia, Teachers Academy Papers. *Accessed Mar.* **2007**, *22*, 2024.
44. Yogarajah, P.; Bhushan, B. Deep Learning Approach to Automated Detection of Dyslexia-Dysgraphia. In Proceedings of the 2020 25th International Conference on Pattern Recognition (ICPR), Milan, Italy, 10–15 January 2021.
45. Hochreiter, S.; Schmidhuber, J. Long Short-Term Memory. *Neural Comput.* **1997**, *9*, 1735–1780. [CrossRef] [PubMed]

applied sciences

MDPI

Article

Area of Interest Tracking Techniques for Driving Scenarios Focusing on Visual Distraction Detection

Viktor Nagy [1,*], Péter Földesi [1,2] and György Istenes [1]

[1] Central Campus Győr, Széchenyi István University, H-9026 Gyor, Hungary; foldesi@sze.hu (P.F.); istenes.gyorgy@ga.sze.hu (G.I.)
[2] Eötvös Loránd Research Network, Piarista u. 4, H-1052 Budapest, Hungary
* Correspondence: nviktor@sze.hu

Abstract: On-road driving studies are essential for comprehending real-world driver behavior. This study investigates the use of eye-tracking (ET) technology in research on driver behavior and attention during Controlled Driving Studies (CDS). One significant challenge in these studies is accurately detecting when drivers divert their attention from crucial driving tasks. To tackle this issue, we present an improved method for analyzing raw gaze data, using a new algorithm for identifying ID tags called Binarized Area of Interest Tracking (BAIT). This technique improves the detection of incidents where the driver's eyes are off the road through binarizing frames under different conditions and iteratively recognizing markers. It represents a significant improvement over traditional methods. The study shows that BAIT performs better than other software in identifying a driver's focus on the windscreen and dashboard with higher accuracy. This study highlights the potential of our method to enhance the analysis of driver attention in real-world conditions, paving the way for future developments for application in naturalistic driving studies.

Keywords: controlled driving study; eye-tracking; gaze patterns; eyes-off-the-road; marker detection

1. Introduction

The evolution of personal transportation is being significantly reshaped by emerging automotive technologies. With the rise of automated and autonomous vehicles, there's a notable shift in User Interface (UI) development for cars, predominantly at SAE level 2 or "Partial Driving Automation" [1]. This progression requires drivers to adapt to more sophisticated Advanced Driving Assistant Systems (ADAS) that manage vehicle dynamics but still rely on the driver for object detection and response, increasing cognitive load. Moreover, current Human–Machine Interfaces (HMI) and Human–Computer Interaction (HCI) concepts designed for manually controlled vehicles may inadvertently escalate manual and visual distractions, challenging the promised safety levels of ADAS [2,3]. In this context, the human driver's situational awareness remains crucial, especially as ADAS, despite advancements, are not infallible and may require human intervention to rectify errors or misjudgments in certain scenarios [4].

1.1. Driving Studies

The categorization of driving research methodologies into Driving Simulators, Naturalistic Driving (ND) studies, Instrumented Vehicle Studies (IVS), and CDS serve as a critical framework for dissecting and understanding the different aspects of driving behavior, vehicle maneuvering, and interactions within the traffic ecosystem. This categorization is instrumental in integrating ET research.

Driving simulators offer a controlled environment for safely assessing driver behavior and cognitive abilities [5,6]. These studies highlight both the absolute and relative validity of simulators in mimicking real-road conditions, albeit with noted limitations in replicating the full spectrum of driving errors, particularly those related to vehicle positioning and speed regulation. The controlled nature of simulators allows for the manipulation of specific variables and the safe assessment of driver responses to hypothetical scenarios, which are impractical or dangerous to test in real-world settings.

ND studies are pivotal for capturing real-world driving behavior by equipping vehicles with cameras and sensors [7]. This unobtrusive data collection approach offers authentic insights into the dynamic interactions between drivers, vehicles, and traffic environments. The strength of ND studies lies in their ability to provide a rich, contextual understanding of driving behavior without the artificial constraints imposed by experimental settings.

IVS are similar to ND studies but utilize real vehicles outfitted with advanced measurement tools [8]. However, IVS can be more focused in their objectives, often geared towards quantifying specific aspects of driving behavior or vehicle performance under naturalistic conditions. This approach enables a detailed analysis of driver strategy, vehicle usage, and decision-making processes. IVS can serve as a bridge between the authentic environments of ND studies and the controlled conditions of driving simulators.

CDS involve the operation of real cars within a managed setting, such as a closed circuit [9]. This method allows researchers to study driving behavior under adjustable conditions, facilitating a focused examination of specific hypotheses about driver performance or the effectiveness of interventions. While lacking the ecological validity of ND studies, controlled driving allows for the precise manipulation of experimental variables, making it a valuable tool for testing specific driving aids or interventions under semi-naturalistic conditions.

1.2. Driver Distraction

Driver distraction, defined as the shift of attention from essential driving tasks to other activities, forms a part of the broader concept of driver inattention [10]. This encompasses several forms, including Driver Diverted Attention, which is synonymous with distraction, whether the focus is on Driving-Related and Non-Driving-Related Tasks (NDRT). Distractions can impede activities necessary for safe driving [11]. Eye tracking and algorithmic analysis of glance behavior help to quantify driver inattention, despite drivers having visual spare capacity or off-target glances [12]. Distractions are classified by the National Highway Traffic Safety Administration into four types: visual, auditory, biomechanical (manual or physical), and cognitive. Visual distractions involve loss of road awareness due to a blocked field of vision or focus on non-road visual targets [13], while auditory distractions come from sounds or auditory signals diverting attention [14]. Manual distractions involve handling devices or interfaces instead of the steering wheel, reducing reaction time [15]. Cognitive distractions are thoughts that limit focus on driving, often caused by external factors or cognitive overload, leading to a "Look at but not see" issue.

The NDRT necessitate the allocation of visual attention and give rise to visual distraction, a phenomenon that can be quantified through gaze tracking techniques and subsequently manifests as Total Eyes-Off-Road Time (TEORT) [16]. TEORT represents the duration during which the driver's gaze is not directed towards the road but is instead focused on the Area of Interest (AOI) represented by the In-Vehicle Information System (IVIS) interface or any other NDRT including phone usage or eating and drinking.

1.3. Eye-Tracking

ET technology is a valuable tool for user testing as it enables the precise assessment of a subject's perception and behavior during task execution. ET is widely used in both real-world and simulated settings for diverse measurements, proving especially beneficial in examining human behavior within the contexts of aviation and vehicular driving [17]. ET is underscored as a crucial method for determining driver distraction through the classification of glance targets. Three primary approaches are present to interpreting ET data in driver attention research [18]: 1. Direction-Based Approach: Evaluates gaze direction (e.g., forward, up, down) to calculate indicators like Eyes-Off-Road. Its limitation lies in not considering the context of the driver's gaze; 2. Target-Based Approach: Identifies objects intersected by the driver's gaze through manual video coding or deep learning. While it distinguishes glance targets, it may overlook the context; 3. Purpose-Based Approach: Focuses on areas deemed essential for driving attentiveness, integrating traffic rules and situational contexts to evaluate gaze relevance and adequacy. These approaches offer varying perspectives on analyzing eye-tracking data for driver attention, each with its strengths and limitations in context sensitivity and specificity. ET systems can record detailed user interactions and provide accurate measurements of gaze shifts, AOI times and pupillometry, even for cognitive abilities. Previous CDS measurements were based on a wearable eye-tracker that provides fixation points of the driver's gaze and detects changes in pupil diameter to monitor distraction and estimate higher cognitive load in comparison tests [19]. Others introduced the Index of Pupillary Activity, a novel ET measure assessing cognitive load via pupil oscillation frequency [20]. The replicable method helps differentiating task difficulty and cognitive load.

1.4. Area of Interest

Several key studies stand out in the literature on AOI detection in various applications. Early research has demonstrated the importance of ET in evaluating interface usability using eye movements, establishing a methodology that has become fundamental in usability studies [21]. This work emphasized the importance of understanding how users interact with interfaces, guiding improvements in design to enhance user experience. In one study researchers highlight differences in gaze patterns between natural environments and lab settings, emphasizing the need to consider natural settings in ET research as it significantly influences gaze behavior [22]. This study underscored the variability of eye movement data and the importance of designing experiments that mimic real-world settings as closely as possible. Another study tackled the area-of-interest problem in ET research by proposing a noise-robust solution for analyzing gaze data, especially when dealing with faces and sparse stimuli. Their methodology significantly contributed to improving the accuracy and reliability of ET analyses across multiple disciplines [23]. Another study introduces a specialized system for ET in video lecture contexts, showcasing its utility in enhancing educational research through engagement analysis and cognitive-process understanding [24]. The research on dynamic AOIs in ET incorporates various methodologies. New methods were introduced for filtering eye movements from dynamic areas of interest, marking a significant advance in real-time ET analysis [25]. The methodology allows for a more precise and automated analysis of gaze data in scenarios where the objects of interest are not static [20]. One study presented guidelines for integrating dynamic AOIs in setups involving moving objects, such as aircraft [26]. This study is crucial for research areas requiring automated and structured analysis of eye movements in dynamic environments, offering a blueprint for setting up such experiments. Another method explores using ArUco fiducial markers to map gaze data in dynamic settings, resolving issues of object occlusion and overlap, and also improves the accuracy of gaze tracking in complex environments [27]. A different approach introduces an open-source software for determining dynamic AOIs, enhancing tracking in studies with moving stimuli [28]. From a signal detection perspective, one study investigates the impact of area of interest (AOI) size on measuring object attention and cognitive processes. The findings contribute to a better understanding of the factors that influence the interpretation of ET data [29]. Some presented a toolkit for wide-screen dynamic AOI measurements using the Pupil Labs Core Eye Tracker, applicable in psychology and transportation research, such as multi-display driving simulators [30]. This toolkit expands the capabilities of researchers to conduct sophisticated analyses of eye movements in diverse and dynamic visual environments. These studies collectively illustrate the diverse applications and advancements in AOI detection using ET technology.

1.5. Image Binarization

Several articles have explored the complexities of image binarization, especially in the context of historical documents. The evolution of methodologies has highlighted the incorporation of machine learning to enhance preservation efforts [31]. One review underscores the challenges faced in preserving and digitizing historical documents, which often suffer from degradation, variable text quality, and background noise. This work is pivotal in guiding future research towards developing more robust and adaptive binarization techniques. The AprilTag 2 system has been developed and optimized for better efficiency and accuracy to present significant improvements in the detection of fiducial markers, which are essential for robotics and augmented reality applications [32]. The AprilTag 2 system improves the detection of fiducial markers. These markers serve as reference points in physical space for various technological applications, including navigation, object tracking, and interaction in augmented reality environments. The presented advancements signify a substantial improvement in the operational capabilities of systems that rely on fiducial markers. This showcases the potential for more seamless integration of virtual and physical elements in technological applications. For instance, in the agricultural sector, researchers have developed an image recognition system for cow identification. This system uses YOLO for cow head detection and CNNs for ear tag recognition, which supports improved herd management in precision dairy farming [33]. By employing advanced image recognition techniques, the study demonstrates the applicability and benefits of such technologies in the agricultural sector, particularly in enhancing the management and welfare of livestock through improved identification and tracking capabilities. These studies demonstrate the increasing range and ongoing enhancement of image analysis technologies, such as binarization and other techniques, in diverse fields.

1.6. Present Study

Recent advancements in ET technology have greatly improved the understanding of driver behavior and distraction, especially on-road, where there are many diverse environmental variables. Although traditional methods can provide valuable insights, they may not fully address the complexities of real-world driving due to reliability issues, and the inability to adapt to the three-dimensional nature of a driver's Field of View (FOV). This gap in the literature underscores a pressing need for innovative solutions capable of overcoming these aggravating factors. Specifically, there exists a critical demand for methodologies that can accurately define and detect AOIs within the cabin space of passenger vehicles, where the windshield's tilt and dashboard architecture introduce unique spatial considerations. Conventional flat-surface marker-based identification systems do not suffice due to potential obstructions, such as the steering wheel or the driver's hands, and external factors like changing light conditions and glare, which compromise detection efficiency. To address these challenges, our study presents a novel approach that utilizes a mathematical model implemented in Matlab. This model is designed to detect markers with exceptional efficiency, accurately identifying complex areas of interest (AOIs) within the driver's operational environment. Our method stands out due to its ability to consider the spatial dynamics of in-vehicle interfaces and the external environmental factors that affect visibility and detection accuracy.

This research aims to bridge the gap in AOI detection methodologies by providing a robust tool that enhances the reliability and applicability of eye-tracking studies in CDS. Our contribution is expected to have a significant impact on the field by offering a practical solution to one of the most pressing challenges in understanding driver distraction and cognitive load in real-world conditions.

2. Methods

This research focused on analyzing driver behavior and distraction levels caused by IVIS, with a particular emphasis on traffic safety. The objective was to conduct data acquisition using an ET device to identify instances of gaze diversion from the road (gaze-off-the-road) and precisely quantify visual distractions from onboard interfaces.

2.1. The Experiment

The visual distraction was measured using an ET system, conducted with 10 volunteer participants (2 females, 8 males, aged 20–44 years), who had varying driving experiences and regularly used IVIS-equipped cars. The test took place on the "High-Speed Handling Course" at the ZalaZONE Test Center, Hungary. The study aimed to assess visual distractions during a brief NDRT using two distinct interface types. Uniform test conditions were maintained (same test car and lighting conditions) for all participants, with task brevity ensuring a minimal environmental impact on the results and comparability of tasks. Conducted on a consistent, straight track section under stable weather conditions, this minimized external distractions like road curvature and variable sunlight. The specific task involved adjusting the car's internal temperature using the climate control system, with each participant receiving standardized verbal and practical instructions on interface use before the test.

2.2. The Measurement System

For detecting visual, manual, and cognitive distractions, the study utilized the Pupil Labs Core, a wearable ET device complemented with high-definition cameras [34]. This head-mounted device, chosen for its superior accuracy compared to alternatives like the SMI ETG 2.6 and Tobii Pro Glasses 2, featured binocular glasses equipped with two infrared eye cameras and a wide-angle Red-Green-Blue (RGB) world-view camera [35]. ET data includes video recordings (with a world-view camera, Eye0, and Eye1) and raw data components (such as time stamps, pupil positions, pupil diameters, and calculated gaze positions marked using x and y coordinates). The setup included an extensible, open-source mobile ET system with software for recording and analyzing data. Calibration was semi-automated, and for enhanced post-processing capabilities, ID-tag markers (AprilTag; tag36h11 family [36]), sized 50 mm × 50 mm and printed on hard plastic, were strategically positioned around the vehicle's dashboard center console and in the driver's windscreen area, as shown in Figure 1. The parameters of the ET system are presented in Table 1.

Figure 1. Test apparatus: Pupil Core eye-tracking device installed on the head of driver; ID tags in the view of driver (around windscreen and center console).

Table 1. Eye-tracking system datasheet.

Feature	Specification
Eye Tracking System	Pupil Core eye-tracking system
Infrared (IR) Eye Cameras	2 cameras, 120 Hz @ 400 × 400 px
RGB World-view camera	1 camera, 30 Hz @ 1080p/60 Hz @ 720p, 139° × 83° wide-angle lens
Recording Management	Pupil Capture software v3.5.1 (Pupil Labs GmbH., Berlin, Germany)
Workstation PC Specifications	11th Gen Intel(R) Core(TM) i7–11800H, 32 DDR4 RAM, NVIDIA GeForce RTX 3050 Ti Laptop GPU
Calibration Process	Semi-automated, using calibration circles
ID-Tag Markers	tag36h11 family printed on 50 mm × 50 mm hard plastic plates (ID tags: 0 to 7)
Post-processing	Pupil Player software v3.5.1 (Pupil Labs GmbH., Berlin, Germany) hereinafter called 'Pupil Labs Software'

2.3. Processing of Measurement

The aim of the measurements is to determine if the driver is looking at the road by tracking their gaze and fixation points using 'Pupil Labs Software'. The gaze is compared with the positions of ID tags on and around the windscreen. While these tags are initially detected with low density, additional post-processing video analysis steps enhance their precision. The critical aspect of ID tag detection is to identify the AOIs, representing the driver's usable field of view and the IVIS. Accurately determining these areas allows the precise assessment of whether the driver's gaze is on the road or looking at the dashboard, providing essential data for measuring eyes-off-the-road times.

2.3.1. Tag Identification

During our previous ET studies, we encountered limitations with the 'Pupil Labs Software' when using Pupil Labs ET glasses. The software was unable to accurately detect tags on the vehicle due to sudden obstructions or distortions in the raw video images. The tags, from the 36h11 family, were initially read using MATLAB's AprilTag function. To mark the corners of the investigated AOIs, the ID tags were positioned as follows and shown in Figure 2:

- Area of driver's view of the road (windscreen); ID tag numbers: 6, 7, 4, 6 (from left to right down).
- Centre console surface (dashboard1); ID tag number: 0, 1, 2, 3, (from left to right down),

One of the challenges encountered was the inconsistent lighting and varying viewing angles, which made it difficult to identify tags in the unedited video. In CDS scenarios, it is difficult to avoid external light variations that may degrade camera images. It has been observed that alterations in lighting conditions may result in flares, optical distortions, and glare. The head-mounted ET glasses move with the subject's head, avoiding distortion of the AOI areas as the ID tag positions constantly shift and change relative to each other. Another problem is when the hand, arm or control unit (e.g., steering wheel) obscures the ID tag. These phenomena are less likely to occur in a simulation environment.

In our research, we devised a novel approach to effectively identify ID tags in video frames; we named our method BAIT. This process involves the initial separation of each video frame into its constituent RGB color components. Subsequently, we implemented a binarization technique on these separated components at varying levels of sensitivity. Binarization here refers to the conversion of the color pixels into a binary format, essentially transforming them into either black or white pixels. The term 'sensitivity' in this context describes the threshold value for the color intensity of a pixel to be considered black. For example, at a sensitivity setting of 0%, only pixels with the maximum color intensity value of 255 are rendered black. Conversely, at a sensitivity of 100%, even a minimal color intensity value of 1 is sufficient to turn a pixel black. The analysis includes examining the original RGB frame, taking a holistic approach. For each set of analyses, one original frame and eighteen binarized frames are considered. There are three sets at six different levels of sensitivity each.

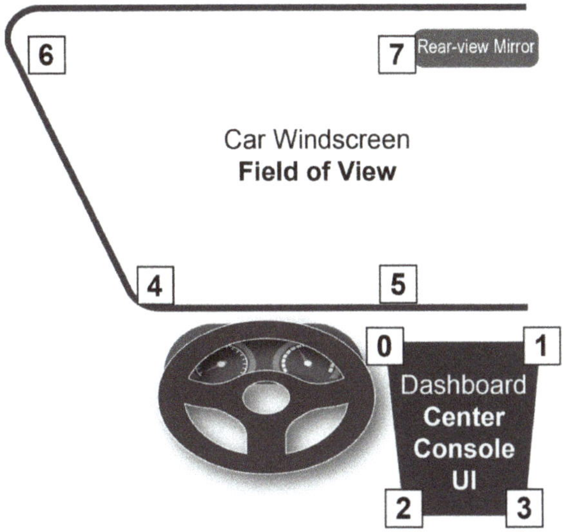

Figure 2. ID tag positioning (around windscreen and center console).

Once the frames have undergone this binarization process, we can then identify the ID tags within each frame. These identifications are conducted separately for each binarized frame, and the findings are subsequently amalgamated. Figure 3 shows the original video frame. Figure 4 show the results of our binarization process on the three separate RGB components of a frame, performed at different levels of sensitivity. The ID tags successfully identified in each iteration are accentuated in black.

Figure 3. The original frame.

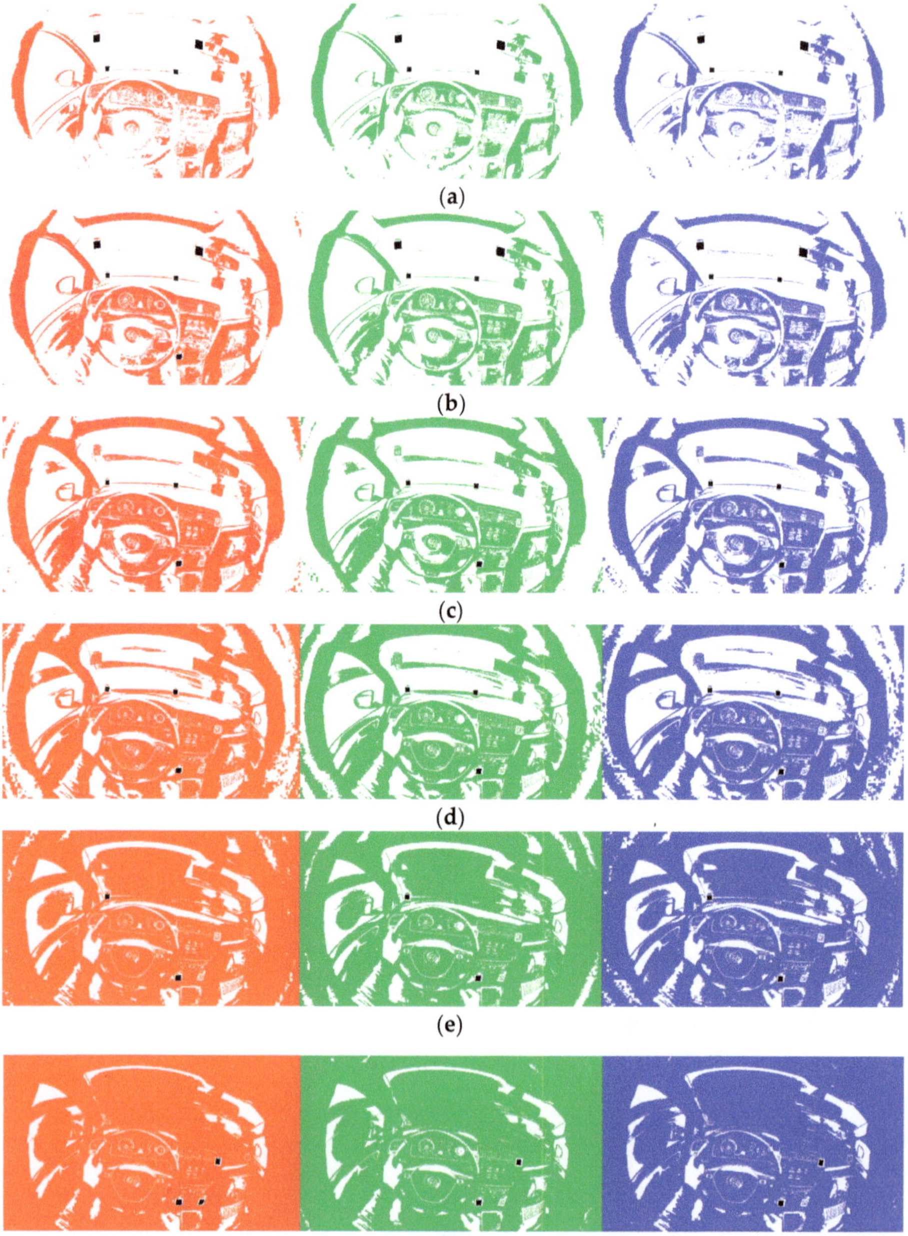

(a)

(b)

(c)

(d)

(e)

(f)

Figure 4. The binary RGB color components with 0% (**a**), 20% (**b**), 40% (**c**), 60% (**d**), 80% (**e**), and 100% (**f**) sensitivity.

Figure 4 underscores the efficacy of our methodology in recognizing ID tags under diverse illumination conditions. This aspect is crucial, as it demonstrates the system's adaptability and reliability in accurately detecting ID tags in a range of lighting environments, a key requirement for consistent AOI detection in dynamic settings. It is important to note that this component of our method is most effective when the ID tags are in clear view and not obscured, even in scenarios where the subject's head is constantly moving while wearing the eye tracking glasses.

2.3.2. Gaze on Road

In our research, we have formulated a method to guarantee effective assessment of driver attention. This involves strategically positioning four ID tags on the windshield, which serve to delineate the driver's road view field as an AOI. These tags are positioned to form a boundary that frames the driver's view of the road. When the driver's gaze is located within the confines of this boundary, it is indicative of the driver's focus on the road. To ascertain the direction of the gaze, we analyze whether it falls to the left of the boundary lines, which are delineated by connecting these tags in a counterclockwise sequence. It is important to note that these ID tags are not situated precisely at the corners of the windshield. Therefore, we have implemented specific adjustments to their placement, which are elaborately described in Figure 5. This adjustment is critical to ensure the accurate determination of whether the driver's gaze is directed towards the road.

Figure 5. Gaze position (yellow circle with green fill), detected tags (blue squares), compensated tag positions (dots in the corners) and "gaze-on-road" indication (dots are green not red).

In our experimental setup, we utilize marking points placed at the four corners of the windshield to define the specific AOI. When the driver's gaze is located within this demarcated area, it is interpreted as focusing on the road ahead, and the visualization shows green color indicators. Additionally, a central green mark is used to signify the actual position of the driver's gaze. The larger diameter green circle with a yellow frame represents the precise and fixation state of gaze identified using the 'Pupil Labs Software', shown in the raw videos that aid visualization, independent of our own analysis.

A key aspect of our methodology is the implementation of an interpolation procedure between successive video frames. This procedure allows us to accurately track the position of these points, even in instances where the associated ID tag is not directly detected in a particular frame. It is important to note, however, that this interpolation technique is most effective when the absence of the tag from the frame is for relatively brief durations. Moreover, our approach accounts for scenarios where the known position of the ID tag may not be within the FOV. In such cases, the previously mentioned points can still be accurately determined based on their known positions relative to the ID tags. A practical demonstration of this scenario is shown in Figure 6, where the effectiveness of the method in tracking gaze position regardless of the direct visibility of ID tags is shown, and the red color of the corner points indicates the gaze-off-road condition. This aspect underscores the robustness of our system in maintaining accurate gaze tracking under various conditions.

Figure 6. Gaze position (yellow circle with green fill), detected tags (blue squares), compensated tag positions (dots in the corners) and "gaze-on-road" indication (dots are red not green).

In our study, as an alternative analytical approach, we consider any gaze that does not fall within the specified boundary (gaze-off-road case) as an "Eyes-Off-The-Road" scenario. This demarcation is essential to identify instances where the driver is not looking at the road, which is a critical factor in monitoring visual distraction when conducting a specific CDS. In cases where the experiment requires the subject to perform complex activities, consideration should be given to modifying the boundaries of the usable FOV (e.g., by adding mirrors) to make the measurement more accurate. Further investigation in this regard involves the measurement of TEORT, which provides a quantitative assessment of the duration for which the driver's attention is diverted away from the road, thereby offering valuable insights for visual distraction monitoring in driving scenarios.

2.3.3. Gaze on Dashboard

In order to improve driver attention monitoring and increase the accuracy of detecting instances when eyes are off the road, it is important to develop a method for examining interactions with the central console controls on the dashboard. In our study, the climate control button array and the integrated touchscreen located on the central console of the passenger car, as UI elements, play a pivotal role. The analysis of the driver's visual distraction during the operation of these controls (NDRTs) is a key focus. To facilitate this, the identification of the central console as an AOI is essential. In our case, the console's slight orientation towards the driver, the perpendicular angle of incidence between the driver's gaze and the plane of the central console, and the positioning of the physical button array and touchscreen on the same plane made it feasible to easily mark the corner points with ID tags. However, typically one ID tag becomes obscured due to the position of the steering wheel or driver's hand. Therefore, the dashboard boundaries were demarcated using only the data from ID tag 1 and ID tag 2. To compensate for the missing left-hand corner points, predefined offsets were applied. The upper offset should be 300 pixels and the lower offset should be 170 pixels, both parallel to the line connecting ID tag 4 and the marked corner points of ID tag 5. Figure 7 provides an example of this approach.

The method can be applied universally, but the specific predefined plane figure and geometric rules used to calculate the position of missing or obscured UI boundary ID tags are determined by the measurement environment. Since the analysis and processing of these points occur post-experiment, the method can be refined based on the specific environmental conditions present. This approach allows for a tailored analysis that accommodates varying dashboard layouts and driver interaction dynamics, ensuring a more accurate assessment of driver attention and UI interaction in diverse driving scenarios.

Figure 7. Incorrect recognition of the dashboard area-gaze position (yellow circle with green fill), detected tags (blue squares), compensated tag positions (dots in the corners) and "gaze on dashboard" indication (red dots).

3. Results

Table 2 presents the success rates of identifying windscreen boundary tags in 10 different measurements. These rates are compared between the standard software provided with Pupil Core ET glasses and the proprietary algorithm developed for the study, highlighting the effectiveness of each method in tag detection under varying conditions.

To compare the performance of 'Pupil Labs software' and 'BAIT', we conducted a comprehensive statistical analysis. We first assessed the normality of our data distributions using the Shapiro–Wilk test. The results showed a significant deviation from normality for both 'Pupil Labs software' ($p = 0.0005$) and 'BAIT' ($p < 0.0001$), indicating that neither dataset followed a normal distribution. This finding highlights the need for caution when using tests that assume normality. Additionally, the Levene's test for the equality of variances indicated a significant difference in variances between the groups ($p = 0.00065$), suggesting a violation of the homogeneity of variances assumption. Based on these preliminary findings, we chose statistical methods that do not depend on the assumption of equal variances between groups for accurate analysis.

Due to the deviations from normality and homogeneity of variances, we opted to use the Wilcoxon Signed-Rank Test for our analysis. The results of the Wilcoxon Signed-Rank Test indicate a highly significant difference in median values between 'Pupil Labs software' and 'BAIT' ($p < 0.00001$), confirming a statistically significant difference in performance between the two conditions. The 'Pupil Labs Software' failed to recognize ID tag 7 in 5 out of 10 instances, while 'BAIT' performed the worst at number 9 due to the participant head movements (looking down) and the camera failing to capture the ID tag. The 'BAIT' consistently outperformed the 'Pupil Labs software' across all measured conditions in accuracy and reliability. It effectively addresses challenges such as brief occlusions or slight angle changes in ID tags, which are common in tracking scenarios. Through sophisticated interpolation techniques, our algorithm compensates for moments when an ID tag is temporarily obscured or viewed from different angles, thereby minimizing errors in tracking and ensuring continuous and precise ID tag identification. This capability is crucial for applications requiring uninterrupted monitoring and exact location tracking.

Table 2. The rates of successful identification of the windscreen boundary ID tags in percentage.

No.	ID Tag No.	Pupil Labs Software (%)	BAIT (%)
1	tag 4	20	99.50
1	tag 5	20	99.75
1	tag 6	20	100
1	tag 7	0	100
2	tag 4	26.15	100
2	tag 5	25.07	100
2	tag 6	26.15	100
2	tag 7	0	100
3	tag 4	23.28	100
3	tag 5	23.53	99.75
3	tag 6	23.77	100
3	tag 7	0	100
4	tag 4	28.26	93.91
4	tag 5	23.91	93.91
4	tag 6	11.30	96.09
4	tag 7	2.83	97.39
5	tag 4	24.52	90.74
5	tag 5	16.89	89.92
5	tag 6	23.98	98.09
5	tag 7	0.27	98.91
6	tag 4	15.99	96.45
6	tag 5	1.27	96.45
6	tag 6	34.01	99.49
6	tag 7	22.84	98.98
7	tag 4	22.54	84.44
7	tag 5	12.38	84.44
7	tag 6	26.98	90.79
7	tag 7	10.48	89.52
8	tag 4	19.30	97.95
8	tag 5	10.53	97.37
8	tag 6	28.95	99.12
8	tag 7	0	100
9	tag 4	1.88	87.76
9	tag 5	1.88	95.53
9	tag 6	32.94	96.94
9	tag 7	8.00	48.24
10	tag 4	0	99.69
10	tag 5	0	98.44
10	tag 6	0	100
10	tag 7	0	94.39

Analysis of the performance data across ID tags 4 to 7 revealed that the mean percentage of success for the 'BAIT' ranged from 92.74% to 98.05%, with relatively low mean deviations and standard deviations, indicating consistent performance across the trials, as shown in Table 3. In contrast, the 'Pupil Labs software' showed lower mean performances with greater variability.

Table 3. Statistical values of the identified ID tags 4 to 7 (windscreen boundaries).

ID Tag No.	Pupil Labs Software (%)				BAIT (%)			
	Mean	Mean Deviation	Standard Deviation	CI 95%	Mean	Mean Deviation	Standard Deviation	CI 95%
tag 4	18.19	7.34	9.75	6.04	95.04	4.66	5.64	3.49
tag 5	13.55	8.33	9.85	6.11	95.56	3.68	5.00	3.10
tag 6	22.81	7.42	10.31	6.39	98.05	2.07	2.91	1.80
tag 7	4.44	5.60	7.50	4.65	92.74	9.55	16.00	9.92

Table 4 compares the effectiveness of 'Pupil Labs software' with a custom-developed algorithm in detecting dashboard boundary tags across 10 distinct measurements. This comparison serves to demonstrate the relative efficiency of each method in ID tag identification under various conditions.

Table 4. The rates of successful identification of the dashboard boundary ID tags in percentage.

No.	ID Tag No.	Pupil Labs Software (%)	BAIT (%)
1	tag 0	0	0
1	tag 1	20	93.75
1	tag 2	8.25	79.5
1	tag 3	19.5	98.25
2	tag 0	0	0
2	tag 1	26.15	84.64
2	tag 2	23.18	77.36
2	tag 3	8.89	77.90
3	tag 0	0	0
3	tag 1	23.28	93.38
3	tag 2	0	31.13
3	tag 3	23.77	73.53
4	tag 0	0	0
4	tag 1	29.78	93.70
4	tag 2	6.74	9.35
4	tag 3	30.65	81.96
5	tag 0	0	0
5	tag 1	26.70	90.19
5	tag 2	31.88	65.12
5	tag 3	10.08	66.49
6	tag 0	0	0
6	tag 1	27.16	85.53
6	tag 2	3.81	65.23
6	tag 3	32.49	72.34
7	tag 0	0	0
7	tag 1	20.95	78.41
7	tag 2	8.25	66.35
7	tag 3	26.98	60.63
8	tag 0	0	0
8	tag 1	26.90	66.67
8	tag 2	23.98	36.55
8	tag 3	3.51	24.85
9	tag 0	0	0
9	tag 1	8	68.71
9	tag 2	8.94	38.82
9	tag 3	24.94	28.94
10	tag 0	0	0
10	tag 1	43.30	98.75
10	tag 2	0	34.27
10	tag 3	37.69	90.03

To evaluate the comparative performance of 'Pupil Labs software' and 'BAIT', we conducted a comprehensive statistical analysis. We ensured the robustness of our findings by first running the Shapiro–Wilk test to assess the normality of our data distributions. The results show that 'Pupil Labs software' did not significantly deviate from a normal distribution ($p = 0.097$), however, 'BAIT' exhibited a significant deviation from normality ($p = 0.011$), suggesting that its data did not follow a normal distribution. Therefore, caution should be exercised when applying tests based on this assumption. The Levene's test for equality of variances revealed a significant difference in variances between the groups ($p = 0.0065$), violating the homogeneity of variances assumption. Therefore, statistical methods that do not rely on equal variances between groups were selected for accurate analysis.

Based on these preliminary findings, we chose to use the Wilcoxon Signed-Rank Test. The results of this test showed a significant difference in median values between 'Pupil Labs software' and 'BAIT' ($p < 0.00001$), clearly demonstrating a statistically significant difference in performance between the two. The 'BAIT' outperformed the 'Pupil Labs software' across all measured conditions in accuracy and reliability. During the measurements, ID tag 0 was always obscured. Table 3 shows that identifying ID tag 3 was also difficult, often because drivers obscured it with their hands while interacting with the dashboard.

The efficacy of the proposed method is contingent on a high rate of ID tag identification and minimal non-identifiable intervals, such as when ID tags are obscured. Consequently, reliable detection of dashboard boundaries throughout the entire measurement was feasible only in measurements 1 and 10. In measurements 2 to 7, detection was only partially successful due to the driver's hand obstructing the dashboard boundary ID tags for extended periods. In measurements 8 and 9, the driver frequently obscured the markers necessary for detection, leading to an inability to determine the dashboard area during these specific measurements.

Upon the analysis of the performance metrics, it is clear that the 'BAIT' software consistently outperformed the 'Pupil Labs Software' for various ID tags, as demonstrated in Table 5, with the exception of ID tag 0, as it was not recognized by any of the solutions after being obscured. The 'BAIT' demonstrated significantly higher mean accuracy rates. Notably, the standard deviations indicated greater consistency in the 'BAIT's performance, with lower variability compared to the 'Pupil Labs software'. The 95% confidence intervals suggest that the true mean performances of the BAIT are significantly higher than those of the 'Pupil Labs software' across all ID tags (except ID tag0), confirming its higher accuracy.

Table 5. Statistical values of the identified ID tags 0 to 3 (dashboard boundaries).

ID Tag No.	Pupil Labs Software (%)				BAIT (%)			
	Mean	Mean Deviation	Standard Deviation	CI 95%	Mean	Mean Deviation	Standard Deviation	CI 95%
tag 0	0	0	0	0	0	0	0	0
tag 1	25.22	5.73	8.84	5.48	85.37	8.61	10.97	6.80
tag 2	11.50	8.91	10.96	6.79	50.37	20.34	23.35	14.47
tag 3	21.85	9.08	11.20	6.94	67.49	17.81	24.00	14.87

Our comparative analysis of ID tag detection algorithms highlights significant performance disparities between the 'BAIT' and 'Pupil Labs software', as shown in Table 6.

Table 6. Statistical values of the comparison.

	Windscreen		Dashboard	
	Pupil Labs Software (%)	BAIT (%)	Pupil Labs Software (%)	BAIT (%)
Mean	14.75	95.35	14.64	50.81
Mean Deviation	10.23	5.04	12.05	32.99
Standard Deviation	11.37	8.82	13.20	36.42
CI 95%	3.52	2.73	4.09	11.29

The results indicate that around the windscreen 'Pupil Labs software' failed to detect some ID tags compared to BAIT. We also observed that ID tag0 remained unidentifiable by all methods, with a recorded value of 0. This presence of extreme values adversely affected the statistical outcomes. However, by implementing a filtering process to exclude the instances with a value of 0, we were able to recalibrate the statistics, as illustrated in Table 7.

Table 7. Filtered statistical values of comparison where 0 values were excluded.

	Windscreen		Dashboard	
	Pupil Labs Software (%)	BAIT (%)	Pupil Labs Software (%)	BAIT (%)
Mean	17.88	95.35	19.53	67.74
Mean Deviation	8.40	5.04	9.89	19.08
Standard Deviation	9.99	8.82	11.65	24.43
CI 95%	3.10	2.73	3.61	7.57

In terms of consistency, the 'BAIT' displayed a more stable performance with lower mean deviations for windscreen scenarios, suggesting a steadier focus detection. This steadiness was particularly evident in the windscreen condition, where the mean deviation of the 'BAIT' was significantly less than that of 'Pupil Labs software'. However, the 'BAIT' demonstrated increased variability in dashboard focus measurements, indicated by a higher standard deviation. The precision of ID tag detection was further characterized by the confidence intervals; the 'BAIT' presented a narrower interval for windscreen focus, implying more reliable estimates. In contrast, its estimates for dashboard focus were less precise, as reflected by a wider confidence interval compared to its windscreen performance and to 'Pupil Labs software'.

Overall, these findings underline the 'BAIT's' robustness in windscreen focus detection while signaling its variable performance in dashboard focus assessment, offering critical insights for its application and potential optimization, as visualized in Figure 8.

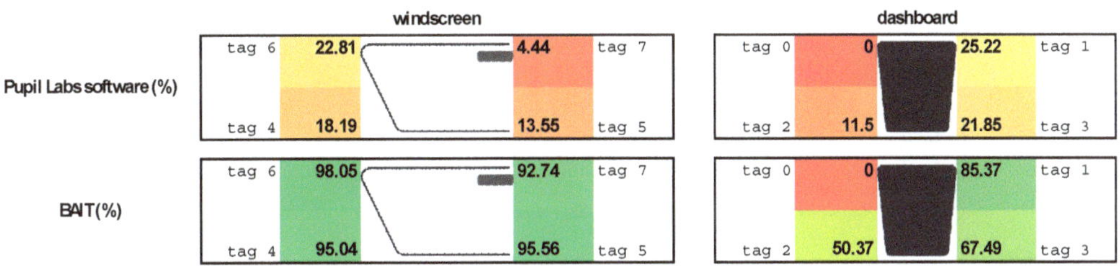

Figure 8. The results are visualized as percentages, with the position of the ID tags reflecting their actual placement.

4. Discussion

In our research, we developed and implemented a bespoke ID tag identification algorithm called BAIT, which exhibited a notably higher level of effectiveness in comparison to conventional, standard software solutions (compared to Pupil Labs software). This enhanced performance was particularly evident in the algorithm's ability to manage and compensate for certain challenges inherent in the ID tag identification process. The following methods were used for higher identification efficiency:

1. Binarization process on the three distinct RGB components of a frame, executed at various sensitivity levels.
2. Interpolation between successive video frames.
3. Adding predefined offset.

A key limitation encountered in ID tag tracking is the obstruction of the ID tag's visibility. Naturally, when an ID tag is completely obscured from the camera's view, its identification becomes unfeasible using direct visual methods. However, our algorithm demonstrates a significant strength in dealing with transient occlusions or minor alterations in the viewing angle during such occlusions. This is achieved through a robust interpolation technique, which is a critical component of our algorithm. The interpolation method employed is designed to predict the position of an ID tag during short periods when it is not visible, using the data from frames where the tag is clearly identified.

Our study evaluates the performance of the 'BAIT' against the 'Pupil Labs software' in attention detection, revealing key differences in accuracy and consistency across different focus areas like the windscreen and dashboard, and highlighting potential areas for further research in algorithm optimization for specific tasks as follows:

- Algorithm Performance: The 'BAIT' demonstrated a markedly higher mean attention percentage on the windscreen, suggesting enhanced detection capabilities in this area compared to the 'Pupil Labs software'. While the 'BAIT' also exhibited a higher mean attention percentage for the dashboard, the increment was not as substantial as observed in the windscreen condition.
- Consistency of Results: The reduced mean deviation in the 'BAIT' for the windscreen condition implies a more consistent measurement of focus across trials than the 'Pupil Labs software'. However, the larger mean deviation in the dashboard condition for the 'BAIT' indicates greater variability, which could be attributed to specific challenges in this setting or inherent algorithmic differences.
- Variability of Data: Standard deviation assessments reveal that the 'BAIT' yields more consistent results for the windscreen condition. Conversely, the 'Pupil Labs software' appears to provide more consistent outcomes when measuring focus on the dashboard.
- Confidence in Estimates: The narrower confidence interval for the 'BAIT' in windscreen observations suggests a higher level of precision in these estimates, potentially reflecting a more reliable performance in this specific task.
- Implications for Future Research: Future research could benefit from further investigation into the conditions and parameters under which each algorithm operates most effectively, as suggested by the observed variability in standard deviation and confidence intervals.
- Algorithmic Suitability: The data suggests that the 'BAIT' may be more suitable for applications requiring precise attention detection on windshields, while the 'Pupil Labs software' may be favored for tasks that demand consistent dashboard focus measurements.

The BAIT algorithm is a significant advancement in ID tag identification and has potential for practical applications. Its robustness and precision make it suitable for integration into research studies in both controlled environments and naturalistic driving scenarios. The BAIT algorithm can significantly enhance the accuracy and reliability of visual distraction measurements in the automotive industry, particularly in semi-naturalistic studies conducted under varying environmental conditions and custom cockpit setups.

The study is limited by its specialized focus and environmental settings, and it only used ET data from 10 participants, each with 8 ID tags. The custom algorithm, tailored for driving scenarios and targeting specific areas like the FOV and UI in cars, may not perform as well in non-driving contexts. Its effectiveness is primarily in driving scenarios used in CDS, limiting its utility in managed settings. Reliance on ET technology and its tuning to specific vehicle interiors and IVIS also constrain its applicability. Furthermore, its focus on visual distraction in driving restricts broader usage beyond driver behavior analysis, impacting its generalizability.

5. Conclusions

In conclusion, this research presents an AOI identification method specifically designed for measuring visual distraction of passenger car drivers while using wearable ET device in CDS. The BAIT algorithm demonstrates superior identification accuracy over the Pupil Labs software, across various ID tags in a driving context. BAIT employs a binarization process on RGB components at multiple sensitivity levels and an innovative interpolation method between video frames to maintain tracking even during transient occlusions.

In our analysis, the BAIT algorithm demonstrates a significant advantage in mean accuracy compared to Pupil Labs software, with 95.35% on the windscreen and 50.81% on the dashboard, suggesting a robust capacity for attention detection in CDS. The algorithm also shows a lower mean deviation, especially on the windscreen, indicating more consistent measurements. A notable limitation for any algorithm, including the BAIT, is the obstruction of visibility of the ID tags. This challenge is particularly acute for dashboard and UI AOI detection, where occlusions are more prevalent and significantly affect tracking accuracy and consistency. However, the BAIT algorithm has greater variability on the dashboard as evidenced by a higher standard deviation (36.42%) compared to the windscreen (8.82%), pointing to a potential area for improvement in complex or variable conditions.

These results indicate that while the BAIT algorithm offers substantial improvements in certain aspects, such as accuracy and consistency for windscreen-focused tasks, it requires further development to enhance its reliability for dashboard-related tasks. Future work should compare BAIT with other ET software and devices, and should focus on refining the algorithm to reduce variability and improve confidence in its dashboard application.

Author Contributions: Conceptualization, V.N., P.F. and G.I.; methodology, G.I.; software, G.I.; validation, V.N. and G.I.; formal analysis, G.I.; investigation, V.N.; resources, V.N.; data curation, V.N.; writing—original draft preparation, V.N. and G.I.; writing—review and editing, V.N.; visualization, V.N. and G.I.; supervision, V.N., P.F. and G.I. All authors have read and agreed to the published version of the manuscript.

Funding: This research received no external funding.

Institutional Review Board Statement: Ethical review was not required as participants joined voluntarily and without compensation, and no personal data was collected or shared. The study prioritised participant privacy and minimised risks, adhering to ethical standards.

Informed Consent Statement: Informed consent was obtained from all subjects involved in the study.

Data Availability Statement: Publicly available datasets were analyzed in this study. This data can be found: https://github.com/viktorbrain/bait, accessed on 2 March 2024.

Acknowledgments: The research was supported by the European Union within the framework of the National Laboratory for Artificial Intelligence. (RRF-2.3.1-21-2022-00004) The research was carried out as a part of the Cooperative Doctoral Program supported by the National Research, Development and Innovation Office and Ministry of Culture and Innovation.

Conflicts of Interest: The authors declare no conflicts of interest.

Abbreviations

ADAS	Advanced Driving Assistant Systems
AOI	Area of Interest
BAIT	Binarized Area of Interest Tracking
CDS	Controlled Driving Study
ET	Eye-tracking
FOV	Field of View
HCI	Human–Computer Interaction
HMI	Human–Machine Interface
ID tag	Identification tag
IVIS	In-Vehicle Information System
IVS	Instrumented Vehicle Study
ND	Naturalistic Driving
NDRT	Non-Driving-Related Task
RGB	Red-Green-Blue
TEORT	Total Eyes-Off-Road Time
UI	User Interface

References

1. Taxonomy and Definitions for Terms Related to Driving Automation Systems for On-Road Motor Vehicles. 2018. Available online: https://www.sae.org/standards/content/j3016_202104/ (accessed on 2 March 2024).
2. Greenlee, E.T.; DeLucia, P.R.; Newton, D.C. Driver Vigilance in Automated Vehicles: Hazard Detection Failures Are a Matter of Time. *Hum. Factors* **2018**, *60*, 465–476. [CrossRef]
3. Strayer, D.L.; Cooper, J.M.; Goethe, R.M.; McCarty, M.M.; Getty, D.J.; Biondi, F. Assessing the Visual and Cognitive Demands of In-Vehicle Information Systems. *Cogn. Res. Princ. Implic.* **2019**, *4*, 18. [CrossRef] [PubMed]
4. Kovács, G. Human Factor Aspects of Situation Awareness in Autonomous Cars—A Psychological Approach. *Acta Polytech. Hung.* **2020**, *18*, 7. [CrossRef]
5. Shechtman, O.; Classen, S.; Awadzi, K.; Mann, W. Comparison of Driving Errors between On-the-Road and Simulated Driving Assessment: A Validation Study. *Traffic Inj. Prev.* **2009**, *10*, 379–385. [CrossRef]
6. Mayhew, D.R.; Simpson, H.M.; Wood, K.M.; Lonero, L.; Clinton, K.M.; Johnson, A.G. On-Road and Simulated Driving: Concurrent and Discriminant Validation. *J. Safety Res.* **2011**, *42*, 267–275. [CrossRef]
7. van Schagen, I.; Sagberg, F. The Potential Benefits of Naturalistic Driving for Road Safety Research: Theoretical and Empirical Considerations and Challenges for the Future. *Procedia Soc. Behav. Sci.* **2012**, *48*, 692–701. [CrossRef]
8. Rizzo, M.; Jermeland, J.; Severson, J. Instrumented Vehicles and Driving Simulators. *Gerontechnology* **2002**, *1*, 291–296. [CrossRef]
9. Bach, K.M.; Jaeger, G.; Skov, M.B.; Thomassen, N.G. Interacting with In-Vehicle Systems: Understanding, Measuring, and Evaluating Attention. In Proceedings of the People and Computers XXIII Celebrating People and Technology (HCI), Cambridge, UK, 1–5 September 2009.
10. Regan, M.A.; Lee, J.D.; Young, K. (Eds.) *Driver Distraction: Theory, Effects, and Mitigation*; CRT Press: Washington, DC, USA, 2008.
11. Regan, M.A.; Hallett, C.; Gordon, C.P. Driver Distraction and Driver Inattention: Definition, Relationship and Taxonomy. *Accid. Anal. Prev.* **2011**, *43*, 1771–1781. [CrossRef]
12. Kircher, K.; Ahlstrom, C. Minimum Required Attention: A Human-Centered Approach to Driver Inattention. *Hum. Factors* **2017**, *59*, 471–484. [CrossRef] [PubMed]
13. Ito, H.; Atsumi, B.; Uno, H.; Akamatsu, M. Visual Distraction While Driving. *IATSS Res.* **2001**, *25*, 20–28. [CrossRef]
14. Victor, T. Analysis of Naturalistic Driving Study Data: Safer Glances, Driver Inattention, and Crash Risk. In *Analysis of Naturalistic Driving Study Data: Safer Glances, Driver Inattention, and Crash Risk*; National Academies: Washington, DC, USA, 2014. [CrossRef]
15. The Royal Society for the Prevention of Accidents (ROSPA). *Road Safety Factsheet Driver Distraction Factsheet*. 28 Calthorpe Road, Edgbaston, Birmingham B15 1RP. 2020. Available online: https://www.rospa.com/media/documents/road-safety/driver-distraction-factsheet.pdf (accessed on 2 March 2024).
16. Purucker, C.; Naujoks, F.; Prill, A.; Neukum, A. Evaluating Distraction of In-Vehicle Information Systems While Driving by Predicting Total Eyes-off-Road Times with Keystroke Level Modeling. *Appl. Ergon.* **2017**, *58*, 543–554. [CrossRef]
17. Madlenak, R.; Masek, J.; Madlenakova, L.; Chinoracky, R. Eye-Tracking Investigation of the Train Driver's: A Case Study. *Appl. Sci.* **2023**, *13*, 2437. [CrossRef]
18. Ahlström, C.; Kircher, K.; Nyström, M.; Wolfe, B. Eye Tracking in Driver Attention Research—How Gaze Data Interpretations Influence What We Learn. *Front. Neuroergonomics* **2021**, *2*, 778043. [CrossRef]
19. Nagy, V.; Kovács, G.; Földesi, P.; Kurhan, D.; Sysyn, M.; Szalai, S.; Fischer, S. Testing Road Vehicle User Interfaces Concerning the Driver's Cognitive Load. *Infrastructures* **2023**, *8*, 49. [CrossRef]
20. Krejtz, K.; Duchowski, A.T.; Niedzielska, A.; Biele, C.; Krejtz, I. Eye Tracking Cognitive Load Using Pupil Diameter and Microsaccades with Fixed Gaze. *PLoS ONE* **2018**, *13*, e0203629. [CrossRef]
21. Goldberg, J.H.; Kotval, X.P. Computer Interface Evaluation Using Eye Movements: Methods and Constructs. *Int. J. Ind. Ergon.* **1999**, *24*, 631–645. [CrossRef]
22. Foulsham, T.; Walker, E.; Kingstone, A. The Where, What and When of Gaze Allocation in the Lab and the Natural Environment. *Vision Res.* **2011**, *51*, 1920–1931. [CrossRef]
23. Hessels, R.S.; Kemner, C.; van den Boomen, C.; Hooge, I.T.C. The Area-of-Interest Problem in Eyetracking Research: A Noise-Robust Solution for Face and Sparse Stimuli. *Behav. Res. Methods* **2016**, *48*, 1694–1712. [CrossRef]
24. Zhang, X.; Yuan, S.M.; Chen, M.D.; Liu, X. A Complete System for Analysis of Video Lecture Based on Eye Tracking. *IEEE Access* **2018**, *6*, 49056–49066. [CrossRef]
25. Jayawardena, G.; Jayarathna, S. Automated Filtering of Eye Movements Using Dynamic AOI in Multiple Granularity Levels. *Int. J. Multimed. Data Eng. Manag.* **2021**, *12*, 49–64. [CrossRef]
26. Friedrich, M.; Rußwinkel, N.; Möhlenbrink, C. A Guideline for Integrating Dynamic Areas of Interests in Existing Set-up for Capturing Eye Movement: Looking at Moving Aircraft. *Behav. Res. Methods* **2017**, *49*, 822–834. [CrossRef] [PubMed]
27. Peysakhovich, V.; Dehais, F.; Duchowski, A.T. ETH Library ArUco/Gaze Tracking in Real Environments Other Conference Item. In Proceedings of the Eye Tracking for Spatial Research, Proceedings of the 3rd International Workshop (ET4S), Zurich, Switzerland, 14 January 2018; pp. 70–71.
28. Bonikowski, L.; Gruszczynski, D.; Matulewski, J. Open-Source Software for Determining the Dynamic Areas of Interest for Eye Tracking Data Analysis. *Procedia Comput. Sci.* **2021**, *192*, 2568–2575. [CrossRef]
29. Orquin, J.L.; Ashby, N.J.S.; Clarke, A.D.F. Areas of Interest as a Signal Detection Problem in Behavioral Eye-Tracking Research. *J. Behav. Decis. Mak.* **2016**, *29*, 103–115. [CrossRef]

30. Faraji, Y.; van Rijn, J.W.; van Nispen, R.M.A.; van Rens, G.H.M.B.; Melis-Dankers, B.J.M.; Koopman, J.; van Rijn, L.J. A Toolkit for Wide-Screen Dynamic Area of Interest Measurements Using the Pupil Labs Core Eye Tracker. *Behav. Res. Methods* **2022**, *55*, 3820–3830. [CrossRef] [PubMed]
31. Tensmeyer, C.; Martinez, T. Historical Document Image Binarization: A Review. *SN Comput. Sci.* **2020**, *1*, 173. [CrossRef]
32. Wang, J. Edwin Olson AprilTag 2: Efficient and Robust Fiducial Detection. In Proceedings of the 2016 IEEE/RSJ International Conference on Intelligent Robots and Systems (IROS), Daejeon, Republic of Korea, 9–14 October 2016; pp. 4193–4198.
33. Zin, T.T.; Misawa, S.; Pwint, M.Z.; Thant, S.; Seint, P.T.; Sumi, K.; Yoshida, K. Cow Identification System Using Ear Tag Recognition. In Proceedings of the LifeTech 2020—2020 IEEE 2nd Global Conference on Life Sciences and Technologies, Kyoto, Japan, 10–12 March 2020; pp. 65–66.
34. Kassner, M.; Patera, W.; Bulling, A. Pupil: An Open Source Platform for Pervasive Eye Tracking and Mobile Gaze-Based Interaction. In Proceedings of the 2014 ACM International Joint Conference on Pervasive and Ubiquitous Computing , Washington, DC, USA, 13–17 September 2014; pp. 1151–1160. [CrossRef]
35. MacInnes, J. Wearable Eye-Tracking for Research: Comparisons across Devices. *bioRxiv* **2018**.
36. Olson, E. AprilTag: A Robust and Flexible Visual Fiducial System. In Proceedings of the IEEE International Conference on Robotics and Automation, Shanghai, China, 9–13 May 2011; pp. 3400–3407.

applied sciences

MDPI

Article

Studying the Role of Visuospatial Attention in the Multi-Attribute Task Battery II

Daniel Gugerell [1,*], Benedikt Gollan [2], Moritz Stolte [1] and Ulrich Ansorge [1,3,4]

1 Faculty of Psychology, University of Vienna, 1010 Vienna, Austria; moritz.stolte@univie.ac.at (M.S.); ulrich.ansorge@univie.ac.at (U.A.)
2 Research Studios Austria, 1090 Vienna, Austria; benedikt.gollan@researchstudio.at
3 Vienna Cognitive Science Hub, University of Vienna, 1010 Vienna, Austria
4 Research Platform Mediatised Lifeworlds, University of Vienna, 1010 Vienna, Austria
* Correspondence: daniel.gugerell@univie.ac.at

Abstract: Task batteries mimicking user tasks are of high heuristic value. Supposedly, they measure individual human aptitude regarding the task in question. However, less is often known about the underlying mechanisms or functions that account for task performance in such complex batteries. This is also true of the Multi-Attribute Task Battery (MATB-II). The MATB-II is a computer display task. It aims to measure human control operations on a flight console. Using the MATB-II and a visual-search task measure of spatial attention, we tested if capture of spatial attention in a bottom-up or top-down way predicted performance in the MATB-II. This is important to understand for questions such as how to implement warning signals on visual displays in human–computer interaction and for what to practice during training of operating with such displays. To measure visuospatial attention, we used both classical task-performance measures (i.e., reaction times and accuracy) as well as novel unobtrusive real-time pupillometry. The latter was done as pupil size covaries with task demands. A large number of analyses showed that: (1) Top-down attention measured before and after the MATB-II was positively correlated. (2) Test-retest reliability was also given for bottom-up attention, but to a smaller degree. As expected, the two spatial attention measures were also negatively correlated with one another. However, (3) neither of the visuospatial attention measures was significantly correlated with overall MATB-II performance, nor with (4) any of the MATB-II subtask performance measures. The latter was true even if the subtask required visuospatial attention (as in the system monitoring task of the MATB-II). (5) Neither did pupillometry predict MATB-II performance, nor performance in any of the MATB-II's subtasks. Yet, (6) pupil size discriminated between different stages of subtask performance in system monitoring. This finding indicated that temporal segregation of pupil size measures is necessary for their correct interpretation, and that caution is advised regarding average pupil-size measures of task demands across tasks and time points within tasks. Finally, we observed surprising effects of workload (or cognitive load) manipulation on MATB-II performance itself, namely, better performance under high- rather than low-workload conditions. The latter findings imply that the MATB-II itself poses a number of questions about its underlying rationale, besides allowing occasional usage in more applied research.

Keywords: pupil dilation; eye-tracking; MATB-II; task demands; attention capture

1. Introduction

1.1. Impact Statement

Human cognitive aptitude for specific applied tasks is often measured with tests or task batteries. These batteries mimic important surface characteristics of the applied task in question. As an example, take the Multi-Attribute Task Battery II (MATB-II). The MATB-II presents components of a flight console on a computer screen, and participants are requested to perform a sequence of subtasks typical for flying (e.g., monitoring for display changes or tracking of moving objects). Batteries such as the MATB-II have potentially high ecological or external validity [1,2]. This is due to their real-world similarity. However, often less is known about their internal validity: it is unclear what underlying human function or mechanism they are measuring because a theoretical model connecting basic human functioning with task performance is lacking. Yet, this is important: to understand the basic functions involved helps to improve displays and training. For example, display signals can be designed to fit to the processing capabilities of the human user. Where this is not possible, known difficulties (e.g., high demands imposed by a faint or peripheral visual signal) could at least be made easier to process for humans by systematic training (e.g., practicing the systematic scanning of the display for the nonsalient signals).

Regarding external versus internal validity, the situation is typically the opposite in a controlled experimental laboratory task. These controlled tasks often measure specific well-described underlying functions and are, therefore, of high internal validity. However, these controlled laboratory tasks are less similar to real-world tasks. Thus, their external and ecological validity is doubtful. It is unclear if they could be used successfully to discriminate individual aptitude in a specific real-world task. For example, the effects of separate cognitive functions or mechanisms (e.g., of memory capacity and inhibition of interference) might not simply add up in a complex real-world task.

In the current study, we, therefore, aimed to understand the connection between performance in MATB-II and one specific experimental task measuring visuospatial attention. Visuospatial attention denotes the selection of locations in the visual environment. This ability is highly relevant for flight performance. For example, visuospatial attention is used to monitor or track different parts of a flight console. However, do individual capabilities of visuospatial attention predict performance in the MATB-II? Or is MATB-II performance driven by other cognitive factors such as memory or the ability to switch between tasks? In addition, maybe humans steer their visuospatial attention in the MATB-II entirely differently from how they do it in a typical visual search task used to measure visuospatial attention under controlled laboratory conditions.

In the current study, in line with the latter possibilities, we did not find any significant correlations between human performance on an experimental task measuring visuospatial attention and the MATB-II. This was also the case for unobtrusive measures of cognitive performance. In summary, thus, the present work was concerned with the internal validity of the MATB-II. Questions regarding the external validity or ecological validity of both the MATB-II and of our controlled measure of visuospatial attention were not addressed. However, the fact that we did not test external validity—for example, that we did not test the sensitivity of the MATB-II for the correct discrimination between experts (pilots) and novices—might have created a caveat. Because we used an opportunity sample consisting of mostly students and a few professional pilots, cognitive performance in this sample might have simply created too little variance (though we varied task difficulty on the MATB-II to create some variance in cognitive performance). Of lesser importance, in the current study, we found interesting and unexpected effects in MATB-II performance as a function of task: performance in the MATB-II increased rather than decreased with increasing task demands (here, the number of subtasks to be performed per unit of time; see Supplement Tables S2 and S3), and we observed that unobtrusive pupillometry could be used to discriminate between stages of subtask performance.

1.2. Theoretical Background

The diagnosis of individual cognitive aptitudes such as that of selective visuospatial attention or working memory capacity can take on different forms, from test batteries, over real-world tasks, to relatively pure tests of individual cognitive functions in controlled experiments [3–7]. In the domain of visuospatial attention, Weichselbaum et al. [8] have recently argued for the usage of experimental tasks because they fulfill two important criteria of diagnostic measurements: They are of high internal validity because they measure different forms of capture of visuospatial attention—top-down dependent capture of visuospatial attention based on current search goals versus bottom-up capture of attention due to high local feature contrasts or salience—in a relatively pure way; that is, free from confounding or contaminating sources of variance such as task shifting, working memory demands, or modality changes. These experimental task measures also showed test-retest reliability in the form of significant correlations between measures of attention across different measurement time points [8,9].

Here, we used the experimental measurement of visuospatial attention to see if relatively pure measures of visuospatial attention can help us to understand performance in an applied test: the Multi-Attribute Task Battery (II, MATB-II) [10]. The MATB-II uses a simplified version of a flight console. The MATB-II can be presented on a computer monitor, and participants must work on different tasks related to the control of the simulated flight console. For their MATB-II performance, participants, thus, have to switch between tasks, with different tasks associated with different areas of the console and with tasks presented in an unforeseeable sequence. For instance, participants have to monitor two buttons in the upper-left hand corner for color changes (from green to gray and from gray to red) and have to respond to the color changes by left-clicking with the mouse on the corresponding changed buttons (system monitoring task). This task is embedded in a sequence of other tasks such as the tracking of a moving crosshair (tracking task) presented to the right of the light and scales, or responses in the lower left of the display to audio presented via headphones (communication task). An in-depth explanation and description of the MATB-II can be found in Section 2.4 below.

Importantly, we chose the MATB-II for an investigation with our experimental visuospatial attention measurement because especially the system monitoring task of salient color changes in the upper left corner during MATB-II performance could benefit either from bottom-up capture of visuospatial attention by salient stimuli, here, color changes, or from top-down control of visuospatial attention, here, to look for particular colors (e.g., the color red) [11–15]. To tell if bottom-up or top-down attention is responsible for MATB-II performance is important. If salient features capture attention in a stimulus-driven or bottom-up fashion, pilots would not need any training and participants would not need any instructions regarding what color changes to look for. A salient color change would capture attention, ensuring that pilots or participants pay attention to the relevant signal. However, the situation is different if top-down control accounts for what pilots and participants pay attention to. Here is an example: Suppose you were to pick up a friend in front of a crowded station. To successfully spot your friend in the crowd, you would have to know what he or she looks like and search for him or her by these known features. In an analogue case during the control of the flight console, pilots and participants would need proper training and instructions to search for and find a critical signal on the console or display. In this case, it would probably also be helpful to use fewer different relevant features to search for across different subtasks in the MATB-II or in flight-console operation, so as not to hinder switching between tasks should a signal onset happen to indicate a necessary task switch (e.g., a blinking lamp to use fuel from a specific pump, see below for details).

In the present study, we correlated performance in the MATB-II with experimental measures of bottom-up versus top-down capture of visuospatial attention. In this way, we were hoping to understand if one of these types of visuospatial attention capture contributes to the performance in the MATB-II in general, and in the system monitoring task of the MATB-II in particular. We present the correlations in Section 3.2.

We also took care to create sufficient performance variance within the MATB-II. This was necessary for the planned correlation or regression analyses because these analyses depend on sufficient variance. To achieve sufficient variance, we varied task demands or cognitive load in the MATB-II in two steps. Specifically, we varied the frequency of tasks and task shifts per unit of time in the MATB-II. Here, a higher frequency of tasks and task shifts per unit of time corresponded to a higher workload. In contrast, a lower frequency of tasks and task shifts per unit of time corresponded to a lower workload.

Obviously, visuospatial attention—the selection of some locations on the console while ignoring others—is involved in MATB-II task performance. For example, one can either track an object with the eyes or look at a changing button for the system monitoring task, but one cannot select both objects with the eyes at the same time. Thus, we would have expected that visuospatial attention and MATB-II task performance are significantly correlated. However, for at least two reasons, we might have failed to find a significant correlation. First, it is not clear if capture of visuospatial attention is the domineering factor for MATB-II task performance. For example, performance on the MATB-II also requires task shifting, and task-shifting abilities that are relatively independent of visuospatial attention could be more decisive than visuospatial attention for overall performance on the MATB-II. Secondly, related to this point, in more applied and real-world tasks such as the MATB-II, the control of visuospatial attention can take on forms that are relatively distinct from the types of capture of visuospatial attention that account for typical visual-search task performance. For example, in many applied and real-world tasks, humans know where things are located and can, thus, systematically shift their attention to a specific location in anticipation of an expected task at this location: if humans expect a task, they could shift attention to a specific location (e.g., to the area of the console at which a cross-hair needs to be tracked). In contrast, no anticipatory attention shifts to a particular location are possible in our experimental visual-search task because, from trial to trial, a to-be-searched-for visual target is equally likely to appear at any possible stimulus location.

In the current study, in addition to the traditional performance measures such as reaction times and numbers of errors, we also looked at pupillary responses. These are known to increase in response to increased task demands or cognitive load [16–22]. For example, Ahlstrom and Friedman-Berg (2016) found that average pupil size increased when controllers used a static storm forecast tool compared to when controllers used a dynamic forecast tool [23]. For the unobtrusive measurement of the pupillary responses, we employed a cognitive load algorithm that automatically models and subtracts size changes due to the pupillary light response based on empirical models of the pupillary light response and camera-based brightness measures, thereby, providing a measure of cognitive load free of this source of pupil size variation [22,24–26]. Here, we did not find any effects of our manipulation of task performance (see Section 3.3). However, when we looked for causes for the lack of an average effect of our load manipulation on pupillary responses, we found that different stages of on-task performance were not all equally correlated with a pupillary response, such that on average, pupillary responses to task-load manipulations might have been washed out (see Section 3.4).

One should also note that the pupil size is related to factors other than workload (or task demands) and light, such as emotions, arousal, memory content, or pharmacological agents [27–29]. We had no reason to suspect that the one or the other of these influences was systematically confounded with the steps of our manipulations. Thus, we did not control for the corresponding influences. However, the broad variety of influences implies the relatively unspecific nature of the pupillary response, meaning that there are also disadvantages to the method besides its advantages (e.g., its unobtrusiveness), such as a relatively high level of noise brought about by the different influences.

2. Materials and Methods

2.1. Participants

The study included 53 participants; 5 were trained pilots (all male), and 49 were psychology students from the University of Vienna (30 female, 19 male). Originally, we intended to include more trained pilots. However, COVID-19 restrictions applied at the time of data acquisition, preventing a larger sample size of trained pilots. The sample has, thus, been gathered opportunistically. It is, therefore, not representative of a wider population. Sample size was based on an a priori calculation assuming a large effect size ($\eta^2 = 0.20$), aiming for a statistical power of 0.8, and allowing an alpha error of 0.05. Regarding the MATB-II, participants were randomly assigned to either the low-workload group

(26 participants, three of which were pilots) or the high-workload group (27 participants, two of which were pilots). Students received partial course credit. Pilots received a small monetary compensation for their time. Prior to the experiment, informed consent was obtained from all participants. Ethical approval (No EK_00644) was obtained from University of Vienna's Ethical Review Board.

2.2. Apparatus

The experiment was conducted in a dimly lit room, where the only relevant light-source was the monitor. The tasks were presented via a 31 cm × 28.5 cm monitor (resolution, 1920 pixels × 1080 pixels; 60 Hz screen refresh rate). Participants were seated in front of the monitor, with their gaze straight ahead, centered on the screen. Viewing direction and distance (60 cm) were supported by a chinrest. Participants wore a mobile, video-based eye-tracker (Pupil Labs, Berlin, Germany; sampling at 60 Hz, with an estimated gaze accuracy of 0.6° (according to manufacturer)). A PC running Windows 10 (Microsoft, Redmond, WA, USA) and Pupil Labs software version 3.4.0 (pupil-labs.com/pupil/, accessed on 9 September 2021) was connected to the eye-tracker for recording of pupil size, eye movements, and the external visual surroundings. A picture of the setup can be seen in Figure 1. This picture only serves illustrative purposes. During testing, the eye-tracker was connected to the computer (not depicted), and the lights were dimmed (which is not the case in this figure).

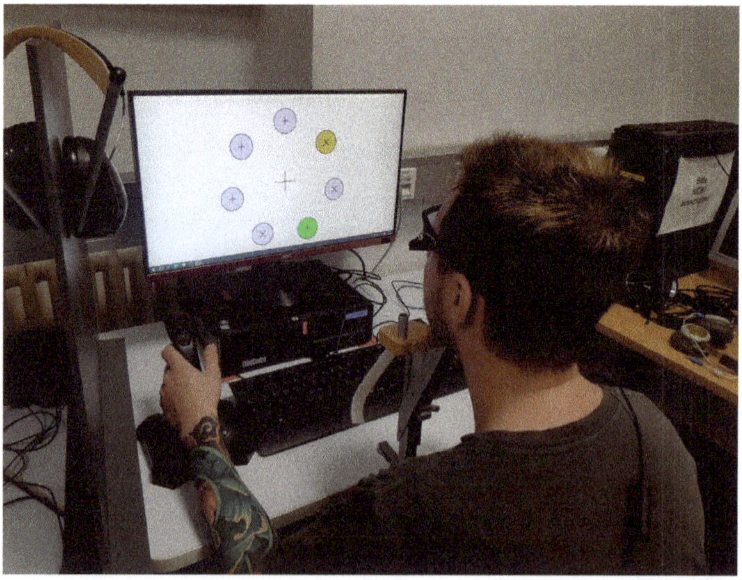

Figure 1. Experimental setup.

Participants also wore stereo headphones (RP-HT265, Panasonic) operating with a standard volume of 25 on a Windows 10 computer.

2.3. Eye-Tracking Data Processing

The pupil data were exported using Pupil Player v3.0.7, with a minimum data confidence of 0.6. Confidence is an assessment by the pupil detector on how sure it is about the measurement. This measurement is taken for each frame and each eye. Pupil Labs suggests that any confidence value exceeding 0.6 is useful data. Further data processing was done using PyCharm Community Edition 2020.2.3. The whole dataset was reduced to a single eye, which was chosen by its higher overall average confidence. The algorithm used a

3D-corrected pupil size measure that takes looking direction into account [25]. To diminish effects of uncontrolled light sources, the overhead lighting in the room was switched off during testing, leaving the monitor in front of the participant as the only light source during testing. The algorithm for the extraction of a pupillary load index used the brightness measured by the scene- or world-camera located over the right eye. The measured brightness was used to model a pupillary light response on an individual basis, separately for each participant. No further weighting of the average measured lightness by the camera (e.g., a stronger weighting of parts of the scene) was applied. The modelled light-elicited response of the pupil was subtracted to arrive at a load measure of the pupillary response.

2.4. Procedure and Task

The experiment consisted of three blocks. The first and third block of the experiment were experimental measurements of capture of visuospatial attention in visual search tasks in which participants had to search for a color-defined target and report the orientation of a cross inside the target (upright or oblique). A singleton distractor was sometimes presented together with the target and away from the target. The singleton distractor could be of a relatively target-similar color or of a relatively dissimilar color, and it was expected to interfere with target search. These blocks consisted of three rounds of 84 trials each. The visual-search task was split into two blocks, one before and one after the second block, so that we could calculate a test-retest reliability of the measures of visuospatial attention. The second block, in-between the visual-search blocks, was the Multi-Attribute Task Battery (MATB-II). Before the experiment started and after each block, the eye-tracker was calibrated for each participant. To ensure proper calibration throughout the experiment, a fixation check was executed at the start of each trial in Blocks 1 and 3. Figure 2 shows an example of a trial used in the visual search task, adapted from Weichselbaum and Ansorge (2018) [9].

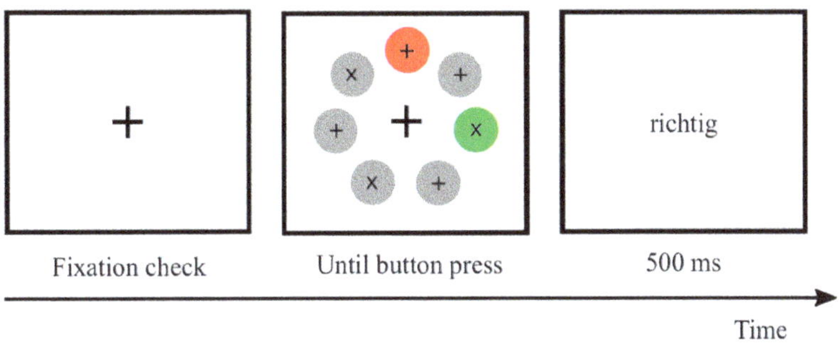

Figure 2. Example of a trial in the visual search task (Blocks 1 and 3).

Before the first block started, participants were shown the target color (below in coordinates of the L*a*b* system; L*: luminance; a*: red/green value; b*: blue/yellow value), which was fixed throughout the experiment and either Red 1 (L*a*b* = 62.7/79.0/65.7), Green 1 (L*a*b* = 62.5/−69.4/52.5), Red 2 (L*a*b* = 62.0/76.7/21.1), or Green 2 (L*a*b* = 62.3/−15.8/52.7), with color balanced across participants. Participants also received an explanation of what the trials would look like, and that their reaction time, as well as the number of correct responses mattered. Each trial started with the presentation of a black fixation cross at screen center for 500 ms. Here, we conducted a fixation check. If necessary, we conducted a drift correction of the eye tracker during the fixation check. Next, the target display was presented. It consisted of seven discs. One disk was in the participant's target color. The other six were either all color-nonsingletons in a neutral, gray color (L*a*b* = 62.0/12.7/−35.8)—these were the distractor-absent trials—or five gray nonsingletons plus one singleton-color distractor—these were the distractor-present trials. Each participant saw two types of distractor-present trials: trials with a target-similar or (top-down) matching singleton-color distractor (e.g., if Green 1 was the target color, the target-similar distractor would have been presented in Green 2); and trials with a target-dissimilar or nonmatching singleton-color distractor (e.g., if Green 1 was the target color, the target-dissimilar distractor would have been presented in Red 1). Distractor-absent, distractor-present/target-similar, and distractor-present/target-dissimilar trials were presented separated in rounds of the first and the last block—that is, those conditions were the same for the 84 trials (e.g., 7 possible target positions × 6 possible distractor positions × 2) of each round (e.g., 84 distractor-absent trials before 84 distractor-present/target-similar trials before 84 distractor-present/target-dissimilar trials). By blocking distractor conditions, we decreased the likelihood of shifts between different top-down search settings even further. This was done to ensure that visuospatial attention rather than task shifting explained visual-search task performance. However, by these runs of different conditions in the visual-search task blocks, we might have also inadvertently encouraged suppression of attention capture, especially by the more target-dissimilar, nonmatching distractor: it is known that repeating distractor colors might help establish proactive suppression of the misleading distractor [30–32]. Throughout the search task, participants had to search for the disk in their instructed target color and respond by clicking either the left or right mouse-button, depending on whether the symbol inside the target disc was a "+" or an "×". After the button press, a feedback display was shown, telling the participants whether they clicked the correct (German word "richtig") or the incorrect (German word "falsch") button. For each participant, there was one target color, a particular order in which the rounds of the distractor-absent, distractor-present/target-similar, and distractor-present/target-dissimilar conditions were realized, and a specific stimulus-to-response mapping (i.e., whether an "×" required the left and the "+" required the right button press, or vice versa). To ensure that participants understood the task, they practiced the search task for at least 20 trials in the distractor-absent condition before data collection started. The task was practiced in the distractor-absent condition, as this was probably the easiest condition.

In the second block, participants were introduced to the MATB-II (see Figure 3). The MATB-II is a computer-based task battery designed to evaluate operator performance and workload with a simplified simulated cockpit console. It requires the simultaneous performance on and unforeseeable switches between several subtasks: system monitoring, tracking, communication, and dynamic resource management tasks (https://matb.larc.nasa.gov/?doing_wp_cron=1649083621.1180279254913330078125, accessed on 3 August 2021). To perform the tasks, participants used a joystick (Model: Logitech Attack 3) and a standard computer mouse.

The colored rectangles in Figure 3 around the task-specific locations were not shown to the participants. They are just helpful illustrations for referencing particular locations. On the upper left, the region surrounded by a red rectangle, numbered 1, as well as the region right below it, surrounded by a blue rectangle with the number 2, is the "System Monitoring" task. The area surrounded by the green rectangle, numbered 3, is the "Tracking" task. Bottom left, the area within the yellow rectangle and the number 4 is the "Communication" task, and to its right, the pink rectangle, numbered 5, is the "Resource Management" task. All tasks will be further explained in the following paragraphs.

System Monitoring: This task requires participants to monitor two warning lights ("F5" and "F6") in the areas within the red boundaries of Figure 3, designated by the number 1. Participants have to monitor that "F5" stays on/green and that "F6" stays out/gray. If either of those states changes ("F5" turns out/gray or "F6" turns on/red), participants must respond by left-clicking the corresponding display button. Additionally, the dark-blue pointers in the scales "F1" to "F4" in the areas of Figure 3, surrounded by blue outlines and designated by the number 2, have to stay within a certain range around the midpoint. If a pointer deviates too much from the midpoint, the participant has to correct/reset its position to the midpoint by left-clicking on the corresponding scale.

Tracking: participants are asked to use a joystick to track the moving circle with the crosshair as a cursor in the area with the green boundary in Figure 3, designated by the number 3.

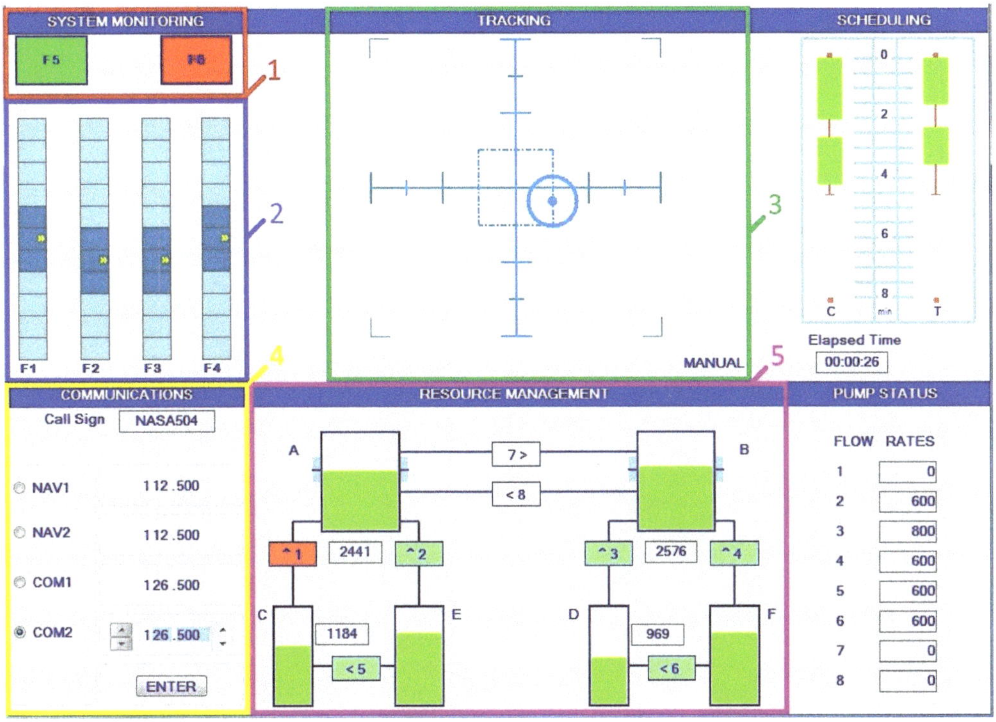

Figure 3. Multi-Attribute Task Battery (MATB-II).

To note, the "Scheduling" timeline to the right of this area is also related to tracking. It shows when the tracking task has to be performed manually and when it switches to "autopilot". The two green bars on the right, above the small "T" (=Tracking), signal to the participant in advance that the tracking task must be performed manually. As soon as the green bar vanishes, leaving behind only the thin orange line, the tracking task was taken over by the autopilot, giving the participants some time to focus on other tasks. The scale in the middle of this sector (located between the "C" and the "T") serves as a timeline in minutes until a tracking ("T") or a communication ("C") task starts. For two reasons, we left this sector out of our coding scheme of areas of interest. First, the sector is related to two different tasks and, hence, gazes directed at this area are difficult to interpret. Second, prompts regarding both tasks—tracking (see above) and communications (see below)—were also evident simply by looking at Sector 3 or by listening to what was communicated via the headphones. In other words, there is no strict necessity to attend to the scheduling area to perform those two tasks.

Communication: This task concerns the area in the bottom left of the displays, inside the yellow border in Figure 3, designated by the number 4. Participants wore headsets during the experiment. Through the headphones, they occasionally heard "calls" from the MATB-II. Foreign callsigns should be ignored, but if the participants' callsign was heard ("NASA504" for each participant), participants had to respond by changing the frequency of a specific radio, as they were told via this call.

Incoming calls can also be anticipated and processed via attending to the "Scheduling" zone. The green bars on the left above the "C" (=Communication) signal indicate to the participant that calls are possible to come in during these critical periods, while phases indicated by the thin orange line only mean that they cannot receive any calls during these periods and can safely ignore audio.

(Dynamic) Resource Management: In this task, which concerns the area inside the violet boundary in Figure 3, designated by the number 5, participants have to keep the filling of the Tanks "A" and "B" above and below defined thresholds (between 2000 and 3000). The tanks are slowly emptying, and participants have to use the pumps (the small areas between the tanks numbered 1 to 8) to refill or empty Tanks "A" and "B". Tanks "E" and "F" have an unlimited amount of fuel, so it is not possible to run out of fuel altogether during the test. Pumps can be activated and deactivated by a single left mouse click. Pumps can also fail (e.g., Pump 1 in Figure 3), which is signaled by the pump turning red. Participants cannot use currently failing pumps, but the failures end after some time.

Participants were randomly assigned to either a low- or high-workload group during the MATB-II block. Within the same total period of time, those participants in the low-workload group had only 3/4 the number of subtasks compared to those in the high-workload group. The total duration of the MATB-II was 5 min in both groups. To make sure that participants understood the tasks of the MATB-II, each group had a 1.5 min trial or practice run before data collection.

The MATB-II ended with the NASA Task-Load Index (NASA-TLX, Figure 4), which asked the participants about their subjectively felt workload during the task. Each subscore came with a verbal clarification. Mental Demand—"Wie mental/geistig anstrengend waren die Aufgaben?" ("How mentally demanding was the task?"). Physical Demand—"Wie physisch/körperlich anstrengend waren die Aufgaben?" ("How physically demanding was the task?"). Temporal Demand—"Wie stressing waren die Aufgaben?" ("How hurried or rushed was the pace of the task?"). Performance—"Wie gut schätzt du deine Leistungen in den Aufgaben ein?" ("How successful were you in accomplishing what you were asked to do?"). Effort—"Wie sehr musstest du dich anstrengen, um diese Leistung zu erbringen?" ("How hard did you have to work to accomplish your level of performance?"). Frustration—"Wie unsicher, entmutigt, irritiert, gestresst oder genervt hast du dich während der Aufgaben gefühlt?" ("How insecure, discouraged, irritated, stressed, or annoyed were you during the task?").

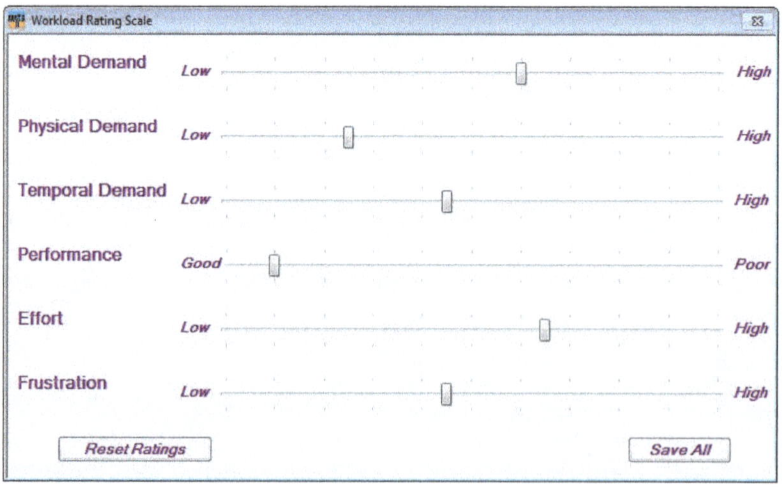

Figure 4. NASA Task-Load Index (NASA-TLX).

3. Results

3.1. *Analyses of Bottom-Up and Top-Down Capture of Visuospatial Attention in the Visual-Search Task*

For the analysis of top-down and bottom-up attention capture, only trials with correct responses were analyzed. Incorrect responses were excluded. Overall, at least 85% of the responses were correct for each participant, while the mean of correct responses was 95% (see Supplementary Table S4).

Two types of scores were calculated: a bottom-up score, which was calculated by subtracting the mean reaction time of all correct responses in the distractor-absent/target-singleton trials, in which no singleton-distractor was presented, from the mean reaction time of all correct responses in the target-dissimilar singleton-distractor trials; and a top-down score, which was calculated by subtracting the mean reaction time of all correct responses in the target-dissimilar singleton-distractor trials from the mean reaction time of all correct responses in the target-similar singleton-distractor trials. A dependent *t*-test of all 49 participants between the bottom-up scores ($M = 13$ ms, $SD = 41$ ms) and the top-down scores ($M = 56$ ms, $SD = 83$ ms) showed a significantly lower bottom-up than top-down score, $t(48) = -2.86$, $p = 0.006$, before the MATB-II task. Similar results were shown after the MATB-II task, with a slight numerical decrease in the bottom-up score ($M = 7$ ms, $SD = 35$ ms) as well as in the top-down score ($M = 37$ ms, $SD = 56$ ms), $t(48) = -2.59$, $p = 0.013$. However, no significant differences were found between the bottom-up scores before and after the MATB-II, $t(48) = 0.81$, $p = 0.421$, or between the top-down scores before and after the MATB-II, $t(48) = 1.87$, $p = 0.077$. These results are in line with those achieved in past research [8].

Next, we calculated linear regressions showing the correlations between bottom-up scores at measurement Time Points 1 and 2 and between top-down scores before and after the MATB-II. Bottom-up scores achieved before the MATB-II correlated significantly with bottom-up scores achieved after the MATB-II, $F(1, 47) = 4.245$, $p = 0.048$, $R^2 = 0.065$, adj. $R^2 = 0.045$. The same was true for top-down scores achieved before and after the MATB-II, $F(1, 47) = 22.75$, $p < 0.001$, $R^2 = 0.326$, adj. $R^2 = 0.312$. Spearman's Rho correlations were, thus, in the same ballpark as in previous studies, with bottom-up scores before and after the MATB-II, $r_s = 0.28$, $p = 0.046$; and with top-down scores before and after the MATB-II, $r_s = 0.57$, $p < 0.001$. See Figure 5.

When correlating the bottom-up scores to the top-down scores before the MATB-II, a significant but negative correlation was found, $F(1, 47) = 7.080$, $p = 0.011$, $R^2 = 0.131$, adj. $R^2 = 0.112$. Again, the same is true when correlating bottom-up scores and top-down scores after the MATB-II, $F(1, 47) = 22.130$, $p < 0.001$, $R^2 = 0.320$, adj. $R^2 = 0.306$. Spearman's Rho correlations between the bottom-up scores and the top-down scores before and after the MATB-II were as followed: $r_s = -0.45$, $p = 0.001$ before the MATB-II; and $r_s = -0.54$, $p < 0.001$ after the MATB-II. See Figure 6.

Lastly, we compared the number of times participants' gaze was distracted by the singleton distractor with the number of times participants were distracted by the nonsingletons (the gray discs). This was done to check if the distractors indeed captured attention or if longer response times (RTs) in trials with a singleton distractor reflected a nonspatial filtering cost [11]. Looking at all distractor-present trials, those with a nonmatching (target-dissimilar) singleton distractor as well as those with a matching (target-similar) singleton distractor present, we observed that participants' eyes fixated the singleton distractors more often ($M = 22.06$, $SD = 13.77$) than the gray nonsingletons ($M = 9.16$, $SD = 8.16$), $t(215) = 11.81$, $p < 0.001$. This was true despite the fact that there was only one singleton distractor in each such display, but five nonsingletons, increasing the likelihood of chance fixations on one of the gray nonsingletons discs compared to the singleton distractors.

Specifically, in nonmatching conditions, with a target-dissimilar singleton distractor, on average, participants fixated the target-dissimilar singleton distractor about 15 times ($M = 14.65$, $SD = 6.96$) and the nonsingletons about nine times ($M = 8.55$, $SD = 8.12$), $t(107) = 5.90$, $p < 0.001$. In matching conditions, with a target-similar singleton distractor present, participants fixated the target-similar singleton distractor about 30 times ($M = 29.46$,

SD = 14.87) and the nonsingletons about 10 times (M = 9.77, SD = 8.15), $t(107)$ = 12.01, p < 0.001. For a more detailed description, see Table 1.

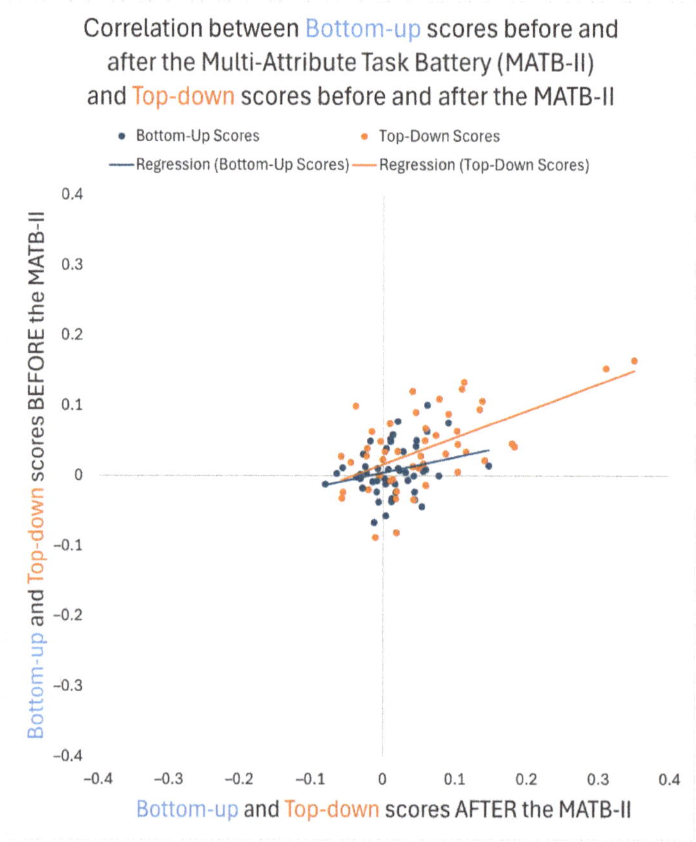

Figure 5. Linear regressions of bottom-up scores after the Multi-Attribute Task Battery (MATB-II) on bottom-scores before the MATB-II, as well as between top-down scores after the MATB-II on top-down scores before the MATB-II. Blue dots and orange dots correspond to individual bottom-up and top-down scores in the visual search task, respectively.

Table 1. Mean fixations of singleton and nonsingleton distractors divided into target color and distractor trial.

Target-Color	Distractor Trial	Mean Target Fixation	SD Target Fixation	Mean Nonsingleton Fixation	SD Nonsingleton Fixation	Degrees of Freedom	T-Value	p-Value
Green-1 (G1)	Dissimilar	18.07	8.41	12.03	10.30	27	1.87	0.038
	Similar	19.75	10.85	13.25	10.35	27	2.25	0.028
Green-2 (G2)	Dissimilar	16.17	5.85	7.26	6.49	29	5.50	<0.001
	Similar	20.67	7.18	10.57	8.02	29	5.06	<0.001
Red-1 (R1)	Dissimilar	11.85	5.25	7.00	6.35	25	2.94	0.005
	Similar	40.08	9.97	5.73	4.98	25	15.41	<0.001
Red-2 (R2)	Dissimilar	14.13	6.97	7.79	7.55	23	2.95	0.005
	Similar	40.29	15.49	9.08	5.82	23	9.04	<0.001

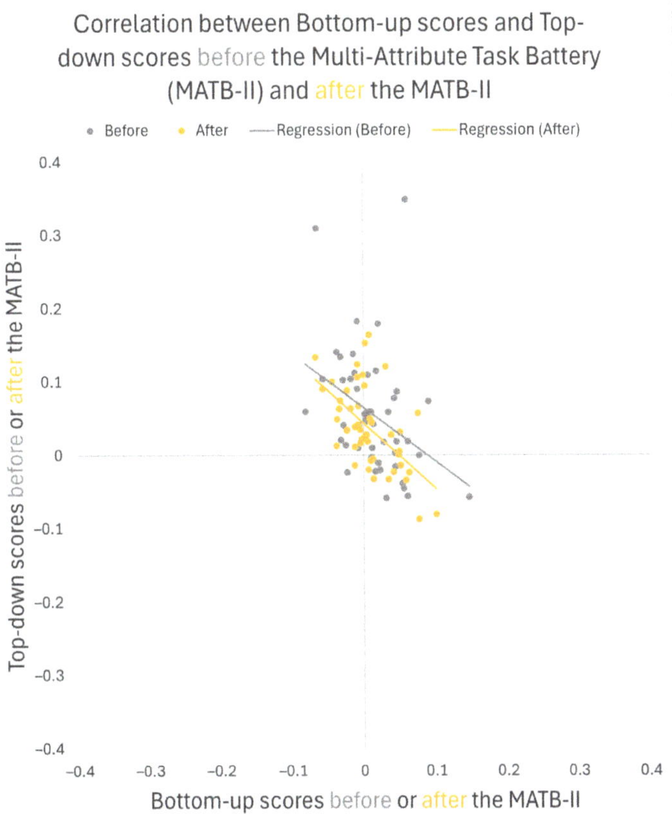

Figure 6. Linear regressions between bottom-up scores and top-down scores before the Multi-Attribute Task Battery (MATB-II), depicted in gray, as well as after the MATB-II, depicted in orange. Gray dots represent individual performance scores on the visual search task before the MATB-II; orange dots represent individual performance scores after the MATB-II.

Since top-down attention-capture scores were calculated as differences in RTs between matching distractor-present trials and nonmatching distractor-present trials, a correlation between the top-down scores and the fixation differences was in order. For the latter, we used the difference between the numbers of times participants looked at a matching singleton distractor versus at a nonmatching singleton distractor, once before and once after the MATB-II (see Figure 7).

Both before and after the MATB-II, we can see a clear correlation between the top-down score of the participants and the difference in the numbers of times participants fixated the matching distractors minus the nonmatching distractors (before the MATB-II: $F[(1, 47) = 27.93$, $p < 0.001$, $R^2 = 0.373$, adj. $R^2 = 0.359$, $r_s = 0.63$, $p < 0.001$; after the MATB-II: $F(1, 47) = 16.27$, $p < 0.001$, $R^2 = 0.257$, adj. $R^2 = 0.241$, $r_s = 0.55$, $p < 0.001$). No such correlations were found between the bottom-up attention-capture score and the same differences between the numbers of times participants fixated the matching singleton distractors minus the nonmatching singleton distractors, both before and after the MATB-II.

One reviewer observed that significant correlations might have been suggested by outliers only. Thus, we repeated the regression analyses without outliers. By using the interquartile range method, we identified two potential outliers—that is, participants with scores higher than the third quartile (Q3) plus 1.5-times the interquartile range (IQR; Q3 + [1.5

× IQR]) in the top-down score category, and two participants who scored higher than that in the bottom-up score category. No participants scored lower than the first quartile minus 1.5-times the interquartile range (Q1 − [1.5 × IQR]).

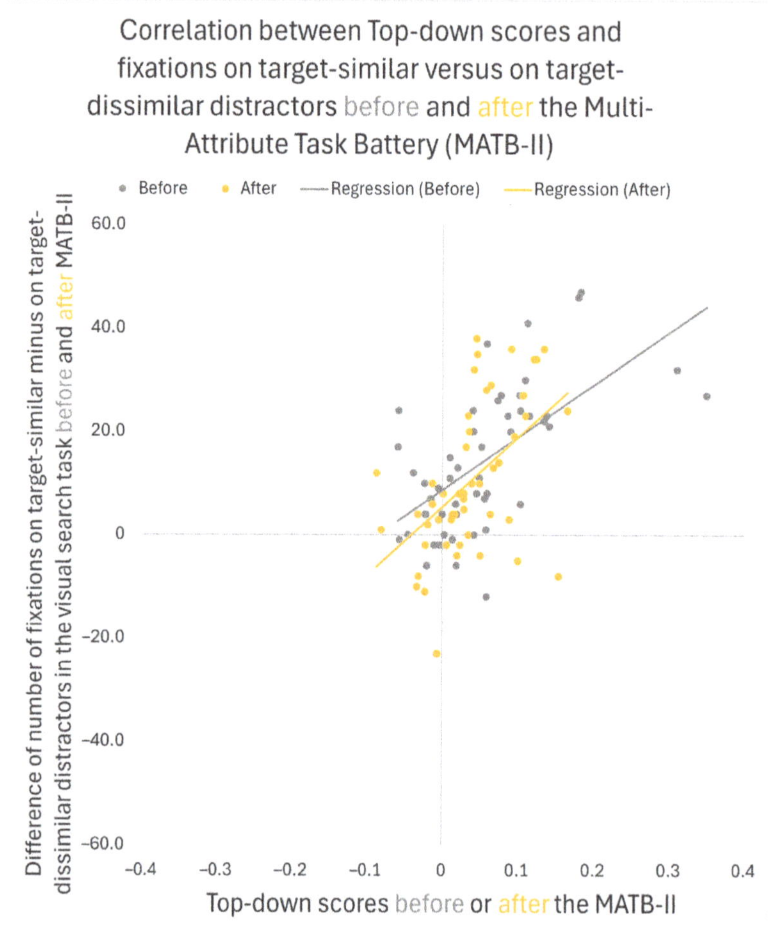

Figure 7. Linear regression of top-down scores on the difference between the number of fixations on target-similar minus on target-dissimilar distractors. The gray dots and the orange dots depict individual data from the visual search task before and after the Multi-Attribute Task Battery II (MATB-II), respectively.

After removing these outliers from the sample, the correlations remained significant, except for the correlations of the bottom-up scores before and after the MATB-II that dropped to a nonsignificant $R^2 = 0.050$, adj. $R^2 = 0.038$, $p = 0.053$. In contrast, we saw a positive correlation of the top-down scores before and after the MATB-II, $R^2 = 0.138$, adj. $R^2 = 0.118$, $p = 0.012$, a negative correlation between the bottom-up scores and the top-down scores before the MATB-II, $R^2 = -0.166$, adj. $R^2 = -0.146$, $p = 0.006$, and a negative correlation between the bottom-up scores and the top-down scores after the MATB-II, $R^2 = -0.340$, adj. $R^2 = -0.324$, $p < 0.001$. We also observed a positive correlation between the top-down score and the fixations on target-similar minus target-dissimilar distractors before the MATB-II, $R^2 = 0.486$, adj. $R^2 = 0.474$, $p < 0.001$, and a positive correlation between the top-down score and the fixations on target-similar minus target-dissimilar distractors after the MATB-II, $R^2 = 0.343$, adj. $R^2 = 0.327$, $p < 0.001$.

3.2. Correlations between Visuospatial Attention in the Experimental Task and Performance on the Multi-Attribute Task Battery

In a next step, we correlated the bottom-up and top-down scores to the overall MATB-II scores, looking for potential correlations between scores in the MATB-II and a top-down or bottom-up capture effect, and came to the following results. A simple regression was used to regress participants' overall score in the MATB-II on the bottom-up capture effect on the one hand, and on the top-down score on the other hand. The bottom-up capture score did not predict MATB-II performance, $r(47) = -0.196$, $p = 0.177$. The same holds true for the top-down score, $r(47) = 0.152$, $p = 0.297$.

A further in-depth analysis of all participant groups (including all participants, only high-workload participants, only low-workload participants, only pilots, and all participants without pilots) regressing MATB-II scores on attention-capture scores was conducted. No significant correlation between either bottom-up or top-down scores and any of the MATB-II subtask performance scores was found, including the system monitoring performance score (see Supplementary Tables S5 and S6).

3.3. Analyses of Pupillary Responses in the Multi-Attribute Task Battery (MATB-II)

The analysis of the pupillary responses was conducted, with the two variables workload (high, low) and performance (high, low). As explained, we used an algorithm to automatically extract a workload measure. Figure 8 shows an example of how this works. Here, one can see how the pupil size of a participant changed during the MATB-II's subtasks, as well as the calculated change in cognitive load, and the calculated light changes that were modelled via the Pupillary-Light-Response (PLR) model [25,26]. This model predicts the pupillary light reflex behavior to brightness via an individually trained empirical model. The model uses brightness measures from the eye tracker's world video data. The algorithm uses the modelled PLR to subtract it from the raw data and arrive at a cognitive load measure.

The top left of Figure 8 shows the changes in pupil diameter over the course of the Multi-Attribute Test Battery (MATB-II; 5 min). Here, the black line corresponds to the pupil diameter in pixels. The colored vertical lines indicate the start and stop of a subtask in the MATB-II. Here, the dotted green line corresponds to a change in the pump's function in the resource-management task ("pump error" = pump cannot be used; "pump repaired" = pump can be used again). A dotted yellow line represents a change in the tracking task ("manual" = participant must control the crosshair; "auto" = the crosshair moves by itself). The dash-dotted blue line indicates the start of a communication task. The blue line corresponds to a participant's response to a communication task. The dash-dotted red line represents the start of a system monitoring task. The red line indicates that the participant responds to a system monitoring task.

The top right of Figure 8 shows the Pupillary-Light-Response (PLR) that was calculated on the basis of the light changes, presented at the bottom right. These PLRs were subtracted from the pupil diameter changes to derive the cognitive or workload changes. The bottom left of Figure 8 shows the cognitive or workload changes during the MATB-II.

Using the raw average pupil diameter sizes in pixels during the MATB-II, no significant differences between the 24 participants in the high workload group ($M = 34.08$, $SD = 6.59$) and the 25 participants in the low workload group ($M = 36.33$, $SD = 7.14$) were found, $t(47) = 1.14$, $p = 0.259$. The same is true for the cognitive load indices derived from the raw data: the average cognitive load of the high workload group ($M = 3.16$, $SD = 1.13$) did not differ significantly from the average cognitive load of the low workload group ($M = 3.46$, $SD = 1.21$), $t(47) = 0.89$, $p = 0.380$. There were also no significant differences in average raw pupil size diameter during the MATB-II between the 24 low performers ($M = 36.22$, $SD = 5.79$) and the 25 high performers ($M = 34.27$, $SD = 7.81$), $t(47) = 0.99$, p = 0.328, and between average cognitive load measures derived from raw pupil sizes between the 24 low performers (*M* = 3.39, *SD* = 1.10) and the 25 high performers (*M* = 3.25, *SD* = 1.26), $t(47) = 0.42$, $p = 0.678$. This latter finding is particularly striking, as clear performance differences and accompanying self-assessments of felt cognitive load or workload were found between the two groups of high versus low performers (see Supplementary Table S1). This means that the average of measured pupil sizes across a task battery such as the MATB-II per se is not very revealing. Among the reasons are possible differences between different tasks and between high versus low performers concerning the rates of saccades and, thus, their contributions to measured pupil sizes. In general, saccades tend to diminish pupil size responses to task characteristics [33]. In addition, pupil size differs for different stages of task-related processing: responses before and after task-related decisions differ [34], such that even a condition-specific average pupil size measure (let alone a measure across conditions) that averages across different processing stages of task performance would not reflect cognitive load or workload, task demands, or overall performance in a complex cognitive test battery. To note, participants have to take a decision prior to each of the overt responses (e.g., a decision to start tracking the moving cursor, or a decision to press a button that turned from green to gray).

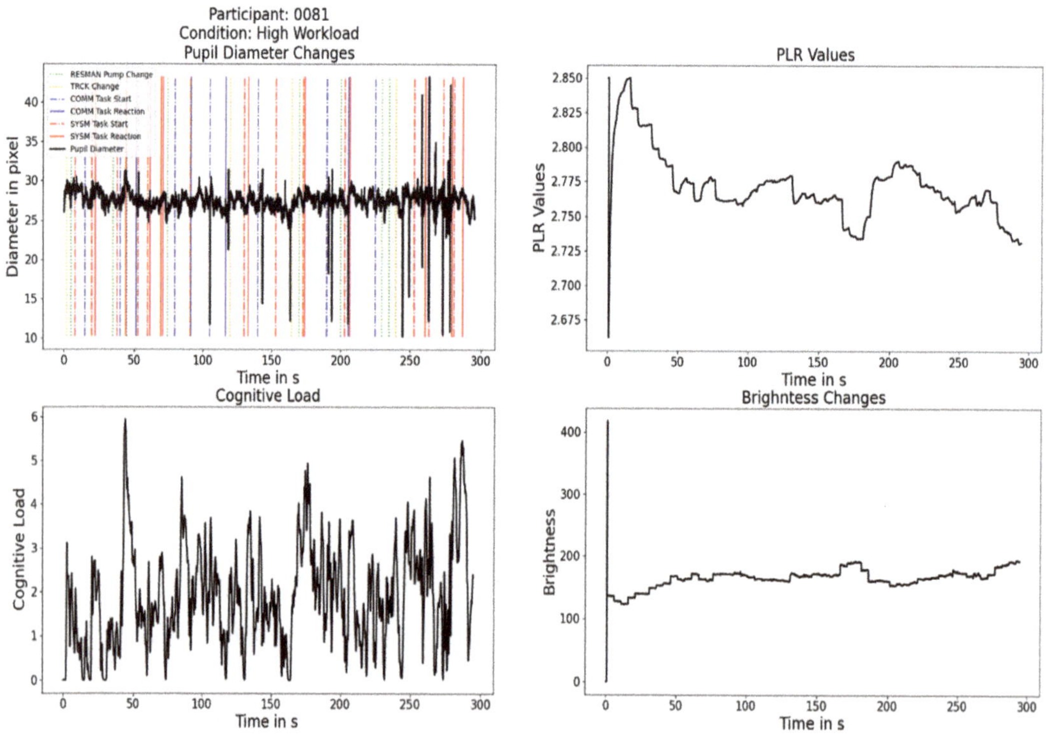

Figure 8. Changes in pupil size and cognitive load of a single participant in the high workload condition.

3.4. Analyses of Pupillary Responses in the System Monitoring Task of the Multi-Attribute Task Battery (MATB-II)

We also analyzed performance in the system monitoring task of the MATB-II more closely because this task has potentially the tightest connection to our experimental measures of top-down versus bottom-up capture. In a first step and in direct continuation of the discussed problems regarding the usage of an average pupil size measure, we analyzed pupillary responses in this task as a function of two stages of the task. For each participant, a "task onset" was defined by the first fixation within the task-specific area of interest following the change of the color of one of the lights/buttons, and a "task response" was defined as the moment at which each participant pressed the light/button (following a color change). The corresponding pupil sizes at these two points in time during the system monitoring task were then evaluated for whether a significant change in diameter could be found between task onset and task response. This was the case: pupil sizes at the time of task onset ($M = 34.29$, $SD = 7.48$) were significantly smaller than pupil sizes at the time of task response ($M = 37.45$, $SD = 8.19$), $t(603) = 19.02$, $p < 0.001$, analogous to past findings [34] showing that pupil size changes reveal the time point of the decision (which has to be taken before the overt manual response is given).

4. Discussion

In the current study, we investigated potential links between experimental measures of top-down and bottom-up capture of visuospatial attention and performance in one cognitive task battery: the MATB-II, a task battery based on operations in a simplified flight console [8]. We did so to understand if one or the other type of directing visuospatial attention—goal-directed, top-down-dependent capture of attention based on matches between visual input and searched for target features [11,35,36]; or bottom-up capture of attention due to the salience or local feature contrast between a visual singleton object and surrounding nonsingletons [13,37–39]—explains performance in the MATB-II in general or in its system monitoring subtask in particular. As performance in the MATB-II requires frequent shifting of attention between different areas on the simulated console (i.e., the monitor), and as especially the system monitoring task could be based on search for changes of lights/buttons to particular colors (i.e., from green to gray and from gray to red), we hypothesized that visuospatial attention could contribute to performance in the MATB-II or its system monitoring subtask. In addition, prior research has shown that both top-down and bottom-up scores of attention capture correlated across time and were negatively correlated with one another, meaning that the experimental task measures of visuospatial attention were not only internally valid, but also relatively stable [8,9].

4.1. Correlation Analyses between Visual-Search Task Measure of Visuospatial Attention and Multi-Attribute Task Battery Scores and between Different Measures of Visuospatial Attention within the Visual Search Task

In the present study, we did not find any of the expected correlations between attention capture and MATB-II task performance. This was the case for the correlations between all (bottom-up and top-down) attention-capture scores and overall MATB-II performance, as well as for the performance scores derived from the different subtasks of the MATB-II. In addition, we replicated the positive correlations between top-down capture scores at measurement Time Points 1 and 2 (here, before and after the MATB-II) and between bottom-up capture scores at measurement Time Points 1 and 2, as well as the negative correlations between top-down and bottom-up capture scores at Time Point 1 and at Time Point 2 [8,9]. Arguably, these correlations provided the upper limit for what could be expected in terms of maximal correlations between attention capture scores and MATB-II task performance because, theoretically, it was to be expected that the correlations between the scores from one and the same task—here, the visual search task—were higher than those between the scores from two different tasks—here, the visual search task and the MATB-II—as the different tasks had less shared sources of performance variance in common [40]. This means underlying psychological functions were more different regarding performance in the visual search task versus the MATB-II than within the visual search task. For example, the task-shifting requirements [41,42] were likely higher in the MATB-II task, whereas suppression of predictable color distractors played probably a larger role in the visual search task [30,31,43]. In the current study, by blocking the different distractor conditions in the visual search task (e.g., by presenting first all trials without a singleton distractor, then all trials with a nonmatching/target-dissimilar distractor, and then all trials with a matching/target-similar distractors), we reduced the residual shift costs that might have theoretically resulted from trying to ignore different specific color singletons from one trial to the next [44,45]. In contrast, task shifts are common in the MATB-II [46]. Likewise, by using different colors to indicate different tasks (e.g., changes from green to gray and from gray to red in the system monitoring tasks) of the MATB-II, we made it very difficult if not impossible for participants to proactively suppress particular irrelevant colors in the test battery [47]. In contrast, using the same singleton-distractor colors for blocks of trials, proactive suppression of distractor interference was probably a factor in the visual search task [31].

Summarizing, it seems that the chances for finding any significant correlations between the experimental visual search task's attention capture scores and the MATB-II performance scores were limited from the start by the less than perfect reliability or temporal consistency (i.e., the correlations < 1.00) of the attention-capture scores in the first place, especially the bottom-up capture score. In addition, there might have been good theoretical reasons why the correlations between attention capture scores and MATB-II performance were low or nonexistent. For example, in the current study, the correlations of the top-down scores were numerically not as low across measurement time points as that of the bottom-up capture scores. Thus, theoretically, there was more space for a correlation of the top-down capture score with the MATB-II performance, especially in a subtask such as system monitoring that participants could have solved by searching for specific colors. However, potential correlations between top-down capture scores and MATB-II task performance that were currently not found could have suffered for theoretical reasons alone. For example, past research has shown that participants have increasing difficulty to proactively search for several relevant colors at the same time [48–52]. However, this was what was required in the MATB-II task. For example, a change from a green to a gray color and a change from a gray to a red color were both task-relevant in the system monitoring task of the MATB-II. In fact, with its fixed positions on the monitor, participants in the MATB-II task could have even used a location-based monitoring (or search) strategy for their task-shifting and subtask performance [53–55]. For example, it is known that participants can exploit their knowledge of likely locations of objects in a scene for their shifts of attention and their eye movements [56–58]. In the present study, considering that specific colors (e.g., the color red) had different meanings depending on where they were located in the display (e.g., they indicated that a button had to be pressed in Areas 1 and 2, see Figure 3, but that a pump failed and can currently not be used to replenish tanks in Area 5, see Figure 3), a location-based strategy or a strategy that looks for conjunctions of specific colors and locations is not unlikely to account for performance in the MATB-II.

4.2. Further Findings of Interest

In addition to these most important findings, we observed surprising effects of cognitive load (or workload) on performance in the MATB-II (see Supplementary Table S2). To increase variance in the MATB-II performance, we used two workload conditions differing in the number of tasks and task shifts per unit of time. Contrary to what we would have expected, however, in the present study, participants' performance was higher in the system monitoring and tracking subtasks under the high- than under the low-workload conditions. Typically, performance in cognitive tasks such as the MATB-II declines with a higher workload [46,59,60]. There are several possible reasons for the presently found deviation from this expected pattern. First, participants in the low-workload condition might not have performed close to capacity, meaning that there could have been spare capacity to prioritize the two subtasks of system monitoring and of tracking, for which we found performance improvements relative to the low-workload conditions. Second, because we used a between-participants design, it is possible that generally better performing participants were placed in the high-workload than in the low-workload group. Third, somewhat related to the first point, general physiological activation in the less demanding conditions might have been too low for optimal performance. It is assumed that emotions experienced in "boring" tasks, imposing too little demands, and the resulting achievement motivation could be too low for optimal cognitive performance [61]. Partly in line with this proposal, early findings suggested, for instance, an inversely u-shaped function relating physiological arousal to task performance [62]. Fourth, a very interesting possibility has recently been suggested when dual-task performance benefits over single-task performance were observed [63,64]. Researchers [63] believe that the necessity to suppress a prepotent response that would naturally occur under some single-task conditions (e.g., not being allowed to look at a target when a spatially compatible manual response to the target is required) could create a single-task cost that is absent when participants are allowed to perform both responses (or "tasks"). According to this reasoning, subtasks in the MATB-II could partly better be integrated with one another in the high-workload condition than in the low-workload condition. For example, alluding to the possibility of a location-based search strategy to look for changes of the stimuli that we discussed above, a higher frequency of the system monitoring task in the high-load conditions could have led to more fixations in this area of the screen (Areas 1 and 2, see Figure 3), and performance on the visually controlled task in the spatially adjacent area (Area 3, see Figure 3, here, the tracking task) could have benefitted from this general looking-direction effect. This type of coupled benefit between performance on these two tasks would be fully in line with our observation of a better performance in these two tasks under high-load conditions (see Supplementary Table S2). It is also in line with a post hoc comparison of the overall higher fixation durations on regions of interest of the tracking tasks under low- than under high-load conditions, suggesting that a higher rate of switching between tasks allowed the participants to be more aware of changes that needed a participant's response. Of the 24 participants in the high-workload condition, only a mean of 36% (SD = 9.64) of the time spent looking at the MATB-II tasks in total was directed at the area of interest of the tracking task, while the 25 participants of the low-workload condition spent a significantly larger mean amount of 42% (SD = 8.75) fixating on the tracking task, $t(49) = 2.09$, $p = 0.047$. Other subtasks of the MATB-II under high-workload conditions might have neither benefited, nor suffered from this dual-task benefit for system monitoring and tracking because these other tasks relied on auditory input (i.e., the communication task) and, thus, would not benefit from visuospatial attention being directed to an adjacent area, or were less dependent on directing visuospatial attention to the particular region of the monitor for other reasons such as being relatively insensitive to the exact time at which the task was handled. The latter would have been the case for the resource management task, for which we did not even analyze reaction times, and which was also least sensitive of all subtasks to the performance difference between high- and low-performers in the MATB-II (see Supplementary Table S7).

4.3. Pupillary Cognitive Load or Workload Responses

A related point of interest concerns the insensitivity of our pupillary cognitive load index to the manipulations of workload, but also to the factual task performance—that is, to the median split of our participants into high versus low performers on the MATB-II. To note, the cognitive load index is a computationally modelled load-elicited pupillary response that is supposed to be free of the luminance-elicited pupillary size change. While we could relatively easily explain the lacking impact of our workload manipulation on the cognitive load index of the pupillary response through the lacking predicted impact of our workload manipulation on performance in the MATB-II, this is not the case for the absence of a difference in the cognitive load index of the pupillary response between high and low performers. The latter groups clearly differed from one another in terms of their performance in the MATB-II in all but one subtask (i.e., the resource management task). Yet, these groups did not differ with respect to their cognitive load index derived from pupillary responses. In addition, high versus low performers also differed regarding their self-assessed workload (see Supplementary Table S8). These significant differences imply that there would have been theoretical reasons to expect a difference in the cognitive load index of the pupillary response. At least three possibilities come to mind explaining the discrepancy between the two measures (objective performance on the MATB-II versus pupil-based load index). First, it is possible that averaging the cognitive load index of the pupillary response across different stages of the subtasks of the MATB-II simply washed out any load differences between high and low performers due to averaging across times of very different sensitivity of the pupils to the load differences. For instance, recent research suggested that indices of pupil sizes could vary depending on the amount of saccades conducted in a task [33]. This was not controlled for in the current study. This general possibility of a watered-down effect of averaging would also be in line with the general observation of stages of different sensitivities of the pupil size for task demands, such as pre- versus postdecisional stages [34]. This possibility of averaging out of the pupillary response to varying degrees would also be supported by the following observation: we observed a difference in the pupillary response at task onset versus at task response. This difference came to light in our more detailed analysis of the system monitoring task performance. Secondly, other studies have also found that different measures of cognitive load such as task performance and pupillary responses do not always converge [60]. In fact, even the performances on different visual tasks that are meant to measure the same aptitude do not necessarily converge [40]. Thirdly, we believe that there is also space for improvement of the estimation of the light-elicited response in spatially articulated displays such as that of the currently used MATB-II. For example, it is known that even subjectively perceived lightness can prompt a light-elicited pupillary response [65,66]. There is arguably room for such illusory lightness in articulated monitor displays [67] such as the ones used in the MATB-II that is currently not ruled out by the automatic measurement and subtraction of the objective light-elicited pupillary response [25,26], so that it is possible that the corresponding artifacts in the pupil size measures could have watered down the true influence of cognitive load on pupil size in the present study's MATB-II, too.

4.4. Limitations

Our discussion already revealed a number of limitations. We pointed out that future studies should take saccade rates into account and that they need to carefully discriminate not only between tasks, but also between stages of task-specific processing to make use of pupil-size measures. In addition, we argued that pupil size measures of workload may also benefit from taking into account more subtle visual brightness effects than are currently measured with the video camera-based brightness measurement. However, we think that controlling for additional influences on pupil size that are relatively independent of workload and brightness (e.g., emotions) is not necessary, unless one has good reasons to assume that such independent effects are confounded with effects of workload.

In addition to these points, more generally, we based our sample size estimates on substantial effect sizes. Certainly, weaker effects were, therefore, impossible for us to detect. Regarding the participants that we tested, we failed to collect more data from experts, in our case, pilots. Instead, our sample consisted of mostly students. This is maybe not ideal in two respects. On the one hand, more pilots could have meant that task-relevant performance variance would have increased, allowing all variance-based measures a better chance to be detected. On the other hand, students might also have been relatively good performers, meaning that especially weaker performers would have been missing, again restricting the overall performance variance in an unnecessary way.

At a theoretical level, one could argue that too little is known yet about how separate cognitive functions such as bottom-up or top-down visuospatial attention play out in more complex applied or real-world tasks. As a consequence, testing for the role in a more applied setting might have been overly optimistic in the first place. This is true, but we would also want to point out that research such as the present study would help to inform these applied or real-world task models by demonstrating if a particular cognitive mechanism or function would have to be taken into account to explain cognitive task performance, yes or no. At a conceptual level, one could also argue that the major purpose of a task battery (e.g., the MATB-II) is its usage in diagnostics. What matters most is if a task or test (battery) could tell people with and without high aptitude from one another. In contrast, understanding the exact working of such tasks or tests would not be necessary for this purpose. Here, we would like to argue, however, that the internal validity of diagnostic tasks or tests is important, even for the practical purposes mentioned above. Knowing what exactly accounts for task or test performance could help to increase task or test sensitivity for the aptitude in question even further. For example, knowing what accounts for task performance would allow one to construct trials or items suited to measure the major performance contributors.

5. Conclusions

In the current study, we found no evidence that measures of top-down or bottom-up capture of visuospatial attention had any bearing on performance in a more applied cognitive task battery. Just as being good at cycling is not sufficient to perform well during a triathlon (which requires one to also run and swim well), visuospatial attention could simply not be decisive for overall performance when operating a flight console. This finding casts doubt on the generalizability of experimental task performance to more applied and real-world tasks. This finding also emphasizes the doubtful ecological validity of many experimental tasks (although they are doubtlessly of high internal validity) [68]. We could also not find any links between MATB-II task performance and cognitive load indices derived from pupillary size. Moreover, we observed surprising effects of workload (or cognitive load) manipulation on MATB-II performance itself. Maybe it is not too surprising that pupillary responses did not react to the task load manipulation because the latter created a paradoxical effect. However, we want to emphasize that there were also no significant correlations between pupillary responses and individual MATB-II performance. These findings imply that the MATB-II itself poses a number of questions about its underlying rationale. These findings also revealed that pupillary responses are not necessarily an ideal tool to tell participants of varying aptitude apart. This conclusion at least holds for the relatively homogenous sample of mostly student participants that we used in the current study. Nevertheless, these types of studies, where concepts with a strong foundation, which in our case would be the bottom-up and top-down search task paradigm, and real-world use-cases are compared toe to toe, are incredibly beneficial for our understanding of limitations of lab studies, as well as possibly finding issues in validity and reliability of a real-world use-case testing apparatus.

Supplementary Materials: The following supporting information can be downloaded at: https://www.mdpi.com/article/10.3390/app14083158/s1, Table S1: t T-Test of all pupil diameter and cognitive load changes during the Multi-Attribute Task Battery (MATB-II) between low- and high-workload groups, as well as between low- and high-performer groups, the latter also split for within the low-workload group and the high-workload group.; Table S2: T-Test of all Multi-Attribute Task Battery (MATB-II) subtasks z-scores, between participants in the low-workload group and the high-workload group, as well as between participants in the low-performance group and participants in the high-performance group.; Table S3: T-Test of all Multi-Attribute Task Battery (MATB-II) subtasks z-scores, between low- and high-performing participants within either the low-workload group or the high-workload group.; Table S4: List of all participants' search-task scores.; Table S5: Pearson Correlation coefficients between Multi-Attribute Task Battery (MATB-II) sub-task performance scores and bottom-up attention-capture scores divided by groups (all participants, all participants - pilots excluded, low-workload group, high-workload group, pilots only); Table S6: Pearson Correlation coefficients between Multi-Attribute Task Battery (MATB-II) sub-task performances and top-down attention-capture scores divided by groups (all participants, all participants - pilots excluded, low-workload group, high-workload group, pilots only); Table S7: X-Y coordinate tracking. Percentages of which area eyes were directed at.; Table S8: T-Test of all NASA Task Load Index (TLX) scores, between participants in the low-workload group and the high-workload group, as well as between participants in the low-performance group and participants in the high-performance group.

Author Contributions: Conceptualization, B.G., M.S. and U.A.; Methodology, D.G., M.S. and U.A.; Software, D.G. and B.G.; Validation, D.G. and B.G.; Formal analysis, D.G.; Resources, U.A.; Data curation, D.G.;

Writing—original draft, D.G. and U.A.; Writing—review & editing, D.G., B.G., M.S. and U.A.; Visualization, D.G.; Supervision, B.G., M.S. and U.A.; Project administration, B.G. and U.A.; Funding acquisition, U.A. All authors have read and agreed to the published version of the manuscript.

Funding: This research was funded by Austrian Research Promotion Agency grant number [880102]. Open Access Funding by the University of Vienna.

Institutional Review Board Statement: The study was conducted in accordance with the Declaration of Helsinki, and approved by the Institutional Review Board (or Ethics Committee) of University of Vienna (protocol code 00644 at the 13. of April 2021). for studies involving humans.

Informed Consent Statement: Informed consent was obtained from all subjects involved in the study.

Data Availability Statement: The data presented in this study are openly available in FigShare at https://doi.org/10.6084/m9.figshare.25540156.

Conflicts of Interest: The authors declare no conflict of interest.

References

1. Kong, Y.; Posada-Quintero, H.F.; Gever, D.; Bonacci, L.; Chon, K.H.; Bolkhovsky, J. Multi-Attribute Task Battery configuration to effectively assess pilot performance deterioration during prolonged wakefulness. *Inform. Med. Unlocked* **2022**, *28*, 100822. [CrossRef]
2. Wang, P.; Fang, W.; Guo, B. A colored petri nets based workload evaluation model and its validation through Multi-Attribute Task Battery-II. *Appl. Ergon.* **2017**, *60*, 260–274. [CrossRef] [PubMed]
3. Fukuda, K.; Vogel, E.K.; Awh, E. Quantity, not quality: The relationship between fluid intelligence and working memory capacity. *Psychon. Bull. Rev.* **2010**, *17*, 673–679. [CrossRef] [PubMed]
4. Robertson, I.H.; Ward, T.; Ridgeway, V.; Nimmo-Smith, I. The structure of normal human attention: The Test of Everyday Attention. *J. Int. Neuropsychol. Soc.* **1996**, *2*, 525–534. [CrossRef]
5. Roque, N.A.; Wright, T.J.; Boot, W.R. Do different attention capture paradigms measure different types of capture? *Atten. Percept. Psychophys.* **2016**, *78*, 2014–2030. [CrossRef] [PubMed]
6. Conway, A.R.A.; Kane, M.J.; Bunting, M.F.; Hambrick, D.Z.; Wilhelm, O.; Engle, R.W. Working memory span tasks: A methodological review and user's guide. *Psychon. Bull. Rev.* **2005**, *12*, 769–786. [CrossRef]
7. Wiegand, I.; Töllner, T.; Habekost, T.; Dyrholm, M.; Müller, H.J.; Finke, K. Distinct Neural Markers of TVA-Based Visual Processing Speed and Short-Term Storage Capacity Parameters. *Cereb. Cortex* **2014**, *24*, 1967–1978. [CrossRef] [PubMed]
8. Weichselbaum, H.; Huber-Huber, C.; Ansorge, U. Attention capture is temporally stable: Evidence from mixed-model correlations. *Cognition* **2018**, *180*, 206–224. [CrossRef]
9. Weichselbaum, H.; Ansorge, U. Bottom-up attention capture with distractor and target singletons defined in the same (color) dimension is not a matter of feature uncertainty. *Atten. Percept. Psychophys.* **2018**, *80*, 1350–1361. [CrossRef]
10. Santiago-Espada, Y.; Myer, R.; Latorella, K.; Comstock, J.R. The Multi-Attribute Task Battery II (MATB-II) Software for Human Performance and Workload Research: A User's Guide. 2011. Available online: https://www.semanticscholar.org/paper/The-Multi-Attribute-Task-Battery-II-(\protect\unhbox\voidb@x\hbox{MATB-II})-for-A-Santiago-Espada-Myer/03048e4a70abc42693148a7b4e24d2a18ab75347 (accessed on 29 August 2023).
11. Folk, C.L.; Remington, R. Selectivity in distraction by irrelevant featural singletons: Evidence for two forms of attentional capture. *J. Exp. Psychol. Hum. Percept. Perform.* **1998**, *24*, 847–858. [CrossRef]
12. Goller, F.; Ditye, T.; Ansorge, U. The contribution of color to attention capture effects during search for onset targets. *Atten. Percept. Psychophys.* **2016**, *78*, 789–807. [CrossRef] [PubMed]
13. Theeuwes, J. Cross-dimensional perceptual selectivity. *Percept. Psychophys.* **1991**, *50*, 184–193. [CrossRef] [PubMed]
14. Theeuwes, J. Perceptual selectivity for color and form. *Percept. Psychophys.* **1992**, *51*, 599–606. [CrossRef] [PubMed]
15. Theeuwes, J. Top–down and bottom–up control of visual selection. *Acta Psychol.* **2010**, *135*, 77–99. [CrossRef]
16. Appel, T.; Scharinger, C.; Gerjets, P.; Kasneci, E. Cross-subject workload classification using pupil-related measures. In Proceedings of the 2018 ACM Symposium on Eye Tracking Research & Applications, Warsaw, Poland, 14–18 June 2018; pp. 1–8. [CrossRef]
17. Chen, S.; Epps, J. Automatic classification of eye activity for cognitive load measurement with emotion interference. *Comput. Methods Programs Biomed.* **2013**, *110*, 111–124. [CrossRef] [PubMed]
18. Chen, S.; Epps, J. Using Task-Induced Pupil Diameter and Blink Rate to Infer Cognitive Load. *Hum. Comput. Interact.* **2014**, *29*, 390–413. [CrossRef]
19. Iqbal, S.T.; Zheng, X.S.; Bailey, B.P. Task-evoked pupillary response to mental workload in human-computer interaction. In Proceedings of the CHI'04 Extended Abstracts on Human Factors in Computing Systems, Vienna, Austria, 24–29 April 2004; pp. 1477–1480.
20. Krejtz, K.; Duchowski, A.T.; Niedzielska, A.; Biele, C.; Krejtz, I. Eye tracking cognitive load using pupil diameter and microsaccades with fixed gaze. *PLoS ONE* **2018**, *13*, e0203629. [CrossRef] [PubMed]
21. Laeng, B.; Ørbo, M.; Holmlund, T.; Miozzo, M. Pupillary Stroop effects. *Cogn. Process.* **2011**, *12*, 13–21. [CrossRef]

22. Stolte, M.; Gollan, B.; Ansorge, U. Tracking visual search demands and memory load through pupil dilation. *J. Vis.* **2020**, *20*, 21. [CrossRef]
23. Ahlstrom, U.; Friedman-Berg, F.J. Using eye movement activity as a correlate of cognitive workload. *Int. J. Ind. Ergon.* **2006**, *36*, 623–636. [CrossRef]
24. Van der Wel, P.; van Steenbergen, H. Pupil dilation as an index of effort in cognitive control tasks: A review. *Psychon. Bull. Rev.* **2018**, *25*, 2005–2015. [CrossRef] [PubMed]
25. Gollan, B. Sensor-based Online Assessment of Human Attention. Ph.D. Thesis, Johannes Kepler University Linz, Linz, Austria, 2018. [CrossRef]
26. Gollan, B.; Ferscha, A. Modeling Pupil Dilation as Online Input for Estimation of Cognitive Load in non-laboratory Attention-Aware Systems. In Proceedings of the COGNITIVE 2016: The Eighth International Conference on Advanced Cognitive Technologies and Applications, Rome, Italy, 20–24 March 2016.
27. Bradley, M.M.; Miccoli, L.; Escrig, M.A.; Lang, P.J. The pupil as a measure of emotional arousal and autonomic activation. *Psychophysiology* **2008**, *45*, 602–607. [CrossRef] [PubMed]
28. Casuccio, A.; Cillino, G.; Pavone, C.; Spitale, E.; Cillino, S. Pharmacologic pupil dilation as a predictive test for the risk for intraoperative floppy-iris syndrome. *J. Cataract. Refract. Surg.* **2011**, *37*, 1447–1454. [CrossRef] [PubMed]
29. Clewett, D.; Gasser, C.; Davachi, L. Pupil-linked arousal signals track the temporal organization of events in memory. *Nat. Commun.* **2020**, *11*, 4007. [CrossRef]
30. Gao, Y.; Theeuwes, J. Learning to suppress a distractor is not affected by working memory load. *Psychon. Bull. Rev.* **2020**, *27*, 96–104. [CrossRef] [PubMed]
31. Stilwell, B.T.; Bahle, B.; Vecera, S.P. Feature-based statistical regularities of distractors modulate attentional capture. *J. Exp. Psychol. Hum. Percept. Perform.* **2019**, *45*, 419–433. [CrossRef] [PubMed]
32. Wang, B.; Theeuwes, J. How to inhibit a distractor location? Statistical learning versus active, top-down suppression. *Atten. Percept. Psychophys.* **2018**, *80*, 860–870. [CrossRef] [PubMed]
33. Burlingham, C.S.; Mirbagheri, S.; Heeger, D.J. A unified model of the task-evoked pupil response. *Sci. Adv.* **2022**, *8*, eabi9979. [CrossRef] [PubMed]
34. Einhäuser, W.; Koch, C.; Carter, O.L. Pupil dilation betrays the timing of decisions. *Front. Hum. Neurosci.* **2010**, *4*, 18. [CrossRef]
35. Bundesen, C. A theory of visual attention. *Psychol. Rev.* **1990**, *97*, 523–547. [CrossRef]
36. Duncan, J.; Humphreys, G.W. Visual search and stimulus similarity. *Psychol. Rev.* **1989**, *96*, 433–458. [CrossRef] [PubMed]
37. Itti, L.; Koch, C.; Niebur, E. A model of saliency-based visual attention for rapid scene analysis. *IEEE Trans. Pattern Anal. Mach. Intell.* **1998**, *20*, 1254–1259. [CrossRef]
38. Li, Z. A saliency map in primary visual cortex. *Trends Cogn. Sci.* **2002**, *6*, 9–16. [CrossRef] [PubMed]
39. Nothdurft, H.-C. Salience from feature contrast: Additivity across dimensions. *Vis. Res.* **2000**, *40*, 1183–1201. [CrossRef] [PubMed]
40. Cappe, C.; Clarke, A.; Mohr, C.; Herzog, M. Is there a common factor for vision? *J. Vis.* **2014**, *14*, 4. [CrossRef] [PubMed]
41. Miyake, A.; Friedman, N.P.; Emerson, M.J.; Witzki, A.H.; Howerter, A.; Wager, T.D. The Unity and Diversity of Executive Functions and Their Contributions to Complex "Frontal Lobe" Tasks: A Latent Variable Analysis. *Cogn. Psychol.* **2000**, *41*, 49–100. [CrossRef] [PubMed]
42. Monsell, S. Task switching. *Trends Cogn. Sci.* **2003**, *7*, 134–140. [CrossRef]
43. Stilwell, B.T.; Vecera, S.P. Learned distractor rejection in the face of strong target guidance. *J. Exp. Psychol. Hum. Percept. Perform.* **2020**, *46*, 926–941. [CrossRef]
44. Reeder, R.R.; Olivers, C.N.; Hanke, M.; Pollmann, S. No evidence for enhanced distractor template representation in early visual cortex. *Cortex* **2018**, *108*, 279–282. [CrossRef]
45. De Vries, I.E.J.; Savran, E.; Van Driel, J.; Olivers, C.N.L. Oscillatory Mechanisms of Preparing for Visual Distraction. *J. Cogn. Neurosci.* **2019**, *31*, 1873–1894. [CrossRef]
46. Gutzwiller, R.S.; Wickens, C.D.; Clegg, B.A. Workload overload modeling: An experiment with MATB II to inform a computational model of task management. *Proc. Hum. Factors Ergon. Soc. Annu. Meet.* **2014**, *58*, 849–853. [CrossRef]
47. Kerzel, D.; Barras, C. Distractor rejection in visual search breaks down with more than a single distractor feature. *J. Exp. Psychol. Hum. Percept. Perform.* **2016**, *42*, 648–657. [CrossRef] [PubMed]
48. Büsel, C.; Pomper, U.; Ansorge, U. Capture of attention by target-similar cues during dual-color search reflects reactive control among top-down selected attentional control settings. *Psychon. Bull. Rev.* **2019**, *26*, 531–537. [CrossRef]
49. Folk, C.L.; Anderson, B.A. Target-uncertainty effects in attentional capture: Color-singleton set or multiple attentional control settings? *Psychon. Bull. Rev.* **2010**, *17*, 421–426. [CrossRef] [PubMed]
50. Grubert, A.; Eimer, M. A capacity limit for the rapid parallel selection of multiple target objects. *J. Vis.* **2018**, *18*, 1017. [CrossRef]
51. Kerzel, D.; Grubert, A. Capacity limitations in template-guided multiple color search. *Psychon. Bull. Rev.* **2022**, *29*, 901–909. [CrossRef]
52. Ort, E.; Fahrenfort, J.J.; Olivers, C.N.L. Lack of Free Choice Reveals the Cost of Having to Search for More Than One Object. *Psychol. Sci.* **2017**, *28*, 1137–1147. [CrossRef]
53. Pereira, E.J.; Castelhano, M.S. Attentional capture is contingent on scene region: Using surface guidance framework to explore attentional mechanisms during search. *Psychon. Bull. Rev.* **2019**, *26*, 1273–1281. [CrossRef]

54. Torralba, A.; Oliva, A.; Castelhano, M.S.; Henderson, J.M. Contextual guidance of eye movements and attention in real-world scenes: The role of global features in object search. *Psychol. Rev.* **2006**, *113*, 766–786. [CrossRef]
55. Wolfe, J.M. Guided Search 6.0: An updated model of visual search. *Psychon. Bull. Rev.* **2021**, *28*, 1060–1092. [CrossRef]
56. Eckstein, M.P.; Drescher, B.A.; Shimozaki, S.S. Attentional Cues in Real Scenes, Saccadic Targeting, and Bayesian Priors. *Psychol. Sci.* **2006**, *17*, 973–980. [CrossRef] [PubMed]
57. Võ, M.L.-H.; Wolfe, J.M. Differential Electrophysiological Signatures of Semantic and Syntactic Scene Processing. *Psychol. Sci.* **2013**, *24*, 1816–1823. [CrossRef] [PubMed]
58. Võ, M.L.; Wolfe, J.M. The role of memory for visual search in scenes. *Ann. New York Acad. Sci.* **2015**, *1339*, 72–81. [CrossRef]
59. Bulikhov, D.; Landry, S.J. The effect of applied effort on MATB-II performance. *Theor. Issues Ergon. Sci.* **2023**, *24*, 233–240. [CrossRef]
60. Muñoz-de-Escalona, E.; Cañas, J.J.; Leva, C.; Longo, L. Task Demand Transition Peak Point Effects on Mental Workload Measures Divergence. In Proceedings of the Human Mental Workload: Models and Applications: 4th International Symposium, H-WORKLOAD 2020, Granada, Spain, 3–5 December 2020; Longo, L., Leva, M.C., Eds.; Communications in Computer and Information Science; Springer International Publishing: Cham, Switzerland, 2020; Volume 1318, pp. 207–226. [CrossRef]
61. Pekrun, R.; Frenzel, A.C.; Goetz, T.; Perry, R.P. The Control-Value Theory of Achievement Emotions. In *Emotion in Education*; Elsevier: Amsterdam, The Netherlands, 2007; pp. 13–36. [CrossRef]
62. Yerkes, R.M.; Dodson, J.D. The relation of strength of stimulus to rapidity of habit-formation. *J. Comp. Neurol. Psychol.* **1908**, *18*, 459–482. [CrossRef]
63. Huestegge, L.; Koch, I. When two actions are easier than one: How inhibitory control demands affect response processing. *Acta Psychol.* **2014**, *151*, 230–236. [CrossRef] [PubMed]
64. Kürten, J.; Raettig, T.; Gutzeit, J.; Huestegge, L. Dual-action benefits: Global (action-inherent) and local (transient) sources of action prepotency underlying inhibition failures in multiple action control. *Psychol. Res.* **2023**, *87*, 410–424. [CrossRef] [PubMed]
65. Laeng, B.; Endestad, T. Bright illusions reduce the eye's pupil. *Proc. Natl. Acad. Sci. USA* **2012**, *109*, 2162–2167. [CrossRef] [PubMed]
66. Laeng, B.; Nabil, S.; Kitaoka, A. The Eye Pupil Adjusts to Illusorily Expanding Holes. *Front. Hum. Neurosci.* **2022**, *16*, 877249. [CrossRef]
67. Bressan, P.; Actis-Grosso, R. Simultaneous Lightness Contrast on Plain and Articulated Surrounds. *Perception* **2006**, *35*, 445–452. [CrossRef]
68. Cavanagh, P.; Alvarez, G. Tracking multiple targets with multifocal attention. *Trends Cogn. Sci.* **2005**, *9*, 349–354. [CrossRef] [PubMed]

applied sciences

MDPI

Article

Video-Based Gaze Detection for Oculomotor Abnormality Measurements

Eran Harpaz †, Rotem Z. Bar-Or *,†, Israel Rosset and Edmund Ben-Ami

NeuraLight Inc., 8 The Green #16790, Dover, DE 19901, USA
* Correspondence: rotem@neuralight.ai
† These authors contributed equally to this work.

Abstract: Measuring oculomotor abnormalities in human subjects is challenging due to the delicate spatio-temporal nature of the oculometric measures (OMs) used to assess eye movement abilities. Some OMs require a gaze estimation accuracy of less than 2 degrees and a sample rate that enables the detection of movements lasting less than 100 ms. While past studies and applications have used dedicated and limiting eye tracking devices to extract OMs, recent advances in imaging sensors and computer vision have enabled video-based gaze detection. Here, we present a self-calibrating neural network model for gaze detection that is suitable for oculomotor abnormality measurement applications. The model considers stimuli target locations while the examined subjects perform visual tasks and calibrate its gaze estimation output in real time. The model was validated in a clinical trial and achieved an axial accuracy of 0.93 degrees and 1.31 degrees for horizontal and vertical gaze estimation locations, respectively, as well as an absolute accuracy of 1.80 degrees. The performance of the proposed model enables the extraction of OMs using affordable and accessible setups—such as desktop computers and laptops—without the need to restrain the patient's head or to use dedicated equipment. This newly introduced approach may significantly ease patient burden and improve clinical results in any medical field that requires eye movement measurements.

Keywords: eye tracking; gaze detection; computer vision; neural networks

1. Introduction

With the development of computational technology and automated machinery, eye movement measurements—specifically, gaze detection and tracking—have gained increasing interest in recent decades. Some applications of gaze detection aim to improve the user interface and engagement with various external complex controlled systems; for example, gaze-based human–computer interactions [1,2] enable the hands-free operation of software, while safety and awareness gaze-based assessments ensure the optimal functionality of drivers [3], pilots [4], and even surgeons [5,6]. Another set of applications intends to harness the remotely detected gaze to map the saliency of selected items in the overall field of view. Advertisement and marketing-oriented studies [7,8] have extensively implemented gaze detection, and tourism researchers have performed gaze detection along with the measurement of other emotional and physical metrics to estimate reactions to particular items or sights [9].

Another rapidly extending set of gaze detection applications is aimed at non-invasive measurement of eye movements in patients with various diseases. As a primary apparent output of the oculomotor system, gaze detection time-series data allow for further derivation and extraction of the eye movement features directly associated with a subject's cognitive and motor functionality, enabling the detection of eye movement abnormalities that may be related to the patient's condition.

Eye movement abnormalities refer to deviations or irregularities observed in the typical characteristic patterns of eye motion in healthy individuals. Such deviations may be indicative of underlying neurological, ophthalmological, or vestibular disorders, making them significant diagnostic indicators for clinicians [10].

The human eye engages in various movement types, including saccades (rapid movements between separate fixation points), smooth pursuit (continuously tracking moving objects), and nystagmus (involuntary rhythmic oscillations of the eyes). Abnormalities in these movements may manifest in various OMs in terms of accuracy, speed, co-ordination, and response patterns with respect to visual stimuli.

Abnormal eye movements may be the result of factors such as damage to the neural pathways governing eye movements [11], dysfunction in the muscles responsible for ocular motion [12], or disruptions in the vestibular system (which processes spatial orientation and balance) [13]. Consequently, eye movement abnormalities are observed across a spectrum of conditions, including those affecting the central nerve system (CNS) such as multiple sclerosis [14,15], Parkinson's disease [16,17], and amyotrophic lateral sclerosis (ALS) [18,19]. Therefore, extracted eye movement features (i.e., OMs) have potential as new biomarkers for the diagnosis of several CNS diseases [16,18,20,21], strongly correlating with the patient's condition and disease progression [22].

Clinicians routinely examine and assess eye movements as a diagnostic tool. Monitoring the accuracy, velocity, and co-ordination of eye movements provides valuable insights into the integrity of neural circuits involved in visual processing and motor control. While clinicians have conducted eye movement examinations for decades, the OMs extracted without specialized equipment or laboratory setup are limited, mainly due to the required temporal and spatial sensitivity. For instance, Saccade movement duration (the time from initialization of the movement until the first stop of the eye) may reach values in the order of 100 ms, posing challenges for the manual detection of eye movement abnormalities. Therefore, the introduction of gaze detection tools with high spatio-temporal accuracies is expected to enable the extraction of the relevant OM, allowing for a more confident observation of eye movement abnormalities.

Although humans can quite accurately detect someone else's gaze visually (i.e., tell where that person looks), the equivalent technology used to locate a human subject's point of regard (PoR) is still lacking. The most commonly used eye trackers at present are Infrared (IR) active sensors, which track the eye's position and orientation to estimate the subject's PoR. These specialized IR eye trackers are currently considered to be the most accurate measurement tool for gaze detection and can be mounted next to a desktop monitor [23] or embedded in wearable head devices (e.g., glasses) [24]. However, even in state-of-the-art IR eye trackers, researchers have observed significant sensitivity to the experimental setup and the diverse characteristics of subjects [25].

Video-based gaze detection has been in development since the 1970s, with many limitations and restrictions imposed on the experimental setup (e.g., fixed head position, an array of mirrors around the subject, multiple camera deployment) and light sources [26,27]. However, advances in hardware since the early 2000s have accelerated the development of video-based gaze detection using standard, affordable web cameras, with their resolution, sensitivity, and frame rate having significantly increased, thus enabling more accurate gaze detection using existing analytical algorithms. In recent years, both computation and storage costs have dropped while data transfer bandwidths have widened, enabling the introduction of efficient and robust neural network (NN) models for video-based gaze detection [28]. This recent leap has encouraged the development of high-accuracy, video-based gaze detection, which may be applied for all the above purposes, with an affordable price tag and a convenient and flexible (ideally seamless) setup.

We introduce and test a gaze detection model that combines several neural network models for eye detection, eye segmentation, and gaze estimation with an ongoing real-time calibration procedure. Our study is aimed at the neurological applications of gaze detection and considers the essential measurement for the extraction of OMs, performed using a simple and affordable setup that presents visual stimulation tasks and processes the video of the gazing subject captured using a webcam. As some OM classes (e.g., saccadic latency) require high spatio-temporal resolution, high accuracy is required when extracting the gaze PoR in each video stream frame.

In this paper, we present our gaze detection model, along with its validation and error estimation results. Section 2 describes the gaze detection model and the clinical study environment, including the experimental setup, examination protocol, and the demographic data of participants. Section 3 provides the results of the video-based gaze detection model, compared to a reference specialized IR eye tracker for validation. In Section 4, we discuss our findings.

2. Materials and Methods

2.1. Gaze Detection Model

The gaze detection model used in this study was developed based on existing published NN models for video-based eye detection, eye segmentation, and gaze detection [22,28], with the addition of information regarding visual stimuli target locations, as depicted in Figure 1.

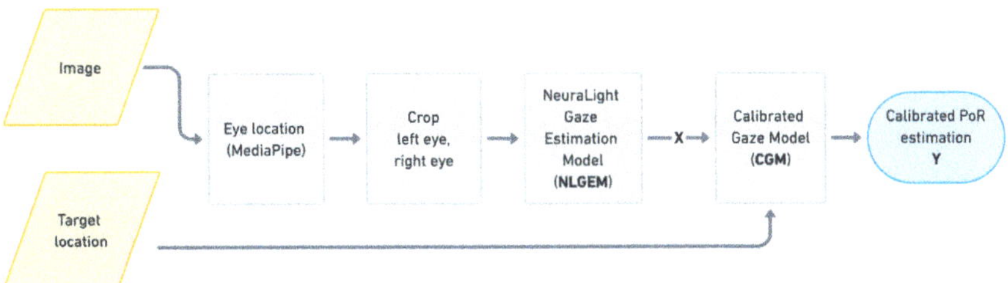

Figure 1. A schematic description of the gaze detection model configuration, where the only input data are the camera-captured image and the stimuli target location on the display. The output Y is the calibrated gaze point of regard (PoR) on the display.

The initial input—namely, an image containing the subject's face—is first processed using the MediaPipe neural network. The MediaPipe Face model [29] detects face landmarks from still images or video; specifically, landmarks around the eyes, such as the iris and the eyelid boundaries. These landmarks are used to extract the eye position in each image. Then, using the eye position information, two smaller images of the left and right eye are cropped from the original image, of which one is horizontally flipped, as is common practice in the field [20], in order to optimize training by assuming symmetry of the extracted features. The cropped eye images, along with the eye position in the image, are then passed into the NeuraLight Gaze Estimation Model (NLGEM), the general architecture of which is shown in Figure 2.

The NeuraLight Gaze Estimation Model is a deep neural network (DNN) composed of three distinct modules: (1) A Convolutional Layers Module, including two equally weighted networks (for the two eyes), which extracts relevant features from eye images using convolutional layers; (2) Fully connected layers (Eye Position Data Module), which generate features based on eye position data (i.e., this module processes spatial information); (3) Integration layers (Combination Module), which utilize fully connected layers to combine the features extracted from the image (module 1) and spatial information (module 2). The output is mapped into the target PoR co-ordinates for each eye, denoted as X.

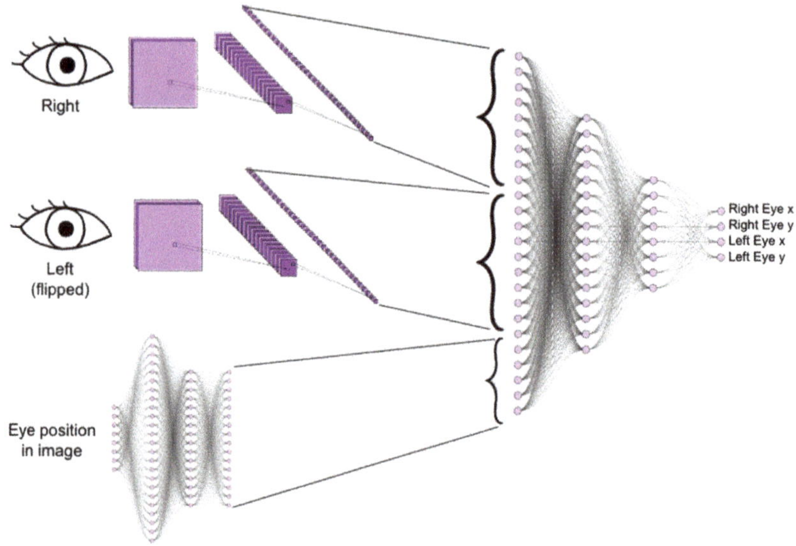

Figure 2. A schematic description of the deep neural network (DNN) gaze detection model, comprising an NN module for eye positioning (lower left, based on the MediaPipe framework) and an NN Gaze Estimation module (right, based on a CNN).

The NLGEM model was trained using 109 subjects as a part of a large healthy subject cohort [30] examined in 925 sessions, with 153,119 frame samples. The NLGEM training cohort included 70 males and 39 females, with a mean age of 41 and a standard deviation of 18.5 years and with the IR eye tracker readings as the training labels.

The NLGEM output gaze point co-ordinates of the two eyes are averaged into a single generic gaze estimation PoR, X, represented with two co-ordinates, which are passed along with the target location into the Calibrated Gaze Model (CGM), which predicts the calibrated gaze PoR, Y, as described in Equations (1)–(3), for multiple frames.

The calibrated gaze matrix **Y** and generic gaze matrix **X** are given as follows:

$$\mathbf{X} = \begin{bmatrix} x_h \\ x_v \end{bmatrix}, \ \mathbf{Y} = \begin{bmatrix} y_h \\ y_v \end{bmatrix} \tag{1}$$

where $\boldsymbol{x_h}$ and $\boldsymbol{x_v}$ are the NLGEM gaze estimation vectors in the horizontal and the vertical axes, respectively, and $\boldsymbol{y_h}$ and $\boldsymbol{y_v}$ are the CGM calibrated gaze estimation vectors in the horizontal and vertical axes, respectively.

For each of N known stimulus target points, a group of calibrated point matrices $\mathbf{Y}_{i=1...N}$ and their corresponding NLGEM generic gaze estimation matrices $\mathbf{X}_{i=1....N}$ are extracted, and the calibrated gaze vector is approximated by solving a regression problem defined according to the following equations.

$$y_{i,h} = E_h(\mathbf{X}_i) \ ; \ y_{i,v} = E_v(\mathbf{X}_i) \tag{2}$$

where $\boldsymbol{E_h}$ and $\boldsymbol{E_v}$ are second-order polynomial regression functions [31–33] of the following forms:

$$\begin{aligned} E_h(\mathbf{X}) &= E_h(x_h, x_v) = a_0 + a_1 \cdot x_h + a_2 \cdot x_v + a_3 \cdot x_h \cdot x_v + a_4 \cdot x_h^2 + a_5 \cdot x_v^2, \\ E_v(\mathbf{X}) &= E_v(x_h, x_v) = b_0 + b_1 \cdot x_h + b_2 \cdot x_v + b_3 \cdot x_h \cdot x_v + b_4 \cdot x_h^2 + b_5 \cdot x_v^2. \end{aligned} \tag{3}$$

Hence, for each calibration point Y_i, with corresponding NLGEM generic gaze estimation matrix X_i, the optimal (least error) coefficients $a_{0...5}$ and $b_{0...5}$ are calculated and further used within the test sequences for ongoing calibration within the examination sequence. This procedure is repeatedly performed during the examination, allowing for supervised learning of the coefficients that may vary between individual subjects, physical setup, and environmental conditions.

2.2. Validation Experiment

The NLGEM and the combination of NLGEM and CGM were validated by comparing the video-based gaze detection results with those of a specialized IR eye tracker (Tobii, Sweden [23]). IR eye tracker and video data were collected from 25 healthy subjects, who were randomly selected from a large cohort of healthy subjects [30].

The validation cohort included 259 subjects: 159 females and 100 males aged 19–86 years, with a mean age of 64 years and a standard deviation of 14 years. A total of 128 of the 259 subjects wore corrective glasses during the test (see Table 1). During the data collection sessions, the subjects sat in front of a monitor, at an approximate distance of 50–70 cm (see Figure 3), and were instructed to complete a set of tasks that included horizontal and vertical reflexive pro-saccades.

Table 1. The validation cohort groups with their corresponding number of participants; age range, mean, and standard deviation; and fraction of participants who wore glasses during the test.

Group	Number	Age [yr] (Min, Max)	Age [yr] (Mean, Std)	Glasses Used/N
Male	100	(19.3, 86.3)	(59.2, 16.6)	44/100
Female	159	(19.3, 83.2)	(65.7, 13.0)	84/159
Total	259	(19.3, 86.3)	(64.5, 13.8)	128/259

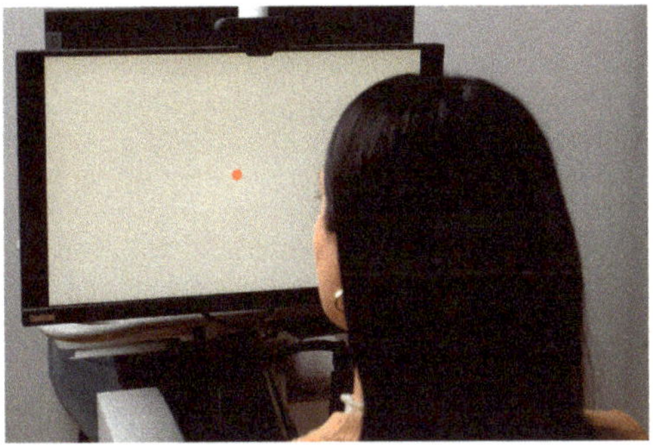

Figure 3. The physical experimental setup in the NeuraLight laboratory. The subject is sitting in front of a display presenting the visual stimulation. Both a video camera (on the top of the monitor) and a specialized IR eye tracker (on the bottom of the monitor) record the subject's eye movements during the examination.

During the pro-saccade task session, the subjects were directed to stare at a red dot when it was presented. The dot appeared at the center of the screen for some (random) time, then immediately disappeared from the screen center and appeared at an angular distance of ~20 degrees or ~13.5 degrees for horizontal or vertical prosaccades, respectively. The dot stayed at its displaced location for 1500 ms and then disappeared. After another 300 ms, where no dot was displayed on the monitor, the central dot reappeared for the next repetition (see Figure 4).

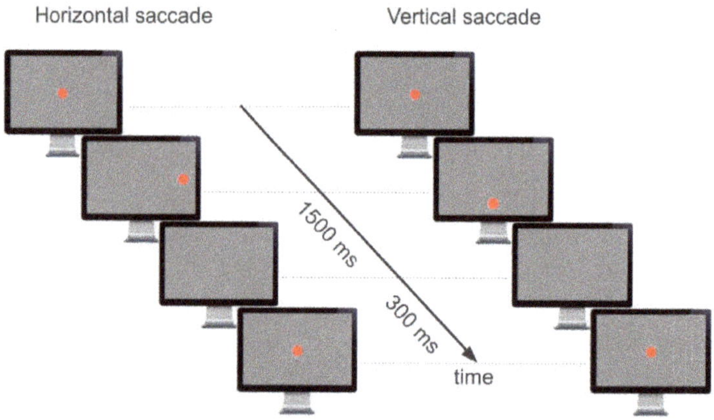

Figure 4. A schematic diagram demonstrating the stimuli displayed during a single horizontal saccade (left panel) and vertical saccade (right panel) task over time. The time interval containing the displaced stimulus is constant and set to 1500 ms, while the time interval in which the monitor is empty between the disappearance of the biased stimulus and the reappearance of the centered stimulus is constant and set to 300 ms.

All tasks were performed on a 1920 × 1080 pixel (52.8 cm × 29.7 cm) monitor presenting a uniform grey background, with a 1.38 cm diameter red circle as the gaze target, representing a target whose angular size (from the subject's location) was 1.35 ± 0.22 degrees. The tests included six 60-s sessions, each containing several pro-saccade stimuli. A break of 30 s was given between the sessions.

While the test sessions were performed, all video and IR eye tracker data were collected using an Apple Mac Mini computer (Apple, designed in Cupertino, CA, USA; manufactured in Malaysia). The stimulus monitor and the webcam timestamps were synchronized, and the data were stored in cloud storage in compliance with HIPAA restrictions. The analysis and preprocessing of data were conducted on an AWS EC2 compute-optimized instance, and the NLGEM training was run on an AWS EC2 gpu-ml-GPU-ML-optimized instance. The Tobii Pro Fusion eye tracker was operated using the Tobii Pro SDK software version 1.9.0 (https://www.tobii.com/products/software/applications-and-developer-kits/tobii-pro-sdk, Tobii, Danderyd, Sweden). The system captured the IR eye tracker gaze data at a sampling rate of 120 Hz and the video stream was captured at 60 frames per second.

3. Results

A total of 469 test sessions of horizontal and vertical pro-saccades were analyzed and validated, for a total of 14,768,320 sample frames. Simple qualitative time-series analyses, as shown in Figure 5, clearly demonstrate the improvement in gaze detection accuracy when the CGM was utilized on top of the NLGEM. While the saccade timing (step function in time) was distinctive in both video-based retrievals, the NLGEM + CGM output was much closer to that of the reference IR eye tracker.

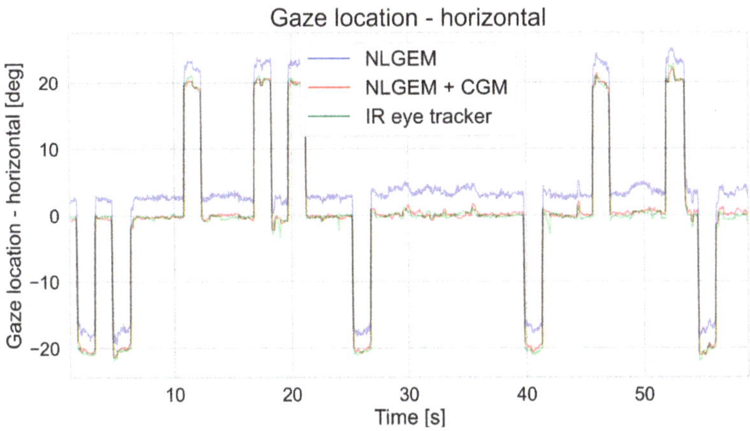

Figure 5. The horizontal gaze location as a function of time of a single subject during a horizontal pro-saccadic session, as measured using a specialized IR eye tracker (green line), video-based NLGEM gaze estimation (blue line), and video-based NLGEM + CGM gaze estimation (red line).

Further quantitative analyses with reference to the IR eye tracker showed that, while the mean absolute error (MAE) of the estimated gaze with the NLGEM itself was 4.71 degrees, the CGM decreased the MAE to 1.80 degrees. This indicates that adding the CGM improved the accuracy by a factor of 2.5, reducing the MAE by 62%. An interesting and distinctive difference was observed between the accuracy levels for the horizontal and vertical gaze detections. Adding the CGM reduced the MAE in the horizontal axis by 58% and in the vertical axis by 65%, achieving MAE values of 0.93 degrees and 1.31 degrees, respectively (see Table 2). When comparing the MAE distributions of the gaze detection based on the two models, we found a significantly narrower MAE distribution when the CGM was applied after the NLGEM, allowing better confidence when aggregating multiple samples (see Figure 6).

Table 2. Mean average error (MAE) calculations (degrees) for the video-based NLGEM and the NLGEM combined with the CGM gaze estimation location compared with the IR eye tracker. The MAE was calculated separately for the horizontal and vertical axes and the absolute error distance (Norm).

Component	MAE NLGEM [deg]	MAE NLGEM + CGM [deg]
Horizontal	2.20	0.93
Vertical	3.70	1.31
Norm	4.71	1.80

A closer look at the error distributions of the vertical and horizontal gaze locations provided by the video-based gaze estimation models (see Figure 7) revealed that the CGM significantly improved the error distribution symmetry, in addition to the MAE values. While the error distribution of the NLGEM estimated gaze locations seemed to be multimodal and to vary with different PoR locations, after the CGM was utilized, the gaze estimation error was characterized by a narrow modal distribution.

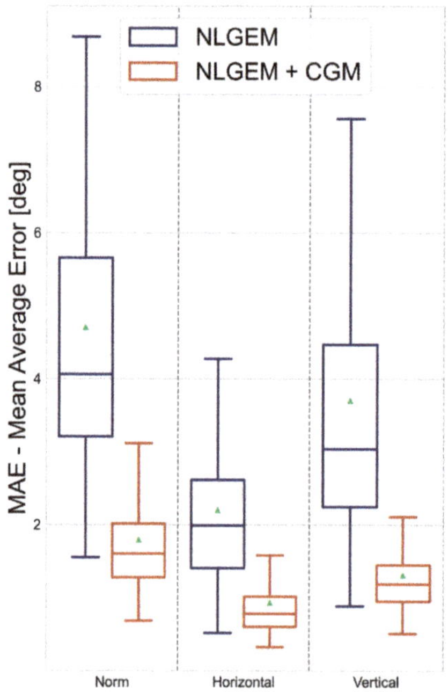

Figure 6. The mean average error (MAE) distributions of the video-based NLGEM gaze estimation (blue) and the video-based NLGEM + CGM gaze estimation (red) in the vertical axis (right panel), in the horizontal axis (center panel), and when calculated for its norm (i.e., the absolute distance from the target; left axis). Each box represents the range between the upper and lower quartiles, and the median is indicated by the inner line. The green triangles represent the mean values. The bars extend 1.5 IQRs from the lower and upper quartiles.

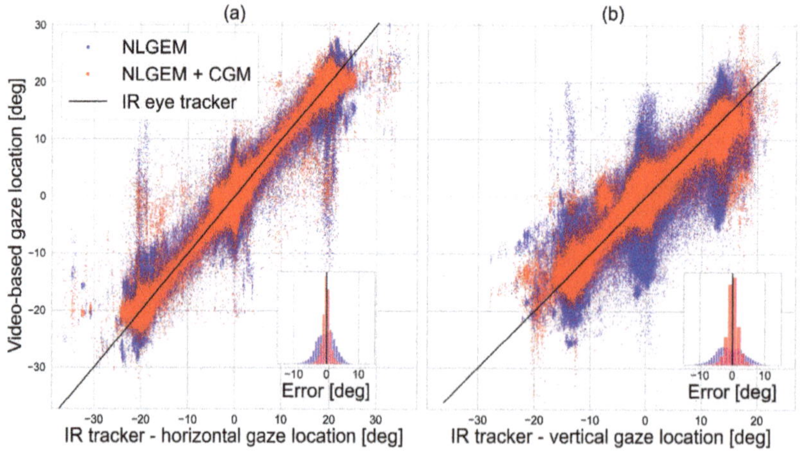

Figure 7. The video-based NLGEM gaze estimation (blue) and the video-based NLGEM + CGM gaze estimation (red) vs. the specialized IR eye tracker gaze estimation (black) during pro-saccade tasks in the horizontal direction (**a**) and vertical direction (**b**). The inner panels show the error distribution of the video-based models, with reference to the IR eye tracker.

The gaze spatial error was calculated as the distance vector between the estimated gaze location and the reference (i.e., the IR eye tracker, in this case). Figure 8 presents the 2D gaze spatial error distribution when implementing NLGEM alone (Figure 8a) and when adding the CGM calculation (Figure 8b), exposing the spatial features of the gaze errors. The gaze estimations produced using the NLGEM were widely distributed in various directions and were characterized by an amorphous pattern whose local maxima were in random locations. This unstructured, clustered distribution may have resulted from biases depending on the individual subjects; for instance, glass lenses may bias passive imaging sensors but would not affect active sensors, such as the IR eye tracker used as a reference in this study.

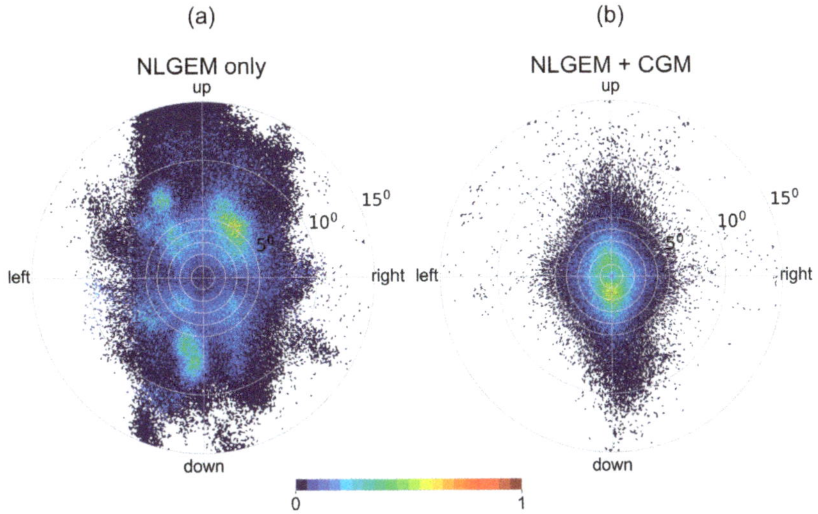

Figure 8. The error spatial normalized distribution of the NLGEM video-based gaze estimation (**a**) and the NLGEM + CGM video-based gaze estimation (**b**), with reference to the specialized IR eye tracker.

Introducing the stimuli target locations and using the CGM in addition to the NLGEM gaze estimations significantly improved the spatial error (Figure 8b). After implementing the CGM, the spatial error pattern was symmetric and centered on the origin, as expected from a calibrated sensor with a normally distributed measurement error.

Additional analysis on the validation cohort results was conducted to estimate the contribution of the CGM to sensitivity to the age of patients, as shown in Figure 9. While the significant advantage of the NLGEM + CGM over the NLGEM was maintained along all patient ages, the MAE for both NLGEM alone and NLGEM + CGM gaze estimation increased with age, at a mean pace of 0.013 $^{deg}/_{yr}$.

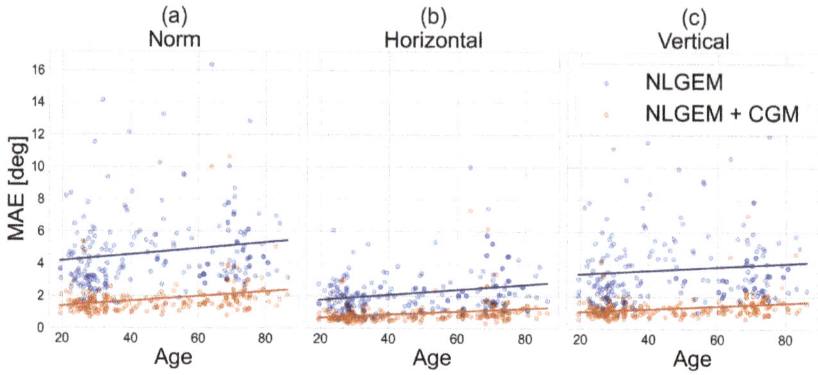

Figure 9. The mean absolute error (MAE) of the video-based NLGEM gaze estimation (blue) and of the video-based NLGEM + CGM gaze estimation (red) as a function of the patient's age: (**a**) The absolute norm error; (**b**) The error in the horizontal axis; (**c**) The error in the vertical axis. The solid lines represent the corresponding linear fits.

4. Discussion

In this study, we introduced a video-based gaze detection model, comprising an independent video-based NeuraLight Gaze Estimation Model (NLGEM) and an additional Calibrated Gaze Model (CGM), which uses the target locations of visual stimuli for ongoing real-time calibration during test sessions. The NLGEM model architecture is based on recently published works (Figure 2) [28], with the exception of training the model on labels measured using an IR tracker and the recruitment of a dedicated cohort for the training and test sets. For validation, we tested our gaze detection model on an independent cohort of 259 participants (see Table 1) who performed horizontal and vertical pro-saccade tasks while sitting at a distance of approximately 60 cm from a display, with no head restraint.

Compared to the use of a specialized IR eye tracker as a reference ground truth, we found that the NLGEM alone achieved an absolute visual angle accuracy (MAE) of 4.80 degrees. While such an accuracy level is comparable to that of some of the leading IR eye trackers available at present [23,24] and may be sufficient for applications that require general visual attention direction or saliency distribution on display, most eye tracking applications require higher accuracy, especially in medical applications (e.g., for the measurement of eye movements in patients with various diseases and oculomotor symptoms).

Most abnormal oculometric measures (OMs) that are present in patients are based on measuring eye movements in response to visual stimulation tasks. Therefore, we added the CGM on top of the NLGEM to leverage the information provided by the visual stimuli, namely the target location. When testing the performance of NLGEM and CGM together (NLGEM + CGM), we achieved an absolute gaze detection accuracy (MAE) of 1.80 degrees in the norm, as well as an MAE of 0.93 degrees in the horizontal direction and 1.31 degrees vertically, as detailed in Table 2. When aiming to measure eye movements, the separation into horizontal and vertical directions is required as, in some movements (e.g., saccades), horizontal and vertical movements involve different pathways [11]. Therefore, the accuracy estimations in this work for the horizontal and vertical axes are useful when assessing OMs based on mechanisms that depend on the movement direction.

The performance of the NLGEM + CGM approach was within the systematic errors of the Tobii Pro Fusion eye tracker (0.3 degrees) when taking into consideration the stimuli target size, which was 1.35 ± 0.22 *deg*. Given the accuracy level of our reference measurement (Tobii, 0.3 degrees) and the size of the target displayed (~1.35 degrees), we suggest that our gaze detection model accuracy fulfils the requirements of various OM extraction applications, such as measuring oculomotor abnormalities in patients with different diseases, using only a retail-grade webcam and without the need to fix the subject's head. With the used video sample rate of 60 frames per second, the maximal error in time for a single sample is 16.6 ms, allowing for the confident detection of abnormalities in OMs, whose time scale is ~100 ms and whose visual angle scale is larger than our calculated errors (e.g., the Square Wave Jerks [34] rate, Saccadic Latency, Saccadic Amplitude, Saccadic Error Rate, and so on).

The impact of age on our video-based gaze detection models was estimated according to an increase in the MAE with the age of the patient, presenting an average rate of 0.013 $^{deg}/_{yr}$. The increase in the gaze estimation MAE with age was similar for the NLGEM and NLGEM + CGM models, as well as in all direction variances examined. The increasing uncertainty in video-based eye tracking with age can be influenced by the effects of aging on the physiology and structure of the eye [35]; for instance, changes in pupil size, lens elasticity, and retinal function may lead to higher variability in these landmarks in aged populations, leading to a continuously increasing error in video-based gaze estimation.

Recent video-based gaze detection models have presented high levels of accuracy for free-head visual stimulation tasks within the range of 2–5 degrees [36–38]. The model introduced in this study yielded better performance under similar experimental settings. Furthermore, unlike the model presented here, all recent studies have mentioned the requirement of a separate dedicated calibration task for each test. The CGM module in our work eliminates the need for this separate calibration task, instead enabling ongoing real-time calibration during the test. The combination of high-accuracy gaze estimation and flexible environmental settings provides new opportunities for advances in the oculometric measurement analysis of patients with various diseases affecting their oculomotor skills, resulting in eye movement abnormalities.

Furthermore, with the capabilities demonstrated in this study, relevant oculometric measures could be extracted and measured easily using a clinical setup, or even remotely in the patient's home, assuming that they have access to a computer equipped with a web camera. The ease of operating these applications would increase the number of examined patients, extending the training set of our models and, hence, their accuracy. An accurate, affordable, and accessible medical standard OM extraction tool may lead to significant scientific progress and potential for many patients who strive for a better diagnosis and monitoring of their disease progress.

Author Contributions: Conceptualization, E.H., I.R., R.Z.B.-O. and E.B.-A.; methodology, E.H.; software, E.H. and I.R.; validation, E.H. and R.Z.B.-O.; formal analysis, R.Z.B.-O.; investigation, E.H.; resources, E.H. and E.B.-A.; data curation, E.H. and E.B.-A.; writing—original draft preparation, R.Z.B.-O.; writing—review and editing, R.Z.B.-O., E.H. and E.B.-A.; visualization, R.Z.B.-O.; supervision, E.H.; project administration, E.B.-A.; funding acquisition, E.B.-A. All authors have read and agreed to the published version of the manuscript.

Funding: This study was fully funded by NeuraLight Ltd.

Institutional Review Board Statement: This study was approved (22 July 2022) by an independent ethics committee (WCG IRB, Puyallup, WA, USA, protocol number HDC/2022-3) and adhered to the tenets of the Declaration of Helsinki.

Informed Consent Statement: Informed consent was obtained from all subjects involved in the study prior to study entry.

Data Availability Statement: Publicly available datasets were analyzed in this study. This data can be found here: https://github.com/Bar-Or/NLGEM_CGM_Gaze.

Acknowledgments: The authors would like to gratefully acknowledge the NeuraLight clinical team and NeuraLight research team. The authors would like to express further gratitude to all healthy subjects who participated in this study.

Conflicts of Interest: E.H., R.Z.B.-O., I.R. and E.B.-A. are employees of NeuraLight. The authors declare that this study received funding from NeuraLight Ltd. The funder had the following involvement with the study: NeuraLight Ltd. has funded the entire operational environment for this study, including examination rooms, software platform, equipment, office supply, data analysis and publication costs.

References

1. Jacob, R.J.K.; Karn, K.S. Eye Tracking in Human-Computer Interaction and Usability Research. In *The Mind's Eye*; Elsevier: Amsterdam, The Netherlands, 2003; pp. 573–605. ISBN 978-0-444-51020-4.
2. Cazzato, D.; Leo, M.; Distante, C.; Voos, H. When I Look into Your Eyes: A Survey on Computer Vision Contributions for Human Gaze Estimation and Tracking. *Sensors* **2020**, *20*, 3739. [CrossRef]
3. Naqvi, R.; Arsalan, M.; Batchuluun, G.; Yoon, H.; Park, K. Deep Learning-Based Gaze Detection System for Automobile Drivers Using a NIR Camera Sensor. *Sensors* **2018**, *18*, 456. [CrossRef]
4. Peißl, S.; Wickens, C.D.; Baruah, R. Eye-Tracking Measures in Aviation: A Selective Literature Review. *Int. J. Aerosp. Psychol.* **2018**, *28*, 98–112. [CrossRef]
5. Atkins, M.S.; Tien, G.; Khan, R.S.A.; Meneghetti, A.; Zheng, B. What Do Surgeons See: Capturing and Synchronizing Eye Gaze for Surgery Applications. *Surg. Innov.* **2013**, *20*, 241–248. [CrossRef]
6. Aggarwal, N.; Saini, B.S.; Gupta, S. The Impact of Clinical Scales in Parkinson's Disease: A Systematic Review. *Egypt. J. Neurol. Psychiatry Neurosurg.* **2021**, *57*, 174. [CrossRef]
7. Santos, R.D.O.J.D.; Oliveira, J.H.C.D.; Rocha, J.B.; Giraldi, J.D.M.E. Eye Tracking in Neuromarketing: A Research Agenda for Marketing Studies. *Int. J. Psychol. Stud.* **2015**, *7*, p32. [CrossRef]
8. Hoffman, D.L.; Moreau, C.P.; Stremersch, S.; Wedel, M. The Rise of New Technologies in Marketing: A Framework and Outlook. *J. Mark.* **2022**, *86*, 1–6. [CrossRef]
9. Scott, N.; Zhang, R.; Le, D.; Moyle, B. A Review of Eye-Tracking Research in Tourism. *Curr. Issues Tour.* **2017**, *22*, 1244–1261. [CrossRef]
10. Leigh, R.J.; Zee, D.S. *The Neurology of Eye Movements*, 5th ed.; Oxford University Press: Oxford, UK, 2015; ISBN 978-0-19-996928-9.
11. Lal, V.; Truong, D. Eye Movement Abnormalities in Movement Disorders. *Clin. Park. Relat. Disord.* **2019**, *1*, 54–63. [CrossRef]
12. Danchaivijitr, C. Diplopia and Eye Movement Disorders. *J. Neurol. Neurosurg. Psychiatry* **2004**, *75*, iv24–iv31. [CrossRef] [PubMed]
13. Johnston, J.L.; Daye, P.M.; Thomson, G.T.D. Inaccurate Saccades and Enhanced Vestibulo-Ocular Reflex Suppression during Combined Eye–Head Movements in Patients with Chronic Neck Pain: Possible Implications for Cervical Vertigo. *Front. Neurol.* **2017**, *8*, 23. [CrossRef]
14. Coric, D.; Nij Bijvank, J.A.; Van Rijn, L.J.; Petzold, A.; Balk, L.J. The Role of Optical Coherence Tomography and Infrared Oculography in Assessing the Visual Pathway and CNS in Multiple Sclerosis. *Neurodegener. Dis. Manag.* **2018**, *8*, 323–335. [CrossRef]
15. Bastien, N.; Chernock, M.; De Villers-Sidani, E.; Voss, P.; Blanchette, F.; Arseneau, F.; Hussein, S.; Ramos, R.; Giacomini, P.S. P.028 Eye Movement Biomarkers for Early Detection of Multiple Sclerosis Disease Progression. *Can. J. Neurol. Sci. J. Can. Sci. Neurol.* **2022**, *49*, S15. [CrossRef]
16. Reiner, J.; Franken, L.; Raveh, E.; Rosset, I.; Kreitman, R.; Ben-Ami, E.; Djaldetti, R. Oculometric Measures as a Tool for Assessment of Clinical Symptoms and Severity of Parkinson's Disease. *J. Neural Transm.* **2023**, *130*, 1241–1248. [CrossRef] [PubMed]
17. Ba, F.; Sang, T.T.; He, W.; Fatehi, J.; Mostofi, E.; Zheng, B. Stereopsis and Eye Movement Abnormalities in Parkinson's Disease and Their Clinical Implications. *Front. Aging Neurosci.* **2022**, *14*, 783773. [CrossRef] [PubMed]
18. Raveh, E.; Ben-Shimon, A.; Anisimov, V.; Kreitman, R.; Ben-Ami, E.; Nechushtan, E.; Birman, N.; Drory, V.E. Correlation between Oculometric Measures and Clinical Assessment in ALS Patients Participating in a Phase IIb Clinical Drug Trial. *Amyotroph. Lateral Scler. Front. Degener.* **2023**, *24*, 495–501. [CrossRef] [PubMed]
19. Becerra-García, R.A.; García-Bermúdez, R.; Joya, G. Differentiation of Saccadic Eye Movement Signals. *Sensors* **2021**, *21*, 5021. [CrossRef] [PubMed]
20. Holzman, P.S. Eye-Tracking Dysfunctions in Schizophrenic Patients and Their Relatives. *Arch. Gen. Psychiatry* **1974**, *31*, 143. [CrossRef] [PubMed]
21. Dadu, A.; Satone, V.; Kaur, R.; Hashemi, S.H.; Leonard, H.; Iwaki, H.; Makarious, M.B.; Billingsley, K.J.; Bandres-Ciga, S.; Sargent, L.J.; et al. Identification and Prediction of Parkinson's Disease Subtypes and Progression Using Machine Learning in Two Cohorts. *Npj Park. Dis.* **2022**, *8*, 172. [CrossRef] [PubMed]
22. Larrazabal, A.J.; García Cena, C.E.; Martínez, C.E. Video-Oculography Eye Tracking towards Clinical Applications: A Review. *Comput. Biol. Med.* **2019**, *108*, 57–66. [CrossRef] [PubMed]
23. Housholder, A.; Reaban, J.; Peregrino, A.; Votta, G.; Mohd, T.K. Evaluating Accuracy of the Tobii Eye Tracker 5. In *Intelligent Human Computer Interaction*; Kim, J.-H., Singh, M., Khan, J., Tiwary, U.S., Sur, M., Singh, D., Eds.; Lecture Notes in Computer Science; Springer International Publishing: Cham, Switzerland, 2022; Volume 13184, pp. 379–390. ISBN 978-3-030-98403-8.
24. Onkhar, V.; Dodou, D.; De Winter, J.C.F. Evaluating the Tobii Pro Glasses 2 and 3 in Static and Dynamic Conditions. *Behav. Res. Methods* **2023**. [CrossRef] [PubMed]
25. Blignaut, P.; Wium, D. Eye-Tracking Data Quality as Affected by Ethnicity and Experimental Design. *Behav. Res. Methods* **2014**, *46*, 67–80. [CrossRef] [PubMed]
26. Chennamma, H.R.; Yuan, X. A Survey on Eye-Gaze Tracking Techniques. *arXiv* **2013**, arXiv:1312.6410.

27. Hansen, D.W.; Ji, Q. In the Eye of the Beholder: A Survey of Models for Eyes and Gaze. *IEEE Trans. Pattern Anal. Mach. Intell.* **2010**, *32*, 478–500. [CrossRef]
28. Valliappan, N.; Dai, N.; Steinberg, E.; He, J.; Rogers, K.; Ramachandran, V.; Xu, P.; Shojaeizadeh, M.; Guo, L.; Kohlhoff, K.; et al. Accelerating Eye Movement Research via Accurate and Affordable Smartphone Eye Tracking. *Nat. Commun.* **2020**, *11*, 4553. [CrossRef] [PubMed]
29. Lugaresi, C.; Tang, J.; Nash, H.; McClanahan, C.; Uboweja, E.; Hays, M.; Zhang, F.; Chang, C.-L.; Yong, M.G.; Lee, J.; et al. MediaPipe: A Framework for Building Perception Pipelines. *arXiv* **2019**, arXiv:1906.08172v1.
30. Rosset, I.; Raveh, E.; Shimon, A.B.; Anisimov, V.; Ben-Ami, E.; Kreitman, R.; Breakstone, M. Validation of a Novel Software-based Platform to Extract Oculometric Measures. *Acta Ophthalmol.* **2022**, *100*. [CrossRef]
31. Lambert, L.S.; Hardt, G.F. Polynomial Regression and Response Surface Analysis. *Oxf. Bibliogr. Manag. Res. Methods* **2018**. [CrossRef]
32. Edwards, J.R. Alternatives to Difference Scores: Polynomial Regression and Response Surface Methodology. *Adv. Meas. Data Anal.* **2002**, 350–400.
33. Rodrigues, A.C. Response Surface Analysis: A Tutorial for Examining Linear and Curvilinear Effects. *Rev. Adm. Contemp.* **2021**, *25*, e200293. [CrossRef]
34. Salman, M.S.; Sharpe, J.A.; Lillakas, L.; Steinbach, M.J. Square Wave Jerks in Children and Adolescents. *Pediatr. Neurol.* **2008**, *38*, 16–19. [CrossRef] [PubMed]
35. Salvi, S.M.; Akhtar, S.; Currie, Z. Ageing Changes in the Eye. *Postgrad. Med. J.* **2006**, *82*, 581–587. [CrossRef] [PubMed]
36. Zhu, W.; Deng, H. Monocular Free-Head 3D Gaze Tracking With Deep Learning and Geometry Constraints. In Proceedings of the IEEE International Conference on Computer Vision (ICCV), Venice, Italy, 22–29 October 2017.
37. Lemley, J.; Kar, A.; Drimbarean, A.; Corcoran, P. Efficient CNN Implementation for Eye-Gaze Estimation on Low-Power/Low-Quality Consumer Imaging Systems. *arXiv* **2018**, arXiv:1806.10890.
38. Wang, D.; Bakhai, A. (Eds.) *Clinical Trials: A Practical Guide to Design, Analysis, and Reporting*; Remedica: London, UK; Chicago, IL, USA, 2006; ISBN 978-1-901346-72-5.

applied sciences

MDPI

Article

Differences between Experts and Novices in the Use of Aircraft Maintenance Documentation: Evidence from Eye Tracking

Florence Paris [1,2,*], Remy Casanova [2,†], Marie-Line Bergeonneau [1] and Daniel Mestre [2,†]

1 Airbus Helicopters, 13700 Marignane, France
2 Aix Marseille University, CNRS, ISM, 13700 Marseille, France; remy.casanova@univ-amu.fr (R.C.); daniel.mestre@univ-amu.fr (D.M.)
* Correspondence: florence.paris@univ-amu.fr
† These authors contributed equally to this work.

Abstract: Maintenance is a highly procedural activity requiring motor and cognitive engagement. The aim of this experimental study was to examine how expertise affects maintenance tasks, in particular, the use of procedural documents. A total of 22 aircraft maintenance technicians were divided into two groups according to their level of expertise. Helicopter maintenance was evaluated in a real work environment, using an eye tracker, a fixed camera, and NASA-TLX to measure workload. Both groups reported a high mental load. Novices showed elevated levels of effort and mental demand. Experts were faster at all levels of the task and spent less time consulting maintenance documentation. The acquisition of procedural information was greater at the start of the task, where the gap between groups was more pronounced. This may be related to the overall planning of the task, in addition, the task was atomized, with frequent back-and-forth between execution and information intake, for all participants. Novices had a longer document consultation duration, spread over a greater number of consultations, but did not have a higher average consultation time. The results indicate a higher mental load for novices, potentially linked to an increased atomization of the task, as shown by the frequency of consultations.

Keywords: aircraft maintenance; procedural documentation; expertise; eye tracking; task load

1. Introduction

1.1. Context

Maintenance refers to a set of tasks aimed at preserving the physical condition of equipment or a system, allowing it to operate in accordance with its specifications [1,2]. The maintenance activity can be understood as the result of a dynamic interaction between external determinants (maintenance task) and internal determinants (maintenance operator) [3,4]. In the aircraft industry context, this activity is crucial in ensuring the airworthiness of aircraft, guaranteeing the safety of passengers, equipment, and people on the ground [5–7]. Various determinants emerge, contributing to the inherent complexity of the task. The aircraft maintenance task, as well as the maintenance task in general, is characterized by hazardous environments, with a high degree of inherent uncertainty and limited repeatability [8–10]. It is important to note the complexity involved in aircraft design. Aircraft consist of multiple interconnected and interdependent systems, each containing sub-systems that are vulnerable to cascading effects. Any malfunction in one system can have an impact on other systems or the whole aircraft [11]. Additionally, access to the part being serviced may also require the removal and re-installation of other systems. Assembly tasks have many parallels with maintenance; indeed, this is because assembly and installation tasks are integral parts of the maintenance task.

1.2. The Procedural Documentation

The complex design of aircraft systems and the severity of the consequences of errors make it subject to stringent regulatory requirements. Maintenance tasks exhibit the attributes of a "well-structured task", as explained by Simon [12]. They are characterized by a testable standard for solutions, descriptions of problem states using objectives and sub-objectives, achievable state modifications, and knowledge integration [12]. The procedure determines the hierarchical structure of the task by sequencing it into sub-tasks with integrated detailed instructions. As a prescriptive document, the aircraft maintenance manual (AMM) explicitly defines all procedures required to maintain an aircraft. Organized into chapters and sub-chapters, this hierarchical document integrates illustrations and text. Managing uncertainty is a significant challenge for safety-critical organizations, such as nuclear power plants, the oil and chemical industries, and aviation [13]. Rules and procedures guide and structure activities by defining objectives, decision-making processes, and constraints, ultimately improving reliability and safety.

1.3. Experts versus Novices

Aircraft maintenance is carried out by aircraft maintenance technicians (AMTs). Given the complexity of the task and safety challenges inherent in the aviation industry, aircraft maintenance is carried out by a highly skilled and specialized workforce [14]. Maintenance requires a wide variety of skills and knowledge [10]. Comprehending the impact of expertise can provide valuable information to identify areas of improvement [15,16].

Expertise has been studied extensively in a wide range of fields [17–19]. The literature highlights the following aspects: expertise is inherently domain-specific because individuals acquire specialized problem-solving strategies within a particular domain through experiences that provide opportunities to use and organize domain-specific information [20]. In their domain, experts often develop an increased ability to perceive significant information patterns that evade those without this skill. For instance, expert electronics technicians were shown to be able to reproduce significant parts of complex circuit diagrams after only a few seconds of exposure, whereas novices were unable to do so [21]. Experts detect specific patterns, which allows them to memorize and process complex information faster than beginners. In Chase and Simon (1973) [22], experts demonstrated enhanced memory for structured stimuli (patterns of chess pieces), but did not show the same ability to recall random unstructured stimuli. These results have been replicated in various fields, including medicine and electronics [21,23,24]. Experts tend to execute actions faster and more efficiently than non-experts [25–28]. Expertise allows individuals to use previously learned rules and procedures, eliminating the need to engage in a step-by-step reasoning process for each task [29]. This phenomenon has implications for cognitive engagement. As individuals gain experience and knowledge within a domain, they construct mental models and heuristics that facilitate more efficient task performance [19,25,29]. Consequently, this leads to a reduction in the mental load required for task completion.

1.4. The Use of Procedural Information

In the context of maintenance, there is a cognitive side of the activity but in contrast to chess, mental calculation, or programming, there is also a physical side of the activity involving the execution of motor tasks. Therefore, the activity must be measured globally, but also through information gathering and execution.

There is a specificity in the cognitive aspects involved in the maintenance activity; indeed, reading a procedure has a pragmatic objective: execution. This directly affects how the procedure is used [30]. The processing of procedural documents occurs in multiple informational contexts, including the user's prior knowledge of the system [31]. In the context of maintenance, unlike other situations where access to the procedural document at the time of the task is difficult or impossible [32,33], the operator refers to the document while performing the procedure [34–36]. A common phenomenon described in the literature on the use of procedure is the "atomization of actions" [37]. The activity is sequenced around two actions: procedural information intake and task execution. Participants interrupt the progression of their actions (execution of instructions) through information-gathering activities carried out on the procedural document. Atomization has been studied in a variety of contexts, including medicine [32,38–40], cooking recipes [37], and the use of everyday objects [41,42]. Atomization would minimize the cognitive cost of translating instructions into actions [37,43]. In multimedia learning, segmenting information into chunks serves as a strategy to reduce the cognitive load on learners engaged in information processing [44–46].

With regard to maintenance, several studies have studied maintenance documentation [34,47–50]. However, to date, no quantitative data have been collected on the use of documentation in a real maintenance task, looking at differences between experts and novices. Moreover, given the complexity of the procedures involved in operational aircraft maintenance tasks, it is expected that the atomization phenomenon will be observed, but we are missing empirical data.

There are various techniques for measuring procedural information use, considering the constraints associated with the maintenance activity. First, the tools used must have the least impact on the operator. For example, the Think-Aloud method is embedded in the context of qualitative research, its main limitation being the direct influence on the execution of the task, which requires the operator to perform a secondary task consisting of the verbal expression of his thoughts [51]. Ganier and his collaborators have developed a specialized software, known as TIP-EXE [32,52]. This software can blur the prescribed document. Therefore, the user can selectively deflect the desired segment of the document with a single click. At the same time, the software generates time data that provide details about the viewing order as well as the time spent exploring each specific segment. This method has many advantages; however, it also generates a cost related to an additional action for the operator and is not adapted to the study of interactions with a non-digital prescription. The method of measuring visual attention through an eye tracker is currently used in expert–novice paradigms and in the context of the study of procedural information intake [51]. As part of the experiments conducted in Jannin's thesis [43] on suture learning, two distinct approaches were adopted to evaluate the use of the procedure: the use of TIP-EXE software and the implementation of an eye-tracking measure. The author underlines the relevance of the eye-tracking method because of its contribution to a more realistic and ecological experience. Other studies have also used eye tracking [53,54] to evaluate the application of the procedure in contexts involving static participants. The adoption of mobile eye-tracking technology offers a relevant solution for assessing the second sequencing between execution and procedure [51]. By measuring the duration of gaze within an area of interest (AOI) [55,56], it is possible to quantify the time and duration during which visual attention is devoted to maintenance documentation, in a non-binding way and via paper format. Eye movement tracking has emerged as the optimal approach for exploring visual cognitive strategies; it allows for accurate measurement in the context of complex tasks within their dynamic environments, extending to fields such as medicine [57], sports [58,59], transport [60–64], and construction [65–67].

1.5. Our Approach

This study is based on a previous study [68,69], and centered on the development of a tool to measure the use of procedure documents in aircraft maintenance. The results from one participant showed an important information intake phase at the beginning of the operation. In this study, one goal is to see if these results are generalizable and if there are specific patterns associated with expertise in procedural information acquisition. The primary aim of our study is to quantify the impact of expertise on procedural information intake in the context of a real maintenance task carried out in a maintenance hangar. The maintenance procedure theoretically provides a comprehensive description of the task, enabling its execution without additional prerequisites [3] and providing the same framework for all AMTs in the maintenance process [34,48]. We intend to measure the operators' activity and workload, to evaluate the effectiveness of procedural documentation in bridging the gap between novices and experts. This investigation was framed by the following research questions and hypotheses:

RQ1. *Is there an impact of expertise on the procedural information intake in the context of a maintenance task?*

H1. *We expect experts to be faster than novices in both the execution and procedural information intake.*

The operationalization of this hypothesis will be based on behavioral indicators (absolute duration, document consultation duration, execution duration, percentage of time spent on the document). To provide a more detailed analysis of the use of the procedure, a closer examination of the atomization phenomenon, as described in the literature, will be proposed.

RQ2. *Is procedural information intake atomization dependent on the expertise level?*

H2. *If the phenomenon of atomization of the task is due to resource-intensive processes associated with procedure execution, then we expect expertise to have an impact on the number of consultations and the average time spent consulting the procedure.*

Finally, we wish to address the workload.

RQ3. *Are there differences in the workload experienced by operators?*

H3. *Maintenance seems to have physical [70–72] and mental dimensions. Based on the literature, the difference between novices and experts is anticipated in the mental dimension.*

2. Materials and Methods

2.1. Participants

The target population for our study is men and women who are helicopter AMTs and over the age of 18. The population consists of 22 participants who have been divided into two groups based on their experience. The inclusion criteria for the study are as follows: (i) be over 18 years of age; and (ii) be actively engaged in AMT work or training at the time of the study. Participants are divided into two groups according to their experience. The expert group consisted of 10 male participants with a mean age of 51.6 years ($SD = 7.6$) and a mean experience of 30 years ($SD = 7.2$). Inclusion in this group required a minimum of 20 years of experience as an AMT. The novice group consisted of 12 participants, with a mean age of 22.7 years ($SD = 3.3$) and a mean experience of 7 months ($SD = 1.8$). Participants in this group were in training at the time of the experiment and had some field experience during their training. Of the 12 participants in the novice group, 67% were male.

2.2. Materials

Data collection included a scene camera, a mobile eye tracker, and a questionnaire. A GoPro Hero 4 camera (GoPro, San Mateo, CA, USA), affixed within the maintenance area (Figure 1), captured the working area surrounding the helicopter at 1080p resolution and 30 frames per second. The Tobii Pro Glasses 2 (Tobii AB, Danderyd, Sweden) was utilized as a head-mounted mobile eye tracker to acquire data on eye fixation, and scene video captured the working area surrounding the helicopter at 1080p resolution and 30 frames per second. The Tobii Pro Glasses 2 was utilized as a head-mounted mobile eye tracker to acquire data on eye fixation and scene video. The device has an accuracy of 0.5° and a sampling rate of 100 Hz. This tool is unobtrusive and suitable for real-world data collection [61,73]. Workload measurement was undertaken using the weighted NASA

Task Load Index [74] questionnaire due to its standardized and validated tool status. The 15 pairwise comparisons of dimensions were presented to the operator. The frequency with which each dimension is chosen determines its weight or importance. These weights are then multiplied by the raw ratings for each dimension, according to the Hart and Staveland procedure [74].

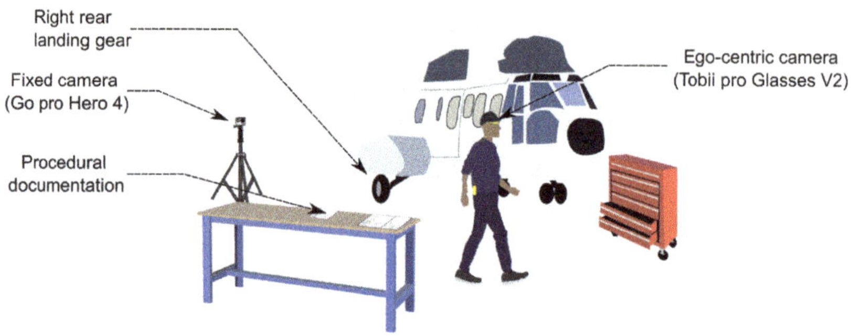

Figure 1. Aircraft maintenance activity analysis setup.

2.3. Protocol

Before starting the experiment, the experimenter provided a detailed explanation of the study and answered any questions the participants might have had. Each participant signed a consent form before being equipped with the eye tracker. During the task, the technician initiated it as soon as they received the procedural document, and participants were free to take as much time as they needed to complete the task.

The validation of maintenance quality was primarily anchored in the successful completion of the task and the final compliance of the helicopter with established navigability standards.

All common maintenance tools and specific tools referenced in the procedural document were available in the hangar. Upon completion, participants signaled the end of the task and were disconnected from the eye tracker. Afterward, they completed the NASA-TLX questionnaire. Aircraft maintenance technicians were tasked with inspecting the components of the right rear landing gear brake unit on an H215/225 helicopter (Airbus Helicopters, Marignane, France). This task involved a removal phase to access the area to be inspected, followed by an installation phase to return the helicopter to its original configuration. The task could be completed by one technician.

The prescribed reference for this task was the aircraft maintenance manual (AMM), which contained the procedure for inspecting brake unit parts on the helicopter model (ensuring the absence of scratches, wear, corrosion, impact marks, leaks, and the verification of their condition). The procedure was 21 pages in a hard copy format, spread over five work cards. The information in the document was either contained entirely in a work card or a chapter within a work card. There were 15 pages of text and 6 pages of figures in the procedural documentation.

2.4. Data Analysis

2.4.1. Previous Result

Prior to this study, we conducted previous research [69] aimed at defining a methodology to characterize the use of procedural documents using an eye-tracking device. It is based on a temporal qualification of the data, allowing us to relate the consultation times within the procedure and the main steps of the tasks materialized by milestones (Figure 2). The methodology developed was tested on the same task as in this experiment with one participant. The division of the task into temporal sequences based on observable milestones makes it possible to enrich the analysis of variables and to compare participants with varying overall task durations.

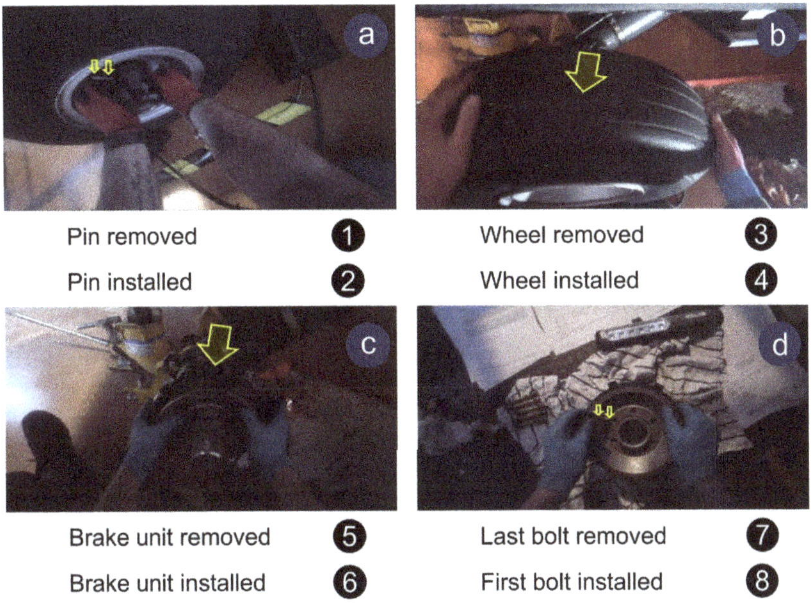

Figure 2. Key parts for task milestones definition: pin (**a**), wheel (**b**), brake unit (**c**), and bolt (**d**). The yellow arrows indicate the location of the part in the image.

The milestones presented in Figure 2 and used in this study were selected because of their succinct yet recognizable actions (observable by priority through the egocentric camera of the eye tracker or by default through the scene camera), and the specific order in which they are realized. Each removal/installation is described in the procedure and was observed for each participant. The visualization of the distribution of the use of the document during the task (Figure 3) allowed us to see the need to characterize the back-and-forth between reading times and execution times. The upper part of the figure shows the breakdown of the task into three phases and nine steps. The three main phases of the maintenance operation are removal, inspection, and installation. The steps are numbered from I to IX. The steps are delimited by the start and end of the operation and by eight numbered milestones whose labels are shown in white frames and presented in Figure 2. The lower part of the figure shows the evolution of the document consultation for a participant based on the data of the previous research [69]. The background is divided into segments colored according to the task step (shown in the upper part). The width of the colored areas in the background shows the relative duration of each step. The gray strips represent the time the participant spent looking at the maintenance document. The black curve represents the cumulative percentage of time the participant spent viewing the document. Based on this observation, we measured the number of consultations and the average consultation duration.

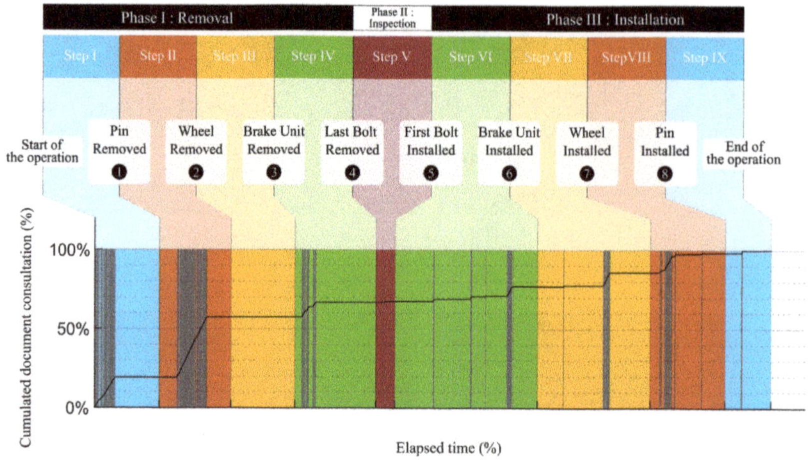

Figure 3. Decomposition of the maintenance operation and evolution of document consultation for one participant.

2.4.2. Variables

We identify four independent variables (expertise, phases, steps, NASA TLX dimensions) and seven dependent variables. The definitions of the dependent variables are presented in Table 1. All dependent variables, except the weighted NASA TLX score, are extracted either globally or for each phase or step.

Table 1. Dependent variables and their definitions.

Variable	Units	Definition
Absolute duration	min	Difference between the timestamps of the milestones bordering the time period studied.
Document consultation duration	min	Sum of gaze fixation duration performed within the AMM during the time period studied
Execution duration	min	Difference between document consultation duration and absolute duration
Percentage of time spent consulting the documentation	%	Ratio between the documentation consultation duration and the absolute duration
Number of consultations	∅	Number of consultations in the time period studied.
Average consultation duration	s	Average duration of consultations over the time period studied.
NASA-TLX scores	∅	The weighted scores on the six dimensions of the NASA-TLX.

2.4.3. Data Quality

One participant did not complete the NASA-TLX questionnaire, resulting in a sample size of 21 for the workload analysis (9 experts and 12 novices). The temporal variables analysis excluded two experts and two novices who had a low gaze sample percentage (<60%) and one novice due to incomplete eye data recording (8 experts and 9 novices). The gaze sample percentages for both groups were as follows: between 60% and 70% for two experts, between 70% and 80% for three experts and one novice, and more than 80%

for three experts and nine novices. The decision to exclude participants demonstrating a gaze sample percentage below 60% was rooted in our commitment to precision and to avoid potential biases in the analysis.

2.4.4. Extraction of Variables Related to Instruction Consultation

To characterize the acquisition of procedural information [75,76], temporal behavioral data were collected to obtain all dependent variables related to the use of procedural documentation. In order to detect document consultation, we used the area of interest (AOI) technique on all eye-tracking data collected in the field. An AOI was defined [56], for all pages of the document, for all participants. We used Tobii Pro Lab 1.152 ® analysis software, which supports both manual and automated AOI mapping. We manually checked fixations for all data collected because a validity test of the automated mapping technique on the previous research [69] yielded unsatisfactory results. The data processing resulted in a time series, indicating when the participants consulted the procedural documents. Gaze fixations were temporally qualified to associate them with the corresponding phase and step (Figure 4). We used a filter threshold on the mapped ocular data to group the fixations made on the document that were spaced less than 3 s apart to form a consultation. We tested a threshold range from 0.5 to 10 s on the data, and we found that the selection of the filter threshold did not affect the inter-participant differences. The decision to use a 3-second threshold was based on the observations made during the previous research [69]. This allowed us to extract the following variables: the number of consultations and average consultation time.

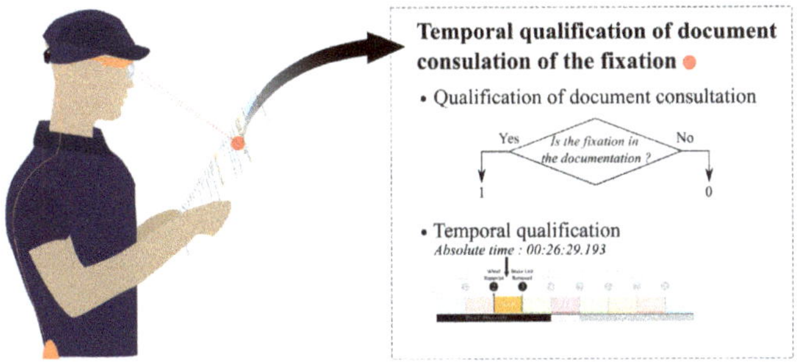

Figure 4. Temporal qualification of document consultation of the fixation. On the left, an illustration of the AMT wearing the mobile eye tracker with the gaze fixation on the maintenance documentation. On the right, the temporal qualification of the document consultation of the fixation is presented, where the first point represents the qualification of the fixation within the documentation and the second point indicates its temporal qualification in the decomposition presented in Figure 3.

2.4.5. Statistical Analysis

We conducted a statistical analysis on the three levels of the maintenance task: entire task, phase level, and step level. To test our hypotheses, we used multiple analyses of variance (ANOVAs) on the dependent variables. At the entire task level, we performed one-way ANOVA with the factor of expertise (novice, expert). At the phase level, we used repeated measure two-way ANOVA with factors of expertise (novice, expert) and phase (removal, inspection, installation). At the step level, we used repeated measure two-way ANOVA with factors of expertise (novice, expert) and Step (I to IX). Similarly, for the weighted NASA TLX scores, we used repeated measure two-way ANOVA with factors of expertise (novice, expert) and dimensions (mental, physical, temporal, performance, effort, frustration). In the case of significant ANOVA results, we conducted post hoc analyses using Student's Newman–Keuls post hoc tests to determine significant differences. A significance level of $\alpha = 0.05$ was used for all analyses.

2.4.6. Data Processing

For data analysis, three software tools were used to process and analyze the data. Tobii Pro Lab (1.152, Tobii AB, Danderyd, Sweden) was used for processing ocular data and raw data exports. Matlab scripts (R2020b, The MathWorks Inc., Natick, MA, USA), were used to obtain dependent variables. Finally, RStudio scripts (1.3.959, RStudio, PBC, Boston, MA, USA) were used to calculate statistical indicators, perform statistical tests, and generate figures.

3. Results

3.1. Workload

This section aims to investigate the effect of expertise on workload. Table 2 presents the mean values and interquartile ranges for the NASA TLX dimension among both experts and novices. The ANOVA revealed no significant effect of expertise on the weighted NASA-TLX. However, the dimension had a significant effect on workload ($F(5, 95) = 14.8, p < 0.001$), with the mental dimension being significantly higher than the other dimensions for all groups (all $p < 0.001$). Additionally, an interaction effect of expertise × dimension was observed ($F(5, 95) = 5.7, p < 0.001$), with novices reporting significantly higher load than experts in the effort ($p < 0.05$) and mental ($p < 0.05$) dimensions.

Table 2. Mean and interquartile range (IQR) values for each NASA TLX dimension (9 experts and 12 novices).

		Mental Demands		Physical Demands		Temporal Demands		Performance		Effort		Frustration	
		Mean	IQR	Mean	IQR	Mean	IQR	Mean	IQR	Mean	IQR	Mean	IQR
Weighted NASA TLX Score	Experts	170.6	175.0	138.9	85.0	88.9	80.0	50.6	50.0	59.4	50.0	29.4	5
	Novices	234.2	197.5	48.3	47.5	43.3	36.25	126.2	30.0	163.3	191.3	28.8	7.5

3.2. Procedural Information Intake

All participants used the AMM during the maintenance task. Table 3 presents the mean values and interquartile ranges for the three variables among both experts and novices.

Table 3. Mean and interquartile range (IQR) values for each of the dependent variables grouped by groups and phases. Each column represents a phase and is divided into two sections, showing the median and interquartile ranges. Similarly, each row represents a dependent variable and is divided into two sections, showing the values for each expertise group (8 experts and 9 novices).

		Removal		Inspection		Installation		Total	
		Mean	IQR	Mean	IQR	Mean	IQR	Mean	IQR
Absolute Duration (min)	Expert	40.6	9.9	11.2	16.2	55.1	20.9	107	33.2
	Novice	78.6	10.9	20.9	9.9	90.4	21.7	189.9	35.9
Execution Duration (min)	Expert	35.0	7.2	9.8	13.4	50.8	16.7	95.7	24.9
	Novice	53.9	16.6	17.8	12.2	77.4	19.5	149.1	18.7
Document consultation duration (min)	Expert	5.6	4.0	1.5	2.7	4.3	3.8	11.5	9.7
	Novice	24.7	8.6	3.1	2.9	12.9	3.2	40.7	15.7
Percentage of time spent on documentation (%)	Expert	14.1	7.9	8.8	12.6	7.6	3.9	10.6	5.0
	Novice	31.4	13.0	20.1	13.0	15.1	6.9	22.0	8.4

3.2.1. Main Effect of Phase/Step

The ANOVA analysis revealed significant effects of the phase on both document consultation duration ($F(2, 30) = 55.2, p < 0.001$) and the percentage of time spent consulting the document ($F(2, 30) = 17.6, p < 0.001$). Post hoc analyses revealed significant differences (all $p < 0.001$) in document consultation duration across all phases. The removal phase exhibited the longest duration, followed by installation and inspection. Additionally, post hoc analysis revealed that the removal phase was significantly higher than the other phases in terms of the percentage of time spent consulting the document ($p < 0.001$).

A main effect of phase was found on both absolute duration ($F(2,30) = 62.1, p < 0.001$) and execution duration ($F(2,30) = 51.2, p < 0.001$). Post hoc analyses revealed significant differences between all phases for both absolute duration ($p < 0.05$) and execution duration ($p < 0.001$). We observed that for both variables, the installation phase had the longest duration, followed by the removal and inspection phases.

On a more microscopic scale, a significant main effect of the step was observed for all four variables: document consultation duration ($F(8,120) = 25.3, p < 0.001$), percentage of time spent on the document ($F(8,120) = 33.8, p < 0.001$), absolute duration ($F(8,120) = 6.4, p < 0.001$), and execution duration ($F(8,120) = 6.2, p < 0.001$). Post hoc analyses revealed that step I exhibited a significantly higher percentage of time allocated to consulting documentation and document consultation duration ($p < 0.001$ for both indicators). Step VII exhibited significantly longer absolute duration and execution duration compared to the other steps ($p < 0.01$ and $p < 0.001$, respectively).

3.2.2. Main Effect of Expertise

Data analysis revealed a significant main effect of expertise on the duration of document consultation ($F(1,15) = 32.2, p < 0.001$), the percentage of time spent consulting documentation ($F(1,15) = 15.5, p < 0.01$), absolute duration ($F(1,15) = 21.1, p < 0.001$), and execution ($F(1,15) = 9.26, p < 0.01$).

3.2.3. Interaction Effect of Phase/Step x Expertise

Regarding the interaction effect between phase and expertise, the results showed no significant interaction effect for execution or the percentage of time spent on documentation. However, a significant interaction effect was observed for the consultation duration ($F(2,30) = 23.6, p < 0.001$) and absolute duration ($F(2,30) = 22.1, p < 0.05$). In a post hoc analysis of the two variables, significant differences in document consultation duration emerged between the novice and expert groups for both the removal and installation phases ($p < 0.001$). During the removal phase, experts showed an average document consultation duration of 5.6 min ($SD = 2.7$ min), while novices showed a significantly longer average of 24.7 min ($SD = 9.7$ min). Similarly, in the installation phase, experts showed an average document consultation duration of 4.3 min ($SD = 2.8$ min), while novices showed an average duration of 12.9 min ($SD = 3.3$ min). Furthermore, a significant difference was observed within the novice group across all phases ($p < 0.001$). This was not observed in the expert group.

When examining the interaction effect of step x expertise, the results show a significant effect on the duration of the consultation ($F(8,120) = 14.6, p < 0.001$), as well as a significant effect on the percentage of time spent on documentation ($F(8,120) = 8.3, p < 0.001$). No interaction effect is found for absolute and execution duration.

Post hoc analyses were conducted for consultation duration and the percentage of time spent on documentation. In relation to the duration of document consultation during Step I (Figure 5), a significant difference was found between the novice and expert groups at this point ($p < 0.001$). Additionally, in terms of the percentage of time spent on documentation during Step I of the task (as shown in Figure 5), both novices ($\sigma = 55.6\%, SD = 14.3\%$) and experts ($\sigma = 22.1\%, SD = 11.8\%$) allocated the highest percentage of time to document consultation. In particular, Step I stands out as significantly higher than all other steps for novices (all $p < 0.001$) and, with the exception of Step II, for experts (all $p < 0.05$).

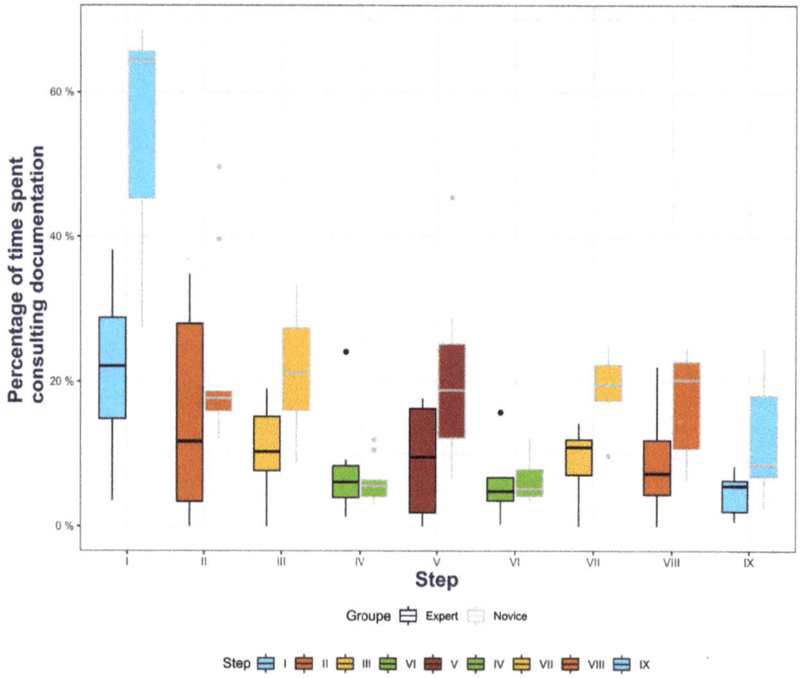

Figure 5. Boxplots of the percentage of time spent consulting documentation per step and expertise group.

In this section, we investigated how expertise influences the variables that compose absolute duration. The results demonstrate that expertise has a significant impact on absolute duration, with a greater impact on consultation than on execution. More specifically, experts perform the maintenance task at an average of 45.8% faster than novices. This distinction becomes more apparent when consulting instructions, where experts are 71.6% faster than novices. For execution, the difference is 35.9%.

3.3. *Atomization*

The analysis focused on indicators measuring the phenomenon of atomization, including the number of consultations and the average duration of consultations.

3.3.1. Main Effect of Phase/Step

For both variables, there are significant main effects on phase, with ($F(2,30) = 25.4$, $p < 0.001$) for consultation and ($F(2,30) = 13.3, p < 0.001$) for average consultation duration. The number of consultations is lower in the inspection phase (all $p < 0.001$). The average consultation duration is longer in removal (all $p < 0.001$). There is also a significant main effect on the step, with ($F(8,120) = 21.4, p < 0.001$) for consultation and ($F(8,120) = 13.7$, $p < 0.001$) for the average consultation duration. There is more consultation on steps V and VII compared to all other steps (all $p < 0.05$). The average consultation duration is longer in Step I ($p < 0.001$).

3.3.2. Main Effect of Expertise

Only the number of consultations was significantly impacted by expertise ($F(1,15) = 22.7$, $p < 0.001$). Novice participants conducted an average of 202 consultations ($SD = 47.2$), while expert participants performed 88 consultations ($SD = 50.8$).

The average consultation duration ($F(1, 15) = 2.1, p > 0.05$) for all participants was 10.8 s, with experts averaging 9.1 s and novices averaging 12.2 seconds.

3.3.3. Interaction Effect of Phase/Step x Expertise

The phase-level ANOVA demonstrated a significant interaction effect solely on the number of consultations ($F(8, 120) = 5.9, p < 0.01$). There is an expert–novice difference in the removal and installation phases (all $p < 0.001$). For novice operators, there is a lower number of consultations during inspection (all $p < 0.001$).

The step-level ANOVA demonstrated a significant interaction effect solely on the average consultation duration ($F(8, 120) = 2.3, p < 0.05$) (Figure 6). For Step I, post hoc analyses indicated that average consultation times were longer than for all other steps. This result applies to both novices (all $p < 0.001$) and experts (all $p < 0.001$), with the exception of Step II for experts.

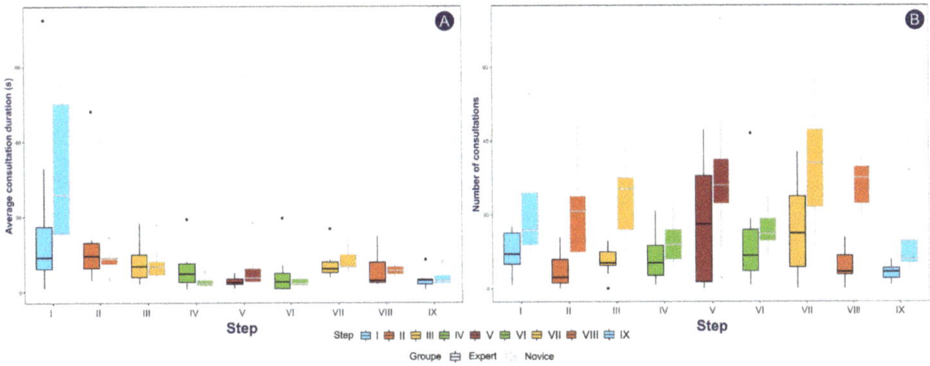

Figure 6. Box plots comparing per step and per expertise group (**A**) the average consultation time, and (**B**) the number of consultations.

4. Discussion

In this study, we investigated the impact of expertise on aircraft maintenance activity.

The key findings of our study can be summarized as follows: Our indicators on activity duration are consistent with the body of literature on the subject [19,26–28,77,78]. Experts have a lower task completion time than novices (H1). The maintenance task encompasses the execution of motor actions that are prescribed by the procedural instructions outlined in the aircraft maintenance manual. Experts are faster on both sides of the task (execution duration and document consultation). Differences between novices and experts are more important in the time dedicated to procedural information intake. On average, novices took 35.9% longer to execute the task and 71.6% longer to consult the documentation. All participants consulted the procedural document, regardless of the level of expertise of the participants, with frequent back-and-forth between the documentation consultation activity and execution throughout the task. These results are consistent with the context of the maintenance task, particularly with the safety aspect inherent in the aviation field, but also with the complexity of the procedures [34] necessary for the maintenance of a helicopter, which makes it impossible to fully memorize it [50]. Expertise has a global effect on all tasks of the maintenance activity, but its effect on document consultation is more complex.

Concerning the NASA-TLX dimensions, novices showed a significantly higher score on both the effort and the mental workload (H3) dimensions as compared to experts. These findings can be explained by considering the influence of the knowledge and skills of the experts on the efficiency of the maintenance activities: both in the extraction of crucial information relative to the current task stage and in the planning of the execution based on the information derived from the procedural document. Our study shows that even if the maintenance activity generates physical constraints (displacement, awkward postures, load bearing) [9,70,72,79], the use of procedures requires a strong mobilization of attentional and cognitive resources, corroborating the findings of [45,50,80–82].

Moreover, our results show that the amount of procedural information intake is not linear during the task. During the removal phase, operators, regardless of their level of expertise, place a greater emphasis on procedural information intake, particularly during the first step of removal for novices and the first and second steps for experts. Removal is theoretically less complicated than installation [83]. Access to certain parts may remain restricted during the removal phase until other components have been deposited. These accessibility constraints are inherent in the system and embody the interdependent relationships that structure the instructions within the procedure. They provide additional information by clarifying the sequence of actions to be followed by the technician. We suggest that the longer duration and greater importance of information gathering at the beginning of a task are not solely related to the execution of instructions during those intervals, but rather to the overall planning of the maintenance task. In this study, procedural information intake would serve two purposes, an execution purpose throughout the task and a general planning purpose at the beginning of the task.

The data relating to the number of consultations and average consultation duration illustrates the phenomenon of atomization in the maintenance task. The aircraft maintenance activity observed for all participants shows a phenomenon observed in the context of other tasks involving a procedural document in other domains [37,40,51]. The whole consultation duration of the document is segmented into multiple short consultations. The maintenance activity consists of multiple processes of information intake and action, resulting in a multitude of specific planning periods linked to the part of instruction consulted.

In our task, novices exhibit a prolonged duration of procedural document consultation, and this extension is manifested in a higher frequency of consultations (H2). However, we do not observe a longer average duration of consultations for novices, if we consider the task in its entirety. These results can be explained by the fact that novices tend to break the overall task into more information acquisition cycles in order to reduce cognitive load, i.e., to process smaller chunks of information at once [45]. Previous work has shown that this process limits the amount of information in working memory in order to reduce the cost of processing instructions [42,80]. However, when focusing on what we identified as the primary planning phase of the task. It is observed that the largest discrepancies between the groups occur in Step I. These discrepancies were observed in terms of consultation duration, the percentage of time devoted to consultation, and the average consultation duration. It is important to note that this effect among novices is not counterbalanced by a decrease in consultation duration during subsequent steps of the task. Our study aligns with the existing literature on the process of forming a mental representation of a problem-solving task environment, referred to as the 'basic problem space' [84,85]. Novices appear to invest more time in procedural information intake for task planning. This suggests that experts, who are familiar with a particular problem type, can efficiently draw upon previous problem spaces and distinguish only necessary information for general planning without going into detailed instructions that will be processed later during execution. This is in contrast to novices who must allocate additional time and effort to construct the problem space from scratch due to their lack of familiarity with the problem type.

4.1. Practical Implications

Our study presents empirical findings on procedural information intake behaviors in the authentic context of maintenance tasks. The research involved using the procedure in its natural paper format, without any imposed restrictions or specific usage instructions. The maintenance task was extensive, lasting over an hour and requiring the execution of multiple instructions from a document comprising numerous pages. Understanding how aircraft maintenance technicians use aircraft maintenance manuals has practical implications for procedural design and AMT training. The information intake within

AMMs is achieved through multiple short consultations, averaging a duration of 10.8 s. Good readers can process information at a rate of 200 to 400 words per minute [86,87]. This indicates that the amount of information absorbed during each consultation is relatively small. In document design, it is important to optimize the physical format to facilitate the efficient location of relevant information [54,88]. Our study highlights the potential challenges faced by novice individuals when initiating the maintenance task; training programs can be designed to emphasize the initial interaction with the global procedural document at the start of a task. Consequently, workers could learn to extract the important cues for planning their entire task. Our study shows that mobile eye tracking is suitable for field studies in the context of aircraft maintenance, even over long periods of measurement with procedural documents in paper format.

4.2. Limitations and Future Studies

There are some limitations associated with this study that need to be mentioned. We believe that the main limitation of this study is our attempt to be as close as possible to real maintenance conditions by not imposing any constraints on the operator's activities. This has implications for methodological choices. The mental workload measurement might have been addressed using physiological indicators [89], such as heart rate or pupil diameter. However, the lighting conditions of our hangar or the movement inherent to maintenance activity made these indicators difficult to set up.

Regarding the depth of the analysis of eye-tracking data, our study considers only basic indicators and procedural documentation in a single object of interest. It would be beneficial to include an analysis of the information extracted from the documentation to further develop the initial contributions presented in this study. For example, it might be interesting to analyze the effect of expertise on document navigation.

Finally, while the primary focus of our study is on procedural aspects, we recognize the importance of including the physical dimension, which may provide a perspective for a more comprehensive understanding of expertise in maintenance tasks.

5. Conclusions

This study investigated the effect of expertise on aircraft maintenance tasks, including the use of procedural documents. The analysis of activity, using step and phase division, as well as the measurement of gaze behavior and workload, enabled us to assess the influence of expertise in a real-life industrial context. The results show that experts are faster than novices at all levels of the task (whole task, phases, steps), as well as in the execution and information intake. The study allowed us to characterize the way procedural information is acquired about a population of AMTs. The results show that the acquisition of procedural information is more important at the beginning of the task and that there is a back-and-forth between execution and information acquisition. This procedural information-gathering time at the beginning of the task can be attributed to the overall planning of the maintenance task prior to the start of its execution. This is when the expert–novice gap is the most important. The extra time spent by novices during this phase is not offset by a less significant use of procedures afterward. The novices had to exert more mental effort than the experts to accomplish the task; it is still important to note that both groups reported a mental dimension that was superior to the other scales measured. The findings indicate that novices experience a higher workload during the maintenance task compared to experts. This could be attributed to novices exhibiting increased task atomization, as evidenced by the greater number of consultations. These results have important implications for AMT training. They demonstrate the importance of focusing on the intake of procedural information and the use of procedures in the planning of maintenance tasks. The findings suggest that training programs for novice AMTs place a strong emphasis on the effective intake of procedural information and the use of procedures in the planning of maintenance tasks. The results suggest that the design of procedures should focus on facilitating the acquisition of procedural information. Our study suggests that the information extraction process within the AMM differs between the planning and completion phases of the task. This could impact the development of procedures. This study paves the way for future research on the effect of expertise on the aircraft maintenance task. Future research could explore the effect of expertise on information gathering within the maintenance procedure.

Author Contributions: Conceptualization, F.P., R.C., M.-L.B. and D.M.; methodology, F.P., R.C. and D.M.; software, F.P.; validation, R.C. and D.M.; formal analysis, F.P., R.C. and D.M.; investigation, F.P.; resources, M.-L.B.; data curation, F.P.; writing—original draft preparation, F.P.; writing—review and editing, F.P., R.C., M.-L.B. and D.M.; visualization, F.P.; supervision, R.C. and D.M.; project administration, D.M.; funding acquisition, R.C., M.-L.B. and D.M. All authors have read and agreed to the published version of the manuscript.

Funding: Florence Paris is employed by Airbus Helicopters under the industrial convention CIFRE n° 2020/0749 between ANRT (Association Nationale de la Recherche et de la Technologie) and Airbus Helicopters. She is affiliated with Aix-Marseille University as a Doctoral Candidate, under collaboration agreement n° IPAH13430 between Airbus Helicopters and Aix-Marseille University (Institute of Movement Sciences).

Institutional Review Board Statement: Not applicable.

Informed Consent Statement: Not applicable.

Data Availability Statement: Data of the resulting values of measurements are not publicly available. For further information regarding the data, contact the authors of this article.

Conflicts of Interest: Florence Paris and Marie-Line Bergeonneau were employed by the company Airbus Helicopters. The remaining authors declare that the research was conducted in the absence of any commercial or financial relationships that could be construed as a potential conflict of interest.

Abbreviations

The following abbreviations are used in this manuscript:

AMM	Aircraft Maintenance Manual
AMT	aircraft maintenance technician
ANOVA	analysis of variance
AOI	area of interest
IQR	interquartile range
MSD	musculoskeletal disorder

References

1. Blaise, J.C.; Levrat, E.; Iung, B. Process approach-based methodology for safe maintenance operation: From concepts to SPRIMI software prototype. *Saf. Sci.* **2014**, *70*, 99–113. [CrossRef]
2. Jasiulewicz-Kaczmarek, M. The role of ergonomics in implementation of the social aspect of sustainability, illustrated with the example of maintenance. In *Occupational Safety and Hygiene*; CRC Press: London, UK, 2013; pp. 1–6. [CrossRef]
3. Leplat, J.; Hoc, J.M. Tâche et activité dans l'analyse psychologique des situations. *Cah. Psychol. Cogn. Anc Cah. Psychol. Marseille* **1983**, *3*, 49–63.
4. Darses, F. Activity analysis: Not what it was! *Trav. Hum.* **2016**, *79*, 193–208. [CrossRef]
5. Latorella, K.; Prabhu, P. A review of human error in aviation maintenance and inspection. *Int. J. Ind. Ergon.* **2000**, *26*, 133–161. [CrossRef]
6. Gunes, T.; Turhan, U.; Açıkel, B. An Assessment of Aircraft Maintenance Technician Competency. *Int. J. Aviat. Sci. Technol.* **2020**, *1*, 22–29. [CrossRef]
7. Hobbs, A. *An Overview of Human Factors in Aviation Maintenance*; Aviation Research and Analysis AR-2008-055; Australian Transport Safety Bureau: Canberra, Australia, 2008; Issue: AR-2008-055.
8. De La Garza, C.; Weill-Fassina, A. Méthode d'analyse des difficultés de gestion du risque dans une activité collective: L'entretien des voies ferrées. *Saf. Sci.* **1995**, *18*, 157–180. [CrossRef]
9. Grusenmeyer, C. *Les accidents liés à la maintenance. Etude bibliographique*; Technical Report NS 248; Institut National de Recherche et de Sécurité (INRS): Paris, France, 2005.
10. Reiman, T. Understanding maintenance work in safety-critical organisations—Managing the performance variability. *Theor. Issues Ergon. Sci.* **2011**, *12*, 339–366. [CrossRef]

11. Federal Aviation Administration. *Aviation Maintenance Technician Handbook–General*; Technical Report FAA-H-8083-30B; U.S. Department of Transportation: Oklahoma City, OK, USA, 2023; Issue: (FAA-H-8083-30B).
12. Simon, H.A. The structure of ill structured problems. *Artif. Intell.* **1973**, *4*, 181–201. [CrossRef]
13. Oedewald, P.; Reiman, T. Special characteristics of safety critical organizations. *Work Psychol. Perspect. VTT Publ.* **2007**, *633*, 1–126.
14. Haritos, T.; Macchiarella, N. A mobile application of augmented reality for aerospace maintenance training. In Proceedings of the 24th Digital Avionics Systems Conference, Washington, DC, USA, 30 October–3 November 2005; Volume 1, pp. 5.B.3–5.1. [CrossRef]
15. Charness, N.; Tuffiash, M. The Role of Expertise Research and Human Factors in Capturing, Explaining, and Producing Superior Performance. *Hum. Factors* **2008**, *50*, 427–432. [CrossRef]
16. Farrington-Darby, T.; Wilson, J.R. The nature of expertise: A review. *Appl. Ergon.* **2006**, *37*, 17–32. [CrossRef]
17. Ericsson, K.A. The Influence of Experience and Deliberate Practice on the Development of Superior Expert Performance. In *The Cambridge Handbook of Expertise and Expert Performance*; Cambridge University Press: Cambridge, UK, 2006; pp. 683–703. [CrossRef]
18. Ericsson, K.; Krampe, R.; Tesch-Roemer, C. The Role of Deliberate Practice in the Acquisition of Expert Performance. *Psychol. Rev.* **1993**, *100*, 363–406. [CrossRef]
19. Chi, M.T.; Glaser, R.; Rees, E.; *Expertise in Problem Solving*; Technical Report ADA100138; University of Pittsburgh, Pa. Learning Researchand Development Center, National Inst. of Education (ED) Washington, DC, USA; Office of Naval Research: Arlington, VA, USA, 1981; Issue: LRDC-1981/3.
20. Voss, J.F.; Greene, T.R.; Post, T.A.; Penner, B.C. Problem-Solving Skill in the Social Sciences. *Psychol. Learn. Motiv.* **1983**, *17*, 165–213. [CrossRef]
21. Egan, D.E.; Schwartz, B.J. Chunking in recall of symbolic drawings. *Mem. Cogn.* **1979**, *7*, 149–158. [CrossRef]
22. Chase, W.G.; Simon, H.A. Perception in chess. *Cogn. Psychol.* **1973**, *4*, 55–81. [CrossRef]
23. Norman, G.R.; Brooks, L.R.; Allen, S.W. Recall by expert medical practitioners and novices as a record of processing attention. *J. Exp. Psychol. Learn. Mem. Cogn.* **1989**, *15*, 1166–1174. [CrossRef] [PubMed]
24. Didierjean, A.; Ferrari, V.; Cauzinille-Marmèche, E. L'expertise cognitive au jeu d'échecs: Quoi de neuf depuis De Groot (1946)? *L'Année Psychol.* **2004**, *104*, 771–793. [CrossRef]
25. Chi, M.T.H.; Glaser, R.; Farr, M.J. *The Nature of Expertise*; Psychology Press: New York, NY, USA, 1988; Google-Books-ID: Nwx8AgAAQBAJ.
26. Haji, F.A.; Khan, R.; Regehr, G.; Drake, J.; de Ribaupierre, S.; Dubrowski, A. Measuring cognitive load during simulation-based psychomotor skills training: Sensitivity of secondary-task performance and subjective ratings. *Adv. Health Sci. Educ. Theory Pract.* **2015**, *20*, 1237–1253. [CrossRef]
27. Judkins, T.N.; Oleynikov, D.; Stergiou, N. Objective evaluation of expert and novice performance during robotic surgical training tasks. *Surg. Endosc.* **2009**, *23*, 590–597. [CrossRef]
28. Kieras, D.; Tibbits, M.; Bovair, S.; Psychology, A.U.T.D.O. *How Experts and Nonexperts Operate Electronic Equipment from Instructions*; Technical Report ADA139451; Department of Psychology, University of Arizona: Tucson, AZ, USA, 1984.
29. Lesgold, A.M. *Acquiring Expertise*; Technical Report PDS-5; University of Pittsburgh, Learning Research and Development Center: Pittsburgh, PA, USA, 1983.
30. Köhler, C.; Kékenbosch, C.; Verstiggel, J.C. La compréhension d'un texte procédural: Un processus à profondeur variable. *Int. J. Psychol.* **2000**, *35*, 258–269. [CrossRef]
31. Ganier, F.; Gombert, J.; Michel, F. Effets du format de présentation des instructions sur l'apprentissage de procédures à l'aide de documents techniques. *Le Trav. Hum.* **2000**, *63*, 121–152.
32. Ganier, F.; de Vries, P. Are instructions in video format always better than photographs when learning manual techniques? The case of learning how to do sutures. *Learn. Instr.* **2016**, *44*, 87–96. [CrossRef]
33. Biard, N. L'apprentissage de procédures médicales par vidéo: Effets de la segmentation et du contrôle du rythme par l'apprenant. Ph.D. Thesis, Université de Bretagne occidentale, Brest, France, 2019.
34. Robin, D. Usages et Bénéfices de la 3D en Maintenance Aéronautique. Ph.D. Thesis, Toulouse II Le Mirail, Toulouse, France, 2012. [CrossRef]
35. Leplat, J. Eléments pour l'étude des documents prescripteurs. In *Repères pour L'analyse de L'activité en Ergonomie*; Le Travail humain, Presses Universitaires de France: Paris, France 2008; pp. 93–130.
36. Anderson, J.R. *Rules of the Mind*; Psychology Press: New York, NY, USA, 2014. [CrossRef]
37. Vermersch, P. Données d'observation sur l'utilisation d'une consigne écrite : L'atomisation de l'action. *Le Trav. Hum.* **1985**, *48*, 161–172.
38. Chaniaud, N.; Natacha, M.; Emilie, L.E.; Olga, M. Impact of the format of user instructions on the handling of a wrist blood pressure monitor. *Cogn. Process.* **2021**, *22*, 261–275.
39. Jannin, L.; Ganier, F.; de Vries, P. Ego or Heterocentric? Effects of The Perspective of Video or Pictures Instructions on Procedural Learning. *L'Année Psychol.* **2022**, *122*, 439–470. [CrossRef]
40. Jannin, L.; Ganier, F.; De Vries, P. Atomized or delayed execution? An alternative paradigm for the study of procedural learning. *J. Educ. Psychol.* **2019**, *111*, 1406–1415. [CrossRef]

41. Duggan, G.B.; Payne, S.J. Interleaving reading and acting while following procedural instructions. *J. Exp. Psychol. Appl.* **2001**, *7*, 297–307. [CrossRef] [PubMed]
42. Ganier, F. Le Traitement Cognitif: Déterminant de la Conception des Documents Procéduraux. Ph.D. Thesis, Université de Bourgogne, Dijon, France, 1999.
43. Jannin, L. Approche Psycho-Ergonomique de L'usage de la Simulation en e-Learning Pour L'apprentissage de Procédures: Le cas du Point de Suture. Ph.D. Thesis, Université de Bretagne occidentale, Brest, France, 2020.
44. Mayer, R.E.; Moreno, R. Nine Ways to Reduce Cognitive Load in Multimedia Learning. *Educ. Psychol.* **2003**, *38*, 43–52. [CrossRef]
45. Fraser, K.L.; Ayres, P.; Sweller, J. Cognitive Load Theory for the Design of Medical Simulations. *Simul. Healthc. J. Soc. Fo Simul. Healthc.* **2015**, *10*, 295–307. [CrossRef]
46. Khacharem, A.; Spanjers, I.A.E.; Zoudji, B.; Kalyuga, S.; Ripoll, H. Using segmentation to support the learning from animated soccer scenes: An effect of prior knowledge. *Psychol. Sport Exerc.* **2013**, *14*, 154–160. [CrossRef]
47. Zafiharimalala, H.; Tricot, A. Text signals in the aircraft maintenance documentation. In Proceedings of the 8th MAD Multidisciplinary Perspectives on Signalling Text Organisation, Moissac, France, 17–20 March 2010.
48. Zafiharimalala, H. Étude Ergonomique Pour la Consultation sur écran de Petite Taille de la Documentation de Maintenance Aéronautique. Ph.D. Thesis, Université Toulouse le Mirail–Toulouse II, Toulouse, France, 2011.
49. Zafiharimalala, H.; Tricot, A. Vers une Prise en Compte de L'utilisateur dans la Conception de Documents en Maintenance Aéronautique. In Proceedings of the Prise en Compte de l'Utilisateur dans les Systèmes d'Information, Toulouse, France, 26 May 2009; pp. 63–74.
50. Cippelletti, E. Aide à la Conception, test de L'usage et de L'acceptation D'un Logiciel de Maintenance. Ph.D. Thesis, Université Grenoble Alpes, Grenoble, France, 2017.
51. Meng, M. Using Eye Tracking to Study Information Selection and Use in Procedures. *IEEE Trans. Prof. Commun.* **2023**, *66*, 7–25. [CrossRef]
52. Ganier, F. 3-Méthodes pour l'étude de la compréhension d'instructions et l'évaluation des documents procéduraux. In *Comprendre la Documentation Technique*; Le Travail Humain, Presses Universitaires de France: Paris, France, 2013; pp. 61–86.
53. Alamargot, D.; Chesnet, D.; Dansac, C.; Ros, C. Eye and Pen: A new device for studying reading during writing. *Behav. Res. Methods* **2006**, *38*, 287–299. [CrossRef]
54. Schmid, S.; Baccino, T. Stratégies de lecture pour les textes à consigne. *Langages* **2001**, *35*, 105–124. [CrossRef]
55. Duchowski, A. Suggested Empirical Guidelines. In *Eye Tracking Methodology: Theory and Practice*; Springer: London, UK, 2007; pp. 171–179. [CrossRef]
56. Jacob, R.J.; Karn, K.S. Commentary on Section 4—Eye tracking in human-computer interaction and usability research: Ready to deliver the promises. In *The Mind's Eye*; Hyönä, J., Radach, R., Deubel, H., Eds.; North-Holland: Amsterdam, The Netherlands, 2003; pp. 573–605. [CrossRef]
57. Bapna, T.; Valles, J.; Leng, S.; Pacilli, M.; Nataraja, R.M. Eye-tracking in surgery: A systematic review. *ANZ J. Surg.* **2023**, *93*, 2600–2608. [CrossRef]
58. Hüttermann, S.; Noël, B.; Memmert, D. Eye tracking in high-performance sports: Evaluation of its application in expert athletes. *Int. J. Comput. Sci. Sport* **2018**, *17*, 182–203. [CrossRef]
59. Espino Palma, C.; Luis del Campo, V.; Muñoz Marín, D. Visual Behaviours of Expert Padel Athletes When Playing on Court: An In Situ Approach with a Portable Eye Tracker. *Sensors* **2023**, *23*, 1438. [CrossRef]
60. Kapitaniak, B.; Walczak, M.; Kosobudzki, M.; Jóźwiak, Z.; Bortkiewicz, A. Application of eye-tracking in drivers testing: A review of research. *Int. J. Occup. Med. Environ. Health* **2015**, *28*, 941–954. [CrossRef]
61. Martinez-Marquez, D.; Pingali, S.; Panuwatwanich, K.; Stewart, R.A.; Mohamed, S. Application of Eye Tracking Technology in Aviation, Maritime, and Construction Industries: A Systematic Review. *Sensors* **2021**, *21*, 4289. [CrossRef] [PubMed]
62. Vrzakova, H.; Bednarik, R. Hard lessons learned: Mobile eye-tracking in cockpits. In Proceedings of the 4th Workshop on Eye Gaze in Intelligent Human Machine Interaction, New York, NY, USA, 26 October 2012; Gaze-In '12, pp. 1–6. [CrossRef]
63. Madlenak, R.; Chinoracky, R.; Stalmasekova, N.; Madlenakova, L. Investigating the Effect of Outdoor Advertising on Consumer Decisions: An Eye-Tracking and A/B Testing Study of Car Drivers' Perception. *Appl. Sci.* **2023**, *13*, 6808. [CrossRef]
64. Madlenak, R.; Masek, J.; Madlenakova, L.; Chinoracky, R. Eye-Tracking Investigation of the Train Driver's: A Case Study. *Appl. Sci.* **2023**, *13*, 2437. [CrossRef]
65. Hasanzadeh, S.; Esmaeili, B.; Dodd, M.D. Measuring Construction Workers' Real-Time Situation Awareness Using Mobile Eye-Tracking. In Proceedings of the Construction Research Congress 2016, San Juan, Puerto Rico, 31 May–2 June, 2016; pp. 2894–2904. [CrossRef]
66. Hasanzadeh, S.; Esmaeili, B.; Dodd, M.D. Examining the Relationship between Construction Workers' Visual Attention and Situation Awareness under Fall and Tripping Hazard Conditions: Using Mobile Eye Tracking. *J. Constr. Eng. Manag.* **2018**, *144*, 1–18. [CrossRef]
67. Fu, H.; Xia, Z.; Tan, Y.; Guo, X. Influence of Cues on the Safety Hazard Recognition of Construction Workers during Safety Training: Evidence from an Eye-Tracking Experiment. *J. Civ. Eng. Educ.* **2024**, *150*, 04023009. [CrossRef]
68. Paris, F.; Casanova, R.; Bergeonneau, M.L.; Mestre, D. Characterizing the expertise of aircraft maintenance technicians using eye-tracking. In Proceedings of the 2022 Symposium on Eye Tracking Research and Applications, Seattle, WA, USA, 8–11 June 2022; ETRA '22, pp. 1–3. [CrossRef]

69. Paris, F.; Casanova, R.; Bergeonneau, M.; Mestre, D. Analysis of the Use of the Maintenance Documentation Using Eye-Tracking: A Pilot Study. In Proceedings of the 1st International Conference on Cognitive Aircraft Systems—ICCAS, Toulouse, France, 1–2 June 2022; Volume 1, pp. 57–60. [CrossRef]
70. Asadi, H.; Yu, D.; Mott, J.H. Risk factors for musculoskeletal injuries in airline maintenance, repair & overhaul. *Int. J. Ind. Ergon.* **2019**, *70*, 107–115.
71. Sugiharto, F.M. The Relationship between Mental Workload and Occupational Stress among Aircraft Maintenance Officers at PT X. *Indones. J. Occup. Saf. Health* **2019**, *8*, 233. [CrossRef]
72. Yazgan, E.; Ozkan, N.F.; Ulutas, B.H. A questionnaire-based musculoskeletal disorder assessment for aircraft maintenance technicians. *Aircr. Eng. Aerosp. Technol.* **2022**, *94*, 240–247. [CrossRef]
73. Duchowski, A.T. A breadth-first survey of eye-tracking applications. *Behav. Res. Methods Instrum. Comput.* **2002**, *34*, 455–470. [CrossRef] [PubMed]
74. Hart, S.G.; Staveland, L.E. Development of NASA-TLX (Task Load Index): Results of Empirical and Theoretical Research. In *Human Mental Workload*; Advances in Psychology; Hancock, P.A., Meshkati, N., Eds.; North-Holland: Amsterdam, The Netherlands, 1988; Volume 52, pp. 139–183. [CrossRef]
75. Ganier, F. Évaluer l'efficacité des documents techniques procéduraux : Un panorama des méthodes. *Le Trav. Hum.* **2002**, *65*, 1–27. [CrossRef]
76. Hegarty, M.; Carpenter, P.A.; Just, M.A. Diagrams in the comprehension of scientific texts. In *Handbook of Reading Research*; Lawrence Erlbaum Associates, Inc.: Hillsdale, NJ, USA, 1991; Volume 2, pp. 641–668.
77. Narazaki, K.; Oleynikov, D.; Stergiou, N. Objective Assessment of Proficiency with Bimanual Inanimate Tasks in Robotic Laparoscopy. *J. Laparoendosc. Adv. Surg. Tech.* **2007**, *17*, 47–52. [CrossRef] [PubMed]
78. Suebnukarn, S.; Phatthanasathiankul, N.; Sombatweroje, S.; Rhienmora, P.; Haddawy, P. Process and outcome measures of expert/novice performance on a haptic virtual reality system. *J. Dent.* **2009**, *37*, 658–665. [CrossRef]
79. Nogueira, H.C.; Diniz, A.C.P.; Barbieri, D.F.; Padula, R.S.; Carregaro, R.L.; de Oliveira, A.B. Musculoskeletal disorders and psychosocial risk factors among workers of the aircraft maintenance industry. *Work* **2012**, *41*, 4801–4807. [CrossRef]
80. Glover, J.A.; Harvey, A.L.; Corkill, A.J. Remembering Written Instructions: Tab a Goes into Slot C, or Does It? *Br. J. Educ. Psychol.* **1988**, *58*, 191–200. [CrossRef]
81. Ganier, F.; Hoareau, C.; Devillers, F. Évaluation des performances et de la charge de travail induits par l'apprentissage de procédures de maintenance en environnement virtuel. *Le Trav. Hum.* **2013**, *76*, 335–363. [CrossRef]
82. Ganier, F. Factors Affecting the Processing of Procedural Instructions: Implications for Document Design. *IEEE Trans. Prof. Commun.* **2004**, *47*, 15–26. [CrossRef]
83. Reason, J.; Maddox, M. Human Error. In *Human Factors Guide for Aviation Maintenance*; Federal Aviation Association (FAA), Ed.; Galaxy Scientific Corporation: Washington, DC, USA 1998; p. 48.
84. Hayes, J.R.; Simon, H.A. Understanding written problem instructions. *Knowl. Cogn.* **1974**, *1* 167–200.
85. Newell, A.; Simon, H.A. *Human Problem Solving*; Prentice-Hall: Englewood Cliffs, NJ, USA, 1972; Volume 104.
86. Brysbaert, M. How many words do we read per minute? A review and meta-analysis of reading rate. *J. Mem. Lang.* **2019**, *109*, 30. [CrossRef]
87. Rayner, K.; Schotter, E.R.; Masson, M.E.J.; Potter, M.C.; Treiman, R. So Much to Read, So Little Time: How Do We Read, and Can Speed Reading Help? *Psychol. Sci. Public Interest* **2016**, *17*, 4–34. [CrossRef]
88. Cellier, J.M.; Terrier, P. Le rôle de la mise en forme matérielle dans le traitement cognitif de consignes. *Langages* **2001**, *35*, 79–91. [CrossRef]
89. Orlandi, L.; Brooks, B. Measuring mental workload and physiological reactions in marine pilots: Building bridges towards redlines of performance. *Appl. Ergon.* **2018**, *69*, 74–92. [CrossRef]

applied sciences

Article

The Impact of Reading Modalities and Text Types on Reading in School-Age Children: An Eye-Tracking Study

Wi-Jiwoon Kim [1], Seo Rin Yoon [1], Seohyun Nam [1], Yunjin Lee [2] and Dongsun Yim [1,*]

[1] Department of Communication Disorders, Ewha Womans University, Seoul 03760, Republic of Korea; juneindec1231@gmail.com (W.-J.K.); srysky@ewhain.net (S.R.Y.); 2646s@ewhain.net (S.N.)
[2] Department of English Language and Literature, Ewha Womans University, Seoul 03760, Republic of Korea; yunjinlee@ewhain.net
* Correspondence: sunyim@ewha.ac.kr; Tel.: +82-2-3277-6720

Abstract: This study examined the eye movement patterns of 317 elementary students across reading conditions (audio-assisted reading (AR) and reading-only (R)) and text types (fiction and non-fiction) and identified eye movement parameters that predict their literal comprehension (LC) and inferential comprehension (IC). Participants, randomly assigned to either reading condition and either text type, answered questions assessing their LC and IC. Average fixation duration (AFD), total fixation duration (TFD), and scanpath length were used as eye movement parameters. The main effects of age were observed on all parameters, along with interaction effects between age and reading condition on TFD and scanpath length. These results indicate that children employ different reading strategies, depending on reading modalities and text types. When controlling for age, TFD had a positive impact on the LC of both text types in the AR, while in the R, it had a negative effect on the IC of both text types. Longer scanpaths predicted the IC of fiction in the AR; the LC and IC of non-fiction under the AR; and the LC of non-fiction within the R. AFD had a negative influence on the IC of fiction in the AR, as well as on the LC and IC of non-fiction in the AR, and the LC of non-fiction under the R. These findings highlight the importance of selecting appropriate reading strategies, based on reading modality and text type, to enhance reading comprehension. This study offers guidance for educators when providing reading instruction to school-age children.

Keywords: eye-tracking; reading modality; audio-assisted reading; text type; reading comprehension; school-age children

1. Introduction

1.1. Reading and Reading Comprehension

Reading is a critical ability in current society, as it enables individuals to successfully acquire information through media and provides opportunities for personal growth, as well as emotional development, through vicarious experiences [1,2]. The importance of reading during the school-age years is particularly prominent, not only because this phase corresponds to the development of one's self-system, which is closely intertwined with reading proficiency [3], but also because reading skills predict academic achievement due to the utilization of text-based educational materials in schools [4].

Reading comprehension is an intricate skill that integrates various linguistic and cognitive components [5,6]. Kim [7] suggested that reading comprehension is directly related to listening comprehension, as well as to word reading skills, which are influenced by linguistic factors, such as phonology, orthography, and semantics, and higher-order cognition and oral language skills, including but not limited to inferring, reasoning, monitoring, syntax, and vocabulary, respectively. Reading comprehension is divided into two types: literal comprehension and inferential comprehension. Literal comprehension involves understanding specific events explicitly presented in the text, while inferential comprehension is achieved through deducing information from the text [8]. Literal comprehension begins to develop at the beginning of school age, primarily supported by word reading and vocabulary skills [9–11]. Inferential comprehension, building upon literal comprehension, is known to be an advanced reading comprehension skill that evolves throughout school age, as it requires the facilitation of background knowledge and integration of information beyond simple word reading [12–14].

1.2. The Effect of Reading Modalities and Text Types on Reading Comprehension

Audio-assisted reading (AR), in which individuals read text while listening to the corresponding audio, is one of the reading modalities proposed to enhance the reading comprehension of poor readers. Previous studies have demonstrated that audio assistance helps them engage more effectively with the text and utilize their cognitive strengths with improved semantic chunking. Under the AR condition, automatic reading, facilitated by the reduced cognitive load of decoding words, allows them to allocate more of their attention to understanding the content of the text when compared to the reading-only (R) condition [15–18]. However, a debate remains regarding whether all school-age children can benefit from AR, as the AR condition could potentially lead to an increased cognitive load by necessitating the simultaneous processing of visual and auditory stimuli [19,20].

The type of text, broadly consisting of two types—fictional (narrative) and non-fictional (expository)—is also acknowledged to have an impact on reading comprehension [21–23]. Fictional text that young readers typically encounter from early childhood is often presented in a sequential manner. This inherent structure helps young children to understand the story more easily, given the similarity between the narrative progression and the development of real-life events they experience [24]. On the other hand, non-fictional text requires more time for reading and comprehension compared to fictional text due to the unfamiliarity of the subject matter and the complexity of sentence structures [25,26]. Hence, it is relatively easier for school-age children to achieve reading comprehension of fictional text as opposed to non-fictional text [22]. Additionally, as children grow older, their comprehension of fictional text can readily improve compared to that of non-fictional text, because recognizing the causal relationship between events is often sufficient for comprehension. In contrast, non-fictional text demands more structured training, including syntactic comprehension and background knowledge, to be effectively comprehended beyond merely understanding causality [27,28].

Chung et al. [29] investigated the impact of various story presentation methods (audio-only, audio-with-text, and text-only) and story types (fiction and non-fiction) on the comprehension of first- and second-grade students. Consistent with previous research, children demonstrated better comprehension of the fictional stories than of the non-fictional stories, and performance of literal comprehension tasks exceeded that of inferential comprehension tasks. Regarding the story presentation methods, overall comprehension scores of the fictional stories in the audio-only condition and the audio-with-text condition were found to be significantly higher than those in the text-only condition. In terms of non-fictional stories, only the audio-with-text condition exhibited higher comprehension scores compared to the condition with reading only. These results suggest that 6- to 8-year-old children can benefit from AR with both fictional and non-fictional stories, surpassing the R condition for both types of stories. Moreover, the effects of the story presentation methods may differ depending on the text type.

1.3. Eye-Tracking Studies on Reading

The eye-tracking technique involves analyzing the dynamic traces created by eye movements to detect one's attention and cognitive processes [30]. According to the eye-mind theory proposed by Just and Carpenter [31], visual processing occurs at the site where gazes are fixated. In the process of reading, during a fixation, readers decode and recognize words and extract the required information, either from a single word or from a semantic chunk consisting of a group of words, while integrating this new information with their exiting knowledge [32]. Subsequently, they make a transition to another word or chunk of text to acquire different information, initiating another fixation. Thus, when applied in reading comprehension tasks, the eye-tracking technique provides insights into the process of information acquisition from text.

Previous research explored the relationship between eye movement patterns and reading proficiency, revealing that shorter fixation duration and fewer fixation counts are indicators of proficient reading [33]. Many studies examined the connection between reading skills and eye movement patterns by comparing children across various age groups and demonstrated that older students exhibit shorter fixations per word, shorter average fixation durations [34,35], and more frequent long saccades [36] compared to their younger counterparts. However, only a few studies consider the spatial aspects of eye movement patterns, and research that investigates a wide age range to observe continuous changes in eye movement patterns over time is limited.

There is scant research related to reading and auditory input using eye-tracking technology. Conklin et al. [37] studied the links between reading proficiency and eye movement patterns under different reading conditions, AR and R, by comparing first language (L1) and second language (L2) speakers. They found that L2 readers showed more frequent fixations and longer fixation durations than L1 readers in the R condition, while there were no significant differences in eye movement parameters between L1 and L2 readers in the AR condition, thus demonstrating the positive effect of audio assistance for developing readers. However, it needs to be determined whether these differences in eye movement patterns under the AR condition directly indicate improved reading comprehension.

Park et al. [38] aimed to determine whether language competency affects the relationship between eye movement patterns and reading comprehension with different reading modalities. They examined reading comprehension of typically developing (TD) children and children with language impairment (LI) in grades 1 and 2 according to reading modalities (AR and R) and the correlations between reading comprehension and eye movement parameters of both groups in each reading condition. Both in the AR and R conditions, TD children performed better in reading comprehension than children with LI. Total fixation duration in the screen; total fixation duration within areas of interest (AOIs), which are sentence areas in the screen; and scanpath length were selected as the eye movement parameters for the study. Total fixation duration within AOIs and scanpath length showed significant positive correlations with story comprehension in the AR condition among TD children, whereas among children with LI, only scanpath length emerged as a significant variable showing a positive correlation with story comprehension. Under the R condition, total fixation durations within the screen and within AOIs showed negative correlations with comprehension scores in the TD group. In contrast, in the LI group, no significant correlations between reading comprehension and eye movement parameters were observed. This disparity in the correlations between comprehension scores and eye movement parameters based on the reading modality implies that children with varying levels of language proficiency may process information in text differently, depending on the availability of audio assistance.

Several studies uncovered how readers approach text based on its difficulty level. In the case of challenging texts, such as those with an enactive style, readers tend to exhibit longer reading time, extended fixation durations, increased fixation counts, and reduced word skipping [35,39]. They also engage in more frequent retrospective glances and allocate more time to revisit prior sentences compared to these behaviors while reading easier texts [40]. Nevertheless, there are limited studies examining how text type influences the eye movements of school-age children and how these eye movement patterns impact their reading comprehension.

1.4. Study Objectives

In this study, we aimed to identify the differences in eye movement patterns, both temporal and spatial, among elementary school students ranging from grades 1 to 6, based on reading conditions (modalities), R and AR; and text types, fiction and non-fiction. Additionally, we sought to understand the impact of these eye movement patterns within each reading condition and text type on their literal and inferential reading comprehension. Therefore, the research questions are as follows:

1. Are there differences in eye movement parameters (average and total fixation durations and scanpath length) among different age groups according to reading conditions and text types?
2. Which eye movement parameters can predict literal and inferential reading comprehension in elementary school children within each reading condition and text type?

2. Materials and Methods

2.1. Participants

A total of 364 children (187 males and 177 females) from grades 1 to 6, who were enrolled in a private elementary school in Seoul, Korea, participated in this study, with an average age of 113 months (SD = 21.13). The study obtained written consent from both parents and children through notices sent to parents. Among these, 40 children were excluded from the research due to not meeting the language proficiency criteria after screening. An additional seven were excluded from the study for not meeting the criteria for non-verbal intelligence after screening. Consequently, the final eligible sample consisted of 317 children who successfully completed the tasks.

The study's inclusion criteria were as follows: (1) enrollment in grades 1 to 6 in an elementary school, (2) achievement of the 10th percentile or higher in both receptive and expressive vocabulary as measured by the Receptive and Expressive Vocabulary Test [41], (3) attainment of a standard score of 85 points or higher in the nonverbal intelligence test component of the Kaufman Brief Intelligence Test-2nd edition [42], (4) demonstration of appropriate reading abilities suitable for engaging with the text in the reading tasks, and (5) no reports from parents or teachers indicating any presence of intellectual, visual, auditory, emotional, behavioral, or neurological problems.

All eligible children participated in two reading tasks, conducted under both the R and AR conditions. The text types employed for these tasks differed depending on the reading condition. For instance, if a child was provided fictional text in the AR condition, non-fictional text was presented in the R condition, and vice versa. These combinations of text types and reading conditions were randomly assigned to participants.

As a result, the initial total sample size amounted to 634 participants. However, due to missing values, attributed to calibration issues or fatigue, a total of 65 samples were excluded from the analysis. The participants' characteristics are presented in Table 1.

Table 1. Participants' characteristics. Values are presented as mean (SD). R: reading-only; AR: audio-assisted reading.

Grade	Reading Condition	Text Type	N	Age (Months)	Non-Verbal Intelligence [1]	Receptive Vocabulary [2]	Expressive Vocabulary [2]
1	R	Fiction	26 (M = 13, F = 13)	81.38 (3.61)	118.47 (13.31)	86.92 (18.06)	84.69 (19.52)
		Non-fiction	12 (M = 2, F = 10)	81.25 (3.36)	115.00 (21.79)	80.25 (13.53)	83.42 (12.60)
	AR	Fiction	11 (M = 1, F = 10)	81.73 (3.07)	115.25 (23.29)	80.64 (14.12)	83.09 (13.16)
		Non-fiction	27 (M = 13, F = 14)	81.33 (3.55)	118.47 (13.31)	87.19 (17.77)	84.44 (19.18)

Table 1. *Cont.*

Grade	Reading Condition	Text Type	N	Age (Months)	Non-Verbal Intelligence [1]	Receptive Vocabulary [2]	Expressive Vocabulary [2]
2	R	Fiction	26 (M = 11, F = 15)	94.23 (3.41)	120.00 (14.65)	104.50 (16.96)	98.50 (15.69)
		Non-fiction	26 (M = 12, F = 14)	94.54 (3.54)	120.22 (14.75)	97.50 (13.98)	95.46 (9.31)
	AR	Fiction	28 (M = 16, F = 12)	94.21 (3.52)	119.13 (14.99)	96.64 (13.93)	94.82 (8.97)
		Non-fiction	27 (M = 15, F = 12)	94.37 (3.58)	120.06 (13.79)	103.37 (17.31)	97.26 (15.41)
3	R	Fiction	22 (M = 13, F = 9)	108.82 (4.41)	123.45 (12.47)	123.18 (19.08)	117.59 (19.43)
		Non-fiction	29 (M = 15, F = 14)	107.52 (3.14)	123.32 (14.47)	118.14 (16.43)	116.97 (19.93)
	AR	Fiction	27 (M = 13, F = 14)	108.00 (3.26)	123.04 (13.47)	120.26 (16.74)	117.74 (19.61)
		Non-fiction	21 (M = 13, F = 8)	108.95 (4.48)	122.71 (12.28)	123.81 (19.32)	117.57 (19.91)
4	R	Fiction	34 (M = 20, F = 14)	119.94 (3.08)	122.15 (11.49)	131.09 (16.66)	130.24 (21.26)
		Non-fiction	26 (M = 14, F = 12)	119.46 (3.52)	121.00 (10.89)	133.81 (15.15)	136.08 (20.56)
	AR	Fiction	24 (M = 13, F = 11)	119.13 (3.38)	120.65 (11.16)	133.63 (15.31)	137.67 (20.62)
		Non-fiction	32 (M = 18, F = 14)	119.91 (3.16)	121.84 (11.66)	130.50 (16.66)	129.78 (21.39)
5	R	Fiction	25 (M = 14, F = 11)	132.32 (2.64)	119.64 (11.38)	148.48 (17.70)	149.56 (16.73)
		Non-fiction	19 (M = 9, F = 10)	133.89 (3.21)	121.00 (14.64)	140.47 (16.90)	148.74 (16.10)
	AR	Fiction	20 (M = 10, F = 10)	133.85 (3.13)	121.16 (14.25)	141.10 (16.68)	149.65 (16.19)
		Non-fiction	25 (M = 14, F = 11)	132.20 (2.48)	119.08 (11.60)	147.76 (16.53)	151.68 (17.55)
6	R	Fiction	15 (M = 10, F = 5)	146.47 (3.48)	120.60 (8.34)	157.67 (16.38)	150.93 (14.38)
		Non-fiction	23 (M = 10, F = 13)	146.09 (4.61)	122.57 (11.59)	154.13 (12.04)	151.78 (12.07)
	AR	Fiction	29 (M = 14, F = 15)	146.28 (4.46)	124.07 (11.32)	154.38 (14.62)	151.31 (13.19)
		Non-fiction	15 (M = 10, F = 5)	146.47 (3.48)	120.60 (8.34)	157.67 (16.38)	150.93 (14.38)

[1] Standardized scores, assessed using the Korean Kaufman Brief Intelligence Test-2 [42], are presented. [2] Raw scores, assessed using the Receptive and Expressive Vocabulary Test [41], are presented.

2.2. Reading Tasks

Six different scripts were used for this study, including three fictional and three non-fictional texts, in order to prevent sharing information about the script among children, as all participants attended the same school. Scripts were randomly assigned to the participants. All participants were native Korean speakers, and all study materials were written and presented in the Korean language.

All scripts were composed by the researchers with reference to the list of recommended books for the first to second graders and were reviewed by a professor of communication disorders and six graduate students in the field of communication disorders. The

KReaD analysis [43], which gauges text difficulty and provides an objective reading level assessment, was performed for each script. The results showed that the fictional texts had a KReaD index of 2.78 grade level and the non-fictional texts had a KReaD index of 5.29 grade level. The length of scripts differed across text types, while the number of sentences within each text type remained consistent. For fictional texts, the average word counts were 803.67 words, with 801, 804, and 806 words for the respective texts, comprising a total of 73 sentences. The non-fictional texts had an average word count of 419.67 words, with 425, 420, and 414 words for each script, and consisted of 37 sentences. The scripts were displayed on a monitor equipped with an attached eye tracker. Each fictional text was divided into 11 slides, and the non-fictional texts were divided into 6 slides, with each slide containing 10 lines of text.

In the R condition, only visual scripts were provided, and the children were required to read the text silently on their own. The researchers observed the child's eye movements, and once they confirmed the completion of the reading, they manually advanced to the next slide. In the AR condition, participants were presented with both the visual script and auditory narration that simultaneously corresponded to the text. They were instructed to read the text while listening to the audio. Once the audio for the slide was complete, the next slide was automatically displayed along with the corresponding audio presentation. The audio files were recorded by a research assistant who held certification as a kindergarten teacher.

2.3. Reading Comprehension Tasks

Following reading or reading while listening to each text, the children were to answer questions about the text to assess their reading comprehension. One professor of communication disorders and six graduate students in communication disorders participated in the development and review of the reading comprehension questions. Additionally, two Level 1 speech-language pathologists evaluated the validity of the questions. If the validity score was 3 or lower on a 5-point scale, the corresponding question was replaced with an alternate question. Reading comprehension assessment questions, created as Microsoft Office PowerPoint files, were displayed on a computer or tablet screen. The researchers read the questions aloud from the screen, and the child verbally provided answers.

The reading comprehension questions encompassed 10 literal questions and 8–9 inferential questions for each text. All items were evaluated on a 2-point scale (0, 1 point) or a 3-point scale (0, 1, 2 points), depending on question complexity and structure. Regarding short-answer questions, 1 point was given if the answer precisely mentioned the relevant information. For open-ended questions, the score ranged from 0 to 2 points. When all contents of the answer were accurate, 2 points were awarded, and if only parts of them were included, 1 point was granted. Fictional texts were assigned a total of 34, 35, and 33 points, and non-fictional texts were scored out of 32, 31, and 32 points, respectively.

After the initial scoring, three research assistants conducted a reassessment of the entire dataset. An evaluation of inter-rater reliability was conducted among evaluators for a randomly selected 10% of the complete dataset, yielding a high level of reliability ($r = 0.98$).

2.4. Eye-Tracking Measurements

The eye-tracking device utilized in this study was the REDn Eye Scientific device, developed by SMI in Germany, with a sampling rate of 60 Hz, an accuracy of 0.4°, and a spatial resolution of 0.03°. The eye-tracking data of the participants during the reading tasks were recorded on a laptop equipped with SMI BeGaze 3.7, the data analysis software. To enhance the accuracy of data collection, all participants underwent calibration for five points on the monitor prior to beginning the task, ensuring that calibration values were within 0.6° before proceeding with the tasks.

Eye-tracking data analysis was conducted using SMI BeGaze 3.7 software. In the reading tasks, the sentences within the presented slide were designated as AOIs. Employing temporal and spatial eye-tracking variables, the gaze exploration processes and the cognitive processing of children during reading were examined [30]. Time-related variables included the total fixation duration (TFD) and average fixation duration (AFD) within the AOI. For a spatial-related variable, the scanpath length was utilized. Fixation refers to sustained gaze on an AOI for about 180–330 ms [44]. The TFD represents the total time (ms) that the AOI was fixated during the reading task, and the AFD is calculated by dividing the TFD within the AOI by the number of fixations. Scanpath length represents the sum of the lengths (in pixels) of gaze movement paths during the tasks, which encompass both progressive and regressive saccades. These fixation durations and scanpath lengths have been shown to be linked to the type of stimuli presented and an individual's reading proficiency [32,45,46].

2.5. Data Analysis

In order to minimize the potential influence of variations in content among different scripts, the average and standard deviation were computed for each group based on the text type and reading condition, and individual performance was then standardized using Z-scores.

Statistical analysis was conducted using *R* (version 4.3.0; R Core Team, 2023). A three-way analysis of variance (ANOVA) was conducted to investigate the differences in eye movement patterns (AFD, TFD, and scanpath length) according to age (first to sixth grades), reading conditions (R and AR), and text types (fictional and non-fictional). Moreover, forward stepwise multiple regression analysis was performed to investigate the eye movement factors that can predict children's literal and inferential comprehension under each reading condition when reading either fictional or non-fictional text, considering age as a controlled variable.

3. Results

This study aimed to explore the differences in eye movement patterns (AFD, TFD, and scanpath length) across age groups, reading conditions (AR and R), and text types (fictional and non-fictional). Furthermore, predictive models were developed to identify the eye movement variables that predict reading comprehension, both literal and inferential, and to investigate whether these predictors varied according to reading conditions and text types while controlling for age. Table 2 displays the reading comprehension performance and eye movement variables based on age, reading conditions, and text types.

Table 2. Descriptive statistics of literal and inferential comprehension and eye tracking variables. Values are presented as mean (SD). All scores are reported in Z-scores. R: reading-only; AR: audio-assisted reading; AFD: average fixation duration; TFD: total fixation duration.

Grade	Reading Condition	Text Type	Literal Comprehension	Inferential Comprehension	AFD	TFD	Scanpath Length
1	R	Fiction	−1.15 (1.31)	−1.21 (1.00)	0.70 (1.36)	0.66 (1.87)	0.20 (1.03)
		Non-fiction	−1.07 (1.36)	−1.30 (0.89)	0.32 (0.76)	0.29 (1.04)	0.40 (1.41)
	AR	Fiction	−0.64 (1.04)	−0.62 (1.07)	0.82 (1.25)	−0.31 (0.81)	−0.81 (1.20)
		Non-fiction	−1.03 (0.90)	−1.24 (0.81)	0.61 (1.13)	−0.13 (1.14)	−0.79 (0.66)
2	R	Fiction	0.23 (0.50)	−0.20 (0.95)	0.37 (1.27)	0.25 (0.80)	0.18 (0.83)
		Non-fiction	−0.75 (0.85)	−0.69 (0.90)	0.36 (1.30)	0.30 (1.08)	−0.06 (0.97)
	AR	Fiction	−0.34 (0.94)	−0.38 (0.97)	0.13 (1.01)	0.52 (1.01)	−0.38 (0.96)
		Non-fiction	−0.35 (0.82)	−0.42 (0.76)	0.13 (0.95)	−0.01 (0.92)	−0.36 (0.79)

Table 2. *Cont.*

Grade	Reading Condition	Text Type	Literal Comprehension	Inferential Comprehension	AFD	TFD	Scanpath Length
3	R	Fiction	0.26 (0.72)	0.25 (0.79)	0.02 (0.81)	−0.10 (0.75)	−0.14 (1.24)
		Non-fiction	0.20 (0.68)	0.27 (0.72)	−0.15 (0.64)	−0.06 (1.10)	−0.19 (1.04)
	AR	Fiction	0.25 (0.70)	0.25 (0.84)	−0.16 (0.87)	0.09 (0.93)	0.29 (0.82)
		Non-fiction	0.14 (0.74)	0.14 (0.63)	0.06 (0.77)	0.04 (0.89)	0.13 (0.83)
4	R	Fiction	0.39 (0.50)	0.62 (0.44)	−0.27 (0.61)	−0.35 (0.51)	−0.27 (0.96)
		Non-fiction	0.46 (0.57)	0.41 (0.58)	−0.19 (0.83)	−0.24 (0.84)	0.09 (0.98)
	AR	Fiction	0.31 (0.62)	0.46 (0.42)	−0.13 (0.78)	0.01 (0.79)	0.29 (0.73)
		Non-fiction	0.49 (0.56)	0.61 (0.47)	−0.35 (0.70)	0.12 (1.14)	0.41 (1.15)
5	R	Fiction	0.36 (0.65)	0.45 (0.60)	−0.55 (0.60)	−0.36 (0.68)	−0.14 (0.85)
		Non-fiction	0.40 (0.64)	0.59 (0.45)	−0.31 (0.60)	−0.21 (0.82)	0.06 (0.81)
	AR	Fiction	0.52 (0.31)	0.29 (0.61)	−0.03 (0.94)	−0.17 (1.11)	0.32 (0.68)
		Non-fiction	0.67 (0.47)	0.65 (0.46)	−0.41 (1.00)	−0.28 (0.89)	0.44 (0.95)
6	R	Fiction	0.49 (0.38)	0.58 (0.47)	−0.50 (0.49)	−0.23 (0.27)	−0.02 (0.97)
		Non-fiction	0.70 (0.44)	0.77 (0.32)	−0.38 (0.55)	−0.26 (0.70)	0.12 (0.84)
	AR	Fiction	0.42 (0.53)	0.57 (0.46)	−0.09 (0.95)	−0.12 (1.04)	0.13 (1.04)
		Non-fiction	0.68 (0.49)	0.83 (0.24)	−0.37 (0.62)	0.13 (0.83)	0.55 (0.90)

3.1. Comparison of Average Fixation Duration According to Age, Reading Conditions, and Text Types

A main effect of age on average fixation duration (AFD) was observed ($F(5, 545) = 14.976$, $p < 0.001$), with a trend towards shorter AFD among older students compared to younger students (see Figure 1). According to the subsequent Bonferroni post hoc test, in the R condition, age-related differences reached statistical significance only when participants were reading fictional text. Significant differences in AFD were observed between grade 1 and grade 4 ($p < 0.001$), grade 1 and grade 5 ($p < 0.001$), grade 1 and grade 6 ($p < 0.001$), as well as between grade 2 and grade 5 ($p = 0.005$) and grade 2 and grade 6 ($p = 0.047$). Within the AR condition, a significant difference in AFD between grade 1 and grade 3 was observed while reading fictional text ($p = 0.041$). When engaging with non-fictional text in the AR condition, significant differences in AFD emerged between grade 1 and grade 4 ($p < 0.001$), grade 1 and grade 5 ($p < 0.001$), and grade 1 and grade 6 ($p = 0.013$).

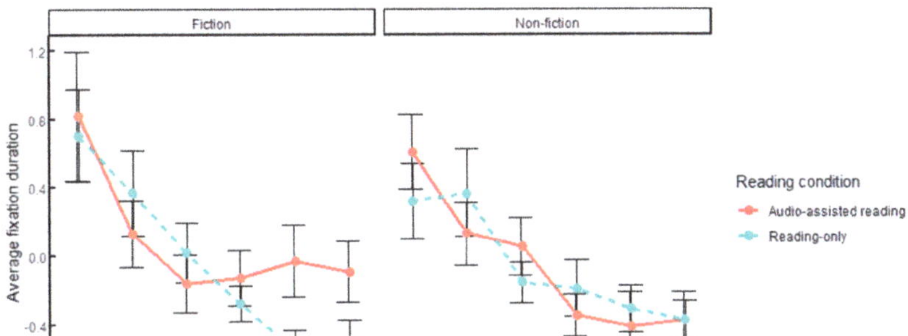

Figure 1. Average fixation duration in each reading condition when reading fictional and non-fictional text.

The results showed no significant main effects for reading condition ($F(1, 545) = 0.313$, $p = 0.576$) and text type ($F(1, 545) = 0.805$, $p = 0.370$). Additionally, no significant interactions were found between age and reading condition ($F(5, 545) = 0.925$, $p = 0.464$), age and text type ($F(5, 545) = 0.279$, $p = 0.925$), or reading condition and text type ($F(1, 545) = 0.700$, $p = 0.043$), and there was no three-way interaction found involving age, reading condition, and text type ($F(5, 545) = 0.989$, $p = 0.424$).

3.2. Comparison of Total Fixation Duration According to Age, Reading Conditions, and Text Types

A main effect of age ($F(5, 545) = 4.086$, $p = 0.001$), as well as an interaction effect between age and reading condition ($F(5, 545) = 2.638$, $p = 0.023$), on total fixation duration (TFD) were observed. A simple main effect test was administered, due to the significant interaction effect. The main effect of age was significant when reading fictional text under both R ($F(5, 545) = 5.22$, $p < 0.001$) and AR ($F(5, 545) = 2.77$, $p = 0.046$) conditions. Within the R condition, age-related differences were observed, showing a decline in TFD with an increase in age. Similarly, while reading fictional text, the AR condition exhibited these age-related differences, with the exception of the results from the first grade children, in which the shortest TFD was observed, deviating from the results for other age groups (see Figure 2). The Bonferroni post hoc test revealed significant differences in TFD between grade 1 and grade 4 ($p = 0.001$) and grade 1 and grade 5 ($p = 0.003$) in the R condition while reading fictional text. The interaction effect between age and reading condition was derived from the significant difference between R and AR conditions in the first grade, with the AR condition demonstrating lower TFD compared to the R condition ($p = 0.006$).

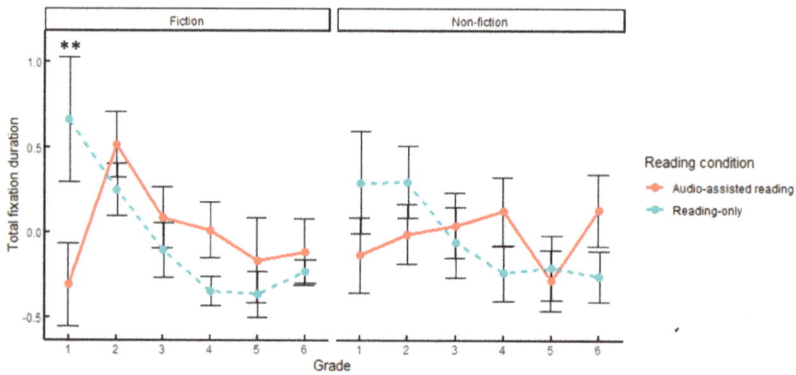

Figure 2. Total fixation duration in each reading condition when reading fictional and non-fictional text. ** $p < 0.01$.

The main effects of reading condition ($F(1, 545) = -0.527$, $p = 0.468$) and text type ($F(1, 545) = 0.054$, $p = 0.816$) were not significant. There were no significant two-way interactions between age and text type ($F(5, 545) = 0.497$, $p = 0.779$) and reading condition and text type ($F(1, 545) = 0.174$, $p = 0.677$), while a three-way interaction among age, reading condition, and text type ($F(5, 545) = 0.853$, $p = 0.513$) also failed to reach statistical significance.

3.3. Comparison of Scanpath Length According to Age, Reading Conditions, and Text Types

A three-way ANOVA revealed a significant main effect of age ($F(5, 545) = 3.286$, $p = 0.006$) and an interaction effect between age and reading condition ($F(5, 545) = 8.634$, $p < 0.001$) in regards to scanpath length. Subsequently, a simple main effect test was performed in response to the observed interaction effect. Irrespective of the text type, a significant main effect of age emerged within the AR condition (fictional text: $F(5, 545) = 4.38$, $p < 0.001$; non-fictional text: $F(5, 545) = 8.66$, $p < 0.001$). In the AR condition, there was a trend of escalating scanpath length as age increased, whereas this age-related tendency was absent within the R condition. Among younger children, the scanpath length was observed to be shorter in the AR condition in comparison to the R condition, regardless of the text type, which is deemed to contribute to the interaction effect between age and reading condition (See Figure 3). The Bonferroni post hoc test was conducted in order to examine the differences in scanpath length across age and reading conditions. Within the AR condition when reading fictional text, there were significant differences in scanpath length between grade 1 and grade 3 ($p = 0.017$), grade 1 and grade 4 ($p = 0.021$), and grade 1 and grade 5 ($p = 0.023$). In the context of non-fictional text under the AR condition, the scanpath length in grade 1 showed a significant difference compared to grade 3 ($p = 0.013$), grade 4 ($p < 0.001$), grade 5 ($p < 0.001$), and grade 6 ($p < 0.001$). Similarly, the scanpath length in grade 2 also exhibited a significant difference compared to grade 4 ($p = 0.027$), grade 5 ($p = 0.036$), and grade 6 ($p = 0.044$). When reading fictional text, significant differences in scanpath length between the R and AR conditions were observed in grade 1 ($p = 0.003$), grade 2 ($p = 0.031$), and grade 4 ($p = 0.025$). Regarding non-fictional text, however, it was only within grade 1 that the significant difference in scanpath length between the two conditions appeared ($p < 0.001$).

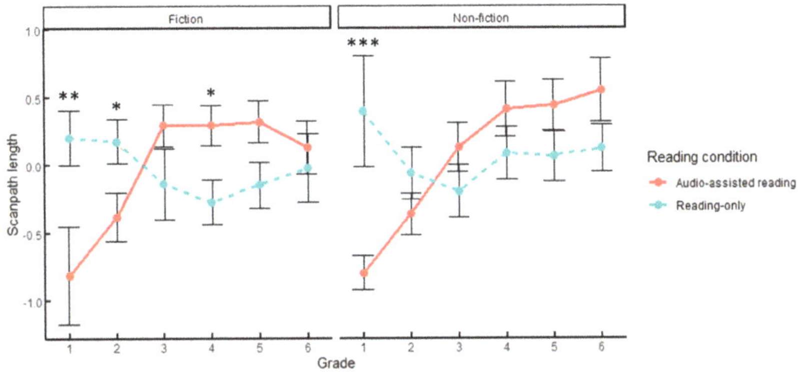

Figure 3. Scanpath length in each reading condition when reading fictional and non-fictional text. * $p < 0.05$; ** $p < 0.01$; *** $p < 0.001$.

Neither reading condition ($F(1, 545) = 0.409$, $p = 0.523$) nor text type ($F(1, 545) = 1.23$, $p = 0.268$) had any significant main effects on scanpath length. The two-way interaction effects between age and text type ($F(5, 545) = 0.78$, $p = 0.562$) and reading condition and text type ($F(1, 545) = 0.01$, $p = 0.919$), as well as a three-way interaction effect among age, reading condition, and text type, were not statistically significant.

3.4. Eye Movement Predictive Models for Reading Comprehension by Reading Conditions and Text Types

First, within the context of fictional reading under the R condition, a predictive model concerning literal comprehension exhibited a statistically significant explanation of 21% of the variance ($F(1, 146) = 40.66$, $p < 0.001$), with no inclusion of eye movement parameters. Only age significantly and positively influenced the variable ($\beta = 0.47$, $t(146) = 6.39$, $p < 0.001$). Regarding inferential comprehension, a predictive model significantly accounted for 37% of the variance ($F(2, 145) = 43.70$, $p < 0.001$). The model encompassed age ($\beta = 0.50$, $t(145) = 7.13$, $p < 0.001$) and TFD ($\beta = -0.22$, $t(145) = -3.21$, $p = 0.002$) as predictors. Both factors were statistically significant, with age displaying a positive and TFD exerting a negative effect on the inferential comprehension scores.

Second, under the R condition during non-fictional reading, a predictive model for literal comprehension significantly explained 37% of the variance ($F(3, 131) = 27.31$, $p < 0.001$). In this model, age ($\beta = 0.53$, $t(131) = 7.32$, $p < 0.001$) and AFD ($\beta = -0.19$, $t(131) = -2.63$, $p = 0.010$) emerged as significant predictors, while scanpath length ($\beta = 0.12$, $t(131) = 1.73$, $p = 0.086$) did not reach statistical significance. Age and scanpath length demonstrated positive associations with literal comprehension, whereas AFD showed a negative impact on the variable. A model predicting inferential comprehension accounted for 47% of the variance ($F(2, 132) = 59.56$, $p < 0.001$), wherein age and TFD appeared as significant factors. Age ($\beta = 0.61$, $t(132) = 9.50$, $p < 0.001$) exhibited a positive influence on the inferential comprehension scores, while the impact of TFD ($\beta = -0.21$, $t(132) = -3.24$, $p = 0.002$) on inferential comprehension was negative.

Next, within the AR condition, while reading fictional text, a predictive model that includes age and TFD significantly accounted for 22% of the variance in literal comprehension ($F(2, 136) = 20.96$, $p < 0.001$). Both age ($\beta = 0.46$, $t(136) = 6.13$, $p < 0.001$) and TFD ($\beta = 0.21$, $t(136) = 2.73$, $p = 0.007$) had a significant positive impact on literal comprehension. For inferential comprehension, on the other hand, a predictive model yielded a significant explanation of 25% of the variance ($F(3, 135) = 16.37$, $p < 0.001$). The variables encompassed in the model were age ($\beta = 0.39$, $t(135) = 5.08$, $p < 0.001$), scanpath length ($\beta = 0.15$, $t(135) = 1.81$, $p = 0.073$), and AFD ($\beta = -0.14$, $t(135) = -1.76$, $p = 0.081$). Age exhibited a significant positive influence on the inferential comprehension scores. Although scanpath length was also positively associated with inferential comprehension, this relationship did not reach statistical significance. AFD negatively affected inferential comprehension, but this effect did not attain statistical significance.

Finally, considering literal comprehension under the AR condition while engaging with non-fictional text, a predictive model significantly explained 45% of the variance, with all three eye movement parameters involved ($F(4, 142) = 30.75$, $p < 0.001$). Age ($\beta = 0.55$, $t(142) = 7.62$, $p < 0.001$) and TFD ($\beta = 0.14$, $t(142) = 2.06$, $p = 0.041$) significantly and positively affected literal comprehension. Scanpath length ($\beta = 0.11$, $t(142) = 1.42$, $p = 0.159$) also displayed a positive impact on literal comprehension, but it was not statistically significant. AFD ($\beta = -0.13$, $t(142) = -1.72$, $p = 0.088$) had a non-significant negative impact on the literal comprehension scores. A model that predicts inferential comprehension included scanpath length and AFD, significantly accounting for 56% of the variance ($F(3, 143) = 63.34$, $p < 0.001$). Age ($\beta = 0.61$, $t(143) = 9.60$, $p < 0.001$) and scanpath length ($\beta = 0.15$, $t(143) = 2.27$, $p = 0.025$) exhibited a positive and significant impact on inferential comprehension, while AFD ($\beta = -0.12$, $t(143) = -1.89$, $p = 0.061$) had a negative and non-significant impact.

The predictive models for literal and inferential comprehension according to reading conditions and text types are presented in Table 3.

Table 3. Eye movement predictive models for reading comprehension in each reading condition and text type. R: reading-only; AR: audio-assisted reading; F: fiction; NF: non-fiction; TFD: total fixation duration; AFD: average fixation duration.

	Dependent Variables	Predictors	β	Std. β	t	p	R^2	Adj. R^2
R_F	Literal comprehension	Age	0.20	0.47	6.39	<0.001	0.22	0.21
	Inferential comprehension	Age	0.02	0.50	7.13	<0.001	0.38	0.37
		TFD	−0.21	−0.22	−3.21	0.002		
R_NF	Literal comprehension	Age	0.02	0.53	7.32	<0.001	0.38	0.37
		AFD	−0.21	−0.19	−2.63	0.010		
		Scanpath length	0.12	0.12	1.73	0.086		
	Inferential comprehension	Age	0.03	0.61	9.50	<0.001	0.47	0.47
		TFD	−0.20	−0.21	−3.24	0.002		
AR_F	Literal comprehension	Age	0.02	0.46	6.13	<0.001	0.24	0.22
		TFD	0.16	0.21	2.73	0.007		
	Inferential comprehension	Age	0.02	0.39	5.08	<0.001	0.27	0.25
		Scanpath length	0.13	0.15	1.81	0.073		
		AFD	−0.12	−0.14	−1.76	0.081		
AR_NF	Literal comprehension	Age	0.02	0.55	7.62	<0.001	0.46	0.45
		Scanpath length	0.10	0.11	1.42	0.159		
		TFD	0.13	0.14	2.06	0.041		
		AFD	−0.13	−0.13	−1.72	0.088		
	Inferential comprehension	Age	0.03	0.61	9.60	<0.001	0.57	0.56
		Scanpath length	0.14	0.15	2.27	0.025		
		AFD	−0.12	−0.12	−1.89	0.061		

4. Discussion

The study aimed to examine the effects of reading conditions—audio-assisted reading and reading only—in fictional and non-fictional texts on 6- to 12-year-old elementary school students' eye movement patterns and their literal and inferential comprehension.

4.1. The Impact of Reading Condition and Text Type on Eye Movement Patterns across Age Groups

First, the AFD, which indicates the speed at which a reader processes a word or a semantic chunk, was analyzed based on age, reading conditions, and text types. The main effect of age showed that, regardless of the reading condition and text type, in general, AFD decreased as age increased. This aligns with the results of previous studies that have explored the relationship between age and fixation duration [47,48].

Results from the Bonferroni post hoc test, which examined differences in AFD across age, revealed variations depending on reading condition and text type. Age differences in AFD were prominent in the R condition when reading fictional text. When it comes to fictional text, older children tend to quickly extract essential information from the text, while younger children take their time in word reading, including decoding and the interpretation of the information, and read the text attentively when asked to read on their own. The reduced age-related gaps in AFD when reading non-fictional text show that older children invest more time and attention to challenging text with complicated sentence structures, while younger children may employ a different approach to processing such text. These findings are consistent with prior research suggesting that text type and difficulty can affect readers' AFD [49].

Unlike the R condition, under the AR condition, the impact of age was pronounced when reading non-fictional text. Despite not reaching statistical significance, the AFD for older children under the AR condition appeared to be longer than that under the R condition for fictional reading, while the contrast was negligible when reading non-fictional text. When provided with audio assistance for reading fictional text, which is typically an easier and more comprehensible text, older children seem to somewhat synchronize their reading pace with the auditory narration while maintaining their own pace. This reading strategy becomes noticeable from the third grade onward, as indicated by the emergence of a plateau at that point. However, when reading non-fictional text, older children in grades 4 to 6 adopt a faster reading strategy to enhance their comprehension.

Second, there is a general decrease in overall TFD with age in both text types, as evidenced by the main effect of age. However, the significance was only exhibited in fictional reading. TFD reflects the time a reader dedicates to comprehensively engaging with the entire text. This age-related trend explains the development of reading fluency as a child grows older [48], and this effect is particularly notable during the reading of fictional text. Furthermore, an interaction effect between age and reading condition was observed, attributed to the substantial drop in TFD observed in grade 1 under the AR condition, unlike the extended TFD observed in the R condition, which could potentially stem from different strategies used by children across age, depending on the reading modalities.

In the R condition, TFD tends to decrease with age, irrespective of text type, but the age effect was significant only when reading fictional text. This effect arises due to the reduced TFD among the first graders when engaging with non-fictional text. Typically, when readers encounter difficult text, there is a tendency for the TFD to rise [25]. However, in the case of young children, text covering unfamiliar topics may affect their focus on the text, potentially leading to a decrease in TFD.

While under the AR condition, the trend of decreasing TFD with age was observed in fictional reading, similar to that observed for the R condition, the TFD for grade 1 children was the shortest among all age groups, and the difference between two reading conditions among first graders was significant. This suggests that first graders actively take advantage of audio assistance during fictional reading. Children in other age groups appear to utilize a combination of visual and audio stimuli, either aligning their reading speed with the speed of audio narration or pacing themselves at a preferable speed.

However, in the case of non-fictional reading under the AR condition, there was no significant change in TFD with age, and it appears to remain relatively constant across different age groups. Given the observed decrease in AFD among older children in the same condition, it can be inferred that older children might engage in repetitive sentence reading while simultaneously listening to the audio. The fact that there were no age-related differences in TFD during non-fictional reading under the AR condition, and that there was no discernible drop causing a significant difference between reading conditions in this context, unlike that observed in fictional reading, implies that younger children maintained their attention throughout the whole text to the same degree as the older children. This finding supports the positive impact of audio assistance on comprehension among young children in regards to reading non-fiction, as revealed by Chung et al. [29].

Finally, scanpath length was analyzed under the AR and R conditions while reading fictional or non-fictional text. The main effect of age was significant under the AR condition, regardless of the text type, with the scanpath length increasing as age increased. In addition, an interaction effect between age and reading condition emerged due to the difference in scanpath length between the AR and R conditions among first and second graders during fictional reading, as well as among first graders during non-fictional reading.

Under the R condition, the scanpath length generally remains consistent across age, with the exception of a slight increases observed among first- and second-grade children in fictional reading, as well as first-grade children in non-fictional reading. Even though these increases did not achieve statistical significance, the extended scanpath length could suggest a need to revisit the previously read text for better comprehension. Decreased AFD in the first graders under the R condition while reading non-fiction may be attributed to their tendency to read words or chunks quickly and to revisit the information previously read in the text. In both fictional and non-fictional reading, first and second graders exhibited longer scanpaths under the R condition than when under the AR condition, and the differences were significant among the first graders during both fictional and non-fictional reading, as well as among the second graders during fictional reading. Younger children more frequently return to the text they have previously read when reading on their own, compared to when they are aided by the audio device.

On the other hand, in the AR condition, there was a trend of increasing scanpath length with age, and this difference across age was apparent during non-fictional reading. The shorter scanpath length among younger children might indicate a preference for utilizing audio assistance or a potentially prolonged word-reading duration that hinders them from covering the complete text. However, the latter possibility can be ruled out, considering that their AFD was not significantly longer under the AR condition. Therefore, it can be inferred that younger, less experienced readers are more inclined to extract information from audio sources rather than the text itself. In contrast, older students exhibit a tendency to engage in repeated back-and-forth reading of the text while simultaneously listening to the audio. This suggests that, under the AR condition, older and more proficient readers read at their preferred pace and revisit the same text multiple times as necessary. This could involve revisiting information they consider important, as well as information presented in the audio, or both. This strategy of repetitive reading is more frequently employed when reading non-fictional text. Similar to the AFD pattern, a plateau is observed from grade 3 onward during fictional reading, whereas the scanpath length continues to increase with age during non-fictional reading. When facing easy and predictable text, such as fiction, skilled readers refrain from allocating excessive attention and effort to repetitive reading. However, when it comes to non-fiction, they often invest more energy in the text by adopting a repeated reading approach.

4.2. Eye Movement Predictive Models for Literal and Inferential Comprehension

When reading fictional text under the R condition, the only significant predictor for literal comprehension was age. However, for inferential comprehension, a shorter TFD emerged as a significant predictor for better performance. These results imply that children tend to naturally develop the ability to understand fictional stories at a literal level as they mature [27], while advancing to inferential comprehension demands more fluent and efficient reading. This difference can be elucidated by the fact that inferential comprehension is based on successful literal comprehension. Proficient readers with greater efficiency possess the cognitive capacity, after understanding the factual events in the text, to engage in critical thinking by integrating background knowledge. This skill is crucial for successful inferential comprehension, extending beyond merely comprehending the factual events in the text [28].

Under the AR condition when reading fictional text, the incorporation of TFD in the predictive model for literal comprehension indicates that allocating additional time to the entire text leads to improved literal comprehension. Regarding inferential comprehension, although it did not reach statistical significance, a longer scanpath length and a shorter AFD were associated with enhanced performance, suggesting that implementing the strategy of repeated reading may contribute to better inferential comprehension.

The predictive model for the literal comprehension of non-fiction under the R condition appeared to be different from that for fictional reading. It included AFD as the significant predictor, alongside scanpath length. This indicates that comprehending non-fictional texts, even at a literal level, requires both efficient and repetitive reading of the text. Processing information promptly remains essential for inferential comprehension in this context as well, as evidenced by TFD emerging as a significant predictor in the model. The pattern showing that shorter temporal factors of eye movements have a positive impact on comprehension in general under the R condition is consistent with the observed negative correlations between TFDs and story comprehension in the work of Park et al. [37].

While reading non-fiction under the AR condition, an increase in TFD, longer scanpath length, and a decreased AFD were associated with improved literal comprehension. Under the AR condition, non-fictional reading, like fictional reading, requires comprehensive engagement with the entire text. Additionally, it necessitates the strategic use of repetitive reading while efficiently extracting information within a single gaze. Similarly, longer scanpaths and a shorter AFD were linked to better inferential comprehension. As with fictional reading in the same reading condition, the practice of repetitive reading plays a crucial role in achieving improved inferential comprehension. The emergence of scanpath length and TFD as factors that positively impact comprehension under the AR condition aligns with the results found in the work of Park et al. [37].

4.3. Research Limitations and Further Investigations

While it is acknowledged that there is an inherent difference in text difficulty and topic between fictional and non-fictional texts, the disparity in reading difficulty levels between the two text types used in this study was substantial. Additionally, there were differences in text length between the two text types. Therefore, it is possible that the observed differences between text types may not be solely attributable to the nature of the texts themselves.

This study primarily focused on reading behaviors in elementary school children, employing identical texts across all age groups. Although this approach facilitated an exploration of age-related variations in reading strategies, a ceiling effect in which older children demonstrated comparable eye movement patterns was observed. Thus, the generalizability of these findings to older or more advanced readers may be limited. Further research should consider examining proficient readers engaging with age-appropriate texts.

The current study only analyzed the behavioral aspects of reading, including voluntary eye movement patterns and reading comprehension scores, in typically developing children. Regarding ocular following responses (OFRs), prior research has revealed that there are no age-related differences in non-voluntary eye movements [50]. Moreover, when comparing preterm children with their peers with dyslexia in the fourth and fifth grades, they showed similar performance in reading comprehension, despite differences in eye movement patterns [51]. Examining both voluntary eye movements and non-voluntary eye movements during reading across children of various age groups, including those with developmental disorders, and assessing their language and higher-older cognition skills that support reading comprehension [7], can enhance understanding of the cognitive mechanisms at play in reading.

The texts used in this study were composed in the participants' native language. Previous research investigating reading processing in adult L1 readers, as well as adult and child L2 learners, has shown that a longer time spent reading is associated with poor comprehension in adult L1 readers. In contrast, extended reading time is linked to improved comprehension for adult L2 readers, and no relationship between eye movements and reading comprehension was observed in child L2 readers [52]. These findings suggest that the results may differ when applied to L2 learners. Therefore, it is recommended that future studies delve into the eye movements and reading performance of L2 learners across various age groups and reading proficiency levels, which could offer valuable insights into the relevance and applicability of the findings in this study in diverse linguistic and educational contexts.

5. Conclusions

The purpose of this study was to identify eye movement patterns in elementary school children under reading-only and audio-assisted reading conditions while reading fictional or non-fictional text, as well as to investigate how these eye movement patterns within each condition, when involved with different text types, affect their literal and inferential reading comprehension.

In general, regardless of reading condition or type of text being read, there is a consistent decrease in average fixation duration as children mature, which serves as an indicator of the development of the ability to read more swiftly over time. However, older and more experienced readers, when encountering easier text such as fiction accompanied by audio assistance, tend to adopt a more relaxed reading pace. The trend of decreasing total fixation duration with age is predominantly observed during fictional reading. Nevertheless, when reading fictional text under the audio-assisted reading condition, a drop in total fixation duration is observed among the first graders. This phenomenon could be due to their preference for extracting information through audio assistance. Scanpath length exhibits a tendency to increase with age under the audio-assisted reading condition, which is different from the pattern observed in the reading-only condition. This implies that as children's reading skills improve, older individuals tend to employ a strategy of rapidly absorbing information from the text while concurrently revisiting it with the assistance of audio. Similar to the results for average fixation duration, however, this increase plateaus beyond the third grade when reading fictional text, indicating that extensive repeated reading is not considered crucial for older children within this context. These findings underscore that younger and older elementary school children employ different reading strategies based on reading modalities and types of text. Younger children appear to lean toward audio narration assistance under the audio-assisted reading condition, while older children opt for a strategy of rapid and repetitive reading. This preference for audio assistance over text among younger children is more evident in fictional reading compared to non-fictional reading, and older children's attentive and repeated reading under the audio-assisted reading condition is more prominent in regards to non-fiction compared to fiction.

Under the reading-only condition, while children acquire skills to understand literal events in fictional text as they grow up, attaining enhanced inferential comprehension of the text requires additional development of rapid and efficient reading abilities. When reading non-fictional text, achieving even literal comprehension calls for efficient reading combined with the revisiting of important information. Furthermore, attaining inferential comprehension in non-fictional text requires quick processing of written information. When audio assistance is provided during fictional reading, devoting sufficient time throughout the text can be adequate for literal comprehension. However, when aiming to comprehend inferential meaning, an efficient and repetitive reading approach becomes essential. Similarly, when reading non-fictional text under the audio-assisted reading condition, both literal and inferential comprehension benefit from reading rapidly and repeatedly.

In order to improve reading comprehension, it is necessary to provide appropriate types of text, along with visual and/or auditory stimuli, taking into consideration the age and reading proficiency of children. The findings of this study could be beneficial for reading instruction among younger children with developing reading skills, as well as for guiding reading strategies among older children.

Author Contributions: Conceptualization, D.Y. and W.-J.K.; methodology, D.Y. and W.-J.K.; software, D.Y. and W.-J.K.; validation, D.Y. and W.-J.K.; formal analysis, W.-J.K.; investigation, W.-J.K., S.R.Y., S.N. and Y.L.; resources, D.Y.; data curation, W.-J.K., S.R.Y., and S.N.; writing—original draft preparation, W.-J.K., S.R.Y., S.N. and Y.L.; writing—review and editing, W.-J.K., S.R.Y. and D.Y.; visualization, W.-J.K.; supervision, D.Y.; project administration, D.Y.; funding acquisition, D.Y. All authors have read and agreed to the published version of the manuscript.

Funding: This research was funded by the Ministry of Science and ICT of the Republic of Korea and the National Research Foundation of Korea, NRF-2022R1A2C1005268.

Institutional Review Board Statement: Not applicable.

Informed Consent Statement: Informed consent was obtained from all subjects involved in the study.

Data Availability Statement: The data presented in the article are available on request from the corresponding author.

Acknowledgments: The authors extend their sincere gratitude to the members of the Child Language Lab at Ewha Womans University for their invaluable contributions and dedicated efforts towards this project.

Conflicts of Interest: The authors declare no conflict of interest.

References

1. Lerner, J.W. From theories to teaching strategies. In *Learning Disabilities: Theories, Diagnosis and Strategies*, 7th ed.; Houghton Mifflin: Boston, MA, USA, 2000; ISBN 978-061-822-405-0.
2. Palani, K.K. Promoting reading habits and creating literate society. *J. Arts Sci. Commer.* **2012**, *3*, 90–94.
3. Bouffard, T. A Developmental study of the relationship between reading development and the self-system. *Eur. J. Psychol. Educ.* **1998**, *13*, 61–74. [CrossRef]
4. Muhammet, B. The structural relationship of reading attitude, reading comprehension and academic achievement. *Int. J. Soc. Sci. Educ.* **2014**, *4*, 931–946.
5. Kamhi, A.G.; Catts, H.W. The language basis of reading: Implications for classification and treatment of children with reading disabilities. In *Speaking, Reading, and Writing in Children with Language Learning Disabilities: New Paradigms in Research and Practice*; Butler, K., Silliman, E., Eds.; Lawrence Erlbaum Associates: Mahwah, NJ, USA, 2002; pp. 45–72. ISBN 978-080-583-366-9.
6. Elleman, A.M.; Oslund, E.L. Reading comprehension research: Implications for practice and policy. *Policy Insights Behav. Brain Sci.* **2019**, *6*, 3–11. [CrossRef]
7. Kim, Y.-S.G. Hierarchical and dynamic relations of language and cognitive skills to reading comprehension: Testing the direct and indirect effects model of reading (DIER). *J. Educ. Psychol.* **2020**, *112*, 667–684. [CrossRef]
8. Kamagi, S. A study on students' ability in literal and inferential comprehension of English texts. *J. Int. Conf. Proc.* **2020**, *3*, 140–144. [CrossRef]
9. Juel, C.; Griffith, P.L.; Gough, P.B. Acquisition of literacy: A longitudinal study of children in first and second grade. *J. Educ. Psychol.* **1986**, *78*, 243–255. [CrossRef]
10. Florit, E.; Roch, M.; Levorato, M.C. Listening text comprehension of explicit and implicit information in preschoolers: The role of verbal and inferential skills. *Discourse Process.* **2011**, *48*, 119–138. [CrossRef]
11. Verhoeven, L.; van Leeuwe, J. Prediction of the development of reading comprehension: A longitudinal study. *Appl. Cogn. Psychol.* **2008**, *22*, 407–423. [CrossRef]
12. Pearson, P.D.; Gordon, C.; Hansen, J. The effect of background knowledge on young children's comprehension of explicit and implicit information. *J. Read. Behav.* **1979**, *11*, 201–209. [CrossRef]
13. Daneman, M.; Carpenter, P.A. Individual differences in working memory and reading. *J. Verbal Learn. Verbal Behav.* **1980**, *19*, 450–466. [CrossRef]
14. Lee, H.J. Listening comprehension ability of school-aged children with specific language impairment using narrative and expository texts. *J. Speech-Lang. Hear. Disord.* **2015**, *24*, 51–62. [CrossRef]

15. Wong, B.Y.L. Problems and issues in the definition of learning disabilities. In *Psychological and Educational Perspectives on Learning Disabilities*; Torgesen, J.K., Wong, B.Y.L., Eds.; Academic Press: Cambridge, MA, UA, 1986; pp. 1–26. ISBN 978-012-695-490-6.
16. Brown, R.; Waring, R.; Donkaewbua, S. Incidental vocabulary acquisition from reading, reading-while-listening, and listening to stories. *Read. A Foreign Lang.* **2008**, *20*, 136–163.
17. LaBerge, D.; Samuels, S.J. Toward a theory of automatic information processing in reading. *Cogn. Psychol.* **1974**, *6*, 293–323. [CrossRef]
18. Chang, A.C.-S.; Millett, S. Improving reading rates and comprehension through audio-assisted extensive reading for beginner learners. *System* **2015**, *52*, 91–102. [CrossRef]
19. Plass, J.L.; Moreno, R.; Brünken, R. Measuring cognitive load. In *Cognitive Load Theory*; Cambridge University Press: Cambridge, UK, 2010; pp. 181–202. ISBN 052-186-023-7.
20. Diao, Y.; Sweller, J. Redundancy in foreign language reading comprehension instruction: Concurrent written and spoken presentations. *Learn. Instr.* **2007**, *17*, 78–88. [CrossRef]
21. Berkowitz, S.; Taylor, B.M. The effects of text type and familiarity on the nature of information recalled by readers. In *Directions in Reading: Research and Instruction*; Pearson, D., Ed.; International Reading Association: Newark, DE, USA, 1981; pp. 157–161.
22. Lehto, J.E.; Anttila, M. Listening comprehension in primary level grades two, four and six. *Scand. J. Educ. Res.* **2003**, *47*, 133–143. [CrossRef]
23. Olson, M.W. Text type and reader ability: The effects on paraphrase and text-based inference questions. *J. Read. Behav.* **1985**, *17*, 199–214. [CrossRef]
24. Kim, E.S.; Hwang, B. The Effects of language intervention based on story grammar for comprehension of written stories in children with intellectual disabilities. *J. Speech-Lang. Hear. Disord.* **2011**, *20*, 89–104. [CrossRef]
25. Bensoussan, M. EFL reading as seen through translation and discourse analysis: Narrative vs. expository texts. *Engl. Specif. Purp.* **1990**, *9*, 49–66. [CrossRef]
26. Sáenz, L.M.; Fuchs, L.S. Examining the reading difficulty of secondary students with Learning Disabilities. *Remedial Spec. Educ.* **2002**, *23*, 31–41. [CrossRef]
27. Graesser, A.; Golding, J.; Long, D.L. Narrative representation and comprehension. In *Handbook of Reading Research*; Barr, R., Kamil, M.L., Mosenthal, P., Pearson, P.D., Eds.; Erlbaum: Mahwah, NJ, USA, 1991; Volume 2, pp. 171–205. ISBN 978-080-585-342-1.
28. McNamara, D.S.; Levinstein, I.B.; Boonthum, C. ISTART: Interactive strategy training for active reading and thinking. *Behav. Res. Methods Instrum. Comput.* **2004**, *36*, 222–233. [CrossRef]
29. Chung, H.E.; Song, H.S.; Cho, Y.R.; Oh, Y.R.; Kim, A.Y.; Joo, H.J.; Yim, D. Story comprehension skills of school-aged children by passage type and question type according to story conditions. *J. Speech-Lang. Hear. Disord.* **2023**, *32*, 49–60. [CrossRef]
30. Lai, M.-L.; Tsai, M.-J.; Yang, F.-Y.; Hsu, C.-Y.; Liu, T.-C.; Lee, S.W.-Y.; Lee, M.-H.; Chiou, G.-L.; Liang, J.-C.; Tsai, C.-C. A review of using eye-tracking technology in exploring learning from 2000 to 2012. *Educ. Res. Rev.* **2013**, *10*, 90–115. [CrossRef]
31. Just, M.A.; Carpenter, P.A. A theory of reading: From eye fixations to comprehension. *Psychol. Rev.* **1980**, *87*, 329–354. [CrossRef]
32. Rayner, K. Eye movements in reading and information processing: 20 years of research. *Psychol. Bull.* **1998**, *124*, 372–422. [CrossRef] [PubMed]
33. Rayner, K. Understanding eye movements in reading. *Sci. Stud. Read.* **1997**, *1*, 317–339. [CrossRef]
34. Rayner, K.; Ardoin, S.P.; Binder, K.S. Children's eye movements in reading: A commentary. *Sch. Psychol. Rev.* **2013**, *42*, 223–233. [CrossRef]
35. Rayner, K. Eye movements and the perceptual span in beginning and skilled readers. *J. Exp. Child Psychol.* **1986**, *41*, 211–236. [CrossRef]
36. Parshina, O.; Lopukhina, A.; Goldina, S.; Iskra, E.; Serebryakova, M.; Vladislava, S.; Zdorova, N.; Dragoy, O. Global reading processes in children with high risk of dyslexia: A scanpath analysis. *Ann. Dyslexia* **2022**, *72*, 403–425. [CrossRef]
37. Conklin, K.; Alotaibi, S.; Pellicer-Sánchez, A.; Vilkaitė-Lozdienė, L. What eye-tracking tells us about reading-only and reading-while-listening in a First and Second Language. *Second. Lang. Res.* **2020**, *36*, 257–276. [CrossRef]
38. Park, W.J.; Yang, Y.; Jeong, E.; Kim, A.; Yim, D. Correlation analysis between eye movement patterns and reading comprehension skills by reading condition in children with typical development and language impairment. *Commun. Sci. Disord.* **2023**, *28*, 39–51. [CrossRef]
39. Magyari, L.; Mangen, A.; Kuzmičová, A.; Jacobs, A.M.; Lüdtke, J. Eye movements and mental imagery during reading of literary texts with different narrative styles. *J. Eye Mov. Res.* **2020**, *13*. [CrossRef] [PubMed]
40. De Leeuw, L.; Segers, E.; Verhoeven, L. Role of text and student characteristics in real-time reading processes across the primary grades. *J. Res. Read.* **2015**, *39*, 389–408. [CrossRef]
41. Kim, Y.T.; Hong, G.H.; Kim, K.H.; Jang, H.S.; Lee, J.Y. *Receptive & Expressive Vocabulary Test (REVT)*; Seoul Community Rehabilitation Center: Seoul, Republic of Korea, 2009.
42. Moon, S.B. *Korean Kaufman Brief Intelligence Test*, 2nd ed.; Hakjisa Publisher: Seoul, Republic of Korea, 2020.
43. Cho, Y.G.; Lee, K.N. Development of the Korean language text analysis program (KReaD Index). *Korean Read. Res.* **2020**, *56*, 225–246.
44. Rayner, K. Eye movements in reading: Models and data. *J. Eye Mov. Res.* **2009**, *2*, 1–10. [CrossRef]
45. Rayner, K.; Pollatsek, A. *The Psychology of Reading*; Prentice-Hall: Hoboken, NJ, USA, 1989; ISBN 978-080-581-872-7.

46. Kliegl, R.; Grabner, E.; Rolfs, M.; Engbert, R. Length, frequency, and predictability effects of words on eye movements in reading. *Eur. J. Cogn. Psychol.* **2004**, *16*, 262–284. [CrossRef]
47. Lee, S.R.; Suh, H. The current status and perspectives of research on reading process using eye-tracker. *Korean Lang. Educ. Res.* **2013**, *46*, 479–503. [CrossRef]
48. Blythe, H.I. Developmental changes in eye movements and visual information encoding associated with learning to read. *Curr. Dir. Psychol. Sci.* **2014**, *23*, 201–207. [CrossRef]
49. Ko, S.R.; Yoon, N.Y. The characteristics of eye-movement in Korean sentence reading: Cluster length, word frequency, and landing position effects. *Korean J. Cogn. Sci.* **2007**, *18*, 325–350. [CrossRef]
50. Miladinović, A.; Quaia, C.; Ajčević, M.; Diplotti, L.; Cumming, B.G.; Pensiero, S.; Accardo, A. Ocular-following responses in school-age children. *PLoS ONE* **2022**, *17*, e0277443. [CrossRef] [PubMed]
51. Bonifacci, P.; Tobia, V.; Sansavini, A.; Guarini, A. Eye-movements in a text reading task: A comparison of preterm children. *Brain Sci.* **2023**, *13*, 425. [CrossRef] [PubMed]
52. Pellicer-Sánchez, A.; Tragant, E.; Conklin, K.; Rodgers, M.; Serrano, R.; Llanes, A. Young learners' processing of multimodal input and its impact on reading comprehension: An eye-tracking study. *Stud. Second. Lang. Acquis.* **2020**, *42*, 577–598. [CrossRef]

applied sciences

MDPI

Article

Exploring the Potential of Event Camera Imaging for Advancing Remote Pupil-Tracking Techniques

Dongwoo Kang [1], Youn Kyu Lee [2] and Jongwook Jeong [3,*]

1 School of Electronic and Electrical Engineering, Hongik University, Seoul 04066, Republic of Korea; dkang@hongik.ac.kr
2 Department of Computer Engineering, Hongik University, Seoul 04066, Republic of Korea; younkyul@hongik.ac.kr
3 Department of Computer Science and Artificial Intelligence, Jeonbuk National University, Jeonju 54896, Republic of Korea
* Correspondence: jwjeong55@jbnu.ac.kr

Abstract: Pupil tracking plays a crucial role in various applications, including human–computer interactions, biometric identification, and Autostereoscopic three-dimensional (3D) displays, such as augmented reality (AR) 3D head-up displays (HUDs). This study aims to explore and compare advancements in pupil-tracking techniques using event camera imaging. Event cameras, also known as neuromorphic cameras, offer unique benefits, such as high temporal resolution and low latency, making them well-suited for capturing fast eye movements. For our research, we selected fast classical machine-learning-based computer vision techniques to develop our remote pupil tracking using event camera images. Our proposed pupil tracker combines local binary-pattern-features-based eye–nose detection with the supervised-descent-method-based eye-nose alignment. We evaluate the performance of event-camera-based techniques in comparison to traditional frame-based approaches to assess their accuracy, robustness, and potential for real-time applications. Consequently, our event-camera-based pupil-tracking method achieved a detection accuracy of 98.1% and a tracking accuracy (pupil precision < 10 mm) of 80.9%. The findings of this study contribute to the field of pupil tracking by providing insights into the strengths and limitations of event camera imaging for accurate and efficient eye tracking.

Keywords: eye tracking; eye detection; event camera; dynamic vision sensor; system latency; Autostereoscopic 3D display; augmented reality; augmented reality 3D head-up display

1. Introduction

Pupil tracking is a fundamental task in computer vision, human–computer interactions, virtual reality (VR), and augmented reality (AR) display systems. It plays a crucial role in enabling various applications, including gaze estimation [1], attention tracking [2], biometric identification [3], and Autostereoscopic three-dimensional (3D) displays, such as AR 3D head-up displays (HUDs) [4]. Eye pupil tracking is also useful in psychology and medicine. Researchers have used it to identify conditions, like stress, by studying how the eyes move and other related body signals [5]. Extensive research has been conducted on head-mounted eye-pupil tracking, a close-range eye-tracking technology primarily designed for wearable devices [6–8]. Additionally, remote eye-tracking has also garnered significant attention in the research community. Remote pupil tracking enables the monitoring and analysis of eye movements from a distance without requiring any physical contact with the user. This non-intrusive technology finds applications in various fields, including human–computer interactions [9], psychological studies [10], Autostereoscopic 3D displays [11], and AR 3D HUDs in automobiles [4], offering valuable insights into users' visual attention and cognitive processes. The advancements in remote eye-tracking techniques have paved the way for more practical and non-intrusive implementations in real-world scenarios. While previous studies have extensively utilized traditional frame-based camera systems, sometimes with the integration of near-infrared (NIR) light, for remote pupil-tracking tasks [11,12], they inherently possess certain limitations, particularly in capturing fast and subtle eye movements that are vital for comprehending cognitive processes and human behavior.

Recently, the emergence of event camera imaging has piqued the interest of the computer vision community due to its unique capabilities for dynamic vision tasks. Event cameras asynchronously capture pixel-level intensity changes, or events, triggered by significant changes in the scene, such as motion. This novel sensing modality offers distinct advantages over conventional frame-based cameras, including a high temporal resolution, low latency, and low power consumption. These properties make event cameras highly attractive for capturing fast eye movements, such as rapid eye movements and subtle eye motions, which are often missed or blurred in frame-based systems [13]. One of the key characteristics of event cameras is their ability to represent motion through positive and negative pixel intensity changes. Positive events represent increases in intensity, while negative events signify decreases. As a result, event cameras provide a sparse representation of the scene, focusing solely on the changes occurring in the environment when motion occurs (Figure 1). This unique feature allows event cameras to excel in capturing dynamic scenes with reduced redundancy and minimized motion blur, making them particularly well-suited for tasks, like pupil tracking, where fast eye movements are critical for accurate analysis [13].

Figure 1. Examples of event camera imaging (**left**) capturing different levels of motion compared to frame-based Complementary Metal-Oxide-Semiconductor (CMOS) camera (**right**). The 1st row shows examples of minimal motion, the 2nd row shows subtle motion, and the 3rd row shows large motion with verifiable eye shape. As depicted in the examples, event cameras effectively capture the pixel-level intensity changes corresponding to motion, providing a clear representation of dynamic events and enhancing the accuracy of pupil-tracking algorithms.

In this paper, considering the potential of event camera imaging, we focus on developing remote pupil-tracking techniques using event cameras for Autostreoscopic 3D displays and AR 3D HUDs. Using knowledge from traditional frame-based eye-tracking, our primary goal is to assess the viability of pupil tracking using event cameras. By integrating event camera data with our previous frame-based methods [4,11], we emphasize the promise of event-camera-based tracking. Through this research, we explore the benefits, challenges, and limits of using event camera imaging for remote pupil tracking.

2. Proposed Method

In our previous work [4,11], we successfully developed an eye-tracking method designed for faces in diverse environments and user conditions. This method involved 11-point eye-nose shape tracking, which was based on the supervised descent method (SDM) [14] for non-occluded faces. Building on the success of our previous work that extensively employed machine-learning-based computer vision algorithms for pupil tracking, we now extend our approach to utilize the unique capabilities of event camera imaging. In this section, we describe how we adapt and apply our previously developed machine-learning-based algorithm to the context of event camera data. Specifically, we present the design of our novel pupil-tracking algorithm, which incorporates feature extraction, eye–nose detection, and alignment methods tailored specifically for event camera imaging. By building upon the principles established in frame-based eye-tracking research and combining them with the insights from our previous work on bare-face eye tracking, we aim to unlock the potential of event camera imaging for more sophisticated and effective pupil tracking. This novel approach holds promise for advancing eye-tracking technologies and expanding their applications in various real-world scenarios.

2.1. Event Camera Imaging

Event cameras stand out due to their asynchronous capture of events—instantaneous pixel intensity variations caused by scene changes. Their defining characteristics and suitability for eye-tracking applications are further detailed in this section.

The key characteristic of event cameras is their asynchronous operation, where they capture pixel-level intensity changes, known as "events," triggered by significant changes in the scene, such as motion. This unique sensing mechanism allows event cameras to react instantly to motion, leading to high temporal resolution and low latency. Unlike frame-based cameras that capture entire frames at fixed time intervals, event cameras produce events in real-time, providing a sparse and efficient representation of dynamic scenes. Another advantage of event cameras is their low power consumption. Traditional cameras often consume substantial power due to continuous image capture and processing, whereas event cameras only generate events when there is motion, significantly reducing power requirements. In terms of the data format, event cameras produce streams of events with precise timestamps, intensity changes, and corresponding pixel locations. This data format contrasts with conventional cameras, which produce sequences of static frames. Event camera data are highly suitable for capturing fast and subtle eye movements, such as rapid eye movements and subtle eye motions, which can be crucial for accurate eye tracking (Figure 2). By leveraging the unique capabilities of event camera imaging, we aim to enhance pupil-tracking performance, particularly in scenarios involving rapid eye movements and real-time applications.

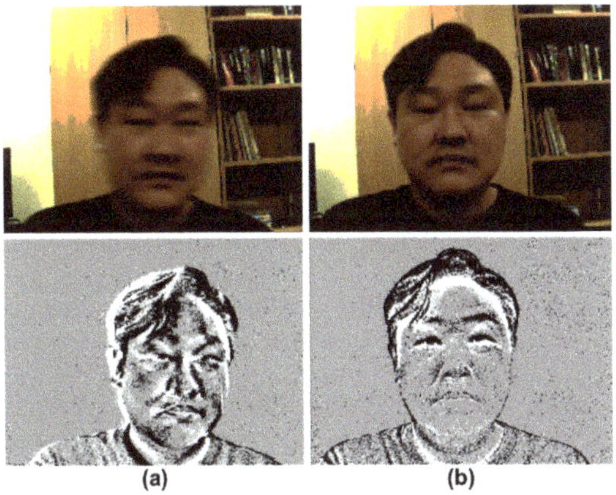

Figure 2. Illustration of the advantages of event cameras over conventional RGB-frame-based cameras. The 1st row shows examples of RGB-frame-based images, and the 2nd row shows corresponding images from the event camera images. (**a**) Rapid movement: while the RGB image shows motion blur due to swift movement, the event camera captures the eye's shape without any motion blur. (**b**) Quick eye movement: demonstrating the capability of the event camera to capture rapid eye movements. During a fast blink, the RGB image lags and still depicts the eye as closed, whereas the event camera swiftly captures the moment, revealing the actual open state of the eye during this time.

Figure 3 showcases the event camera used in our proposed method: the DAVIS 346 by Inivation [15]. This state-of-the-art event camera plays a crucial role in our research, enabling us to capture pixel-level intensity changes with exceptional precision. The DAVIS 346 event camera operates asynchronously, allowing it to respond instantaneously to motion events. Specifically, it processes a bandwidth of 12 million events per second, and its minimum latency is approximately 20 microseconds. Moreover, when converting these events for visualization purposes, they are typically aggregated to form event frames at a user-defined rate, similar to the event frame concept that accumulates events over a predefined interval to visualize them in a 2D image format. For our experiments, we chose to visualize these frames at 30 fps. The DAVIS 346 offers a resolution of 346 × 260 pixels, a dynamic range of 120 dB, minimum latency of 20 µs, and 180 mA power consumption at 5V DC. For our training and testing purposes, the images captured with the DAVIS 346 were resized to a resolution of 640 × 480 pixels to optimize the performance of our algorithms.

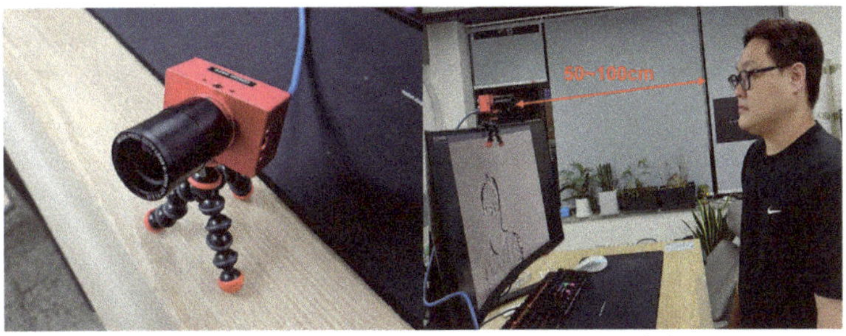

(**left**) (**right**)

Figure 3. The event camera used in our proposed method: Inivation's DAVIS 346 (**left**) [15]. The experimental setup for remote pupil tracking, demonstrating the distance range between the event camera imaging device and the user's face, spanning from 50 to 100 cm (**right**).

In addition to presenting the event camera itself, Figure 3 also illustrates the experimental setup we used for remote pupil tracking. The distance range between the event camera imaging device and the user's face spans from 50 to 100 cm. Designed for Autostereoscopic 3D PC displays and vehicular AR 3D HUD systems, this distance was selected to guarantee the best pupil-tracking results in these settings. In our evaluations, participants with eyeglasses posed no issues for our methodology; however, sunglasses that occlude the eyes were excluded. Our system, developed for both Autostereoscopic 3D displays and AR 3D HUDs and utilizing the high dynamic range of event cameras, is expected to function efficiently outdoors. Yet, direct outdoor evaluations were not part of this study. This setup ensures that we can efficiently monitor and analyze the eye movements from a certain distance without the need for physical contact with the user. The remote pupil-tracking approach offers non-intrusive and user-friendly eye-tracking solutions for various real-world scenarios. With the DAVIS 346 event camera's capabilities and the remote pupil tracking setup, we are well-equipped to explore the potential of event camera imaging for advanced pupil-tracking tasks. These features enable us to effectively capture and analyze eye movements, especially in challenging conditions, thereby paving the way for more accurate and efficient eye-tracking solutions.

2.2. Pupil-Tracking Algorithm

In our research, the creation of event frames is an important step. By accumulating events over a 33 ms interval, we translate this information into a visual format familiar to standard frame-based systems. The flowchart in Figure 4 starts with data from the event camera. These data are collected over the 33 ms period to form the event frame. Once the frame accumulates events for the set 33 ms interval, it is passed on to the next stage for processing. After forming the event frame, our method first identifies and localizes the eye–nose region within the frame. This detection step utilizes cascaded Adaboost classifiers with multi-block local binary patterns (LBPs) for the robust and efficient recognition of the eye region. Upon successful detection of the eye–nose region, our system activates the SDM-based eye–nose shape alignment. The next tracking checker block ensures that our tracking is maintained over consecutive frames and verifies the validity of the tracking. For the tracking checker, we utilize Scale-Invariant Feature Transform (SIFT) features extracted around 11 landmarks on bare faces and use a support vector machine (SVM) to ascertain the success of tracking. When the eye tracking fails, it restarts the detection mode, which scans the whole image to find the eye–nose area with a relatively lower speed (16 ms), compared to the tracking mode (5 ms), which utilized a small region of interest from the eye tracking success in the previous camera frame. Therefore, it is desirable to maintain the tracking mode at each frame without the execution of the detection module, in terms of the overall system latency. The above processes yield the final eye coordinates, allowing our system to effectively and efficiently track pupils in dynamic environments. The entire process, from event frame formulation to the extraction of the final eye coordinates, is illustrated in Figure 4.

We are expanding on the success of our previously developed eye-tracking method [4,11], which demonstrated effectiveness in diverse environmental settings and with different users. The foundation of our previous approach relied on 11-point eye–nose shape tracking, employing SIFT features [16], the SDM [14]. A concise list of the main features we employed includes the following: (1) 11-point eye-nose shape tracking—this technique selects the most significant landmark points within the entire facial structure, chosen specifically for their role in enhancing the accuracy of eye alignment, (2) SDM regression with the SIFT feature—optimized for central processing unit (CPU) efficiency; SDM uses a 4-stage regression to transition from an average to an optimal facial shape. SDM focuses on a series of descent directions to minimize non-linear square functions of landmarks. This regression-based approach not only reduces computational cost but also enhances the alignment accuracy, presenting shape alignment as an optimization task. We efficiently regress the initial pupil positions from the detected eye nose regions to their optimal pupil center positions, along with other eye–nose landmark points, enabling swift and accurate tracking. Given the demands of real-time applications and the challenges posed by various light conditions, eye occlusion, head movements, and limited computing resources, we opted for a comprehensive and efficient machine-learning-based computer vision approach. This approach includes utilizing the speed advantage of the SDM [14] and cascaded Adaboost classifiers [17,18] with multiblock LBP [19] for eye–nose region detection, offering a robust alternative to more computationally intensive methods.

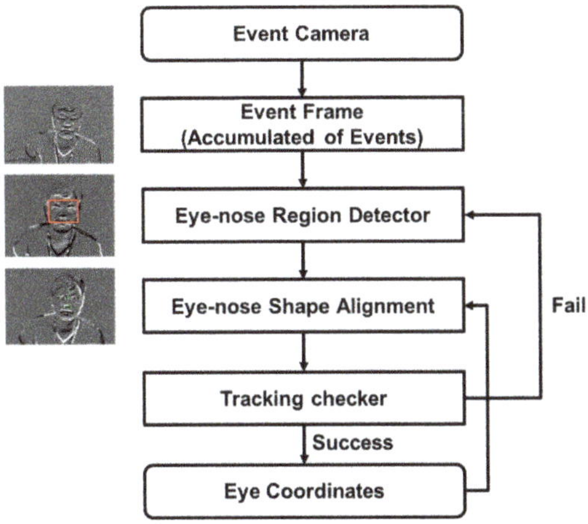

Figure 4. Flowchart of the proposed pupil-tracking method based on event camera imaging. This visual representation details the process, starting from event frame generation, moving to eye–nose detection and alignment, and ending with the tracking checker.

Furthermore, our previous studies [4,11] have demonstrated the substantial speed advantage of the SDM-based eye tracking method over various convolutional neural-network (CNN)-based algorithms. While CNNs exhibit remarkable performance in computer vision tasks, they often demand significant computational resources and result in longer processing times, making them less suitable for real-time applications. In contrast, our chosen approach, which utilized a multi-block LBP-based detector and SDM-based aligner, exhibited faster and more efficient performance, particularly on conventional CPUs in PCs or mobile tablets with limited graphic processing unit (GPU) resources [4,11]. The LBP-based detector enabled straightforward and practical eye–nose region detection, while the SDM-based aligner ensured accurate and real-time eye center position tracking. This capability was essential for capturing rapid eye movements during pupil-tracking tasks. Our previous studies [4,11] highlighted that the SDM-based eye tracking achieved an impressive speed of 4 ms per 640 by 480 image resolution with CPU usage. In comparison, various CNN-based algorithms, such as ESR (15 ms, CPU) [20], DVLN (15 ms, CPU) [21], and LAB (2.6 s, CPU) [22], required significantly more time under the same conditions. The superior speed and efficiency of our method make it highly suitable for real-time eye-tracking applications, especially when dealing with rapid eye movements, dynamic environments, and limited computing resources.

In the context of event camera imaging, we have adapted and applied our previously developed machine-learning-based computer vision algorithm for pupil tracking. Our new algorithm is specifically designed to work with event camera data and includes feature extraction, eye–nose detection, and alignment methods. By combining insights from frame-based eye-tracking research with our knowledge from bare-face eye tracking, our goal is to effectively utilize the unique capabilities of event camera imaging. The main components of our tracking system are divided into three stages: (1) eye–nose region detection from event camera images, which accumulate asynchronous events during a fixed time, (2) tracking the eye center position based on the detected eye–nose region, and (3) a tracker-checker for fast tracking. For eye–nose region detection, we employ the error-based learning (EBL) method [11], using cascaded Adaboost classifiers with multiblock LBP. This approach is designed to make optimal use of standard CPUs found in personal computers (PCs) or mobile tablets with limited GPU resources. Upon successful eye–nose region detection, the eye center position tracking mode is activated. We use a coarse-to-fine strategy to infer the pupil center location through the use of the SDM with SIFT features, followed by pupil position refinement through the pupil-segmentation module. The SDM-based shape alignments rely on 11 landmark points that cover the eyes and nose areas.

To enhance pupil-tracking performance using event cameras, we developed a specialized event camera image database (DB) and implemented efficient learning methods. The DB was created by capturing real-world videos using the DAVIS 346 event camera, and the videos were categorized into three motion levels as shown in Figure 1: minimal motion, subtle motion, and large motion with verifiable eye shape. For training the eye–nose region detector, we utilized images from both the subtle and large motion categories. We employed the EBL method to efficiently detect eye–nose regions from the event camera images. Typically, the EBL method, which is inherently iterative, progresses through three stages refining and reducing large datasets to essential samples. Due to the limited number of images available in the DB, we focused on the early and middle stages of the EBL training process, leaving out the final matured stage [11]. As for the eye–nose region aligner, we concentrated solely on the large motion category for training. The aligner needs to accurately handle eye shapes under significant motion, making the large motion DB more suitable for this purpose. The specialized event camera image DB played a crucial role in training both the eye–nose region detector and aligner. By incorporating distinct motion categories, we ensured that the algorithms could effectively adapt to different motion levels and diverse eye shapes encountered in real-world scenarios. As a result, while the performance may not be considered superior, our fine-tuned detector and aligner have shown great potential in leveraging event camera imaging for pupil tracking. Indeed, one of the most notable achievements of our event-camera-based pupil-tracking method is its ability to capture rapid eye movements that are challenging for traditional RGB-frame-based systems. The event camera's asynchronous operation and high temporal resolution allow it to detect and respond instantly to pixel-level intensity changes triggered by motion events. This unique sensing mechanism enables us to accurately track fast eye movements, which are often difficult for conventional frame-based cameras to capture.

3. Experimental Results

To evaluate the performance of event camera-based pupil tracking, we conducted comprehensive experiments using a diverse dataset that includes various eye movement scenarios and lighting conditions. We compared the results obtained from our proposed event-camera-based method with our previous frame-based eye-tracking algorithms [11]. The experimental results convincingly showcased the potential of event camera imaging in significantly enhancing the accuracy and robustness of pupil tracking, especially during rapid eye movements. Our proposed method was implemented using C^{++} and tested solely based on CPU computations on a Windows PC. Remarkably, the algorithms achieved an impressive speed of 200 frames per second at a 640×480 resolution with a 2.0 GHz CPU, showcasing their real-time capabilities and practical suitability for various applications. Table 1 summarizes the pupil-tracking specification. The eye–nose detection uses a cascaded Adaboost classifier combined with multiblock LBP, incorporating nine boosting substages. For pupil localization, the aligner adopts an SDM-based 11-point eye–nose-alignment technique that integrates SIFT features through a 4-step regression. These predefined 11 points include the left eye's outer and inner corners, its center; the right eye's outer and inner corners, its center; and the nasion, pronasale, left alare, subnasale, and right alare. We assessed the precision of our algorithm by computing the disparity between the ground truth and the tracked pupil centers. This method provides a direct quantitative measure of the algorithm's performance by identifying how closely our tracking aligns with known truth values. To relate these disparities to real-world measurements, we utilized the inter-pupil distance (IPD) as a reference. Assuming an IPD of 65 mm, which is a general average for adults, we converted pixel distances into physical distances, enabling us to accurately estimate the positions of the pupils in real-world units. Consequently, our event-camera-based pupil-tracking method achieved a detection accuracy of 98.1% and a tracking accuracy (pupil precision < 10 mm) of 80.9%. The detection accuracy was on par with existing RGB-frame-camera-based pupil-tracking methods, while the tracking accuracy, though slightly lower than frame-camera-based algorithms, proved reasonable and promising for an initial exploration of event-camera-based pupil tracking. A summary of these results is provided in Table 2.

Table 1. Pupil tracking specification.

Parameter	Details
Tracked Shape Points	11 Eye-nose Points (3 left eye, 3 right eye, 4 nose)
Distance between camera and users (cm)	50 to 100
Computing System	2.0 GHz CPU
Event Camera Model	DAVIS 346 (Inivation)
Event Camera Resolution	346 × 260 (resized to 640 × 480)
Event Camera Latency	20 μs
Event Frame Speed (event aggregation time)	30 fps

Table 2. Performance of the proposed event-camera-based pupil-tracking method. For a comparison, previous RGB-frame-camera-based method [11] performance is also shown.

Method	Light Condition	Detection Accuracy	Tracking Accuracy (Pupil Precision < 10 mm)	Speed
Content-aware [11] (CIS RGB Camera)	Normal Light (100~400 lux)	99.4%	99.4%	200 fps (CPU)
Proposed Method	Normal Light (100~400 lux)	98.1%	80.9%	200 fps (CPU)

The dataset employed for our proposed method was thoughtfully constructed, consisting of real-world videos captured using the DAVIS 346 event camera. To train the eye–nose region detector, we used a combination of images from both the subtle and large motion categories of the event camera dataset. We efficiently detected eye–nose regions in the event camera images using the EBL method [11]. Due to the limited number of available images in the dataset, our focus was on the early and middle stages of the EBL training process, excluding the final matured stage. Specifically, the detector training incorporated 3608 event camera images along with 3949 negative non-face background images. For the eye–nose region aligner, we exclusively concentrated on the large motion category of the event camera dataset during training. The aligner's primary task was to accurately handle eye shapes under significant motion, making the large motion DB particularly well-suited for this purpose. The event camera alignment training comprised 2273 events with verifiable eye shape.

By constructing and utilizing this specialized event camera dataset, we ensured the algorithms' adaptability to challenging real-world scenarios involving various eye movements and head poses. The proposed algorithm was evaluated based on a video DB captured in a normal office environment with illumination ranging from 100 to 400 lux, using the DAVIS346 event camera. The DB consisted of videos categorized into three distinct motion levels, each having a verifiable eye shape. To assess the algorithm's performance, a test set comprising 474 face images with large movements was utilized. These rigorous tests allowed us to validate the algorithm's capabilities in handling real-world scenarios with different motion levels and lighting conditions, particularly emphasizing its proficiency in accurately tracking pupils during rapid eye movements (Figure 5). Table 3 provides a summary of the training and testing DBs used for the evaluation of our algorithm.

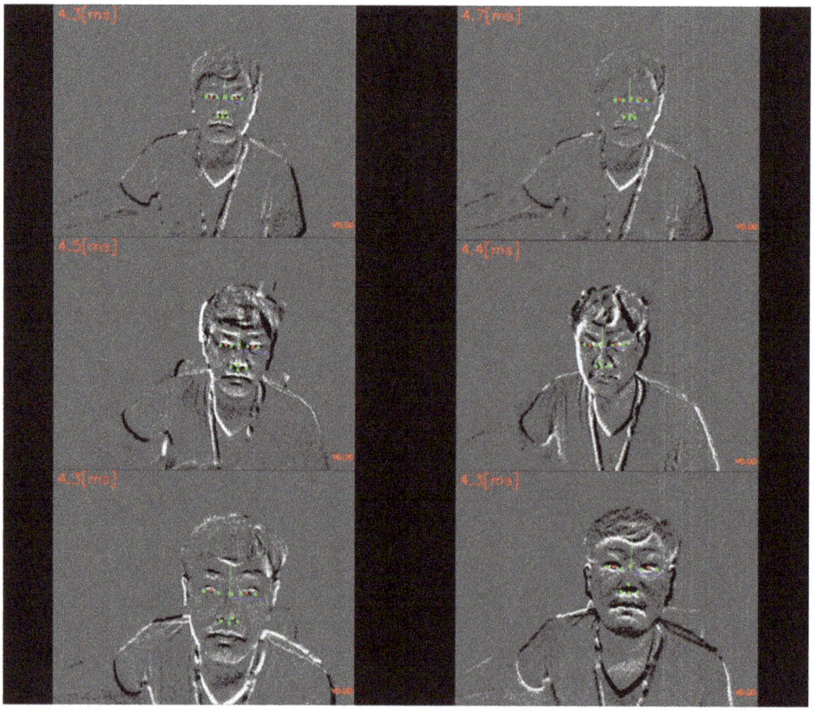

Figure 5. Experimental results obtained from event camera face images with verifiable eye shapes due to large movements. The pupil-tracking algorithm demonstrated successful performance across various face motions.

Table 3. Training and testing DB for the proposed event-camera-based pupil-tracking method.

Training DB (Detector)	DB Type	DB Number
Real Event Camera Images	Face Images with Subtle and Large Movement (Image with verifiable eye shape)	3608
	Non-face Background Images	3949
Training DB (Aligner)	DB Type	DB Number
Real Event Camera Images	Face Images with Large Movement (Image with verifiable eye shape)	2273
Test DB (Pupil Tracking)	DB Type	DB Number
Real Event Camera Images	Face Images with Large Movement (Image with verifiable eye shape)	474

4. Discussion

In this study, the primary objective was assessing how existing algorithms perform when applied to event camera imaging. Our approach used machine-learning-based computer vision methods, including a multi-block LBP-based detector and SDM-based aligner, to achieve real-time and efficient pupil-tracking performance. For our experiments, we aggregated events into frames at 30 fps to accurately represent eye movements. This rate was chosen for its visual clarity and its compatibility with our SDM-based keypoint alignment. Our algorithm, utilizing the SDM, showed optimal performance with data aggregated at this rate. We evaluated the algorithm's capabilities using a comprehensive dataset that included various eye movement scenarios, and we compared the results with our previous frame-based eye-tracking algorithms. While our event camera-based approach achieved a nearly equivalent detection accuracy of 98.1%, closely matching the 99.4% achieved by traditional RGB frame camera methods [11], there was a noticeable decline in the tracking accuracy. The tracking accuracy dropped from 99.4% with the RGB-frame-camera-based method [11] to 80.9% in our proposed approach. To further quantify our results, we computed the precision and recall for our method. The precision achieved was 100%, and the recall was 80.89%. Based on our testing, the confusion matrix related to our approach has been detailed in Figure 6. Our true negative value was zero, consistent with our test dataset that did not contain any images without pupils. A notable point from our results is the zero false positives. This can be attributed to the intrinsic nature of event cameras, which do not output any pixel value in static backgrounds. Hence, there is no activation unless there is motion. This characteristic eliminates the chances of false positive detections in areas with no movement, showing one of the significant advantages of utilizing event cameras. Since event cameras might not consistently provide uniform shape information, SDM can sometimes fail in its regression tasks, leading to less precise tracking. Moreover, our tracker checker tends to discard tracking instances when the shape information is unclear, especially during non-insufficient movements. Our choice of the AdaBoost-based eye–nose detection combined with the SDM-based pupil alignment was intentionally selected. This conventional method was chosen driven by our primary aim: to examine the feasibility of well-established remote eye-tracking algorithms on rapidly functioning event cameras. As demonstrated in our previous research on RGB-frame-based cameras [11], while advanced deep learning methods may offer improved results, our technique can operate efficiently on CPUs, eliminating the necessity for high-priced GPUs. However, methods, like AdaBoost and SDM, have limitations when confronting outliers, noise, occlusions, and other challenging scenarios compared to newer deep learning techniques. A further study focusing on deep neural networks designed for event cameras is required.

Figure 7 showcases some failure cases of the proposed method. In Figure 7a, we observe a scenario with minimal movements and an obscured eye shape, leading to the detector's failure in detecting the eye–nose region. Similarly, Figure 7b presents a case where the eye shape is visible, but the algorithm encounters challenges in the alignment and tracker-checker components, resulting in tracking failure. These instances illustrate the complexities and limitations associated with event camera imaging, particularly when dealing with scenarios involving minimal movements and obscured eye shapes. Additionally, Table 4 summarizes our algorithm's performance across movement levels. In the large movement category, we achieved a detection accuracy of 98% and a tracking accuracy of 80.9%, illustrating our system's ability to track pupils during quick eye motions. For a range from minimal to large movements, the detection accuracy was reduced to 69.1% and tracking to 52.7%, emphasizing the tracking challenges with varying motion intensities. A comparison between our proposed event-camera-based method and state-of-the-art RGB-frame-camera-based techniques [22–25] is also listed in Table 5.

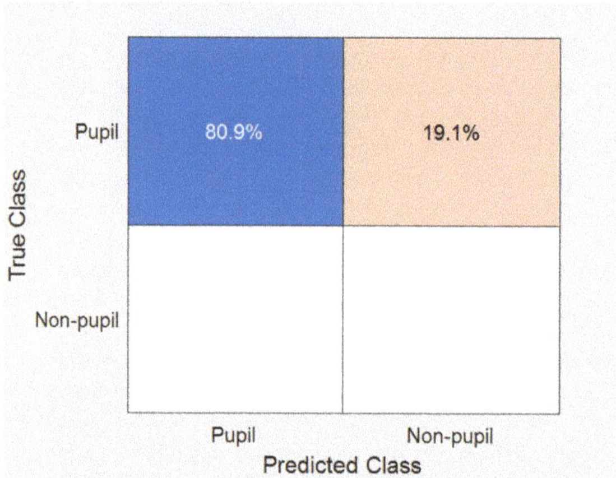

Figure 6. Confusion matrix for the proposed pupil localization.

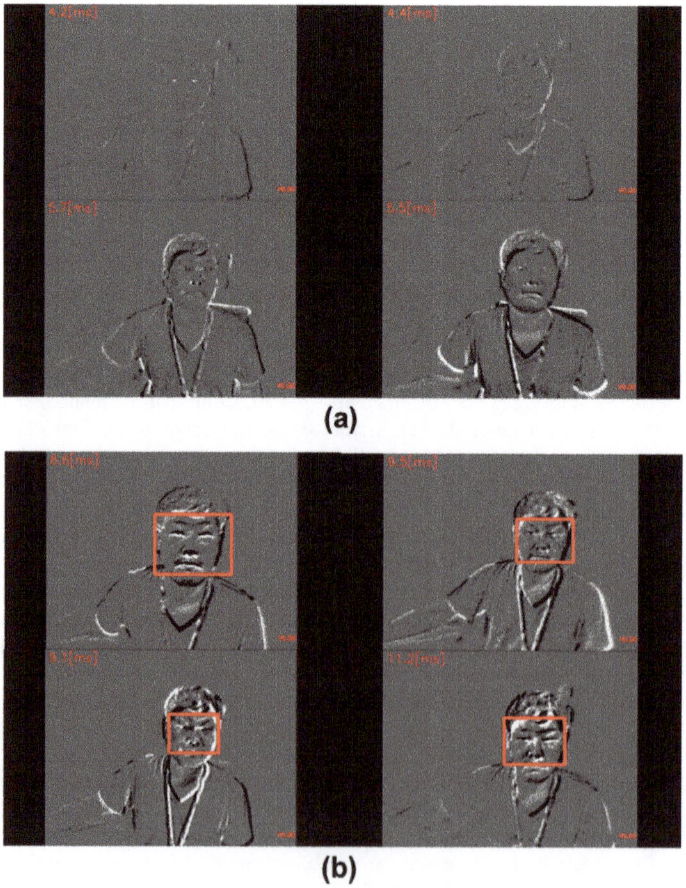

Figure 7. Failure cases of the proposed event-camera-based pupil tracking method. (**a**) Minimal movements with obscured eye shape, leading to a failure in eye–nose region detection. (**b**) Visible eye shape, but failure in the alignment and tracker-checker components.

Table 4. Performance comparison of the proposed event-camera-based pupil-tracking method on different movement levels.

Test DB	DB Type	Detection Accuracy	Tracking Accuracy (Pupil Precision < 10 mm)
Real Event Camera Images Indoor Office (100~400 lux)	Large Movement (Image with verifiable eye shape)	98.1%	80.9%
	Various Movement (minimal to large movement)	69.1%	52.7%

Table 5. Comparison between previous RGB-frame-camera-based studies and the proposed method.

Method	Sensor Type	Test Dataset	Keypoint Number	Speed	GFLOPs
LAB [22]	RGB frame camera	Public DB (WFLW [22])	98	60 ms (GPU)	29.1
Wing [23]			98	343 ms (GPU)	5.5
Awing [24]			98	41 ms (GPU)	26.7
AVS + SAN [25]			98	16 ms (GPU)	62.8
Ours	Event camera	In-house DB	11	4 ms (CPU)	N/A

Despite the algorithm's successes in handling rapid eye movements and achieving real-time capabilities, there are areas for improvement. One notable limitation is the reduced accuracy when dealing with subtle or minimal movements. When there is minimal-to-no head movement, the nature of event cameras, which primarily respond to changes in the scene, might produce sparse events, complicating eye–nose detection. Our research successfully detected pupil movements across a 1 m range using event cameras, as evidenced in the Figure 1, Figure 5, and Figure 6 shown in the manuscript. However, we recognize the resolution limitation of the DAVIS 346 and anticipate improvements with next-generation high definition (HD) event cameras. These situations may lead to partial occlusion or insufficient motion cues, making it challenging for the algorithm to accurately detect and track pupils. Furthermore, the algorithm's performance was dependent on the quality and availability of data in the training dataset. The limited number of available images in the event camera dataset for training the detector and aligner may have influenced the algorithm's performance on certain motion levels. Another consideration is the trade-off between speed and accuracy. While our proposed method achieved remarkable real-time performance at 200 frames per second at a 640 $\times$ 480 resolution with a 2.0 GHz CPU, there is room for improving the accuracy at the expense of processing speed. For specific applications that require higher precision, optimizations to balance speed and accuracy should be explored. In this study, our primary goal was to assess the feasibility of using event cameras for remote eye tracking, positioning our work as a preliminary exploration in this domain. We acknowledge that a comprehensive comparison with other eye-tracking methods and a more extensive validation were not undertaken. Additionally, to overcome these limitations and further enhance the algorithm's performance, several strategies can be considered. In this research, we emphasized computational efficiency, favoring methods, like SDM, Adaboost, and LBP. However, to further optimize the performance of our algorithm, considering diverse strategies is important. As deep learning continues to develop with new lightweight networks coming out, adapting or customizing these networks specifically for event cameras could be beneficial. By using recent advanced deep neural networks [26,27], the algorithm could potentially handle subtle movements more effectively and enhance its robustness in challenging scenarios with obscured eye shapes. Additionally, utilizing the graph structure, especially through approaches, like the graph Fourier transform as discussed in ref. [28], can be adopted to improve tracking capabilities, offering a richer representation of data relationships. Moreover, efforts to expand the training dataset with a more diverse range of event camera data could be undertaken. By collecting data from various real-world environments and users, the algorithm can better adapt to different motion levels and lighting conditions, ultimately leading to improved generalization and performance.

5. Conclusions

In conclusion, our proposed event-camera-based pupil-tracking algorithm demonstrated promising results in accurately tracking pupils during rapid eye movements, with real-time capabilities. Specifically, our method reached a detection accuracy rate of 98.1% and a tracking accuracy, where the pupil difference was less than 10 mm, at 80.9%. However, there are challenges to overcome, particularly in handling subtle movements and occluded eye shapes. Future research could focus on expanding the dataset for training and investigating new machine learning techniques to improve the algorithm's performance across diverse eye movement scenarios and lighting conditions. By addressing these challenges, event-camera-based pupil tracking holds great potential for advancing eye-tracking technologies and enabling new applications in various real-world settings.

Author Contributions: Conceptualization, D.K. and J.J.; methodology, D.K. and Y.K.L.; software, D.K.; validation, D.K. and Y.K.L.; formal analysis, J.J.; investigation, Y.K.L.; resources, D.K.; data curation, J.J.; writing—original draft preparation, D.K.; writing—review and editing, Y.K.L. and J.J.; visualization, Y.K.L.; supervision, J.J.; project administration, D.K.; funding acquisition, D.K. All authors have read and agreed to the published version of the manuscript.

Funding: This work was supported by the National Research Foundation of Korea (NRF) grant funded by the Korea government (MSIT) (No. 2022R1F1A1074056); this work was supported by the 2023 Hongik University Research Fund. This work was supported by the Ministry of Education (MOE) and a Korea Institute for Advancement of Technology (KIAT) grant funded by the Korea Government (MOTIE) (P0022165, High-Speed Semiconductor IC Design and Test/Signal Integrity Professional Training Project).

Institutional Review Board Statement: Not applicable.

Informed Consent Statement: Informed consent was obtained from all subjects involved in the study.

Data Availability Statement: Not applicable.

Conflicts of Interest: The authors declare no conflict of interest.

References

1. Yiu, Y.-H.; Aboulatta, M.; Raiser, T.; Ophey, L.; Flanagin, V.L.; Zu Elenburg, P.; Ahmadi, S.-A. DeepVOG: Open-source pupil segmentation and gaze estimation in neuroscience using deep learning. *J. Neurosci. Methods* **2019**, *324*, 108307. [CrossRef] [PubMed]
2. Skaramagkas, V.; Giannakakis, G.; Ktistakis, E.; Manousos, D.; Karatzanis, I.; Tachos, N.S.; Tripoliti, E.; Marias, K.; Fotiadis, D.I.; Tsiknakis, M. Review of eye tracking metrics involved in emotional and cognitive processes. *IEEE Rev. Biomed. Eng.* **2021**, *16*, 260–277. [CrossRef] [PubMed]
3. Asish, S.M.; Kulshreshth, A.K.; Borst, C.W. User identification utilizing minimal eye-gaze features in virtual reality applications. *Virtual Worlds* **2022**, *1*, 42–61. [CrossRef]
4. Kang, D.; Ma, L. Real-Time Eye Tracking for Bare and Sunglasses-Wearing Faces for Augmented Reality 3D Head-Up Displays. *IEEE Access* **2021**, *9*, 125508–125522. [CrossRef]
5. Yousefi, M.S.; Reisi, F.; Daliri, M.R.; Shalchyan, V. Stress Detection Using Eye Tracking Data: An Evaluation of Full Parameters. *IEEE Access* **2022**, *10*, 118941–118952. [CrossRef]
6. Ou, W.-L.; Kuo, T.-L.; Chang, C.-C.; Fan, C.-P. Deep-learning-based pupil center detection and tracking technology for visible-light wearable gaze tracking devices. *Appl. Sci.* **2021**, *11*, 851. [CrossRef]
7. Bozomitu, R.G.; Păsărică, A.; Tărniceriu, D.; Rotariu, C. Development of an Eye Tracking-Based Human-Computer Interface for Real-Time Applications. *Sensors* **2019**, *19*, 3630. [CrossRef] [PubMed]
8. Thiago, S.; Fuhl, W.; Kasneci, E. PuRe: Robust pupil detection for real-time pervasive eye tracking. *Comput. Vis. Image Underst.* **2018**, *170*, 40–50.
9. Majaranta, P.; Bulling, A. Eye tracking and eye-based human–computer interaction. In *Advances in Physiological Computing*; Springer: London, UK, 2014; pp. 39–65.
10. Zheng, L.J.; Mountstephens, J.; Teo, J. Emotion recognition using eye-tracking: Taxonomy, review and current challenges. *Sensors* **2020**, *20*, 2384.
11. Kang, D.; Heo, J. Content-Aware Eye Tracking for Autostereoscopic 3D Display. *Sensors* **2020**, *20*, 4787. [CrossRef] [PubMed]

12. Braiden, B.; Rose, J.; Eizenman, M. Hybrid eye-tracking on a smartphone with CNN feature extraction and an infrared 3D model. *Sensors* **2020**, *20*, 543.
13. Gallego, G.; Delbruck, T.; Orchard, G.; Bartolozzi, C.; Taba, B.; Censi, A.; Leutenegger, S.; Davison, A.J.; Conradt, J.; Danilidis, K.; et al. Event-based vision: A survey. *IEEE Trans. Pattern Anal. Mach. Intell.* **2020**, *44*, 154–180. [CrossRef] [PubMed]
14. Xuehan, X.; De la Torre, F. Supervised descent method and its applications to face alignment. In Proceedings of the IEEE Conference on Computer Vision and Pattern Recognition, Portland, OR, USA, 23–28 June 2013; pp. 53–539.
15. DAVIS346. Available online: https://inivation.com/wp-content/uploads/2019/08/DAVIS346.pdf (accessed on 1 August 2023).
16. Lowe, D. Distinctive image features from scale-invariant keypoints. *Int. J. Comput. Vis.* **2004**, *60*, 91–110. [CrossRef]
17. Paul, V.; Jones, M.J. Robust real-time face detection. *Int. J. Comput. Vis.* **2004**, *57*, 137–154.
18. Paul, V.; Jones, M. Rapid object detection using a boosted cascade of simple features. In Proceedings of the 2001 IEEE Computer Society Conference on Computer Vision and Pattern Recognition, CVPR, Kauai, HI, USA, 8–14 December 2001.
19. Zhang, L.; Chu, R.; Xiang, S.; Liao, S.; Li, S.Z. Face detection based on multi-block lbp representation. In Proceedings of the International Conference on Biometrics, Seoul, Korea, 27–29 August 2007; pp. 11–18.
20. Cao, X.; Wei, Y.; Wen, F.; Sun, J. Face alignment by explicit shape regression. *Int. J. Comput. Vis.* **2014**, *107*, 177–190. [CrossRef]
21. Wenyan, W.; Yang, S. Leveraging intra and inter-dataset variations for robust face alignment. In Proceedings of the IEEE Conference on Computer Vision and Pattern Recognition Workshops, Honolulu, HI, USA, 21–26 July 2017; pp. 150–159.
22. Wu, W.; Qian, C.; Yang, S.; Wang, Q.; Cai, Y.; Zhou, Q. Look at boundary: A boundary-aware face alignment algorithm. In Proceedings of the IEEE Conference on Computer Vision and Pattern Recognition, Salt Lake City, UT, USA, 18–23 June 2018; pp. 2129–2138.
23. Feng, Z.H.; Kittler, J.; Awais, M.; Huber, P.; Wu, X.J. Wing loss for robust facial landmark localisation with convolutional neural networks. In Proceedings of the IEEE Conference on Computer Vision and Pattern Recognition, Salt Lake City, UT, USA, 18–23 June 2018; pp. 2235–2245.
24. Wang, X.; Bo, L.; Fuxin, L. Adaptive wing loss for robust face alignment via heatmap regression. In Proceedings of the IEEE/CVF International Conference on Computer Vision, Seoul, Republic of Korea, 27 October–2 November 2019; pp. 6971–6981.
25. Qian, S.; Sun, K.; Wu, W.; Qian, C.; Jia, J. Aggregation via separation: Boosting facial landmark detector with semi-supervised style translation. In Proceedings of the IEEE/CVF International Conference on Computer Vision, Seoul, Republic of Korea, 27 October–2 November 2019; pp. 10153–10163.
26. Kujur, A.; Raza, Z.; Khan, A.A.; Wechtaisong, C. Data Complexity Based Evaluation of the Model Dependence of Brain MRI Images for Classification of Brain Tumor and Alzheimer's Disease. *IEEE Access* **2022**, *10*, 112117–112133. [CrossRef]
27. Khan, A.A.; Madendran, R.K.; Thirunavukkarasu, U.; Faheem, M. D2PAM: Epileptic Seizures Prediction Using Adversarial Deep Dual Patch Attention Mechanism. 2023. Available online: https://ietresearch.onlinelibrary.wiley.com/action/showCitFormats?doi=10.1049%2Fcit2.12261 (accessed on 24 July 2023).
28. Belda, J.; Vergara, L.; Safont, G.; Salazar, A.; Parcheta, Z. A New Surrogating Algorithm by the Complex Graph Fourier Transform (CGFT). *Entropy* **2019**, *21*, 759. [CrossRef] [PubMed]

applied sciences

MDPI

Article

Investigating the Effect of Outdoor Advertising on Consumer Decisions: An Eye-Tracking and A/B Testing Study of Car Drivers' Perception

Radovan Madlenak *, Roman Chinoracky, Natalia Stalmasekova and Lucia Madlenakova

Faculty of Operation and Economics of Transport and Communications, University of Žilina, Univerzitná 8215/1, 010 26 Žilina, Slovakia

* Correspondence: radovan.madlenak@fpedas.uniza.sk

Abstract: This study aims to investigate the impact of outdoor advertising on consumer behaviour by using eye-tracking analysis while drivers travel specific routes in Žilina, Slovakia. This research combines questionnaire inquiry and A/B testing to assess the conscious and subconscious effects of outdoor advertising on consumer decisions. The findings of this study have important implications for businesses providing outdoor advertising spaces, as well as those using outdoor advertising as a form of advertisement. Additionally, the study provides insights into the role of transportation background and how it influences consumer behaviour in relation to outdoor advertising.

Keywords: eye tracking; outdoor advertising; car drivers' perception

1. Introduction

Outdoor advertising is a form of marketing that uses public spaces as a platform for advertising messages [1–3]. It involves placing ads on outside structures, such as billboards, bus stops, and bus shelters, and in public spaces, such as parks, streets, and transit stations [4,5]. The aim of outdoor advertising is to capture the attention of potential customers, to create brand recognition, and to increase sales [6,7]. The main characteristic of outdoor advertising is its ability to reach a wide variety of people in a short amount of time. It is often used in combination with other forms of marketing channels, such as television, radio, and print. In other words, outdoor advertising can also be used to support other marketing activities such as digital, radio, and television by creating a unified message [8,9].

The main advantages of outdoor advertising for businesses are the following:

- Cost-effective: Outdoor advertising is often more cost-effective than some forms of advertising. This is because the cost of producing the ad is lower than other forms of advertising, such as television and radio [10,11].
- Reach: Outdoor advertising such as billboards and posters can reach a large and diverse audience [12,13].
- Visibility: Outdoor ads are highly visible, especially if placed in a high-traffic area. This visibility helps to ensure that message reaches more people [14,15].
- Flexibility: Outdoor advertising allows for considerable flexibility when it comes to design, content, and placement [16].
- Immediate: Outdoor advertising's immediacy is one of its most attractive features. Message is seen immediately and can be changed quickly if needed [17,18].
- Branding: Outdoor advertising can be used to reinforce brand identity and to create an impression on potential customers [19,20].

Considering the benefits mentioned, it is possible to list the drawbacks of outdoor advertising:

- Cost: Even if it may be cost-effective in comparison with some forms of marketing, outdoor advertising is still a relatively expensive form of advertising and may not be affordable for some businesses [21,22].
- Limited Reach: Outdoor advertising can only reach people who are within the vicinity of the advertisement. It is not possible to target a specific audience with outdoor advertising [23,24].
- Short-Lived: Outdoor advertisements are often only visible for a few seconds or minutes before the person passes by. As a result, it is not possible to leave a lasting impression on the viewer [25,26].
- Environmental Impact: Outdoor advertising can have a negative environmental impact if not managed properly. Excessive billboards and signs can create visual clutter and pollution in an area [27,28].

The history of outdoor advertising dates back to times when merchants used painted signs and other forms of advertising to promote their wares. Since the 1920s, billboard companies have used a variety of techniques to create eye-catching displays, including painted signs, neon lighting, and even 3D displays [29].

In general, and as it was already mentioned, standard outdoor advertising includes billboards, bus wraps, bus benches, murals, neon signs, yard signs, street banners, digital displays, and vehicle wraps. Billboards are typically placed on major highways and are large and captivating. Bus wraps are one of the most popular forms of outdoor advertising, and involve wrapping a bus in an advertisement. Bus benches are placed in high-traffic areas and allow commuters to sit and observe the ad that is a part of the bench while they wait for the bus. Murals are large, eye-catching paintings that are placed in high-traffic areas. Neon signs, yard signs, and street banners are also popular forms of outdoor advertising and are usually part of the overall composition of city streets. Digital displays, such as digital billboards and digital signs, are also becoming increasingly popular. Vehicle wraps are used to turn cars and other vehicles into moving billboards [30,31].

There are several factors impacting the use of outdoor advertising from the point of view of advertisers. Most vocal are the following:

- Location: Outdoor advertising is most effective when it is placed in areas where it will be seen by the largest number of people. High-traffic areas, such as major highways and intersections, are the most common location for outdoor advertising [32,33].
- Visibility: Outdoor advertising must be seen in order to be effective. Factors such as size, brightness, and contrast can all influence how visible an advertisement is [34,35].
- Weather: Weather can impact the visibility of outdoor advertising, as well as how long it lasts. Rain and wind can cause signs to fade or become damaged over time, reducing their effectiveness [36].
- Cost: Outdoor advertising can be expensive, and this can be a major factor in determining whether a company opts to use it [21,24].
- Target Audience: Companies should consider the demographics and interests of their target audience when selecting their outdoor advertising locations. This will help ensure that the advertisement reaches the right people [37,38].

Outdoor advertising can have a powerful impact on consumer behaviour. It can serve as a reminder of brand presence, create brand awareness, and influence brand recognition and loyalty. Outdoor advertising can also encourage impulse buying and provide information about special offers, new products, and services. Additionally, it can be used to increase customer engagement and to create a sense of urgency. Outdoor advertising can also create positive associations with a brand, making it more likely that consumers will think of the brand when making purchase decisions. It can drive traffic to a website or physical location and increase overall sales [39,40].

Several determinants of outdoor advertising play a role in consumer decision making, including the location of the advertisement, the message conveyed, the size and design of the ad, and the target audience. The location of an advertisement can have a significant effect on the visibility of the ad, as well as its ability to reach the intended audience. The message an ad conveys is also important, as it helps to shape the consumer's perception of the product or service being advertised. The size and design of an ad can also influence its effectiveness, as an ad that stands out and is easily recognizable can have a greater impact. The target audience of an ad is also critical, as it can influence the types of images, language, and overall message used to appeal to the intended demographic [16,41,42].

Based on a review of the open access publications that we conducted in this article, we can summarize the scope of research regarding outdoor advertising as follows:

Many studies deal with the right placement of outdoor advertising, its visuals, costs, and regulation [11,12,15,16,21,32,41].

A lot of authors perceive outdoor advertising as visual smog and deal with its negative impact on the environment and society [10,13,20,27,28].

Other studies deal with how outdoor advertising promotes the language and culture of chosen regions such as Malaysia [18], the disparities of the outdoor advertising when aimed on different racial and ethnic groups in the USA or Indonesia [19,25,37], or unethical content in outdoor advertising and its negative social impact [33,34].

Further research is focused on the impact of outdoor advertising on driving or riding experience [14,36].

We found only three articles that examined the influence of outdoor advertising on purchasing decisions and the targeting of outdoor advertising for the right customer [26,38,40].

This means that, as a conclusion from the conducted analysis of given articles, we identified the following research information gaps dedicated to the impact of outdoor advertising on consumer behaviour:

1. Lack of data on the long-term impact of outdoor advertising on consumer behaviour;
2. Lack of information on the influence of outdoor advertising on different demographic groups;
3. Insufficient data on how outdoor advertising is perceived by consumers in different regions;
4. Limited research on how outdoor advertising affects the purchase decision of consumers;
5. Lack of research into the effectiveness of outdoor advertising compared with other forms of advertising.

By merging statements two and three, we formulated our research basis. Our research is centred around the research problem of understanding how various outdoor advertisements influence consumer behaviour in a particular city in Slovakia. As such, the main objective of this paper is to evaluate the effects of outdoor advertising on consumer behaviour in a chosen city in Slovakia, with a focus on online shopping. By fulfilling the information gaps, we provide an insight into the topic, which may be beneficial not only to the scientific community but also to the practitioners of outdoor advertising.

2. Materials and Methods

There are several methods with which we can analyse the impact of outdoor advertising on consumer behaviour. A mapping service is a technology that can be used to determine the location of outdoor advertising, as well as to analyse data from various sources such as census data, traffic patterns, and demographics. Another method of heat mapping is a technique used to identify the most effective locations for outdoor advertising. Data such as traffic patterns, demographic information, and other relevant details can be used to identify areas that are more likely to be exposed to an advertisement. An eye-tracking analysis is another method that involves the use of eye-tracking technology to measure where viewers are looking when they encounter outdoor advertising. This can provide valuable insight into which elements of an advertisement are most effective. By tracking the eye movements of viewers, researchers can determine which elements of the ad are attracting attention, how long viewers are looking at different parts of the ad, and how the ad is affecting their overall impression. Classic marketing methods of surveys can also be used. Surveys can be conducted to determine the effectiveness of outdoor advertising. Questions can be asked to gauge how viewers responded to specific elements of an advertisement, as well as to determine if the ad was memorable [43–45].

In this study, we combined and used all of these methods, and thus, we created a sequence of steps in which the usage of methods is highlighted (Figure 1). Following each of these steps contributed to reaching the main goal of the article.

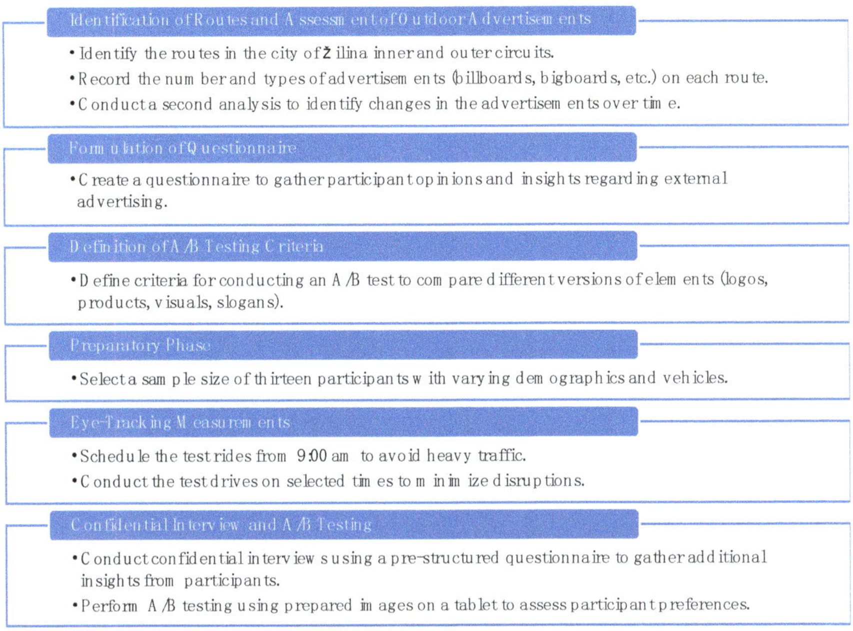

Figure 1. Methodology of the research.

The first step consists of the identification of routes of the selected city, which is the city of Žilina. Identifying the routes of the Slovakian city of Žilina, we employed Google Maps to distinguish the external and internal circuits. Our subsequent task was to assess the density of outdoor advertisements by personally traversing the predetermined sections of the outer and inner circuits. Our analysis of the situation in Žilina allowed us to determine the prevalence of outdoor advertisements.

The inner circuit consists of the following streets (Figure 2): Legionárska–J. M. Hurbana–Kálov–P. O. Hviezdoslava–1. Mája–Veľká Okružná. In the inner circuit, 29 large-format advertisements were recorded: 28 billboards and 1 bigboard.

Over time, some outdoor advertising can disappear due to many factors, such as weather damage, vandalism, or changes in the environment. The materials used in outdoor advertising are usually not designed to last forever, so they can deteriorate over time. Thus, we conducted a second analysis that revealed that 4 billboards had been removed in the meantime. Of the 25 large-format advertisements located on route, compared with the original analysis, the following was recorded: 10 same advertisements; 8 advertisements from the same advertiser but different advertisements (the company remained the same, but the product, visual, etc. changed); and 7 other advertisements.

The outer circuit consists of the following streets (Figure 3): Košická–Na Horevaží–Ľavobrežná–Estakáda–Rajecká. This circuit had 72 large-format advertisements, of which 55 were billboards, 16 were bigboards, and 1 was a megaboard.

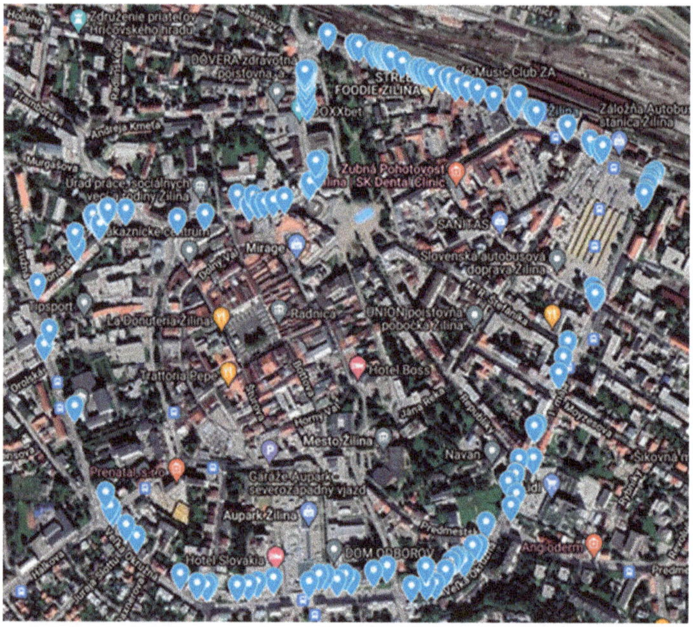

Figure 2. Inner circuit of selected roads.

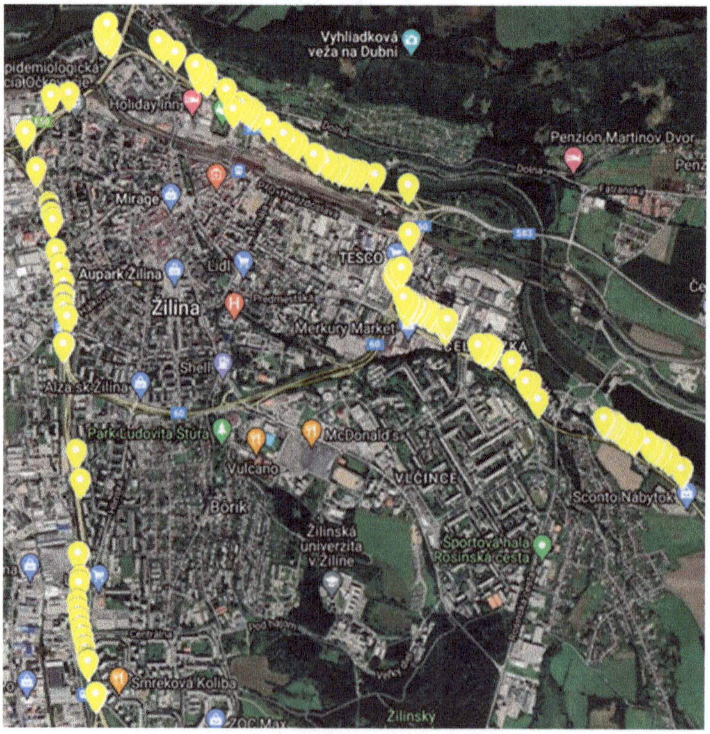

Figure 3. Outer circuit of selected roads.

Again, due to the same assumption as for the inner circuit, we conducted a second analysis. The analysis revealed that 4 billboards had been removed. Compared with the original analysis, the outer circuit now had 15 same advertisements; 10 advertisements from the same advertiser but a different advertisement; and 43 other advertisements or empty advertising carriers. It is evident that the advertisements on the outer circuit have changed significantly during the period between the first and second analyses. Almost 80% of the 72 analysed advertisements were changed or removed.

The outer circuit of Žilina connects the city from north to south and from east to west, while the inner circuit creates a circular connection between the outer suburbs and the city centre. Together, these roads are essential for the functioning of the city. Žilina is an indispensable transportation hub in the northern part of Slovakia, boasting a large central railway station and numerous significant railway lines. Furthermore, Žilina is also a crucial crossroads for road traffic, with major highways leading to the Czech Republic, Poland, and Austria.

The positive aspects of both circuits are the placement of advertisements on both sides of the road. There are also many billboards and bigboards on the selected routes, as well as large-format banners placed on buildings and various banners. The necessary variety of outdoor advertising is provided by the location of the individual routes, since the research took place in the centre of the city, in its outskirts, and on highway exits (so-called freeways).

The second step in the research process was the formulation of a questionnaire for the participants to complete. Querying their opinions, the questions sought to identify: (1) whether the individual is conscious of external advertising while driving; (2) what aspect of external advertising most catches their eye (graphics, slogan, logo, colours, size of the carrier, etc.); (3) the level of awareness of the impact of external advertising on their buying behaviour; (4) whether their purchasing decisions are swayed by external advertising; and (5) the frequency of their online shopping habits (daily, weekly, monthly, etc.).

The questionnaire was filled out after the research commenced. The research itself centred on examining the effect of external advertising placed on selected routes on the attention of research participants while driving a car. Attention can be understood in terms of how it alters drivers' perception of the environment.

The third step in the process was to define the criteria for conducting an A/B test. A/B testing is a scientific approach to comparison, in which two versions of a particular element—such as a logo, product, graphic visual, or slogan—are evaluated against each other to determine which version performs better [46]. The randomly assigned participants of the study were presented with elements A and B after the completion of their drive, both on the outer and inner circuits. Subsequently, the drivers were asked four questions to assess which variant was more appealing: (1) Which option do you prefer when making a purchase—A or B? (2) What led you to choose this option? (This was an open question.) (3) Did you register the selected logo or product during the test drive? (Answers were limited to yes/no.) (4) Is there a specific product associated with the logo you saw? (Answers were limited to yes/no, and this question was applicable only to the logos of companies.)

Due to the substantial amount of outdoor advertising on both the inner and outer circuits, we carefully selected a specific set of advertisements for A/B testing and its correlation with eye-tracking research. We chose these ads for their visibility to drivers on both circuits, which were all in the form of billboards. Billboards on the outer circuit were labelled as TR4-005, TR4-006, TR4-017, TR4-029, TR4-039, TR4-055, TR4-059, TR4-075, TR4-079, TR4-092, TR4-097, TR4-114, TR4-115, TR4-119, TR4-121, TR4-122, TR4-143, TR4-151, TR4-155, TR4-156, TR4-157, and TR4-158. As for inner circuit, the billboards were identified as TR1-002, TR1-030, TR1-031, TR1-032, TR1-033, TR1-040, TR1-041, TR1-042, TR1-043, TR1-044, TR1-045, TR1-074, TR1-075, TR1-076, TR1-088, TR1-100, TR1-103, TR1-115, and TR1-116.

In the fourth step of the preparatory phase of the research, all relevant aspects of our research were formulated. Thirteen participants of varying genders, ages, and vehicles drove various routes—a sample size much larger than the recommended 6 by the Nolsen Norman Group's publication "How to Conduct Eyetracking Studies" [44]. Consequently, the results of the research could be accurately interpreted and applied to further knowledge acquisition. Seven women and six men aged 21 to 37 droves on an inner and outer circuit over three days, in varying weather and traffic conditions. Using the SMI Eye Tracking Glasses 2 (Wireless Analysis) version, we tracked the attention of the drivers towards external advertising with eye tracking.

The SMI EyeTracking Glasses 2 (ETG 2) is a wearable eye-tracking system that allows us to capture and analyse real-world visual attention and gaze behaviour. ETG 2 was designed as a lightweight and unobtrusive pair of glasses. The eye-tracking hardware is integrated into the glasses frame, along with miniature cameras, sensors, and other components required for eye tracking. The ETG 2 system utilizes high-resolution cameras mounted on the glasses to capture the wearer's eye movements. The glasses include two cameras (one for each eye) to provide binocular tracking and more accurate measurements. To ensure robust eye tracking in various lighting conditions, the ETG 2 uses infrared illumination. Near-infrared light is emitted from the glasses frame, illuminating the eyes without causing discomfort or interfering with the wearer's vision. The cameras in the ETG 2 capture images of the wearer's eyes at a frame rate 60 Hz. These images are processed in real time using sophisticated algorithms to detect and track important features such as the pupil, corneal reflections, and eye movements. Before starting an eye-tracking session (measurement), the driver needs to go through a calibration procedure. This involves looking at specific calibration targets and following researcher's instructions while the eye-tracking system records the eye movements. The calibration process establishes the relationship between the recorded eye movements and the actual point of gaze in the driver's field of view. During the eye-tracking experiment, the ETG 2 continuously records eye movement data, including gaze coordinates, pupil diameter, and eye movement velocity. The data were transmitted by the cable to a connected notebook for real-time analysis [47].

SMI provides dedicated software BeGaze for analysing the recorded eye-tracking data. The BeGaze software allows researchers to visualize and analyse gaze patterns, to generate heatmaps or gaze plots, and to extract various metrics related to fixations, saccades, and other eye movement parameters. These analysis tools help researchers gain insights into visual attention, cognitive processes, and user behaviour.

The SMI EyeTracking Glasses 2 technology enables to study eye movements in real-world environments, making it well-suited for applications such as market research, usability testing, sports performance analysis, and human factors research. Its portable and unobtrusive design allows for natural and ecologically valid eye-tracking studies in a wide range of settings and scenarios [48].

This eye tracker does not significantly affect the cognitive abilities of the drivers and is advantageous for field measurements as it creates a natural and normal environment for the driver.

Steps five and six are implementation stages. The implementation stage of research is the process of executing the research activities. This stage consists of enacting the research plan (steps one to four), collecting data, examining the data, interpreting the results, and drawing conclusions.

In the fifth step, the actual eye-tracking measurements took place. Measurements were conducted from 9:00 a.m., with a schedule set so that each ride was allotted thirty minutes. To avoid morning and afternoon traffic rush in the city, the selection of times for test rides was carefully considered. Rides at this time should proceed without disruption from traffic jams. During the test drive, the driver had a calibrated eye-tracking device mounted on their head. On the passenger seat, the researcher calibrated the device before the drive and continuously monitored the data obtained on the computer during the journey. Another researcher occupied the back seat, observing the entire ride and measurement (Figure 4).

Figure 4. Eye-tracking testing and verifying data.

Eye-tracking measurements are focused on specific indicators that can be measured by an eye tracker: fixations, saccadic movements, and blinks. Fixation refers to the period when the eyes are relatively still, focusing on a specific point of interest. During fixation, visual information is gathered and processed. Fixations typically last around 200–300 milliseconds and allow the brain to extract detailed information from the visual scene [48]. Fixations indicate what a person has noticed, how long they looked at it, and the order in which they viewed different elements in a scene. Saccadic movements, on the other hand, are rapid and involuntary eye movements that shift the gaze from one point to another. These movements allow us to explore the visual environment by redirecting our focus to new points of interest. Saccades occur between fixations and typically last around 20–50 milliseconds. They are crucial for scanning the visual scene and are involved in acquiring new visual information [45]. Saccadic movements measure the speed and accuracy with which the eyes move from one point to the next, providing insight into the user's cognitive and perceptual processes. Blinks are brief closures of the eyelids that occur regularly to keep the eyes moisturized and protected. Blinks are essential for maintaining the health and function of the eyes. During a blink, the visual system is momentarily interrupted, and visual information is not processed. Blinks typically last around 100–150 milliseconds, but their frequency can vary depending on factors such as task demands, attention levels, and individual differences [45]. Blinks are used to gauge a person's attention and engagement with a particular stimulus and can even reveal visual fatigue and distraction.

The last stage of the research (sixth step) entailed a confidential interview (questionnaire) and an A/B testing between the researcher and the driver (steps two and three). This took place in a secluded atmosphere, free from any third-party interference. The interviewer used a pre-structured questionnaire, noting down the responses into their laptop. For the A/B testing, the researcher presented the driver with a tablet containing the prepared images which they were required to go through. Upon completion of the interview, the measurement was also concluded and the research progressed to the subsequent driver.

Considering the data obtained from the research, the results are interpreted via tables and graphs. The tables provide an in-depth analysis of the examined variables that were gathered using the eye tracker. The graphs illustrate the frequent responses given by the research participants following the rides.

3. Results

3.1. Drive on Inner Circuit

Drivers on the inner circuit during testing drives scarcely observed the billboards selected for A/B testing. A captivating fact about this route is that none of the six drivers noted the advertisement when driving into the car park at the Lidl supermarket (near Kálov Street) where the rides concluded. Not a single driver also directed their gaze to the large and conspicuously visible billboard fashioned on the edifice. Concerning the single billboard on this route, only one driver focused his gaze on it.

The first drive took place in light, early morning traffic, with few cars on the road. The sky was grey and overcast, yet there was no rain. While driving, the driver kept his eyes on the road ahead. He paid close attention to traffic signs and kept his gaze fixed upon the traffic lights at intersections. While stopped at an intersection, a clearly visible billboard advertisement was in the line of sight, directly behind the traffic light. However, the driver never diverted his eyes, keeping them fixed on the road. Aside from the stop at the intersection, the ride was uninterrupted. On one occasion, the driver did briefly focus his gaze on a billboard located on the opposite side of the road, which was not part of the test. Table 1 provides a clear summary of the key performance indicators (KPIs) derived from the eye-tracking device.

Table 1. Measurement results—Driver 1.

Indicator	Fixation	Saccadic Movements	Blinks
Total number	1594	1461	122
Average	171	156	13

The second driver kept his gaze fixed on the road ahead, glancing occasionally towards the tachometer on the dashboard, amid a backdrop of smooth traffic and cloudy but dry weather. At one point, a red traffic light necessitated a brief stop, but otherwise, the journey was uninterrupted. Driver 2 exhibited a far lower number of fixations than Driver 1, suggesting that the eye tracker was better calibrated (Table 2). Nevertheless, the gathered data were sufficient to warrant its evaluation within the research.

Table 2. Measurement results—Driver 2.

Indicator	Fixation	Saccadic Movements	Blinks
Total number	789	473	70
Average	82	49	7

The third drive happened with a greater number of cars on the route than the previous two drives, and the sky was somewhat cloudier, which made the scenery darker. There were three pauses during the drive: two times to give way to pedestrians at the intersection, and once due to a red light at the traffic lights. Unfortunately, the results from this driver cannot be processed due to the calibration of the eye tracker (see results from Table 3), though the data from the questionnaire inquiry and testing can be partially utilized for the research. The only issue is with question three from the A/B testing, as it is impossible to confirm or validate the answer with a video recording from the eye tracker.

Table 3. Measurement results—Driver 3.

Indicator	Fixation	Saccadic Movements	Blinks
Total number	77	41	34
Average	8	4	3

Traffic in the fourth drive was similar to what had been experienced before; however, the sky was much clearer. As one of the few drivers, he was acutely aware of outdoor advertisements. The driver had turned his gaze to the numerous billboard advertisements placed in a visible position for the cars leaving the Lidl supermarket, where the test drives began and ended. The driver paid close attention to the road ahead. During the ride, he repeatedly focused on the advertisement placed on the back of the bus he was following for a certain period of time. Possibly, there were issues with the eye tracker calibration, as there were repeated long fixations or no fixation registered on the recording in some sections. This is also reflected in the measured data (Table 4).

Table 4. Measurement results—Driver 4.

Indicator	Fixation	Saccadic Movements	Blinks
Total number	977	897	56
Average	96	88	5

Driver 5 embarked on his journey on a drizzly Saturday morning, in place of the previously missed Wednesday ride. The roads were surprisingly free of impediments, with only a few cars traversing the route. The dismal weather was a constant companion, with heavy rain and dark clouds hanging above. Nevertheless, Driver 5 made it to his destination without a hitch, carefully observing the cars in front of him or the rear-view mirrors. Although he had limited experience with the route, as he had only previously driven on other roads in Žilina, he kept his concentration on the task at hand. Along the way, Driver 5 noticed only a single billboard advertisement and a single city light. Table 5 summarises the analysed key performance indicators obtained from the eye-tracking device.

Table 5. Measurement results—Driver 5.

Indicator	Fixation	Saccadic Movements	Blinks
Total number	1582	1412	149
Average	163	146	15

On Saturday, during supplementary measurements for Driver 3, the downpour had ceased and the clouds had started to dissipate. The traffic in the sixth drive was a bit heavier than it was during the previous ride, but there were only two pauses at red lights at crossroads. Driver 6 followed the highway and the areas immediately adjacent to it, taking particular notice of the cars in front of him. During the journey, the driver mentioned that his eyes had been drawn to the bright digital advertisements. This was evident right from the start of the ride, when he was the only one to spot the digital ad while leaving the Lidl store and heading downtown. Additionally, the driver noticed several billboards in close proximity. The key performance indicators obtained from the eye-tracking device are summarized in Table 6.

Table 6. Measurement results—Driver 6.

Indicator	Fixation	Saccadic Movements	Blinks
Total number	1605	1510	58
Average	166	156	6

3.2. Drive on Outer Circuit

Driving along the outer circuit has resulted in a spike in recorded external advertising by drivers. This can be attributed to the extended journey, the opportune positioning of advertisements, as well as the reduced external stimuli compared with driving through the city centre. Many drivers fixed their gaze on the sizable advertisement in the form of a banner on a building. Notably, these were banners on a football stadium and a banner promoting the Lidl supermarket, which is easily visible to drivers traveling down L'avobrežná Street towards the city centre.

The first attempt at riding was unsuccessful due to an inaccurate calibration of the eye tracker. As a result, a second ride was taken with the same measurements, potentially altering the driver's perception. On a Saturday at noon, Driver 7 embarked on the second ride. The sky was cloudy with a wet roadway, and the roads were quite empty. The ride was smooth, except for one interruption at a red light. The driver focused on the street and traffic signs, as well as advertisements. In addition to the pre-selected ads for testing, the driver also noted a large-format banner advertisement hung up at the football stadium. Interestingly, the driver's gaze repeatedly fixated on this particular advertisement. Table 7 presents the data obtained from the eye tracker during the measurement.

Table 7. Measurement results—Driver 7.

Drive	Indicator	Fixation	Saccadic Movements	Blinks
1	Total number	1001	546	162
	Average	50	27	8
2	Total number	3621	3312	308
	Average	183	167	15

Despite their unsatisfactory calibration results, Driver 8 managed to remain composed and deliver a smooth ride with no stops. Traffic conditions were favourable, with a moderate amount of vehicles on the road. The sky was clear, granting excellent visibility. Due to the unsatisfactory calibration results, the data from this eye tracking measurement (see Table 8) were not used for next evaluation.

Table 8. Measurement results—Driver 8.

Indicator	Fixation	Saccadic Movements	Blinks
Total number	520	301	160
Average	27	15	8

The ninth drive was first employed for eye tracking with a yellow filter, resulting in a notable improvement in tracking and motion accuracy, simplifying the calibration process. Environmentally, the conditions remained the same as in the prior measurement, with a steady flow of traffic and a cloudless sky. Although there were a greater number of cars on the road than usual, two stops at intersections due to red lights were observed. On the return trip, a queue formed on Košická Street towards Martin, adding to the overall journey time. Driver 9 was very vigilant, driving carefully and attentively scanning the road for the specified advertisements as well as various billboards and bigboards on either side of the road. On a stop at a traffic light intersection on Košická Street, a bigboard and megaboard were visible on the opposite side of the intersection. While the queue was forming, the driver also noticed several other billboards at the stop and in the slow-moving line. Table 9 presents the data collected from the eye-tracking device during the measurement.

Table 9. Measurement results—Driver 9.

Indicator	Fixation	Saccadic Movements	Blinks
Total number	3809	3102	570
Average	142	115	21

As the number of vehicles swelled along Košická and L'avobrežná streets, the sky began to cloud over. When passing through the intersection where the green light had just flickered on, there was a momentary hiccup in the traffic, yet the voyage remained unhindered. Driver 10 kept in his lane and followed the procession of vehicles in front of him, as well as those trailing behind. Despite the sluggish pace of the queue, his attention was scarcely drawn to the outdoor advertising, but he did take note of a few billboards and bigboards. Table 10 presents the data acquired from the eyetracker during the measurement process.

The eleventh ride took place before the sun reached its peak, so the roads were already becoming congested with a large number of vehicles. At one stop, the driver paused at a red-light intersection. Visibility was good, and the weather was suitable. The driver noted the smaller advertisements on the side of the street, but when he followed behind a larger vehicle, his focus shifted only to it. During the ride, the driver mentioned noticing a number of exterior ads on the sides of the road, and this was confirmed by the vast amount of attention he gave to the various outdoor ads, such as those on the opposing side of the street or the large billboards on buildings. Table 11 presents the comprehensive data acquired from the eye-tracker during the measurement process.

Table 10. Measurement results—Driver 10.

Indicator	Fixation	Saccadic Movements	Blinks
Total number	3600	3081	515
Average	150	128	21

Table 11. Measurement results—Driver 11.

Indicator	Fixation	Saccadic Movements	Blinks
Total number	3907	3401	496
Average	178	155	22

The roads, during the twelfth drive, were tranquil, with nearly no traffic. At a crossroads, there was a single halt as the light turned red. The atmosphere was cloudy, but not rainy, just with a light mist. Driver 12 mainly kept their eyes on the road ahead, yet also monitored the roadside advertisements and traffic signs on the right. During the test drive, the driver's gaze was frequently directed to the experimental advertisements, as well as those that were not included in the experiment. Most of them were placed beside the road on the driver's side. This driver recorded the highest count of external advertisements from all of the measurements. Table 12 displays the data acquired during the eyetracking measurement for driver 12. The table presents a comprehensive summary of the collected information.

Table 12. Measurement results—Driver 12.

Indicator	Fixation	Saccadic Movements	Blinks
Total number	3406	3165	496
Average	159	148	23

An extra trial drive (thirteenth) was carried out as a substitute for the journey with poor calibration. The weather had improved since the prior ride. The drizzle subsided, and the skies began to brighten up. Traffic stayed consistent, and the roads were nearly deserted. The drive paused twice due to a stop at an intersection. Driver 13 carefully monitored the road and traffic signals. He was intent on driving. Occasionally, he would glance away from the road. Just like the prior driver, he noticed a substantial amount of advertisements, but mainly on his side of the street. Table 13 displays the eye-tracking measurement data obtained from the latest driver (driver 13). This data provides insights into their eye movements and gaze patterns during the drive.

Table 13. Measurement results—Driver 13.

Indicator	Fixation	Saccadic Movements	Blinks
Total number	2875	2375	399
Average	132	109	18

4. Results of Questionnaire Inquiry

The questionnaire results (Table 14) indicate that a majority of participants, specifically 62%, reside in or near Žilina, while the remaining 38% live in different areas or cities. All drivers included in the study are familiar with Žilina and have experience driving in the town. Among these drivers, 77% have driven low-seated cars, while 23% have driven high-seated vehicles. Consequently, the majority of tests and measurements were conducted using small cars, such as hatchbacks or sedans.

Table 14. Opinions and insights about outdoor advertising.

Drivers	Residence	Perception of Outdoor Advertising	Driver's Attention: Aspect of Outdoor Ads	Awareness of the Impact of Outdoor Ads on Consumer Behaviour	Impact of Outdoor Ads on Consumer Behaviour	Online Shopping Frequency
Driver 1	Podbiel'	Yes	Graphics	No	No	2 × year
Driver 2	Žilina	Yes	Graphics	No	No	1 × month
Driver 3	Žilina	Yes	Ad size	No	Yes	1 × month
Driver 4	Žilina	Yes	Graphics	No	No	2 × month
Driver 5	Žilina	No	Ad content	No	No	1 × month
Driver 6	Teplička	Yes	Flashing	Yes	No	2 × month
Driver 7	Teplička	Yes	Ad size	No	No	1 × month
Driver 8	Teplička	Yes	Colours	No	No	Not shopping
Driver 9	Belá	Yes	Colours	No	No	2 × year
Driver 10	Kubíková	Yes	Ad size	No	No	1 × month
Driver 11	Brodno	Yes	Ad size	Yes	No	2 × month
Driver 12	Považská Bystrica	No	Colours	No	No	1 × month
Driver 13	Považská Bystrica	Yes	Graphics	No	No	1 × month

The initial question inquired about drivers' perception of outdoor advertising, including billboards, bigboards, banners, flags, and signs. A significant proportion of drivers, up to 85%, reported being aware of outdoor advertisements while driving. A small percentage, 15%, indicated that they were unable to perceive such advertising.

The responses to the open-ended question were categorized into five sections. Thirty-one percent of drivers agreed that graphics and the size of the advertisement were the most effective in capturing their attention.

This suggests that the size of the advertisement plays a crucial role in attracting drivers' attention. Moreover, careful consideration of the visual elements can also be effective in drawing attention. Colours or colourfulness (23%) were identified as having a pleasing and visually appealing effect on drivers. Consequently, selecting the appropriate hues can enhance the advertisement's reach and increase the likelihood of attracting more drivers. Additionally, drivers were enticed by the content of the advertisement (7%) and flashing elements (8%), particularly in digital outdoor advertising.

The third question investigated the impact of external advertising on drivers' shopping habits. Fifteen percent of respondents acknowledged being influenced by external advertising, while eighty-five percent stated that they were not affected. This indicates that drivers are either not swayed by external advertising or are unaware of its influence on their purchasing decisions.

The subsequent inquiry aimed to determine whether external advertising can significantly influence drivers to choose a specific option from various choices when making an online purchase. The responses to this question overwhelmingly leaned towards a negative response. A notable 92% of drivers answered "No", indicating that external advertising does not heavily influence their online purchasing decisions, while only 8% responded with a "Yes".

The fifth and final question sought to ascertain the frequency of online shopping among the surveyed drivers. A total of 54% of participants reported shopping online at least once a month, and 23% revealed shopping twice a month. This indicates that 77% of the drivers surveyed are frequent online shoppers, which is a positive outcome. However, there were still outliers, with 15% and 8% of drivers stating that they shop online only once every six months or never shop online, respectively. The latter figure is rather unexpected, especially considering that the majority of Slovaks, particularly younger generations, are expected to engage in regular online shopping.

5. Results of A/B Testing

The A/B testing results provided the fundamental data that could be further used and developed. This testing consisted of 18 choices in the inner circuit and 22 choices in the outer circuit, with each selection being presented with four questions. During the testing, each driver was instructed to simulate the online shopping experience and make decisions accordingly. Their responses were recorded based on their autonomous answers, free from any external pressure or influence from the researcher. During the duration of the research, some of the advertisements were altered, such as TR1-002 in the inner circuit and TR4-039, TR4-055, TR4-059, TR4-075, TR4-115, and partially TR4-005 in the outer circuit. The latter was modified between the first and second measurements. These data were used in the research wherever feasible. Additionally, there were calibration issues with Driver 3 and Driver 8, meaning their data were only used where possible and were excluded from the eye-tracking evaluation.

Question 1 of the test focused on the selection of an option (A or B) that the driver prefers or selects when purchasing. The driver chose according to their personal inclination or preference. The responses for the inner and outer circuits were evaluated independently. The question was about which option, A or B, you would choose when purchasing. The answers were mainly categorized as Correct and Incorrect to enable the recognition of individual answers of the drivers when evaluating Question 1. The answer Correct means that tested subject chose the option that was placed on the billboard and had the opportunity to see it while driving. The answer Incorrect means that the tested subject chose an option not displayed on the billboards along the road. This appraisal was then be employed for further processing, thus necessitating the differentiation of the drivers' individual answers.

On the inner circuit, five drivers (data from Driver 3 were not usable for further research) yielded 90 responses, of which 12 were correct and 6 were incorrect selections, with the highest success rate being for Driver 1 and the best result being TR1-088, chosen correctly by all. When evaluating the ads, 62% of the responses proved correct, while 38% were incorrect (Table 15).

Table 15. Results of A/B testing for identification of preferred options—inner circuit.

Outdoor Adverts	Results					
	Driver 1	Driver 2	Driver 3	Driver 4	Driver 5	Driver 6
TR1-002	Correct	Correct	N/A	Incorrect	Correct	Correct
TR1-030	Correct	Correct	N/A	Correct	Incorrect	Correct
TR1-031	Incorrect	Correct	N/A	Correct	Correct	Incorrect
TR1-032	Correct	Incorrect	N/A	Correct	Correct	Correct
TR1-033	Incorrect	Correct	N/A	Correct	Incorrect	Incorrect
TR1-040	Correct	Incorrect	N/A	Incorrect	Correct	Correct
TR1-041	Correct	Correct	N/A	Correct	Incorrect	Incorrect
TR1-042	Incorrect	Incorrect	N/A	Correct	Correct	Incorrect
TR1-043	Correct	Correct	N/A	Correct	Incorrect	Incorrect
TR1-045	Correct	Correct	N/A	Incorrect	Correct	Correct
TR1-074	Correct	Incorrect	N/A	Incorrect	Incorrect	Correct
TR1-075	Incorrect	Correct	N/A	Incorrect	Correct	Correct
TR1-076	Incorrect	Incorrect	N/A	Incorrect	Correct	Incorrect
TR1-088	Correct	Correct	N/A	Correct	Correct	Correct
TR1-100	Correct	Incorrect	N/A	Incorrect	Correct	Incorrect
TR1-103	Incorrect	Correct	N/A	Correct	Correct	Correct
TR1-115	Correct	Incorrect	N/A	Correct	Incorrect	Correct
TR1-116	Correct	Correct	N/A	Correct	Incorrect	Correct

On the outer circuit, six drivers (data from Driver 8 were not usable for further research) amassed 132 responses, with Driver 10 being the most successful, with 17 correct and 5 incorrect options. The results were determined to be evenly split, with a 53% to 47% ratio of correct to incorrect answers (Table 16).

Table 16. Results of A/B testing for identification of preferred options—outer circuit.

Outdoor Adverts	Results						
	Driver 7	Driver 8	Driver 9	Driver 10	Driver 11	Driver 12	Driver 13
TR4-005	Correct	N/A	Incorrect	Correct	Incorrect	Incorrect	Incorrect
TR4-006	Correct	N/A	Incorrect	Correct	Incorrect	Incorrect	Correct
TR4-017	Incorrect	N/A	Incorrect	Incorrect	Incorrect	Correct	Incorrect
TR4-029	Incorrect	N/A	Correct	Correct	Correct	Correct	Correct
TR4-039	Incorrect	N/A	Correct	Correct	Incorrect	Incorrect	Incorrect
TR4-055	Incorrect	N/A	Incorrect	Correct	Incorrect	Incorrect	Incorrect
TR4-059	Incorrect	N/A	Incorrect	Correct	Incorrect	Incorrect	Correct
TR4-075	Correct	N/A	Correct	Correct	Correct	Correct	Correct
TR4-079	Incorrect	N/A	Correct	Correct	Incorrect	Correct	Incorrect
TR4-092	Incorrect	N/A	Incorrect	Incorrect	Correct	Incorrect	Incorrect
TR4-097	Correct	N/A	Correct	Correct	Incorrect	Incorrect	Correct
TR4-114	Correct	N/A	Incorrect	Correct	Incorrect	Correct	Incorrect
TR4-115	Incorrect	N/A	Incorrect	Incorrect	Incorrect	Incorrect	Incorrect
TR4-119	Correct	N/A	Correct	Incorrect	Correct	Incorrect	Correct
TR4-121	Correct	N/A	Incorrect	Correct	Incorrect	Correct	Incorrect
TR4-122	Correct	N/A	Correct	Incorrect	Correct	Incorrect	Incorrect
TR4-143	Correct	N/A	Incorrect	Correct	Correct	Correct	Correct
TR4-151	Correct	N/A	Incorrect	Correct	Correct	Incorrect	Correct
TR4-155	Correct	N/A	Correct	Correct	Correct	Correct	Correct
TR4-156	Correct	N/A	Correct	Correct	Incorrect	Correct	Correct
TR4-157	Incorrect	N/A	Correct	Correct	Correct	Correct	Incorrect
TR4-158	Incorrect	N/A	Correct	Correct	Correct	Incorrect	Incorrect

Joint evaluation of the data yielded a final outcome of 57% correct answers to 43% incorrect answers. However, it is unclear whether the results were influenced by the perception of the external advertisement or if drivers were simply choosing based on personal preference.

Another question from the questionnaire probes whether drivers noticed or registered the chosen logo or product during their test drive. This is a closed question with the options Yes or No. The results were once more divided for inner circuit and outer circuit separately, yet were also evaluated together. For this evaluation, the results from the altered advertisements were no longer taken into account since the answer is irrelevant (TR-002 in the inner circuit and the TR4-005, TR4-039, TR4-055, TR4-059, TR4-075, TR4-115 in the outer circuit). The drivers were unable to see advertisements that were not on the route during the test drive.

The inner circuit recorded a total of 85 responses (Table 17), with 12 being positive and 73 being negative, giving an overall ratio of 14% Yes to 86% No. This is an interesting result, as more than half of drivers on this route chose the "correct" option in the A/B test. The highest number of positive responses (4) were given for advertisement TR1-075. Driver 2 indicated that he noticed or registered logos or products 7 times, while 10 times, he did not see them.

Meanwhile, the outer circuit yielded the same result, with 14% Yes responses and 86% No responses (Table 18). The most positive responses (2) were given for the advertisements TR4-097, TR4-121, TR4-156, and TR4-157. Notably, Driver 7 gave the most Yes responses, 8 times, and 8 times, he answered No.

Table 17. Results of A/B testing for noticing the logo or product while driving—inner circuit.

Outdoor Adverts	Results					Σ	
	Driver 1	Driver 2	Driver 4	Driver 5	Driver 6	Yes	No
TR1-030	No	No	No	No	No	0	5
TR1-031	No	No	No	No	No	0	5
TR1-032	No	No	No	No	No	0	5
TR1-033	No	No	No	No	No	0	5
TR1-040	No	Yes	Yes	No	No	2	3
TR1-041	No	No	No	No	Yes	1	4
TR1-042	No	Yes	No	No	No	1	4
TR1-043	No	Yes	No	No	No	1	4
TR1-045	No	No	No	No	No	0	5
TR1-074	No	Yes	No	No	No	1	4
TR1-075	Yes	Yes	No	No	Yes	3	2
TR1-076	No	No	No	No	No	0	5
TR1-088	No	Yes	No	No	Yes	2	3
TR1-100	No	No	No	No	No	0	5
TR1-103	No	No	No	No	No	0	5
TR1-115	No	No	No	No	No	0	5
TR1-116	No	Yes	No	No	No	1	4
Σ ("Yes")	1	7	1	0	3	12	73

Table 18. Results of A/B testing for notice of the logo or product while driving—outer circuit.

Outdoor Adverts	Results						Σ	
	Driver 7	Driver 9	Driver 10	Driver 11	Driver 12	Driver 13	Yes	No
TR4-006	Yes	No	No	No	No	No	1	5
TR4-017	No	No	No	No	No	No	0	6
TR4-029	Yes	No	No	No	No	No	1	5
TR4-079	No	No	No	No	No	Yes	1	5
TR4-092	No	Yes	No	No	No	No	1	5
TR4-097	Yes	No	Yes	No	No	No	2	4
TR4-114	No	No	No	No	Yes	No	1	5
TR4-119	Yes	No	No	No	No	No	1	5
TR4-121	Yes	No	No	Yes	No	No	2	4
TR4-122	No	No	No	No	No	No	0	6
TR4-143	No	No	No	No	Yes	No	1	5
TR4-151	Yes	No	No	No	No	No	1	5
TR4-155	No	No	No	No	No	No	0	6
TR4-156	Yes	No	Yes	No	No	No	2	4
TR4-157	Yes	No	No	No	No	Yes	2	4
TR4-158	No	No	No	No	No	No	0	6
Σ ("Yes")	8	1	2	1	2	2	16	80

From the overall assessment for both routes, the ratio is 15.5% for Yes and 84.5% for No. Indeed, the answer Yes was registered 28 times, while the answer No was documented 153 times. This analysis could be indicative of participating drivers only slightly perceiving and monitoring outdoor advertising while driving. Nonetheless, there is also a chance that drivers perceive outdoor advertising subconsciously and thus respond to the question negatively. Additional accurate findings were available once the eye tracker measurement had been evaluated.

The last question from the A/B testing was asked drivers to assess whether they associated the given logo or brand with a particular product. This focused on the experience or knowledge of a specific product or service that the driver knows is offered or sold by the company. If the driver chose an aquarist logo, the answer that they sell fish would not be positively evaluated; rather, it should be a specific product purchased or mediated directly from the aquarist. This question was asked only for selections that included the company logo, excluding those with specific products. All responses, including those from drivers without the results of eye-tracking measurement and changed advertisements, were evaluated together and separately for both routes to determine if there exists a correlation between product knowledge and purchase decisions.

On the inner circuit, 85 selections have been evaluated, with 20 connections to a specific product, and 65 times, it was not connected, resulting in a ratio of 24% to 76% in favour of the No answer. The most successful selections were TR1-002 and TR1-075, each with six Yes answers. Driver 6 had the most product brands connected to them, with Yes answered five times. The outer circuit evaluation totalled 96 data, with a near balanced distribution of 46 positive and 50 negative answers, representing 48% Yes answers and 52% No answers. TR4-115 had the highest number of Yes answers (7). Driver 7 had the highest tally of all drivers on the outer circuit, with 10 Yes answers.

The joint evaluation of both routes yielded 66 affirmative answers and 115 negative ones, resulting in a total of 181. The ratio of affirmative to negative answers was an unfavourable 36.5% to 63.5%, indicating that nearly two-thirds of respondents may have been influenced by their familiarity with a certain service or product linked to the logo.

6. Results of Eye-Tracking Analysis

Previous conclusions and outcomes were meticulously scrutinized on the basis of the subjective responses of individual drivers (A/B testing results). The evaluation of measurements and records from the eye tracker provided the requisite value to the earlier outcomes, which were then supported by tangible evidence. The recordings from the measurements with the eye tracker served as the essential foundation for the research and work done overall. An important indicator of the success of the eye-tracking measurement is the fixation and saccadic eye movements values. Table 19 evidently shows the drivers for whom the results of the eye tracker measurement were inadequate (Driver 3 and Driver 8).

Table 19. Average number of fixations and saccadic eye movements.

Indicator	Fixation (per Minute)	Saccadic Movements (per Minute)	Blinks (per Minute)	Duration of Ride (in Minutes)
Driver 1	171	156	13	9:19
Driver 2	82	49	7	9:34
Driver 3	8	4	3	9:11
Driver 4	96	88	5	10:08
Driver 5	163	146	15	9:39
Driver 6	166	156	6	9:38
Driver 7	183	167	15	19:47
Driver 8	27	15	8	19:04
Driver 9	142	115	21	26:48
Driver 10	150	128	21	23:55
Driver 11	178	155	22	21:52
Driver 12	159	148	23	21:19
Driver 13	132	109	18	21:42
Average (Drivers 3 and 8 excluded)	147	129	15	

It is evident from the table that Driver 3 and Driver 8 had extensive difficulty in calibrating the eye tracker, rendering their measurements unusable for research, thus necessitating their exclusion from any further research regarding the eye-tracking data. Driver 2 and Driver 4 too presented substantially lower fixation and saccadic movement values compared with the remainder of the sample, yet these figures were satisfactory for research purposes; accordingly, they will be included in the research for the eye-tracking measurements. All the values in Table 19 have been recalculated per minute, considering each driver's test drive was of a different duration. Driver 7 ostensibly had the most desirable results. Nevertheless, it is imperative to point out that an excessive amount of fixations or saccadic movements while driving can cause agitation and unease. The average fixation value for the participating drivers was 147 per minute, while the average saccadic movement value was 129. This results in an average of over two fixations and saccadic movements per second for the driver.

Eye fixation is a critical component of research, particularly when it comes to outdoor advertising. An eye tracker can be used to measure each single fixation on the outdoor advertisement chosen for testing, as well as all other large-format advertisements excluded from the experiment. Within the inner circuit, 25 large-format advertisements were studied, resulting in a mere six fixations—a ratio of 5%. The outer circuit had a slightly better outcome, with 108 fixations—representing a ratio of 13% out of the total number of possible views.

For elucidation, the assessment in Table 20 is directed at all the outdoor advertisements located on the test routes. All the test drives tallied up to 557 ads, of which drivers noted 65. The total fixation rate from all the ads was 12%. To put it another way, during the test drives, the driver on average recorded one out of every ten large-format outdoor advertisements.

Table 20. Evaluation of outdoor advertisements seen during test drives.

Inner Circuit	Outdoor Advertising (OA)	Seen OA	View Ratio of OA on Total Number of OA	Outer Circuit	Outdoor Advertising (OA)	Seen OA	View Ratio of OA on Total Number of OA
Driver 1	25	3	12%	Driver 7	72	13	18%
Driver 2	25	0	0%	Driver 9	72	5	7%
Driver 4	25	2	8%	Driver 10	72	4	6%
Driver 5	25	0	0%	Driver 11	72	12	16%
Driver 6	25	1	4%	Driver 12	72	14	19%
Σ	125	6	5%	Driver 13	72	11	15%
				Σ	432	59	14%

The ultimate step in data evaluation and assessment is the fusion of eye tracking and A/B testing of the participating drivers. For both pathways, the external ads integrated in the trial were individually examined. However, the results were much less successful when all the ads on the routes were evaluated. After analysing the modified advertisement, 17 external ads were present on the inner circuit that was subjected to the testing. Since measurements were taken from five to six drivers, this accounts for 85 advertisements in total. Surprisingly, only four were registered by the drivers, and no fixations of the gaze were recorded for 81 of them. This generated a ratio of 5% for observed ads. Two drivers were unsuccessful in noting any fixations on the specified ads. From the viewpoint of advertisements, this corresponds to one fixation for 4 advertisements and zero fixations for 13 advertisements across five test drives.

The outcomes of the outer circuit evaluation were markedly different from those of the inner circuit. Measurements of 6 drivers and 16 ads were used in the assessment. Out of the 96 outdoor ads visible on route, 24 were noted by drivers. On average, the total fixation rate was 25%. The most fixations (3) were recorded for ads TR4-155 and TR4-157 (Figure 5). Driver 12 was the one with the highest number of recorded ads, having seen six ads overall. This gave a total ratio of 16% seen and 84% without fixation on both routes.

After a thorough assessment of the advertising tracking, a comparison between the drivers' subjective responses from the A/B testing and the measured values from the eye tracker was made. Three variants were then produced:

- Response Yes and Saw—evaluation based on the driver's answer of Yes to the question on whether they noticed the logo or product they selected during the test drive, and the eye tracker recording that they saw the advertising used for that choice in the A/B testing.
- Response Yes and Not seen—evaluation based on the driver's answer of Yes to the question on whether they noticed the logo or product they selected during the test

drive, and the eye tracker recording that they did not witness the advertising used for that choice in the A/B testing.
- Response No and Saw—evaluation based on the driver's answer of No to the question on whether they noticed the logo or product they selected during the test drive, and the eye tracker recording that they saw the advertising used for that choice in the A/B testing.

Figure 5. Outdoor adverts TR4-155 and TR4-157, outer circuit.

The evaluation of conditions was conducted according to the criterion of selecting TRUE or FALSE. When both conditions were fulfilled, the response was marked as TRUE. However, if one or both of the conditions were not satisfied, the result was labelled FALSE. The first variant evaluated was Answer Yes and Saw. The aim was to determine how often the driver reported that they noticed the chosen option and actually focused their gaze on it during the trial. The evaluation of this variant on the inner route revealed that only in two cases was the result TRUE, which signifies that in these two situations, both conditions were fulfilled. In terms of percentage, this outcome accounts for only 2% of the entire sample. The outer route was evaluated as TRUE in 5 cases out of a total of 96 options. Here, it is 5% of the entire sample. The overall ratio of fulfilment of this variant from both routes is 7 out of 181, which constitutes 1% of the entire sample.

The second variant with slight changes was Answer Yes and Not Seen. This was a situation in which the driver during the testing indicated that they saw the chosen logo or product during the test drive, but no fixation was recorded in the eye tracker data. On the inner circuit, these conditions were fulfilled in 10 out of 85 possible cases, representing 11.8% of the total sample. On the outer circuit, the conditions for the variant were met in 9 cases, representing 9.4% of all possibilities. From the overall evaluation of both routes together, the conditions were fulfilled in 10.5% of all possibilities.

The intriguing variant for investigation was answer No and Saw; from an investigative point of view, this is especially interesting. The assessment of this variant provides insight into the potential effect of external advertising on buying decisions. In this context, the driver claimed they did not notice the selected logo during the trial run, but in fact, they had it in focus. On the inner path, two cases fulfilled the conditions, representing 2.3% of the overall sample evaluated. On the outer route, the results were much better; twenty options were accurately evaluated, equating to 20.8% of all possibilities. Once both routes were taken into consideration, 22 of 181 options met the conditions, making up 12.2% of the total sample.

The third variant of evaluation was combined with A/B testing to determine any potential correlation between the perception of the advertisement and its influence on purchase decisions. This evaluation combines two previous evaluations, the A/B test based on "correct" and "incorrect" choices out of the options presented to the drivers among the individual choices in the test and the evaluation of the No Answer and Seen option. The aim was to identify instances wherein the driver might have registered the advertisement with the selected logo or product, while stating they did not see it during the test drive. If these three conditions are met, it can be concluded that there is a relationship between the driver's making a purchase decision based on the registration of an external advertisement. In the assessment of the inner circuit, no correlation possibilities were discovered. Of the 85 possibilities, none fulfilled all three specified criteria. This can be partially attributed to the limited number of advertisements witnessed by drivers along the route. Nonetheless, the evaluation of the outer circuit uncovered nine scenarios in which all conditions were satisfied. Specifically, this accounts for 9% of the total sample evaluated. For these nine instances, it can be hypothesized that the visible outdoor advertising had a bearing on the purchasing decisions of certain drivers.

7. Discussion

This article aims to comprehensively understand the magnitude of external advertising's influence on customer decision-making in the digital domain. To enhance the precision of the research and data, this study measures the effects of external advertising on drivers and their decision-making processes. To simulate the online environment, the researchers employed A/B testing, wherein drivers were promptly presented with two options after driving. This testing method was designed to elicit a choice between the brand and the product itself, resembling the process of online shopping. To ensure that drivers would adapt their behaviour and preferences accordingly, they were given prior notification of this experimental setup.

To elucidate conscious consumer preferences, an extensive interview was conducted. The primary objective of this interview was to ascertain the frequency with which the participating drivers engage in online purchasing. It is worth noting that over two-thirds of the sample reported engaging in monthly online transactions. This substantial figure lends credence to the research outcomes and their relevance in the context of consumer behaviour within the digital landscape. Given drivers' familiarity with this form of shopping, their decision-making is inherently connected to the online realm.

Following a meticulous interview process and subsequent A/B testing, it was revealed that most drivers did not consciously perceive external advertising while driving. Nevertheless, the measurements obtained from the study unveiled that drivers are most strongly attracted to advertisements featuring visually appealing graphics, appropriate sizes, and captivating colours. This finding is paramount for advertisers, as it enables them to effectively engage consumers through three key mechanisms: establishing contact, capturing attention, and placing advertisements in optimal locations. Armed with this knowledge, advertisers can leverage visually appealing graphics, appropriately sized ads, and captivating colours to ensure that their advertisements are seen and noticed by drivers.

The subsequent inquiry pertains to the impact of external advertising on drivers' purchasing behaviour. Most participants reported limited awareness of the influence exerted by such advertising on their decision-making. However, it is important to note that further investigation and comprehensive assessment utilizing additional tools would be required to corroborate or refute this observation definitively. It is pertinent to acknowledge that the research presented in this article was conducted from the driver's perspective, with data collection facilitated by an eye tracker, thus limiting the scope of aspects that could be evaluated. When questioned regarding the influence of external advertising on their purchasing decisions, nearly all drivers asserted that it does not affect their decision-making process. The collected measurements partially substantiate this finding. Nonetheless, the impact of external advertising on drivers' purchasing decisions, albeit minor, warrants further exploration and investigation.

7.1. Research Limitations

Throughout the research process, various key issues emerged that directly impacted the study and its components. Noteworthy influences were observed during the research.

One crucial factor that affected the research pertained to the selection of drivers. Gender was taken into consideration to ensure a relatively balanced sample of participants. Age diversity was also considered, with a range of 20 years. It is plausible to suggest that if the sample had predominantly consisted of one gender or age group, the obtained results may have differed from those obtained.

The utilization or lack thereof of a yellow filter on the eye tracker during measurements proved to be a significant factor. Insufficient calibration occurred without the filter, leading to unsuitable results for further evaluation (Drivers 3 and 8).

The selection of suitable routes played a crucial role in influencing the overall results. Comparing the two routes used in the research, significant differences in driving style and perception of outdoor advertising were observed, aligning with the intended purpose of route selection. Despite the exclusion of Drivers 3 and 8, the scenarios presented (inner circle and outer circle) yielded valuable findings.

The research presented in this article holds promise for the future, offering ample opportunities for further enhancements and the discovery of correlations. By incorporating additional technologies such as brain activity measurement and eye tracking for option selection, this research, which already utilizes A/B testing and eye trackers, can be further enriched. These methods can provide novel insights into shopping behaviour, including the order in which the eyes fixate on specific points. Furthermore, investigating the same routes for drivers and passengers may unveil a potentially greater impact of external advertising on passengers than on drivers.

The extensive scope of outdoor advertising and its substantial influence on consumer behaviour warrants further investigation and research. While this research draws upon a wealth of data and remains relevant, there is always room for improvement and refinement of the outcomes. It can be concluded, however, that outdoor advertising does exert a certain influence on customers' decisions. Nevertheless, the research findings suggest that the impact of outdoor advertising on motor vehicle drivers is relatively minimal.

7.2. Agenda for Future Research

The A/B testing conducted in this study elicited responses to four questions associated with selections made for each circuit. The results demonstrated comparable success rates across both circuits, suggesting a lack of discernible influence of advertising on decision-making. Notably, many drivers make choices based on personal preferences, encompassing elements such as brand recognition, visually appealing stimuli, and other unspecified factors. Although a fraction of respondents acknowledged some impact of advertisements, these responses were subjective, thus necessitating caution in their interpretation. It is plausible to posit that the influence of advertising may operate at a subconscious level.

The analysis of participants' responses revealed that drivers consciously register minimal outdoor advertisements. This limited conscious registration can be attributed to the fleeting nature of their exposure, characterized by an average fixation time of merely 0.3 s and often restricted to a single fixation. Consequently, the advertised logo or product often goes unnoticed, resulting in a lack of conscious recognition during decision-making. The evidence suggests that decisions are predominantly guided by personal experiences with specific goods or services and by the influence of word-of-mouth reviews from others. Consequently, it appears that outdoor advertising exerts only a marginal impact on individuals' decision-making processes.

The eye-tracking measurements employed in this research are pivotal for assessing its validity, as they guarantee the accuracy of the collected data. Notably, a significant disparity exists between the measurements obtained from the inner and outer circuits. The "urban" inner circuit records considerably fewer outdoor advertisements compared with the "circular" outer circuit. Nevertheless, it is observed that, on average, drivers notice approximately one-tenth of the large-format outdoor advertisements encountered. It is important to acknowledge that this value is contingent upon numerous factors. Nonetheless, it can be stated that a lower number of recorded ads corresponds to a weaker impact on purchase decisions.

By evaluating measurements conducted under three different conditions, certain instances reveal the potential for external advertising to sway driver choices. However, it is important to note that this potential remains relatively weak when compared with the overall number of ads surveyed. This observation underscores the need for further measurements and exploration. Notably, all instances of possible influence were registered on the outer circuit, indicating the influence exerted while driving in town. Conversely, within the city, specifically on the inner circuit, no instances of possible impact through external advertising were recorded. It is crucial to avoid unequivocal assertions of the absence of influence; nonetheless, determining the magnitude of impact solely based on eye-tracking measurements is inherently challenging.

7.3. Research Implications

Based on the meticulous analysis of the data, it becomes evident that the driver's perception, and hence the impact of external advertising on the driver, is subject to a multitude of factors. Notably, the examination of eye movement patterns in both the inner and outer circuits reveals a substantial decrease in the number of fixations and saccadic movements within the inner circuit. Furthermore, the level of traffic in urban centres and arterial roads outside the city exerts a discernible influence on the driver's attentional capacity; in denser traffic conditions, the driver's vigilance is heightened, consequently diminishing the likelihood of noticing external advertising. Consequently, it is impractical to target advertising campaigns towards city centres when aiming to reach drivers effectively. Instead, the strategic focus should encompass sections with fewer points of conflict, such as extended linear segments characterized by low traffic intensity. In areas with high traffic density, the impact of external advertising is notably diminished.

The visibility of outdoor advertising exhibits a profound dependence on its placement. Within the inner circuit, advertisements are frequently concentrated in inconspicuous locations where drivers direct their attention predominantly towards the traffic rather than peripheral objects. However, advertisements positioned along extensive, unobstructed roads that afford long-distance visibility possess an enhanced potential to capture the driver's attention. Consequently, the degree of influence on the consumer is directly proportional to the positioning of the advertisement. Furthermore, the influence exerted by the advertisement can be significantly modulated by the consumer's pre-existing opinion of the advertised product or service. Favourable past experiences with the brand or product increase the likelihood of being swayed towards making a purchase, thus augmenting the impact of the advertisement. Conversely, unfavourable experiences may prompt the consumer to opt for a competitor, thereby still exerting an influence on the efficacy of the advertisement.

In summary, the findings of this research can be succinctly encapsulated in the assertion that outdoor advertisements possess the potential to influence a driver's purchasing decisions. Although the driver's primary focus remains on operating the vehicle, instances arise wherein the route and prevailing traffic conditions allow for conscious notice of the advertisements. While this occurrence is not ubiquitous, if it does transpire, there exists the possibility of the advertisement exercising some sway in the eventual decision-making process.

8. Conclusions

The findings from this research provide clarity on various aspects of the influence of outdoor advertising on customers' purchasing decisions. It becomes evident that the impact of outdoor advertising on drivers is minimal during the experimental testing. Factors such as prevailing road conditions and traffic volume significantly influence drivers' perception of advertising. Consequently, it can be concluded that outdoor advertising is better suited for pedestrians or passengers in vehicles, especially in specific locations such as urban settings.

This study aimed to determine the impact of outdoor advertising on customers' purchasing behaviour by employing A/B testing and assuming the role of drivers of personal vehicles. The research and experimental outcomes shed light on the extent of influence exerted by outdoor advertising on customers' purchasing decisions, particularly in the online realm. The study identified nine instances where a clear correlation between outdoor advertising and specific purchase decisions was evident, suggesting some (albeit low) likelihood of the influence of outdoor advertising on customer decisions.

The results of the pre-experimental questionnaire highlight the significant factors that can impact customer decision-making and attention, including advertisement dimensions, colour schemes, and placement. In the online environment, customers' decision-making processes can be influenced by subtle details, especially when encountering unfamiliar brands or products. Outdoor advertising can have a similar effect on customers, but it requires the advertisement to be initially perceived and processed subconsciously.

Marketers and advertising agencies need to consider various factors when devising strategies for outdoor advertising. The location and visually captivating nature of billboards, for example, can have a considerable influence on consumer purchasing decisions. However, the effectiveness of this impact depends on the advertisement being perceived by the consumer. Therefore, careful attention should be given to directing individual advertisements to drivers or pedestrians through precise site selection, appropriate frequency, and visually distinct content.

For future research endeavours, it is recommended to leverage diverse technologies, such as EEG (electroencephalography) and FEA (functional eye-tracking analysis), to gather a greater volume of data. This research utilized an eye-tracking device, which collected data from a specific region. By harnessing multiple technologies, data can be obtained from various sensors, enabling comprehensive evaluation, comparison, and the identification of potential correlations. The intersection of marketing, advertising, and eye-tracking in the transportation field presents an intriguing and relatively unexplored area, offering ample room for further research and valuable measurements. The remarkable potential of outdoor advertising necessitates continual exploration and investigation.

Author Contributions: Conceptualization, R.M.; methodology, R.M.; software, R.M.; validation, R.M., R.C., N.S. and L.M.; formal analysis, R.C.; investigation, R.C. and N.S.; resources, R.M. and L.M.; data curation, R.C. and N.S.; writing—original draft preparation, R.C. and N.S.; writing—review and editing, R.C. and N.S.; visualization, R.M.; supervision, R.M.; project administration, R.M.; funding acquisition, R.M. All authors have read and agreed to the published version of the manuscript.

Funding: This publication was created as a part of research projects the Operational Program Integrated Infrastructure 2014–2020 for the project: Innovative solutions for propulsion, energy, and safety components of means of transport, with ITMS project code 313011V334, co-financed from the resources of the European Regional Development Fund.

Institutional Review Board Statement: Not applicable.

Informed Consent Statement: Not applicable.

Data Availability Statement: The data of the resulting values of measurements are not publicly available. For further information regarding the data, contact the authors of this article.

Conflicts of Interest: The authors declare no conflict of interest.

References

1. Nelson, R.; Sykes, A. *Outdoor Advertising*; Routledge: London, UK, 2013.
2. Barry, P. *Advertising Concept Book 3E: Think Now, Design Later*, 3rd ed.; Thames & Hudson: New York, NY, USA, 2016.
3. Bernstein, D. *Advertising Outdoors: Watch This Space!* 1st ed.; Phaidon Press: London, UK, 1997.
4. Sutte, D.T. *The Appraisal of Outdoor Advertising Signs*; Appraisal Institute: Chicago, IL, USA, 1994.
5. Arens, W.; Weigold, M.M. *Advertising*, 3rd ed.; McGraw Hill: New York, NY, USA, 2017.
6. Kotler, P.T.; Armstrong, G. *Principles of Marketing Global Edition*; Pearson: London, UK; New York, NY, USA, 2021.
7. Portella, A. *Visual Pollution: Advertising, Signage and Environmental Quality*, 1st ed.; Routledge: Burlington, VT, USA, 2014.
8. Sullivan, L. *Hey Whipple, Squeeze This: The Classic Guide to Creating Great Advertising*, 6th ed.; Wiley: Hoboken, NJ, USA, 2022.
9. Kotler, P.; Keller, K. *Marketing Management, Global Edition*, 16th ed.; Pearson: London, UK, 2021.
10. Czajkowski, M.; Lekka, M.; Kiełczewska, A.; Lekki, M. Valuing externalities of outdoor advertising in an urban setting-the case of Warsaw. *J. Urban Econ.* **2022**, *130*, 103452. [CrossRef]

11. Hiranuma, Y.; Fujita, S.; Wada, Y. Multiobjective Optimization of Outdoor Advertisements Focusing on Impression, Attention, and Memory. *Int. J. Affect. Eng.* **2017**, *16*, 157–163. [CrossRef]
12. Huang, M.; Li, X.; Liang, X.; He, J.; Li, H. Interest-Driven Outdoor Advertising Display Location Selection Using Mobile Phone Data. *IEEE Access* **2019**, *7*, 30878–30889. [CrossRef]
13. Pluciennik, M.; Heldak, M. Outdoor Advertising in Public Space and its Legal System in Poland over the Centuries. In Proceedings of the 3rd World Multidisciplinary Civil Engineering, Architecture, Urban Planning Symposium (Wmcaus 2018), Prague, Czech Republic, 18–22 June 2018; IOP Publishing Ltd.: Bristol, UK, 2019; Volume 471, p. 112046. [CrossRef]
14. Izadpanah, P.; Omrani, R.; Koo, S.; Hadayeghi, A. Effect of Static Electronic Advertising Signs on Road Safety: An Experimental Case Study. *J. Orthop. Trauma* **2014**, *28*, S33–S36. [CrossRef]
15. Morera, Á.; Sánchez, Á.; Moreno, A.B.; Sappa, Á.D.; Vélez, J.F. SSD vs. YOLO for Detection of Outdoor Urban Advertising Panels under Multiple Variabilities. *Sensors* **2020**, *20*, 4587. [CrossRef]
16. Leonova, I.A.; Khramova, M.M.; Zaichkina, N.V. Advertising Design of Urban Development. *Galact. Media* **2022**, *4*, 81–93. [CrossRef]
17. Murwonugroho, W.; Yudarwati, G.A. Exposure to Unconventional Outdoor Media Advertising. *Pertanika J. Soc. Sci. Hum.* **2020**, *28*, 3407–3424. [CrossRef]
18. Tajuddin, S.A.; Zulkepli, N. An Investigation of the Use of Language, Social Identity and Multicultural Values for Nation-Building in Malaysian Outdoor Advertising. *Soc. Sci.* **2019**, *8*, 18. [CrossRef]
19. Zahid, N.; Fung, L.; Reynoso, M.; Schillinger, D.; Mejia, R. Socioeconomic disparities in outdoor branded advertising in San Francisco and Oakland, California. *Prev. Med. Rep.* **2022**, *27*, 101796. [CrossRef]
20. Urban, M.; Mirosław, K.; Krzysztof, K.; Karolina, P. Artificial, Cheap, Fake: Free Associations as a Research Method for Outdoor Billboard Advertising and Visual Pollution. *Hum. Aff.* **2020**, *30*, 253–268. [CrossRef]
21. Zhang, Y.; Liu, X.; Shi, C.; Liu, Y.; Guo, J.; Zhang, Z.; Jiang, Y. Optimizing Impression Counts for Outdoor Advertising. In Proceedings of the 25th ACM SIGKDD International Conference on Knowledge Discovery & Data Mining (KDD '19), Anchorage, AK, USA, 4–8 August 2019; Association for Computing Machinery: New York, NY, USA, 2019; pp. 1205–1215. [CrossRef]
22. Zahradka, J.; Machova, V.; Kucera, J. What Is the Price of Outdoor Advertising: A Case Study of the Czech Republic? *Ad. Alta-J. Interdiscip. Res.* **2021**, *11*, 386–391. [CrossRef]
23. Novak, M.; Kincl, T. Reaching Specific Audiences by Television Advertising Scheduling-the Case of the Czech Republic. In *Vision 2020: Sustainable Growth, Economic Development, and Global Competitiveness*; Soliman, K.S., Ed.; Int Business Information Management Assoc-Ibima: Norristown, PA, USA, 2014; Volumes 1–5, pp. 1290–1299.
24. Zhang, P.; Liu, C.; Chen, C.; Cheng, Y.; Li, X. Trajectory-driven Influential Billboard Placement. In Proceedings of the 24th ACM SIGKDD International Conference on Knowledge Discovery & Data Mining, New York, NY, USA, 19–23 August 2018; Association for Computing Machinery: New York, NY, USA, 2018; pp. 2748–2757. [CrossRef]
25. Megatsari, H.; Ridlo, I.A.; Amir, V.; Kusuma, D. Visibility and Hotspots of Outdoor Tobacco Advertisement around Educational Facilities without an Advertising Ban: Geospatial Analysis in Surabaya City, Indonesia. *Tob. Prev. Cessat.* **2019**, *5*, 32. [CrossRef]
26. Volle, P. The short-term effect of store-level promotions on store choice, and the moderating role of individual variables. *J. Bus. Res.* **2001**, *53*, 63–73. [CrossRef]
27. Nikolaeva, Z.V. "Slow" Visual Environment in the Urban Landscapes. *Galact. Media-J. Media Stud.-Galakt. Media-Zhurnal Media Issled.* **2022**, *4*, 85–99. [CrossRef]
28. Savchuk, V. Image Out of Place. *Galact. Media-J. Media Stud.-Galakt. Media-Zhurnal Media Issled.* **2022**, *4*, 35–46. [CrossRef]
29. Young, M. *Ogilvy on Advertising in the Digital Age*; Bloomsbury: New York, NY, USA, 2018.
30. Madleňák, R.; Madleňáková, L. Vizuálne Znečistenie Cestnej Infraštruktúry. 2022. Available online: https://www.researchgate.net/publication/354826470_Vizualne_znecistenie_cestnej_infrastruktury (accessed on 22 February 2023).
31. Wakil, K.; Hashim, N.; Mahdi, N.; Nayan, N.; Hanafiah, M.H. Mitigating Urban Visual Pollution through a Multistakeholder Spatial Decision Support System to Optimize Locational Potential of Billboards. *ISPRS Int. J. Geo-Inf.* **2021**, *10*, 60. [CrossRef]
32. Liu, B.; Liu, F. Positioning Analysis of Urban Outdoor Advertising. In Proceedings of the International Conference on Economics and Management Innovations (ICEMI 2017), Ho Chi Minh, Vietnam, 22–24 February 2017; Yue, X.G., McAleer, M., Eds.; Volkson Press: Kuala Lumpur, Malaysia, 2017; Volume 1, pp. 415–416. [CrossRef]
33. Egli, V.; Ross, N.A.; Winters, M. Viewing obesogenic advertising in children's neighbourhoods using Google Street View. *Geogr. Res.* **2019**, *57*, 84–97. [CrossRef]
34. Adams, J.; Ganiti, E.; White, M. Socio-economic differences in outdoor food advertising in a city in Northern England. *Public Health Nutr.* **2011**, *14*, 945–950. [CrossRef] [PubMed]
35. Roux, T.; Waldt, D.L.R.V.D.; Ehlers, L. A Classification Framework for Out-of-Home Advertising Media in South Africa. Communicatio-South African. *Communicatio* **2013**, *39*, 383–401. [CrossRef]
36. Moore, P.; Helbich, M. Cycling through the Landscape of Advertising in Amsterdam: A Commuters Perspective. *Sustainability* **2020**, *12*, 5719. [CrossRef]
37. Kwate, N.O.A.; Lee, T.H. Ghettoizing Outdoor Advertising: Disadvantage and Ad Panel Density in Black Neighborhoods. *J. Urban Health* **2007**, *84*, 21–31. [CrossRef] [PubMed]
38. Anagnostopoulos, A.; Petroni, F.; Sorella, M. Targeted interest-driven advertising in cities using Twitter. *Data Min. Knowl. Discov.* **2018**, *32*, 737–763. [CrossRef]

39. Robertson, J.; Li, X.; Huang, Z.; Sun, Y.; Luo, W.; Yin, J. How Deep Is Your Love? The Brand Love-Loyalty Matrix in Consumer-Brand Relationships. *J. Bus. Res.* **2022**, *149*, 651–662. [CrossRef]
40. Gulmez, M.; Karaca, S.; Kitapci, O. The Effects of Outdoor Advertisements on Consumers: A Case Study. *Stud. Bus. Econ.* **2010**, *5*, 70–88.
41. Wilson, R.T.; Till, B.D. Effects of outdoor advertising: Does location matter? *Psychol. Mark.* **2011**, *28*, 909–933. [CrossRef]
42. Efrat, K.; Souchon, A.L.; Dickenson, P.; Nemkova, E. Chutzpadik advertising and its effectiveness: Four studies of agencies and audiences. *J. Bus. Res.* **2021**, *137*, 601–613. [CrossRef]
43. Holmqvist, K.; Nyström, M.; Andersson, R.; Dewhurst, R.; Jarodzka, H.; Van de Weijer, J. *Eye Tracking: A Comprehensive Guide to Methods and Measures*; Oxford University Press: Oxford, UK, 2015.
44. Nielsen, J.; Pernice, K. *Eyetracking Web Usability*; New Riders Pub: Berkeley, CA, USA, 2009.
45. Duchowski, A.T. *Eye Tracking Methodology: Theory and Practice, 3rd ed*; Springer: Berlin/Heidelberg, Germany, 2017.
46. Siroker, D.; Koomen, P. *A/B Testing: The Most Powerful Way to Turn Clicks into Customers*, 1st ed.; Wiley: Hoboken, NJ, USA, 2015.
47. Madlenak, R.; Hudak, M.; Madlenakova, L. Measurement of Visual Smog Influence to Driver in Real and Laboratory Conditions. In Proceedings of the 21st International Scientific Conference on Transport Means (Transport Means), Juodkrante, Lithuania, 20–22 September 2017; pp. 177–180.
48. Hooge, I.T.C.; Niehorster, D.C.; Hessels, R.S.; Benjamins, J.S.; Nyström, M. How robust are wearable eye trackers to slow and fast head and body movements? *Behav. Res.* **2022**, 1–15. [CrossRef]

applied sciences

MDPI

Article

Evaluation of an Eye-Tracking-Based Method for Assessing the Visual Performance with Progressive Lens Designs

Pablo Concepcion-Grande [1,*], Eva Chamorro [1], José Miguel Cleva [1], José Alonso [1] and Jose A. Gómez-Pedrero [2]

[1] Clinical Research Department, Indizen Optical Technologies, 28002 Madrid, Spain
[2] Applied Optics Complutense Group, Optics Department, Optics and Optometry Faculty, Complutense University of Madrid, 28049 Madrid, Spain
* Correspondence: pconcepcion@iot.es

Abstract: Due to the lack of sensitivity of visual acuity (VA) measurement to quantify differences in visual performance between progressive power lenses (PPLs), in this study, we propose and evaluate an eye-tracking-based method to assess visual performance when wearing PPLs. A wearable eye-tracker system (Tobii-Pro Glasses 3) recorded the pupil position of 27 PPL users at near and distance vision during a VA test while wearing three PPL designs: a PPL for general use (PPL-Balance), a PPL optimized for near vision (PPL-Near), and a PPL optimized for distance vision (PPL-Distance). The participants were asked to recognize eye charts at both near and distance vision using centered and oblique gaze directions with each PPL design. The results showed no statistically significant differences between PPLs for VA. However, significant differences in eye-tracking parameters were observed between PPLs. Furthermore, PPL-Distance had a lower test duration, complete fixation time, and number of fixations at distance evaluation. PPL-Near has a lower test duration, complete fixation time, and number of fixations for near vision. In conclusion, the quality of vision with PPLs can be better characterized by incorporating eye movement parameters than the traditional evaluation method.

Keywords: high contrast visual acuity; progressive power lenses; eye-tracking; eye fixations

1. Introduction

Presbyopia is an age-related condition that prevents focusing on near objects; it is a natural part of the aging process and begins to develop around age 40 [1]. Progressive power lenses (PPLs) are a popular solution for presbyopes, as they provide a gradual transition of spherical power between distance and near vision, allowing wearers to see clearly at all distances by changing their gaze direction [2]. Due to the power variation along the vertical main meridian, usually an umbilical curve, unwanted astigmatic and spherical power variations appear in the lateral areas of the lens and affect the quality of vision [3,4]. Some proposed methods to evaluate the quality of vision with PPLs are based on the representation of theoretical power distribution maps obtained with lens mappers [5,6] or calculated using exact ray tracking to obtain user-perceived power distribution maps [7,8]. They are based on geometrical magnitude calculations that estimate the theoretical fields of view [5,6,9]. Although theoretical representations could be useful to characterize PPLs, the quality of vision varies depending on the subjective visual perception of the user. In order to gain a better understanding of this topic, several studies have been carried out to evaluate the quality of vision with PPLs using different methods such as satisfaction questionnaires [10–13], contrast sensitivity [14], reading performance [11,15], skew distortion [16], or high contrast visual acuity (VA) [12,17–19]. High-contrast VA is one of the main ways to assess the quality of vision with PPLs. VA refers to the ability to discern object details subtending a certain angle and is commonly employed in clinical practice to measure vision quality. It is also the standard measure to assess the quality of an optical correction [1]. The measurement of VA has been extensively used to evaluate the impact of lateral refractive errors in PPLs on visual performance. Legras et al. [17] evaluated differences in VA with 2 different PPLs and reported worse VA values when viewing through the lateral regions of the lens in comparison with the central region. Villegas et al. [19] also evaluated the effect of off-axis refractive errors in a PPL and showed a reduction in VA at off-axis gaze directions in comparison with centered gaze directions. However, these studies have not found significant differences in VA scores between different types of PPLs. This could be because the VA score does not consider other factors that impact visual perception, such as the time needed to recognize the optotypes. For this reason, this work proposes the assessment of the visual quality provided by PPLs by means of parameters such as recognition speed or the number of eye fixations while recognizing the optotypes.

Video-based ETs allow the monitoring and recording of gaze positions by sending infrared light to the subject's eye and recording with a camera the light reflected from it [20,21]. The bright pupil and the corneal reflections are processed using advanced image-processing software to obtain the instantaneous gaze direction with high accuracy and to calculate eye movements as saccades and fixations [21–23]. Thanks to these systems, it is possible to study the influence of factors such as text characteristics [24] or blur on eye movements [25]. In the field of PPLs, this technology has been widely used to study how lateral refractive errors of PPLs affect eye fixations. Han et al. [26,27] analyzed differences in eye fixations when reading with PPLs vs. single-vision lenses. Concepcion-Grande et al. [28] studied differences in eye fixations while reading on a monitor screen with two different PPL designs. Rifai et al. [29] studied differences in eye fixations while driving between PPL users in comparison with non-PPL users. All of them demonstrated that lateral unwanted refractive errors of PPLs affect eye fixation characteristics. For that reason, this study aims to evaluate an eye-tracking-based method for assessing the quality of vision with progressive power lenses by analyzing test duration and eye fixation characteristics during a high-contrast visual acuity test.

2. Materials and Methods

Study Design: A prospective, observational, longitudinal, double-masked study was carried out to evaluate test duration and characteristics of eye fixation when performing VA tests with 3 different PPL types. The factors analyzed were eye chart size, gaze direction, and lens design. The study followed the principles of the Declaration of Helsinki. Full study approval was obtained from the Complutense University of Madrid Committee Review Board (CE_20210715-3_SAL). All participants provided written informed consent before the start of the study, and at the end of the study, subjects were compensated with one pair of glasses.

Participants: The study sample was made up of presbyopic participants of both genders who were older than 44 and had worn PPLs for at least six months before the start of the study. The inclusion criteria were: (1) Refractive error range of −6.00 D to +5.00 D with astigmatism less than or equal to 2.50 D. (2) Near addition power from +1.00 D to +3.00 D. (3) Best-corrected VA is better than 0.1 logMAR monocularly and 0.05 logMAR binocularly. (4) Anisometropia below 1.50 D. Subjects were rejected if they had any ocular diseases, non-compensated binocular vision anomalies, medical conditions that could affect vision, or if they were undergoing any pharmacological treatments that might have affected the subjects' visual function. The sample size was calculated based on data from a preliminary study with five participants who met the same inclusion criteria as above. The calculation was performed using the GRANMO sample size calculator, version 7.12 (Institut Municipal d'Investigació Mèdica, Barcelona, Spain). Two-tailed testing with an alpha risk of 0.05, a beta risk of 0.1, and a dropout rate of 30% was set to estimate a sample size of 37 participants.

Procedure: All participants underwent a full optometric assessment to check whether they met the inclusion criteria. The visual examination included VA measurement using the PVVAT test (Precision Vision, La Salle, III), subjective refraction at a distance and near vision, stereo acuity assessment by the Titmus test, the Worth test, the Cover test, and ocular motility examination. After the optometrists determined the participant met the inclusion criteria, the fitting parameters and position of wear for the eye-tracker glasses were measured: pupillary position, segment height, back vertex distance, frame wrap angle, and pantoscopic tilt. Once these data were collected, the PPL study lenses were ordered. VA measurements incorporating an eye-tracking system for three different PPL designs at far and near distances were recorded in two different day visits with a duration of two hours. During the first visit, far-distance VA recordings were collected for the three different PPLs at three different gaze directions, and a two-minute break was taken between each experimental condition to minimize the participant's fatigue. In a similar way, during the second visit, near-distance VA measurements were collected for the three different PPLs and three gaze directions, including two-minute breaks between each experimental condition to minimize visual fatigue.

Progressive Power Lenses: Three different individualized free-form PPL designs were used for this study: (1) a balanced design, PPL-Balance (Endless Steady Balance, IOT, Madrid, Spain); (2) a lens with a wider field of view for near vision, PPL-Near (Endless Steady Near, IOT, Madrid, Spain); and (3) a lens with a wider field of view for distance vision, PPL-Distance (Endless Steady Distance, IOT, Madrid, Spain). The PPL's technical characteristics (cylinder and mean power distribution maps) for a plano prescription, addition 2D, using standard position-of-wear parameters are shown in Figure 1. The lenses were placed on a specific clip-on frame that was attached to the eye-tracker glasses. This configuration allows for direct pupil registration without any interference from the PPL. Lenses were calculated using an advanced lens calculation software (FreeForm Designer, IOT, Madrid, Spain) considering the fitting parameters of the PPLs attached to the ET glasses to reduce oblique aberrations and maintain a stable field of view regardless of the prescription and the additional power of each participant.

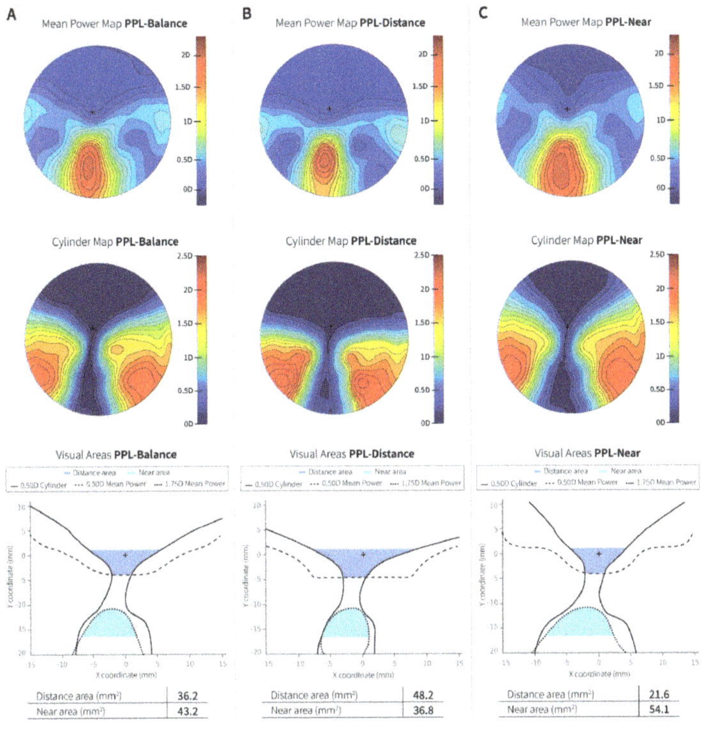

Figure 1. Mean power, cylinder power maps distribution, and visual areas according to Sheedy's criteria [6] for a Plano prescription, addition 2D with default parameters. (**A**) PPL-Balance. (**B**) PPL-Distance. (**C**) PPL-Near. Reprinted with permission from Ref. [30]. 2023, Concepcion-Grande et al.

Eye tracking recording: Binocular pupil position was recorded using a wearable eye-tracker system (Tobii Pro Glasses 3, Tobii AB, Stockholm, Sweden) with a sampling rate of 50 Hz. Recordings were made while participants were performing VA tests at a distance and near vision using eye charts with logMAR (logarithm of the minimum angle of resolution) unit notation and a scoring criterion that assigns to the subject the VA corresponding to a given line when at least three letters are correctly recognized [31,32]. The eye charts were composed of black optotypes over a white background with a luminance of 160 cd/m^2. Measurements were performed under photopic conditions (70 lux) in a uniformly illuminated room. Each eye chart was made up of a single row of five randomized optotypes (Sloan letters). The VA increments between eye charts were 0.10 logMAR. Subjects were asked to read the entire row of letters from left to right, beginning with an eye chart with a letter size two steps greater than their best-correction VA until the maximum VA was reached. VA measurements were done for each of the three PPLs at three different gaze directions in the following sequence: centered, 12.5° off-axis dominant eye side, and 12.5° off-axis non-dominant eye side. The order of measurements for each PPL was randomized. Far-distance VA was recorded using three eye charts shown on a screen monitor (Asus LCD Monitor VP228HE 21.5″) located at 5.25 m. Each of the letters on each eye chart was separated from the other by an angle of 1°. To evaluate off-axis positions, participants were seated on top of a big rotating platform with a chin rest to prevent head motion and ensure that all participants were looking through the same area of the lens. Near-distance VA was assessed at 0.37 m using three eye charts for each gaze direction displayed on a screen (Microsoft Surface PRO 4, 12.3″). The angular separation between letters in the same eye chart was 6.4°. Off-axis gaze directions were evaluated by moving the screen to three different positions. To prevent head motion and ensure participants used the central and lateral regions of the PPL, a table with a chin rest was used.

Recordings were processed to calculate fixations using Tobii Pro Lab software (Tobii AB, Stockholm, Sweden) and the Tobii I-VT fixation filter [33,34]. The velocity threshold was set according to a pilot study on 10 emmetropic non-presbyopic participants with the same experimental set-up as in the present work. Participants were asked to look at 5 optotypes of 0.4 logMAR size at 5.25 m and 0.37 m. A velocity threshold of 40°/s was set for the near-distance VA task, and 6°/s was set for the far-distance VA task (Figure 2). To ensure the quality of the recordings, a data quality analysis was performed. The data quality of each recording was calculated as the number of time points in each recording for which valid gaze data was collected, divided by the number of time points in the recording. The data quality of each recording was computed as the percentage of valid gaze data points relative to the total number of points recorded. As in other studies requiring very good quality in data recording [21,35], we set a threshold for data loss of 10%. Those participants with all recordings and valid data of 90% or more were included in the study.

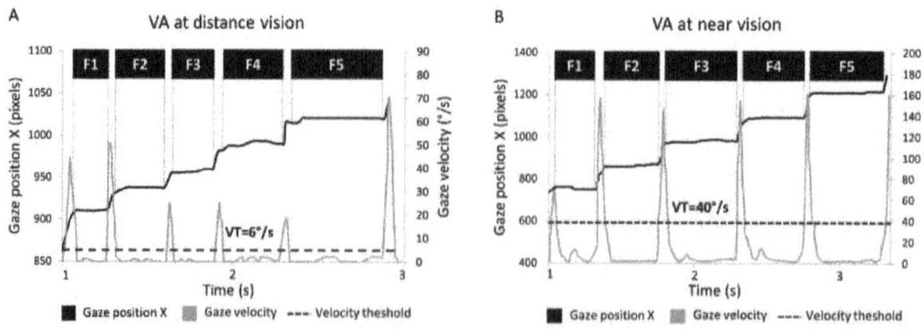

Figure 2. Fixation classification examples from a gaze position signal during VA test at distance vision (**A**) and near vision (**B**). The velocity threshold was set to allow the algorithm to recognize the five fixations corresponding to the five optotypes displayed on the screen (F1–F5).

Statistical Analysis: All the statistical analyses performed in this study were carried out with Python 3.8.8 software using the statsmodels library [36]. A three-way repeated measures ANOVA was used to assess differences in eye movements depending on the eye chart size, gaze direction, and PPL design, both for distance and near-distance VA measurements. To evaluate differences in VA scores depending on the gaze direction and the PPL design, a two-way repeated measure ANOVA was performed. The level of significance was set at 0.05 and the statistical power at 0.8. A Tukey HSD post-hoc test was used to determine which means differ significantly from each other. The variables analyzed were VA, test duration, complete fixation time, and the number of fixations.

3. Results

3.1. Sample Characteristics

A total of 42 subjects were enrolled in the study. Eye-tracking recordings were not attempted on 3 of them due to dry eyes (n = 1) and damaged lenses (n = 2). Eye-tracking recordings were collected from a total of 39 subjects; 13 of them did not meet the 90% valid data threshold for all recordings and were discarded from the data analysis (Figure 3). The final sample consisted of 27 subjects (15 men and 12 women), ranging in age from 44 to 65 years old (54 ± 6). The average mean refractive error of the participants was −0.8 ± 2.6 D (ranging from −6 D to +4.62 D). There were 12 myopic participants, 10 participants with hyperopia, and 5 emmetropic participants. The participants' addition powers ranged from 0.75 D to 2.50 D, with an average of 1.9 ± 0.5 D. The average mean percentage of valid data was 99.6 ± 1.2 (ranging from 91.1 to 100) for far-distance VA recordings and 99.7 ± 1.1 (ranging from 90.8 to 100) for near-distance VA recordings.

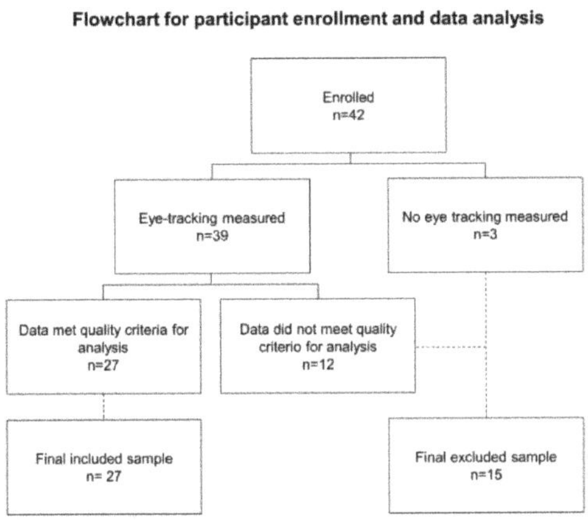

Figure 3. Flowchart for participant enrollment and data analysis.

3.2. Far-Distance VA

The results showed no statistical differences in distance vision for VA between PPLs and gaze direction (Table 1).

Table 1. Detailed statistics for visual acuity (VA) analysis at distance vision. Two-way repeated measures ANOVA.

PPL-Balance VA (Mean ± SD)	PPL-Distance VA (Mean ± SD)	PPL-Near VA (Mean ± SD)	SS	MS	Df	F-Ratio	*p*-Value
−0.06 ± 0.06	−0.06 ± 0.06	−0.05 ± 0.07	0.005	0.002	2	2.205	0.120
Centered VA (Mean ± SD)	**Dominant eye VA (Mean ± SD)**	**Non Dominant Eye VA (Mean ± SD)**	**SS**	**MS**	**Df**	**F-Ratio**	***p*-Value**
−0.06 ± 0.06	−0.06 ± 0.06	−0.05 ± 0.07	0.004	0.002	2	1.833	0.170

However, statistically significant differences in eye movements were found for the three factors analyzed: eye chart size, gaze direction, and PPL design. No statistically significant interactions were found between the analyzed factors. For the eye chart size, it was expected that when the letter became smaller, the task difficulty increased, thus affecting the eye movements. The results confirmed that with a smaller optotype size, there was a statistically significant longer test duration, longer fixation time, and higher fixation count. Regarding the gaze directions, as the participant is forced to look through the lateral areas of the lens with blur, we would expect the increased recognition effort to affect eye movement. Statistically significant differences in longer test duration, longer complete fixation time, and a greater number of fixations were found for off-axis gaze directions relative to the central one. Finally, it was observed an effect of PPL design on eye movements. When the participants were using the PPL optimized for distance vision, statistically lower test durations, lower duration of fixations, and a lower number of fixations were found. (Figure 4 and Table 2).

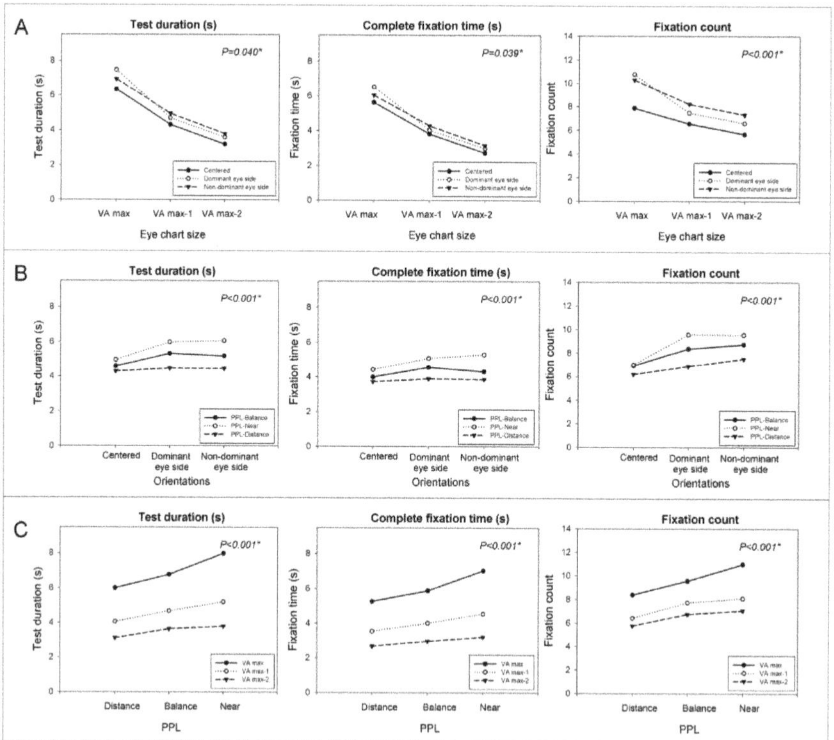

Figure 4. Variations in test duration, complete fixation time, and fixation count depend on the interactions of eye chart size and gaze direction (**A**), the gaze directions and PPL (**B**), and PPL and eye chart (**C**) for far-distance VA tasks. * Shows significance at the 0.05 level.

Table 2. Detailed statistics for Figure 4. Three-way repeated measures ANOVA test with pos-hoc comparisons using Tukey HSD method. * Shows significance at the 0.05 level.

	ANOVA Test for Eye Chart Size				Tukey HSD Comparisons for Eye Chart Size (*p*-Value)		
	Df	**Mean Square**	**F-Ratio**	***p*-Value**	**AVmax/Avmax-1**	**AVmax/Avmax-2**	**AVmax-1/Avmax-2**
Test duration	2	725.671	55.82	<0.001 *	<0.001 *	<0.001 *	<0.001 *
Fixation time	2	606.413	61.16	<0.001 *	<0.001 *	<0.001 *	<0.001 *
Fixation count	2	628.898	17.07	<0.001 *	<0.001 *	<0.001 *	0.1476
	ANOVA test for gaze direction				**Tukey HSD comparisons for gaze direction (*p*-value)**		
	Df	**Mean square**	**F-ratio**	***p*-value**	**Centered/dominant**	**Centered/Non dominant**	**Dominant/Non**
Test duration	2	31.62	6.09	0.040 *	0.066	0.079	0.996
Fixation time	2	16.24	3.45	0.039 *	0.172	0.2069	0.995
Fixation count	2	252.45	12.17	<0.001 *	0.003 *	<0.001 *	0.782
	ANOVA test for lens design				**Tukey HSD comparisons for lens design (*p*-value)**		
	Df	**Mean square**	**F-ratio**	***p*-value**	**Balance/Distance**	**Balance/Near**	**Distance/Near**
Test duration	2	96.87	13.82	<0.001 *	0.066	0.065	<0.001 *
Fixation time	2	74.62	14.86	<0.001 *	0.163	0.031 *	<0.001 *
Fixation count	2	211.79	8.18	<0.001 *	0.047 *	0.331	<0.001 *

3.3. Near-Distance VA

The results for near vision were similar to those for distance vision. No statistically significant differences for VA were found regarding PPL or gaze direction (Table 3).

Table 3. Detailed statistics for VA analysis at near vision. Two-way repeated measures ANOVA.

PPL-Balance VA (Mean ± SD)	PPL-Distance VA (Mean ± SD)	PPL-Near VA (Mean ± SD)	SS	MS	Df	F-Ratio	*p*-Value
0.09 ± 0.09	0.09 ± 0.09	0.08 ± 0.09	0.008	0.004	2	1.140	0.146
Centered VA (mean ± SD)	**Dominant eye VA (mean ± SD)**	**Non dominant eye VA (mean ± SD)**	**SS**	**MS**	**Df**	**F-ratio**	***p*-value**
0.08 ± 0.09	0.08 ± 0.08	0.09 ± 0.09	0.004	0.002	2	1.150	0.330

However, eye-tracker data showed statistically significant differences for the three factors analyzed: eye chart size, gaze direction, and progressive lens design. No statistically significant interactions were found between factors. Smaller eye chart sizes resulted in longer test duration, longer fixation time, and more fixations compared to larger ones. Participants had more difficulty recognizing eye charts in off-axis gaze directions, resulting in longer test duration, complete fixation time, and more fixations compared to the central ones. Finally, regarding the PPL design, when participants used the PPL optimized for near vision, the results showed a reduction in test duration, total fixation time, and number of fixations compared to PPL-Balance and PPL-Near. (Figure 5 and Table 4).

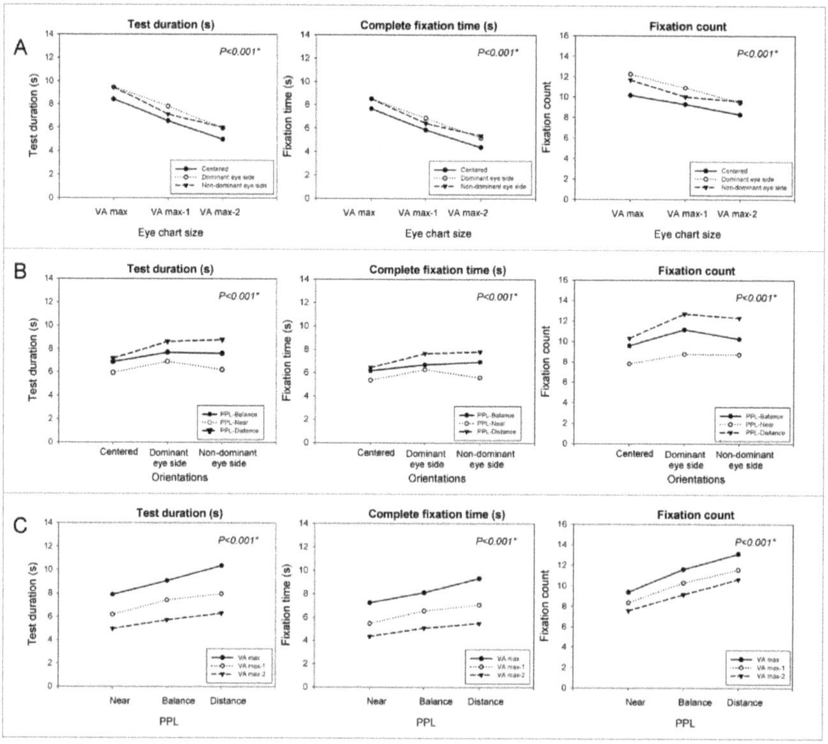

Figure 5. Variations in test duration, complete fixation time, and fixation count depending on the interactions of eye chart size and gaze direction (**A**), the gaze directions and PPL (**B**), and PPL and eye chart (**C**) for near-distance VA task. * Shows significance at the 0.05 level.

Table 4. Detailed statistics for Figure 5. Three-way repeated measures ANOVA test with pos-hoc comparisons using Tukey HSD method. * Shows significance at the 0.05 level.

	ANOVA Test for Eye Chart Size				**Tukey HSD Comparisons for Eye Chart Size (*p*-Value)**		
	Df	**Mean Square**	**F-Ratio**	***p*-Value**	**AVmax/Avmax-1**	**AVmax/Avmax-2**	**AVmax-1/Avmax-2**
Test duration	2	722.45	43.58	<0.001 *	<0.001 *	<0.001 *	<0.001 *
Fixation time	2	644.19	47.40	<0.001 *	<0.001 *	<0.001 *	<0.001 *
Fixation count	2	312.56	10.96	<0.001 *	0.040 *	<0.001 *	0.176
	ANOVA Test for Gaze Direction				**Tukey HSD comparisons for gaze direction (*p*-value)**		
	Df	**Mean square**	**F-ratio**	***p*-value**	**Centered/dominant**	**Centered/Non dominant**	**Dominant/Non dominant**
Test duration	2	78.87	9.19	<0.001 *	0.003 *	0.024 *	0.778
Fixation time	2	58.05	7.94	<0.001 *	0.009 *	0.021 *	0.949
Fixation count	2	171.51	6.41	<0.001 *	0.007 *	0.073	0.687
	ANOVA test for lens design				**Tukey HSD comparisons for lens design (*p*-value)**		
	Df	**Mean square**	**F-ratio**	***p*-value**	**Balance/Distance**	**Balance/Near**	**Distance/Near**
Test duration	2	209.73	13.71	<0.001 *	0.037 *	0.003 *	<0.001 *
Fixation time	2	150.08	10.37	<0.001 *	0.045 *	0.010 *	<0.001 *
Fixation count	2	679.62	27.38	<0.001 *	0.019 *	0.001 *	<0.001 *

4. Discussion

In this paper, we present a way of assessing the quality of vision provided by PPLs with different power distributions using an eye-tracking-based system during the VA measurement. It is important to note that VA is subjective and depends on the participant's answer, whereas eye-tracking data is objective and provides quantitative data about eye movements, adding more information about the quality of vision with PPLs compared to the traditional VA evaluation method. The method proposed is based on the analysis of test duration, fixation time, and the number of fixations required to recognize the different optotypes of standard eye charts. The study showed that when evaluating the far-distance VA of participants using a PPL design with a wider far-distance visual area, the test duration, fixation time, and the number of fixations are reduced. Similarly, a PPL design with a wider near area provided a lower test duration, a lower fixation time, and a lower number of fixations during the evaluation of near-distance VA. It should be noted that the values of standard VA obtained with different PPL designs were not different with statistical significance.

Although VA is considered a gold standard for the evaluation of optical quality, it seems insufficient alone to evaluate the quality of vision [17]. It is well known that sometimes clinicians report patients with high VA complaining about poor vision quality. Specifically, regarding the performance of PPLs, several studies have tried to evaluate differences in VA between different PPL designs without success. Legras et al. [17] evaluated differences in VA at eight different off-axis positions on 20 presbyopic participants with two different PPL designs and did not find differences in VA between them. On the other hand, Han et al. [12] measured VA in the far and near regions in 95 presbyopic patients with a customized and a non-customized PPL design, and, once again, the results did not show differences in VA between both PPLs.

Additionally, having a method that can determine differences in the visual performance provided by different PPL designs could help lens designers develop better lenses. Based on previous studies, we presume that the evaluation of eye movements during the performance of a specific task could be a sensitive indicator of the quality of vision provided by these lenses. In another study, Han et al. [27] evaluated differences between single-vision lenses and PPLs on 11 presbyopes. The subjects were required to read aloud a copy of printed text placed along their midline at 0.60 m. Eye movements were analyzed using the ISCAN computer-based system. The results showed an increase in fixation numbers when participants used PPLs compared to single-vision lenses. On the other hand, the study from Concepcion-Grande et al. [28] recorded the eye movements of 38 presbyopes using the Tobii X3-120 eye tracking system while participants were using two different PPL designs. Participants were asked to read aloud a text displayed on a monitor screen at centered and off-axis gaze directions located at 0.67 m. The results showed greater fixation time and the number of fixations in off-axis gaze directions in comparison with the central position. Finally, the study from Concepción-Grande et al. [30] recorded eye movements using a Tobii Pro Glasses 3 device on 28 participants using different PPLs. Participants were asked to read the text at far and near distances. The results showed that fixation time and the number of fixations were affected by the PPL design. All of these studies showed statistically significant differences in eye movements associated with the unwanted refractive errors present in the lateral areas of the PPLs. However, all these methods are based on reading tasks whose difficulty could vary from one experiment to another. To eliminate this uncertainty, we have used, as a reading test, the standard eye charts that are used to evaluate visual acuity under the same standardized conditions in which VA is clinically measured. So, in this paper, we propose a simple way to enhance the gold standard evaluation of VA by incorporating new metrics based on the characteristics of eye movements. To our knowledge, this is the first time an eye-tracking system is used while measuring VA and while using different PPL designs, and this method has proven to be sensitive enough to identify differences between designs and gaze direction.

In this study, we also incorporated the analysis of two well-known factors that affect visual performance. Firstly, it is obvious that recognition difficulty depends on the eye chart size. In this sense, when the letter became smaller, the task difficulty increased. As expected, results confirmed that with a smaller optotype size, there was a statistically significant longer test duration, longer fixation time, and higher fixation count than eye charts with a larger optotype size. Secondly, it is well known that unwanted refractive results showed statistically significant longer test duration, longer complete fixation time, and a greater number of fixations for off-axis gaze directions in comparison with the central gaze direction.

Future studies could improve the experimental setup by incorporating changes that enable the evaluation of eye movements in a more natural setting. Currently, the assessment of far-distance VA involves using a 21.5-inch screen positioned 5.25 m away from the subject's eyes, resulting in a narrow horizontal field of view of 4.2°. To assess a wider field of view, the subject must be rotated in three different gaze directions while using a chin rest to prevent head motion, which adds complexity to the experiment. Instead, a larger screen with a head tracking system would be a better alternative to the current rotation platform with a chin rest, as it would provide a wider field of view and eliminate the need for rotation. As explained in the flowchart for participant enrollment, 30% of participants were discarded because their recordings did not meet the quality criteria. It would be interesting to study the reasons for the data loss and account for them in future work and also to redefine a quality criterion that could be implemented in the optical practice without compromising the results.

5. Conclusions

In conclusion, the proposed eye-tracking method for assessing the quality of vision during a VA test can assess differences in test duration and eye fixation characteristics between PPL with different power distributions and is a more sensitive indicator of the quality of vision provided by the lenses than the standard VA evaluation. Although this method has been tested for the evaluation of the quality of vision provided by PPLs, it could be used in any other field in which the sheer capacity of letter recognition does not provide enough information about visual performance. Additionally, some examples could be the study of some visual conditions (i.e., cataracts) or specific visual tasks (i.e., night driving) in which the visual quality is reduced but the visual acuity does not decrease.

6. Patents

The results described in this manuscript have been the subject of a patent issued to José Miguel Cleva, Eva Chamorro, Pablo Concepcion-Grande, and José Alonso. The patent covers merit functions for lens optimization in which eye-tracker parameters describing visual performance are used, which is related to the research presented in this manuscript.

Author Contributions: Conceptualization, E.C. and J.M.C.; methodology, P.C.-G., E.C. and J.M.C.; formal analysis, P.C.-G., E.C. and J.M.C.; investigation, P.C.-G., E.C. and J.M.C.; data curation, P.C.-G.; writing—original draft preparation, P.C.-G.; writing—review and editing, J.A.G.-P., E.C., J.M.C. and J.A.; supervision, J.A.G.-P., E.C., J.M.C. and J.A.; project administration, E.C. and J.M.C. All authors have read and agreed to the published version of the manuscript.

Funding: The research was supported by Indizen Optical Technologies SL.

Institutional Review Board Statement: The study was conducted in accordance with the Declaration of Helsinki and approved by the Institutional Review Board of the Complutense University of Madrid (CE_20210715-3_SAL).

Informed Consent Statement: Informed consent was obtained from all subjects involved in the study.

Data Availability Statement: The data presented in this study are available on request from the corresponding author.

Acknowledgments: The authors acknowledge the support of Indizen Optical Technologies SL. They also thank the anonymous participants and the optometrists in charge of the measurements.

Conflicts of Interest: The authors of this work include P.C.-G., E.C., J.M.C. and J.A., who are all employees of Indizen Optical Technologies and have also authored the patent resulting from this research. The funders had no role in the study design, data collection, analysis, the decision to publish, or the preparation of the manuscript. The remaining authors do not have any conflict of interest to disclose.

References

1. Millodot, M. *Dictionary of Optometry and Visual Science E-Book*, 7th ed.; Elsevier Health Sciences: London, UK, 2014.
2. Raasch, T.W.; Lijuan, S.; Yi, A. Whole-Surface Characterization of Progressive Addition Lenses. *Optom. Vis. Sci.* **2011**, *88*, 217–226. [CrossRef] [PubMed]
3. Alonso, J.; Gómez-Pedrero, J.A.; Quiroga, J.A. *Modern Ophthalmic Optics*, 1st ed.; Cambridge University Press: Cambridge, UK, 2019.
4. Sheedy, J.E.; Campbell, C.; King-Smith, E.; Hayes, J.R. Progressive Powered Lenses: The Minkwitz Theorem. *Optom. Vis. Sci.* **2005**, *82*, 916–922. [CrossRef] [PubMed]
5. Sheedy, J.E. Progressive addition lenses—Matching the specific lens to patient needs. *Optometry* **2004**, *75*, 83–102. [CrossRef] [PubMed]
6. Sheedy, J.E. Correlation analysis of the optics of progressive addition lenses. *Optom. Vis. Sci.* **2004**, *81*, 350–361. [CrossRef]
7. Arroyo, R.; Crespo, D.; Alonso, J. Influence of the Base Curve in the Performance of Customized and Classical Progressive Lenses. *Optom. Vis. Sci.* **2013**, *90*, 282–292. [CrossRef]
8. Arroyo, R.; Crespo, D.; Alonso, J. Scoring of Progressive Power Lenses by Means of User Power Maps. *Optom. Vis. Sci.* **2012**, *89*, E489–E501. [CrossRef]
9. Sheedy, J.E.; Hardy, R.F. The optics of occupational progressive lenses. *Optom. J. Am. Optom. Assoc.* **2005**, *76*, 432–441. [CrossRef]
10. Boutron, I.; Touizer, C.; Pitrou, I.; Roy, C.; Ravaud, P. The VEPRO trial: A cross-over randomised controlled trial comparing 2 progressive lenses for patients with presbyopia. *Trials* **2009**, *9*, 54. [CrossRef]
11. Mateo, B.; Porcar-Seder, R.; Solaz, J.S.; Dürsteler, J.C. Experimental procedure for measuring and comparing head–neck–trunk posture and movements caused by different progressive addition lens designs. *Ergonomics* **2010**, *53*, 904–913. [CrossRef]
12. Han, S.C.; Graham, A.D.; Lin, M.C. Clinical Assessment of a Customized Free-Form Progressive Add Lens Spectacle. *Optom. Vis. Sci.* **2011**, *88*, 234–243. [CrossRef]
13. Forkel, J.; Reiniger, J.L.; Muschielok, A.; Welk, A.; Seidemann, A.; Baumbach, P. Personalized Progressive Addition Lenses: Correlation between Performance and Design. *Optom. Vis. Sci.* **2017**, *94*, 208–218. [CrossRef]
14. Selenow, A.; Bauer, E.A.; Ali, S.R.; Spencer, L.W.; Ciuffreda, K.J. Assessing Visual Performance with Progressive Addition Lenses. *Optom. Vis. Sci.* **2002**, *79*, 502–505. [CrossRef] [PubMed]
15. Selenow, A. Progressive lenses: New techniques for assessing visual performance. In *Vision Science and Its Applications*; Optical Society of America: Washion, DC, USA, 2000; p. MD4.
16. Habtegiorgis, S.W.; Rifai, K.; Lappe, M.; Wahl, S. Experience-dependent long-term facilitation of skew adaptation. *J. Vis.* **2018**, *18*, 7. [CrossRef] [PubMed]
17. Legras, R.; Vincent, M.; Marin, G. Does visual acuity predict visual preference in progressive addition lenses? *J. Optom.* 2022. [CrossRef]
18. Chamorro, E. Lens Design Techniques to Improve Satisfaction in Free-Form Progressive Addition Lens Users. *J. Optom.* **2018**, *6*, 91–99. [CrossRef]
19. Villegas, E.A.; Artal, P. Visual Acuity and Optical Parameters in Progressive-Power Lenses. *Optom. Vis. Sci.* **2006**, *83*, 672–681. [CrossRef] [PubMed]
20. Duchowski, A.T.; Duchowski, A.T. *Eye Tracking Methodology: Theory and Practice*; Springer: Berlin, Germany, 2017.
21. Holmqvist, K.; Andersson, R. *Eye-Tracking: A Comprehensive Guide to Methods, Paradigms and Measures*, 2nd ed.; Lund Eye-Tracking Research Institute: Lund, Sweden, 2017.
22. Hooge, I.T.C.; Niehorster, D.C.; Nyström, M.; Andersson, R.; Hessels, R.S. Fixation classification: How to merge and select fixation candidates. *Behav. Res. Methods* **2022**, *54*, 2765–2776. [CrossRef] [PubMed]
23. Holmqvist, K.; Örbom, S.L.; Hooge, I.T.; Niehorster, D.C.; Alexander, R.G.; Andersson, R.; Benjamins, J.S.; Blignaut, P.; Brouwer, A.M.; Chuang, L.L.; et al. Eye tracking: Empirical foundations for a minimal reporting guideline. *Behav. Res. Methods* **2023**, *55*, 364–416. [CrossRef]
24. Rayner, K.; Pollatsek, A.; Ashby, J.; Clifton, C., Jr. *Psychology of Reading*; Psychology Press: London, UK, 2012.
25. Grisham, D.; Powers, M.; Riles, P. Visual skills of poor readers in high school. *Optometry* **2007**, *78*, 542–549. [CrossRef]
26. Han, Y.; Ciuffreda, K.J.; Selenow, A.; Ali, S.R. Dynamic Interactions of Eye and Head Movements When Reading with Single-Vision and Progressive Lenses in a Simulated Computer-Based Environment. *Investig. Ophthalmol. Vis. Sci.* **2003**, *44*, 1534–1545. [CrossRef]

27. Han, Y.; Ciuffreda, K.J.; Selenow, A.; Bauer, E.; Ali, S.R.; Spencer, W. Static Aspects of Eye and Head Movements during Reading in a Simulated Computer-Based Environment with Single-Vision and Progressive Lenses. *Investig. Ophthalmol. Vis. Sci.* **2003**, *44*, 145–153. [CrossRef] [PubMed]
28. Concepcion-Grande, P.; González, A.; Chamorro, E.; Cleva, J.M.; Alonso, J.; Gómez-Pedrero, J.A. Eye movements as a predictor of preference for progressive power lenses. *J. Eye Mov. Res.* **2022**, 15. [CrossRef] [PubMed]
29. Rifai, K.; Wahl, S. Specific eye-head coordination enhances vision in progressive lens wearers. *J. Vis.* **2016**, *16*, 5. [CrossRef] [PubMed]
30. Concepcion-Grande, P.; Chamorro, E.; Cleva, J.M.; Alonso, J.; Gómez-Pedrero, J.A. Correlation between reading time and characteristics of eye fixations and progressive lens design. *PLoS ONE* **2023**, *18*, e0281861. [CrossRef] [PubMed]
31. Bailey, I.L.; Jackson, A.J. Changes in the clinical measurement of visual acuity. *J. Phys. Conf. Ser.* **2016**, *772*, 012046. [CrossRef]
32. Ng, J.S.; Wong, A. Line-by-line visual acuity scoring equivalence with letter-by-letter visual acuity scoring. *Clin. Exp. Optom.* **2022**, *105*, 414–419. [CrossRef]
33. Olsen, A. The Tobii I-VT fixation filter. *Tobii Technol.* **2012**, *21*, 4–19.
34. Tobii Technology, A.B. *Determining the Tobii I-VT Fixation Filter's Default Values: Method Description and Results Discussion;* Tobii® Technology: Danderyd Municipality, Sweden, 2012.
35. Wass, S.V.; Forssman, L.; Leppänen, J. Robustness and precision: How data quality may influence key dependent variables in infant eye-tracker analyses. *Infancy* **2014**, *19*, 427–460. [CrossRef]
36. Seabold, S.; Perktold, J. Statsmodels: Econometric and statistical modeling with python. In Proceedings of the 9th Python in Science Conference, Austin, TX, USA, 28 June–3 July 2010; pp. 10–25080.

applied sciences

MDPI

Article

The Effect of 3D TVs on Eye Movement and Motor Performance

Chiuhsiang Joe Lin [1], Retno Widyaningrum [2] and Yogi Tri Prasetyo [3,4,5,*]

[1] Department of Industrial Management, National Taiwan University of Science and Technology. No. 43, Sec. 4, Keelung Rd., Da'an Dist., Taipei City 10607, Taiwan
[2] Department of Industrial and System Engineering, Institut Teknologi Sepuluh Nopember, Kampus ITS Sukolilo, Surabaya 60111, Indonesia
[3] International Bachelor Program in Engineering, Yuan Ze University, 135 Yuan-Tung Rd., Chung-Li 32003, Taiwan
[4] Department of Industrial Engineering and Management, Yuan Ze University, 135 Yuan-Tung Rd., Chung-Li 32003, Taiwan
[5] School of Industrial Engineering and Engineering Management, Mapúa University. 658 Muralla St., Intramuros, Manila 1002, Philippines
* Correspondence: yogi.tri.prasetyo@saturn.yzu.edu.tw; Tel.: +886-3-4638800 (ext. 2422)

Abstract: Three-dimensional TVs have been commercialized in recent few years; however, poor visual and motor performances may have an impact on consumer acceptance of 3D TVs. The purpose of this study was to investigate the effects of 3D TVs on eye movement and motor performance. Specifically, the effect of stereoscopic display parallax of 3D TVs and movement task index of difficulty (ID) on eye movement was investigated. In addition, the effect of stereoscopic display parallax of 3D TVs and movement task ID on motor performance was also investigated. Twelve participants voluntarily participated in a multi-directional tapping task under two different viewing environments (2D TV and 3D TV), three different levels of stereoscopic depth (140, 190, 210 cm), and six different Index of Difficulty levels (2.8, 3.3, 3.7, 4.2, 5.1, 6.1 bit). The study revealed that environment had significant effects on eye movement time, index of eye performance, eye fixation accuracy, number of fixations, time to first fixation, saccadic duration, revisited fixation duration, hand movement time, index of hand performance, and error rate. Interestingly, there were no significant effects of stereoscopic depth on eye movement and motor performance; however, the best performance was found when the 3D object was placed at 210 cm. The main novelty and contributions of this study is the in-depth investigations of the effect of 3D TVs on eye movement and motor performance. The findings of this study could lead to a better understanding of the visual and motor performance for 3D TVs.

Keywords: 3D TV; stereoscopic displays; virtual reality; depth

1. Introduction

Three-dimensional TVs have been commercialized in recent years. The objective of this commercialization is to replicate the experience achievable in 3D cinematic presentations in a more intimate home setting [1]. 3D TVs are affordable, aesthetically pleasing, and can provide users with a sense of presence [2]; therefore, the commercialization has been accompanied by the increasing availability of 3D TVs broadcast channels or even 3D home cinema [3]. Engineers and academicians are continually engaged in the assessment of 3D TV, aiming to maximize the image quality while also minimizing the side effects [4–6]. To fully optimize 3D TVs, it is necessary to gain a better understanding of the impact of 3D TVs on the Human Visual System (HVS) [3].

Three-dimensional TVs generate 3D images by creating depth. Depth, also widely known as parallax in 3D stereoscopic display [7,8], was defined as the binocular disparity in the human visual system that gives a 3D stereoscopic effect of depth with each eye receiving a similar image, but not identical, to that of a real spatial vision by horizontal disparity [9]. The user can experience the depth of 3D TVs by wearing 3D glasses [10]. Ideally, 3D TVs should be able to detect 3D glasses positions and change the depth immediately so the users can perceive the image comfortably [3].

One common device to evaluate the depth perception in the stereoscopic display is an eye tracker [2,7]. It has been extensively used to collect and analyze HVS in the stereoscopic display [11]. Eye trackers are able to capture the eye movement, which provides evidence of visual attention as a fundamental system in visual perception [12]. Eye trackers have been widely used in many research disciplines, such as measuring cognitive load during the driving task [13], assembly task [14], software screen complexity [15], and even military camouflage [16]. In the context of 3D interface design, an eye tracker has the potential to improve many existing 3D interaction techniques [2].

Despite the numerous papers related to 3D TVs in recent years, very limited research has investigated the effect of 3D TV environments on eye movement and motor performance. Most studies which utilized 3D TVs mostly only investigated the subjective assessment of visual discomfort. Read et al. [17] investigated the changes in vision, balance, and coordination associated with normal home 3D TVs viewing in the 2 months after first acquiring a 3D TV. Read [18] also investigated the subjective experience in-home 3D TVs over 8 weeks by using symptoms questionnaire, while Lambooij et al. [19] investigated the three different assessments for visual discomfort: (1) single assessment score for each stimulus sequence, (2) continuous assessment, and (3) retrospective assessment for the entire test. Similarly, Lee et al. [20] investigated the effect of stimulus width on visual discomfort by measuring visual discomfort and binocular fusion time, while Chang et al. [21] and Chang et al. [22] only examined the physical properties of 3D glasses. Furthermore, a more recent study by Zang et al. [23] compared the difference in visual comfort between 3D TVs and VR glasses. Finally, Urvoy et al. [24] proposed a comprehensive review of visual fatigue and discomfort based on physiological and psychological processes enabling depth perception.

Some of the most recent studies related to 3D TVs generally incorporated physiological responses of the human while watching the stimuli on a 3D TV. For instance, Chen et al. [25] investigated the effect of 3D TVs on human brain activity. In addition, Manshouri et al. [26] and Chen et al. [27] utilized EEG to investigate the effect of 3D TVs on brain waves. However, the effects of the 3D TVs on eye movements and motor performance are still clearly underexplored. Generally, poor visual and motor performances may have an impact to consumer acceptance of 3D TV. A further in-depth investigation of eye movement and motor performance are needed to enhance the performance in 3D TV.

Our previous studies investigated the effect of parallax on eye movement parameters in the projection-based stereoscopic display [8,28–30]. Eye movement parameters which consisted of eye movement time, fixation duration, time to first fixation, number of fixations, and eye gaze accuracy were evaluated under three different levels of depth. The results revealed that depth had significant effects on all eye movement parameters in projection-based stereoscopic displays [28,29]. The participants were found to have longer eye movement time, longer fixation duration, longer time to first fixation, larger number of fixations, and less eye gaze accuracy when the target was projected at 50 cm in front of the screen compared to projected at 20 cm in front of the screen or projected at the screen [28].

The purpose of this study was mainly intended to investigate the effects of 3D TV environments on eye movement and motor performance. Using a similar approach to our previous studies [8,28,29,31–33], we utilized an eye tracker to explore a comprehensive analysis regarding the effect of 3D TVs on selected eye movement parameters and motor performance. We also discussed the effect of depth and index of difficulty, since both variables could influence eye movement and motor performance in a stereoscopic environment [34]. This study is one of the first studies that investigated the effect of 3D TVs on eye movement and motor performance simultaneously. The findings of this study could lead to better understanding of the visual and motor performance for 3D TVs.

2. Materials and Methods

2.1. Participants

Twelve healthy graduate students (6 male and 6 female) from National Taiwan University of Science and Technology were voluntary participated in the current study (Mean: 25 years; standard deviation: 3 years). All participants reported normal or corrected to normal visual acuity (1.0 in decimal unit). Prior to the study, the participants were required to fill out a consent form and screened for the capability to see the 3D object clearly on a 3D TV.

2.2. Apparatus and Stimuli

A Tobii X2-60 eye tracker (Tobii, Stockholm, Sweden) was utilized to collect the eye movement data. The accuracy was 0.4 degrees of visual angle and the sampling rate was 60 Hz [22]. The screen recording media element from Tobii Studio cannot be applied in this experiment because we created the parallax setting of the 3D object from a 3D Vision IR Emitter NVIDIA. Therefore, a Logitech webcam C-920 (Logitech International S.A., Lausanne, Switzerland) was utilized to record the eye movement and eye fixation point on the screen display. This webcam was integrated with a Tobii eye tracker. All equipment was fixed using adhesive tape and marked. As recommended by Salvucci and Goldberg [35] and Goldberg [15], the raw fixation data were filtered using Velocity Threshold Identification (I-VT) and the velocity threshold was set to 30 o/s. Tobii Studio eye tracking version 3.3.2 was used for the analysis of raw fixation data. The entire experiment was conducted in a dark room (3.6 m × 3.2 m × 2.5 m) covered by dark curtains and walls to create an excellent stereoscopic environment.

During the experiment on a 3D stereoscopic display, participants sat at a distance of 60 cm in front of the Tobii Eye Tracker (Figure 1). In addition, a Sony 3D TV Bravia was placed at 210 cm distance from the participant's eyes. All participants were instructed to wear active 3D glasses to perceive the 3D environment by utilizing a pair of Sony TDG-BT500A (Sony Group Corporation, Tokyo, Japan). These Sony 3D glasses were integrated with a 3D TVs Sony Bravia (ViewSonic PJD6251 DLP) (Sony Group Corporation, Tokyo, Japan) and a 3D Vision IR Emitter NVIDIA which adapted the 3D TV system with depth image-based rendering [36].

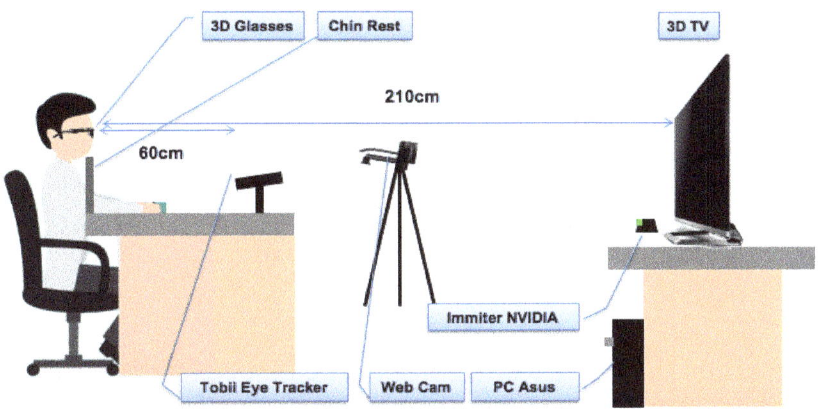

Figure 1. An illustration of the current study.

2.3. Independent Variables

Similar to [18], the environment was designed with two different levels: a 2D and 3D environment (Figure 2). In the 2D environment, the participant performed the tapping task on the screen display. In the 3D environment, participant performed the multidirectional tapping task; 3D TVs were integrated with NVIDIA to create a stereoscopic viewing environment.

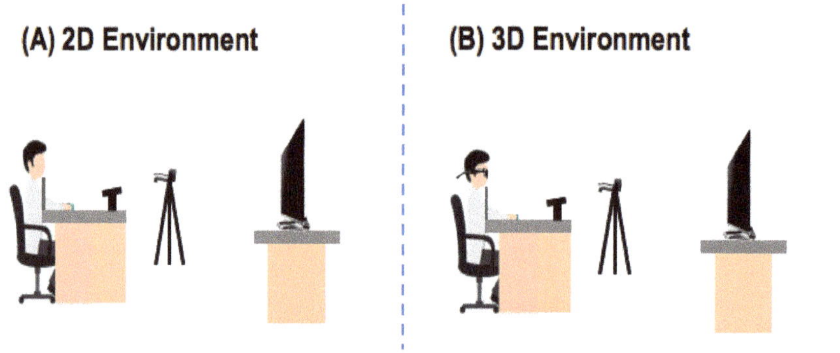

Figure 2. The illustration of two different environments. (**A**) Participant performed tapping task in a 2D environment. (**B**) Participant utilized 3D glasses to perform the multi-directional tapping task in a 3D environment. 3D TVs were integrated with NVIDIA to create a stereoscopic viewing environment.

The depth was varied into three levels: 210 cm, 190 cm, and 140 cm (Figure 3). The term "depth" was preferred over "parallax" in this study because we compared the effect of a 2D and 3D environment. In the 2D environment, we did not create a binocular disparity that creates a 3D effect. Thus, the participant asked to move closer to the screen in order to create an equal target distance as the experiment in the 3D environment (Figure 4).

The index of difficulty (ID) was defined as the task difficulty and precision level measured by object width and movement distance [37]. The unit of index of difficulty consisted of bits that equated to a quantity of information transmitted to measure the difficulty of the pointing tasks. This was explained that the pointing reduced due to higher information processing task. Following our previous publications [8,28,29] and ISO 9241-9, which classified precision task to measure the accuracy into three levels, i.e., low, medium, and high, ID and task precision level are presented in Table 1. There were two levels of environment, three levels of depth, and six levels of ID in the current study. Thus, we adopt a within-subject design with 36 combinations.

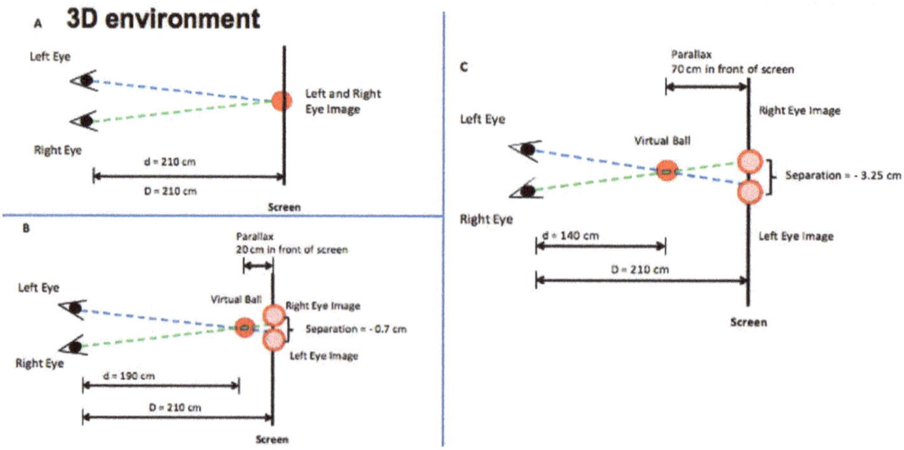

Figure 3. An illustration of the horizontal separation of two images on a 3D TV with three different levels of depth [5].

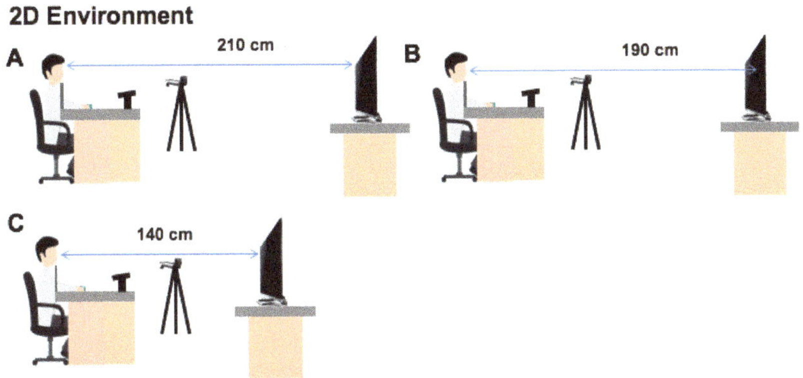

Figure 4. Participant performed the experiment in a 2D environment with distances of (**A**) 210 cm, (**B**) 190 cm, and (**C**) 140 cm.

Table 1. ID and task precision level [8].

Distance (Unity Unit)	Width (Unity Unit)	ID (Bits)	Task Precision Level
40	3.3	3.7	Low
40	2.3	4.2	Medium
40	0.6	6.1	High
20	3.3	2.8	Low
20	2.3	3.3	Low
20	0.6	5.1	Medium

2.4. Dependent Variables

Following two of our previous publications [8,28], there were two categories of dependent variables in the current study: eye movement and motor performance. The first category, eye movement, consists of eye movement time, index of performance eye, number of fixations, time to first fixation, saccade duration, revisited fixation duration, and eye gaze accuracy. The second category, motor performance, consists of hand movement time, index of performance hand, and error rate. The definition of each independent variables is presented in Table 2.

Table 2. Dependent variables and each definition.

Category	Variable	Definition	Supported by
Eye Movement	Eye movement time (EMT)	The elapsed time from the fixation point of the eye on the starting ball to the fixation point on the destination ball.	Lin & Widyaningrum [8]
	Index of eye performance (IP eye)	ID/EMT. IP eye shows the global index of eye performance, which considers speed and accuracy.	MacKenzie [38]
	Number of fixations	A total number of fixations counted starting from the origin virtual to destination virtual ball.	Lin et al. [29]
	Time to first fixation	An elapsed time from the slide presentation until the first fixation on the virtual target.	Goldberg [15]
	Saccade duration	A sum of saccadic time spent within an AOI.	Lin & Widyaningrum [8]
	Revisited fixation duration	A sum of revisited fixation durations within an AOI.	Lin & Widyaningrum [8]
	Eye gaze accuracy	The distance between the recorded fixation locations and the actual location of the projection of the image as a performance evaluation. The *x*-axis was measured from left to right and the *y*-axis was measured from bottom to the top.	Lin & Widyaningrum [28]

Table 2. *Cont.*

Category	Variable	Definition	Supported by
Motor Performance	Hand movement time (HMT)	Time taken from the starting ball to the destination ball.	Lin & Widyaningrum [8]
	Index of hand performance (IP hand)	ID/HMT. IP hand shows the global index of hand performance, which considers speed and accuracy.	MacKenzie [38]
	Error rate	A click outside the target ball. Since the total number of clicks was 12, the error rate was calculated as: Error rate = (N − 12)/12.	Lin et al. [34]; Lin & Widyaningrum [8]

2.5. Experimental Procedure

The current study was conducted according to the ethical guidelines published by National Taiwan University Research Ethics Committee. Prior to the experiment, participants were required to perform a visual acuity test and stereo vision check. The visual acuity of each participant was measured by utilizing a Snellen test [39]. In addition, each participant was also required to pass a stereo vision check to ensure that they were capable of perceiving the 3D target. Finally, they were required to fill out a consent form which consisted of confidential data of the participants and the detailed descriptions of experimental tasks.

During the experiment on 3D display, participants were asked to wear the Sony 3D glasses and sit on an adjustable chair. In addition, all participants were also to keep their head on a chin rest. At the beginning of the experiment, a calibration was performed for each participant to ensure that Tobii eye tracker detected the participant's eye movement. Regular calibration setting with five red dots from Tobii eye tracker was used as a default to capture participants' eye gaze binocularly. They were instructed to look at the five red calibration dots as accurately as possible until each red dot disappeared. The qualifying participants were included in the experiment.

A multidirectional tapping task was selected as a task in this study, as suggested by ISO 9241-9. Similar to our previous studies [28–30], participants were instructed to perform a tapping task by clicking 12 virtual balls in concentric circles with a mouse as fast and accurate as possible (Figure 5). The virtual red ball was programmed on the Unity 3D platform version 4.3.4 and projected as a 3D object.

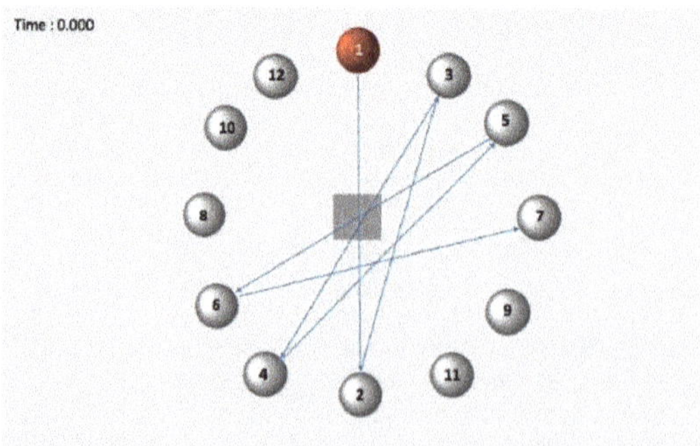

Figure 5. The pointing sequence of virtual red balls during multidirectional tapping task (shown as ball 1) [8].

Note that the ISO 9241-9 tapping task is performed on a 2D plane. Although visually the targets are displayed in 3D, the movement is on a plane. This situation is common for interactions in a 3D visual environment, where 3D input devices are not necessarily available or only planar movements are involved, such as pointing between menu items [2]. In this study, we used a desk mouse to tap between the targets, and therefore, the hand movement was limited to 2D motion. The cursor of the mouse is displayed in 3D but only moves on the vertical display plane, because the actual mouse moves on the horizontal desk plane. The mapping is a very common practice with the usual desktop computer setup. No additional learning is necessary. The effect under investigation, if any, would only come from the 3D visual display of the targets and the cursor, and would not be confounded with the effect of 3D movement of the cursor, which would be a much more complex interaction situation and is not within the scope of this study.

At the beginning, the 3D cursor was set at the center cube. To start the experiment, each participant was asked to click the center cube. One virtual red ball would appear at a time and participant was instructed to hit the virtual red ball by utilizing 3D cursor. After the red ball was hit, the color would turn white and the next virtual red ball would appear in red. Figure 5 shows the sequence of the virtual red ball. The changing color of the ball guided the participant to look at the balls in concentric circles until all 12 balls were clicked. Each participant completed all six levels of ID in one of thhree depth conditions (140 cm, 190 cm, and 210 cm) under two different environments (2D TV and 3D TV).

2.6. Data Processing and Analysis

Hand movement time (HMT) was recorded based on the 3D cursor clicks in the tapping task. On the other hand, eye movement data needed to be analyzed by using our previous algorithm [8]. The index of eye performance (IP eye) and index of hand performance (IP hand) was calculated by dividing the ID by the movement time [38]. Therefore, while analyzing the effects of environment, depth, and ID on IP eye and IP hand, the ID was removed from the RM-ANOVA table, since there was a direct correlation between ID and IP.

The repeated measures analysis of variance (RM-ANOVA) was employed with $\alpha = 0.05$ to test the significance of each independent variables and its interactions to each dependent variable. In addition, the significance criteria were adjusted according to the sequential Bonferroni (Bonferroni–Holm) correction algorithm for multiple comparisons. We also conducted a post-hoc Tukey HSD test to analyze the differences occurred between pairs of group means in the RM-ANOVA analysis.

3. Results

3.1. Eye Movement

3.1.1. Eye Movement Time

Table 3 presents the means, SDs, ANOVA, and Tukey HSD test results of the eye movement time. The environment was found to have a significant effect on eye movement time ($F_{1,11} = 5.732$, *p*-value = 0.036). The Tukey HSD test showed a significant difference between hand movement time in screen displays and stereoscopic displays. Eye movement time increased when participants performed the tapping task in stereoscopic displays. There were no significant interactions between depth and eye movement time ($F_{2,22} = 1.372$, *p*-value = 0.385), even though the eye movement time increased when the object was close to participants' eyes. The main effect for the index of difficulty ($F_{5,55} = 65.138$, *p*-value = 0.001) was significant on eye movement time. The result of the repeated measures ANOVA reported that there was no significant difference in the interactions between the environment and depth ($F_{2,22} = 0.161$, *p*-value = 0.852), the environment and index of difficulty ($F_{5,55} = 2.219$, *p*-value = 0.065), parallax and ID ($F_{10,110} = 1.722$, *p*-value = 0.085), and the environment, depth, and ID ($F_{10,110} = 0.599$, *p*-value = 0.811).

3.1.2. Index of Eye Performance

The result of the repeated measures ANOVA in Table 4 reported that there were significant interactions between the index of eye performance and the environment ($F_{1,11} = 5.249$, *p*-value = 0.043). Moreover, the Tukey HSD showed a significant difference between screen and stereoscopic displays. However, there was no significant difference between depth and the index of eye performance ($F_{2,22} = 1.317$, *p*-value 0.288). The interaction between the environment and depth ($F_{2,22} = 1.364$, *p*-value = 0.277), interaction between depth and ID

($F_{10,110}$ = 1.520, *p*-value = 0.142), and the interaction between the environment, depth, and ID ($F_{10,110}$ = 0.789, *p*-value = 0.640) were not significantly different from the index of eye performance. However, the interaction between the environment and index of difficulty was significantly different ($F_{5,55}$ = 2.497, p = 0.041).

Table 3. Means, SDs, ANOVA, and Tukey HSD test results of eye movement time.

	Eye Movement Time					
	Level	**Mean (s)**	**Group [a]**	**SD**	$F_{n,m}$	***p*-Value**
Environment	2D Screen Displays	0.474	A	0.185	$F_{1,11}$ = 5.732	p = 0.036
	3D Stereoscopic Displays	0.635	B	0.334		
Depth	210 cm	0.525	A	0.260	$F_{2,22}$ = 1.372	p = 0.385
	190 cm	0.566	A	0.312		
	140 cm	0.571	A	0.269		
ID	2.8 bits	0.435	A	0.158	$F_{5,55}$ = 65.138	p = 0.001
	3.3 bits	0.479	B	0.262		
	3.7 bits	0.594	C	0.247		
	4.2 bits	0.580	C	0.225		
	5.1 bits	0.540	B, C	0.305		
	6.1 bits	0.699	D	0.374		
Environment * Depth					$F_{2,22}$ = 0.161	p = 0.852
Environment * ID					$F_{5,55}$ = 2.219	p = 0.065
Depth * ID					$F_{10,110}$ = 1.722	p = 0.085
Environment * Depth * ID					$F_{10,110}$ = 0.599	p = 0.811

Table 4. Means, SDs, ANOVA, and Tukey HSD test results of eye performance.

	Index of Eye Performance					
	Level	**Mean (bits/s)**	**Group [a]**	**SD**	$F_{n,m}$	***p*-Value**
Environment	2D Screen Display	10.712	A	6.999	$F_{1,11}$ = 5.249	p = 0.043
	3D Stereoscopic Display	8.360	B	4.824		
Depth	210 cm	10.078	A	6.836	$F_{2,22}$ = 1.317	p = 0.288
	190 cm	9.665	A	6.361		
	140 cm	8.728	A	5.153		
Environment * Depth					$F_{2,22}$ = 1.364	p = 0.277

3.1.3. Number of Fixations

The main effect of the index of difficulty ($F_{5,55}$ = 15.022, *p*-value = 0.000) was significant for the number of fixations (Table 5). Post-hoc analysis with a Tukey HSD test revealed that there was a significant different when index of difficulty varied from low to high. The Tukey HSD test divided the index of difficulty levels into three groups as shown in Table 5. Similarly, the interaction of the environment and the index of difficulty was significantly different for number of fixations ($F_{5,55}$ = 3.171, *p*-value = 0.014). We did not find a significant difference in number of fixations for the environment ($F_{1,11}$ = 1.726, *p*-value = 0.216), depth ($F_{2,22}$ = 0.064, *p*-value = 0.938), interaction of the environment and depth ($F_{2,22}$ = 1.055, *p*-value = 0.365), interaction of depth and the index of difficulty ($F_{10,110}$ = 0.973, *p*-value = 0.471), and interaction of the environment, depth, and the index of difficulty ($F_{10,110}$ = 0.660, *p*-value = 0.759).

Table 5. Means, SDs, ANOVA, and Tukey HSD test results of number of fixations.

	Number of Fixations					
	Level	**Mean**	**Group** [a]	**SD**	$F_{n,m}$	***p*-Value**
Environment	2D Screen Displays	2.686	A	0.481	$F_{1,11} = 1.726$	$p = 0.216$
	3D Stereoscopic Displays	2.899	A	0.822		
Depth	210 cm	2.813	A	0.791	$F_{2,22} = 0.064$	$p = 0.938$
	190 cm	2.777	A	0.657		
	140 cm	2.745	A	0.583		
ID	2.8 bits	2.580	A	0.430	$F_{5,55} = 15.022$	$p = 0.000$
	3.3 bits	2.543	A	0.587		
	3.7 bits	2.883	B	0.449		
	4.2 bits	2.875	B	0.518		
	5.1 bits	2.627	A, B	0.871		
	6.1 bits	3.249	C	0.831		
Environment * Depth					$F_{2,22} = 1.055$	$p = 0.365$
Environment * ID					$F_{5,55} = 3.171$	$p = 0.014$
Depth * ID					$F_{10,110} = 0.973$	$p = 0.471$
Environment * Depth * ID					$F_{10,110} = 0.660$	$p = 0.759$

3.1.4. Time to First Fixation

Overall, the environment influenced time to first fixation ($F_{1,11} = 4.965$, *p*-value = 0.048). A longer time to first fixation occurred when a virtual target appeared on 3D TV displays (Table 6). Furthermore, the Tukey HSD test showed that time to first fixation on 2D TV screen displays differed from time to first fixation on a 3D TV. However, there was no significant difference between time to first fixation and depth ($F_{2,22} = 0.398$, *p*-value = 0.677), index of difficulty ($F_{5,55} = 0.408$, *p*-value = 0.841), interaction of environment and depth ($F_{2,22} = 0.392$, *p*-value = 0.681), interaction of environment and index of difficulty ($F_{5,55} = 0.853$, *p*-value = 0.518), interaction of depth and index of difficulty ($F_{10,110} = 1.365$, *p*-value = 0.206), and interaction of environment, depth, and index of difficulty ($F_{10,110} = 0.906$, *p*-value = 0.531).

Table 6. Means, SDs, ANOVA, and Tukey HSD test results of time to first fixation.

	Time to First Fixation					
	Level	**Mean (s)**	**Group** [a]	**SD**	$F_{n,m}$	***p*-Value**
Environment	2D Screen Displays	0.076	A	0.060	$F_{1,11} = 4.965$	$p = 0.048$
	3D Stereoscopic Displays	0.105	B	0.083		
Depth	210 cm	0.085	A	0.068	$F_{2,22} = 0.398$	$p = 0.677$
	190 cm	0.093	A	0.070		
	140 cm	0.096	A	0.083		
ID	2.8 bits	0.094	A	0.090	$F_{5,55} = 0.408$	$p = 0.841$
	3.3 bits	0.083	A	0.053		
	3.7 bits	0.090	A	0.063		
	4.2 bits	0.097	A	0.086		
	5.1 bits	0.088	A	0.077		
	6.1 bits	0.091	A	0.070		
Environment * Depth					$F_{2,22} = 0.392$	$p = 0.681$
Environment * ID					$F_{5,55} = 0.853$	$p = 0.518$
Depth * ID					$F_{10,110} = 1.365$	$p = 0.206$
Environment * Depth * ID					$F_{10,110} = 0.906$	$p = 0.531$

3.1.5. Saccadic Duration

The results of repeated measures ANOVA in Table 7 revealed that there were significant difference on the environment ($F_{1,11}$ = 8.481, *p*-value = 0.014), the index of difficulty ($F_{5,55}$ = 18.512, *p*-value = 0.000), interaction of the environment and depth ($F_{2,22}$ = 9.915, *p*-value = 0.001), interaction of depth and the index of difficulty ($F_{10,110}$ = 4.875, *p*-value = 0.000), and interaction of the environment, depth, and index of difficulty ($F_{10,110}$ = 2.047, *p*-value = 0.035). However, the analysis revealed there was no significant main effect for depth ($F_{2,22}$ = 1.271, *p*-value = 0.300) as well as for the index of difficulty ($F_{5,55}$ = 0.890, *p*-value = 0.494).

Table 7. Means, SDs, ANOVA, and Tukey HSD test results of saccadic duration.

	Saccadic Duration					
	Level	Mean (s)	Group [a]	SD	$F_{n,m}$	*p*-Value
Environment	2D Screen Displays	0.535	A	0.182	$F_{1,11}$ = 8.481	*p* = 0.014
	3D Stereoscopic Displays	0.652	B	0.304		
Depth	210 cm	0.617	A	0.282	$F_{2,22}$ = 1.271	*p* = 0.300
	190 cm	0.581	A	0.256		
	140 cm	0.546	A	0.231		
ID	2.8 bits	0.436	A	0.173	$F_{5,55}$ = 18.512	*p* = 0.000
	3.3 bits	0.484	A	0.182		
	3.7 bits	0.665	B	0.220		
	4.2 bits	0.638	B	0.193		
	5.1 bits	0.613	B	0.286		
	6.1 bits	0.724	B	0.332		
Environment * Depth					$F_{2,22}$ = 9.915	*p* = 0.001
Environment * ID					$F_{5,55}$ = 0.890	*p* = 0.494
Depth * ID					$F_{10,110}$ = 4.875	*p* = 0.000
Environment * Depth * ID					$F_{10,110}$ = 2.047	*p* = 0.035

3.1.6. Revisited Fixation Duration

Repeated measures ANOVA in Table 8 results revealed that there was a significant main effect of the environment ($F_{1,11}$ = 6.122, *p*-value = 0.031), the index of difficulty ($F_{5,55}$ = 47.224, *p*-value = 0.000), and the interaction of environment and depth ($F_{2,22}$ = 12.463, *p*-value = 0.000) on revisited fixation duration. We have not found a significant difference between revisited fixation duration with depth ($F_{2,22}$ = 0.604, *p*-value = 0.556), interaction of the environment and the index of difficulty ($F_{5,55}$ = 1.955, *p*-value = 0.100), interaction of depth and index of difficulty ($F_{10,110}$ = 1.035, *p*-value = 0.419), and interaction of the environment, depth, and the index of difficulty ($F_{10,110}$ = 1.841, *p*-value = 0.062).

3.1.7. Eye Fixation Accuracy

The repeated measures ANOVA results in Table 9 shows that there was a significant difference between eye fixation accuracy in screen displays and stereoscopic displays ($F_{1,11}$ = 8.559, *p*-value = 0.014). Moreover, the Tukey HSD showed a significant difference between screen and stereoscopic displays. Similarly, it shows that there was a significant accuracy difference for six levels index of difficulty ($F_{1,11}$ = 13.799, *p*-value = 0.000). The Tukey HSD results divided six levels of index of difficulty into three groups (see Table 9). However, there were no significant accuracy differences between depth ($F_{2,22}$ = 2.131, *p*-value = 0.143), the environment and depth ($F_{2,22}$ = 4.785, *p*-value = 0.677), the environment and the index of difficulty ($F_{5,55}$ = 23.500, *p*-value = 0.620), depth and the index of difficulty ($F_{10,110}$ = 8.759, *p*-value = 0.928), and interactions of the environment, depth, and index of difficulty ($F_{10,110}$ = 28.604, *p*-value = 0.354).

Table 8. Means, SDs, ANOVA, and Tukey HSD test results of revisited fixation duration.

Revisited Fixation Duration						
	Level	**Mean (s)**	**Group [a]**	**SD**	$F_{n,m}$	***p*-Value**
Environment	2D Screen Displays	0.974	A	0.274	$F_{1,11} = 6.122$	$p = 0.031$
	3D Stereoscopic Displays	1.114	B	0.401		
Depth	210 cm	1.027	A	0.358	$F_{2,22} = 0.604$	$p = 0.556$
	190 cm	1.042	A	0.341		
	140 cm	1.101	A	0.353		
ID	2.8 bits	0.762	A	0.216	$F_{5,55} = 47.224$	$p = 0.000$
	3.3 bits	0.947	B	0.234		
	3.7 bits	0.960	B	0.270		
	4.2 bits	0.967	B	0.265		
	5.1 bits	1.324	C	0.318		
	6.1 bits	1.303	C	0.388		
Environment * Depth					$F_{2,22} = 12.463$	$p = 0.000$
Environment * ID					$F_{5,55} = 1.955$	$p = 0.100$
Depth * ID					$F_{10,110} = 1.035$	$p = 0.419$
Environment * Depth * ID					$F_{10,110} = 1.841$	$p = 0.062$

Table 9. Means, SDs, ANOVA, and Tukey HSD test results of eye fixation accuracy.

Accuracy						
	Level	**Mean (%)**	**Group [a]**	**SD**	$F_{n,m}$	***p*-Value**
Environment	2D Screen Displays	94.443	A	4.432	$F_{1,11} = 8.559$	$p = 0.014$
	3D Stereoscopic Displays	92.220	B	6.820		
Depth	210 cm	92.452	A	6.331	$F_{2,22} = 2.131$	$p = 0.143$
	190 cm	94.160	A	5.020		
	140 cm	93.383	A	6.036		
ID	2.8 bits	92.489	A	5.320	$F_{5,55} = 13.799$	$p = 0.000$
	3.3 bits	91.904	A	4.938		
	3.7 bits	96.071	B	5.772		
	4.2 bits	96.280	B	3.377		
	5.1 bits	90.098	A, C	5.248		
	6.1 bits	93.148	A	7.283		
Environment * Depth					$F_{2,22} = 4.785$	$p = 0.677$
Environment * ID					$F_{5,55} = 23.500$	$p = 0.620$
Depth * ID					$F_{10,110} = 8.759$	$p = 0.928$
Environment * Depth * ID					$F_{10,110} = 28.604$	$p = 0.354$

3.2. Motor Performance

3.2.1. Hand Movement Time

Table 10 presents the means, SDs, ANOVA, and Tukey HSD test of hand movement time. The mean average of hand movement time increased in stereoscopic displays. The ANOVA shows there is significant difference in the environment ($F_{1,11} = 15.879$, *p*-value = 0.002). The Tukey HSD test revealed a significant difference occurred between hand movement time in screen displays and stereoscopic displays. A longer hand movement time occurred with the object in stereoscopic displays. The mean of hand movement time increased with depth. When the object was close to participants' eyes, it resulted in a longer hand movement time. However, ANOVA results show that there is no significant difference for different depth level ($F_{2,22} = 0.996$, *p*-value = 0.385). The index of difficulty affected hand movement time ($F_{5,55} = 144.887$, *p*-value = 0.000). The result of the

Tukey HSD test reported a significant difference in index of difficulty (see Table 10). The ANOVA results revealed that a significant difference occurred between the interaction of the environment and depth ($F_{2,22}$ = 13.115, *p*-value = *p* = 0.000), interaction of environment and ID ($F_{5,55}$ = 3.177, *p*-value = 0.014), the interaction of the depth and index of difficulty ($F_{10,110}$ = 2.684, *p*-value = 0.003), and the interaction of the environment, depth, and ID ($F_{10,110}$ = 2.157, *p*-value = *p* = 0.026).

Table 10. Means, SDs, ANOVA, and Tukey HSD test results of hand movement time.

Hand Movement Time						
	Level	Mean (s)	Group [a]	SD	$F_{n,m}$	*p*-Value
Environment	2D Screen Displays	1.539	A	0.371	$F_{1,11}$ = 15.879	*p* = 0.002
	3D Stereoscopic Displays	1.689	B	0.451		
Depth	210 cm	1.594	A	0.388	$F_{2,22}$ = 0.996	*p* = 0.385
	190 cm	1.617	A	0.399		
	140 cm	1.673	A	0.467		
ID	2.8 bits	1.160	A	0.247	$F_{5,55}$ = 144.887	*p* = 0.000
	3.3 bits	1.403	B	0.266		
	3.7 bits	1.602	C	0.241		
	4.2 bits	1.572	C	0.281		
	5.1 bits	1.881	D	0.344		
	6.1 bits	2.068	E	0.377		
Environment * Depth					$F_{2,22}$ = 13.115	*p* = 0.000
Environment * ID					$F_{5,55}$ = 3.177	*p* = 0.014
Depth * ID					$F_{10,110}$ = 2.684	*p* = 0.003
Environment * Depth * ID					$F_{10,110}$ = 2.157	*p* = 0.026

3.2.2. Index of Hand Performance

There was a significant main effect of environment and index of hand performance ($F_{1,11}$ = 22.317, *p*-value = 0.001) (Table 11). The Tukey HSD test reported significantly higher index of hand performance for screen displays. There was no significant effect of depth on the index of hand performance ($F_{2,22}$ = 1.53, *p*-value = 0.238). The Tukey HSD test showed a significant difference between each level of index of difficulty.

Table 11. Means, SDs, ANOVA, and Tukey HSD test results of index of motor performance.

Index of Hand Performance						
	Level	Mean (bits/s)	Group [a]	SD	$F_{n,m}$	*p*-Value
Environment	2D Screen Display	2.772	A	1.278	$F_{1,11}$ = 22.317	*p* = 0.001
	3D Stereoscopic Display	2.539	B	0.520		
Depth	210 cm	2.700	A	0.680	$F_{2,22}$ = 1.532	*p* = 0.238
	190 cm	2.625	A	0.434		
	140 cm	2.695	A	0.528		
Environment * Depth					$F_{2,22}$ = 13.207	*p* = 0.000

3.2.3. Error Rate

The repeated measures ANOVA results in Table 12 revealed a significant main effect of index of difficulty ($F_{5,55}$ = 9.920, *p*-value = 0.000) and interaction between the environment and depth ($F_{2,22}$ = 6.428, *p*-value = 0.006). However, there were no significant interactions between the environment ($F_{1,11}$ = 0.084, *p*-value = 0.777), depth ($F_{2,22}$ = 0.296, *p*-value = 0.747), the environment and index of difficulty ($F_{5,55}$ = 1.245, *p*-value = 0.301), depth and index of difficulty ($F_{10,110}$ = 1.683, *p*-value = 0.094), and the environment, depth, and index of difficulty ($F_{10,110}$ = 0.456, *p*-value = 0.915).

Table 12. Means, SDs, ANOVA, and Tukey HSD test results of index of error rate.

	Level	Mean	Group [a]	SD	$F_{n,m}$	*p*-Value
		Error Rate				
Environment	2D Screen Displays	0.068	A	0.097	$F_{1,11}$ = 0.084	*p* = 0.777
	3D Stereoscopic Displays	0.070	A	0.099		
Depth	210 cm	0.065	A	0.086	$F_{2,22}$ = 0.296	*p* = 0.747
	190 cm	0.067	A	0.097		
	140 cm	0.073	A	0.111		
ID	2.8 bits	0.029	A	0.053	$F_{5,55}$ = 9.920	*p* = 0.000
	3.3 bits	0.050	A	0.068		
	3.7 bits	0.046	A	0.075		
	4.2 bits	0.053	A	0.074		
	5.1 bits	0.137	B	0.142		
	6.1 bits	0.097	C	0.107		
Environment * Depth					$F_{2,22}$ = 6.428	*p* = 0.006
Environment * ID					$F_{5,55}$ = 1.245	*p* = 0.301
Depth * ID					$F_{10,110}$ = 1.683	*p* = 0.094
Environment * Depth * ID					$F_{10,110}$ = 0.456	*p* = 0.915

Finally, Table 13 shows the experimental results summary in this study. This table represents all main effects of environment, depth, and index of difficulty on eye movement measures. In addition, Table 13 also shows the main effects of environment, depth, and index of difficulty on motor performance.

Table 13. Summary of the findings.

No	Dependent Variable	Environment	Depth	Index of Difficulty
1	Eye Movement Time (second)	*p* = 0.036, $F_{1,11}$ = 5.732	*p* = 0.385, $F_{2,22}$ = 1.372	*p* = 0.274, $F_{5,55}$ = 12.760
2	Index of Eye Performance (bits/second)	*p* = 0.043, $F_{1,11}$ = 5.249	*p* = 0.288, $F_{2,22}$ = 1.317	*p* = 0.000, $F_{5,55}$ = 11.353
3	Number of Fixations	*p* = 0.216, $F_{1,11}$ = 1.726	*p* = 0.938, $F_{2,22}$ = 0.064	*p* = 0.000, $F_{5,55}$ = 15.022
4	Time to first Fixation (second)	*p* = 0.048, $F_{1,11}$ = 4.965	*p* = 0.677, $F_{2,22}$ = 0.398	*p* = 0.841, $F_{5,55}$ = 0.408
5	Saccadic Duration (second)	*p* = 0.014, $F_{1,11}$ = 8.481	*p* = 0.300, $F_{2,22}$ = 1.271	*p* = 0.000, $F_{5,55}$ = 18.512
6	Revisited Fixation Duration (second)	*p* = 0.031, $F_{1,11}$ = 6.122	*p* = 0.604, $F_{2,22}$ = 0.556	*p* = 0.000, $F_{5,55}$ = 47.224
7	Eye Fixation Accuracy	*p* = 0.014, $F_{1,11}$ = 8.559	*p* = 0.677, $F_{2,22}$ = 13.799	*p* = 0.000, $F_{5,55}$ = 13.799
8	Hand Movement Time (second)	*p* = 0.002, $F_{1,11}$ = 15.879	*p* = 0.385, $F_{2,22}$ = 0.996	*p* = 0.000, $F_{5,55}$ = 144.887
9	Index of Hand Performance (bits/second)	*p* = 0.001, $F_{1,11}$ = 22.317	*p* = 0.238, $F_{2,22}$ = 1.532	*p* = 0.000, $F_{5,55}$ = 28.899
10	Error Rate (%)	*p* = 0.777, $F_{1,11}$ = 0.084	*p* = 0.747, $F_{2,22}$ = 0.296	*p* = 0.000, $F_{5,55}$ = 9.920

4. Discussion

4.1. The Effect of Environment (3D TV)

The result of a repeated measures ANOVA revealed that environment had significant effects on eye movement time, index of eye performance, time to first fixation, saccade duration, revisited fixation duration, eye gaze accuracy, hand movement time, and index of hand performance. However, there were no significant main effects of environment on number of fixations and error rate. Participants were found to have longer eye movement time, lower index of eye performance, longer time to first fixation, longer saccade duration, longer revisited fixation duration, lower eye gaze accuracy, longer hand movement time, and lower index of hand performance when the target was presented in a 3D environment.

Theoretically, eye movement should be faster than hand movement. Participants assured the position of the target until they decided to move their hand to click the target. Eyes will guide the hand to click target when the eyes fixate on the position of the target [40]. In this study, participants required a longer time to click the virtual target in the 3D environment compared with the target in the 2D environment. It appears that in the 2D environment, participants perceived the target clearly without any difficulty and confusion, and therefore, the participants could determine the target in screen displays faster and more effectively than the virtual target in the 3D environment.

The index of eye performance was higher than the index of hand performance because the extraocular muscles that shift the eye are the fastest muscle in the human body [41]. Therefore, the speed gain of the eye made a difference over the hand for the same distances and resulted a higher index of eye performance. Our study is consistent with [42], which reported that eye performance was much higher than hand click performance.

The index of hand and eye performances in the 3D environment was lower than in the 2D environment. This condition happened because the movement time in the 3D environment was longer than movement time in the 2D environment. The index of performance was the result of the index of difficulty divided by the movement time; therefore, a longer movement time would result in a lower index of difficulty.

In the 3D environment, participants had longer hand and eye movement times with a lower index of hand and eye performances. This condition might have been caused by the accommodation-vergence conflict when participants perceived a virtual target in the 3D environment [20,24,43]. This conflict might influence the binocular ability vision of participants to focus on the virtual target. Moreover, this conflict might have affected the speed and accuracy of the task [44].

Eye fixation accuracy declined when the participants performed in the 3D environment. Eye fixation accuracy was determined as the percentage deviation between eye fixation location and the projected images of the target in the 2D environment. Participants performed precisely when they perceived the target in the 2D environment. Participants encountered difficulty to fixate accurately on the projected images of the virtual target. High difficulty levels of cognitive processing might be a factor of lower accuracy in the 3D environment. Holmqvist et al. [11] stated that a microsaccade, an eye fixation movement tremor, and drift could happen due to a high difficulty level of cognitive processing. Moreover, low accuracy could have occurred because of perceived depth error [45]. Therefore, eye fixation accuracy became lower in the 3D environment.

A longer time to first fixation happened when participants performed in the 3D environment. This was not surprising since participants required more processing time in the 3D environment to recognize and to identify the location of the virtual ball. In order to perceived the virtual target clearly, participants needed longer eye adaptation and accommodation processes.

Based on the saccadic duration and revisited fixation duration, the results showed that saccadic duration and revisited fixation duration in the 3D environment were longer than those in the 2D environment. In the 3D environment, participants spent significantly more time in revisited fixation. Depth perception was required to perceive the virtual target in stereoscopic displays [46,47]. Difficulty to perceive the virtual target could affect the revisited fixation duration. Moreover, some participants reported that they found it more difficult to perceive the virtual target in the 3D environment compared to the 2D environment.

The error rate was not significantly different from the environment. Overall, the error rate calculation was below 7%. The results implied that there was no speed–accuracy trade-off in this study. Therefore, the hand and eye movement results could be acknowledged as being truly an effect of the visual environment.

4.2. The Effect of Depth

The results of the repeated measures ANOVA revealed that there was no significant difference between depth and hand and eye movement times, the index of hand and eye performances, error rate, eye fixation accuracy, number of fixations, time to first fixation, saccadic duration, and revisited fixation duration. Even though the results showed no significant difference, there were trends in the results when participants performed the task in three different levels of depth.

Participants had longer eye movement time, longer hand movement time, longer saccadic duration, and longer revisited fixation duration when the target was presented closer to their eyes. Although depth was found not significantly affect most of the independent variables, the index of eye and hand performances were found lower at a depth of 140 cm compared to 190 cm and 210 cm. Moreover, participants had a higher error rate when the target was brought closer to the participants' eyes at a depth of 140 cm.

Psychophysical research reported that the implication of depth perception could affect human perception to see the target clearly. The compilation of experiment results about depth judgment reported misjudgment made by participants. They judged the depth distance to be smaller than the actual depth of target [48–51]. Therefore, depth could contribute to a longer hand and eye movement time, saccadic duration, and revisited fixation duration a lower index of hand and eye performance, and a higher error rate when the target projected closer to the participants' eyes.

4.3. The Effect of Index of Difficulty (ID)

The result of the repeated measures ANOVA reported that hand movement time, index of hand and eye performance, error rate, eye fixation accuracy, number of fixations, saccadic duration, and revisited fixation duration had a significant difference in six different levels of index of difficulty. However, there was no significant effect of index of difficulty on eye movement time and time to first fixation. Our previous study applied structural equation modeling (SEM) to analyze the interrelationship among ID and selected eye movement parameters [29]. We also found that ID had significant effects on eye movement time and number of fixations. In addition, we also revealed that ID had no significant effect on time to first fixation. Despite it being a different statistical technique, the repeated measures ANOVA analysis matches with the previous SEM analysis. Moreover, post-hoc analysis in one-way repeated ANOVA could reveal significant differences among the group which could not be obtained by utilizing an SEM analysis.

Hand and eye movement times increased when the index of difficulty increased. Similarly, saccadic duration and revisited fixation duration were longer when the index of difficulty level increased. Many researchers reported higher correlations between movement time and the index of difficulty [52–56]. Similarly, in this study, the index of difficulty significantly affected hand and eye movement time as well as saccadic duration and revisited fixation duration.

Hand and eye movement times were related to the index of hand and eye performance. The increase of movement time would be compensated for by the increase in the index of difficulty and decrease the value of the index of performance [38]. However, in this study, the results reported that participants had a higher index of hand and eye performances when they performed the tapping tasks at a higher level of index of difficulty. This occurred because of the slightly different in value between eye and hand movement times for each level of index of difficulty. Thus, the index of hand and eye performances would be high when the short movement time was divided by the high-level index of difficulty. Longer movement times have been consequently associated with the number of fixations [38]. In line with this study, longer movement times, caused by a higher level index of difficulty, lead to a higher number of fixations.

The index of difficulty influenced the error rate made by the participant in this experiment. Higher levels of index of difficulty caused a higher error rate and eye fixation accuracy. Wade et al. [57] and Card et al. [58] reported that decreasing target width caused a higher error rate. The smaller target width increased the difficulty level for the participants to perceive the target location, which would lead to an inaccuracy in the tapping task.

4.4. Practical Implications

Generally, poor visual and motor performances may have an impact on consumer acceptance of 3D TVs. This study provided a general implication for users to perceive virtual objects in 3D TVs or stereoscopic displays. The results revealed that poor visual and motor performances may have an impact on the acceptance of 3D TVs due to visual discomfort or fatigue. The variation of depth had no significant difference at different levels on any independent variable. The visual and motor performance was good in combination with depth in the experiment. However, the distance from the user to the display (3D TV) revealed that the depth of 210 cm had the best eye movement and motor performance compared with the distance (190 cm and 140 cm). The depth (210 cm) should minimize the vergence accommodation conflict for the users. In addition, the smallest depth (140 cm) would affect the visual phenomenon that occurs when the brain receives mismatching cues between vergence and accommodation of the eye. Thus, depth should be considered in order to minimize visual discomfort and vergence accommodation conflict.

4.5. Limiations and Future Research Directions

Despite the substantial contributions of this study, we would like to mention several limitations in this study. First, we purely investigated the effect of 3D TVs on eye movement and motor performance. Future research should propose a new technical solution to capture the physical and psychological changes simultaneously when a person watches a 3D TV. Second, the statistical analysis was RM-ANOVA, which could not investigate the effect of one independent variable on two or more dependent variables simultaneously. Future research that incorporates structural equation modeling or data mining techniques would be a promising direction. Finally, curved display TVs are currently becoming available on the market. Using our approach, future research could investigate the effect of curved display TVs on eye movement and motor performance.

5. Conclusions

Three-dimensional TVs have been commercialized in recent years; however, the commercialization of them has faced difficulties on the market. The purpose of this study was mainly to investigate in depth the effects of 3D TV environments on eye movement and motor performance. We also discussed the effect of parallax and index of difficulty, since both variables could influence eye movement and motor performance.

The results showed that the environment had significant effects on eye movement time, index of eye performance, eye fixation accuracy, number of fixations, time to first fixation, saccadic duration, revisited fixation duration, hand movement time, index of hand performance, and error rate. Participants were found to have longer eye movement time, lower index of eye performance, longer time to first fixation, longer saccade duration, longer revisited fixation duration, lower eye gaze accuracy, longer hand movement time, and lower index of hand performance when the target was presented in a 3D environment.

Interestingly, no significant effects of environment were found on the number of fixations and error rate. Regarding ID, the results showed that there were significant main effects between index of difficulty and hand movement time, index of hand and eye performances, error rate, eye fixation accuracy, saccadic duration, and revisited fixation duration. Finally, no significant differences were found between different levels of depth on any independent variables, although bigger depth (210 cm) mostly had the best eye movement and motor performance compared with smaller depth (190 cm and 140 cm).

This study is the first in-depth investigations of the effect of 3D TVs to eye movement and motor performance. The parameters could be beneficial for developers [35,36] and virtual reality researchers [59–63] to enhance the human performance of 3D TVs.

Author Contributions: Conceptualization, C.J.L. and R.W.; methodology, C.J.L. and R.W.; software, R.W.; validation, C.J.L. and Y.T.P.; formal analysis, C.J.L., R.W. and Y.T.P.; investigation, C.J.L., R.W. and Y.T.P.; resources, R.W.; writing—original draft preparation, R.W. and Y.T.P.; writing—review and editing, C.J.L.; supervision, C.J.L.; funding acquisition, Y.T.P. All authors have read and agreed to the published version of the manuscript.

Funding: This work was supported by the Ministry of Science and Technology of Taiwan (MOST 103-2221-E-011-100-MY3) and Mapúa University Directed Research for Innovation and Value Enhancement (DRIVE).

Institutional Review Board Statement: The current study was conducted according to the ethical guidelines published by the National Taiwan University Research Ethics Committee.

Informed Consent Statement: Informed consent was obtained from all subjects involved in the study.

Data Availability Statement: The data presented in this study are available on request from the corresponding author.

Acknowledgments: The researchers would like to extend their deepest gratitude to all participants in this study.

Conflicts of Interest: The authors declare no conflict of interest.

References

1. Minoli, D. *3D Television (3DTV) Technology, Systems, and Deployment: Rolling out the Infrastructure for Next-Generation Entertainment*; CRC Press: Boca Raton, FL, USA, 2010.
2. Bowman, D.; Kruijff, E.; LaViola, J.J., Jr.; Poupyrev, I.P. *3D User Interfaces: Theory and Practice, CourseSmart eTextbook*; Addison-Wesley: Boston, MA, USA, 2004.
3. Fernando, A.; Worrall, S.T.; Ekmekciolu, E. *3DTV: Processing and Transmission of 3D Video Signals*; John Wiley & Sons: Hoboken, NJ, USA, 2013.
4. Zhou, J.; Wang, L.; Yin, H.; Bovik, A.C. Eye movements and visual discomfort when viewing stereoscopic 3D content. *Digit. Signal Process.* **2019**, *91*, 41–53. [CrossRef]
5. Teather, R.J.; Stuerzlinger, W. Pointing at 3d target projections with one-eyed and stereo cursors. In Proceedings of the SIGCHI Conference on Human Factors in Computing Systems, Paris, France, 27 April–2 May 2013; pp. 159–168.
6. Machuca, M.D.B.; Stuerzlinger, W. Do stereo display deficiencies affect 3D pointing? In Proceedings of the Extended Abstracts of the 2018 CHI Conference on Human Factors in Computing Systems, Montreal, QC, Canada, 21–26 April 2018; pp. 1–6.
7. Lin, C.J.; Prasetyo, Y.T.; Widyaningrum, R. Eye movement measures for predicting eye gaze accuracy and symptoms in 2D and 3D displays. *Displays* **2019**, *60*, 1–8. [CrossRef]
8. Lin, C.J.; Widyaningrum, R. Eye pointing in stereoscopic displays. *J. Eye Mov. Res.* **2016**, *9*. [CrossRef]
9. Fuchs, P. *Virtual Reality Headsets—A Theoretical and Pragmatic Approach*; CRC Press: Boca Raton, FL, USA, 2017.
10. Sharples, S.; Cobb, S.; Moody, A.; Wilson, J.R. Virtual reality induced symptoms and effects (VRISE): Comparison of head mounted display (HMD), desktop and projection display systems. *Displays* **2008**, *29*, 58–69. [CrossRef]
11. Holmqvist, K.; Nyström, M.; Andersson, R.; Dewhurst, R.; Jarodzka, H.; Van de Weijer, J. *Eye Tracking: A Comprehensive Guide to Methods and Measures*; OUP Oxford: Singapore, 2011.
12. Artal, P. *Handbook of Visual Optics*; CRC Press, Taylor & Francis Group: Boca Raton, FL, USA, 2017.
13. Čegovnik, T.; Stojmenova, K.; Jakus, G.; Sodnik, J. An analysis of the suitability of a low-cost eye tracker for assessing the cognitive load of drivers. *Appl. Ergon.* **2018**, *68*, 1–11. [CrossRef] [PubMed]
14. Bækgaard, P.; Jalaliniya, S.; Hansen, J.P. Pupillary measurement during an assembly task. *Appl. Ergon.* **2019**, *75*, 99–107. [CrossRef] [PubMed]
15. Goldberg, J.H. Measuring software screen complexity: Relating eye tracking, emotional valence, and subjective ratings. *Int. J. Hum.-Comput. Interact.* **2014**, *30*, 518–532. [CrossRef]
16. Lin, C.J.; Chang, C.-C.; Lee, Y.-H. Evaluating camouflage design using eye movement data. *Appl. Ergon.* **2014**, *45*, 714–723. [CrossRef]
17. Read, J.C.; Godfrey, A.; Bohr, I.; Simonotto, J.; Galna, B.; Smulders, T.V. Viewing 3D TV over two months produces no discernible effects on balance, coordination or eyesight. *Ergonomics* **2016**, *59*, 1073–1088. [CrossRef]
18. Read, J.C. Viewer experience with stereoscopic 3D television in the home. *Displays* **2014**, *35*, 252–260. [CrossRef]
19. Lambooij, M.; IJsselsteijn, W.A.; Heynderickx, I. Visual discomfort of 3D TV: Assessment methods and modeling. *Displays* **2011**, *32*, 209–218. [CrossRef]
20. Lee, S.-I.; Jung, Y.J.; Sohn, H.; Speranza, F.; Ro, Y.M. Effect of stimulus width on the perceived visual discomfort in viewing stereoscopic 3-D-TV. *IEEE Trans. Broadcast.* **2013**, *59*, 580–590. [CrossRef]
21. Chang, J.; Jung, K.; Kim, W.; Moon, S.K.; Freivalds, A.; Simpson, T.W.; Baik, S.P. Effects of weight balance on a 3D TV shutter type glasses: Subjective discomfort and physical contact load on the nose. *Int. J. Ind. Ergon.* **2014**, *44*, 801–809. [CrossRef]

22. Chang, J.; Moon, S.K.; Jung, K.; Kim, W.; Parkinson, M.; Freivalds, A.; Simpson, T.W.; Baik, S.P. Glasses-type wearable computer displays: Usability considerations examined with a 3D glasses case study. *Ergonomics* **2018**, *61*, 670–681. [CrossRef]
23. Zang, B.; Zhou, J.; Xiong, J. What is the 3D comfort difference experienced via VR glasses and 3D-TV. In *Digital TV and Multimedia Communication, Proceedings of the International Forum on Digital TV and Wireless Multimedia Communications, Shanghai, China, 20–21 September 2018*; Springer: Singapore, 2019; pp. 261–272.
24. Urvoy, M.; Barkowsky, M.; Le Callet, P. How visual fatigue and discomfort impact 3D-TV quality of experience: A comprehensive review of technological, psychophysical, and psychological factors. *Ann. Telecommun.* **2013**, *68*, 641–655. [CrossRef]
25. Chen, C.; Wang, J.; Li, K.; Liu, Y.; Chen, X. Visual fatigue caused by watching 3DTV: An fmri study. *BioMed. Eng. OnLine* **2015**, *14*, S12. [CrossRef]
26. Manshouri, N.; Maleki, M.; Kayikcioglu, T. An EEG-based stereoscopic research of the PSD differences in pre and post 2D&3D movies watching. *Biomed. Signal Process. Control* **2020**, *55*, 101642.
27. Chen, C.; Li, K.; Wu, Q.; Wang, H.; Qian, Z.; Sudlow, G. EEG-based detection and evaluation of fatigue caused by watching 3DTV. *Displays* **2013**, *34*, 81–88. [CrossRef]
28. Lin, C.J.; Widyaningrum, R. The effect of parallax on eye fixation parameter in projection-based stereoscopic displays. *Appl. Ergon.* **2018**, *69*, 10–16. [CrossRef]
29. Lin, C.J.; Prasetyo, Y.T.; Widyaningrum, R. Eye movement parameters for performance evaluation in projection-based stereoscopic display. *J. Eye Mov. Res.* **2018**, *11*. [CrossRef] [PubMed]
30. Prasetyo, Y.T.; Widyaningrum, R.; Lin, C.J. Eye gaze accuracy in the projection-based stereoscopic display as a function of number of fixation, eye movement time, and parallax. In Proceedings of the 2019 IEEE International Conference on Industrial Engineering and Engineering Management (IEEM), Macao, China, 15–18 December 2019; pp. 54–58.
31. Prasetyo, Y.T.; Widyaningrum, R. Error rate as mediators of the relationships among 2D/3D TV environment, eye gaze accuracy, and symptoms. In Proceedings of the 21st Congress of the International Ergonomics Association (IEA 2021), online, 13–18 June 2021; pp. 756–761.
32. Prasetyo, Y.T.; Widyaningrum, R. Eye-hand movement in 3D displays: A structural equation modeling approach. *IOP Conf. Ser. Mater. Sci. Eng.* **2021**, *1072*, 012059. [CrossRef]
33. Prasetyo, Y.T.; Widyaningrum, R. Eye ballistic phase time and eye correction phase time as mediators of the relationships among 2D/3D TV environment, eye gaze accuracy, and symptoms. In *Convergence of Ergonomics and Design*; Advances in Intelligent Systems and Computing; Springer: Cham, Switzerland, 2021; pp. 399–408.
34. Lin, C.J.; Ho, S.-H.; Chen, Y.-J. An investigation of pointing postures in a 3D stereoscopic environment. *Appl. Ergon.* **2015**, *48*, 154–163. [CrossRef]
35. Salvucci, D.D.; Goldberg, J.H. Identifying fixations and saccades in eye-tracking protocols. In Proceedings of the 2000 Symposium on Eye Tracking Research & Applications, Palm Beach Gardens, FL, USA, 6–8 November 2000; pp. 71–78.
36. Frick, A.; Koch, R. LDV generation from multi-view hybrid image and depth video. In *3D-TV System with Depth-Image-Based Rendering*; Springer: Berlin/Heidelberg, Germany, 2013; pp. 191–220.
37. Park, Y.-G.; Jung, H.-C.; Park, M.-K.; Kang, T.-Y.; Kim, B.-M.; Kim, H.-J. Method for Providing a User Interface Using Motion and Device Adopting the Method. U.S. Patent US20120151415A1, 24 August 2012.
38. MacKenzie, I.S. Fitts' law as a research and design tool in human-computer interaction. *Hum.-Comput. Interact.* **1992**, *7*, 91–139. [CrossRef]
39. *Guide Méthodologique pour le Dépistage Visuel (Test Snellen): Programme Santé des Jeunes d'Age Scolaire*; Centre Hospitalier Maisonneuve-Rosemont: Montréal, QC, Canada, 1984.
40. Neggers, S.F.; Bekkering, H. Gaze anchoring to a pointing target is present during the entire pointing movement and is driven by a non-visual signal. *J. Neurophysiol.* **2001**, *86*, 961–970. [CrossRef] [PubMed]
41. Bobick, J.; Balaban, N. *The Handy Anatomy Answer Book*; Visible Ink Press: Canton, MI, USA, 2008.
42. Vertegaal, R. A Fitts Law comparison of eye tracking and manual input in the selection of visual targets. In Proceedings of the 10th International Conference on Multimodal Interfaces, Chania, Greece, 20–22 October 2008; pp. 241–248.
43. Watt, S.J.; Akeley, K.; Ernst, M.O.; Banks, M.S. Focus cues affect perceived depth. *J. Vis.* **2005**, *5*, 7. [CrossRef]
44. Hoffman, D.M.; Girshick, A.R.; Akeley, K.; Banks, M.S. Vergence–accommodation conflicts hinder visual performance and cause visual fatigue. *J. Vis.* **2008**, *8*, 33. [CrossRef] [PubMed]
45. Deering, M. High resolution virtual reality. In Proceedings of the 19th Annual Conference on Computer Graphics and Interactive Techniques, Chicago, IL, USA, 26–31 July 1992; pp. 195–202.
46. Liu, L.; van Liere, R.; Nieuwenhuizen, C.; Martens, J.-B. Comparing aimed movements in the real world and in virtual reality. In Proceedings of the 2009 IEEE Virtual Reality Conference, Lafayette, LA, USA, 14–18 March 2009; pp. 219–222.
47. Woodworth, R. *The Accuracy of Voluntary Movement Columbia University Contributions to Philosophy, Psychology and Education*; Columbia University: New York, NY, USA, 1899.
48. Caudek, C.; Proffitt, D.R. Depth perception in motion parallax and stereokinesis. *J. Exp. Psychol. Hum. Percept. Perform.* **1993**, *19*, 32. [CrossRef]
49. Domini, F.; Caudek, C. Perceiving surface slant from deformation of optic flow. *J. Exp. Psychol. Hum. Percept. Perform.* **1999**, *25*, 426. [CrossRef] [PubMed]

50. Loomis, J.; Eby, D. Relative motion parallax and the perception of structure from motio. In Proceedings of the Workshop on Visual Motion, Irvine, CA, USA, 20–22 March 1989; pp. 204–211.
51. Todd, J.T.; Bressan, P. The perception of 3-dimensional affine structure from minimal apparent motion sequences. *Percept. Psychophys.* **1990**, *48*, 419–430. [CrossRef]
52. Drury, C.G. Application of Fitts' law to foot-pedal design. *Hum. Factors* **1975**, *17*, 368–373. [CrossRef]
53. Fitts, P.M.; Peterson, J.R. Information capacity of discrete motor responses. *J. Exp. Psychol.* **1964**, *67*, 103. [CrossRef]
54. Kerr, B.A.; Langolf, G.D. Speed of aiming movements. *Q. J. Exp. Psychol.* **1977**, *29*, 475–481. [CrossRef]
55. Knight, A.; Dagnall, P. Precision in movements. *Ergonomics* **1967**, *10*, 321–330. [CrossRef]
56. Kvålseth, T.O. An alternative to Fitts' law. *Bull. Psychon. Soc.* **1980**, *16*, 371–373. [CrossRef]
57. Wade, M.G.; Newell, K.M.; Wallace, S.A. Decision time and movement time as a function of response complexity in retarded persons. *Am. J. Ment. Defic.* **1978**, *83*, 135–144. [PubMed]
58. Card, S.K.; English, W.K.; Burr, B.J. Evaluation of mouse, rate-controlled isometric joystick, step keys, and text keys for text selection on a CRT. *Ergonomics* **1978**, *21*, 601–613. [CrossRef]
59. Long, Z.; Liu, L.; Yuan, X.; Zheng, Y.; Niu, Y.; Yao, L. Assessment of 3D visual discomfort based on dynamic functional connectivity analysis with HMM in EEG. *Brain Sci.* **2022**, *12*, 937. [CrossRef]
60. Lin, P.-H.; Jin, Y.-M. Applying fuzzy theory in selecting the image quality factors of 3D televisions. *Int. J. Ind. Ergon.* **2019**, *74*, 102841. [CrossRef]
61. Park, S.; Kyung, G.; Yi, J.; Choi, D.; Lee, S. Curved tvs improved watching experience when display curvature radii approached viewing distances: Effects of display curvature radius, viewing distance, and lateral viewing position on TV watching experience. *PLoS ONE* **2020**, *15*, e0228437. [CrossRef] [PubMed]
62. Wahl, S.; Dragneva, D.; Rifai, K. Digitalization versus immersion: Performance and subjective evaluation of 3D perception with emulated accommodation and parallax in digital microsurgery. *J. Biomed. Opt.* **2019**, *24*, 106501. [CrossRef]
63. Yu, M.; Li, Y.; Tian, F. Responses of functional brain networks while watching 2D and 3D videos: An EEG study. *Biomed. Signal Process. Control* **2021**, *68*, 102613. [CrossRef]

applied sciences

MDPI

Article

Eye-Tracking Investigation of the Train Driver's: A Case Study

Radovan Madlenak *, Jaroslav Masek, Lucia Madlenakova and Roman Chinoracky

Faculty of Operation and Economics of Transport and Communications, University of Žilina, Univerzitná 8215/1, 010 26 Žilina, Slovakia
* Correspondence: radovan.madlenak@uniza.sk

Abstract: This article investigates the utilization of eye-tracking methodology to monitor the driver's activities and attention during the arrival and departure procedures of train operations on Slovak Railway (ŽSR) line no. 120, Bratislava–Žilina. Previous studies conducted in 2020 formed the basis of the current research, which focused on two train stations and two railway stops located on the Žilina–Púchov track section. The results of the experiment allowed for a greater understanding of the driver's cognitive processes, thereby leading to increased safety and sustainability in the railway transport system. It is noteworthy that the employed measurement methodology and technology had no detrimental effect on train operation, or operational and thus passenger safety. Thus, the results of this experiment provide a sound foundation for further exploration into human–machine (driver–train) interaction in actual traffic conditions.

Keywords: train driver's behavior; eye tracking; railway safety; human-machine interaction

1. Introduction

The essential tools for achieving a sustainable transport vision are global strategic objectives based on the "Strategic Plan for Transport Development in the Slovak Republic until 2030" [1] and the "Roadmap to a Single European Transport (White Paper)" [2]. These documents delineate the trends and requirements defined in European and national strategies. The document comprises several strategic global objectives that can be identified as main goals of sustainable railway transport. This study is concerned with the objective of increasing the safety and security of transport, which necessitates the provision of safe mobility through secure infrastructure and advanced technologies/procedures, incorporating preventive and control mechanisms [3].

Railway transport performance in the conveyance of passengers has seen continual growth and is the safest mode of transportation. The key criterion for any system of transportation is its security [4].

Rail transport is an ecologically sustainable mode of transportation, as evidenced by its contribution of only 0.5% of total EU greenhouse gas emissions in 2017, according to the European Environment Agency [5]. Passenger kilometers in the EU-28 have grown from 375 billion in 2004 to 441 billion in 2014, translating to an increase of 17% in the modal share of rail travel from 6.1% to 6.9%. Such an increase in rail transportation has resulted in a decrease in congestion, air pollution, and greenhouse gas emissions in and around the larger cities within the EU. Eurostat reported in 2018 that the railway sector in the EU had a transport performance of 471,701.6 million passenger kilometers and almost ten billion passengers, with a 1.5% increase compared to 2017 figures [6,7].

Railway transport safety is highly reliant on the signaling and safety systems employed. These systems are typically divided into four distinct categories: station interlocking equipment, crossing interlocking devices, train protection systems, and line signaling equipment. Station interlocking equipment ensures that the railway infrastructure is in a safe state, crossing interlocking devices protect rail crossings from potential collisions, train protection systems reduce the risk of derailment, and line signaling equipment enhances the visibility of railway signals. All of these distinct systems are essential in providing a high level of safety in railway transport [8].

Rail transport safety is substantially enhanced by the incorporation of modern safety systems and the continuous modernization thereof. Traffic conditions, means of transport and human factors are the primary determinants of sustainable transport safety. The condition of the infrastructure and the level of signaling and safety systems, as well as weather conditions and other external factors, all contribute to the overall safety of rail transport. Additionally, the technical state of the means of transport, as well as the safety level, are fundamental determinants of safety. Finally, human factors, which constitute one of the most prominent causes of transport accidents, must be taken into account. The failures of infrastructure personnel, train drivers, and third parties can all have significant ramifications on transport safety [9].

Various definitions of human factors can be identified. Several authors describe it as an area of research that assesses human psychological, social, physical, and biological characteristics, synthesizes the data collected, and applies the findings to the design, operation, or utilization of products or systems with the aim of maximizing human performance, health, safety, and/or habitability [10–12].

According to the International Ergonomics Association, the discipline of Human Factors is devoted to the scientific examination of human–system interactions. This field of inquiry centers on the aptitude of human beings to engage with tasks, equipment, technologies, and the environment in order to understand and evaluate these connections [13]. The Transport Research Board (TRB) additionally indicates that the study of human factors is a multidisciplinary science that scrutinizes the interrelation between humans and devices, products, and systems. This branch of investigation is a fusion of behavioral science, engineering, and other disciplines, striving to establish the principles that ensure the usability of devices and systems by their designated users [14].

When evaluating the impact of the human element on the railway system, the quality of education and training of railway personnel, their level of experience, and their state of health and wellbeing must be taken into consideration. Factors such as the quality of educational and training programs, the degree of expertise of railway personnel, and the current physical and psychological condition of employees such as fatigue, hunger, thirst, and overwork can all have significant implications [15].

Ensuring the sustainability of rail transport necessitates the assurance of its safety, wherein the human element plays an essential role. Numerous railway safety regulations exist in the context of railway safety and accidents [16]. For example, the Commission Directive 2014/88 EC EU of 9 June 2014 amended Directive 2004/49/EC of the European Parliament and the Council concerning common safety indicators and common methods for determining the magnitude of harm in the instance of accidents, and included a Corrigendum to Commission Directive 2014/88/EU of 9 June 2014. June 2014 amended Directive 2004/49/EC of the European Parliament and the Council regarding common safety indicators and common methods for determining the amount of damage in the event of accidents, and the Decision of 11 December 2013 C (2013) 8780. This Decision established common safety targets (CSTs) for the interval 2011–2015 for all Member States. The European Railway Agency (ERA) is responsible for their computation and adherence to safety levels. Varying national regulations are also in place, based on European safety rules.

The issue of railway accidents relating to the train driver's culpability is of importance due to the particular type of accidents indicated in Table 1 sourced from the Czech Rail Safety Inspection Office. The data in Table 1 encompass the exclusive category of incidents (exceeding the main/shunting stop signal). Drivers are responsible for 99% of this type of crash. An inquiry from the Czech Rail Safety Inspection Office established that the primary causes for drivers' errors are fatigue, overwork, and inadequate driving techniques and experience. There is no exact protective system in rail transport for evaluating drivers' driving capabilities, wise/poor practices or vigilance [17].

Table 1. Unauthorized driving (violation of traffic signs) through the stop signal, including subsequent collision or derailment on sidings, regional, and national lines [17].

	2018			2019			2020		
	Accidents	Train	Shunting	Accidents	Train	Shunting	Accidents	Train	Shunting
January	12	8	4	14	12	2	15	10	5
February	15	11	4	21	12	9	15	9	6
March	6	4	2	20	15	5	11	8	3
April	8	5	3	11	8	3	10	7	3
May	19	16	3	7	5	2	7	7	0
June	12	10	2	14	10	4	18	13	5
July	13	9	4	10	4	6	14	9	5
August	12	7	5	11	7	4	9	7	2
September	23	20	3	6	5	1	13	6	7
October	11	7	4	7	6	1	12	8	4
November	15	11	4	17	13	4	13	7	6
December	2	2	0	11	7	4	12	10	2
Summary	148	110	38	149	104	45	149	101	48

The average age of train drivers employed by Company ZSSK (national passenger operator in Slovakia) in 2019 was 46 years, whereas for Company ZSSK Cargo (national cargo operator in Slovakia), the average age was 49 years. A noteworthy fact is that the Czech railway sector, whose companies operate in Slovakia as well, faced a significant shortfall of 330 drivers in 2020, and the average age of those employed was 49.6 years, with 11% being over the age of 65.

Investigation into human–machine interactions is an effective way to ascertain the variables that have an influence on human performance when operating machines. Identifying the critical contributing factors (positive and/or negative) that affect human behavior can lead to enhanced transport safety [18].

Edkins D. G. and Pollock M.C. conducted a pioneering comprehensive examination of train drivers' vigilance in 1997. They commenced their investigation with the proposition that railway operations necessitate that train drivers remain alert, oftentimes in tedious conditions, and act quickly to unforeseen critical signals. They scrutinized 112 rail accidents in Australia between 1990 and 1994, and determined that the drivers' attention was implicated in 70% of the accidents. Moreover, the researchers observed that train driver errors commonly involved skill-based behavior [19].

Lorenz's dissertation thesis examines the utility of modern technology in facilitating route knowledge acquisition among inexperienced train drivers. He highlights the importance of Human–Machine Interaction (HMI), which is defined as the communication between a human and a machine via a user interface. User interface encompasses the use of input devices and software, and the human eye is one of the primary input media, providing 80 to 90 percent of information gleaned from the outside world. To gain insight into a user's gaze point, eye tracking is employed as an experimental research method. Consequently, this research contributes to a better understanding of the effectiveness of modern technology in propagating route knowledge with regard to train driving [20–22].

The study of human interaction and behavior in safety-critical environments is a focal point of human factors research [23]. Traditional techniques for quantifying human performance typically incorporate metrics such as response time and accuracy. Performance measures are thus generated. Furthermore, to gain a better understanding of task progression, an examination of the underlying processes must be conducted. This necessitates the utilization of procedural measures, and in this regard, eye movements are particularly advantageous due to their ability to provide insights into the visual, cognitive, and perceptual aspects of human performance [24,25].

Investigation of human factors utilizing the user testing method is a viable approach for exploring the level of interaction between humans and machines. To maximize the efficacy of usability testing, a representative sample of the targeted user group should be chosen and the data collection techniques must be capable of capturing the demands associated with the activities performed. Eye-tracking technology provides a unique opportunity for user testing as it is capable of measuring the perception and behavior of the tested subject while they are completing the assigned tasks. The usefulness of eye-tracking in transport systems is evident, as it has been employed for various measurements in both real and simulated environments and is especially advantageous for the analysis of human behavior in aviation and vehicle driving.

Eye trackers have been employed in flight simulators for the purpose of aviation experiments, as demonstrated by the studies of Kocian and Longridge [26,27]. An example of effective utilization of eye-tracking technology in a flight simulator was provided by Anders [28]. In the course of the experiment, eye and head movements of professional pilots were recorded by eye-tracking equipment in a simulated flight environment. This enabled an analysis of the interaction between the pilot and the Human–Machine Interface (HMI) with regard to the selection and management of information, situational and mode perception in an aircraft cockpit. The experiment was performed in a full flight simulator Airbus 330 certified for airline training. The cockpit was divided into twelve fields of interest, and pilots had to perform flights beginning from a specified altitude, followed by descent and landing. This experiment shows how eye movements effectively inform the assessment of pilots' performance, as well as the instruction of novice pilots.

The application of eye trackers within driving simulators has been acknowledged to be an efficient method of recognizing the nature of the driving task and improving driver training strategies, as well as preventing road traffic accidents. Chapman and Underwood's study demonstrated that inexperienced drivers were observed to have a more protracted fixation on stimuli than experienced drivers. This indicates that novices require additional time to process visual information from the scene [29]. The research of Dishart and Land showed that the use of the road section with tangent points increases with experience and then decreases as drivers learn to optimize the pattern of their visual surveillance and search [30].

Ho's driving study investigates the impact of environmental factors such as clutter, illumination, and age on the visual search for traffic signs in images of driving scenes. Results from the study revealed considerable differences in the number of errors, reaction times, number of fixations, and average fixation duration between older and younger participants. Due to the rapidly aging driving population, the authors recommend reducing the number of advertisements near roads, removing superfluous traffic signs, and making them more prominent for the drivers, thereby augmenting road safety [31]. Recarte and Nunes's research on mental activity during driving suggests the advisability of raising drivers' awareness about the possible effects of driving. At the same time, the study indicates that fixation on thoughts unrelated to driving could be reduced by diminishing the windows and mirrors in the car, which would result in a decreased probability of detecting traffic events [32].

An analysis of driving behavior revealed that eye-tracking technology was primarily employed in aviation and automotive experiments, with a lack of experiments devoted to other modes of transportation. A survey of the Web of Science database uncovered a few studies on the evaluation of driver behavior with user testing technology in railway transport systems:

- Luke et al. explored the visual task of train driving by utilizing a corneal dark eye-tracking system to track the visual search and scanning patterns of train drivers. Data collected from the system included the duration and frequency of glances towards different aspects of the dynamic scene both inside and outside the train cab. The primary focus of the experiment was the visual scene in front of the train [33].

- Madlenak et al. conducted an in-depth examination of the driver's attention during train operation. The study analyzed two common processes during the train driver's work: locomotion on the tracks (without stops) and locomotion through the train station (with stops at the station) [9].
- Rjabovs and Palacin investigate the performance-shaping factors associated with holistic design considerations of metro systems, and further evaluate their influence on driver behavior through the implementation of eye-tracking techniques in a case study [34].
- Yan et al. investigated the particularity of train drivers' fatigue in a high-speed railway context [35].
- Naghiyev et al. conducted an explorative eye-tracking study in a real-world setting with conventional and European Rail Traffic Management System drivers on their regularly scheduled routes. The results of this study offered a more comprehensive qualitative examination of the cause of the transition in the standard visual attentional strategy from observation of the tracks to speed information inside the cab [36].
- Guo et al. investigated the role of image velocity and complexity on the dynamic visual field of high-speed train drivers, with eye movement analysis demonstrating that image velocity had a significant impact, whereas complexity did not [37].
- Vera Verstappen conducted a pilot study to investigate the effect of a fellow passenger on train drivers' performance and attention allocation. Utilizing a train simulator, the results of the study revealed that the presence of an inconsiderate individual in the driver's cabin had a detrimental effect on driving performance, with tasks being completed more successfully when the driver was alone. These findings are of paramount importance to the optimization of train drivers' performance and the enhancement of railway safety [38].
- Brandengurger et al. (2020) conducted a study to determine the duties and responsibilities of a locomotive engineer who operates an ultra-modern, high-velocity passenger train. The outcomes of the investigation suggest that the engineer must maintain a persistent level of mental effort and sustained concentration in order to acquire cognitive information and monitor the environment continuously. Consequently, the role of the train driver is set to evolve into that of a train operator in the coming years [39].

This analysis clarifies the limited implementation of real-world eye-tracking research devoted to examining train driver behavior and operations under specific circumstances. Despite the potential of utilizing eye-tracking technology to gain insight into the cognition and decision-making of train drivers, research in this area has been limited. To date, only a few studies have been conducted, and even those have primarily featured highly controlled, simulated environments. While such research is valuable, the results are not applicable to the dynamic and unpredictable conditions of the real world. It is therefore necessary to develop additional research initiatives that incorporate real-world train operations. Such research could involve collecting data from drivers in diverse operational contexts and varying levels of complexity. In addition, the data should be analyzed to reveal how different factors (e.g., weather, train speed, and passenger load) can affect the decision making of train drivers.

Therefore, the goal of this study is to explore the potential of utilizing eye-tracking technology to gain insight into the cognition and decision making of train drivers and to develop additional research initiatives that incorporate real-world train operations in order to better understand the cognitive processes involved in train operations and ultimately, improve the safety of the rail system.

2. Materials and Methods

According to the results of a literature review and the requirements for determining optimal practices for the operations of a train driver in certain situations, we have established the primary objective to achieve the goal defined at the end of the article's introduction: to analyze the approaches to arriving at and departing from several types of train stations, and to identify the most effective practices from the perspective of the train driver. The overall process of conducting the research (research methodology) is presented in Figure 1. The key sections related to the research are presented in Sections 2.1 and 2.2.

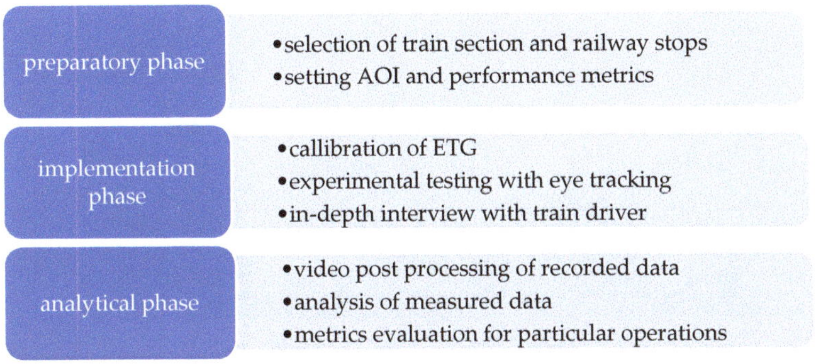

Figure 1. Methodology of research.

2.1. Research Conditions

In the spring of 2020, an experimental investigation was conducted under real railway traffic circumstances. The primary stage of the study included the determination of an appropriate location for the experiment, which was the railway infrastructure line. After an appraisal of potential railway lines near Žilina, the Žilina-Púchov railway track was chosen due to its recent reconstruction, high-quality condition, modernized safety and train control system, and its widespread representation of Slovak railway characteristics such as double-tracking, electrification, traction system, high density of traffic, safety, and control system. Ten stops were located on the selected track section, from which two train stations and two railway stops were chosen for the analysis. Subsequently, the essential characteristics of the selected train stations and railway stops were identified:

- Horný Hričov railway stop is located on the ŽSR line no. 120 Bratislava hl.st.—Žilina, in the interstation section Dolný Hričov—Žilina. The stop position on the track is located at kilometer 195,042, with exits to the right side, in the direction of travel, and the double track is electrified by 3 kV DC.
- Dolný Hričov station (Žilina district) is located on the double-track electrified (3 kV DC) line no. 120 Žilina—Bratislava, between Žilina and Bytča at kilometer 193,073. The station has seven transport tracks and one manipulation track. The station building is located on the left side, in the direction of Bratislava.
- Bytča railway station is located on the double-track electrified line ŽSR no. 120 Bratislava—Žilina, track kilometer 185,275; 3 kV DC electrifies the track. The station building is located on the right side, in the direction of Bratislava. The station has seven transport and four manipulation tracks.
- Predmier railway stop is located on the ŽSR no. 120 Bratislava hl. st.—Žilina, in the interstation section Považská Teplá—Bytča, track kilometer 183,620. The track is a double track, electrified by 3 kV DC. The location of the building is to the left, in the direction of Bratislava hl. st.

Our case study utilized the Škoda Transportation-manufactured electric double-decker multiple-unit series 671 (EPJ), which was utilized in a prior experiment [9], and is depicted in Figure 2. This multiple-unit rolling stock includes one electric traction wagon, one wagon, and one control wagon.

Figure 2. Electric double-decker multiple-unit series 671 [40].

A case study was conducted on Railway Track No. 120: Bratislava-Žilina, situated in the section of Žilina-Púchov of Slovak Railways (ŽSR) (see Figure 3). This double-track, 3 kV DC electrified railway line measures 44 km and is part of the V Corridor [41].

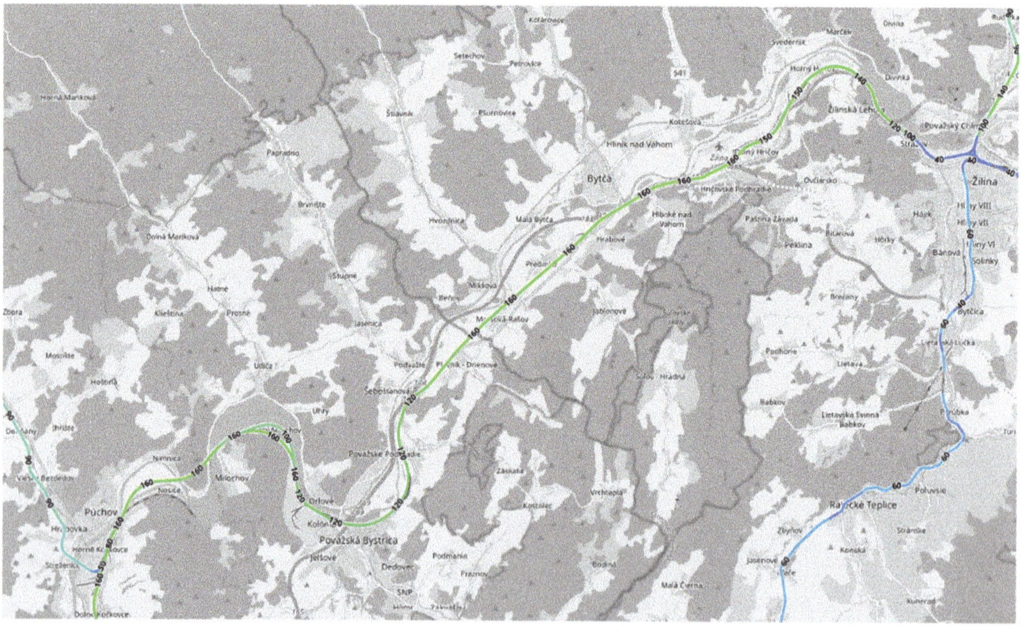

Figure 3. Track section Žilina—Púchov with speed limitations.

The track section has undergone a full overhaul, resulting in the maximum speed for conventional trains being raised to 120–160 km/h (as illustrated in Figure 4). The utilization of the European Train Control System Level 2 (ETCS Lvl. 2) has enabled tilting trains to achieve higher speeds. The completion of the reconstruction of the Púchov–Zilina lines will make ETCS level 2 fully functional, with it only being employed by compatible vehicles; the Automatic Signal Block system, however, will continue to be used due to the lack of compatible equipment in the carriers' vehicle fleets. Additionally, a new traction system, signaling apparatus, and information equipment have been installed [42–44]. Moreover, a mobile radio network and new telecommunication technology have been implemented to provide a direct radio link between the dispatcher and the moving trains, with the entirety of the track section being regulated from the central transport control center in Púchov [41].

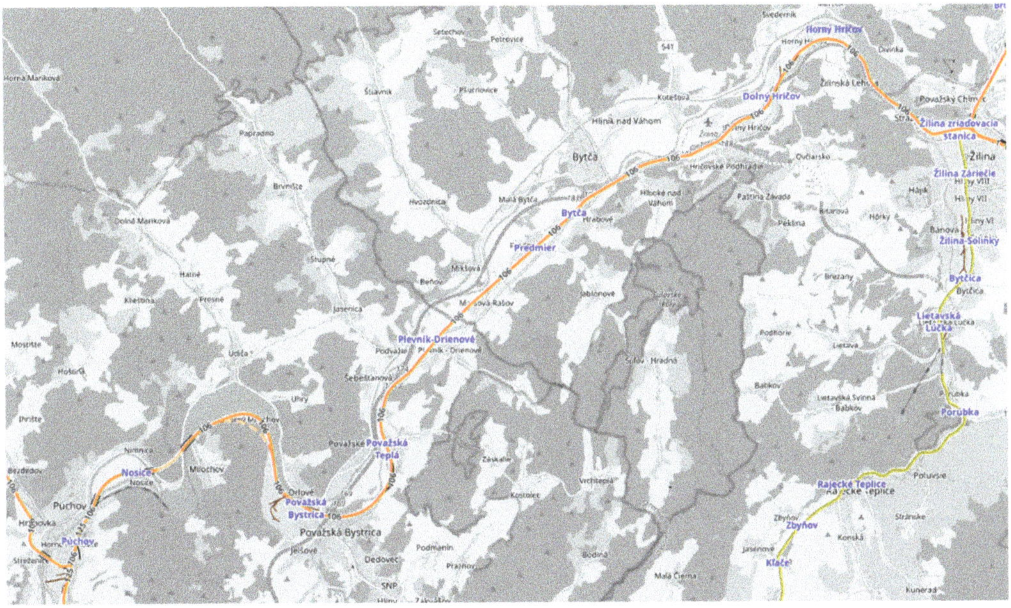

Figure 4. Track section Žilina–Púchov with railway stops and train stations.

Between 2014 and 2018, a 22,702 km railway section from Považská Teplá to Žilina underwent full reconstruction, which included the installation of a new traction line, an automatic signal block, an ETCS Level 2 European Train Control System, and an information device. Additionally, the stations and stops are now compliant with the requirements for full accessibility by individuals with reduced mobility.

2.2. *Eye-Tracking Technology*

Investigation of human factors utilizing the user testing method is a viable approach for exploring the level of interaction between humans and machines. To maximize the efficacy of usability testing, a representative sample of the targeted user group should be chosen and the data collection techniques must be capable of capturing the demands associated with the activities performed. Eye-tracking technology provides a unique opportunity for user testing as it is capable of measuring the perception and behavior of the tested subject while they are completing the assigned tasks. The usefulness of eye tracking in transport systems is evident, as it has been employed for various measurements in both real and simulated environments and is especially advantageous for the analysis of human behavior in aviation and vehicle driving.

The application of eye-tracking technology was utilized to analyze the train driver's behavior with great accuracy while in operation. The SMI ETG 2W head-mounted eye-tracking glasses with software iViewETG version 2.8 were selected to procure raw data. This device was specifically designed to capture the visual conduct of the subject in real-time scenarios. Equipped with three high-speed cameras, two infrared cameras were used to record the subject's pupils' movement and position in both eyes, while the third high-definition scene camera with a resolution 1280 × 960 p @24 fps captured the surrounding environment. Additionally, a smartphone was connected to the glasses for data recording purposes. The SMI ETG 2W provides eye tracking with a sampling frequency of 60 Hz throughout the field of view and guarantees precise data with a tracking range of 80° horizontal, 60° vertical, and a gaze tracking accuracy of 0.5° over all distances [45].

The SMI BeGaze software 3.7.59 (produced by SensoMotoric Instruments (SMI), Teltow, Germany) was employed to conduct an in-depth analysis of the raw data collected by the SMI ETG 2W. This comprehensive application provided a range of analytical functionalities, including Scan Path, which illustrated the map of the driver's gaze fixations and the order in which they occurred. The most beneficial analytical tool for our research, included in the BeGaze software, was the AOI (Areas of Interest) analysis. In this analysis, user-defined metrics were extracted from the pre-defined regions in the visual stimulus. To identify the areas of train control and operation, the AOI editor was used to designate the main AOIs in the train cabin. As a result, thirteen AOIs (panels) were identified (see Figure 5).

Figure 5. Area of interests (panels) identified in the EPJ 671 train cabin.

The Areas of Interest (AOI) displayed in the figure are numerically coded from A to M, each representing a distinct aspect of the train's operation:

- A stands for the view of the external environment, encompassing front, right, and left windows.
- B stands for the left and right rear-view mirrors.
- C denotes railway signals.
- D is indicative of the actual speed, as shown in Panel D.
- E is the main train operating window.
- F corresponds to the cab signaling and the train protection system Mirel
- G is for the brake system pressure.
- H refer to the set of train driving controllers.
- I is the automatic train speed controller.
- J is the main train controller, controlling both acceleration and braking.
- K is the timetable sheet.
- L is for notes pertaining to the section, such as speed restrictions.
- M is the signaling of safety closure of the train doors.

Observe that the cab display of the European Train Control System (ETCS) is depicted in Figure 5, with the black window located above region K. Nonetheless, since the ETCS is not in use, it has been deactivated.

In order to acquire pertinent information from eye-tracking recordings, the fixation-to-fixation coding technique was utilized. This video-coding procedure enabled the generation of a reference image from a segment of the scene (train cabin) camera video, and successive clicks in the reference image at the identical position as the fixation within the superimposed scene video, once for each fixation in the data [46].

The Human–Machine Interaction Laboratory (HMI-LAB) of the University of Zilina is located at the University Science Park and is equipped with both software and hardware. The primary purpose of the HMI-LAB is to conduct research and testing related to human-machine interactions in a variety of settings. This lab was used to evaluate data for their final publication.

The experiment was conducted to evaluate the behavior of a train driver during daylight on a chosen stretch of track. A climatized train cabin was utilized, free from any external interferences. A 51-year-old train driver, with 30 years of experience in regional, long-distance national, international, and railway transport, was engaged in the experiment; he had been absent from any category A or B railway accident (as classified by international railway safety standards) [9]. The train driver's task was to drive the train in the usual way. He wore eye-tracking goggles to record his interaction with the locomotive's controls and surroundings. He had no information about the variables to be evaluated during the measurement. He passed through 9 stations during his journey. Measurements on the same track were repeated 6 times, and the results presented in the paper are the average values of indicators from four selected types of stations.

It should be emphasized that there are no standardized tasks that a driver must abide by. The two main regulations governing Slovak railways are the Regulation: Z1 Railway Operation Rules and Regulation: Performance of the driver's activities ZSSK V2. The Railway Operation Rules (Z1) is an extensive (more than 500 pages) set of regulations on transport activities and train operation on railways managed by ŽSR. The Regulation on the Performance of Train Driver Activities ZSSK V2 details technological procedures and activities related to work activity and drive management of rolling stock. Despite their scope, neither regulation contains detailed processes and work procedures for the oper-ational actions of the train driver during the arrival of the train to the station/stop and the departure of the train from the station/stop.

In order to obtain optimum raw data, SMI eye-tracking glasses were used to monitor the driver's visual attention. The following three steps were essential prior to measurement: establishing a connection between the eye-tracking glasses and the recording device (smartphone); configuring the experiment for the subject being tested in the recording device; and, completing the calibration process of the eye-tracking glasses and initiating the recording of the subject's gaze.

The experiment has a critical analytical component that is designed to evaluate metrics that delineate the operation of the train and the interaction between the driver and the train's cabin control systems and panels during specialized operations. This research aims to elucidate the location, duration and frequency of the driver's gaze directed towards the areas of interest [47,48]. The metrics to be established for each of the areas of interest in the cabin are as follows:

- Dwell time is defined as the period of time from a participant's entry to their exit in a particular AOI. In some human factor research, dwell is referred to as glance or gaze duration. Dwell time is generally the aggregate of fixation and saccades durations during the stay in an AOI. The recorded dwell time for an AIO is contingent upon the AOI semantics and the participant's task. Dwell time is indicative of the attention paid to an AOI or the informative nature of said AOI. It may be presented in an absolute (time in milliseconds) or relative format (% of total time).
- The number of fixations is defined as a period when the eye is relatively stationary; yet, certain definitions incorporate visual intake as an auxiliary parameter on fixations. During the period inside of the AOI, the number of fixations has also been referred to as fixation density. The number of ocular fixations indicates the significance of the AOI for the subject under examination.

- Average fixation duration is a measure commonly employed in eye-tracking research, with variation in duration across different tasks and stimuli being observed. It is generally accepted that longer fixations denote a more intensive and strenuous cognitive process. This measure can be expressed quantitatively in terms of absolute time in milliseconds.
- Revisits denote a transition from one AOI to another; the number of revisits can provide insight into the subject's attentional focus with respect to a particular AOI. The frequency of revisits is thus indicative of the amount of time the subject devoted to a given AOI.

In order to guarantee the correct conduct of the research and interpretation of the acquired data, we employed a variety of scientific techniques. Initial research and extraction of extant bibliographic resources, the amalgamation of knowledge obligatory for experimental assessment, observation during the experiment period, analysis, comparison, induction, deduction, statistical techniques in the investigative period, and graphical techniques for representing the data aided each stage of the completed research.

For the purpose of linking conscious and unconscious perceptions of the situation with which the driver is confronted, the eye-tracking research is complemented by the implementation of an in-depth interview.

An in-depth interview is a type of qualitative research method that involves conducting an in-depth, semi-structured conversation with a participant to explore their thoughts, feelings and experiences on a particular topic. It is usually conducted after conducting eye tracking analysis to provide an additional layer of understanding of how and why the test participants interacted with a situation with which they are confronted. In-depth interviews can help identify user needs, uncover motivations and uncover how the user interacts with the product or medium [49].

3. Results

In the methodological component of our investigation, we identified and subsequently concentrated on two particular locomotive operations (train arriving at stations and train leaving the station) at two distinct locations (train station and railway stop). The assessment was partitioned into four trials, and each trial was divided into two operations.

3.1. *Trial 1—Railway Stop Horný Hričov*

At this railway station, the average total time for arriving and departing was 200 s. The mean period of entry was 120 s (Table 2), while the mean duration of the departure procedure was 80 s (as illustrated in Table 3).

Table 2. The arrival procedure's average statistic for railway stop Horný Hričov.

Metric	Top Three AOI According to Best Values		
Average dwell time (%)	window section AOIs (56%)	panel E AOI (7.6%)	mirror section AOIs (6%)
The average number of fixations	window section AOIs (225)	panel E AOI (44)	panel D AOI (15)
Average fixation duration (ms)	mirror section AOIs (546.3 ms)	panel F AOI (308.2 ms)	window section AOIs (275.3 ms)
Average revisits	window section AOIs (23)	panel E AOI (16)	panel D AOI (8)

Table 3. The departure procedure's average statistic for railway stop Horný Hričov.

Metric	Top Three AOI According to Best Values		
Average dwell time (%)	window section AOIs (33.3%)	panel E AOI (31%)	panel D AOI (20.6%)
The average number of fixations	window section AOIs (79)	panel E AOI (68)	panel D AOI (41)
Average fixation duration (ms)	panel K AOI (688.2 ms)	panel G AOI (551.9 ms)	mirror section AOIs (509.4 ms)
Average revisits	window section AOIs (23)	panel E AOI (16)	panel D AOI (8)

3.2. Trial 2—Train Station Dolný Hričov

The aggregate duration of the arrival and departure processes at this train station was 215 s on average. The mean length of the entry process was 140 s (see Table 4), and the mean duration of the departure process was 75 s (as shown in Table 5).

Table 4. The arrival procedure's average statistic for train station Dolný Hričov.

Metric	Top Three AOI According to Best Values		
Average dwell time (%)	window section AOIs (49.7%)	panel E AOI (14.7%)	panel D AOI (7.7%)
The average number of fixations	window section AOIs (216)	panel E AOI (87)	panel D AOI (48)
Average fixation duration (ms)	panel K AOI (303.6 ms)	window section AOIs (301.1 ms)	railway signal AOI (295.0 ms)
Average revisits	window section AOIs (44)	panel E AOI (34)	panel D AOI (29)

Table 5. The departure procedure's average statistic for train station Dolný Hričov.

Metric	Top Three AOI According to Best Values		
Average dwell time (%)	window section AOIs (44.0%)	mirror section AOIs (16.1%)	panel E AOI (12.1%)
The average number of fixations	window section AOIs (81)	panel E AOI (40)	panel D AOI (25)
Average fixation duration (ms)	mirror section AOIs (698.9 ms)	panel I AOI (429.4 ms)	panel K AOI (425.9 ms)
Average revisits	window section AOIs (22)	panel E AOI (13)	panel D AOI (12)

3.3. Trial 3—Train Station Bytča

The average amount of time taken for people to enter and exit this railway station was 170 s. As seen in Table 6, the mean duration of the entry process was 100 s and the mean duration of the exit process was 70 s (Table 7).

Table 6. The arrival procedure's average statistic for train station Bytča.

Metric	Top Three AOI According to Best Values		
Average dwell time (%)	window section AOIs (54.6%)	panel E AOI (12.7%)	panel D AOI (8.2%)
The average number of fixations	window section AOIs (166)	panel E AOI (58)	panel D AOI (37)
Average fixation duration (ms)	mirror section AOIs (522.8 ms)	panel H AOI (315.1 ms)	window section AOIs (304.4 ms)
Average revisits	window section AOIs (28)	panel E AOI (23)	panel D AOI (16)

Table 7. The departure procedure's average statistic for train station Bytča.

Metric	Top Three AOI According to Best Values		
Average dwell time (%)	panel E AOI (36.2%)	window section AOIs (32.9%)	panel D AOI (10.5%)
The average number of fixations	panel E AOI (85)	window section AOIs (55)	panel D AOI (32)
Average fixation duration (ms)	railway signal AOI (428.1 ms)	window section AOIs (404.9 ms)	mirror section AOIs (403.0 ms)
Average revisits	panel E AOI (22)	window section AOIs (22)	panel D AOI (19)

3.4. Trial 4—Railway Stop Predmier

The mean duration for the arrival and departure operations at this railway station was 75 s. Table 8 reveals that the average time for the arrival process was 40 s and Table 9 indicates that the average time for the departure process was 35 s.

Table 8. The arrival procedure's average statistic for railway stop Predmier.

Metric	Top Three AOI According to Best Values		
Average dwell time (%)	window section AOIs (28.0%)	panel E AOI (23.2%)	panel D AOI (11.9%)
The average number of fixations	window section AOIs (40)	panel E AOI (35)	panel D AOI (19)
Average fixation duration (ms)	panel K AOI (428.0 ms)	panel F AOI (361.2 ms)	panel I AOI (282.1 ms)
Average revisits	window section AOIs (11)	panel E AOI (11)	panel D AOI (11)

Table 9. The departure procedure's average statistic for railway stop Predmier.

Metric	Top Three AOI According to Best Values		
Average dwell time (%)	panel E AOI (58.5%)	window section AOIs (15.0%)	panel D AOI (11.4%)
The average number of fixations	panel E AOI (52)	window section AOIs (14)	panel D AOI (13)
Average fixation duration (ms)	panel K AOI (697.4 ms)	panel E AOI (364.5 ms)	window section AOIs (361.5 ms)
Average revisits	panel E AOI (11)	window section AOIs (7)	panel D AOI (7)

The results of the eye-tracking experiment demonstrate that the most pertinent panels in the train cabin are panel E (train operating window) and panel D (information concerning the train's speed). It is evident that the driver's attention is differently devoted to the AOIs (based on dwell time, number of fixations, and revisits) between the arrival and departure scenarios. During arrival, the driver's focus is mainly on the front and side windows, then panel E and panel D; whereas, during the departure, the driver's attention is mainly concentrated on panel E.

The train driver stated the following: "Ensuring safety and the safety of others was paid attention to during the drive by following the rules of the railway, monitoring speed and the speed of other trains, and being aware of surroundings. The traffic around, including other trains, track-side objects, and any other objects on the track were monitored, as well as railway signals, crossings, and any changes in the environment".

Eye-tracking research revealed that the driver's gaze was particularly attentive to the safety elements of the cockpit, and that he was able to quickly and accurately identify the controls he needed to ensure the safety of the train. Furthermore, the research revealed that the driver had strong cognitive abilities and was able to quickly and accurately identify the controls he needed to operate the train.

The disparities between the arrival and departure procedures can be discerned in the AOI Sequence Chart. This chart displays the temporal order in which the AOIs were canvassed by the train driver's line of sight. The colored bars symbolize the individual AOIs that were perused. The AOIs' labels are located along the y-axis, while the x-axis shows the extent of time in milliseconds.

Figure 6 illustrates the average train driver's gaze trajectory upon nearing a railway station. On average, nine seconds prior to the train coming to a halt, the driver began to scrutinize panels F, G, and H (respectively pertaining to the train safety system, the pressure in the brake system, and other train driving controllers). Just before the train stops (an average of three seconds prior), the driver surveyed the mirror and side window for any potential hazards. Finally, one second before the train's stop, the driver checked the timetable and compared the actual time to the train's schedule. What the train driver did while passengers are getting on and off the train is not part of the measurements.

The Figure 7 AOI sequence chart illustrates the train driver's operational procedure during departure. Initially, the driver assessed the automatic speed controller and panels E and D, alongside his notes pertaining to the upcoming train section. Subsequently, he surveyed the side window for any potential late passenger boarding, while also analyzing the panels containing preliminary information concerning train operations and the actual speed. Following this, the driver inspected the timetable with the train schedule and information regarding the safety of the train doors. Finally, the train was set in motion, and the driver's attention oscillated between panels E/D and the front window, as the arrival procedure began.

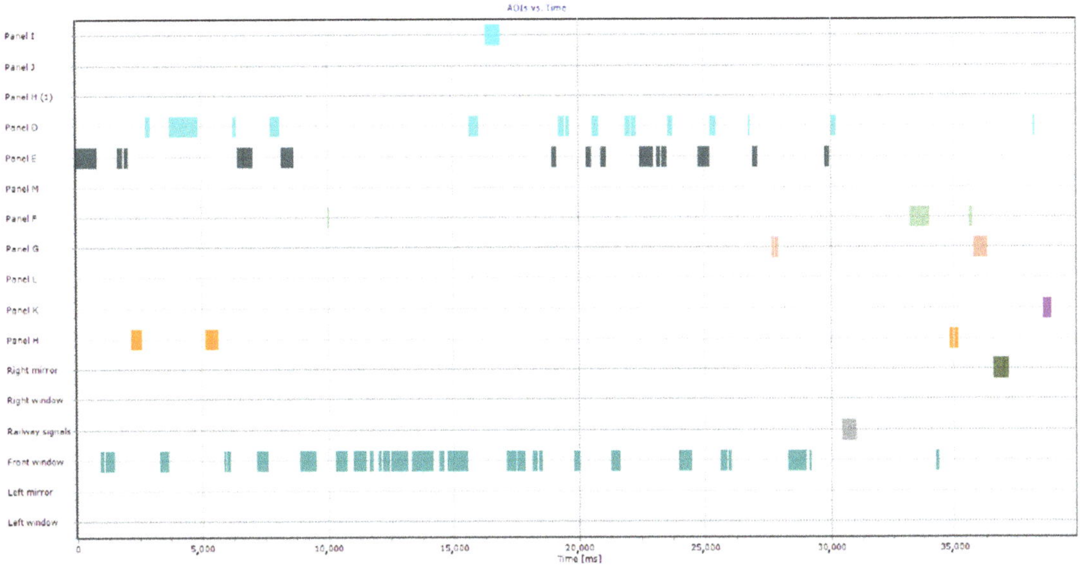

Figure 6. AOI sequence chart of average arrival procedure to railway stop Predmier.

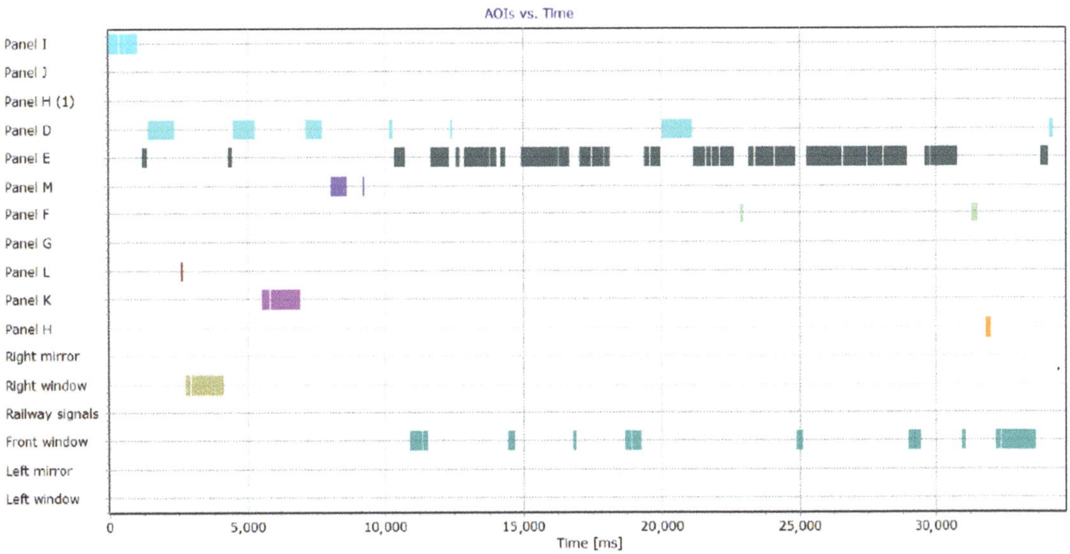

Figure 7. AOI sequence chart of average departure procedure from railway stop Predmier.

3.5. Comparison of Arrival and Departure Procedures

In the concluding section of the article, we presented particular outcomes from eye-tracking examinations focused on the train driver conduct during the arrival and departure operations in railway halts and train stations. It is imperative to appraise the outcomes from a more comprehensive point of view. Thus, we constructed an overall dataset that elucidates arrival and departure procedures. The dataset comprises the mean information from train driver behavior testing during four arrivals and four departures of the train, repeated during the six train runs at the same track. The average outcomes collaborate with data sets from twenty-four assessments for the arrival procedure and twenty-four assessments for the departure procedure.

During all arrivals at the stations, the driver directed his gaze to the window section (front window, side windows, and mirrors) for an average of 49.9% dwell time, to the panel section (29.9% of the dwell time), and to the railway signal section (1.15% of the dwell time) (see Figure 8). The correlation between the number of fixations on a particular Area of Interest (AOI) and the dwell time metric was noted. A greater number of fixations on a certain AOI indicates that the AOIs are more salient (or the AOI content is regularly fluctuating) and are more perceptible to the driver than others. On the whole, the average number of fixations on the whole window section was 168.75, on the panel section 108.75, and on the railway signal section only 4.5. This is likely due to the fact that the scenery on the main window is constantly changing, and the driver must direct most of his attention to the window section.

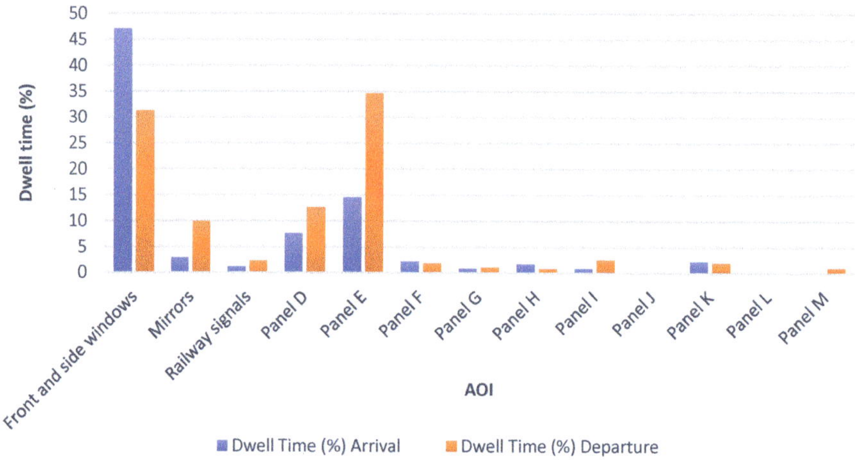

Figure 8. The comparison of the average dwell time between arrival and departure procedures.

The mean fixation time for the AOI displays a range of 119.8 milliseconds (panel I) to 397.3 milliseconds (mirrors). This variance can be attributed to the varying levels of complexity between the two stimuli, the buttons of the automatic speed controller (panel I) being easier to evaluate than the presence of passengers boarding and staying on the platform (mirrors). This is illustrated in Figure 9.

The ultimate metric is the average revisits, which reflects the number of times the driver's gaze has been directed at the specified Area of Interest (AOI) through all trials. This statistic elucidates the magnitude of importance associated with the designated AOI. In the context of train arrival procedures, the most common revisits were the front and side window sections (27).

Various categories of train driver operations are the techniques of leaving the station. We studied all actions of the train driver in all four departures from two railway halts and two railway stations throughout the six measurements and established the average characteristics. During the departure processes, the train driver directed his gaze towards the window sector for 41.2% of the overall duration, to the control panel section for 56.3% of the total span, and towards the railway signal sector for 2.2% of the whole period on average (see Figure 8).

The quantified values of dwell time demonstrate that the locomotive engineer devoted more attention to the manipulation of the panel than to the surveillance through windows or mirrors. Upon analyzing the mean number of fixations on the sections, the total window section had 70.8 and the panel section 107.3, with only five fixations on the railway signal section. This higher mean figure of fixations on the panel section of the cabin reveals the requirement to manipulate, control, and operate the panel controls during the train departure procedure during all trials of the experiment.

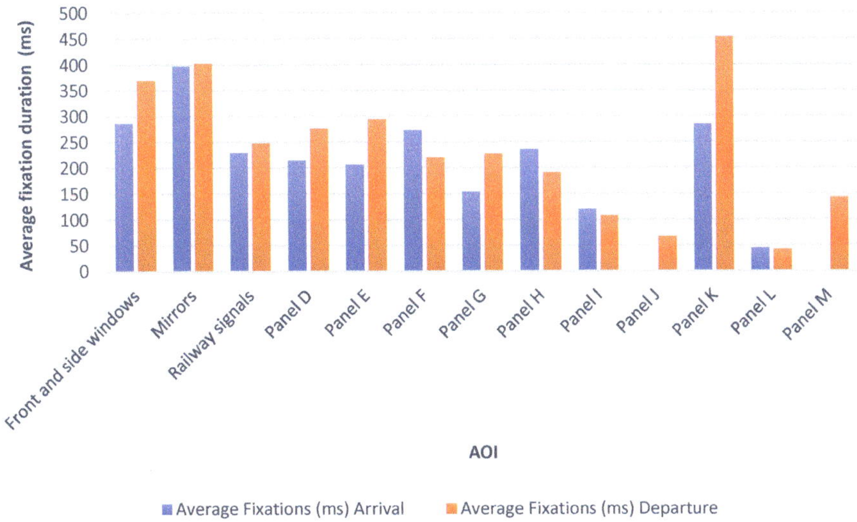

Figure 9. The comparison of the average fixation duration between arrival and departure procedures.

Upon assessment of the average fixation time during all train departures, the minimum average fixation time was 41.5 ms (panel L). The greatest average fixation time of 452.9 ms was identified on panel K (refer to Figure 9). All the necessary data pertaining to the train schedule (as a comprehensive train schedule, and arrival and departure times for each stop at the train section) were situated on panel K. Notations situated on panel L merely served an informative purpose. Consequently, the average fixation duration was insignificant. Nevertheless, the timetable located on panel K had a fundamental role in driving and operating the train; thus, the average fixations were the most prolonged (the cognitive process when the train driver was deciphering the text content from the timetable).

Investigation of the particular Area of Interest (AOI) during train departures demonstrated the magnitude of its impact. In the course of the operation on the railway line, the highest mean values of return visits were observed in the window (front and side windows) region (18.5), Panel E (16.3), and Panel D (13.5). This more detailed analysis enabled distinguishing the disparities in the driver's actions in distinct (arrival and departure of the train) circumstances. Ultimately, it must be affirmed that the employed procedures and measuring equipment had no influence on the security of the train operations during the experimentation.

In order to further investigate the patterns of driver behavior during the operation of a train arriving and departing from a station, we conducted an in-depth analysis of the activities performed. The aim of the analysis was to identify patterns of train operation based on the test subject's fixations on objects in the cab and around the train. The initial analysis showed a high degree of fragmentation of the train operator's views on the different panels in the train cab, so we decided to generalize the areas of interest to the following:

- Front window, which will include everything in the driver's view in front of the train cab (AOI: A—Front Window and C—Railway signals)
- Side windows, which will contain everything in view to the right and left of the train cab (AOI: A—Left and right windows, B—Left and right mirrors)

- Control panels, which contains the set of control panels in the train cab (all panels in the train cab. AOI: panel D to panel M)
- White space, representing the fixation of the train driver on the area outside our investigation.

We analyzed the average values of fixations on our defined regions of interest obtained during the six measurements in each station. The length of fixations on each region of interest over time shows the pattern of cognitive actions of the train driver during the arrival and departure of the train from the stations and railway stops. Stations and railway stops are marked in figures as A "railway stop Predmier", B "station Dolný Hričov", C "railway stop Horný Hričov" and D "station Bytča". We also normalized the length of the analyzed processes and took into account the activities that took place 35 s before the train stopped in the station and 35 s after the train left the station.

In Figure 10, it is possible to identify the behavior of the driver when the train arrives at the station. The operations performed by the train driver can be divided into three phases. In the initial phases, the driver's gaze is directed to the situation of what is in front of the train, i.e., the Front Window area. In the middle phase, the driver alternates his attention between the Front window and the Control panels. The driver starts to check the real speed and braking status of the train with the instruments located in the Control panels area. There is a sequence of rapid saccades between the Front window and the Control panels. In the final phase, the driver monitors the situation on the sides of the train through the side windows and mirrors (AOI Side windows). He also focuses his vision on the Control panels area, where he checks the full stop status of the train. Again, a sequence of fast saccades between Control panels and Side windows can be identified.

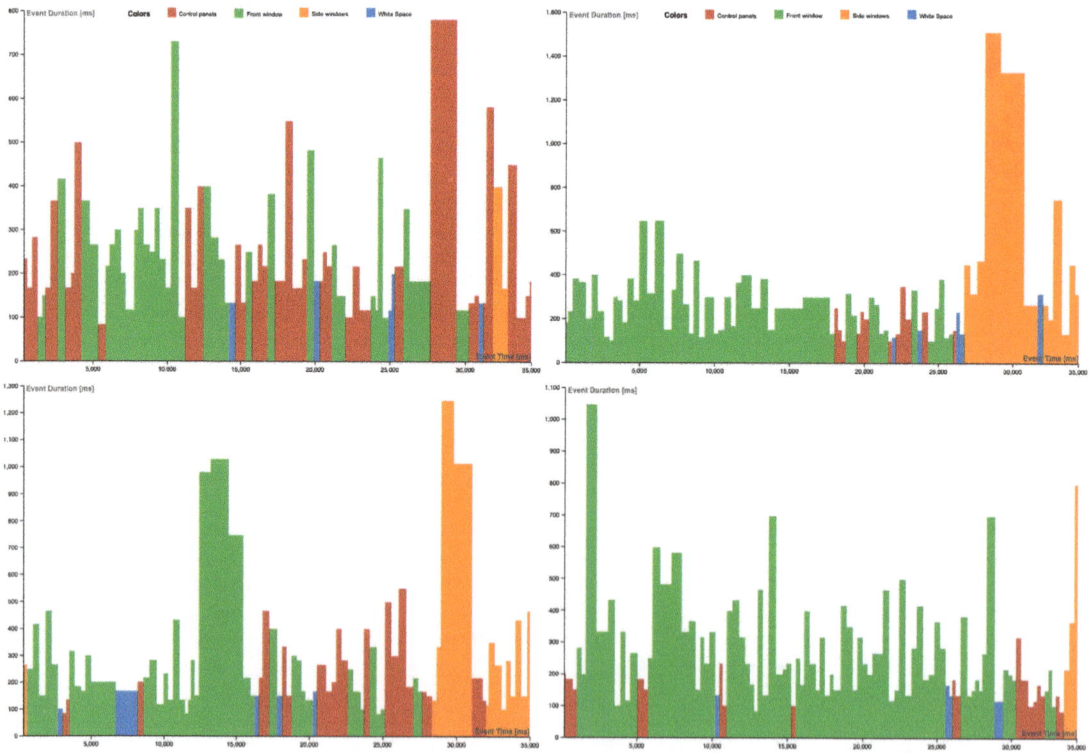

Figure 10. Analysis of fixations during train arrival at the station.

Figure 11 shows the flow of procedures that the train driver performs when leaving the station. In principle, they can be divided into 2 phases, depending on the speed of the train and the distance from the station. In the initial phase, a visual check of the situation on the side of the train (platform) takes place, as the train driver's gaze is directed to the Side windows area, and only after the train has started to move does the driver also focus his attention on the Control panels area. At this stage it is possible to identify a significant length of eye fixation on the monitored area of interest. In the second part of the process of the train leaving the station, the tracking of the situation in front of the train starts. It is possible to identify frequent alternation of the driver's gaze between the Control panels and the Front window. The train at this point is already completely outside the station environment.

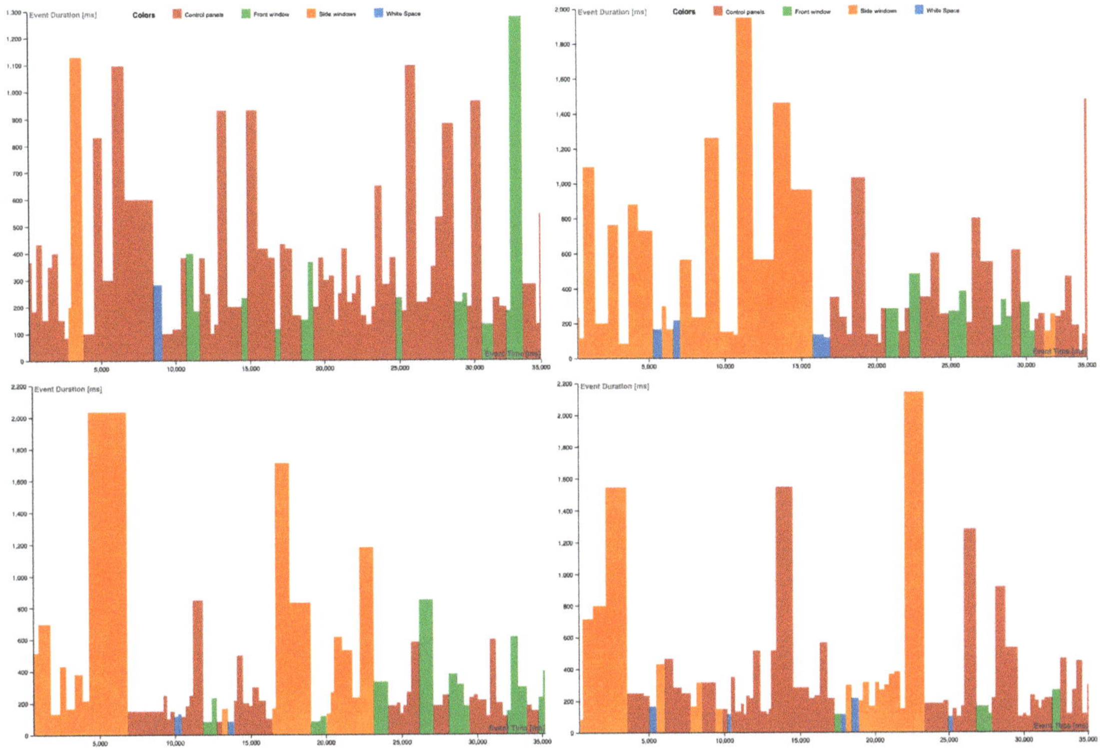

Figure 11. Analysis of fixations during train departure from the station or a railway stop.

Examining the duration of fixations during the arrival and departure of a train from the station provides us with a unique perspective on driver behavior. Oftentimes, fixations are a means of extracting information, and longer fixations indicate a more complex cognitive process. On average, fixations last 200–300 ms. Analyzing the average fixation durations (see Figure 12), the highest values are seen in the Side windows area. This is likely due to the increased rate of movement in the vicinity of the train during its arrival and departure. When the train arrives at the station (Figure 12A1–D1), the Frontal window area of interest (AOI) has a higher fixation length value than the Control panels, as identifying potential hazards in front of the train is of utmost importance. Conversely, when the train departs the station (Figure 12A2–D2), the Control panels gain more attention than the Frontal Window, as the train driver needs to interact with the train controls in order to set the train in motion.

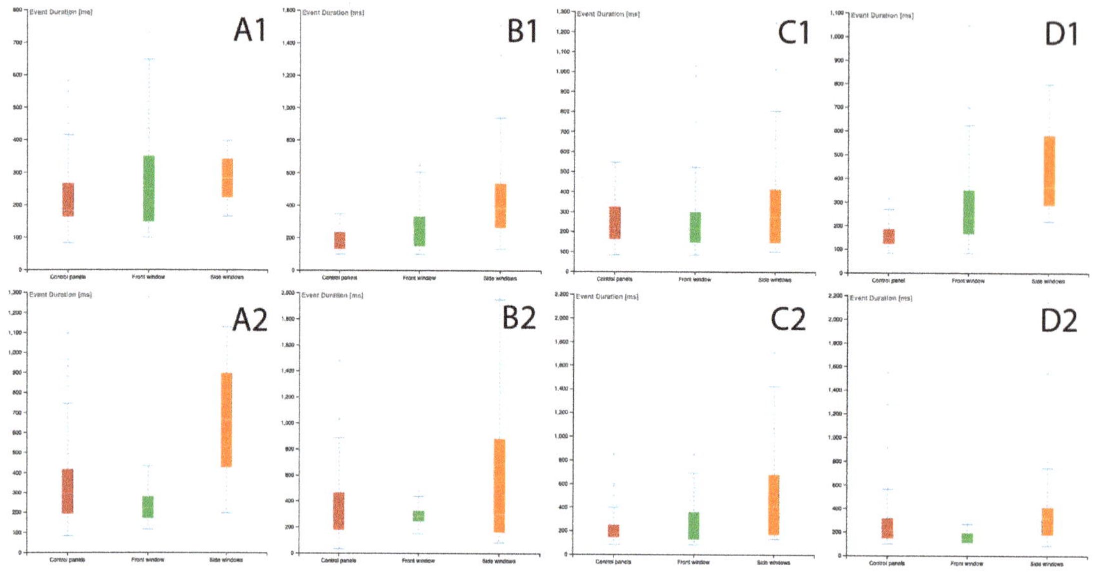

Figure 12. Analysis of the length of fixations at the AOI during the arrival and departure of the train from the station or from the railway stop.

3.6. In-Depth Interview

The eye-tracking measurement was additionally complemented by an in-depth interview with the driver. The conclusions of this interview are as follows:

The train driver stated: "Ensuring safety and the safety of others was paid attention to during the drive by following the rules of the railway, monitoring speed and the speed of other trains, and being aware of surroundings. The traffic around, including other trains, track-side objects, and any other objects on the track were monitored, as well as railway signals, crossings, and any changes in the environment".

Each railway operative must develop and adhere to comprehensive protocols and routines derived from their own experiences and conduct, which can be time consuming and costly as well as encouraging the acquisition of substandard railway operating behaviors and precipitating hazardous situations and collisions.

To sum it up, eye-tracking research revealed that the driver's gaze was particularly attentive to the safety elements of the cockpit, and that he was able to quickly and accurately identify the controls he needed to ensure the safety of the train. Furthermore, the research revealed that the driver had strong cognitive abilities and was able to quickly and accurately identify the controls he needed to operate the train.

4. Discussion

Sustainable security in rail transportation systems is a critical issue, directly impacting the sustainability of the entire rail transport sector. To mitigate the increasing number of tragic railway accidents, train operators and infrastructural providers must implement various signaling and train protection systems. According to Edkins and Pollock's research on railway traffic accidents, the behavior of train drivers is the most significant factor [19]. In our research, we employed user testing with eye-tracking technology to study the activities and behavior of drivers in real traffic conditions. This innovative method has great potential for future use in the railway sector. The results of the measurement of the train driver's actions can be utilized to better comprehend the driver's work and to recognize beneficial practices and skills. As Lorenz's work stipulates, recognizing route knowledge and sharing it with other drivers is essential for enhancing railway safety [20].

The aforementioned measurement and its outcomes provide evidence of the authors' research into railway safety. The investigation was conducted by a highly experienced driver, with an impeccable safety record, in real-world conditions, on a genuine track, with passengers on board (not in a simulated environment). This experiment confirmed the proof of concept and validated the methods and methodology in actual operation. We have identified a set of driver attention sequences that are applicable to different types of rail stations, which we consider to be the best practice based on the extensive practical experience of train drivers. Additionally, we are exploring the importance of the interior equipment (panels) in the train cabin for the driver during the arrival and departure of the train. This level of significance is reflected in the average dwelling time and the average duration of the driver's gaze on a particular panel. During the aforementioned train operations, the cognitive process of the driver was measured by the average time spent fixating on a specific panel within the cabin. By comparing the average data collected in the arrival and departure procedures, we have been able to demonstrate the various levels of importance of the panels and the duration of the driver's cognitive processes. All these results will be used as a reference for further research.

Research Limitations of this study can be summed as following:

- The number of participants limits the study. Although we conducted the measurement six times, we had only one participant. Increasing the number of participants can help ensure better validity and reliability of the research results.
- The study was conducted on only two train stations and two railway stops, which may limit the generalizability of the results.
- The study used eye-tracking methodology, which is limited to visual attention and may not capture all aspects of the driver's cognitive processes.
- The methodology and technology may not be applicable to all railway systems, and further research is needed to assess its applicability in different systems.

Future research in our field of driver activity measurement (as seen in other modes of transport [26–32]) will involve the following stages:

- Testing the behavior, attentiveness and activity of drivers in an anomalous work environment through the implementation of eye-tracking technology and comparing the results to a reference benchmark established by the experiment.
- Exploring the activities of various driver profiles and collecting and classifying data regarding their psychological characteristics, capabilities and experiences through a combination of eye-tracking and electroencephalography (EEG) technology.
- Revising existing teaching approaches for novice train drivers and devising novel methods of assessing train driver skills.
- Disseminating the "route knowledge" of experienced train drivers to rookie drivers or novices with a particular focus on the attention sequences in the train cabin.

Verification of the efficacy of the proof of concept and validation of the techniques and methods in actual operation should proceed in forthcoming research with experimentally altered internal (inside the cabin) and external (climatic, luminous) circumstances, with various competent and experienced drivers' operation circumstances. The upcoming research offers numerous new chances and should result in examination for a superior comprehension of the driver's means of operating and amplify the railway transport system's sustainability and security.

Author Contributions: Conceptualization, R.M. and J.M.; methodology, R.M.; validation, L.M. and R.C.; formal analysis, J.M.; investigation, R.M.; resources, J.M.; data curation, L.M. and R.C.; writing—original draft preparation, R.M and J.M.; writing—review and editing, R.C.; visualization, L.M.; supervision, R.M.; funding acquisition, R.M. All authors have read and agreed to the published version of the manuscript.

Funding: This publication was created as a part of research projects the Operational Program Integrated Infrastructure 2014–2020 for the project: Innovative solutions for propulsion, energy, and safety components of means of transport, with ITMS project code 313011V334, co-financed from the resources of the European Regional Development Fund.

Institutional Review Board Statement: Not applicable.

Informed Consent Statement: Not applicable.

Data Availability Statement: Data of the resulting values of measurements are not publicly available. For further information regarding the data, contact the authors of this article.

Conflicts of Interest: The authors declare no conflict of interest.

References

1. Ministry of Transport and Construction of the Slovak Republic. Strategic Plan for the Development of Transport in the Slovak Republic until 2030. Available online: https://www.opii.gov.sk/ (accessed on 28 December 2020).
2. White Paper. Roadmap to a Single European Transport Area—Towards a Competitive and Resource Efficient Transport System. Available online: https://ec.europa.eu/transport/themes/european-strategies/white-paper-2011_en (accessed on 29 December 2020).
3. Ministry of Transport and Construction of the Slovak Republic. Public Passenger Transport 2030. Available online: https://www.mindop.sk/en (accessed on 30 December 2020).
4. European Environment Agency. Greenhouse Gas Emissions from Transport in Europe. Available online: https://www.eea.europa.eu/data-and-maps/indicators/transport-emissions-of-greenhouse-gases (accessed on 29 December 2020).
5. Poelman, H.; Dijkstra, L.; Ackermans, L. *Rail Transport Performance in Europe: Developing a New Set of Regional and Territorial Accessibility Indicators for Rail*; Publications Office of the European Union: Luxembourg, 2020.
6. Čamaj, J.; Ponický, J.; Pečený, L.; Meško, P.; Zeman, K. Current problems in extraordinariness situations with the impact on the management of rail transport under the conditions of Slovak railways. In *Horizons of Railway Transport 2018*; Édition Diffusion Presse Sciences: London, UK, 2018; pp. 1–5.
7. Kampf, R.; Stopka, O.; Bartuška, L.; Zeman, K. Circulation of vehicles as an important parameter of public transport efficiency. In Proceedings of the Transport Means 2015, 19th International Scientific Conference on Transport Means, Kaunas, Lithuania, 23–25 October 2015; pp. 143–146.
8. Černá, L.; Dolinayová, A.; Daniš, J. Identification of risks in railway transport and the proposal for their price evaluate. In Proceedings of the 20th International Scientific Conference. Transport Means, Juodkrante, Lithuania, 5–7 October 2016; pp. 414–419.
9. Madleňák, R.; Mašek, J.; Madleňáková, L. An experimental analysis of the driver's attention during train driving. *Open Eng.* **2020**, *10*, 64–73. [CrossRef]
10. Stramler, J. *The Dictionary for Human Factors: Ergonomics*; Routledge: New York, NY, USA, 1993. [CrossRef]
11. Re, A.; Macchi, L. From cognitive reliability to competence? An evolving approach to human factors and safety. *Cogn. Process.* **2010**, *12*, 79–85. [CrossRef]
12. Neumann, W.P.; Winkelhaus, S.; Grosse, E.H.; Glock, C.H. Industry 4.0 and the Human Factor—A Systems Framework and Analysis Methodology for Successful Development. *Int. J. Prod. Econ.* **2021**, *233*, 1079912. [CrossRef]
13. International Ergonomics Association. What Is Ergonomics? Available online: http://www.iea.cc/01_what/What%20is%20Ergonomics.html (accessed on 17 January 2021).
14. National Research Council. *Health Care Comes Home: The Human Factors*; The National Academies Press: Washington, DC, USA, 2011. [CrossRef]
15. Hudak, M.; Madlenak, R. The research of driver's gaze at the traffic signs. In *CBU International Conference Proceedings 2016: Innovations in Science and Education*; Central Bohemia University: Prague, Czech Republic, 2016; pp. 896–899.
16. Andrejszki, T.; Torok, A.; Csete, M. Identifying the utility function of transport services from stated preferences. *Transp. Telecommun.* **2015**, *16*, 138–144. [CrossRef]
17. The Czech Rail Safety Inspection Office—Safety Statistics 2018–2020. Available online: https://www.dicr.cz/ (accessed on 5 October 2020).
18. Hoc, J.M. From human-machine interaction to human-machine cooperation. *Ergonomics* **2000**, *43*, 833–843. [CrossRef] [PubMed]
19. Edkins, D.G.; Pollock, M.C. The influence of sustained attention on railway accidents. *Accid. Anal. Prev.* **1997**, *29*, 533–539. [CrossRef] [PubMed]
20. Lorenz, A. Möglichkeiten zum Streckenkenntniserwerb in Deutschland: Empirische Untersuchungen, Analyse und Diskussion. Ph.D. Thesis, Technische Universität Carolo-Wilhelmina zu Braunschweig, Braunschweig, Germany, 2017. [CrossRef]
21. Chang, R.F.; Chang, C.W.; Tseng, K.H.; Chiang, C.L.; Kao, W.S.; Chen, W.J. Structural planning and implementation of a microprocessor-based human-machine interface in a steam-explosion process application. *Comput. Stand. Interfaces* **2011**, *33*, 232–248. [CrossRef]

22. Duchowski, A.T. *Eye Tracking Methodology*, 3rd ed.; Springer: Cham, Switzerland, 2017; pp. 281–299.
23. Jacob, R.J.K.; Karn, K.S. Eye tracking in human-computer interaction and usability research: Ready to deliver the promises. In *Mind's Eye: Cognitive and Applied Aspects of Eye Movement Research*; Elsevier: Amsterdam, The Netherlands, 2003; pp. 573–605.
24. Hudak, M.; Madlenak, R. The Research of Driver Distraction by Visual Smog on Selected Road Stretch in Slovakia. *Procedia Eng.* **2017**, *178*, 472–479. [CrossRef]
25. Madlenak, R.; Hudak, M. The Research of Visual Pollution of Road Infrastructure in Slovakia. In *Challenge of Transport Telematics, Tst 2016*; Mikulski, J., Ed.; Springer Int. Publishing Ag: Cham, Switzerland, 2016; Volume 640, pp. 415–425.
26. Kocian, D. Visual world subsystem. In *Industry Days: Super Cockpit/virtual Crew Systems*; Cockpit, S., Ed.; Air Force Museum, Wright-Patterson AFB: Dayton, OH, USA, 1987.
27. Longridge, T.; Thomas, M.; Fernie, A.; Williams, T.; Wetzel, P. Design of an eye slaved area of interest system for the simulator complexity testbed. In *Area of Interests/Field of View Research Using ASPT*; Air Force Human Resources Laboratory: San Antonio, TX, USA, 1989; pp. 275–283.
28. Anders, G. Pilot's attention allocation during approach and landing—Eye- and head-tracking research in an A330 full flight simulator. In Proceedings of the 11th International Symposium on Aviation Psychology, Columbus, OH, USA, 5–8 March 2001.
29. Chapman, P.R.; Underwood, G. Visual search of dynamic scenes: Event types and the role of experience in viewing driving situations. In *Eye Guidance in Reading and Scene Perception*; Underwood, G., Ed.; Elsevier: Amsterdam, The Netherlands, 1998; pp. 369–394.
30. Dishart, D.C.; Land, M.F. The development of the eye movement strategies of learner drivers. In *Eye Guidance in Reading and Scene Perception*; Underwood, G., Ed.; Elsevier: Amsterdam, The Netherlands, 1998; pp. 419–430.
31. Ho, G.; Scialfa, C.T.; Caird, J.K.; Graw, T. Visual search for traffic signs: The effects of clutter, luminance, and aging. *Human Factors* **2001**, *43*, 194–207. [CrossRef] [PubMed]
32. Recarte, M.A.; Nunes, L.M. Effects of verbal and spatial-imagery tasks on eye fixations while driving. *J. Exp. Psychol. Appl.* **2000**, *6*, 31–43. [CrossRef] [PubMed]
33. Luke, T.; Brook-Carter, N.; Parkes, A.; Grimes, E.; Mills, A. An investigation of train driver visual strategies. *Cogn. Technol. Work* **2005**, *8*, 15–29. [CrossRef]
34. Rjabovs, A.; Palacin, R. Investigation into Effects of System Design on Metro Drivers' Safety-Related Performance: An Eye-Tracking Study. *Urban Rail Transit* **2019**, *5*, 267–277. [CrossRef]
35. Yan, R.H.; Wu, C.; Wang, Y.M. A Preliminary Study for Exploring High-speed Train Driver Fatigue Using Eye-gaze Cue. In Proceedings of the 2016 2nd International Conference on Artificial Intelligence and Industrial Engineering (Aiie 2016), Beijing, China, 20–21 November 2016; Volume 133, pp. 187–190.
36. Naghiyev, A.; Sharples, S.; Ryan, B.; Coplestone, A.; Carey, M. Real World Verbal Protocol Data Analysis of European Rail Traffic Management System Train Driving and Conventional Train Driving. In Proceedings of the 2016 IEEE International Conference on Intelligent Rail Transportation (Icirt), Birmingham, UK, 23–25 August 2016; pp. 191–196.
37. Guo, B.Y.; Mao, Y.J.; Hedge, A.; Fang, W.N. Effects of apparent image velocity and complexity on the dynamic visual field using a high-speed train driving simulator. *Int. J. Ind. Ergon.* **2015**, *48*, 99–109. [CrossRef]
38. Verstappen, V. The performance of Dutch train drivers based on the impact of the presence of a second person in the cab. *Proc. Inst. Mech. Eng. Part F J. Rail Rapid Transit* **2017**, *231*, 1130–1140. [CrossRef]
39. Brandenburger, N.; Hormann, H.J.; Stelling, D.; Naumann, A. Tasks, skills, and competencies of future high-speed train drivers. *Proc. Inst. Mech. Eng. Part F J. Rail Rapid Transit* **2017**, *231*, 1115–1122. [CrossRef]
40. Skoda Transportation-Technical Characteristics of EPJ Series 671. Available online: https://www.skoda.cz/ (accessed on 19 October 2020).
41. Slovak Railways (ŽSR). Track, No.120 Technical Information. Available online: https://www.zsr.sk/ (accessed on 17 October 2020).
42. Meško, P.; Gašparík, J.; Lalinská, J. Railway capacity issues on Slovak international corridors. In Proceedings of the Transport Means 2017—Proceedings of the International Conference, Juodkrante, Lithuania, 20–22 September 2017; Volume 2017, pp. 436–441.
43. Ľupták, V.; Bartuška, L.; Hanzl, J. Assessment of connection quality on transport networks applying the empirical models in traffic planning: A case study. In Proceedings of the Transport Means—Proceedings of the International Conference, Trakai, Lithuania, 3–5 October 2018; Volume 2018, pp. 236–240.
44. Vojtek, M.; Kendra, M.; Stoilova, S. Optimization of railway vehicles circulation in passenger transport. *Transp. Res. Procedia* **2019**, *40*, 586–593. [CrossRef]
45. Madlenak, R.; Hudak, M. Analysis of Roadside Advertisements on Selected Road Stretch in Zilina. In *Proceedings of the 20th International Scientific Conference Transport Means 2016*; Kaunas Univ Technology Press: Kaunas, Lithuania, 2016; pp. 618–621.
46. Vaculik, J.; Tengler, J.; Maslak, O.; Tanger, L. How Can New Technologies to Improve The Delivery Process. In Proceedings of the CLC 2013: Carpathian Logistics Congress—Congress Proceedings, Cracow, Poland, 9–11 December 2013; pp. 236–242.
47. Madudova, E.; Corejova, T.; Valica, M. Economic Sustainability in a Wider Context: Case Study of Considerable ICT Sector Sub-Divisions. *Sustainability* **2018**, *10*, 2511. [CrossRef]

48. Stalmasekova, N.; Genzorova, T.; Corejova, T.; Gasperova, L. The impact of using the digital environment in transport. *Procedia Eng.* **2017**, *192*, 231–236. [CrossRef]
49. Tekin, H.H. In-Depth Interview as a Data Collection Technique in Qualitative Research Method. *Int. J. Environ. Res. Public Health* **2006**, *3*, 101–116.

applied sciences

MDPI

Article

Parameters of Optokinetic Nystagmus Are Influenced by the Nature of a Visual Stimulus

Peter Essig [1,*], Jonas Müller [1] and Siegfried Wahl [1,2]

[1] Institute for Ophthalmic Research, University of Tübingen, 72076 Tübingen, Germany
[2] Carl Zeiss Vision International GmbH, 73430 Aalen, Germany
* Correspondence: peter.essig@uni-tuebingen.de

Abstract: Studies on contrast sensitivity (CS) testing using optokinetic nystagmus (OKN) proposed adjusting the stimulus presentation duration based on its contrast, to increase the time efficiency of such measurement. Furthermore, stimulus-specific limits of the least OKN gain might reduce false negatives in OKN detection procedures. Therefore, we aimed to test the effects of various stimulus characteristics on OKN and to propose the stimulus-specific limits for the OKN gain and stimulus presentation duration. We tested the effect of contrast (C), spatial frequency (SF), and color on selected parameters of robust OKN response, namely its onset and offset time, amplitude, and gain. The right eyes of fifteen emmetropes were tracked with an infrared eye tracker during monocular observations of sinusoidal gratings moving over the horizontal plane with a velocity of (21 °/s). The available contrast levels were C: 0.5%, 2.0%, 8.2%, 16.5%, 33.0%, and 55.5% presented in a random order for ten times in all measurements of SF: 0.12, 0.25, 0.5, and 1.00 cycles per degree and grating type: luminance, red-green, and blue-yellow. This study showed a significant effect of the stimulus characteristics on the OKN onset, offset and gain. The effect of SF was insignificant in OKN amplitude; however, it indicated significance for the C and grating type. Furthermore, the OKN gain and offset limits were proposed as functions of contrast for the luminance and chromatic gratings. This study concludes the characteristics of a visual stimulus have an effect on the OKN gain and onset and offset time, yet do not affect the eye-movement amplitude considerably. Moreover, the proposed limits are expected to improve the time efficiency and eye-movement detection in OKN-based contrast sensitivity measurements.

Keywords: eye tracking; detection; optokinetic nystagmus; contrast sensitivity; color; adjustments

1. Introduction

Measurements of contrast sensitivity (CS) provide an insight into the patient's visual performance and its examination is necessary in the detection of various eye diseases, for example glaucoma [1], cataracts [2], retinal diseases [3], or in measurements of the performance of amblyopia treatment [4]. Furthermore, the color (or chromatic) contrast sensitivity (CCS) was proposed as an extension of a classical CS to color vision [5], which has been assessed using eye movements recently as well [6]. Because the measurements of CS are performed in the clinical practice in a subjective way, the already commenced research searches for possible objective measurements. In order to gain objective information about the patient's visual performance, various types of eye movements such as microsaccades [7–10], smooth pursuit eye movements [11], optokinetic nystagmus (OKN) [6,12–14], or reflexive (reactive) saccades [15] have been used in the past. Moreover, it has been stated that performing eye movement-based tests for appraisal of visual performance may help examine non-communicative participants [11]. Here, the current study was focused on the OKN—a reflexive eye movement occurring in instances of a moving scenario observation.

This eye movement consists of two phases, first a slow phase (OKN-SP) respecting the direction of a moving scenario, followed by a quick phase (OKN-QP), occurring in a saccade-like fashion in the direction against the stimulus. Although the previous research showed the OKN-QP to be in a similar velocity range compared to normal saccades [16], no attentional input was found to be a trigger of the OKN-QP and therefore the statement of OKN-QP to be same as normal saccades was not supported [17]. Nonetheless, the velocity-based algorithms for saccade detection [18] were successfully implemented [14,19].

Since the OKN occurrence is dependent on contrast and spatial frequency of a target, previous studies proposed this type of eye movement as a reliable tool for CS appraisal [13,14,19], although the contrast sensitivity functions (CSFs) were shown to be shifted over the x-axis to the left due to the velocity of a moving target [20]. In OKN-based CS measurements, the CSFs were shown to correlate with a subjective judgment of the direction the visual stimulus moved in [13] or were shown to be tending toward lower values in conditions of defocused vision, especially in measurements of higher spatial frequencies [14]. This effect was considered a successful replication of the clinical measurements of CS under defocus, as shown in some previous works [21–23]. Moreover, Tatiyosyan et al. performed a CS appraisal using a VR headset and simulated low-vision conditions [19]. On top of that, the previous research showed a possible implementation of adaptive psychometric procedures in methods of searching for the contrast thresholds for future creation of OKN-based CSFs, making the testing adaptive and time-efficient, but requiring advanced skills in programming [14].

In this context, another way to possibly increase the time efficiency of the OKN-based CS testing might be useful, while avoiding the already established live-detection method. To reach this aim, we targeted the optimization of the stimulus presentation duration based on its parameters: SF, C, and type (luminance/chromatic). The rationale of this idea is an early finding of OKN onset time (starting time of the 1st OKN-QP) to be dependent on the contrast level in a low-speed drifting grating, showing a faster onset (shorter latency) with increasing contrast [24]. In the current study, we re-tested this effect and as the stimulus duration limit based on its parameters was sought, we also examined the offset time of the robust OKN response (two OKN movements occurring in the respective direction to the direction of the moving stimulus [14,25]) for visual stimuli of various spatial frequencies, contrast levels, and types. Here the OKN offset time was defined as the ending time of the third OKN-QP.

Moreover, some of the already established procedures for OKN detection use the least OKN gain to successfully detect the eye movement event [13,14]. This approach might, however, lead to events of false-negative detection (no OKN detected, although there was a visible OKN pattern) when using just one fixed parameter. As suggested in the previous work [14], using detection limits for the OKN gain based on the stimulus parameters might be a possible solution. The motivation behind this idea is the finding of Rinner et al., who found a linear correlation between the OKN gain and the contrast on a $\log C$ scale [26] in a zebrafish model. In the current study, we aimed to replicate this effect in emmetropic participants tested with visual stimuli of various C, SF, and types.

The last parameter of the robust OKN eye movement we evaluated with respect to the visual stimulus parameters was the OKN-SP amplitude. Here the analysis of the OKN amplitude was performed for all parameters of the visual stimulus used in the current study, first for its potential influence on the robust OKN offset time and second to complete the range of the eye movement parameters presented in the current study. As the study aimed to test the effects of chromatic gratings and also to propose the limits for the OKN gain and the presentation duration for such kinds of visual stimuli, two chromatic gratings were used in addition to the luminance grating. The two chromatic gratings were red-green (R-G) and blue-yellow (B-Y) presented in the same range of spatial frequencies and contrast levels as the luminance stimulus. These color combinations were used first because they have been already used in several works in the past [5,27–29] and to accommodate clinical measurements. Moreover, as it was already performed in previous works, the data were collected under monocular stimulation conditions [10,14], performing by patching one eye with an infra-red filter. This approach was used to follow clinical conditions for contrast sensitivity testing, without having a significant impact on the eye-tracking quality, while gaining the information from both eyes [10].

2. Materials and Methods

2.1. Participants

Fifteen emmetropic participants with a mean age of 24.7 ± 3 (4 male and 11 female), participated in the current study. We considered emmetropia as a refractive error smaller than ±0.5 D in spherical equivalent of their tested (right) eye, measured by the wavefront-based autorefraction (ZEISS i.Profiler plus, Carl Zeiss Vision, Aalen, Germany). All participants had a negative history of ocular, systemic, or neurological disease, amblyopia, or trauma. Prior to the testing, all participants underwent a standard color testing using the 24-plate Ishihara test (Kanehara Trading Inc., Tokyo, Japan) in order to guarantee no abnormalities in the tested group. Furthermore, to consider a comparable level of tiredness in every subject in the two measurement sessions we conducted, the pause between measurements was exactly one week in all subjects, with the same starting time of the two experimental parts. The study protocol followed the Declaration of Helsinki. In addition, the study was approved by the ethics committee of the Faculty of Medicine of the University Tuebingen (Institutional Review Board number: 881/2017B02), and signed informed consent was obtained from all participants prior to the experiment. All recruited participants were students of the University of Tuebingen and were financially reimbursed for taking part in the experiment.

2.2. Visual Stimulus and Eye Tracking

For the OKN stimulation, we used a vertically oriented sinusoidal grating drifting over the horizontal plane with a constant velocity of $v = 21\,^{\circ}/\mathrm{s}$, which was comparable to a previous work focused on contrast sensitivity using OKN [30]. Because no clear effect of the gain of OKN has been found between the two horizontal directions [31], the grating drifted either nasally or temporally in a random order, in an equal number of trials. The stimuli were created in MATLAB (MATLAB2018b; MathWorks, Natick, MA, USA) using the Psychtoolbox-3 extension [32,33] and covered the entire Viewpixx screen (VIEWPixx; VPixx Technologies Inc., Saint Bruno, Quebec, Canada), refreshing at a rate of 120 Hz. Because the screen provided a resolution of 1920 × 1200 pixels with a pixel pitch of 0.252 mm, the covered visual field from the viewing distance of 75 cm was $\approx 36°$ and $\approx 23°$ in the horizontal and vertical planes, respectively. Furthermore, the screen provided a bit depth of 12 bits, and the luminance nonlinearity was corrected via gamma correction. The spatial frequencies (SFs) calculated for the observing distance were $SF = 0.12, 0.25, 0.5, 1.0$ cycles per degree (cpd). These were selected for their relevance, considering the velocity of the stimulus [20]. The contrast of the stimulus for each trial was randomly selected from the 6 available levels (0.5%, 2.0%, 8.2%, 16.5%, 33.0%, 55.5%), while every contrast level was always presented ten times in every measurement defined by the SF and the grating type (luminance, R-G, B-Y). These contrast levels were selected upon consideration that this range was relevant in contrast sensitivity testing. The motion of the contrast stimulus was aborted at time $t = 2\,\mathrm{s}$ after stimulus onset. After every presentation of the stimulus, a gray cross of 1.25° in size appeared in the center of the screen for $t = 4\,\mathrm{s}$, while during its presentation the participants were asked to blink and rest their vision. During the presentation of the stimulus, the participants were instructed to fixate on the center of the stimulus to stimulate the stare OKN, as performed in previous studies examining CS with OKN [13,14]. The workflow of the stimulus with all its phases is shown in the Figure 1.

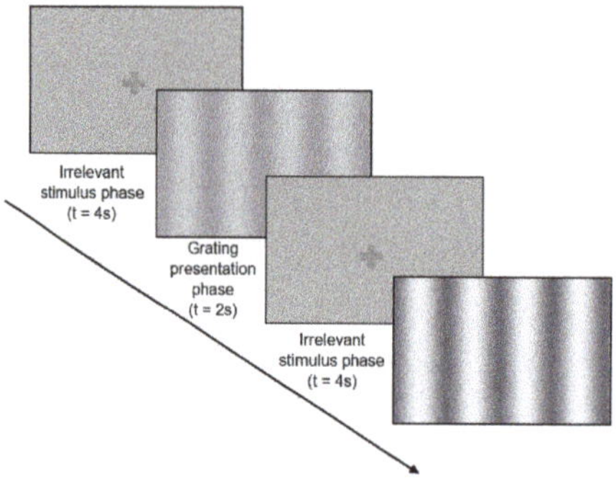

Figure 1. The workflow of the stimulus presentation consisted of the following phases.

Because the current study targeted testing of the effects in normal and chromatic visual stimuli, three types of sinusoidal gratings were used. The first grating was a commonly used sinusoidal luminance grating for standard contrast sensitivity measurements. Secondly, we used two chromatic gratings (R-G and B-Y), following previous studies [5,27,28,30,34], as shown on the Figure 2. Here, the chromatic gratings of the R-G or B-Y modulation were created as the sum of red and green or blue and yellow luminance-modulated monochromatic gratings with a phase difference of 180° between them. The nature of the three gratings was such that the luminance grating converged towards a gray value of the background (middle gray value), whereas the chromatic gratings converged towards black, with decreasing contrast as depicted in the Figure 2. We used the convergence to the middle grey value in the luminance target as we aimed to use an iso-luminant stimulus. In the chromatic stimuli, this approach was not applicable, as even the low-contrast stimuli would have elicited the eye movement by the respective color difference. For this reason, we let the gratings converge towards black. The color gratings were created with the use of a predefined color lookup table computed for the gamma correction, similarly as done by Neumann et al. [35] for cone-specific stimuli. Furthermore, the standard luminosity function $v(\lambda)$ functioned as the baseline for the monitor calibration.

The eye-tracking was performed in a head-fixed condition, using the EyeLink 1000 Plus eye tracker (SR Research, Kanata, ON, Canada) with a fixed sampling rate of 1000 Hz. All data have been captured under monocular stimulation conditions to follow clinical measurements of CS. Here the left eye was covered by an IR filter (ePlastics, San Diego, CA, USA) with a transmission of $T > 90\%$ for $\lambda > 800$ ms, allowing tracking of both eyes while presenting the stimulus only to the right eye. Furthermore, this filter was shown not to significantly affect the eye-tracking quality [10] and was used in OKN-based CS measurements before [14]. Prior to every measurement, a nine-point calibration procedure of the eye tracker was performed. All data collection has been performed in a testing laboratory while the lights were switched off.

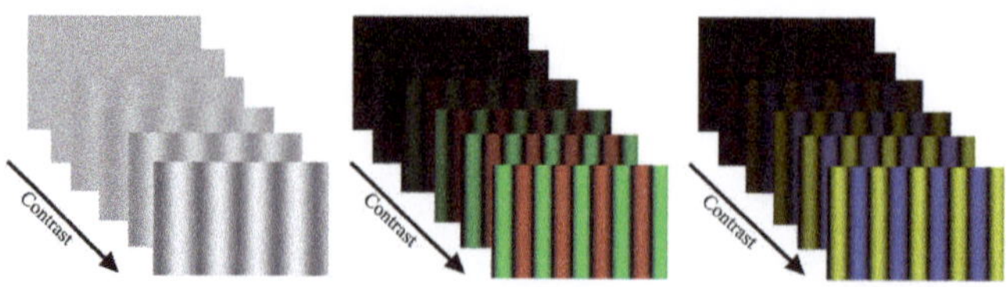

Figure 2. The visual stimuli shown in the contrast levels used in the current study (0.5%, 2.0%, 8.2%, 16.5%, 33.0%, 55.5%) for the luminance as well as for the two chromatic gratings.

2.3. Data Analysis

The data of the tested (right) eye of all participants were treated manually in an offline way with the following steps. First, we sought the trials in which a robust OKN response was visible (at least two OKN patterns) [14,25] that occurred in the correct direction, respectively to the direction of the stimulus drift. An example of such a sequence containing a robust OKN response is depicted in Figure 3. These filtered sequences of gaze data were labeled by a combination of a subject, spatial frequency, grating type, and the contrast level, separately for the ten repetitions of every contrast level. Prior to the gaze data analysis, blinks (epochs of the missing pupil) were discarded with a buffer of 50 ms to protect our analysis from potential blink-related artifacts. From every data sequence we derived the onset and offset time of the OKN, the gain, and amplitude as follows. The starting time of the first OKN-QP was considered as the OKN onset time, as done in a previous study [24]. Here the OKN gain was calculated as the average ratio of the OKN-SP and the velocity of the stimulus of the two consequent OKN patterns. Next, the amplitude of the OKN was calculated as the average distance the eye had traveled in the two OKN-SPs of the two consequent OKN patterns. Next, the OKN offset time was determined as the ending time point of the third OKN-QP. Finally, we calculated the average value of the respective parameter for every combination of a participant, spatial frequency, grating type, and contrast level across the ten repetitions of the contrast-specific stimulus. For the analysis of the OKN parameters, we used the first two OKN events as depicted in Figure 3, first in order to have a comparable amount of data across conditions and second to provide the two limits for the robust OKN response, since this has been considered in the past [14,25].

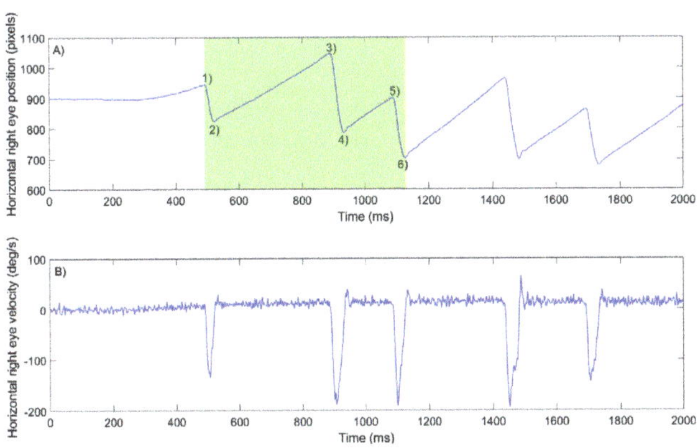

Figure 3. (**A**) OKN pattern for one typical subject for the 2 s grating presentation. Please note that we analyzed the data of the first two OKN patterns (up to the 3rd OKN-QP). Here the numbers 1 to 6 represent the following time points. (1) onset time of the OKN, (2) start time of the 1st OKN-SP (end time of the 1st OKN-QP), (3) start time of the 2nd OKN-QP (end time of the 1st OKN-SP), (4) start time of the 2nd OKN-SP (end time of the 2nd OKN-QP), (5) start time of the 3rd OKN-QP (end time of the 2nd OKN-SP), and (6) end time of the 3rd OKN-QP. The green area represents the gaze data used for the analysis (first two OKN events). (**B**) The derived horizontal eye velocity.

The statistical analysis was conducted using linear mixed-effects models with the statistics software JMP (JMP®, Version 16. SAS Institute Inc., Cary, NC, USA, 1989–2022) in order to analyze the significance of the effects of the visual stimulus parameters on the OKN onset, offset, amplitude, and gain. We run a single model for every of the tested OKN parameter, where the corresponding parameter acted as a dependent variable, with the participant as a random effect and three fixed effects: spatial frequency, grating type, and the contrast level. The selected method of all these models was the standard least squares. The variables of subject number, spatial frequency, grating type, and the contrast level were set as nominal with the respective OKN parameter (onset, offset, gain, amplitude) as a continuous variable. Prior to utilizing the results of the models, we verified the model by visual inspection of the normality of the distribution of the residuals, as well as by statistical testing the homoscedasticity of the variances of residuals using the Brown–Forsythe test and reported in cases of violation. The significance level was set to $\alpha = 5\%$.

Furthermore, because the aim of the current study was to propose the visual stimulus-specific limits for the OKN gain (threshold of the least gain of an OKN-SP considered in eye movement detection procedures) and the OKN offset time (the limit for the visual stimulus presentation duration), we first calculated the respective percentiles from the respective data sets. Because the limit for the OKN gain is considered as the least relative OKN-SP velocity to the stimulus velocity, the eye movement has to yield to be detected, we sought the 5th percentile values. In contrast to that, because we considered the OKN offset time as the maximum duration of the visual stimulus presentation, the 95th percentile was sought.

On top of that, for possible application of these limits to a larger population, we applied the respective percentile levels on the inverse cumulative distribution function ($iCDF$) given for our data. This approach consisted first of searching for the appropriate distribution model of the offset and gain values for the corresponding parameters of visual stimuli using the $fitmethis$ function. in the MATLAB environment. Here the distribution model with the lowest AIC coefficient was applied. Moreover, we created arrays of rational numbers (for the OKN gain we set bounds to 0 and 1, and for OKN offset 200 ms and 2000 ms). Last, we applied the $iCDF$ derived from our original data on the array values and sought the respective percentile levels applied in testing the OKN gain and offset once again in order to get the distribution-based limit values.

3. Results

3.1. Onset and Offset Time of the OKN

In a previous study the influence of contrast and spatial frequency of the OKN onset time was already tested, showing a shorter latency with increasing contrast level and suggesting adjusting the stimulus presentation time upon the parameters of the stimulus [24]. Here in the current study, we aimed to replicate this effect for a grating of a higher velocity as well as for other grating types. To get the first insight we show a box plot (Figure 4), containing combined data of all subjects for the three gratings as an example of one spatial frequency. Here the expected trend was confirmed and thus replicated the effect of the contrast–onset relationship for a higher visual stimulus velocity.

In testing the OKN onset time, the linear mixed-effects model ($n = 1037; R^2 = 0.72$) revealed significant effects of SF (F(3,1012) = 35.32; $p < 0.0001$), color (F(2,1012) = 31.84; $p < 0.0001$) and contrast (F(5,1012) = 192.97; $p < 0.0001$) on the the onset time.

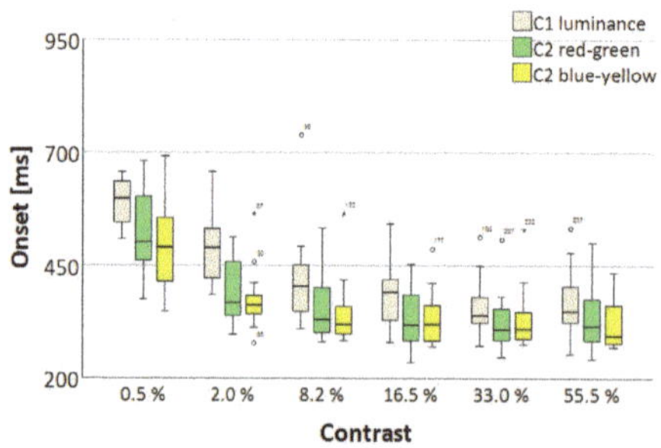

Figure 4. Box plots of the OKN onset time are shown as a function of contrast for the three gratings (luminance, R-G, B-Y) as an example of one spatial frequency ($SF = 0.12$ cpd). The circle and the asterisk indentify outliers, while the circle denotes a "standard out", considered a value laying outside the 3rd quartile + 1.5*interquartile range or 1st quartile – 1.5*interquartile range; and asterisk denotes a "far out" value, considered a value laying outside the 3rd quartile + 3*interquartile range or 1st quartile - 3*interquartile range; The respective number is the indentifier (observation in the data set).

In testing the OKN offset time (box plot shown in Figure 5), the linear mixed-effects model ($n = 1037; R^2 = 0.70$) revealed significant effects of SF (F(3,1012) = 48.10; $p < 0.0001$), color (F(2,1012) = 74.89; $p < 0.0001$), and contrast (F(5,1012) = 152.48; $p < 0.0001$) on the offset time.

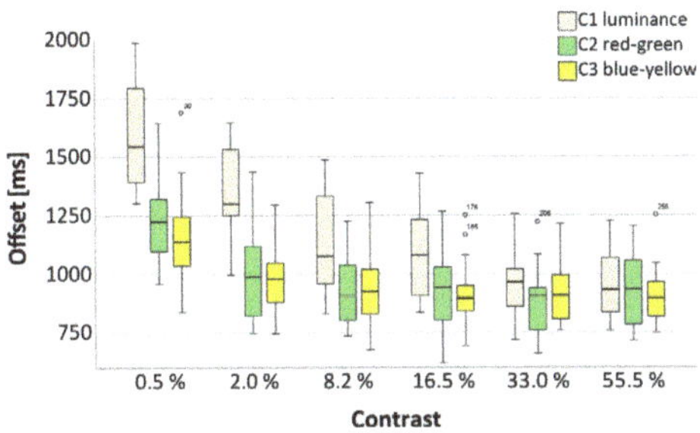

Figure 5. Box plots of the OKN offset time are shown as a function of contrast for the three gratings (luminance, R-G, B-Y) as an example of one spatial frequency ($SF = 0.12$ cpd). The circle and the asterisk indentify outliers, while the circle denotes a "standard out", considered a value laying outside the 3rd quartile + 1.5*interquartile range or 1st quartile – 1.5*interquartile range; and asterisk denotes a "far out" value, considered a value laying outside the 3rd quartile + 3*interquartile range or 1st quartile - 3*interquartile range; The respective number is the indentifier (observation in the data set).

At the last point, we report the violation of homoscedasticity of the residuals in cases of testing both, the OKN onset and offset time, as the Brown–Forsythe test revealed statistical significance. Please note that the problem of heteroscedasticity of the residuals is discussed below in the respective section.

3.2. Amplitude of OKN

The linear mixed-effects model ($n = 1037; R^2 = 0.60$) revealed an insignificant effect of SF (F(3,1012) = 2.08; $p = 0.1$). Grating type and contrast showed significant effects as (F(2,1012) = 10.50; $p < 0.0001$) and (F(5,1012) = 4.09; $p = 0.0011$), respectively. The box plot showing the change in OKN-SP amplitude over the used contrast levels is shown in Figure 6.

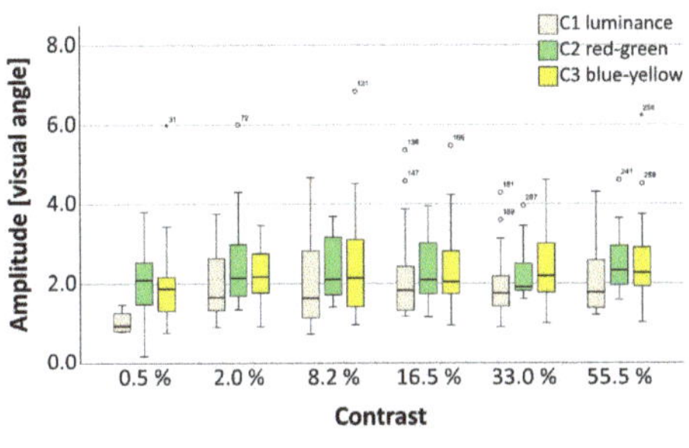

Figure 6. Box plots of the OKN-SP amplitude are shown as a function of contrast for the three gratings (luminance, R-G, B-Y) as an example of one spatial frequency ($SF = 0.12$ cpd). The circle and the asterisk indentify outliers, while the circle denotes a "standard out", considered a value laying outside the 3rd quartile + 1.5*interquartile range or 1st quartile – 1.5*interquartile range; and asterisk denotes a "far out" value, considered a value laying outside the 3rd quartile + 3*interquartile range or 1st quartile - 3*interquartile range; The respective number is the indentifier (observation in the data set).

3.3. Gain of the OKN-SP

On the one hand, the OKN gain obtained for the luminance stimulus showed a continuous increase with increasing contrast levels. On the other hand, the OKN gain showed saturation for the chromatic stimuli for contrast levels higher than 2%, while generally the gain was found to be higher for the two chromatic stimuli, compared to the luminance grating. Here the linear mixed-effects model ($n = 1037$; $R^2 = 0.62$) revealed significant effects of SF (F(3,1012) = 16.15; $p < 0.0001$), color (F(2,1012) = 81.85; $p < 0.0001$), and contrast (F(5,1012) = 50.70; $p < 0.0001$) on the OKN-SP gain. The box plot (Figure 7) shows the OKN-SP gain over the range of contrast levels.

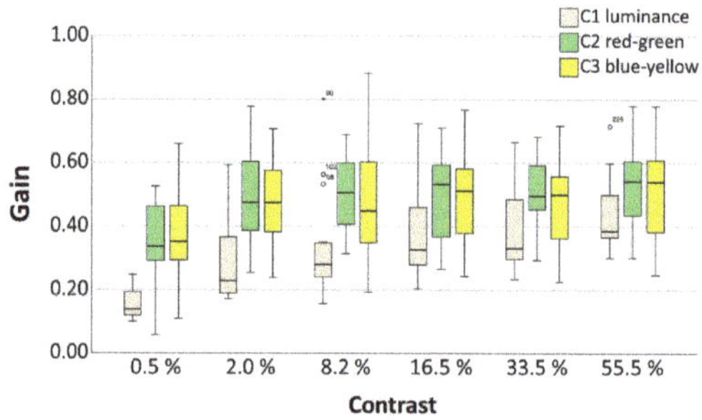

Figure 7. Box plots of the OKN gain are shown as a function of contrast for the three gratings (luminance, R-G, B-Y) as an example of one spatial frequency ($SF = 0.12$ cpd). The circle and the asterisk indentify outliers, while the circle denotes a "standard out", considered a value laying outside the 3rd quartile + 1.5*interquartile range or 1st quartile – 1.5*interquartile range; and asterisk denotes a "far out" value, considered a value laying outside the 3rd quartile + 3*interquartile range or 1st quartile - 3*interquartile range; The respective number is the indentifier (observation in the data set).

3.4. Visual Stimulus-Related Limits of the OKN Gain and Offset Time

Besides providing the statistical testing for the potential influence of various parameters of the visual stimulus on the selected OKN parameters, the target of the current study was to suggest adjusted limit values for the grating presentation time (offset of the robust OKN response) and for the OKN detection procedure (gain of the OKN-SP).

First, although the spatial frequency revealed a statistically significant effect on both the offset and gain, the clinical relevance was due to its low difference being considered to be negligible, as shown in the tables below (Tables 1 and 2) for the three gratings. Second, following an earlier suggestion [14], we propose the limits for every individual contrast level and grating type, combining all spatial frequencies for each of them. Furthermore, the proposed limits for the two chromatic gratings (R-G and B-Y) are shown in a combined way as well as the post hoc Tukey's test revealed an insignificant effect of the two different chromatic gratings on the significance level of $\alpha = 5\%$. Finally, the proposed limits for the OKN offset and gain, derived in two described ways (percentile levels applied once directly to the data and once to the $iCDF$), are depicted in Figure 8.

Table 1. Median (mean ± SD) of the OKN gain values were calculated over all subjects and contrast levels, individually for the three gratings and the four spatial frequencies.

–	SF = 0.12 cpd	SF = 0.25 cpd	SF = 0.5 cpd	SF = 1 cpd
C1 (luminance)	0.33 (0.36 ± 0.15)	0.38 (0.4 ± 0.15)	0.44 (0.44 ± 0.13)	0.39 (0.41 ± 0.15)
C2 (R-G)	0.49 (0.48 ± 0.14)	0.5 (0.5 ± 0.15)	0.5 (0.5 ± 0.12)	0.45 (0.44 ± 0.13)
C3 (B-Y)	0.48 (0.48 ± 0.18)	0.48 (0.47 ± 0.14)	0.51 (0.48 ± 0.14)	0.48 (0.46 ± 0.14)

Table 2. Median (mean ± SD) of the OKN offset time values were calculated over all subjects and contrast levels, individually for the three gratings and the four spatial frequencies. All values in the table are provided in ms.

–	SF = 0.12 cpd	SF = 0.25 cpd	SF = 0.5 cpd	SF = 1 cpd
C1 (luminance)	1077 (1114 ± 250)	1022 (1070 ± 267)	999 (1031 ± 234)	1036 (1066 ± 231)
C2 (R-G)	963 (987 ± 204)	892 (926 ± 172)	868 (937 ± 200)	949 (1041 ± 265)
C3 (B-Y)	952 (973 ± 180)	894 (925 ± 152)	908 (972 ± 200)	1010 (1080 ± 262)

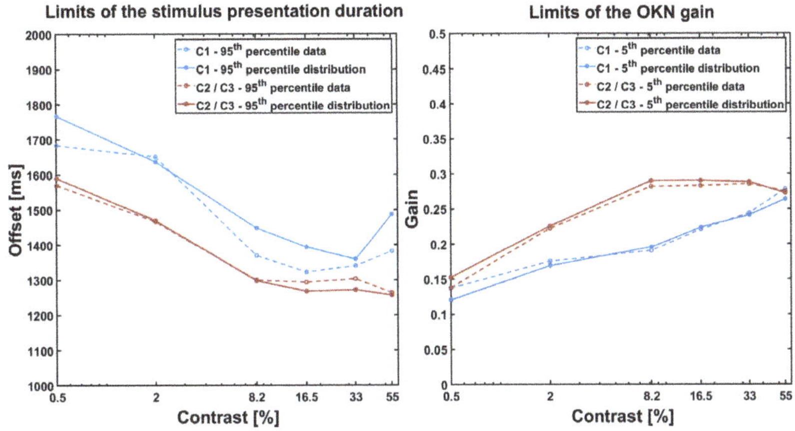

Figure 8. Proposed limits as a function of contrast for the luminance and chromatic gratings.

4. Discussion

The current study aimed to test the effects of contrast, spatial frequency, and grating type on four selected OKN parameters, namely the onset and offset time, amplitude, and gain. Furthermore, the current study aimed to propose limits for optimized contrast sensitivity testing using the OKN responses. In this context, the OKN offset time limit was ratiocinated to be used as a maximum grating presentation time in OKN-based contrast sensitivity testing to increase the time efficiency of such measurement [24], while avoiding any live-detection procedure [14]. Second, we aimed to propose limits of the OKN gain based on parameters of the visual stimulus targeting prevention from false negative eye movement detection [14].

In a previous work investigating the relationship of the OKN onset time and contrast [24], the resulting function showed shorter latency with increasing contrast level as well. Here a latency range from approximately 361 to 525 ms for contrast levels ranging from 58% to 0.1% in low-speed stimuli (2.5 deg/s) was found. In the current study, we confirmed this trend for luminance as well as the R-G and B-Y gratings drifting with a higher velocity. In contrast to a previous study [24], we found a statistically significant effect of the spatial frequency. This could be first due to a different velocity and range of spatial frequencies of the grating used in the current study. More importantly, however, we used linear mixed-effects models for the statistical evaluation considering the nature of our data. As the models have been violated by the heteroscedasticity of the variance of residuals, we consider a potential effect on the statistical results, although a previous study allows such statistical testing even with the residuals being heteroscedastic [36]. Similarly to the dependence of the OKN onset time on contrast, this effect can also be observed for the onset (latency) of other types of eye movements as microsaccades [7] or reflexive (reactive) saccades [37,38]. Furthermore, the relative eye velocity to the target velocity in smooth pursuit eye movements was found to be higher in contrast-rich stimuli [39]. The described contrast dependence can be attributed to the higher recognizability of the stimulus due to the increase in contrast [38]. Moreover, comparing the onset time of OKN stimulated by the two types of our grating, the two chromatic gratings yield a faster OKN response faster compared to the luminance visual stimulus. As the relative-to-fixation sensitivity for chromatic gratings in smooth-pursuit eye movements was previously shown to be increased compared to a luminance grating, ref. [30], the authors assume faster OKN onset due to the enhanced sensitivity in the initial tracking phase (before the first OKN-QP).

Similarly, the offset time of OKN, defined as the end time of the third OKN-QP (end of the robust OKN response [14,25]) was found to be influenced by the contrast of our visual stimuli as well, following a comparable trend function to the OKN onset time. Here the spatial frequency and color showed a statistical significance and, as with the OKN onset time, the linear model for statistical analysis contained heteroscedasticity of variance of the residuals. Interestingly, although the trend of the offset time over the tested contrast levels has been found to be similar to the onset time, the visually inspected standard deviation was found to be bigger in the offset time. This effect could be due to the unequal amplitude in every OKN pattern. Furthermore, similarly to the onset time, the offset time of the OKN stimulated by the two chromatic gratings was found to be shorter compared to the luminance visual stimulus. We consider the reason for this effect to be enhanced sensitivity during the tracking phases in stimulation with chromatic stimuli, resulting in higher gain [30]. Furthermore, we found the amplitude of the OKN-SPs and the OKN gain to be influenced by the grating type (chromatic or luminance), both having generally higher values in simulations with the chromatic visual stimuli.

In terms of the OKN amplitude, Wang et al. found a trend of saturation in the OKN amplitude for grating beyond a luminance of 2×10^{-5}cd/m^2 in one defined spatial frequency (0.1 cpd) [40] in scotopically simulated OKN. In comparison to this study, we found a similar trend in stimulation with the luminance as well as with the two chromatic gratings, giving the first evidence the eye movement amplitude is influenced by contrast only in the low-contrast range.

The gain of the OKN showed an expected trend of increasing its value with increasing contrast of a visual stimulus. However, this effect was already shown in the past, for an animal (zebra-fish) model [26]. In addition, the current study supports the result of Rinner et al. [26] of spatial frequency having an impact on the OKN gain, although both studies provide only an initial evidence. In this context, the authors suggest further investigations, as all the selected spatial frequencies in the current study were around the peak of the expected CS function for the selected stimulus velocity [20]. Furthermore, the OKN gain obtained for the stimulation with chromatic gratings showed saturation for contrast levels higher than 2%, while generally in visual inspection the gain was found to be higher for the two chromatic stimuli compared to the luminance grating. We expect this effect to originate in the enhanced sensitivity for chromatic targets, as already addressed [30].

In further connection to the previous research, the OKN gain has not only been found to be a function of contrast or spatial frequency but was also found to be dependent on the size of the simulating area on the retina, indicating a possibility to use the OKN gain in investigations of visual field loss [41].

Equally important to the statistical testing of the effect of various stimulus parameters on selected parameters of the OKN eye movement, this study proposes limits, allowing optimized OKN-based contrast sensitivity testing. As an example of the potential effect of the stimulus duration limitation, one measurement of one SF consisting of ten presentations of the six contrast levels from this study, each lasting for 2 s, would result in a 120 s long measurement, whereas in utilization of the proposed limits the duration of the test will be reduced by approximately 33%, considering equal testing of high and low contrast levels. However, since the equal amount of presentations of low and high contrast levels is not expected in a clinical testing of a healthy patient, conducting the test rather in a low-contrast range, the method of the adjusted presentation duration upon the stimulus contrast might be even more relevant. The respective limits for the OKN offset time and gain have been derived as percentiles (95th and 5th, respectively), as the data did not follow a normal distribution. In the OKN offset time limit proposal (Figure 8) an unexpected trend occurred in the stimulation of luminance grating (offset in the $C = 55\%$ is delayed compared to the $C = 33\%$). We assume that this effect might come from the selected percentile levels we used for the analysis, as the related box plots (Figure 5) show a continuous trend. Furthermore, this unexpected tail in the contrast–offset function was reduced when using the data distribution approach, making this effect negligible for clinical implementation. Nonetheless, we assume that utilization of such a limit approach could be helpful also in the future examinations of CS using OKN responses in VR environment [19] or other mobile devices with sufficient eye-tracking quality [42].

As the last point, the authors aim to report the limitations of the current study. First, since a wide range of velocities for the stimulus movement has been used in the past [6,13,14,30,43], a future study may also take the varying velocity as a parameter to extend the usability of the limits also for other paces of a stimulus. Second, the standard luminosity function was not obtained individually for each study participant, which may consequently lead to a slight imbalance among subjects in the brightness perception of the different test stimuli. Third, as reported above, the statistical testing of OKN onset and offset time using the linear mixed-effects models were not supporting the homoscedasticity of the variance of the residuals, which might have an influence on the reported significance of the tested effects. Lastly, the current work did not consider the possible effect of melanopsin, stimulated partially by the B-Y stimulus and the change in the pupil sizes resulting from various luminance levels across the six contrasts of the two chromatic gratings. This approach was selected as the authors aimed to provide a clinically applicable approach to optimize optokinetic nystagmus-based contrast sensitivity testing. However, to maintain a comparable level of tiredness in the two measurement events of each participant, each participant underwent the respective measurement on the same weekday at the same time. As shown previously in [44], the effect of pupil size on contrast sensitivity has been found to be significant; however, it is clinically irrelevant for its small difference and lack of a tendency in emmetropic conditions, as well in conditions of defocus. Furthermore, since the two of the chromatic gratings converged towards black with decreasing contrast resulting in a decreasing retinal luminance, the authors state a potential effect on contrast sensitivity [45]. However, this method was selected on purpose to cancel the OKN response in the low-contrast stimuli. Moreover, the clinical relevance of the difference in contrast sensitivity under the two extreme mean retinal luminances, given by the maximum and minimum contrast level for the respective chromatic grating, is questionable.

5. Conclusions

The current study showed the effects of stimulus spatial frequency, contrast, and type on selected parameters of optokinetic nystagmus (OKN). These eye movement parameters were namely the onset, offset, amplitude, and gain, giving a systematic overview of how OKN changes with various parameters of a visual stimulus. Furthermore, in the current study we propose limits for the OKN gain with respect to the visual stimulus contrast, which could be potentially used to reduce false negatives in OKN detection (OKN-SP assessment). Additionally, we propose the maximum stimulus presentation duration, based on the offset time of the robust OKN response. Here the aim was to enhance the time efficiency, while avoiding the live OKN detection method, requiring advanced skills in programming. All these limits have been proposed for a wide range of contrast levels and for luminance as well as chromatic gratings.

Author Contributions: Conceptualization, P.E., J.M. and S.W.; methodology, P.E., J.M. and S.W.; formal analysis, P.E. and J.M.; investigation, P.E. and J.M.; data curation, J.M.; writing—original draft preparation, P.E., J.M. and S.W.; writing—review and editing, P.E., J.M. and S.W.; visualization, P.E. and J.M.; supervision, S.W.; project administration, S.W. All authors have read and agreed to the published version of the manuscript.

Funding: Funding was received from Eberhard-Karls-University Tuebingen (ZUK 63) as part of the German Excellence initiative from the Federal Ministry of Education and Research (BMBF). Further funding was received from Deutsche Forschungsgemeinschaft and the Open Access Publishing Fund of the University of Tuebingen. S.W. is a scientist at the University of Tuebingen and is employed by Carl Zeiss Vision International GmbH. The funders did not have any additional role in the study design, data collection and analysis, decision to publish, or manuscript preparation. P.E.: none; J.M.: none; S.W. Carl Zeiss: Vision International GmbH (E,F).

Institutional Review Board Statement: The Ethics Committee at the Medical Faculty of the Eberhard Karls University and the University Hospital Tübingen approved to carry out the study within its facilities (Institutional Review Board number: 881/2017B02). The study followed the tenets of the Declaration of Helsinki.

Informed Consent Statement: Written informed consent was obtained from all participants after the content and possible consequences of the study had been explained.

Acknowledgments: The authors gratefully acknowledge the helpful support of Carl Zeiss Vision International GmbH, Aalen, and the support by the Open Access Publishing Fund of the University of Tübingen.

Conflicts of Interest: The authors P.E. and J.M. declare no potential conflicts of interest regarding this study. S.W. is a scientist at the University of Tübingen and is employed by Carl Zeiss Vision International GmbH. There is no conflict of interest regarding this study.

References

1. Atkin, A.; Bodis-Wollner, I.; Wolkstein, M.; Moss, A.; Podos, S.M. Abnormalities of central contrast sensitivity in glaucoma. *Am. J. Ophthalmol.* **1979**, *88*, 205–211. [CrossRef] [PubMed]
2. Hess, R.; Woo, G. Vision through cataracts. *Investig. Ophthalmol. Vis. Sci.* **1978**, *17*, 428–435.
3. Wolkstein, M.; Atkin, A.; Bodis-Wollner, I. Contrast sensitivity in retinal disease. *Ophthalmology* **1980**, *87*, 1140–1149. [CrossRef] [PubMed]
4. Zhou, Y.; Huang, C.; Xu, P.; Tao, L.; Qiu, Z.; Li, X.; Lu, Z.L. Perceptual learning improves contrast sensitivity and visual acuity in adults with anisometropic amblyopia. *Vis. Res.* **2006**, *46*, 739–750. [CrossRef] [PubMed]
5. Mullen, K.T. The contrast sensitivity of human colour vision to red-green and blue-yellow chromatic gratings. *J. Physiol.* **1985**, *359*, 381–400. [CrossRef]
6. Taore, A.; Lobo, G.; Turnbull, P.R.; Dakin, S.C. Diagnosis of colour vision deficits using eye movements. *Sci. Rep.* **2022**, *12*, 7734 [CrossRef]
7. Bonneh, Y.S.; Adini, Y.; Polat, U. Contrast sensitivity revealed by microsaccades. *J. Vis.* **2015**, *15*, 11. [CrossRef]
8. Scholes, C.; McGraw, P.V.; Nyström, M.; Roach, N.W. Fixational eye movements predict visual sensitivity. *Proc. R. Soc. B Biol. Sci.* **2015**, *282*, 20151568. [CrossRef]
9. Denniss, J.; Scholes, C.; McGraw, P.V.; Nam, S.H.; Roach, N.W. Estimation of contrast sensitivity from fixational eye movements. *Investig. Ophthalmol. Vis. Sci.* **2018**, *59*, 5408–5416. [CrossRef]
10. Essig, P.; Leube, A.; Rifai, K.; Wahl, S. Microsaccadic rate signatures correlate under monocular and binocular stimulation conditions. *J. Eye Mov. Res.* **2020**, *11*. [CrossRef]
11. Mooney, S.W.; Hill, N.J.; Tuzun, M.S.; Alam, N.M.; Carmel, J.B.; Prusky, G.T. Curveball: A tool for rapid measurement of contrast sensitivity based on smooth eye movements. *J. Vis.* **2018**, *18*, 7. [CrossRef] [PubMed]
12. Cetinkaya, A.; Oto, S.; Akman, A.; Akova, Y. Relationship between optokinetic nystagmus response and recognition visual acuity. *Eye* **2008**, *22*, 77–81. [CrossRef] [PubMed]
13. Dakin, S.C.; Turnbull, P.R. Similar contrast sensitivity functions measured using psychophysics and optokinetic nystagmus. *Sci. Rep.* **2016**, *6*, 34514. [CrossRef] [PubMed]
14. Essig, P.; Sauer, Y.; Wahl, S. Contrast Sensitivity Testing in Healthy and Blurred Vision Conditions Using a Novel Optokinetic Nystagmus Live-Detection Method. *Transl. Vis. Sci. Technol.* **2021**, *10*, 12. [CrossRef]
15. Essig, P.; Sauer, Y.; Wahl, S. Reflexive Saccades Used for Objective and Automated Measurements of Contrast Sensitivity in Selected Areas of Visual Field. *Transl. Vis. Sci. Technol.* **2022**, *11*, 29. [CrossRef]
16. Garbutt, S.; Harwood, M.R.; Harris, C.M. Comparison of the main sequence of reflexive saccades and the quick phases of optokinetic nystagmus. *Br. J. Ophthalmol.* **2001**, *85*, 1477–1483. [CrossRef]
17. Hanning, N.M.; Deubel, H. Unlike saccades, quick phases of optokinetic nystagmus (okn) are not preceded by shifts of attention. *J. Vis.* **2019**, *19*, 53c. [CrossRef]
18. Engbert, R.; Kliegl, R. Microsaccades uncover the orientation of covert attention. *Vis. Res.* **2003**, *43*, 1035–1045. [CrossRef]
19. Tatiyosyan, S.A.; Rifai, K.; Wahl, S. Standalone cooperation-free OKN-based low vision contrast sensitivity estimation in VR-a pilot study. *Restor. Neurol. Neurosci.* **2020**, *38*, 119–129. [CrossRef]
20. Burr, D.C.; Ross, J. Contrast sensitivity at high velocities. *Vis. Res.* **1982**, *22*, 479–484. [CrossRef]

21. Marmor, M.F.; Gawande, A. Effect of visual blur on contrast sensitivity: Clinical implications. *Ophthalmology* **1988**, *95*, 139–143. [CrossRef] [PubMed]
22. Green, D.; Campbell, F. Effect of focus on the visual response to a sinusoidally modulated spatial stimulus. *JOSA* **1965**, *55*, 1154–1157. [CrossRef]
23. Jansonius, N.; Kooijman, A. The effect of defocus on edge contrast sensitivity. *Ophthalmic Physiol. Opt.* **1997**, *17*, 128–132. [CrossRef] [PubMed]
24. Essig, P.; Sauer, Y.; Wahl, S. OKN-onset is influenced by the contrast level of a visual stimulus. *Investig. Ophthalmol. Vis. Sci.* **2021**, *62*, 3330–3330.
25. Turuwhenua, J.; Yu, T.Y.; Mazharullah, Z.; Thompson, B. A method for detecting optokinetic nystagmus based on the optic flow of the limbus. *Vis. Res.* **2014**, *103*, 75–82. [CrossRef]
26. Rinner, O.; Rick, J.M.; Neuhauss, S.C. Contrast sensitivity, spatial and temporal tuning of the larval zebrafish optokinetic response. *Investig. Ophthalmol. Vis. Sci.* **2005**, *46*, 137–142. [CrossRef]
27. Van Der Horst, G.J.; De Weert, C.M.; Bouman, M.A. Transfer of spatial chromaticity-contrast at threshold in the human eye. *JOSA* **1967**, *57*, 1260–1266. [CrossRef]
28. Rovamo, J.M.; Kankaanpää, M.I.; Kukkonen, H. Modelling spatial contrast sensitivity functions for chromatic and luminance-modulated gratings. *Vis. Res.* **1999**, *39*, 2387–2398. [CrossRef]
29. Chwesiuk, M.; Mantiuk, R. Measurements of contrast sensitivity for peripheral vision. In Proceedings of the ACM Symposium on Applied Perception 2019, Barcelona, Spain, 19–20 September 2019; pp. 1–9.
30. Schütz, A.C.; Braun, D.I.; Gegenfurtner, K.R. Chromatic contrast sensitivity during optokinetic nystagmus, visually enhanced vestibulo-ocular reflex, and smooth pursuit eye movements. *J. Neurophysiol.* **2009**, *101*, 2317–2327. [CrossRef]
31. Van den Berg, A.; Collewijn, H. Directional asymmetries of human optokinetic nystagmus. *Exp. Brain Res.* **1988**, *70*, 597–604. [CrossRef]
32. Brainard, D.H.; Vision, S. The psychophysics toolbox. *Spat. Vis.* **1997**, *10*, 433–436. [CrossRef] [PubMed]
33. Kleiner, M.; Brainard, D.; Pelli, D.; Ingling, A.; Murray, R.; Broussard, C. What's new in Psychtoolbox-3? *Perception* **2007**, *36*, 1–16.
34. Braun, D.I.; Schütz, A.C.; Gegenfurtner, K.R. Visual sensitivity for luminance and chromatic stimuli during the execution of smooth pursuit and saccadic eye movements. *Vis. Res.* **2017**, *136*, 57–69. [CrossRef] [PubMed]
35. Neumann, A.; Leube, A.; Nabawi, N.; Sauer, Y.; Essig, P.; Breher, K.; Wahl, S. Short-Term Peripheral Contrast Reduction Affects Central Chromatic and Achromatic Contrast Sensitivity. *Photonics* **2022**, *9*, 123. [CrossRef]
36. Bathke, A. The ANOVA F test can still be used in some balanced designs with unequal variances and nonnormal data. *J. Stat. Plan. Inference* **2004**, *126*, 413–422. [CrossRef]
37. Ludwig, C.J.; Gilchrist, I.D.; McSorley, E. The influence of spatial frequency and contrast on saccade latencies. *Vis. Res.* **2004**, *44*, 2597–2604. [CrossRef]
38. Carpenter, R. Contrast, probability, and saccadic latency: Evidence for independence of detection and decision. *Curr. Biol.* **2004**, *14*, 1576–1580. [CrossRef]
39. Haegerstrom-Portnoy, G.; Brown, B. Contrast effects on smooth-pursuit eye movement velocity. *Vis. Res.* **1979**, *19*, 169–174. [CrossRef]
40. Wang, L.; Soderberg, P.G.; Wang, L. Frequency and amplitude in scotopically stimulated optokinetic nystagmus. *Graefe's Arch. Clin. Exp. Ophthalmol.* **1995**, *233*, 8–12. [CrossRef]
41. Doustkouhi, S.M.; Turnbull, P.R.; Dakin, S.C. The effect of simulated visual field loss on optokinetic nystagmus. *Transl. Vis. Sci. Technol.* **2020**, *9*, 25–25. [CrossRef]
42. Leube, A.; Rifai, K. Sampling rate influences saccade detection in mobile eye tracking of a reading task. *J. Eye Mov. Res.* **2017**, *10*. [CrossRef] [PubMed]
43. Leguire, L.; Zaff, B.; Freeman, S.; Rogers, G.; Bremer, D.; Wali, N. Contrast sensitivity of optokinetic nystagmus. *Vis. Res.* **1991**, *31*, 89–97. [CrossRef] [PubMed]
44. Strang, N.C.; Atchison, D.A.; Woods, R.L. Effects of defocus and pupil size on human contrast sensitivity. *Ophthalmic Physiol. Opt.* **1999**, *19*, 415–426. [CrossRef] [PubMed]
45. Rovamo, J.; Mustonen, J.; Näsänen, R. Modelling contrast sensitivity as a function of retinal illuminance and grating area. *Vis. Res.* **1994**, *34*, 1301–1314. [CrossRef]

applied sciences

MDPI

Article

Use of a DNN in Recording and Analysis of Operator Attention in Advanced HMI Systems

Zbigniew Gomolka [1,*], Ewa Zeslawska [1,*], Boguslaw Twarog [1], Damian Kordos [2] and Pawel Rzucidlo [2]

1 College of Natural Sciences, University of Rzeszow, Pigonia St. 1, 35-959 Rzeszow, Poland
2 Department of Avionics and Control, Faculty of Mechanical Engineering and Aeronautics, Rzeszow University of Technology, al. Powstancow Warszawy 12, 35-959 Rzeszow, Poland
* Correspondence: zgomolka@ur.edu.pl (Z.G.); ezeslawska@ur.edu.pl (E.Z.)

Abstract: The main objective of this research was to propose a smart technology to record and analyse the attention of operators of transportation devices where human–machine interaction occurs. Four simulators were used in this study: General Aviation (GA), Remotely Piloted Aircraft System (RPAS), AS 1600, and Czajka, in which a spatio-temporal trajectory of system operator attention describing the histogram distribution of cockpit instrument observations was sought. Detection of the position of individual instruments in the video stream recorded by the eyetracker was accomplished using a pre-trained Fast R-CNN deep neural network. The training set for the network was constructed using a modified Kanade–Lucas–Tomasi (KLT) algorithm, which was applied to optimise the labelling of the cockpit instruments of each simulator. A deep neural network allows for sustained instrument tracking in situations where classical algorithms stop their work due to introduced noise. A mechanism for the flexible selection of Area Of Interest (AOI) objects that can be tracked in the recorded video stream was used to analyse the recorded attention using a mobile eyetracker. The obtained data allow for further analysis of key skills in the education of operators of such systems. The use of deep neural networks as a detector for selected instrument types has made it possible to universalise the use of this technology for observer attention analysis when applied to a different objects-sets of monitoring and control instruments.

Keywords: eye tracking; deep neural network; attention trajectory; HMI systems

1. Introduction

The eye-tracking equipment market lacks objective systems to determine the level of training of those operating multitasking mechanical equipment (and more). Existing mobile eyetracker software does not provide seamless AOI analysis in recorded video streams. The products of leading eye-tracking system manufacturers do not provide such functionality [1–3]. This paper extends earlier research's related with pilot attention tracking during key procedures, i.e., take-off and landing, which was carried out using the SMI RED 500 and Tobii T60 stationary eyetrackers and the Tobii Glasses mobile eyetracker. Stationary eyetrackers allow video streams to be recorded and further analysed using the environments provided by SMI—BeGaze and Tobii Studio. In addition, the analysed example of the study of the assessment of the relationship between eye-tracking measurements and the perceived workload in robotic surgical tasks was the problem described in the article [4]. Another analysed study aimed to review eye-tracking concepts, methods and techniques by developing efficient and effective modern approaches such as machine learning (ML), Internet of Things (IoT) and cloud computing. These approaches have been in use for over two decades and are used heavily in the development of the latest eye-tracking applications [5]. In another study, the authors developed three artificial intelligence techniques, namely machine learning, deep learning, and a hybrid technique between them, for the early diagnosis of autism. The first technique, feedforward neural networks (FFNN) and artificial neural networks (ANN), the second technique using the pre-trained convolutional neural network model (CNN, GoogleNet and ResNet-18), and the third technique used the hybrid method between deep learning (GoogleNet and ResNet-18) and machine learning (SVM), called GoogleNet + SVM and ResNet-18 + SVM, and these achieved high performance and accuracy [6]. For example, work to develop observer attentional statistics for a 3 min video sequence (MJPG2000, 640 × 480 pixels at 30 fps) covering the location of nine instruments in the cockpit requires at least 48 h of user effort see Figure 1.

Figure 1. General view of the pilot attention measurement strategy during fly.

The effect of this engagement is one-off and requires redefining the AOI both when changing the operator and the flight task being recorded. This functionality is important, especially in the case of complex Human–Machine Interfaces (HMI) systems, where it is indispensable to transfer large amounts of data in the shortest possible time, e.g., production line operators or operators of ground air traffic control stations of unmanned systems [7–11]. The approach proposed in this paper is based on well-known and used eye-tracking systems which, due to their universality and targeting a different audience, do not allow for application in the areas and tasks that are the purpose of this paper. The authors hypothesise that the use of a deep pre-trained neural network supporting a mobile eye-tracking system will enable both the intelligent location of AOI areas throughout the video sequence and the obtaining of appropriate observation histograms for individual AOIs defined for a given HMI.

The process of detecting the position of individual instruments in the recorded video stream was carried out using the pre-trained Fast R-CNN deep neural network. The training vector for the network was realised using a modified KLT algorithm, which optimised the labelling of cockpit instruments. A deep neural network allows you to keep track of instruments in situations when classical algorithms stop their work due to digital noise. Among the available machine learning methods, we can also use the AutoML automated learning system. AutoML was designed as an artificial intelligence-based solution to the growing demand of applying machine learning. The high degree of automation in AutoML aims to allow non-experts to make use of machine learning models and techniques without requiring them to become experts in machine learning. As big data become ubiquitous across domains, and more and more stakeholders aspire to make the most of their data, demand for machine learning tools has spurred researchers to explore the possibilities of automated machine learning (AutoML). AutoML tools aim to make machine learning accessible for non-machine learning experts (domain experts), to improve the efficiency of machine learning, and to accelerate machine learning research. In this review article, the authors introduce a new classification system for AutoML systems, using a seven-tiered schematic to distinguish these systems based on their level of autonomy [12]. In another article, the authors examine the readiness of popular AutoML frameworks from the perspective of machine learning practitioners. Their goal is to demonstrate how the growing AutoML trend will affect the future job responsibilities of scientists, researchers, and human data practitioners [13]. In article [14], the authors try to investigate the interaction between data cleansing and other ML pipeline hyperparameters for supervised binary classification tasks. They use AutoML for both the dirty and clean state of all CleanML datasets. Because AutoML optimises the entire pipeline, you can avoid measurement artifacts related to static preprocessing. The method proposed in this paper for recording and analysing operator attention is a key added value and its light motive.

2. Research Methods

2.1. HMI Stations

For purposes of the research work carried out, workstations were selected and configured using HMIs in which it was possible to record the observer's attention. The data collected in this way will allow received video streams to be processed using a Deep Neural Network (DNN) and thus enable the level of training of the operators of selected HMI systems to be assessed [15–17]. In particular, this will apply to operators of manned and unmanned aircraft and operators of means of a road transport. For this purpose, four sets of devices using HMIs were prepared (see Figure 2):

- GA flight simulator equipped with standard analogue instrumentation, configured to type FNTP II MCC as a twin-engine piston aircraft, with analogue-equipped retractable landing gear, providing an alternative for pilots practically training in the air;
- Flying laboratory Czajka MP02A, which is a two-crew (pilot + passenger) high-wing monoplane with tricycle landing gear of carbon–polymer laminate construction (span 9.72 (m), width 1.215 (m)) with engine propulsion type Rotax 912 ULS with a traction propeller. An aeroplane adapted to and capable of providing flight tests of the avionics equipment and solutions was used. A laboratory equipped with a research control and navigation system was developed under the LOT project;
- RPAS ground station as a simulated electric-powered aircraft with a span of 2.6 (m) and take-off weight of 2.5 (kg);
- The AS 1600 truck simulator with a 6-degree-of-freedom motion platform (based on a SCANIA truck cab).

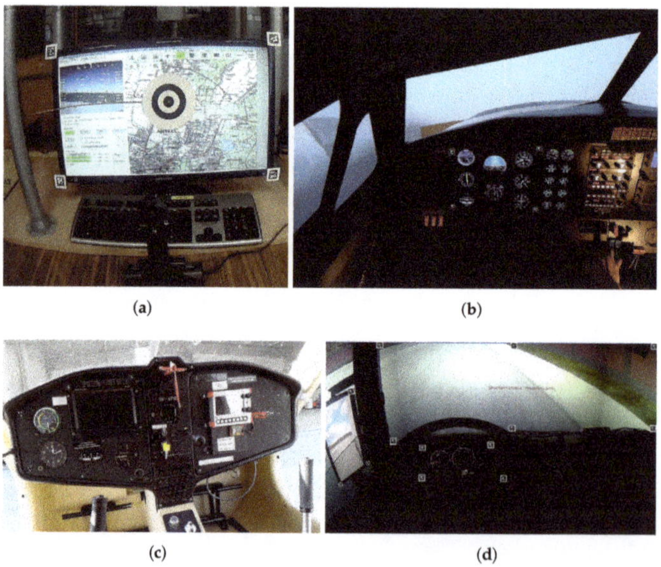

Figure 2. Observer attention recording and analysis stand (**a**) RPAS, (**b**) GA simulator (cockpit view), (**c**) flying lab (cockpit view), (**d**) truck simulator (cockpit view).

In the course of the research carried out on individual simulators, each station was equipped with a prototype of a mobile eye-tracking system along with dedicated components allowing for the process of calibration, validation and recording of video sequences.

2.2. An Eye-Tracking System for Attention Recording

The study used the open source eye-tracking system Pupil Core v2.0.182 equipped with a camera recording the observed scene and two cameras recording eye movement in infrared. This is a typical system that is subject to calibration at the initial stage and is a key element in determining the accuracy of the recorded coordinates of the operator's observations [18–21]. In order to achieve high accuracy of the attentional measurements, 5-point calibration using a screen, calibration using a calibration tag/marker and natural calibration made possible by the use of Apriltags were used interchangeably. Due to the nature of the research, calibration for the flight simulator and the Czajka aircraft was carried out using a calibration marker. The eye-tracking system employed the 2D Gaze Mapping eye coordinate detection model, which maintains accuracy within a visual error limit of $<1^{\circ}$. The use of the 2D Gaze Mapping model works mainly in systems where participants do not have to move their heads and the experiment time is relatively short [22–25].

2.3. Tasks for HMI Station Operators

During the execution of each test, subjects in the experiments were asked to perform the following tasks:

- GA simulator. Execution of a precision instrument approach as indicated by the Instrument Landing System (ILS). This approach provides vertical and horizontal guidance to the Decision Altitude (DA). The barometric height DA is related to the local pressure prevailing at medium sea level—QNH (Q Nautical Height). Glide performed under minimum weather conditions for CAT I ILS, i.e., visibility along runway RVR 550 m and cloud base at 200 ft AGL (Above Ground Level). Atmospheric conditions allow flights only under IFR (Instrument Flight Rules), which means that pilots can navigate solely on the basis of on-board instruments. The flight takes place in windless conditions on a configured aircraft with three-point retractable landing gear. The aircraft configuration includes flaps in the landing position, landing gear released, and power close to minimum. Flights are performed at the EPRZ—Rzeszow Jasionka airport on runway 27 with an available landing length of 3192 m and width of 45 m. The airport elevation is 693 ft, and the magnetic heading of the runway is 265 degrees. The flight starts at 7 NM from the runway threshold and at a barometric altitude of 3000 ft ft AMSL (Above Medium Sea Level). The task ends when a Decision Height (DH) of 200 ft is reached.
- Flying laboratory Czajka MP02A. Flight operations under Visual Flight Rules (VFR). Flight operations were divided into three main stages: take-off from the EPRJ OKL airport (Aviation Training Centre) (magnetic runway heading 265 degrees), building a traffic pattern according to instructions from the air traffic control tower after reaching 1000 ft AMSL, and landing at the EPRJ airport. The aircraft on which the simulator tasks are performed is fully configured and adapted to perform a given phase of flight.
- RPAS ground station. Performing a flight in BVLOS mode (Beyond Visual Line of Sight—operations beyond the visual range of the UAV operator) in the EPML airport area. The system operator uses a hand-held mini control panel, an on-board camera image, an integrated pilot-navigation display system and an interactive map to perform a manual take-off. The take-off and initial climb was on the 09 direction. After reaching an altitude of 100 m AGL, a 90-degree turn to the left was followed by a course to the north and a further climb to an altitude of 150 (m) AGL. Then, there was another turn to the left on a course of 270 degrees in order to build a traffic pattern. This part of the flight was already in manual-assisted mode, which was characterised by the protection of the flight parameter envelope, in particular the angles of spatial orientation. After the third turn, the descent begins, which is followed by a final turn to bring the aircraft straight ahead for landing. The entire landing process, including the landing roll, was carried out in assisted manual mode.
- Truck simulator. Driving a lorry in urban conditions where during the journey, the driver pays attention to the correct observation of junctions and crossings with traffic

lights, pedestrians and other road users, and observes speed limits and road signs. A simulation was carried out under different weather and day conditions.

Once the group of people taking part in the experiment had been formed, the research was carried out on a test group of pilots and drivers with varying degrees of training and experience in aviation and operators of road transport vehicles. The experiment lasted no longer than 30 min in order to preserve the correct perception of the subject and to limit the influence of fatigue. This allowed them to focus their attention better. The research was conducted on two groups of people: in the flying task, Group I included people with less than 80 h of flying experience considered as a group of inexperienced pilots (NONPILOT). Group II (PILOT), on the other hand, is made up of people with >80 h flight experience. In the truck control task, a distinction was made between Group I (those with less than 10 h driving experience) and Group II (those with more than 10 h driving experience).

3. Operator Attention Tracking System Using a DNN

Figure 3 presents the modular structure of a designed workstation for recording and analysing the attention of operators of advanced systems using an HMI. Within Module A are sets of infrared sensors to detect the position and orientation of the observer's pupil (1) and scene observation cameras (2). The module is responsible for acquiring the video stream of the observed scene and recording the spatial position of the observer's pupils. Module B performs the tasks of attentional coordinate detection (3) and fixation detection (5). Module C performs AOI detection tasks in the video stream with the trained DNN [26–30]. Its main component (4) performs the task of detecting in the video stream the presence of instruments that are part of the HMI in use. This is completed by using the trained weight set obtained from the set of interface components (4a). The direct instrument recognition block (4b) in the video stream uses a deep neural network (4bb).

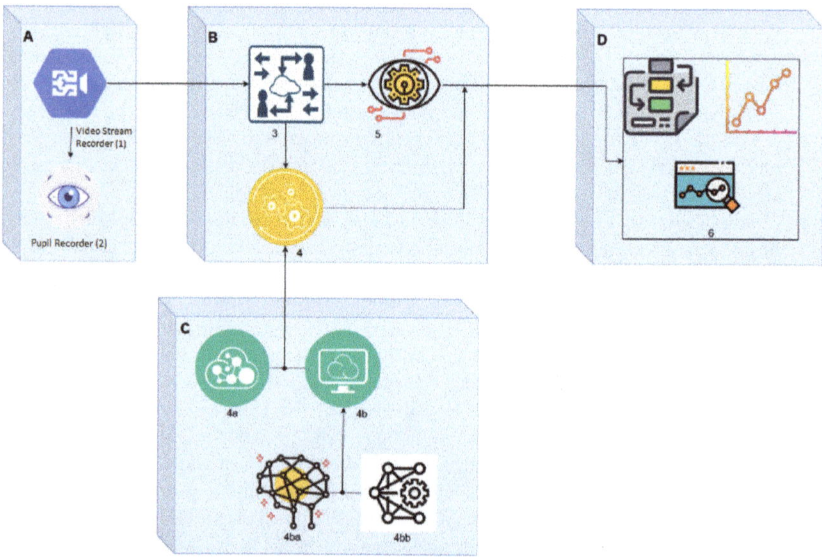

Figure 3. Schematic diagram of a modular workstation structure for recording and analysing operator attention in advanced HMI systems. (**A–D**) denotes consecutive modules for signal processing in the system.

The authors assumed that a set of pre-trained architectures provided by the DNN Toolbox Matlab® library environment would be used in the DNN simulation studies. A modified KLT algorithm (see Algorithm 1) was implemented to prepare a training set that would contain a series of video frames of the operator cockpit instruments of a given station. Its task is to match the template image $T(x)$ with the input image $I(x)$. The vector x contains the coordinates of the image $[x, y]T$.

Algorithm 1 Image characteristic point detector tracker–KLT algorithm

Input: $I(x), \varepsilon$
Output: p
begin
do{
warp $I(x)$ with $W(x,p) \rightarrow I(W(x,p))$
the error $T(x) \rightarrow I(W(x,p))$
warped gradients $\nabla I = [I_x, I_y]$ evaluated at $W(x,p)$
the Jacobian of the warping $\frac{\partial W}{\partial p}$
steepest descent $\nabla I \frac{\partial W}{\partial p}$
inverse Hessian $H^{-1} = \left[\sum_{x \in T} \left[\nabla I \frac{\partial W}{\partial p}\right]^T \left[\nabla I \frac{\partial W}{\partial p}\right]\right]^{-1}$
multiply steepest descend with error:
$\sum_{x \in T} \left[\nabla I \frac{\partial W}{\partial p}\right]^T [T(x) - I(W(x,p))]$
compute Δp
update parameters $p \leftarrow p + \Delta p$
}**while** $(\Delta p < \varepsilon)$
end;

In matrix notation form, it can be represented accordingly:

$$W(x,p) = \begin{bmatrix} x + p_1 \\ x + p_2 \end{bmatrix} \quad (1)$$

$$\Delta p = H^{-1} \sum_{x \in T} \left[\nabla I \frac{\partial W}{\partial p}\right]^T [T(x) - I(W(x,p))] \quad (2)$$

$$H = \sum_{x \in T} \left[\nabla I \frac{\partial W}{\partial p}\right]^T \left[\nabla I \frac{\partial W}{\partial p}\right] \quad (3)$$

In this form, the algorithm was introduced as a tracker function into VideoLabeler, which allowed the generation of a sequence of images into the GroundTruth variable that constitutes the training set for each simulator. It should be noted that if tracked points are lost from the field of view (see Figure 4), it is unable to re-determine their location when they reappear—hence the need to use machine learning for object recognition.

An example of video recording showing the loss of ROI3 when the operator performs hand movements—the lost Region of Interest (ROI) is marked with a dashed line (left bottom corner of the cockpit image on Figure 4). The data obtained in the marking session exported to the GroundTruth object (see Table 1, Figure 5) contain, among other things, information about the time (in seconds since the beginning of the video) and the position of rectangular object envelopes in the form of centre coordinates and dimensions (in pixels): $[x, y, W, H]$

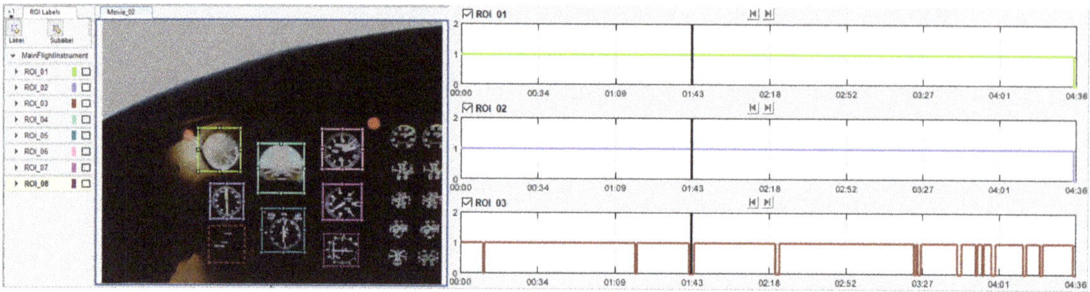

Figure 4. Example video recording showing the loss of ROI3 when the operator performs hand movements—the lost ROI is marked with a dashed line.

Table 1. GroundTruth with properties.

Simulator Type	Data Source	Label Definitions	Label Data
RPAS	[1 × 1 GroundTruth]	[4 × 5 table]	[11,417 × 4 timetable]
AS 1600	[1 × 1 GroundTruth]	[3 × 5 table]	[9568 × 3 timetable]
GA	[1 × 1 GroundTruth]	[8 × 5 table]	[1545 × 8 timetable]
Czajka MP02A	[1 × 1 GroundTruth]	[6 × 5 table]	[1843 × 6 timetable]

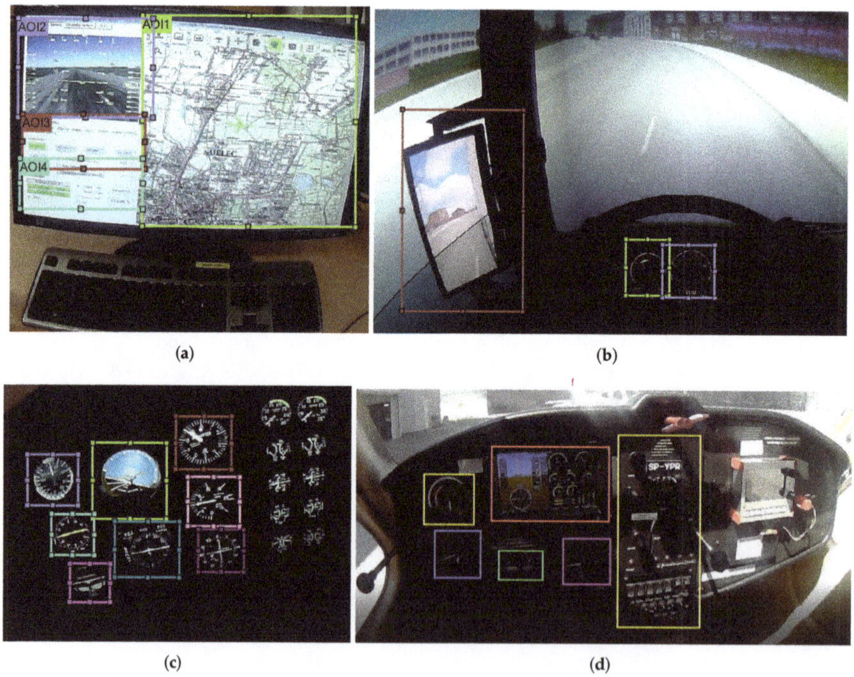

Figure 5. List of areas of interest that were used to build a training set for DNN networks, RPAS cockpit (**a**), truck simulator cockpit (**b**), GA cockpit (**c**) and flying lab cockpit (**d**).

As we already know, only a few layers in a deep neural network are responsible for selecting image features. In order to make easier observations of the input convolutional layer that extracts basic image features, such as the area or edge, it has been visualised in the form of a weight filter in Figure 6. Processing these features by deeper layers of the net enables the extraction of further image features with a higher degree of cocpit instruments details. In order to emphasise the changes taking place during the training of the pre-trained RCNN network, a visualisation of the weight matrix of the convolutional layer has been included after completing the training process Figure 6a. Due to subtle differences in the details of the obtained weight distribution, a visualisation of the difference in the weight matrix before and at the end of the training process is presented in Figure 6b. The visualisation of the obtained difference demonstrates the influence of the training sequence used in the training process on the form of the weight matrix distribution in the convolutional layer. In this way, we can observe the influence of the applied training sequence in the learning process on the form of the input layer weight matrix and primitive features extraction process.

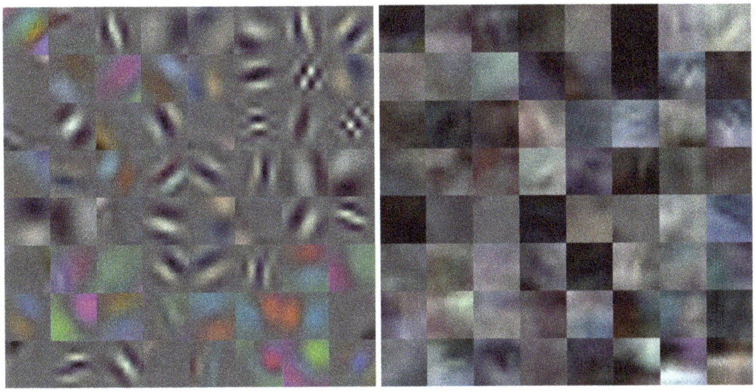

(a) (b)

Figure 6. The visualisation of the weight filter from the input convolutional layer in the R-CNN net after training (**a**) and difference with pretrained weight matrix (**b**).

4. Results and Discussion

Two object detection techniques using convolutional neural networks were selected: YOLO and R-CNN. Off-the-shelf GoogLeNet and SqueezeNet structures were implemented in each of them as modules responsible for detecting the position of instruments visible in the field of observation of the HMI system operator (see Table 2). They were then trained on prepared training data sets consisting of randomly selected and shuffled 500 frames (video stream, frame: 640 × 480 × 3, 30 fps) from four different simulators, in which the position of the ROI was manually determined. In the experimental and measurement part, a series of tests have been carried out with the participation of 20 people who successively performed tasks defined by experts conducting training classes on individual simulators. For the GA and Czajka flight simulator, it was the task of landing on instruments (IFR) at the EPRZ Jasionka airport (the international ICAO code for civil airports annotations) in night conditions. For the RPAS simulator, it was a mission to perform an unmanned aerial vehicle flying in a defined geographical location around the airport in EPML Mielec. For the A1600 simulator, the operator's task was to perform a ride in a virtual city scenery, taking into account the road infrastructure and pedestrian traffic. For each recorded video stream, the appropriate video sequences were selected containing full imaging of the simulator instruments, the use of which by the operator will be further analysed. Using the modified KLT algorithm, which was described in the previous chapter, a training sequence was generated consisting of ROI coordinates for individual instruments tracked in the observed scene along the time axis of individual image frames for all selected video sequences. A total of 5000 training sets was created for each simulator, which were split on 70–20–10% parts, respectively, i.e., into training, validation and test sets in order to avoid the possible overfitting effect. Detection performance was tested on a video stream not included in the training and validation sets. It was observed that for the adopted network models, the generation of region proposals is faster and better adapted to the data compared to other R-CNN models. In Table 3, the fourth and final stage of the learning process is presented.

Table 2. The network architectures considered in the experimental part of the study.

	R-CNN GoogLeNet	R-CNN SqueezeNet	YOLO GoogLeNet	YOLO SqueezeNet
Input type	Image	Image	Image	Image
Output type	Classification, Object detection	Classification, Object detection	Object detection	Object detection
Number of layers	155	78	105	42
Number of classifications	183	87	122	45

Table 3. Re-training Fast R-CNN using updated RPN.

Epoch	Iteration	Time Elapsed (hh:mm:ss)	Mini-Batch Loss	Mini-Batch Accuracy (%)	Mini-Batch RMSE	Base Learning Rate
1	1	00:00:00	0.1412	96,88	0.10	0.0050
1	100	00:00:18	0.1430	100.00	0.14	0.0050
1	200	00:00:37	0.1068	98.44	0.14	0.0050
1	300	00:00:56	0.1377	93.75	0.08	0.0050
1	400	00:01:15	0.1731	95.31	0.09	0.0050
1	500	00:01:34	0.1245	100.00	0.11	0.0050
2	600	00:01:52	0.1997	93,75	0.11	0.0050
2	700	00:02:11	0.0565	100.00	0.08	0.0050
2	800	00:02:30	0.1225	96.88	0.10	0.0050
2	900	00:02:49	0.0942	98.44	0.10	0.0050
2	1000	00:03:07	0.0852	96.88	0.06	0.0050

For such a trained network, tests were carried out for individual simulators. The fixation coordinates indicated by the eyetracker were entered into the coordinate system of the individual video frames of the recorded stream. The neural network that conducted the detection of the presence of areas of interest in each frame of the video stream provided the position coordinates of the recognised instruments. During the learning process, it was found that for video frames containing a high concentration of instruments, the effect of incorrect identification of the type of instrument appeared. Therefore, as the assessment of the efficiency considered net architectures, we have obtained the R_2 coefficient values which have been ranging between 0.82 and 0.94. Since R_2 is highly sensitive to the presence of falsly identified instruments, we reported two more robust metrics for model performance evaluation: RMSE and MAPE. The R-CNN model showed lowest errors with RMSE ranged between 0.92 and 0.96 and MAPE ranged between 5.50% and 8.45%, respectively. The final result of the system is an observation histogram constructed by detecting the coincidence of fixation coordinates and coordinates of detected instruments, as shown in Figure 7. To construct the spatio-temporal trajectory, the mechanism of coincidence detection and contour blurring of the observed instruments described in [1,2] was used. Each frame from the recorded video stream can be used as the background of the resulting graph, regarding limitations that all instruments used by the operator involved in attention trajectory analysis are displayed correctly. The extracted contour lines show the individual ROIs defined in the analysed scene. The vertical axis of the chart shows the time of the observations, while the rising points represent successive, chronologically appearing fixations in the fields of individual instruments. The lines connecting the points are a virtual representation of the real saccades taking place in real time in successive frames of the recorded video stream. The space-time course of fixations is the basis for further expert analysis of the acquired efficiency of the system monitoring and control by the operator. From the point of view of the effectiveness of the training of operators of the systems involved in this work, it is important to carry out measurements under real operating conditions of the operator, taking into account the accompanying time deficit for making important operating decisions.

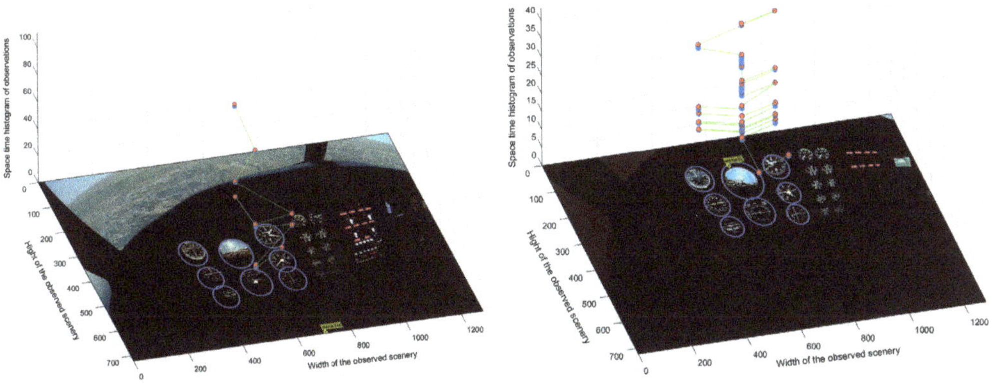

(a) (b)

Figure 7. Spatio-temporal trajectory of the observer's attention fixation for a GA class simulator for VFR (**a**) and IFR conditions (**b**) respectively.

5. Conclusions

Using the video stream from the PupilLabs device and the DNN network architectures considered in this work, it is possible to construct a suitable training set to detect, in a video stream, the coordinates of instruments located in the operator's field of observation of selected HMI systems. A deep neural network allows for sustained instrument tracking in situations where classical algorithms stop their work due to introduced noise. To use R-CNN detectors in a real-time system, hybrid solutions should be sought, for example combining DNNs with tracking algorithms such as the Point Tracker KLT used in the paper. A neural network could initially or periodically recognise objects that appear in the field of view, while the Point Tracker could track their position with small movements of objects. For the YOLO SqueezeNet architecture, despite its high speed, no results were obtained to enable its effective use, as its efficiency was unsatisfactory. The Faster R-CNN architecture showed the highest identification efficiency. The disadvantage of this solution was the drastic increase in processing time for a single frame of the video stream. This fact significantly hinders its use in real-time object tracking solutions. The proposed system makes it possible to check the verification of practical skills at different stages of training. Using DNNs and the contour blurring mechanism, it is possible to detect in a video stream the locations of selected objects and, on this basis, effectively construct spatio-temporal fixation statistics. The key advantage of the developed method is the relatively fast and precise transfer of as much information as possible to the operator using systems where there is a need to control both machines in the broadest sense and processes. The three-dimensional time course of the observation coordinates, which is the actual trajectory of the operator's attention, provides the basis for assessing the level of training of the subject. This strategy universalises the proposed technology to different application areas and allows the ergonomics of different HMIs to be evaluated. However, the proposed method allows for an effective analysis of the observer's attention trajectory, so some of its limitations can be identified. The first one is the difficulty of implementing the proposed method in the real-time regime with the use of more complex deep neural network architectures due to the high computational complexity of the algorithm. Moreover, the question remains whether for the applied methods of network architectures and simulator sets it is possible to easily include other HMI platforms without reducing the achieved effectiveness of the currently trained network. Taking into account the above, it is necessary to conduct further experiments regarding other simulators using the HMI system. A natural development of the research presented in this paper may be the use of the proposed technology to detect anomalies in the HMI system operator's work, for example their fatigue, improper chronology of activities checking the correct operation of the system and its control, etc. In particular, the proposed measurement method using DNN can be tested with the participation of flight controllers, during training on simulator stations. Currently, new directions of studies are concentrated on the use of non-invasive eyetrackers, which enable remote registration of the observer's attention in a way that does not require additional activity related to the need of use a specific type of glasses or micro camera sets for the operator.

Author Contributions: Conceptualisation, Z.G., E.Z., B.T., D.K. and P.R.; methodology, Z.G., E.Z., B.T., D.K. and P.R.; software, Z.G., E.Z., B.T., D.K. and P.R.; validation, Z.G., E.Z., B.T., D.K. and P.R.; formal analysis, Z.G., E.Z., B.T., D.K. and P.R.; investigation, Z.G., E.Z., B.T., D.K. and P.R.; resources, Z.G., E.Z., B.T., D.K. and P.R.; data curation, Z.G., E.Z., B.T., D.K. and P.R.; writing—original draft preparation, Z.G., E.Z., B.T., D.K. and P.R.; writing—review and editing, Z.G., E.Z., B.T., D.K. and P.R.; visualisation, Z.G., E.Z., B.T., D.K. and P.R.; supervision, Z.G.; project administration, Z.G., E.Z., B.T., D.K. and P.R. All authors have read and agreed to the published version of the manuscript.

Funding: This research received no external funding.

Institutional Review Board Statement: Not applicable.

Informed Consent Statement: Not applicable.

Data Availability Statement: Not applicable.

Conflicts of Interest: The authors declare no conflict of interest.

Abbreviations

The following abbreviations are used in this manuscript:

AGL	Above Ground Level
AMSL	Above Medium Sea Level
ANN	Artificial Neural Networks (ANN)
AOI	Area Of Interest
BVLOS	Beyond Visual Line of Sight
CNN	Convolutional Neural Betwork
DA	Decision Altitude
DH	Decision Height
DNN	Deep Neural Network
FFNN	Feedforward Neural Networks
GA	General Aviation
HMI	Human–Machine Interfaces
IFR	Instrument Flight Rules
ILS	Instrument Landing System
IoT	Internet of Things
KLT	Kanade–Lucas–Tomasi
ML	Machine Learning
RPAS	Remotely Piloted Aircraft System
QNH	Q Nautical Height
VFR	Visual Flight Rules

References

1. Gomolka, Z.; Kordos, D.; Zeslawska, E. The Application of Flexible Areas of Interest to Pilot Mobile Eye Tracking. *Sensors* **2020**, *20*, 986. [CrossRef] [PubMed]
2. Gomolka, Z.; Twarog, B.; Zeslawska, E.; Kordos, D. Registration and Analysis of a Pilot's Attention Using a Mobile Eyetracking System. In *Engineering in Dependability of Computer Systems and Networks. DepCoS-RELCOMEX 2019*; Advances in Intelligent Systems and Computing; Zamojski, W., Mazurkiewicz, J., Sugier, J., Walkowiak, T., Kacprzyk, J., Eds.; Springer: Cham, Switzerland, 2020; Volume 987.
3. Kasprowski, P.; Harężlak, K.; Skurowski, P. Implicit Calibration Using Probable Fixation Targets. *Sensors* **2019**, *19*, 216. [CrossRef] [PubMed]

4. Wu, C.; Cha, J.; Sulek, J.; Zhou, T.; Sundaram, C.P.; Wachs, J.; Yu, D. Eye-Tracking Metrics Predict Perceived Workload in Robotic Surgical Skills Training. *Hum. Factors* **2020**, *62*, 1365–1386 [CrossRef] [PubMed]
5. Klaib, A.F.; Alsrehin, N.O.; Melhem, W.Y.; Bashtawi, H.O.; Magableh, A.A. Eye tracking algorithms, techniques, tools, and applications with an emphasis on machine learning and Internet of Things technologies. *Expert Syst. Appl.* **2021**, *166*, 114037. [CrossRef]
6. Ahmed, I.A.; Senan, E.M.; Rassem, T.H.; Ali, M.A.H.; Shatnawi, H.S.A.; Alwazer, S.M.; Alshahrani, M. Eye Tracking-Based Diagnosis and Early Detection of Autism Spectrum Disorder Using Machine Learning and Deep Learning Techniques. *Electronics* **2022**, *11*, 530. [CrossRef]
7. Wang, F.; Wolf, J.; Farshad, M.; Meboldt, M.; Lohmeyer, Q. Object-gaze distance: Quantifying near-peripheral gaze behavior in real-world applications. *J. Eye Mov. Res.* **2021**, *14*. [CrossRef] [PubMed]
8. Orzeł, B. *The Eye-Tracking Usage for Testing Customers' Gaze on Conformity Marks Placed on Products Packages*; Silesian University of Technology Scientific Papers, Organization and Management Series; Silesian University of Technology: Gliwice, Poland, 2021.
9. Li, J.; Li, H.; Wang, H.; Umer, W.; Fu, H.; Xing, X. Evaluating the impact of mental fatigue on construction equipment operators' ability to detect hazards using wearable eye-tracking technology. *Autom. Constr.* **2019**, *105*, 102835. [CrossRef]
10. Korek, W.T.; Mendez, A.; Asad, H.U.; Li, W.C.; Lone, M. Understanding Human Behaviour in Flight Operation Using Eye-Tracking Technology. In *Engineering Psychology and Cognitive Ergonomics. Cognition and Design. HCII 2020*; Lecture Notes in Computer Science; Harris, D., Li, W.C., Eds.; Springer: Cham, Switzerland, 2020; Volume 12187.
11. Zhang, X.; Sun, Y.; Zhang, Y.; Su, S. Multi-agent modelling and situational awareness analysis of human-computer interaction in the aircraft cockpit: A case study. *Simul. Model. Pract. Theory* **2021**, *111*, 102355. [CrossRef]
12. Santu, S.K.K.; Hassan, M.M.; Smith, M.J.; Xu, L.; Zhai, C.; Veeramachaneni, K. AutoML to Date and Beyond: Challenges and Opportunities. *ACM Comput. Surv.* **2021**, *54*, 8.
13. Siriborvornratanakul, T. Human behavior in image-based Road Health Inspection Systems despite the emerging AutoML. *J. Big Data* **2022**, *9*, 96 [CrossRef] [PubMed]
14. Neutatz, F.; Chen, B.; Alkhatib, Y.; Ye, J.; Abedjan, Z. Data Cleaning and AutoML: Would an Optimizer Choose to Clean? *Datenbank Spektrum* **2022**, *22*, 121–130. [CrossRef]
15. Kondratenko, Y.; Sidenko, I.; Kondratenko, G.; Petrovych, V.; Taranov, M.; Sova, I. Artificial Neural Networks for Recognition of Brain Tumors on MRI Images. In *Information and Communication Technologies in Education, Research, and Industrial Applications. ICTERI 2020*; Communications in Computer and Information Science; Bollin, A., Ermolayev, V., Mayr, H.C., Nikitchenko, M., Spivakovsky, A., Tkachuk, M., Yakovyna, V., Zholtkevych, G., Eds.; Springer: Cham, Switzerland, 2021; Volume 1308.
16. Feng, D.; Lu, X.; Lin, X. Deep Detection for Face Manipulation. In *Neural Information Processing. ICONIP 2020*; Communications in Computer and Information Science; Yang, H., Pasupa, K., Leung, A.C.-S., Kwok, J.T., Chan, J.H., King, I., Eds.; Springer: Cham, Switzerland, 2020; Volume 1333.
17. Zhong, J.; Sun, W.; Cai, Q.; Zhang, Z.; Dong, Z.; Gao, M. Deep Learning Based Strategy for Eye-to-Hand Robotic Tracking and Grabbing. In *Neural Information Processing. ICONIP 2020*; Lecture Notes in Computer Science; Yang, H., Pasupa, K., Leung, A.C.-S., Kwok, J.T., Chan, J.H., King, I., Eds.; Springer: Cham, Switzerland, 2020; Volume 12533.
18. Szewczyk, G.; Spinelli, R.; Magagnotti, N.; Tylek, P.; Sowa, J.M.; Rudy, P.; Gaj-Gielarowiec, D. The mental workload of harvester operators working in steep terrain conditions. *Silva Fennica* **2020**, *54*, 10355. [CrossRef]
19. Kasprowski, P. Identifying users based on their eye tracker calibration data. In *ACM Symposium on Eye Tracking Research and Applications (ETRA '20 Adjunct)*; Association for Computing Machinery: New York, NY, USA, 2020; Article 38, pp. 1–2.
20. Harezlak, K.; Augustyn, D.R.; Kasprowski, P. An Analysis of Entropy-Based Eye Movement Events Detection. *Entropy* **2019**, *21*, 107. [CrossRef] [PubMed]
21. Edewaard, D.E.; Tyrrell, R.A.; Duchowski, A.T.; Szubski, E.C.; King, S.S. Using Eye Tracking to Assess the Temporal Dynamics by Which Drivers Notice Cyclists in Daylight: Drivers Becoming Aware of Cyclists. In *ACM Symposium on Eye Tracking Research and Applications (ETRA '20 Short Papers)*; Association for Computing Machinery: New York, NY, USA, 2020; Article 36, pp. 1–5.
22. Szewczyk, G.; Spinelli, R.; Magagnotti, N.; Mitka, B.; Tylek, P.; Kulak, D.; Adamski, K. Perception of the Harvester Operator's Working Environment in Windthrow Stands. *Forests* **2021**, *12*, 168. [CrossRef]
23. Neverova, N.; Wolf, C.; Lacey, G.; Fridman, L.; Chandra, D.; Barbello, B.; Taylor, G. Learning Human Identity From Motion Patterns. *IEEE Access* **2016**, *4*, 1810–1820. [CrossRef]
24. Li, J.; Li, H.; Umer, W.; Wang, H.; Xing, X.; Zhao, S.; Hou, J. Identification and classification of construction equipment operators' mental fatigue using wearable eye-tracking technology. *Autom. Constr.* **2020**, *109*, 103000. [CrossRef]
25. Kasprowski, P.; Harezlak, K. Using mutual distance plot and warped time distance chart to compare scan-paths of multiple observers. In *Proceedings of the 11th ACM Symposium on Eye Tracking Research & Applications* (*ETRA '19*); Association for Computing Machinery: New York, NY, USA, 2019; Article 77, pp. 1–5.
26. Gomolka, Z.; Twarog, B.; Zeslawska, E. Fractional Order Derivative Mechanism to Extract Biometric Features. In *Theory and Engineering of Dependable Computer Systems and Networks. DepCoS-RELCOMEX 2021*; Advances in Intelligent Systems and Computing; Zamojski, W., Mazurkiewicz, J., Sugier, J., Walkowiak, T., Kacprzyk, J., Eds.; Springer: Cham, Switzerland, 2021; Volume 1389.
27. Khan, M.N.; Ahmed, M.M. Trajectory-level fog detection based on in-vehicle video camera with TensorFlow deep learning utilizing SHRP2 naturalistic driving data. *Accid. Anal. Prev.* **2020**, *142*, 105521. [CrossRef]

28. Samaraweera, W.; Premaratne, S.; Dharmaratne, A. Deep Learning for Classification of Cricket Umpire Postures. In *Neura Information Processing. ICONIP 2020*; Communications in Computer and Information Science; Springer: Cham, Switzerland, 202(Volume 1333.
29. Maggu, J.; Majumdar, A.; Chouzenoux, E.; Chierchia, G. Deep Convolutional Transform Learning. In *Neural Information Processing ICONIP 2020*; Communications in Computer and Information Science; Springer: Cham, Switzerland, 2020; Volume 1333.
30. Jayech, K. Deep Convolutional Neural Networks Based on Image Data Augmentation for Visual Object Recognition. In *Intelligent Data Engineering and Automated Learning – IDEAL 2019. IDEAL 2019*; Lecture Notes in Computer Science; Yin, H., Camacho, D., Tino, P., Tallón-Ballesteros, A., Menezes, R., Allmendinger, R., Eds.; Springer: Cham, Switzerland, 2019; Volume 11871.

MDPI AG
Grosspeteranlage 5
4052 Basel
Switzerland
Tel.: +41 61 683 77 34

Applied Sciences Editorial Office
E-mail: applsci@mdpi.com
www.mdpi.com/journal/applsci

www.ingramcontent.com/pod-product-compliance
Lightning Source LLC
Chambersburg PA
CBHW061829210926
51850CB00006B/843
9783725860470